A
SOCIO
OF
AUSTRALIAN
SOCIETY

CU00871785

INTRODUCTORY READINGS

A SOCIOLOGY OF AUSTRALIAN SOCIETY

INTRODUCTORY READINGS

EDITED BY
Jake M. Najman and John S. Western
University of Queensland, St Lucia

M

© J. M. Najman and J. S. Western and contributors 1988

All rights reserved.
No part of this publication
may be reproduced or transmitted
in any form or by any means,
without permission.

First published 1988 by
THE MACMILLAN COMPANY OF AUSTRALIA PTY LTD
107 Moray Street, South Melbourne 3205
6 Clarke Street, Crows Nest 2065
Reprinted 1988, 1989 (twice)

Associated companies and representatives
throughout the world

National Library of Australia
cataloguing in publication data

A Sociology of Australian society.

Includes index.
ISBN 0 333 43079 4.
ISBN 0 333 43080 8 (pbk.).

1. Sociology – Australia. 2. Australia – Social conditions.
I. Najman, J. M. (Jackob Moses). II. Western, John S. (John Stuart),
1931–

301'.0994

Set in Plantin by Graphicraft Typesetters, Hong Kong
Printed in the People's Republic of China

Contents

v

Part III: Current Issues and Concerns

Notes on Contributors

Don S. Anderson is Professorial Fellow in the Research School of Social Sciences at the Australian National University. His current research preoccupation is a sociological study of the public/private divide in education systems.

John Braithwaite is a Senior Research Fellow, Department of Sociology, Research School of Social Sciences, Australian National University. He is known particularly for his research on white collar crime.

Lois Bryson is currently an Associate Professor in the School of Sociology at the University of New South Wales. She has published widely on aspects of Australian life, with a major focus on social policy, inequality, family and feminist issues.

Don Edgar gained his PhD at Stanford University and was Assistant Professor at the University of Chicago before returning to Monash University. He was Reader in Sociology at La Trobe University before becoming foundation Director of the Australian Institute of Family Studies.

Stephen Hill is Foundation Professor and Head of the Department of Sociology, and Director of the Centre for Technology and Social Change at the University of Wollongong. He was educated in physical science, business administration and sociology. Professor Hill has written over seventy research articles and several books on technology, science and society, and his last book, *Future Tense? – Technology in Australia* is now in its third edition.

David Ip is a Lecturer in Sociology at the University of Queensland. His teaching and research interests include leisure and recreation, and social impact assessment.

Adam Jamrozik is a Senior Research Fellow at the Social Welfare Research Centre, University of New South Wales, where he has published a number of research monographs on social policy, the labour market and child and family welfare.

James Jupp is currently a Senior Fellow at the Australian National University and General Editor of the Bicentennial *Encyclopedia of the Australian People*. He is the author of a number of books on Australian politics and immigration, and in 1984 edited *Ethnic Politics in Australia* (Allen & Unwin).

Ian Keen after a period as an art teacher in London and Oxford, gained an honours degree in anthropology from University College, London, and the PhD at the Australian National University. He has carried out field work in north-east Arnhem Land and other parts of the Northern Territory.

David Kemp is Professor of Politics at Monash University, Victoria. He is the author of *Society and Electoral Behaviour in Australia* and numerous articles and chapter in works on Australian politics. His most recent study, *Politics and Authority: Australia* is forthcoming.

Pat Mullins is a Senior Lecturer in Sociology at the University of Queensland. He has published widely in the area of urbanisation.

Jake Najman is a Senior Lecturer, jointly appointed to the Departments of Anthropology and Sociology, and Social and Preventive Medicine, at the University of Queensland. He has published widely in the fields of health care evaluation and medical sociology.

Michael Pusey is Senior Lecturer in Sociology at the University of New South Wales. His publications include *The Dynamics of Bureaucracy*, articles and chapters on education, critical theory, public policy and organisation, and, most recently, a book on the social theory of Jurgen Habermas.

Roman Tomasic is Principal Lecturer in Law at the Canberra College of Advanced Education. He holds doctorates in sociology (University of New South Wales) and law (University of Wisconsin-Madison). His most recent publication is *The Sociology of Law* (Sage, London, 1985).

John Western is Professor of Sociology at the University of Queensland. He has published widely in the fields of social class and inequality, the media, health and welfare.

Mark Western is an honours graduate undertaking his doctorate studies at the University of Queensland. His major interests are in Marxist and neo-Marxist conceptions of class.

Claire Williams, Senior Lecturer in Sociology at Flinders University, South Australia, is the author of *Open Cut.* She is an industrial sociologist who has just completed a study of Telecom technicians, flight attendants and bank workers in Australia.

Tables and Figures

Preface

This reader introduces the basic concepts, methods and subject matter of sociology. We have taken for the major focus a structural approach to Australian society. We would argue that there are five structural bases to this society, and these we have designated as class, gender, race, ethnic origin and age. They are important because beliefs, behaviours and access to scarce and valued resources are, in part, derived from them.

We also stress the importance of the institutions or institutional areas that characterise society. It is commonly argued that any society comprises five major institutional areas. The first of these has been described as the polity, or the political institutions of that society – the parliament, political parties, pressure groups and the public service: indeed, the whole range of groups which provides for the government. The second major institutional area is the economy, which is concerned with the production and distribution of goods and services. Religion is the third major area: how does it affect the social order, and are religious beliefs, values and ideas connected with other features of the society? These are questions of concern to sociologists. A celebrated account of the relationship between religion and the economy was provided by Max Weber, the nineteenth-century European social scientist. Weber argued that the Protestant ethic, which comprised a set of values and behaviours supporting hard work and achievement, was an important factor in the development of nineteenth-century capitalism.

Sociologists also see family and marriage as a central institutional area of society. To what extent is its institution of marriage changing in the latter part of the twentieth century? Is the frequency of marriage changing, or the age at which marriage takes place? Again, these are all questions which sociologists address. Finally, there is education. What is its function? Does it provide knowledge or does it equip individuals with particular beliefs which enable them to fit easily into the existing social order? In this sense does education serve to limit social change in society?

A third approach to sociology comes from an interest in the dominant social issues of a period: unemployment, health, the appropriateness of welfare services, as well as conservation, and the changing nature of political beliefs. Typically, sociologists address these latter concerns from a structural and institutionally oriented approach.

This reader, then, is loosely divided into three sections. Firstly, there are the contributions which take a structural perspective and provide a framework for understanding society in general, and Australian society in particular. Secondly, there are readings which consider the current state of some institutions in Australian society. Thirdly, the contributors discuss a number of contemporary social issues.

The reader reflects, we believe, the current state of the discipline of sociology in Australia. It is notable that the contributors approach their task from different perspectives, using varying theoretical approaches and methodologies. This diversity of approach warrants some comment.

Many of the social sciences manifest such approaches to their subject matter. In this context we would suggest that each chapter reflects something of the author's personal qualities, as well as of the topic being discussed. A key tenet of science is that research is reproducible; that the personal qualities of researchers intrude only to a very limited extent into their research. Indeed, scientists rely on this reproducibility of findings to determine the level of credibility they place on a particular body of knowledge.

Does the limited agreement within sociology on theories and methods mean that it and the other social sciences are unscientific? Is sociology gradually moving to a more agreed-upon set of theories and methods? Again on this, as on other issues, there are different points of view. We would argue that sociology should become more scientific than it is; that theories and methods, as well as substantive findings, should be subjected to scientific criteria and then accepted or rejected.

Not all will share this view; even more interestingly, some sociologists would deny the possibility of *knowing* social reality. They would suggest that our understandings are largely moulded by our prior experiences and that we can only *imagine* a particular version of reality. We here take the view that there is an objectively knowable reality. We suggest that it is appropriate to accept the assumption that it is, for example, a chair upon which we sit, not a construction which exists only in our minds.

Sociology, then, is concerned with understanding society and this involves understanding people's conceptions of reality.

Despite the conflicting perspectives and the tentative nature of much sociological knowledge, sociology provides a compelling and personally involving approach to understanding not only society, but oneself. It raises important questions about 'truths' which may previously have been taken for granted. It provides a great deal of factual information about the social world. A sociological approach, we suggest, enables people to make better decisions about their lives, and be more understanding of those with whom they come in contact.

This reader provides an indication of the growth of sociology in Australia. However, it also suggests that much remains to be done before we can claim to have an adequate understanding of Australian society. We invite the reader to join with us in building this understanding.

John S. Western
Jake M. Najman
University of Queensland,
St Lucia

Part I
Basic Structures and Concepts

Chapter One

Sociology: The Study of Social Structures and Cultural Reproduction

Jake M. Najman

This chapter has two tasks. The first is to describe the discipline of sociology and identify some of its subject matters, its theories and methods. The second is to introduce some of the readings which follow and identify their common thrust and purpose.

The subject matter of this chapter is perhaps the most fundamental of sociological questions: that is, how society, as we individually experience it, comes to exist. The sociological response to this question begins by noting that an individual is structurally located within a sector of the social system, and emphasises that he or she is a product of this system. In the above context what appear to be individual experiences are more properly seen as those which a group may reportedly have in common. The dominant foci for sociological explanations of human behaviour are various aggregations (groups) in society, their circumstances and interactions.

What is Sociology?

We, with others, define sociology as the *scientific study of society*. There are two key words in this definition, 'scientific' and 'society'. Sociology is scientific because it relies on the methods of science to provide data which may be sociologically interpreted. Sociologists eschew anecdotal, idiosyncratic and personal judgements in their analyses of society. The methods used by sociologists provide for the collection of verifiable and, in principle, reproducible information. Society is the subject matter of sociology, and this term includes aggregate groups within a geographically delineated nation state, groups which have a social-structural location.

Individuals, it could be argued, do not experience the total social system but a particular manifestation of it refracted by the group to which they belong. Women, the aged, migrants, Aborigines and the economically disadvantaged are examples of groups in Australian society which have experiences in common, as a consequence of their group membership. These common experiences shape a group's perception of the 'real' world. The individual, from the sociological perspective, is a product of a social process and it is towards an understanding of this process that this analysis is directed.

The Sociological Perspective

Perhaps one of the most difficult of all concepts to comprehend is the extent to which the world is perceived through a particular set of 'glasses'. The metaphor of the three blind people in search of what an elephant looks like, forming their images on the basis of the different parts they touch, is useful in an illustrative sense. Psychologists, historians, philosophers and geographers all see society through 'glasses' created by their chosen discipline. It should not be surprising, therefore, that various disciplines can inspect the same world but concentrate upon different elements of it, and come to somewhat different conclusions about it.

Where sociological explanations differ from, and possibly compete with, those of other disciplines, two interpretations should be considered. Firstly, the explanations might be seen to challenge each other, and the weaker explanation (chosen by whatever criteria) may be rejected. Alternatively, the explanations might be seen to be complementary. Consistent with this latter view it is relevant to note that much social research may proceed using the best available, but nevertheless imperfect, methods, and that most quantitative explanations can claim to explain only a modest proportion of observed variations in behaviour. While sociologists may sometimes write as if they have a comprehensive explanation of a particular social concern (e.g. unemployment, poor health, urban development) they generally implicitly, or sometimes explicitly, can only legitimately claim to offer partial explanations. This is not to suggest that these partial accounts are unimportant or that they may be disregarded, but rather that they are incomplete and not always in conflict with similarly directed accounts from other disciplines.

A distinctive feature of sociology is that it seeks to explain social behaviour by examining social institutions (sets of generally agreed upon rules associated with various functions performed in society) and the membership of social groups in society. This is often described as a structural perspective, and it explicitly involves locating individuals within a social matrix. In the above sense sociology differs from disciplines which seek to explain behaviour by considering the biological characteristics or individual experiences of people.

Sociologists attend to institutions – economic, political, legal and educational – and the socio-demographic characteristics of individuals (e.g. gender, class, ethnicity and race), as these reflect unique patterns of socialisation. Sociologists are particularly interested in the manner and extent to which institutionally derived beliefs, values and behaviours are learnt as a consequence of an individual's location in the social order. This concern is addressed in a number of chapters which follow (see Williams, Chapter 4, Anderson, Chapter 8, and Edgar, Chapter 14) and is also discussed in greater detail later in this chapter.

Illustrations of the Structural Perspective

Sociologists generally argue that human behaviour is learned and occurs in patterns associated with one's position in the social structure. Homans (1986: xxv) defines social structure as 'more or less enduring practices followed by a number of persons, whether or not these practices are made explicit ... or defended by sanctions'. The term 'social structure' is used to refer to various groups within either the broader society (distinguished by their socio-demographic characteristics) or within these groups, sub-groups characterised by common experiences, beliefs and/or behaviours (e.g. a university department may include sub-groups with different approaches to their personal or academic activities).

Because this sociological emphasis on structural explanations differs from that which may be both intuitively preferable and more generally familiar, the following two illustrations are taken from the chapters which follow in this book. The examples concern unemployment levels and changes in marriage rates in Australian society.

Sociologists are frequently interested in, and wish to explain, social concerns such as unemployment. In seeking to explain such a phenomenon the personal or individual qualities of the unemployed would generally receive less attention than associations between structurally derived forces and unemployment levels. A sociological approach to unemployment could begin with the observation that about 9 per cent of the Australian population is registered as unemployed. The unemployment rate, it could be argued, remains the same irrespective of who is unemployed at a specific time. In this sense the unemployment rate is a characteristic of the society, and will vary from time to time. Jamrozic, in Chapter 15, shows that unemployment levels have changed over time in Australia and that some groups in Australian society experience higher rates of unemployment.

The available data confirm the recent increase in unemployment rates. Hill's Chapter 9 attributes the present high unemployment level to features of the capitalist economic system and our colonialist past. He argues that successive Australian governments spurned intervention in manufacturing industry and instead were content to allow Australian primary products to be sold and manufactured overseas. As primary and manufacturing industry became more efficient and employment levels declined, the absence of prior planning meant that, except for the service sector, unemployment levels increased.

Of course, as Jamrozic points out, not all groups in Australian society are equally liable to experience unemployment. Those who are young, unskilled and/or Aboriginal have the highest unemployment rates. Older males are a relatively small proportion of the total unemployed, but experience long periods of unemployment. While it is not yet possible to explain fully why the young and unskilled are unable to obtain employment, it does appear that there are increasingly fewer jobs suitable for unskilled people, and that increased employment opportunities are generally to be had in jobs requiring higher levels of education.

A similar structural approach is evident when we examine changes in marriage and divorce rates, as Edgar has in Chapter 14. Thus, over time, an increasing proportion of Australians have chosen to marry but there has also been an increase in the proportion of those who have chosen to end their marriages (and who usually remarry). Serial marriages, where a person may change partners as his/her circumstances change, have become more common.

While in individual cases it may be possible to argue that a marriage failed because of the personal characteristics of the participants, the observation that rates of divorce have recently increased many times suggests that other explanations must be considered. Thus improved methods of contraception; legal changes which simplify divorce; the availability of child-care; the decline in the extended family; the increased rate of female workforce participation; and a decline in religiosity, all may contribute to increases in rates of marital dissolution.

According to both these explanations, what appear to be 'individual troubles', that is, unemployment or marital breakdown, are more correctly interpreted as consequences of the structural arrangements and institutional norms which prevail within a society (e.g. the legal system, welfare and child-care services or developments in medical technology). In the above context the sociologist is less interested in why a particular marriage failed, than in why the institution of marriage is no longer accepted to the extent that may have been the case previously: that is, why the institution of marriage is failing to meet the needs of many in contemporary society.

Variations in Sociological Perspectives

The foregoing should not be taken, of course, to suggest that there is a single sociological view or approach to which all, or even most, sociologists subscribe. Indeed, various studies show that sociology is characterised by a diversity of theories and methods. In comparing disciplines according to the level of agreement or conflict over theories, methods and findings, Lodahl and Gordon (1972) circulated a questionnaire to staff in 80 university departments (20 each in physics, chemistry, sociology and political science). Physics was consistently ranked as having the most consensus while sociology and political science had the least.

A similar result comes from Gareau (1985), who has compared the sociological orientations of scholars in various countries. As he points out, there is no German physics or French chemistry, but it *is* meaningful to distinguish between Russian and American sociology. Some prefer to conceive of sociology as action oriented and concerned with redressing fundamental inequalities in society. Others perceive its mandate in more narrow terms, as concerned with understanding society. Some are interested in 'grand' theories of society, and others with understanding the day-to-day interactions which dominate people's lives. Sociology, then, is typified by a diversity of theories, methods and often conflicting conclusions. This diversity, even within a single country like Australia, is reflected in the chapters which follow.

For a student of sociology, there is a need to consider carefully the arguments presented by various authors, the quality of the evidence they bring to bear, and to determine whether the weight of proof points to one or other conclusion. In the above context, sociologists and those studying sociology have two specific tasks. The first is to examine the varieties of ideas and findings which

bear upon a particular subject, and the second is to make public –
in the sense that the assessments made can be explained and
justified – judgements about this literature and that state of
knowledge.

The acknowledged diversity of the sociological effort does not
deny the existence of some common themes which bind together
the various contributions to this book. This is an Australian
reader, specifically concerned with national events and issues.
Most contributors acknowledge a need for both historically based
and economically derived (in a Marxist sense) analyses of the
Australian condition. Most use quantitative and qualitative data to
support and/or illustrate their arguments. Many refer implicitly or
explicitly to policy implications of the analyses they have presented.
All appear to share Homans' (1970: 27) view that the

> ... most interesting theoretical task will remain that of showing
> how structures, relative enduring relationships ... are created and
> maintained by individual human choices, choices constrained by the
> choices of others, but still choices.

Most of the chapters manifest an interest in the social system as
a whole and the extent to which this system, into which an
individual is born, moulds and shapes his or her perceptions,
knowledge and behaviours. The system may become, as we will
observe in the pages which follow, a source of specific behavioural
preferences and a set of underlying values and beliefs which
influence decision making in a range of situations not previously
encountered.

The Patterning of Values, Beliefs and Behaviour

As we have argued, sociologists seek to understand and explain
structurally distinguishable groups in society and their patterns of
values, beliefs and behaviours. What are such patterns in Australian society? Two examples will be considered; male/female
variations and those associated with socio-economic (social class)
inequalities.

Male/female differences have generated an intense and, to some
extent, unresolved debate for many social scientists. Williams in
Chapter 4 goes so far as to suggest that there are male and female
ways of 'knowing'. In one cross-national study involving 2,800
university students in 28 countries, comparisons of stereotypes of
male and female behavioural differences were sought (Williams
and Best 1982). Interestingly, males and females were generally

found to agree that males were active, assertive, confident, forceful, logical, solid and wise (this is only a partial list) while females were typically perceived as affected, charming, emotional, kind, sensitive, soft-hearted and weak (1982: 77). Similar findings emerged from a review of ethnographic reports of socialisation practices in 110 cultures. In such reports, girls were typically socialised to nurturance of others, obedience and responsibility, while males were more often socialised towards achievement and self-reliance (Barry, Bacon and Child 1973: 153). Australian studies have provided results consistent with those from other countries.

In one study in Melbourne, schoolgirls more often aspired to occupations with an altruistic component, while boys appeared more interested in 'exciting' occupations (Musgrave 1984: 205). A survey of students at a Sydney college suggested that while females were somewhat willing to assume some non-traditional domestic and work roles, males rejected these alternatives in greater number (Albury, Chaples and Stubbs 1977: 136). Not only are males and females believed to differ in a number of their social characteristics, but their achievement levels are also markedly different.

Thus, while approximately equal numbers of males and females enter the Australian Mathematics Competition (AMC), males gain more of the top awards. Indeed, on a 30-item paper, males score on average between 1 and $1\frac{1}{2}$ more correct answers. One interesting aspect of this difference is that females appear less willing than males to guess at an answer when they are penalised for an incorrect guess (Edwards 1984).

Inequalities in achievement are further evident when we compare the male and female achievement levels within occupational groups. Thus, in Victoria 55 per cent of teachers but only 16 per cent of high school principals are female (Bottomley and Sampson 1977: 137). Of all full-time female university staff members, 1.3 per cent are at professorial level (males, 11.9 per cent), while 30.3 per cent are at tutor level (males, 8.9 per cent) (Sargent 1983: 110). When males enter largely segregated female occupations (nursing, secretarial, teaching) they tend to be promoted rapidly to senior positions (Currie 1982: 181–82). There is then general agreement that males and females differ in their values, beliefs and performance. It is, however, less clear why such differences are found so consistently.

One group would tend to ascribe the above inequalities to male and female biological differences. Certainly such biological differences exist and should not be dismissed. One study of 75 animal species, including crustaceans, reptiles, birds and mammals, found that, almost without exception, there was (as there is in humans), inferior male longevity (reported in Retherford 1975: 9). The human female advantage is partly attributable to biological factors, the protection from atherosclerosis provided by oestrogen hormones (Retherford 1975: 15). Further, females as a consequence of their child-bearing, may be better biologically equipped to perform integrative/expressive functions (Williams and Best 1982: 241), though the evidence for (or against) this is unconvincing.

Regardless of the specific biological differences which may arguably distinguish males from females, there is little doubt that the process of socialisation serves to exaggerate these differences and to greatly limit the alternatives available to both women and, to a lesser extent, men. Thus, in a study of Euro-American children in the United States, there was clear evidence that children acquired these stereotypes with age as they were exposed to the dominant culture (see Table 1.1). One of the consequences of this process, as Edgar (1980) in an Australian study has shown, is 'that girls ... had a lower estimation of their own competence even when their measured verbal intelligence was superior to boys' (Edgar 1980: 163).

It is important here to grasp the subtle but pervasive nature of gender stereotypes. Thus, in one study children who were shown a videotape of a female doctor and a male nurse, when asked to recall the content of the tape, remembered a male doctor and a female nurse (reported in Williams and Best 1982: 24). A similar point emerges from the following reported exchange:

A psychologist overheard her four-year-old son trying to explain her occupation to a young friend.
SON: 'My mother helps people. She's a doctor.'
FRIEND: 'You mean a nurse.'
SON: 'No. She's not that kind of doctor. She's a psychologist. She's a doctor of psychology.'
FRIEND: 'I see. She's a nurse of psychology.'
(William and Best 1982: 302)

Another instance of socially patterned behaviour may be associated with socio-economic inequalities in society (see Western and Western, Chapter 3, for a more detailed analysis of these inequalities).

Income inequalities provide unambiguous evidence of structurally determined constraints on human behaviour. The 1984 Australian Household Expenditure Survey (1986) provides evidence of major differences in lifestyle associated with one's socio-economic position. The lowest 10 per cent of income earners spend $24 a week on housing compared with the $70 spent by the top 10 per cent. Twenty-four dollars comprises 17 per cent of the total

income of the lowest income group while $70 is only 10 per cent of
the total income of the highest income group.

Table 1.1 Ages at which Children acquire Sex Stereotypes

	Stereotypes of Males	Stereotypes of Females
At 5 years of age	strong, aggressive, dominant	gentle, affectionate
By 8 years of age	disorderly, cruel, coarse, adventurous, ambitious, loud, boastful	weak, emotional, appreciative, excitable, gentle, soft-hearted, sophisticated, submissive
By 11 years of age	confident, steady, jolly	talkative, rattle-brained, complaining

Source: Williams and Best 1982: 25

The wealthy spend more, both absolutely and relatively, on
alcohol, clothing, transport and recreation. Lower income people
spend a greater proportion of their incomes on housing, fuel,
power and food – that is, essentials – and they appear to have little
remaining for discretionary activities. These are not simply differences in spending power, but could be expected to influence a
person's perception of the world and his or her place in it.

Gary Marks has provided the following data from the Brisbane
component of the Class Structure of Australia Project (see Table
1.2). Marks has compared the values and attitudes of people who
are located at different levels of the class hierarchy. His work
suggests that we live in a society in which the social class to which
people belong influences their attitudes and feelings about the
social world. Manual and clerical workers, in contrast with their
higher class counterparts, express greater feelings of alienation and
lesser feelings of work satisfaction, and also express much less
positive attitudes about their work. Managers/owners, a higher
class group, not surprisingly, support a free market philosophy and
overwhelmingly reject government intervention in the day-to-day
functioning of society.

Economic inequalities in Australian society have their starkest
consequences when we compare the 'life chances' of those who are
socio-economically advantaged and disadvantaged. As Taylor *et
al.* (1983), McMichael (1985) and Siskind *et al.* (1987) have shown,
those who are lowest on the socio-economic hierarchy have higher

Table 1.2 Attitudes and Beliefs of Brisbane Residents by their Occupational Class

	Significance P-Value	I Manager/Owner	II Self-employed	III Professional/Managerial	IV Clerical/Sales	V Manual Workers
		% most strongly agreeing with scale items				
1. Alienation	0.001	29	39	22	41	63
2. Work Satisfaction	0.001	37	33	36	25	8
3. Work Attitudes	0.001	66	39	43	23	14
4. Government Intervention	0.001	17	33	24	37	63
5. Free Market	0.01	54	28	24	21	26

1. A scale which measures feelings of powerlessness; an inability to influence events and circumstances
2. A scale measuring conditions at work including pay, hours and interactions with others
3. A scale measuring general attitudes to work and whether respondent's work is perceived as important and useful
4. A scale measuring respondent's reaction to government intervention in a range of industrial and social matters
5. A scale measuring respondent's reaction to 'New Right' views, emphasising that the government should not intervene in most areas

Source: Marks, Class Structure of Australia Project

adult and infant mortality rates and, interestingly, these differences are evident for most causes of death. These findings
suggest major variations in the structurally determined patterning
of social behaviour associated with mortality differences.

Edgar (1980) provides some interesting Australian illustrations
of the manner in which children of varying economic circumstances are reared, which partly account for the behaviour, lifestyle
and health differences noted above. He notes that overseas studies
have suggested that middle class parents seek to communicate
particular values which the child is expected to internalise and,
presumably, apply as circumstances arise. By contrast, working
class parents tend to focus on specific behaviours and to punish
their children if they transgress. These findings were reinforced by
his Australian research (1980: 163) which showed that:

> Non-manual fathers liked their children to be interested in how and
> why things happen, considerate of others and self-controlled and
> responsible. The manual fathers ranked more highly good manners,
> being neat and clean, obeying parents and conforming to appropriate
> sex roles.

Here it is important to note that not only values, beliefs and
behaviours are communicated, but a particular orientation to the
culture of the society. This is likely to include perceptions of a
desirable partner, expectations of future employment, and a view
about the appropriateness of academic and other achievements.
Indeed, while acknowledging that IQ scores (particularly verbal
IQ scores) may partly reflect cultural values as well as innate
ability, there is evidence to show that children born into a poverty
environment but reared by adopting middle class parents manifest
substantially higher IQ scores than similar children who remained
in their original environment (Scarr and Weinberg 1976). Children
reared in a more middle class environment appear more often to
manifest personal qualities which will enable them to 'succeed' in
contemporary industrial societies like Australia.

Socialisation

In describing male/female and socio-economic differences in
values, beliefs and behaviours (associated with one's structural
location), we have noted that sociologists generally attribute these
differences to the socialisation process. In this section we will
consider this process in greater detail and explore both the various
ways it is believed to occur and its implications for understanding

stability and change in society.

While there is general agreement that socialisation is a process which communicates societal, sub-cultural and familial knowledge and values, there are different emphases evident in writings on the subject. Denisoff and Wahrman (1975) and Baldridge (1975) take the view that infants are largely moulded by the socialisation process and made into beings which fit into the existing social order. By contrast, Douglas (1973) and Sites (1975) suggest that socialisation is an interactive process which leads to changes in all the participants, adults and children. These approaches are labelled respectively the normative and interactionist views of socialisation. These are complementary approaches to understanding the process of socialisation – that is, of the interaction of the individual and society.

According to the normative view, children in a particular sector of society are taught the culture – which includes knowledge, beliefs, morals, customs, habits etc. – of that society. The culture is successively communicated by the representatives of the society with whom the child comes into contact, the agents of socialisation. Thus, parents and close family members control initial socialisation, then peer groups, the media (see Western, Chapter 18, for additional details) and school (see Anderson, Chapter 8, for more details) followed by significant others – that is, people with whom there is a close relationship. Institutions like the legal system provide formal sanctions for deviation, in that they reflect the dominant ideology and are frequently communicated by the agents of socialisation. Children, it is argued, are taught a set of norms (rules of behaviour) associated with their roles (position in the social structure). Successful socialisation involves the internalisation of these norms (the belief that the rules of behaviour come from within the individual).

An important aspect of the normative view is the assumption that the child simply becomes the sum total of his or her experiences. This is argued not only on the basis that the new member of the society responds as required in order to avoid sanctions, but also because beliefs about right and wrong and the values underlying decision making are also acquired during the socialisation process. A logical extension of this view of socialisation is that humans are essentially similar products of their society, their choices being constrained by their experiences.

Evidence for the validity of the normative view can be found in at least two sets of data. The first is derived from simple observation and survey research. Thus, in addition to the gender and class patterns of belief and behaviour we have noted, it is possible to observe a variety of ethnic and racial groups, and their similarities of appearance and behaviour. Indeed as Jupp points out in Chapter 6, migrants will frequently choose to live in parts of Australian cities with others of similar origin, retaining many of their cultural practices, presumably because they find foreign cultures less agreeable.

The second type of evidence comes from experimental research and emphasises the extent to which people appear to be willing to conform to the demands made upon them by others. In the first experiment of relevance, Asch (1955) took 7 (or sometimes 9) college students and showed them 2 large white cards. One had a vertical black line and the other 3 lines of different length. Each of the participants was asked publicly which of the 3 lines was the same length as the single line. A test administration showed that outside the experimental situation there were less than 1 per cent of errors.

In the experimental situation, the first 6 people were, on instruction, required to consistently state an incorrect line was the same size as the single line. The subject was the seventh person and the aim of the experiment was to determine whether people would yield to group pressure to deny the reality they could unambiguously observe.

Some 37 per cent of 'errors' were made in the experimental situation, suggesting that a substantial minority of participants yielded to group pressure. One-quarter of the subjects appeared to give answers which indicated they were behaving independently of the group, while some others agreed with the group the whole time. Maximum conformity appeared to occur with 7 to 9 opponents and after about 4 trials.

Thus the experiment by Asch suggested that some, but by no means all, people yielded to group pressure. It would be simplistic to interpret these findings totally at face value. Some persons may have agreed with the others in the group to avoid conflict, and may not have been reporting what they believed they saw. This contextual behaviour (behaving in one way with one group and another way elsewhere) has its counterpart in many real life situations. Regardless of the motives of the experimental subjects and accepting the possibly temporary nature of the phenomena, Asch's studies raise some important questions.

Thus, it is interesting to speculate about how much more conformity might have been observed had the participants been friends (a peer group), rather than strangers, and whether a high level of conformity to peer pressure characterises much human behaviour.

In the second experiment of interest Milgram (1974) inserted an advertisement in a New Haven, Connecticut paper, inviting the public (especially mentioned were factory workers, businessmen, construction workers etc.) to participate in a 1-hour project involving memory and learning. The participants were paid a fee on entry and told that the money was now theirs, no matter what. Two participants and an instructor were ostensibly involved in each experiment. The 2 participants would draw lots and one was allocated the task of teaching the other (the subject) a set of word pairs. The learner was taken to a room where he was strapped to a chair, to prevent movement. The teacher was taken to another room (a glass partition separated the 2 rooms in the main version of the experiment). In the latter room, there was an electric shock generator with 30 level-type switches. Under each switch (they went up in units of 15 volts, from 15 to 450 volts) was a label with the higher voltages, having the words strong *shock, danger: severe shock* and, after 400 volts, just red Xs.

The teacher was told that the aim of the experiment was to assess the impact of punishment on learning. Consequently, every time the subject made an error, he was to receive a shock, with 15-volt increments for every error until he received 450 volts. In the key experiment the subject appeared to make frequent errors and, when shocked, responded loudly, yelling, screaming and, at 150 volts, refusing to continue in the experiment. The subject-learner was a stooge in the pay of the researchers; there were no shocks and the aim of the experiment was to determine the extent to which an average member of the community was prepared to obey an instruction to harm or hurt another person.

In the situation described above, 16 of 40 'teachers' administered shocks all the way to 450 volts. In another version of the experiment, where the subject could be heard but not seen, 25 'teachers' administered the maximum possible shock. When the subject could be neither seen nor heard, all 40 teachers administered 300 volts and, of these, 26 went all the way to 450 volts. In another version of the experiment where the 'teacher' was in the same room and had to arm-wrestle the victim's hand on to the electric pad, 12 of 40 participants administered the maximum shock. The final version of the experiment, of particular interest, involved a variation where the 'teacher' read out the words and a third party pulled the lever to administer the shock, the subject becoming a small part of the task. In this latter case 37 of 40 people continued to 450 volts. (The study was also carried out in Germany, with the finding that Germans were no more or less obedient than Americans.)

This study raises some important questions which are relevant to the normative view of socialisation, and which warrant discussion. The 'teachers' in the above experiment appeared to be prepared to follow orders, despite the fact that these were given by strangers and that they could leave the experiment with their money and without fear of harm to themselves. Given that we generally receive our 'orders' from people with whom we have a relationship, what is our own level of conformity?

The 'teachers' in the above experiment appeared to fear how they would be perceived if they did not obey. Presumably the fear of embarrassment was greater than the discomfort created by administering a severe electric shock to an apparently innocent and unwilling (but powerless) subject.

While there is a body of observational, survey and experimental data which suggests that much human behaviour involves a level of conformity or obedience, it is important to also consider some contrary evidence. Firstly, it is clear that behaviours of both individuals and groups change over time, sometimes over relatively short periods. Thus, in the last fifty years, the nature of work and leisure have changed greatly (see Hill, Chapter 9), as has the structure of the family in Western industrial societies (see Edgar, Chapter 14). Such levels of change would not be possible if those who subscribe to the normative view of socialisation were completely correct. Secondly, while both Asch (1955) and Milgram (1974) identified a level of conformity or obedience, they also found experimental subjects who appeared to choose not to obey, though one might argue that these latter people may have been conforming to other influences. This raises the third reservation that, in the real world, as distinct from the findings of laboratory-type experiments, people are exposed to a wide variety of influences, many of which will conflict in whole or part. Behaviour consistent with one influence necessarily leads to the disregard of another.

The second approach to understanding socialisation, deals more specifically with the process itself and the manner in which the socialisation process transforms the self. This interactionist view begins by noting that socialisation is a lifelong process. As adults move either geographically or through time (i.e. they age), and they are exposed to a changing variety of factors which, to a greater or lesser extent, contribute to their personal qualities. Further, interaction is a two-way process, and even in the example of a child where the parent is largely in control, the child's behaviour can influence the parents' subsequent actions. As parents seek to control their infants, so it is possible to observe these infants experimenting with a variety of actions (sulking, bargaining, shows of temper) which appear to have the aim of influencing the parent.

Studies of the process of socialisation tend to focus upon communication at both the verbal and non-verbal level. Indeed some studies now suggest that non-verbal communication conveys the majority of information. Non-verbal communication includes physical proximity, facial expression, posture, voice tone, rate of speech and body position. Non-verbal communication has received considerable mass media attention, and been popularised under the heading of body language.

The subtlety of this communication process is exemplified by a study of the impact of one involuntary response, the size of the pupils of the eye (Hess 1975). In this study a group of subjects was shown two photographs of a woman. The pictures were identical except that the woman's pupils were larger in one picture than the other. The group were then asked to report in which of the two photographs the woman appeared more sympathetic, happy, warm and attractive. There was a tendency for the group to attribute more positive qualities to the woman with the larger pupils.

These studies reinforce the early observations of Charles Horton Cooley (1964) and George Herbert Mead (1934, 1964) who suggested that we are continually 'reading' the cues of the persons with whom we interact. As a result of these real or imagined reactions of others to us, we build an image of who we are and where we fit into the total human mosaic. It is this image which then determines how we react to, and interact with, others, and they in turn, relate to us.

This process goes some way to explaining why Edgar (1980: 162) found, in research on Australian school children, that girls had a lower estimate of their competence than boys. He argues (1980: 140) that:

> If our experience ... shows us to be members of a competent, respected, successful group with some status in society, then we are likely to approach life confident ... if our parents are poor, of low status and exercise little control in the wider scheme of things, our horizons will be limited, our self-image will be less confident, our scope for initiatives more constrained.

The interactionist view of socialisation points to the importance of the ongoing nature of the socialisation process, the reciprocal effects of communication and interaction, the creation of a perception of self and the subtle, often unwanted and unplanned consequences of this process.

Which view of socialisation has greater credibility? The normative view suggests that we become what those who are important to us make of us. The interactionist view, contrarily, argues that we make society in the process of being made by it. The answer to this question is clearly that each approach adds to our understanding of society, and that the utility of each will vary depending upon the specific circumstances/situations we wish to explain. We are made, to some extent, in the image of an existing social structure, but in the process we have the capacity to influence and change that structure.

Further, behaviour change may result from technological changes which may physically transform human societies. As examples, the motor car increased mobility and ultimately contributed to the decline in the extended family; the contraceptive pill influenced sexual practices and ultimately altered the nature of marriage.

Accordingly, we may conclude that we are socialised by the agents of socialisation, but that this process varies somewhat from individual to individual and from one historical period to another. At the same time we react to, and influence, those around us. The society which results is then a product of many forces, some acting in concert, some in competition, some deliberately, some unintentionally. We become, nevertheless, the sum total of these experiences and interactions.

Conclusion

This chapter began by identifying the subject matter of sociology. Sociology, it has been argued, seeks to understand how society comes to be as it is, and how it changes. Sociological explanations of behaviour begin with the axiom that human behaviours are (partly) determined by one's location within a social structural setting. One's social structural position is important primarily because it reflects both the content and the manner in which one is socialised.

Sociology should not be (some would say cannot be) an abstract and impersonal science. Sociology is intimately concerned with how we come to be as we are. In accounting for the behaviour of those in society, it provides an interpretation which we may compare with our own experiences. Ultimately it is for the student of sociology to weigh the evidence and to make an informed judgement about the validity of the explanations which sociology offers.

Sociology has the capacity to influence individuals by altering their perceptions of themselves. It has demonstrated a capacity to transform the structure of society by providing pertinent data and insightful analyses (e.g. the move for Affirmative Action comes partly from sociological research and analysis).

Above all, three qualities are required of the successful student of sociology. The first is a scepticism, a willingness to question the evidence of supposed authorities and one's own senses. The second is a receptiveness to a wide variety of sometimes apparently extraordinary and diverse ideas. This means reading widely, and considering as much of the pertinent data as possible. Thirdly, an interest in the world as it is frequently perceived by the underclass in society, those who usually have no voice, is required. This is the humanistic dimension of sociology which is inextricably related to the sociologist's interest in social, political and economic inequalities, and their possible elimination.

Of course, many relevant issues have been left undiscussed (e.g. questions of the exercise of power, the extent to which the social system in which we live services the interests of some but not others and the extent to which the institutions of society are essentially conservative and perpetuate inequalities which already exist), but these are addressed in the chapters which follow.

References

Albury, R.M., Chaples, E.A. and Stubbs, K. (1977) 'Sexism Among a Group of Sydney Tertiary Students', *ANZJS* 13 (2): 133–36.
Asch, S.E. (1955) 'Opinions and Social Pressure' *Scientific American*, November.
Baldridge, J.V. (1975) *Sociology*. New York: John Wiley and Sons.
Barry, H., Bacon, M.K. and Child, I.L. (1973) 'A Cross-Cultural Survey of Some Sex Differences in Socialization' in S. Scarr-Salapatek and P. Salapatek (eds) *Socialization*. Columbus, Ohio: Charles E. Merrill.
Bottomley, M. and Sampson, S. (1977) 'The Case of the Female Principal: Sex Role Attitudes and Perceptions of Sex Differences in Ability', *ANZJS* 13 (2): 137–40.
Cooley, C.H. (1964) *Human Nature and the Social Order*. New York: Schocken Books.
Currie, J. (1982) 'The Sex Factors in Occupational Choice', *ANZJS* 18 (2): 180–95.
Denisoff, R.S. and Wahrman, R. (1975) *An Introduction to Sociology*. New York: Free Press.
Douglas, J.D. (ed.) (1973) *An Introduction to Sociology*. New York: Free Press.
Edgar, D. (1980) *Introduction to Australian Society*. Sydney: Prentice-Hall.
Hess, E.H. (1975) 'The Role of Pupil Size in Communication', *Scientific American* 110–19.
Homans, G.C. (1970) 'A Life of Synthesis' in I.C. Horowitz *Sociological Self-Images*. Oxford: Pergamon Press.
———(1986) 'Fifty Years of Sociology,' *Annual Review of Sociology* 12 (XIII–XXX). Annual Reviews Inc., Palo Alto, California.

Edwards, J. (1984) 'Raelene, Marjorie and Betty', *The Australian Mathematics Teacher* 40 (2): 11–13.

Gareau, F.H. (1985) 'The Multinational Version of Social Science', *Current Sociology* 33 (3): 169.

Household Expenditure Survey Australia 1984 (1986) Canberra: Australian Bureau of Statistics.

Lodahl, J.B. and Gordon, G (1972) 'The Structure of Scientific Fields and the Functioning of University Graduate Departments', *American Sociological Review* 37 (1): 57–72.

McMichael, A.J. (1985) 'Social Class (As Estimated by Occupational Prestige) and Mortality in Australian Males in the 1970s', *Community Health Studies* 9 (3): 220–30.

Mead, G.H. (1934) *Mind, Self and Society*. Chicago: University of Chicago Press.

———(1964) *On Social Psychology*. Chicago: University of Chicago Press.

Milgram, S. (1974) *Obedience to Authority*. London: Tavistock.

Musgrave, P.W. (1984) 'The Moral Values of some Australian Adolescents: A Report and Discussion', *ANZJS* 20 (2): 197–217.

Retherford, R.D. (1975) *The Changing Sex Differential in Mortality*. Westpoint, Connecticut: Greenwood Press.

Rosenthal, R. and Jacobson, L.F. (1968) 'Teacher Expectations for the Disadvantaged', *Scientific American*, April.

Sargent, M. (1983) *Sociology for Australians*. Melbourne: Longman Cheshire.

Scarr, S. and Weinberg, R.A. (1976) 'IQ Test Performance of Black Children Adopted by White Families', *American Psychologist* 31, October: 726–39.

Siskind, V., Najman, J.M. and Copeman, R. (1987) 'Infant Mortality in Socio-economically Advantaged and Disadvantaged Areas in Brisbane', *Community Health Studies*, xi (1): 24–30.

Sites, P. (1975) *Control and Constraint*. New York: Macmillan.

Taylor, R. *et al.* (1983). *Occupation and Mortality in Australian Working Age Males, 1975–77*. Melbourne: Health Commission of Victoria and Department of Social and Preventive Medicine, Monash University.

Williams, J.E. and Best, D.L. (1982) *Measuring Sex Stereotypes*. Beverly Hills: Sage.

Chapter Two

State and Polity

Michael Pusey

> An intellectual sea change is under way in comparative social
> science ... A diverse set of scholars with wide-ranging substantive
> concerns has begun to place the state, viewed as an institution and
> social actor, at the centre of attention.
>
> (Evans *et al.* 1985: 347)

Australia is an English-speaking federation made up of former
British colonies, and now a nation that is firmly set within the
cultural, economic and political sphere of influence of the United
States. Given also that most Australian sociologists and political
scientists were trained, if not in Australia, then almost certainly in
the United States and/or the United Kingdom, we should not be in
the least surprised that British and American intellectual traditions
and tastes have influenced, and even fixed, the priorities for
research in many areas of Australian studies.

It is for this reason, among others, that Australians have, quite
inappropriately and at some cost to our own self-understanding,
grown used to looking at the Australian polity and State from
perspectives that come to us from two nations in which the State
has, *comparatively speaking*, had a smaller historical, cultural, and
intellectual importance. The United Kingdom is a very old nation
and a nation with a territory, a people, and a monarchical and
parliamentary government, which predates the modern State by
some several centuries. Although the United States was the 'first
new nation' (Lipset 1963)[1] it is old by comparison with Australia.
The United States was founded in a political and intellectual
setting that was profoundly hostile to the modern State as it is
understood today in the wider community of nations, and these
deeply rooted attitudes remain part of the American political and
intellectual consciousness to the present day. Although Australia
shares a common inheritance with the United States and the
United Kingdom, the differences between these and the Australian
State are at least as important as the similarities. What follows
below is an outline, in a comparative and historical perspective, of

the essential characteristics of the Australian State in a way that will stress the important and much neglected differences rather than the commonalities. But first some basic definitions and qualifications are necessary.

There is no definitive way of drawing the line between polity, society, economy and State: each term refers to something basic and throws the other into sharper view. Another difficulty is that usage varies according to whether the author travels on a British, American or continental European passport – and whether he or she is a political scientist or a sociologist. Yet, despite the difficulties, the concept of 'the State' is the only one that satisfactorily gathers up the military, the police, the constitution, and more importantly, the government, the bureaucracy and the legislature, and joins them all into a single entity. The relation of the State so defined with the other categories of 'society', 'polity' and 'economy' raises absolutely basic theoretical assumptions and problems that cannot be dealt with here. A few further points of definition and perspective must suffice.

'Society' is clearly the most general and basic term: neither 'the economy' nor 'the State' fall ready made from the sky into history; nor do they obediently obey and supposedly independent laws of economic or political behaviour. As sociologists and historians must insist, State and economy are both socially constructed and situated in the history of particular nations. Since any discussion of the State raises clashes between Weberian, Marxist, and pluralist assumptions, I should add that my perspective makes the basic, and I think widely-shared assumptions, that in every capitalist society there is a structurally given three-cornered competition among three actors for the wealth and Gross National Product of the nation: the first, and usually the strongest, actor is capital (which is shorthand for 'business interests', 'free enterprise' or 'the private sector'); the second is labour (which for most purposes simply means wage and salary earners), and the third is 'the State' – to avoid confusion I shall spell 'State' with a capital 'S' when the term is being used in the general sense above to refer inclusively to government, legislature and bureaucracy and I shall use it with a small case to refer to the states – of Victoria and Tasmania etc. – in the Australian federation. There is a mutually constitutive though unequal relationship between State, capital and labour. This means among other things that the boundaries between them are never fixed and that, for example, the State through industrial and arbitration legislation and other means, structures and defines the relationship between capital and labour.

In what follows the State is not treated, as it is in many Marxist perspectives, as a simple extension of the power of capital: on the contrary, the State is such a fascinating area for study precisely because it has some 'relative autonomy'[2] from those who own the nation's productive resources. In other words the causal arrows between economy and State run in both directions: they shape each other and the same is true of the relationship between State and polity. The State is of course shaped by polity and politics but so also are politics and the polity conditioned by the particular features of the State. 'Polity' is the general term we use to refer to all political expression and to political norms and attitudes that are manifest in that part of society usually called 'civil society' because it lies outside the formal structures of the State (the constitution, the government, and the bureaucracy). Many of these meanings are manifest in everyday usage. For example, when members of the business community rail against 'state intervention' they are usually referring not simply to a specific law but to a whole complex of political, legal, and economic actions and structures of the State that impinge directly and indirectly on the economy. Similarly, the distinction between civil society and the State is made in practice all the time by those people who want to protect 'civil liberties' from 'intrusions by the State'.

Birthmarks: the Legacy of Foundation

Australia, like the United States, developed in its own territory from early British colonial settlements. Similarly it was also geographically far removed from continental Europe and from the various struggles for emancipation from old aristocracies which so deeply marked the political constitution and temper of such continental European nations as France, Germany and Italy. The great difference is that the two settlements were separated in time by some one hundred and fifty years. America was 'born liberal' in the sense that its political institutions crystallised the liberal creeds which its early settlers took from England in the second half of the seventeenth and the eighteenth centuries. The American settlers defined themselves above all as individuals who were, according to John Locke and other notable English liberals of the period, endowed by God with natural rights to 'the enjoyment of life, liberty and property'. Government was only a contrivance, almost a necessary evil, or perhaps at best 'a subordinate practical convenience' (Held *et al.* 1983: 13), but certainly not a focus of value in itself. The purpose of political life is purely to secure 'the conditions for freedom so that the *private* ends of individuals might be met in civil society (Held *et al.* 1983: 13). This was the creed of a middle class, with its back turned against the despotism of an old monarchy, and bent now on prosperity and individual enterprise freed from unwanted interference and restraint; bent 'on the enjoyment of property' (which Locke defined very broadly). This creed, and the political norms and structures which it legitimated, solidified *before* the industrial revolution and amid a population in which as many as four-fifths of the people who worked were owners of their own means of livelihood (Mayer 1964). These people, property owners and small entrepreneurs, living in a bountiful land before the era of the factory, quickly rationalised the inequalities that they themselves would create with a pseudo-egalitarian doctrine of equality of opportunity (Badie and Birnbaum 1964: 203–10) – some might rise like Horatio Alger, from 'rags to riches' but, no matter how extreme the differences between rich and poor, all are equal in as much as they begin with an equal chance – (which they never do!) One need only add the religious premiss that God chooses only those who are worthy, to find the rudiments of what Hofstadter (1963) called the 'evangelical egalitarianism' of the American charter myth.

The contrasts with Australia are quite striking. Australia's early settlers were for the most part the victims of the industrial revolution and of the ugliest period of militant British capitalism. They are described (McNaughtan 1955: 103) as 'the outpourings of the unions and poor houses of the United Kingdom', and it is clear, as Rosecrance (1964: 280) puts it, that they 'were largely a homogenous group of city folk of humble economic and social origins'.

These people were about as far estranged from the liberal American ideal of the intimate self-governing community as any English-speaking population ever could be. Whether convict or free settler, from the day of arrival their political experience was typically of a gubernatorial military government in a penal colony, and hence of a State that was, from its first moments, very much a 'strong state'.[3]

There are several features of this early formative period of Australian history, dating from the full development of the penal system in the 1820s to the depression of the 1890s, which shaped the ethos and the structures of the Australian State.

Firstly, the Aborigines were quickly overwhelmed and pushed out of white Australian history and consciousness. Because they were largely nomadic hunter-gatherers who had not 'mixed their labour with the land' in a way that Europeans of the time could recognise as 'productive', they were judged to be completely uncivilised and without legal rights to their land. The continent had been declared a *terra nullis*, in effect a vacant land, and there was therefore no legal or cultural foundation to secure a place for the Aboriginal in the political and institutional history of the white population. The point of these remarks is obvious: foundation institutionalised a basic 'structural inequality'. At the same time it estranged the white population from the cultural and historical universe of the original inhabitants and deepened their sense of geographical isolation and general vulnerability.

Secondly, with the exception of South Australia, all the Australian states began as penal colonies. Just under 200,000 convicts were brought to Australia before transportation to the eastern states was abandoned in 1850. This would have its effects on the character of the colonial states in a number of ways.

> The indiscriminate use of the lash undermined the essential belief in the possibility of just authority. More than this, the attempt to reproduce in Australia a social hierarchy in which the legal code could achieve the more general significance it possessed in England was doomed to failure.
>
> (MacIntyre 1985: 14)

Moreover, the hopes for decent self-government of the freed convicts, of 'the emancipists' as they were called, and of the greatly increased population of free settlers who had come with the gold rushes of the 1850s, were clearly irreconcilable with repressive laws and the military disciplines of penal colonialism. The consequence was that,

> legal and political disabilities were the overriding concern of the reformers, overshadowing all other complaints ... The Australian radicals of the 1840s and 1850s were so preoccupied with political issues, so steeped in the doctrines of liberalism and constitutional democracy, that they came to look upon the state as an instrument of popular sovereignty
>
> (MacIntyre 1985: 18)

In short, the brutality and human degradation of the convict system destroyed the legitimacy of the old order and made new structures of government a pre-condition for independence. And, perhaps most importantly, this experience focused all attention on *political* reform and the benefits of a reformed – and still strong – State.

Thirdly, just as American settlers defined themselves with political aspirations that were progressive in their own time, so the early white Australians, and certainly the rump of poor free settlers who followed the convicts from the 1830s to the gold rushes of the 1850s, brought with them the Chartist demands for political reform of the capitalist economic and social order of their time. The Chartist movement, so named after the People's Charter published in London in May 1838, embodied the resentments of the working class against the Corn Laws, the Poor Laws of 1834, the long factory working hours and the tenuous legality of trade unions. It demanded universal male suffrage, equal electoral districts, ballot voting, the payment of members of parliament and the abolition of property qualifications for membership of parliament. In 1842 these demands were put in a second petition – with 3,000,000 signatures – to a parliament which ignored it, defeated the movement and banished many of its leaders to Australia. Nearly all the demands were won in Australia only a decade later.

Although Chartism was for the most part not a revolutionary movement, it was driven by deep resentment of both the privileges of the British aristocracy and the terrible *social* inequalities of the Industrial Revolution. The Chartists did not succeed in making Australia a haven of popular socialism but, on the other hand, their bitter experience of *laissez-faire* capitalism and of the ugliest side of 'private enterprise' has contributed to the birth of an Australian State that was,

> born modern ... in the sense that ... Australians believed that the state, far from encroaching upon individual rights would be the most likely protector of rights against other agencies of social coercion. Unlike the doctrinaire liberals of Europe, Australians believed that the major constraints on individual liberty were not public, but private.[4]

The point is that, at least for these reformists, and for the working class of the time, *laissez-faire* capitalism had already lost its legitimacy. 'Economic development' was not an end in itself and would not of itself overcome the bitterly resented social inequalities.

Fourthly, and of equal importance, is the intellectual and political complexion of the next generation of reformists from the 1850s to Federation in 1900. There is no doubt that the radical voices of the two preceding decades from the 1830s to the gold rushes of 1850s were inspired by the Chartists. But what has been missed in the 'romantic socialist' view of this early history is that the more radical and popular socialist demands of the time (for social justice and for the equitable apportionment of the land) were first mediated and then largely subsumed into the prevailing liberalism of an increasingly influential class of successful emancipists, liberal merchants and, especially, lawyers and other professional people who would take an ever-stronger role in the articulation of popular demands, first for self-government in the 1850s and then in leading the movement for the creation of a new federation.

These Australians were secular, pragmatic and utilitarian. The traditional and religious metaphysical shroudings had disappeared with the break with the old world, and the political ideology which found institutional expression through these reformers was strongly coloured by the utilitarian liberalism of Jeremy Bentham (Collins 1985). The anti-intellectualism of Australian political ideology originates at least in part from an ethical and intellectual scepticism that is anti-utopian and that, in Bentham's words, shuns 'the perplexity of ambiguous and sophistical discourse that, while it distracts and eludes the apprehension, stimulates and inflames the passions'.

The more important consequence may be that this pragmatic, utilitarian and materialist strain of liberalism cast the State more as a neutral instrument for the efficient organisation of the economic, political and legal-administrative structures of society. It would easily allow the more limited ideal of fair political representation to replace the quest for social justice. Put more bluntly it would not be unfriendly to modern capitalism in as much as it helped to steer the political and institutional reforms leading to Federation into a course that would allow labour and land to be more easily treated as commodities.

State and Economy

Liberalism is every bit as slippery a notion as any other 'ism'. Indeed Tim Rowse (1978: 41–42) rightly insists that liberalism is a 'psychologically promiscuous', 'protean and flexible' doctrine that can be invoked 'to defend a wide range of political arrangements'. Liberal principles are of course always invoked either to justify or to defend every change in the relationship between State, capital and labour.

Yet, the relationship between State and capital does have an underlying pattern and here the German political scientist Claus Offe provides a convenient way of describing the constraints and requirements which the private sector normally imposes on the State in what are commonly known today as liberal capitalist societies. According to Offe's (1975) descriptive model these constraints and requirements are summarised in four 'principles' which he identifies as: 'exclusion', 'maintenance', 'dependence' and 'legitimation'. 'Exclusion' means simply that the 'State has no authority to control production or to make private investment decisions, because in a 'free enterprise' = capitalist economy production must be 'free' and this means that the State is *excluded* from control of private capital. The second distinguishing characteristic of the State, especially in modern, 'developed', 'late-capitalist' societies, is that it has to *maintain*, support and protect, the capital accumulation process (with state financed or provided education, transport, communications, electricity, land and labour etc.). The third principle is dependency: the State is *dependent* on the taxes which must be levied directly (e.g. company tax, payroll tax), and indirectly (e.g. income and sales taxes), from the capital accumulation process of a private economy that it cannot command but 'must' maintain. And, fourthly, the State 'must' *legitimate* itself *and* its relation with private interests by either hiding or justifying its role and its decisions in a way that is adequate to sustain mass popular support for both State *and capital*.

Although these 'principles'[5] describe present-day realities, they can usefully be kept in the background of our following discussion as a way of clarifying some of the distinctive features of the Australian State from the 1840s to the present.

While Britain in the time of Gladstonian liberalism was coming to the peak of its industrial and commercial power in the last quarter of the nineteenth century, Australia was comprised of six fledgling colonies in which the institutions and role of the State were developing their own form in the very different social and political conditions of the colonies of the period. In as much as the British State was involved in the maintenance of capital accumulation, the involvement was largely indirect: domestically the coercive apparatus of the State – the courts and the police – were deployed both to repress the social unrest produced by the industrial revolution and to discipline the labour force. Externally its great imperial military power was used to protect British possessions, markets, sea lanes and trading interests overseas. Within its own territory Britain was, as the comparative literature (Nettl 1968: 574, 577, 582; Evans *et al.* 1985) insists, still the liberal 'stateless' society *par excellence* – the same was, and still is, true of the United States. Capital alone was the great engine and structuring force in society. The relationship between capital and the State summarised in Offe's four principles is above all a description of this British and American model of liberal capitalism.

In the colonies everything was different. Capitalism of a particular rural/pastoral form had preceded industrialisation. In contrast with the American frontier the Australian hinterland was suited to grazing rather than to small farming. Vast holdings of grazing land were taken up by squatters and graziers who were interested only in amassing personal wealth – mostly they had no care for the future of the colonies, with which they did not identify, because most of them intended to leave when their pockets were full (Rosecrance 1964: 289). Their monopoly over the land together with an insatiable demand for wool from the textile mills of northern England had produced a rural 'staples economy'[6] centred on the production of wool. In contrast with the American frontier the Australian frontier produced a 'rural proletariat' of 'shepherds, boundary riders and shearers'. Although the first Australian capitalists, the squatter 'Wool Kings', would fight strongly to protect their own interests, they were successfully opposed by a working class with vivid memories of the miseries they had left behind them and by a growing reformist middle class of emancipists, merchants and professional people. These people were determined that a journey halfway round the globe must lead to something more than a leap from the frying pan to the fire.

> Accordingly they would harbour little good will for the squatter; for here, after all, were the English industrialists and the perpetrators of the Corn Laws rolled into one. If economic liberalism was not fully adequate as a social gospel, how much less tolerable would be the creation of a class which reeked of landed privilege? Indeed, many Australians qua Britons had had to fight the *ancien regime* before they arrived in Sydney; they were scarcely likely to put up with an Australian version of the old enemy.
>
> (Rosecrance 1964: 287)

Without 'state intervention' Australia would be destined to develop rather as a poor Third World 'comprador' economy,[7] entirely dependent on cash crops and with a State designed only to maintain whatever measure of repression its foreign sponsors would demand. With a form of State-led capitalism, and with State intervention on a scale that was unthinkable in Britain itself, the colonies would develop on a broader base that might accommodate the aspirations of a larger population whose voice was somehow heard in London by a relatively enlightened Colonial Office that had learned something from the errors of its own heavy-handed responses to earlier popular demands in the United States and in Canada. By the 1860s most of the Chartist demands were won and the colonies had universal male suffrage and popularly elected semi-independent governments which severely curbed the political power of large landholders.

The government was *not excluded* from the private economy but rather joined with it in a relationship of strong partnership which, in the last decade of the nineteenth century, had secured for Australians the highest per capita incomes in the world and set a pattern of relationship between state, polity and economy that would shape the federation and its future for many decades to come. As Butlin puts it,

> Traditionally, Australian colonial government during the second half of the nineteenth century performed what was, in effect, a *general management role* in their economies. In its essence, 'colonial socialism' entailed *direct action* by governments to attract foreign (British) resources of capital and labour, through public borrowing overseas and large-scale programmes of publicly-assisted migration; the investment of British capital in publicly-owned taxed assets in Australia; the concentration of this investment in public business undertakings, primarily in transport and communications; and the delivery of market services by these public enterprises.
>
> (Butlin *et al*. 1892: 320)

State investments in the economy were roughly equal to those of the private sector until the 1930s.

And so, clearly, in the *formative period* of modern Australia up until as late as the 1930s, the pattern of relationships between State and capital defies the ordinary 'principles' of liberal capitalism proposed in the Offe model. The underlying reality is still that Australia was a relatively small, economically dependent nation locked into the larger world economy by its still semi-colonial economic dependence upon the markets and capital resources of the United Kingdom. Yet the sheer scale of government involvement in the Australian economy contradicts the liberal principles. The State could not be excluded from private investment decisions because local capital and manufacturing interests were so dependent upon it: in so many vital areas such as railways, port construction and the like, the State *led* and capital *followed* (in America it was typically the other way around). The purpose of state action was not to compete with the private economy and certainly not to build a parallel state economy on socialist or other principles. Instead, the intention was clearly to attract and support the private economy by providing the missing infrastructure for development. Yet the scale of state investment, together with the historical context in which it had developed, institutionalised a measure of state authority in economic matters that looked more like equal co-sponsorship of production than the subordinate maintenance function of the normal liberal capitalist pattern.

There are four fairly constant factors which seem to explain much of what is most important in the relations between State and economy in Australia from its foundation to the present day. Firstly Australia and its economy have always been dependent and vulnerable. The vulnerability is accentuated by a simultaneous dependence on favourable conditions for specialised pastoral/

farm products and raw materials *exports* and, on the other hand, a need to spend large proportions of foreign earnings to pay for imported manufactured goods. To this day Australia remains a trading nation with only a small population and a correspondingly small market for its own manufacturing industries, one that is heavily dependent on the vicissitudes of commodity markets and of a world economy that is always entirely beyond its control. Secondly, in its relations with both State and labour, capital in Australia has always been divided. On one side there were the large producers and collectors of raw materials for the overseas markets – mining, pastoral and shipping companies – that are generally capital-intensive rather than labour-intensive, and usually dependent on swings in demand and price in their foreign markets. On the other side of capital in Australia are the local domestic manufacturing and service industries whose interests are governed much more by wage costs and the threat of competing imported products.[8] Thirdly, there has always been economic rivalry among the states along with basic differences over economic policy. The form of the federation, and especially of its industrial and tariff powers were influenced by long-standing conflicts between Victorian interests that were, and to some extent still remain to this day, more protectionist; on the other hand, New South Wales has traditionally favoured more free market/low tariff policies. Fourthly, industrialisation in Australia was a relatively late phenomenon occurring mainly in the early to middle decades of this century, and so at a time when labour had already achieved strong political representation and considerable defensive strength (Connell and Irving 1980: 279).

The interplay of these factors, set against the legacy of foundation, provide some broad historically contextualised specifications of what is distinctive about the Australian State and its relation to the economy.

Immigration
The first white Australians were brought to Botany Bay and Risdon Cove on 'assisted passages' of a very particular kind. In stark contrast with the larger established nations of Europe, immigration had, from the first white settlements of Australia, remained a centrally important function of the State. Immigration policies have reflected Australia's cultural identifications and the fears – so clearly manifested in the pre-war White Australia Policy – of a dependent nation with a vast territory. State-sponsored immigration produced the ethnic homogeneity of the white foundation population as well as the social and political cleavages that

were to shape the nation and the later federation. Immigration
policies have continued to shape the ethnic, social, cultural and
political characteristics and disposition of the population. They
have also affected foreign policy, and, although opinions differ as
to whether immigration policies have on balance weakened or
strengthened labour in Australia, it is clear that they have always
had an importance (whether in threat or action) as a potential instrument for reducing wage costs by increasing the supply of cheap
labour from abroad. The wider economic importance of immigration policies is well underlined by Butlin in the following terms;

> The acquisition of foreign capital through government action was a
> correlative of this population aim: to combine increasing inputs of
> overseas capital and migrant labour with domestic natural resources
> in order to establish the conditions for enlarged foreign trade and
> domestic activity.
>
> (Butlin 1983: 83)

Tariff Protection

Australia's economically dependent situation within the world
economy produced deeply-engrained conflicts of interests between
large, and mainly foreign-owned, enterprises and the domestic
manufacturing sector. 'Big' (foreign-owned) capital trading and
production interests have always pressed for low tariff protection
and low exchange rates. Domestic capital, on the other hand, has a
common interest with labour in pressing for high tariff barriers to
protect local industry from foreign competition. The State was
therefore cast into the role of arbiter and broker in a triangle of
conflict between these two sections of capital and labour. The
complexity of these conflicts was further complicated after Federation by continued competition between the states for capital
investment. The role of the State, and more especially of the new
federal State, was in this respect reconstituted and vividly demonstrated in the famous Harvester Judgment of 1907 in which the
Federal Arbitration Court under Mr Justice Higgins enforced the
requirement that, under the laws of the 'New Protection' policy,
'fair and reasonable wages' must be paid to the workers of the
Harvester Company as a condition for tariff protection (MacIntyre
1983: 106–10).[9] This was a classical example of the way these
conflicts have given the State the leeway to play the actors off
against each other and thus extract concessions that would otherwise be unobtainable: in short they have given added strength to
the Australian State and enhanced its relative autonomy.

Industrial Arbitration and Wage Fixation

The maritime strike of the 1890s and the armed clashes involving police and militia in 1891, 1892 and 1894 ended in the defeat of the waterside workers, miners, transport industry workers, and some 20,000 shearers who had all joined the strike. On the face of it the defeat was an important gain for the large early 'pre-industrial' pastoral, mining and transport capital interests, which were bent on driving down wage levels by employing non-union labour at lower and lower rates. But this was a Pyrrhic victory and, in the longer perspective, really a defeat, because it led to a consolidation of labour's political and parliamentary strength, gave impetus to the development of wage fixing and arbitration legislation in the colonial states; influenced the terms on which industrial and arbitration laws would be written into the new federation; and, perhaps most importantly, persuaded local domestic industrial interests, during the crucial formative pre-war years, that their interests lay in accepting state-determined wage levels in return for protective tariffs.

> 'New Protection' found sufficient agreement between the craft workers and their employers to outweigh the interests of capital producing for the export market and ensured industrialisation would proceed within the economic framework established by the new Commonwealth.
>
> (MacIntyre 1983: 111)

Between Federation in 1901 and World War I the primary function of state industrial arbitration (in both the Commonwealth and the states) was to protect employed union labour by raising wage standards towards judicially declared minimum levels and to encourage the general development and re-formation of union organisations and the development of federal unions (Butlin 1983: 91). Some unions would see the arbitration system as 'the legal machinery of the capitalist class as it holds the working class sheep tight while he is being shorn by the boss' (Connell and Irving 1980: 282), while some of the more aggressive employers fought it as a violation of 'freedom of contract, upon which no self-respecting employer will ever listen to discussion'. But, despite opposition, the arbitration system was in due course accepted by both sides and cemented into the structures of the Australian State. It has to the present day institutionalised, contained and to some extent pacified, conflicts between labour and capital.

This very brief sketch captures some of the defining character-istics of the relation between State and capital in Australia from foundation to the end of World War II. In terms of the modern debates that are 'bringing the state back in' (Evans *et al.* 1985) we see a strong State that has secured considerable authority and relative autonomy in its relations with capital; taken a nation-building role; led rather than followed private enterprise in national economic development and secured high living standards for the wage and salary-earning majority of its population.

In many respects this image still holds up against present-day realities and in some it is even strengthened by developments in the forty years since the war. Yet forty years is a long time in the life of a young nation and developments over this period raise serious questions about the durability of many of these classical features of relations between State and capital. During this period under predominantly conservative governments led by Menzies, Holt, Gorton, McMahon and Fraser, the Australian State provision in such areas as welfare and education declined to the point where it now looks meagre by comparison with the OECD nations such as France and the Scandinavian countries. During the long post-war boom, the wages and salaries proportion of Gross National Product fell slightly from 1948 to 1966 (*Yearbook Australia* 1968: 628). More significantly, the wages and salaries share of total income fell by approximately 7 per cent from 1975–76 to 1985–86 at a time when the income share of the corporate sector has increased (Treasury Roundup 1986: 11). In this period foreign and mainly American multi-national capital has captured large sections of the Australian economy while domestic manufacturing industries have fallen into rapid decline.

> The total of foreign capitalists' investment in Australia rose from about 500 million [pounds sterling] in the late 1940s to about $10,000 million in the early 1970s, the American share having risen to near par with the British. By then a quarter of the fifty largest companies in the country were subsidiaries of multi-national corporations; official inquiries, when finally made, reckoned that foreign capital held between a quarter and a third of the entire corporate business of the country. Japanese investment followed American in the 1960s. From being an appendage of one, Australia had graduated economically to a field for the play of forces from several of the international centres of capitalism.
>
> (Connell and Irving 1980: 294)

The short-lived Whitlam reformist Labor government demonstrated, among other things, that the State was not strong enough to nationalise anything profitable: it was defeated in attempts to nationalise industry and take control over minerals and resource production, as well as in an attempt to control prices and incomes. In the succeeding Fraser years tax minimisation and evasion schemes were protected by the government and the High Court to permit a massive shift of the total taxation burden (that is the running costs of the State) from the corporate sector to the wage and salary earners.[10] As Butlin summarises,

> legal support for monoplistic or oligopolistic structures offered by all governments contributed to this increase in private influence. From this development flowed the extension of monopolistic practices of almost every sort, with greater or less active assistance but almost always with legal permission given by the Federal and State governments.
>
> (Butlin 1983: 96)

In short the overall picture since World War II, and especially over the last decade, is of a strong assertion of capital at the expense of labour *and of the State,* and accordingly, a closer approximation to the liberal pattern of relations between capital and State in which the latter is increasingly excluded from the effective planning and direction of capital investments and at the same time committed to deploying an increasing share of the State's resources for their maintenance and legitimation without regard for the longer-term national interest. The pattern is nowhere better exemplified than in the manner in which BHP, Australia's largest company, extracted massive capital support from several governments to subsidise the Whyalla steel works. This way of converting public resources into private returns to shareholders is what Szelenyi (1980) calls, with only a little exaggeration, 'the state mode of production'.

The Federal Structure and Bureaucracy in Australia

A comparative sketch points to the distinctiveness and the complexity of State power in Australia. In one relatively 'Stateless' society, the United States, power is exerted principally on the one hand, through a political process of patronage and bargaining between central and local levels, and on the other hand by the courts which dominate almost every aspect of State administration. Sovereignty in the United States[11] is quintessentially embodied in the law and especially in the Constitution and the Supreme Court which together massively overshadow the importance of their equivalents in Australia. In the United States the law is, at least in social matters, the enabling vehicle and focus for most significant changes, and certainly those that raise explicit conflicts of interest. The law, the Constitution, and the Supreme Court are the guarantors of 'individual rights' and together they form a legal structure with an authority that towers over the other sectors of the State including, in many respects, the federal government itself, which Americans curiously perceive as a rather distant, abstract, and almost foreign entity to which newspaper articles refer in such phrases as 'the Dispute between City Hall and the United States'. In the United Kingdom, in which there is of course a monarchy, no written constitution, and a much more inward-looking legal system, it is Her Majesty's elected government which is the focus of State power. In France, traditionally the model of the 'strong' State, sovereign power is concentrated in a much more integrated State apparatus, that Birnbaum (1977) describes as 'la République des Fonctionnaires': in France both the law and the elected government – no matter whether of de Gaulle or of Mitterand – are perceived as emanations of a State dominated by its centralised, elaborate and highly professionalised bureaucratic apparatus. (In French 'l'Etat' (the State) is significantly *always* written with a capital 'E'!)

Against this background we see some of the more obvious aspects of the Australian case. Like the United States, Australia is a federation. But it's a federation in which, at least since the 1930s and 1940s, the central, federal government and administration have a far greater importance. In as much as the law and the Constitution overshadow administration in the United States, the reverse is true in Australia. The most obvious contrast with the United Kingdom is of course that Australia is a federation with a constitution. The similarity is that, under the Westminister system, in the United Kingdom as in Australia, the elected party is subject to a strict discipline of government and Cabinet, a system that has marginalised the ordinary elected member of Parliament and concentrated interest group representation at the doors of ministers and senior officials. Yet in Australia the bureaucracy is far more conspicuous than in the United Kingdom and more readily accepted as a strong centre of legitimate state power: in this, as in many other respects, Australia is again closer to France and to the other states of continental Europe. Certainly one of the distinctive features of the Australian case is that it combines a federal structure with a comparatively strong State, and one in which bureaucracy and administration have a distinctive character. It is these two distinguishing aspects of the Australian State, its federal structure and its reliance on bureaucracy, that we should now examine more closely.

The Federal Structure

The Commonwealth Constitution formally allocates some exclusive powers to the federal government. In addition to the obvious responsibilities for defence and external affairs, these exclusive powers include, in Brian Head's (1983: 7) summary, 'overseas trade, immigration; customs and excise; issuing of currency; interstate industrial arbitration; postal and other communications; corporations and aspects of banking'. Whereas the states and territories are responsible for 'the administration of most routine services as well as key areas of economic activity; they regulate or have potential power to control most aspects of industry, energy supply, prices, courts, prisons, police, mineral exploration and development, land use, environment, welfare services, consumer affairs, ports, water resources, some forms of taxation, and most aspects of criminal, civil and commercial law'. The relative size of the three levels of the State in Australia are reflected in their shares of total civilian employment and of public revenues. In 1982 the six states and the Northern Territory together employed over 65 per cent of the civilian workforce of public employees but, during the 1970s they spent about 46 per cent of total public outlays. However, the actual and potential predominance of the federal government is reflected in the fact that, since World War II, it has had a monopoly over income tax powers and now, with this power, collects over 80 per cent of all public revenues. A large proportion of this income is redistributed to the states but in the years since the war it has become ever clearer that the federal government's hold over the purse strings and its power under the Constitution to fix the terms of its grants to the states have steadily increased its financial dominance. The federal government employed 26 per cent of all public employees in 1982 and during the 1970s it spent about 48 per cent of total public outlays. Local government, the third tier in the structure, has always had a comparatively marginal importance in Australia and this shows in its meagre share of only 8 per cent of the civilian workforce and its 6 per cent of total public revenues in the 1970s (Head 1983: 7).

How does the federal structure of the Australian State mark the character of state power and the pattern of politics in Australia? We only have space to offer two comments in response to this important, but extremely complex question.

Firstly, the powers of the federal government in relation to the states have grown steadily in the eighty-six years since Federation and this great increase in its power has acted as a kind of force field which has gradually conditioned and shaped political and economic life in Australia since then. The federation was created at the turn of the century in a time when governments everywhere were very small by today's standards – in 1870 for example the British civil service totalled just over 50,000 men and women, whereas by 1970 this figure had grown by a factor of 16 to number some 800,000 employees (Aberbach *et al.* 1981: 2). And so when the Australian federation was created, it was generally assumed that it would have only a restricted role and some notables of the period 'even anticipated that the major legislative business of the new parliament would be transacted once and for all in a fairly brief period' (MacIntyre 1983: 106). This increase in the powers of the federal government was greatly accelerated during World War II, which shifted attention from the governments in the six states to a federal government charged both with emergency powers and the fateful responsibilities of defending a nation. It emerged from the war with a monopoly of income tax powers which it never relinquished to the states, and with its prestige and authority massively enhanced. Since then the increasing complexities of economic management and the acceptance of Keynesian econo-mic policies have forced the increasing centralisation of power in Canberra.

Secondly, the federal structure of the Australian State has *shaped the opposing positions and strategies of the major political parties*. In addressing this question it is important to note that the structure itself is by no means neutral. The idea of a federation originates not from socialist ideas, but on the contrary from Madison and other prominent liberal 'Federalists' who shaped the American federal constitution in 1787 and 1788. Accordingly, the Australian federal structure embodies most of the great normative principles of liberal thought; in its division of powers, in the provision of constitutionally secured 'checks and balances', in the primacy which it gives to private over public enterprise, and to the limitation of state power. Horne (1985) and others argue that the federation has an inherently conservative bias because it protects 'free trade' against competing notions of the general interest of the population and because it allows the flagrantly undemocratic practices of some of the state governments to continue behind the usually contrived excuse that the Commonwealth has no power to intervene. To this one must add a second contextual observation that, over the eighty-six years of the federation's existence, Labor governments have ruled only for some twenty-four years, in generally short and precarious terms of office in which they were either blocked by hostile senates or were governing in the shadow of war.

Yet, within this context the contrasting ways in which Labor and conservative governments have used the federal structure are fairly obvious. Labor governments have in the main been *centra-list*. Labor's centralism has been:

> ... inspired by its desire to intervene actively in the economy to promote growth, foster rising living standards and full employment, equality of opportunity, and, on occasion, a more equitable distribution of income and wealth, combined with the belief that these objectives can only be effectively achieved from the centre because this eliminates the opposition which would otherwise come from conservative state governments.
>
> (Groenwegen 1983: 188)

It is hardly surprising that non-Labor governments have, on the contrary, sought to use the federal government to thwart social reforms and any redistribution of either profits or state revenues in favour of wage and salary earners. As Greenwood noted some fifty years ago, and as Groenwegen has recently reiterated, it is therefore to be expected that the conservative preferences would be legitimated by appeals to the liberal principles embodied in the federation:

> ... the defence of state rights and federalism by conservative governments, although cloaked by the ideology that federalism is essential for the preservation of individual liberty and freedom of choice, is largely designed to put a brake on ... excessive government intervention and thereby safeguard what it calls the rights of free private enterprise ... Continuing conservative support for the institutions of federalism is also inspired by the fact that in Australia at least, they constitute real barriers against socialism, imagined or otherwise.
>
> (Groenwegen 1983: 188)

Bureaucracy

Alan Davies' (1964: 1) frequently quoted remark that 'Australians have a talent for bureaucracy' points to an essential trait of Australian society that has in various ways attracted the attention of every major historical, sociological and economic study of Australian politics and society. Encel underlines the point by listing some of the great number and variety of functions that have at various times been performed by State enterprises: they include the acquisition and export of farm products, air transport, aluminium production, bakeries, banking, brick and pipe making, broadcasting and – the list goes on – home building, insurance, meat production and distribution, port administration, shipping and shipbuilding (Encel 1970: 64). We have already noted above that public capital outlays were larger than those of the private sector until as late as 1930 (Butlin 1983: 84) and that in Australia the state has at various times taken a pioneering role in opening up new areas of development. However, the true significance of bureaucracy as a feature of the Australian State lies elsewhere and beyond considerations of its relative size or even the unusual variety of its enterprises.

As we have intimated from the beginning, the really distinctive and important feature is the relation and place which bureaucracy occupies in the total make-up of the State in Australia. What matters is the relative importance of bureaucracy *in relation to* the political processes of government, and to the other aspects of the state (the Constitution and the federal structure) as these interface with the polity. In Britain and America 'allocative'[12] conflicts (over who gets what) are normally assumed to find resolution through 'the political process'. The polity, anchored as it is in civil society, must 'speak' through its elected politicians who carry the 'the voice of the people' across some invisible boundary line between the polity and the State. It is these elected representatives of the people who issue directives to what is seen in the classically liberal way as the grey and mechanical world of administration and bureaucracy- a world that is either despised (as in the United States) or taken for granted (as in the United Kingdom) because in both countries it is commonly assumed in theory, despite all the evidence to the contrary, to work as a neutral instrument for the implementation of *politically determined policies* – it ostensibly makes no distinctive and valuable contribution of its own.[13] It is this which, by contrast, points to what is distinctive about the Australian case.

Australia is distinguished by its enormously extensive and long-standing use of semi-judicial and other statutory and administrative authorities. The examples are everywhere: fisheries and forestry commissions, water boards, the Industries Assistance Commission, the various state and Commonwealth arbitration commissions and tribunals, the Schools Commission, the Australian Broadcasting Corporation, etc. etc. Australians place greater trust in the deliberative and interest-mediation processes of these bodies (Parker 1965, Miller 1954), more so than do most other people. The other side of the coin is that they not only mistrust politicians – that is common everywhere – but, more significantly, they mistrust the *political process itself*. For example, in the lead-up to the election of the first Whitlam government in 1972, the Labor Party successfully insisted that a new (and very large) statutory authority, the Australian Schools Commission, would be created by a Labor government because 'the education of our children was so important that it should not become a "political football"'. This is a very Australian attitude. The underlying assumptions carry strong echoes of Australia's foundation: the State is a more reliable guardian of the common good than private interests or their political representatives. Similarly, there are other reasons for this Australian preference for bureaucracy that also have their roots in earlier periods of our history. In Australia the polity is not, as in the United Kingdom and the United States, supported and formed by a centuries-old middle class political tradition of 'gentlemanly debate'. The vast distances and the virtual absence of local government in Australia have played their part in as much as politics in Australia was never an intimate and familiar aspect of neighbourhood life, but rather something that is done 'out there' by self-seeking people with 'private' – in Australia that means 'vested' – interests. In the United Kingdom, which is still the only modern country where one finds working class Tories in substantial numbers, large majorities have proven with their votes that they have some trust in the principle of *noblesse oblige*, and some confidence still that the established upper and middle classes will govern in the common interest. And similarly in the United States, where there has never been a Labour working class party in the normal European sense, there is still a general belief that the congressmen, senators and presidents – who must all prove a strict fidelity to the interests of capital and business as a precondition for political office! – will somehow govern 'for the people'. By contrast, the Australian distrust of the political process and the preference instead for administrative and semi-judicial allocative structures continues because from their first years Australians have never found reason to trust their élites and political leaders, who are still, as Stretton argues, of consistently low stature (Stretton 1985). Another important factor – and one that is both cause and consequence of the Australian reliance on judicial and bureaucratic-administrative state authorities – is that although there is certainly a strong abiding preoccupation with equity and a 'fair go', Australian civil society and polity don't have a 'moral vocabulary capable of connecting social realities with political institutions (Collins 1985). Accordingly, the political process is either eclipsed or truncated as social needs are more directly translated into bureaucratic-administrative programmes.

In Australia there is also, as we have intimated, an important and paradoxical relation between the pressure for egalitarianism and social justice on the one hand and bureaucracy on the other: a paradox in as much as,

Bureaucracy 'is the very model of the regime which acts by the rule of equality'. Herein lies the paradox of egalitarianism in Australia: the search for equality of the redistributive kind breeds bureaucracy; bureaucracy breeds authority; and authority undermines the equality which bred it.

(Encel 1970: 57)

In other words, the State, the centre of institutionalised power in society gathers more power, and creates further hierarchical divisions, as its power is mobilised to redress inequalities. But is this an unavoidable consequence of state administration action? Or are the proliferating hierarchies – of educational grades and certificates, levels and classifications of employment, of government benefits, of fee scales and residential areas – the preferred forms which business and capital interests impose on all state action as a condition for their co-operation (Connell and Irving 1980)?

Conclusion

Now, as before, Australians continue to face the world from their situation as a relatively small and dependent nation, an island continent lacking strong economically protective regional associations. It was Australia's dependency on the British Empire which took battalions of its young men to fight for 'God, King and Country' on the other side of the globe and which also structured its economic relations and provided a shell within which the institutions of the Australian State would develop in their own characteristic form. The British Empire dissolved with World War II, the national independence movements of its former colonies, and the entry of the United Kingdom into the European Economic Community. The single most important fact about the Australian State and nation, namely its dependency, was shifted, from Britain, to a radically new empire, the United States. This now represents a greater danger to the Australian people than did the old British Empire, or the other new empire, the USSR, which represses the satellite nations of Eastern Europe.

Australia was settled by a population which emigrated from the heartland of an empire that was ready to grant formal independence to its own British foundation population on fairly easy terms. In the new relationship with the United States the familial ties are absent, whereas the means of military and economic coercion are immeasurably stronger. The State in present-day capitalist societies depends, as does just about everything else, on the vagaries of economic life, and so the future of the Australian State is likely to be shaped through its economic dependence on a world economy that is politically controlled ever more tightly by transnational corporations based in the United States and other centres of world capital. This represents an especially acute danger for Australia not only because in contrast to the member countries of the EEC it is unprotected by regional ties but also, and much more importantly, because multi-national capital continues to overwhelm local capital interests as it presses ever more relentlessly for a greater share of GNP. This process goes on at the expense not only of local capital and of Australian wage and salary earners, but at the expense also of the third actor, the State, which is the only one with the power to protect Australian assets and to secure an equitable distribution of the nation's wealth. These dangers are already clearly announced in ideological campaigns for 'deregulation' and 'privatisation' and, as other observers (Albinski 1985; Head 1984, 1986) have noted, in threats to the long-term stability of the Australian federation which accrue from sharpening conflicts of interest in the face of challenges mainly from the less industrialised states of Queensland, Western Australia, the Northern Territory and Tasmania that are willing to serve as vehicles for multi-national bids to capture Australian mineral, timber, energy and land resources.

Australia was born modern in a second important respect in as much as it has always used bureaucracy and administration to do creative nation-building work. In the United States and the United Kingdom there is consternation and alarm at the discovery that administration is no longer a neutral instrument and passive appendage of government and politics and that it now plays at least as strong a role in the *creation* of policies as do elected politicians. In several Western democracies, and most especially in the United States and the United Kingdom, the now unavoidable scale and weight of a massively expanded state administrative apparatus are experienced not only as limitations on capital but also as potentially threatening challenges to tenaciously held but irredeemably old-fashioned myths about the relation between State, polity, economy and society (Aberbach *et al.* 1981). Australians, on the other hand, are more used to the idea that society is administered.

In Australia there are therefore fewer cultural obstacles to *positive* reappropriations not only of the State in general, but more particularly of its bureaucracy and administration. In this respect Australia is more like France in as much as bureaucracy and administration have an empowering legitimacy that is deeply engrained in the long-held practice and belief that the administrative apparatus of the State (Royal Commissions, unroyal commissions, statutory authorities, tribunals, boards, committees of inquiry, etc.) *can and should* serve and respresent the general interest.[14] Like France, Australia now has, at least since the last war, an élite modern and highly professionalised public service in Canberra. It is true that whole sectors of it were captured by business interests[15] and that there is a general bias in as much as the bureaucracy does not respond well to reformist governments (Wilenski 1979, Renouf 1981). Yet, whatever the shortcomings, it is not a socially isolated club or caste like the top echelons of the British civil service, nor is it a despised and fettered instrument of capital as in the United States,[16] nor is it, despite many similarities with the French case, cluttered and partly paralysed by the 'decision overloads' (Crozier *et al*. 1965: 11–20, Crozier 1970) that accrue in the French system from the deep and complex social and political cleavages that shape French politics.

In short, Canberra has most of the essential prerequisites of a modern state apparatus with considerable relative autonomy. Yet only the future will tell whether the Australian State has the strength to protect and advance the larger interests of the Australian people in the face of the again accumulating pressures of isolation, dependency and vulnerability in a new age of militant world capitalism. Too much optimism would be foolish.

Acknowledgement

I wish to express my gratitude in particular to four people, Tim Rowse, Robert van Krieken, Trevor Matthews and Brian Head, who read the draft of this chapter and gave me some much-needed and extremely constructive criticism. I would also like to thank Kees Steps and Alec Puscy for their editorial assistance. The responsibility for the flaws that remain is all mine.

Notes

1. See Chapter 5 for comparisons with Australia and note Lipset's very American perspective that gives almost no importance to the State.
2. 'Relative autonomy' is a term originally coined by Poulantzas and taken up in a debate with Miliband in the early 1970s. Although it is now a commonly accepted term the notion still occasions much debate – see for example the discussion between Theda Skocpol and Ralph Miliband that can be taken up through Ralph Miliband's 'State Power and Class Interests', *New Left Review* 138, 1983: 57–68; and Skocpol's 'Political Response to Capitalist Crisis: Neo-Marxist

Theories of the State and the Case of the New Deal', *Politics and Society* 10, 1980: 155–201.

3. The important distinction between 'strong' and 'weak' states is generally attributed to Stephen Krasner. See his excellent review article, 'Approaches to the State: Alternative Conceptions and Historical Dynamics', *Comparative Politics* 16 (2), January 1984: 223–44; and follow the connections backwards to its origins in the pathbreaking article by J.P. Nettl, 'The State as a Conceptual Variable', *World Politics* 20, July 1968: 557–84; and then follow the thread forwards to Skocpol's work, mentioned above.

4. See Rosecrance, p. 310.

5. The quotation marks for 'principles' here as for 'must' in the preceding paragraph are intended to indicate that there is nothing inexorably given about these 'principles'. They are, as I indicated, descriptive and not normative laws. There is not independent 'functional necessity'.

6. 'Staples economies' are those such as Canada, the Argentine and Australia which are or were heavily dependent on the world economy as producers of staples such as wheat, wool, meat etc. Malcolm Alexander, who explains the relevance of staples theory and its relevance to Australia, attributes it to Canadian political economists and principally to the work of Harold Innis. See Alexander in Head.

7. Contrasts and similarities with the early development of Canada, Argentina and Brazil are available in an interesting discussion by M.L. Alexander: 'Australia in the Capitalist world Economy', In Head, B., (ed.) *State and Economy in Australia*, Oxford University Press, 1983.

8. In this discussion I am heavily indebted to Stuart MacIntyre's excellent chapter, 'Labour, Capital and Arbitration 1890–1920', in Head, B. (ed.) *State and Economy in Australia*, Oxford University Press, 1983, and also to MacIntyre's *Winners and Losers*, Allen & Unwin, 1985.

9. Although the judgment was subsequently overturned by the High Court it is of no less significance as a watershed in the linkage forged through the state between wage and tariff policies. This is discussed by MacIntyre in the Head collection, referred to above, pp. 106–10 and in Chapter 3, 'A Fair Wage' in MacIntyre's *Winners and Losers*.

10. This shift, which only caught public attention in the Fraser years, had been going on for years. Connell and Irving (1980: 306) show that even in 1969, at the peak of the boom years, as many as one-third of the 150,000 registered companies in Australia recorded no profits in their annual returns.

11. It is Nettl (1968) who first treated the locus of sovereignty as an important variable among different states and within this context dealt with these characteristics of the United States. The point has been taken up by Skocpol and Krasner, among others.

12. Politics as 'the authoritative allocation of values' (of all kinds, both material and non-material) is a widely used and largely liberal notion that comes from Easton, D., *The Political System* (Knopf, 1953), and

it is clearly explained in the context of the State in Poggi, G., *The Development of the Modern State*, Chapter 1 (Stanford University Press, 1978).

13. The attitude of British liberalism is nowhere more beautifully expressed than in the words of Lord Palmerston to Queen Victoria in 1837, 'Bureaucracy is a bad European system of government, created by the use of permanent public officials, a system that does not, should not, and cannot exist in England' (quoted in Encel 1970: 58).

14. In French the phrase *l'intérêt général* conveys this with a special authority and is the legitimating idea *par excellence* of the French bureaucratic system. The roots of course go back to Rousseau, the Revolution, and the consolidation of the Napoleonic bureaucratic state.

15. This has been a pervasive process of which the most conspicuous case is the Department of Trade and Customs that was virtually annexed by business interests under the auspices of its minister Sir John McEwen. See Matthews (Head 1983: 139).

16. There is consensus on these findings. Nettl (1968: 580) says of the British lot, 'Its autonomy is an attribute of a caste rather than the administrative emanation of a state.' See also Badie and Birnbaum, pp. 196–211, and the detailed empirical analyses in the seven-nation study of Aberbach *et al.* (1981).

References

Aberbach, J.D., Putnam, R.D. and Rockman, B.A. (1981) *Bureaucrats and Politicians in Western Democracies*. Cambridge: Harvard University Press.

Albinski, H (1985) 'Australia and the United States' in *Australia: The Daedalus Symposium*. Sydney: Angus & Robertson.

Badie, B. and Birnbaum, P. (1983) *The Sociology of the State*. Chicago: Chicago University Press.

Birnbaum, P. (1977) *Les Sommets de l'Etat*. Paris: Editions du Seuil. (Translated as *The Heights of Power*, Chicago University Press.)

Butlin, N.G. (1983) 'Trends in Public/Private Relations, 1901–75' in Head, B. (ed.) *State and Economy in Australia*. Melbourne: Oxford University Press.

——, Barnard, A., Pincus, J.J. (1982) *Government and Capitalism*. Sydney: Allen & Unwin.

Collins, H. (1985) 'Political Ideology in Australia: The Distinctiveness of a Benthamite Society', *Australia: The Daedalus Symposium*. Sydney: Angus & Robertson.

Connell, R.W. and Irving, T.H. (1980) *Class Structure in Australian History*. Melbourne: Longman Cheshire.

Crozier, M. (1970) *The Stalled Society*. New York: Viking Press.

——, Hungtington, P., Watanuki, J. (eds) (1965) *The Crisis of Democracy*. New York: New York University Press.

Davies, A.F. (1964) *Australian Democracy.* Melbourne, London and New York: Longman Green.

Easton, D. (1953). *The Political System.* New York: Knopf.

Encel, S. (1970) *Equality and Authority.* Melbourne: Longman Cheshire.

Evans, P., Rueschemeyer, D. and Skocpol, T. (eds.) (1985) *Bringing the State Back In.* New York: Cambridge University Press.

Groenwegen, P. (1983) 'The Political Economy of Federalism, 1901–81' in Head (ed.).

Head, B.W. (ed.) (1983) *State and Economy in Australia.* Melbourne: Oxford University Press.

———(1984) 'Fragmentation, Federalism and Resources: the Australian State in the 1980s', *Australian and New Zealand Journal of Sociology,* November 1984.

———(ed.) (1986) *Politics of Development in Australia.* Sydney: Allen & Unwin.

Held, D. *et al.* (eds) (1983) *States and Societies.* Oxford: Martin Robertson.

Hofstadter, R. (1963) *Anti-Intellectualism in American Life.* New York: Alfred Knopf.

Horne, D. (1985) 'Who Rules Australia?' in Graubard, S. (ed.) *Australia: The Daedalus Symposium.* Sydney: Angus & Robertson.

Lipset, S.M. (1963) *The First New Nation.* Basic Books.

MacIntyre, S. (1983) 'Labour, Capital and Arbitration, 1890–1920', in Head (ed.).

———(1985) *Winners and Losers.* Sydney: Allen & Unwin.

McNaughtan, I.D. (1955) 'Colonial Liberalism, 1851–92' in *Australia: A Social and Political History.* Sydney.

Matthews, T. (1983) 'Business Associations and the State' in Head, B.W. (ed.) *State and Economy in Australia.* Melbourne: Oxford University Press.

Mayer, K. 'Social Stratification in two Equalitarian Societies', *Social Research* 31: 435–65.

Miller, J.D.B. (1954) *Australian Government and Politics.* London: Gerald Duckworth and Co.

Miliband, R. (1983) 'State Power and Class Interests', *New Left Review* 138: 57–68.

Nettle J.P., 'The State as a Conceptual Variable', *World Politics* 20, July 1968: 557–84.

Offe, C. (1975) 'The Theory of the Capitalist State and the Problem of Policy Formation' in Leon N. Linberg *et al.* (eds) *Stress and Contradiction in Modern Capitalism.* Lexington Books.

Parker, R.S. (1965) 'Power in Australia' *The Australian and New Zealand Journal of Sociology,* October: 85–96.

Poggi, G. (1978) *The Development of the Modern State.* Stanford: Stanford University Press.

Renouf, A. (1981) 'The Public Servant', *Australian Journal of Public Administration,* December: 359–62.

Rosecrance, R. (1964) 'The Radical Culture of Australia' in Louis Hartz (ed.). *The Founding of New Societies.* New York: Harcourt, Brace.

Rowse, T. (1978) *Australian Liberalism and National Character*. Melbourne: Kibble Books.

Skocpol, T. (1980) 'Political Response to Capitalist Crisis: Neo-Marxist Theories of the State and the Case of the New Deal', *Politics and Society* 10: 155–201.

Szelenyi, I. (1980) 'The Relative Autonomy of the State or State Mode of Production' in M. Dear and M. Scott (eds) *Urbanisation and Urban Planning in Capitalist Society*. London: Methuen.

Treasury Roundup (1986) Canberra: Australian Government Printer.

Wilenski, P. (1979) 'Political Problems of Administrative Reform', *Australian Journal of Public Administration*, December: 347–61.

Yearbook Australia, 54 (1968) Canberra: Commonwealth Bureau of Census and Statistics.

Chapter Three

Class and Inequality: Theory and Research

Mark C. Western and John S. Western

There are few more controversial issues in sociology today than those dealing with social class and social status. This is despite the fact that the two concepts have been widely used for many years and indeed had their origin in the writings of several of the most prominent early authors in the field of sociology.

That the concepts have attracted as much attention as they have is not surprising. Perhaps one of the most distinguishing features of society is its group structure. One can, for example, identify groups representing the interests of workers on the one hand and business interests on the other; political groupings are also clearly apparent as are those based on religious and ethnic grounds. This is far from an exhaustive list of the groups which comprise a society but it serves to make the point that groups are all-pervasive. Two matters suggest themselves for our attention. First, what is the basis of group formation. Second, do groups differ in terms of their relative significance within society?

These deceptively simple questions need to have a little more said about them. We will take the second one first. The question of whether groups differ in terms of their relative significance within society in the sense that some developed at an earlier historical time and that other groups are derivatives from them has been a central concern of those who have addressed the issue of the conditions for change and stability within society. There would, we believe, be fairly general agreement as to the fact of the primacy of certain groups. There would be less agreement on their identification. The concepts of class and status, and the structures within society to which they refer have been prominent in these debates. The concepts have been central to sociological concern, then, because in part they have drawn attention to structures which are basic and fundamental to the existence of society. They are seen as underpinning the social structure of the society; all else is derived from them.

The first question posed earlier concerning the bases of group formation is of course related to the one we have just been discussing. It is not sufficient to be able to identify the basic group structure of society; we also need to understand how groups come into existence. What is the basis of group formation? It is important to be able to answer this question because an understanding of it will provide us with an understanding of the factors making for group stability and group change. This, in turn, will provide us with an explanation of the broader patterns of societal change and stability. Writers in the field of class and status have also addressed these questions with considerable enthusiasm.

This chapter, then, is devoted to the important issues of class and status. It is divided into three major sections. In the first the manner in which the two concepts develop in the writings of Marx and Weber are considered. We see that Marx's understanding of class develops from his early writings in the *Communist Manifesto*, through his historical writings, to the more mature form as represented by *Capital*. We see that in *Capital* he identified many of the issues that presently preoccupy modern Marxist writers.

Weber's approach is both similar to, and different from, that developed by Marx. In common with Marx he stresses the importance of economic factors for class formation but is inclined to emphasise different features of the economy. He also argues for the importance of social status or social honour, a notion to which Marx pays very little attention.

In the second section we examine the contribution of Australian authors to the debate and note that there are both theoretical and empirical accounts. In this section the work of an American, Erik Wright, is also discussed, as it has been the starting point for a large-scale study of class in Australian society. Finally, in the last section of the chapter we draw the threads of the different arguments together and propose a way of looking at class in Australian society which integrates the major themes of the arguments we have discussed.

The Origins of Class and Status

Marx on class

Any discussion of social class must necessarily start with a discussion of the work of Karl Marx, complex and ambiguous though Marx's understanding of class proves to be. As nearly every writer in the area feels compelled to note, Marx himself never provided an explicit definition of the concept although, as Hall (1977) argues, nearly all of his writing is in one way or another concerned with class. The lack of a straightforward definition coupled with the pivotal importance of class for Marx's social analysis have served to ensure that 'what Marx actually said about class' has become the subject of considerable debate.

In spite of this, however, there is general agreement that a Marxist concept of class contains two elements: an objective economic situation in which people at work can be located, and a subjective consciousness (Ossowski 1963, Bottomore 1966). The first of these elements is defined in terms of the social relations of production, that is, the various relationships between people involved in producing economic goods and services. The second concerns the various understandings and conceptions that individuals in different social classes possess about the nature of society, and the way in which these conceptions are tied to class struggle and social change. In other words, Marx's theory of class is one which attempts to explain 'the interplay between the real situation of individuals in the process of production, on one side, and the conceptions which they form of their situation and of the lines of social and political action which are open to them on the other' (Bottomore 1966: 17)

In general it is possible to identify three models of class analysis in Marx's work. The first is found most clearly in the *Communist Manifesto*, although it also informs the analysis present in other texts written up to and including *The Economic and Philosophical Manuscripts of 1844*. The second is the type of analysis found in Marx's historical writings, particularly *The Class Struggles in France* and *The Eighteenth Brumaire of Louis Bonaparte*. This represents a significant departure from the earlier writings. The third model of analysis, in which Marx laid the groundwork for much of the current literature on the workings of class relations in contemporary societies, is to be found in the *Grundrisse* and *Capital*. We will consider each of these three models briefly in turn.

The analysis of the relations between social classes contained in the *Communist Manifesto* is that which is most often presented as Marx's view of class. Here the 'bourgeois epoch' (a term referring to nineteenth-century European capitalism) is characterised by the opposition of two social classes, bourgeoisie and proletariat. As owners and controllers of the means of production – that is, property used in production such as land, physical equipment, machinery in factories – the bourgeoisie obtain from wage labourers (the proletariat) labour power, their ability to work, which is essential for the production of goods and services. On the other hand, the proletariat cannot survive without working for the bourgeoisie because they lack other assets of their own from which income could be derived (Marx and Engels 1955). These two classes exist in an interdependent, almost all would say, oppositional relationship. The existence of one class (owners) implies the existence of the other (workers): it is impossible for the classes to exist independently of each other. Each class is defined in terms of its relationship to the means of production, and to the other social class. The *Manifesto* explains it in this way:

> By bourgeoisie is meant that class of modern capitalists, owners of the means of social production and employers of wage labour. By proletariat, the class of modern wage labourers who, having no means of production of their own, are reduced to selling their labour power in order to live.
>
> (Marx and Engels 1955: 51)

For Marx, writing in the *Manifesto*, all of society was gradually being split into these two classes. With industrial development, production increases rapidly and wealth and ownership of capital become increasingly concentrated in the hands of fewer and fewer large capitalists. Small owners and others who cannot compete are forced into the proletariat. As the inevitable polarisation of classes continues, the middle class, an intermediate stratum of trades-people, craftworkers and shopkeepers, gradually 'sinks' into the proletariat. Nineteenth century Europe was seen as gradually splitting into 'two great hostile camps' (Marx and Engels 1955: 53). Eventually Marx argued, society would reach a point where the two classes could no longer co-exist. The social relations of production, the relationships between people involved in production that define the existence of classes, would become incompatible with the forces of production, the way goods and services are produced in society. As the forces of production (level of technology, kinds of equipment used, production methods, etc.) change and develop, the relations between people involved in production which had been formed before the new forces of production had emerged no longer fit as well as they once did (Marx and Engels 1976b).

Marx would say that a contradiction exists between the forces of production and the social relations of production. Whereas initially the technical methods of production of nineteenth century European capitalism led to the development of the social class that owned the means of production and paid a class of workers to use these to produce goods, further industrial development led to the class division between the bourgeoisie and the proletariat becoming the most pronounced and basic division within society. This polarisation of social classes, as it is called, creates a situation in which capitalism can no longer continue. The working class becomes organised politically and conscious of its unity as a class, and of its opposition to the capitalists. There results a proletarian revolution in which the old form of society is abolished along with the conditions which themselves produced social classes (Marx and Engels 1955).

In this first model of analysis Marx felt that the objective position of the working class with respect to the means of production would produce a revolutionary working class consciousness which would translate directly into political action, leading to the overthrow of the existing structure of society. Class consciousness and class struggle were the direct by-products of the proletariat's objective position in the class structure. For Marx, there existed a direct correspondence between class location and class consciousness and struggle.

However, in his later writings Marx modified this position. Using this simple model of class analysis we cannot explain the presence of the 'middle class', that large number of people, professionals, managers, technocrats, clerical and sales workers, in modern capitalist society who cannot be placed unambiguously either in the working class or the capitalist class. Additionally, in the first model all political and social conflict is directly attributable to conflicts between social classes, with a proletarian revolution being the inevitable outcome of the contradictory structural features of capitalist society. Yet there have been no working class revolutions anywhere of the type envisaged by Marx in this early analysis. At the same time, the direct presence of social classes in current political events often appears negligible. Ethnic background, gender and level of education often seem to be more important than class in determining how people respond to political situations. The form of class analysis outlined up to this point cannot address these issues.

In his historical analyses Marx begins to consider some of these problems. By contrast to the *Manifesto* which is a political work concerned with the processes that will produce a socialist revolution, *The Class Struggles in France* and *The Eighteenth Brumaire of Louis Bonaparte* are empirical examinations of historical struggles. They represent Marx's attempt to explain French history from 1848 to 1852 within a framework based on the struggles between classes, and fractions of classes, for political power.

However, their main usefulness for us lies in the way in which they demonstrate how the complexities of actual political events are explicable in terms of patterns of class relations.

For Marx, two events marked the beginning and end of this period of French history. In February 1848 the monarchy of King Louis Philippe, whose reign began in July 1830, was overthrown by an uprising of the Paris National Guard. In its place was a new provisional government, a Liberal-Socialist coalition of the bourgeoisie, proletariat and *petit bourgeoisie*. In December 1851 Louis Napoleon Bonaparte, the first Bonaparte's nephew, who had been President of France since December 1848, assumed sole power by overthrowing the French Parliament. He ruled as president for another ten years. Between the February 1848 revolt and the December 1851 coup, French history is marked by political instability and social change (Marx 1969a, 1969b).

Marx's analyses of this period make several important points that are not contained within his earlier writings on class analysis. Amongst these are the realisations that fractions (segments of the class) from within a single class may struggle with each other for political power; that the significant political actors are not necessarily whole classes or class fractions, but temporary and shifting coalitions; that classes may be represented politically by people who are not members of that class; that the role of the state is crucial to an understanding of political events; and, finally and most importantly, that class struggle must be understood within a set of specific historical conditions (Hall 1977, Clegg, Boreham and Dow 1986). For Marx the conclusion that follows from this final point is that the proletarian revolution, far from being simply the inevitable outcome of the conflict between capitalists and the working class (as was argued in the *Manifesto*), depends on certain preconditions having been met. Without the existence of certain factors within capitalist society, a substantial decline in the living conditions of the proletariat, for example, the socialist revolution, cannot occur (Marx 1969a, 1969b). The recognition of this is probably the most significant development contained in Marx's historical work.

Marx's most expanded model of class analysis occurs in his latest works, notably the *Grundrisse* and *Capital*. In the *Manifesto*, class struggle simply reflected a polarised class structure which was itself an expression of a fundamental contradiction between the forces and relations of production. In the empirical works it was possible to analyse politics when apparently whole classes were not directly involved but in the *Grundrisse* and *Capital*, Marx goes beyond these forms of analysis.

In this last model Marx identifies a number of 'class effects'.

These represent the outcome of the historical development of the labour process, the process by which raw materials are turned into products for sale. For Marx, the organisation of production under capitalism passed through three stages. It began with craft workers employed by single capitalists and no division of labour. The next step involved the introduction of a division of labour and then, finally, machinery, until the predominant form of production is that which is machine-based and centred in large factories (Marx 1976a). The class effects of this process include the emergence of an industrial working class or proletariat excluded from ownership and control of the means of production, 'free' instead to sell its labour power and exposed to the competition of the labour market. Work is progressively 'deskilled' as an increasingly extensive division of labour based on the use of machinery emerges and traditional craft skills disappear. Finally, there is the growth of white collar workers not directly involved in production. Some of these are book-keepers, clerks, secretaries and lawyers, who have a role in the distribution and circulation of goods produced. Others occupy managerial and supervisory positions and are responsible for co-ordinating production (Marx 1976a).

Two important theoretical reorientations are contained in the later works. In the first place Marx clarifies his position with respect to the economic spheres of production, distribution, exchange, circulation and consumption of goods. Exchange, distribution, consumption and circulation cannot occur without production. Therefore it is impossible to understand the economic and social organisation of capitalist society by focusing on the market which is the context for exchange, distribution, consumption and circulation. Instead one must begin with the most fundamental element, the system of production (Marx 1973, 1976a). This idea is basic to Marx's mature economic writings.

The second major reorientation in approach characteristic of the *Grundrisse* and *Capital* concerns the clarification of the concepts of labour and labour power. This represents Marx's attempt to explain how and why capitalist societies are continually able to produce a surplus of goods and services. It is from this surplus that capitalist profits are derived. If labour is merely a 'commodity', something which the worker sells in the labour market to the capitalist, then the cost of production is the sum of the prices of machinery, raw materials, labour (wages) and other associated production costs. If these costs equal the cost of the commodity produced, no profit is made by the capitalist. If an arbitrary profit percentage is fixed above the cost of production, then the capitalist's gain derives from whoever buys the commodity. It is merely a transfer from one to the other. Similarly, if it is argued that the capitalist underpays the worker, then a related argument holds. Once again the capitalist acquires only what the worker loses and no overall additional surplus is generated (Nicolaus 1967, 1968).

What then, Marx asks, is the source of this additional surplus or this additional value? The answer is labour or, more precisely, labour power. Labour power, unlike other commodities, has the capacity to create value. This argument can be clarified in the following way. In the transaction between worker and capitalist, what the worker sells is labour power, the ability to turn raw materials into commodities which can be sold. In exchange for this, capitalists pay wages, buying the workers' labour power for a certain length of time. There are two processes occurring in this exchange. On the one hand, capitalists pay wages. The value of these must be sufficient to pay for the commodities (food, clothing, shelter, perhaps certain kinds of consumer goods, etc.) which workers need to sustain and reproduce themselves and their families. This reproduction need not necessarily be only at a subsistence level but is determined by historically specific social factors – for instance, whether or not capitalists require trained and educated workers or whether workers have been able to enforce better minimum standards (for example, wages and working conditions) through organised political activity (Edel 1981).

On the other hand, in exchange for wages the capitalist receives a certain number of hours' labour time. The value of goods that workers produce in this period is determined by the development of the forces of production (levels of technology and knowledge, technical production methods, etc.) and the rhythm and pace of work established by the employer. In general, Marx argued, workers will produce more in a day, for example, than is required for their reproduction, with the surplus value accruing to the capitalists (Edel 1981, Marx 1973, 1976a). Thus if, in an eight hour day, it takes workers two hours to produce commodities equivalent to the value of their wages, for the remaining six hours they are creating surplus value. The process by which workers produce surplus value and capitalists take possession of it, Marx defined as exploitation.

Several points have been made in this very abbreviated account of Marx's analysis of social class which need to be kept in mind. It is important to note that the analysis is 'historical' in the sense that it displays a development sequence which reflects Marx's increasing awareness of the complexity of the phenomenon he was studying. His first approximation at class analysis resulted in the identification of two basic social classes, the proletariat and the bourgeoisie or middle class defined in terms of their social relations to the means of production. This relationship was inherently contradictory and its resolution would follow from a proletarian revolution which would result in the overthrow of the bourgeoisie and the emergence of a classless society. In the historical work which followed, Marx recognised both the complexity of the bourgeoisie with its conflicting factions and the emergence of a middle class which refused to 'sink' into the proletariat or become indistinguishable from the bourgeoisie. Finally, in the third period characterised by the *Grundrisse* and *Capital,* the important concept of exploitation based on surplus value was developed. It is important to note that capitalist exploitation of workers is not a value judgement about the nature of work in capitalist society. It is an objective feature of the relationship between capitalists and workers. To say that 'capitalists exploit workers' means they are able to extract more labour power from them than they pay for. It is an objective statement about the classes' respective positions in the social relations of production.

Marx's legacy for an understanding of the class structure of contemporary capitalist society is, therefore, not simply in terms of a simplistic proletariat-bourgeoisie structure which demonstrably has not led to the overthrow of the existing regime, but rather in drawing attention to the importance of an emerging diverse middle stratum, and the analytic significance of the concept of exploitation. We will have more to say about these matters when we come, shortly, to the Australian scene.

Weber on Class, Status, and Party
While Marx's work provides the basis for many contemporary analyses of social classes and their role in capitalist societies today, there is also a significant body of theory and research that has its origins in the work of Max Weber. Weber was writing at almost the same time as Marx and was, in part, influenced by Marx's ideas. Indeed, there is a widespread tendency, as Turner (1981: 5) notes when writing of Marx and Weber, to situate them in 'a nice opposition'. Marx, with his clear understanding of the importance of objective structural elements (e.g. economic class relations in a capitalist society) in shaping human behaviour and action, is contrasted with Weber and his focus on socially meaningful intentions which are the basis of human action. Marx's structural determinism is contrasted with 'a Weberian commitment to the freedom of individual will' (Turner 1981: 5).

This counterposing of Marx and Weber does have some validity, for there is in Weber's writings a strong emphasis on understanding the meanings individuals attach to their behaviour (Weber 1964). However, it can also be argued that the role of social structures in constraining and influencing human behaviour was not something Weber chose to ignore. He has a very real sense of the way in which capitalist society develops according to structural imperatives 'regardless of the subjective preferences of individual capitalists and workers' (Turner 1981: 11). Thus, like Marx, Weber is not unaware of the importance of structural relations in influencing and affecting human behaviour. Unlike Marx, however, Weber's writings do not stress the centrality of classes and class analysis for an understanding of the development of capitalist societies (Crompton and Gubbay 1977, Western 1983).

Weber directly addresses the question of what constitutes a class in two places, although these are incomplete treatments of the topic (Giddens and Held 1982). His point of departure is the manner in which power is distributed in societies. For Weber, society is made up of privileged and disprivileged groups, and he is concerned to elaborate the various criteria under which power is allocated and group membership determined. By power he refers to 'the chance of man or a number of men to realise their own will in a social action, even against the resistance of others who are participating in the action' (Weber 1982a: 60).

This is obviously a very general definition and Weber is quick to argue that power should not simply be thought of in economic terms. While power undoubtedly has an economic dimension, it may also be expressed or distributed in other ways. It may be reflected in the social honour or prestige that certain kinds of groups enjoy, and the basis for identifying these groups need not necessarily be economic. For instance, ethnic groups and racial groups may be differentially accorded prestige in society so that the question of whether these groups are powerful or powerless rests on an examination of other than economic factors.

When the distribution of power in a society is tied to the economic order, that is, the system of distributing and using goods and services, Weber speaks of social classes. When power is related to social honour and the existence of groups that share particular non-economic qualities (for example ethnic groups, racial groups or gender-based groups) Weber uses the term status groups. A third basis for the distribution of power, party, is less significant than the preceding two, and we will deal briefly with it later. The existence of classes, status groups and parties reflects how power is structured in society.

In order to understand how Weber's use of the term class differs from Marx's concept, it is first necessary to clarify what Weber means by life chances. In simplistic terms, life chances refer to the opportunities that people have to acquire material and non-material rewards over their lifetime (Crompton and Gubbay 1977).

When a group of people's life chances are determined or caused by certain kinds of economic factors they constitute a class (Weber 1982a). Specifically, Weber is concerned with the kinds of resources people possess which are used primarily in the labour market to determine their access to various kinds of rewards (Weber 1982a, Parkin 1972). Class position or class situation in Weberian terms is therefore equivalent to market situation. The kinds of goods and services that people command and can exchange for rewards in the labour market determine their class situation.

In common with Marx, Weber sees the basic determinant of class situation as ownership of property. However, this does not mean that Weber and Marx and have an identical understanding of class. For Marx, the ownership of property or lack thereof is important in defining classes only if property relates to production. For Weber, property is the determinant of class situation not within the context of production but in terms of the market and exchange relations. The ownership of property gives privileged classes a kind of bargaining power which can be used in the market either to generate income or to acquire various kinds of rewards, such as expensive consumer goods (Weber 1982a). Classes with no property have no assets to bring to bear in the market. Their limited life chances reflect this lack of property. However, Weber also realised that rewards need not be determined solely by property ownership or the lack of it. Individuals may lack property but they may be able to offer services or have 'marketable skills' for which there is a demand. Classes which derive from services offered or skills possessed Weber described as commercial classes. Examples of positively privileged commercial classes include various kinds of entrepreneurs – for example, bankers, financiers and merchants, professionals with sought-after skills, such as doctors and lawyers, or certain kinds of skilled workers (Weber 1982b).

The notion of class situation as dependent not only on property ownership but on the possession of various kinds of skills or services is a pluralistic conception of classes (Giddens 1981). Weber adds to the complexity by further differentiating on the basis of the kinds of property and kinds of skills or qualifications possessed. In addition, he says that between the privileged and unprivileged classes exist middle classes. While he is not particularly clear about who belongs to these, the examples he provides include public and private officials, some professionals, and highly-skilled workers and craftspeople. The implication is that the class situation of the middle classes is to some extent reliant upon arbitrary judgements about individual privilege.

While the differentiation on the basis of property is fundamental to class situation and represents the pure case in the completely free *laissez-faire* market, as capitalism develops, commercial classes are particularly significant. In capitalist society today, it is often argued, opportunities for material rewards such as income, employment security, promotional opportunities etc. are less a function of property ownership and more directly attributable to the kinds of skills possessed, qualifications held and the like (Parkin 1972, 1979). How rewards are distributed and allocated is tied very closely to the distribution of marketable skills and the qualifications or credentials which accompany these.

As we have described it so far, class situation is for Weber purely an objective feature of an individual's position in the market. There is no clear sense of the subjective side of class: that common class situations produce an association amongst class members, along with shared ideas and understandings (Weber 1982a). As a consequence, classes are not fundamental agents of social change. Individuals with a common class situation may under certain circumstances react in the same way; however, more frequently they do not (Weber 1982a). For social action to be class action, other kinds of social conditions must be present. Unlike Marx, Weber assigns classes no basic priority as agents of social change.

For Weber, status groups are an alternative basis for group formation and mobilisation. They are typically communities, that is, groups of people who have a common lifestyle and who are distinguished from others on the basis of some shared quality (Weber 1982a). Where classes may be characterised as an objective feature of the individual's market situation, status groups have a subjective dimension to them that is embodied in mutual feelings of belonging together and similar ways of life. Possible bases for status group formation include such features as age, occupation, race, gender, religion and ethnicity.

Crucial to Weber's concept of status is his assumption that the status situation of people is determined by estimations of social honour or prestige. Within status groups, honour or prestige is expressed in a particular lifestyle which is expected of all members of the group. Once this lifestyle limits behaviour and social interaction – for example, by confining marriage to members within the status circle, and is consequently accepted by members of the group – then the emergence of the status group as a distinct and, to a certain extent closed, community has begun (Weber 1982a).

As with class, status also affects life chances. Membership of the status group may confer certain kinds of monopolistic privileges on members with respect to various goods or opportunities. 'Honorific preferences' may include such things as rights to wear special clothes, or eat particular foods, but status groups may also monopolise material privileges such as particular trades or crafts (Weber 1971). By employing their monopolistic rights status groups can actively exclude non-members from the group. Conversely, this monopolistic privilege may also mean that to maintain their way of life status groups are specifically excluded from certain kinds of goods or opportunities. The existence of typical lifestyles does mean, however, that status groups are characterised by particular specific patterns of consumption of goods (Weber 1982a).

Class and status represent two possible bases of group formation and mobilisation within society. In times of rapid technological and economic change, such as under capitalism, rewards are determined primarily by market allocation, and power is allocated along class lines. In times of economic and technological stability status stratification and non-market considerations dominate (Crompton and Gubbay 1977, Parkin 1979). Class and status are in one sense separate and autonomous bases of stratification.

However, while class and status are independent and while class stratification predominates within contemporary capitalism, processes of status group formation do cross-cut or intersect market relationships. The professional occupations of law and medicine, for instance, monopolise particular skills which are legally and socially recognised via credentials or qualifications. These groups also operate collectively through professional organisations and are allocated social prestige on the basis of occupation. They are, according to Weber, status groups, yet the possession of a qualification like a medical degree undoubtedly enhances an individual's market situation. It is a determinant of class situation. Similarly, the social evaluation of qualities such as gender or ethnicity may affect the individual's market capacity. Gender or ethnic background may be seen as positive or negative, influencing the bargaining position of people within the labour market. Status factors may thus be superimposed on economic or class considerations. Nevertheless, most neo-Weberians would argue, market situation and the economic order is the predominant mechanism by which power is allocated in a capitalist society today (Parkin 1972, Goldthorpe 1983, 1984).[1]

For Weber, the way power is distributed in society is reflected primarily in the existence of classes and status groups of various kinds. With respect to the economic order, power is distributed in the market and produces privileged and disprivileged classes with varying market advantages that determine life chances. Status groups are defined outside the market within the social order, and inequalities are exemplified in specific lifestyles, monopolistic privileges and rights, and prestige or social esteem. Classes or status groups may be characterised by patterns of association and provide the basis for the formation of significant social groupings. For both classes and status groups, power is indirectly evident in the existence of privileged groups with advantages of certain kinds and disprivileged groups excluded from or denied those advantages.

Parties, unlike classes and status groups, are explicitly concerned with power. By this Weber means that parties are organised social groupings with a specified goal, which act in an organised and collective fashion to achieve their goals (Weber 1982a). Parties need not simply be political parties in the contemporary sense of the word. Any association of people which aims at acquiring control over some organisation constitutes a party in the Weberian sense of the term. Parties may form in organisations like social clubs as well as in the wider political sphere. Classes and status groups may be represented by parties but often parties will stand for interests that are a combination of both class and status-type interests.

It should be clear from our treatment of both Marx and Weber that there are significant differences in their approaches to class, social change and capitalism. For Marx, class relations are fundamentally relations of production, that is relationships between people who fill various positions in the production of goods and services. The development of the labour process under capitalism results in the increasing separation of workers from the entire production process and the emergence of a 'middle class' of white collar workers of various kinds. Classes, whether acting as class fractions or alliances, or whole classes acting collectively, are seen to be the major agent of social change.

Weber, on the other hand, has a conception of class based on the market. Class situation is a feature of the kinds of assets, properties, skills, or qualifications which can be bargained with for material reward. There is no reason to expect from a Weberian perspective that classes will act collectively in any way. Status groups are typically groups whose members share some subjective qualities – similar ideas, lifestyles, and patterns of consumption. Status criteria may cross-cut or reinforce class divisions. Finally, parties represent organised social groups with specific social and personal goals.

In recent times a great number of sociologists and other social scientists have attempted to analyse modern industrial society from both Marxist and Weberian perspectives. As might be expected, Australian society has had its share of such analyses. In the next section of the chapter we will discuss the contribution made by a number of commentators from both perspectives to an understanding of this society.

Class in Australian Society

Marxist Analyses
There is a considerable body of literature which examines Australian society from a Marxist perspective. If we take disciplinary boundaries as a criterion, it is possible to find analyses within political science, history, economics, English, geography and anthropology as well as sociology all of which have been influenced in some way by Marxist analyses. In the present chapter there is little chance of a comprehensive coverage of this material; consequently, we propose to focus on several of the specifically sociological accounts which have highlighted the processes of class relations. It will become apparent that even within a Marxist perspective there exists disagreement about what actually constitutes class relations and how these should be empirically investigated.

Nevertheless some commonalities do exist. There is general agreement that Australia is a capitalist society in which the economy is predominantly based upon private ownership of the means of production with profit making as the primary objective. Economic activities are regulated through the commodity and labour markets. Profits are appropriated by capitalists and taxed by the state, and workers are free to sell their labour power. These features of the economy are a result of the interplay between the forces and social relations of production that we considered in an abstract way earlier.

While the economy is significantly dominated by private ownership and capital, this ownership is fundamentally corporate in nature and commonly of a transnational character (Berry 1984). These large transnational corporations are linked by interlocking directorships with key individuals simultaneously sitting on the boards of directors of more than one corporation. The increasing monopolisation of capital into fewer and fewer large corporations has been matched by extensive government intervention and regulation of business and industry. Corporate capitalism as it exists thus demonstrates an empirical complexity that is some distance from the abstract analysis of capitalist society contained within Marx's *Capital*.

The organisation of Australian society from a Marxist perspective in terms of the existence of two fundamentally antagonistic social classes, broadly an ownership class and a working one, means class conflict has not only economic, but also political and ideological expressions. It is the interplay of economic relations of production and ideological and political conflicts upon which writers within this tradition focus.

R.W. Connell is a leading figure. In *Ruling Class, Ruling Culture*, Connell (1977) sets out to analyse class relations in Australia by focusing upon the 'ruling class'. He is concerned with the structure and internal complexity of the Australian ruling class, the way class relations influence political events, and the impact of class on ideology, culture and consciousness.

In *Ruling Class, Ruling Culture* Connell's analysis begins with the idea that class relations constitute the generative structure of capitalist society. In other words, all social relations throughout society are in some way ordered by class relations (Connell 1977, 1983a). The point of departure for the elaboration of the structure of the ruling class – the 'core' class for Connell's analysis – is the private ownership of productive resources (Connell 1977). However, of itself, the focus on private ownership is of little value for, as Connell reminds us, there are approximately one million Australians who are shareholders in corporations and companies of various sizes. Furthermore, within this class of owners, shares are frequently traded and therefore circulate, attenuating the relationship of owners to companies. In addition, the circulation of ownership occurs via companies as well as people. Companies often own shares in other companies and this further attenuates the relationship between owners and enterprises. The mere fact of private ownership is therefore not enough to be able to speak usefully about a ruling class.

In order to elaborate the structure of the ruling class it is necessary to analyse ruling class activity. For Connell, such activity involves the exercise of power and control that is embodied in profit making, corporate growth and ruling class mobilisation and resistance to working class politics (Connell 1977). Within the ruling class it is possible to identify a leadership or élite of active and influential members. This comprises a business élite of upper level executives and business owners who are able to 'mobilise and direct the use of property as capital' (Connell 1977: 49). These people are generally self-appointed and mobilise capital and capital accumulation without opposition from other ruling class members. When they are opposed it is generally by rival entrepreneurs who are also able to mobilise sufficient capital to mount significant corporate challenges.

While the business leadership co-ordinates the conduct of

business within the ruling class, there exists alongside the business élite a political one. As with the business leadership, the political leadership consists of enterpreneurs, but they mobilise political support rather than capital and their activity takes place within state organisations rather than in the sphere of economic activity (Connell 1977). The political leadership consists of leaders in the Liberal and Country, now National, Parties. Political activity of the ruling class is financed by the business leadership.

In order to complete his analysis of the structure of the leadership of the ruling class, Connell next turns his attention to the state bureaucracy. Top public servants are bureaucratic entrepreneurs in a parallel way to politicians and business entrepreneurs. However, the power of civil servants is not class-based, relying as it does on the organised administrative structure of the state. Although similar in social background, lifestyles, attitudes, and work patterns to the business élite, top public servants are not part of the ruling class (Connell 1977). Their routine decisions, however, affect the population as a whole in a way unmatched by executives of even the largest corporations. To sum up: from Connell's perspective Australia has a ruling class based on private ownership and productive resources, with a business and political leadership.

To a large extent, Connell's argument is confined to an analysis of economic domination and competition within the ruling class; the working class is not only silent but absent. In Connell's terms, class is an event of history which seems to be happening only to the ruling class. The reason for this is that, in addition to economic and political domination, there exists ideological or cultural domination. Connell devotes particular attention to the role of the mass media in creating the ideological conditions under which conservative politics may flourish (Connell 1977). The media does this by the production of a set of middle class cultural categories which imply a definite interpretation of the way the world operates. What is important and newsworthy are the day-to-day activities of 'middle class' and ruling class people such as politicians, senior public servants and businessmen. If blue collar workers are mentioned at all, it is not for their normal occupational activities but for unusual events in their lives: sporting successes, being the victim or instigator of a crime or suffering some kind of personal catastrophe, for example.

Support for this analysis is provided in Connell and Irving's historical study *Class Structure in Australian History* (1980). They identify four distinct periods in Australian history, from 1788 to 1975, marking out the main stages of development of capitalist class relations. In the first period they identify, 1788–1840, the foundations for capitalism were established. Close links between the colonial state and an emerging pastoral ruling class typically comprising free settlers with English capital, coupled with the availability of assigned convict labour, laid the basis for capitalism in Australia today. The second period, from 1840–1890, saw the contraction of state activity, while convict transportation ceased and pastoral employment declined relative to urban mercantile employment and gold mining, and the colony became self-governing (Connell and Irving 1980). With the advent of responsible government, political control became an important basis for economic power. During this period conflict in the ruling class first becomes apparent. Politics centred around struggles for control over colonial governments between a coalition of urban, commercial and merchant capitalists on the one hand, and rural pastoral capitalists on the other.

It is not until the end of this period, around the 1880s and 1890s that working class mobilisation actually began to challenge the domination of commercial capital. Mobilisation was greatest in cities and towns which were centres of commerce rather than manufacturing. Working class suburban communities of people who lived and worked together made for a solidarity that translated effectively into political activity. In the pastoral districts, non-metropolitan ports and mining areas, class awareness and militancy were reflected in the new unionism of bush workers, miners and transport workers. Increasing organisation by workers and the corresponding spread of the union movement enabled in the 1890s a new form of working class opposition – the development of a political party, the Australian Labor Party. The parliamentary representation that resulted from the emergence of the Labor Party institutionalised working class opposition.

The ruling class response to working class mobilisation during this period centred around the organisation and formation of various employer groups and federations. However, their activities were initially confined to supporting the entry of businessmen into Parliament and acting as pressure groups. There was no attempt to develop a mass-based conservative party in opposition to the Labor Party (Connell and Irving 1980).

The third period in the development of Australian class relations takes us to World War II. Industrialisation slowly emerged, and by the late 1930s accounted for 25 per cent of the workforce and about 18 per cent of GDP (Connell and Irving 1980). One of the major consequences of industrialism was a change in the labour process. Work became routinised and regular – a feature of the factory production we have already considered in our treatment of Marx. There was a separation of management from workers and the emergence of new groups of technocrats, technical workers increasingly important to the production process. Politically, this period represented a period of ruling class reorganisation against the working class mobilisation just described. The first response was the creation of a mass political party although this met with varying success until the formation of the Liberal Party in 1944 under Menzies.

Following World War II, Australia began to reintegrate into world capitalism and its allegiance began to shift to the United States. This final period also witnessed the increasing penetration of the Australian economy by foreign capital, particularly from the United States, and later from Japan. Foreign investment was especially significant in mining, steel making and the motor industry (Connell and Irving 1980).

This analysis brings us to the point of departure of *Ruling Class, Ruling Culture.* Australia is locked into a system of world capitalism and dominated by transnational capital. Class relations demonstrate a ruling class domination, although the ruling class is itself dominated by internal competition and struggles for corporate power. The working class is politically quiescent and fragmented.

In *Open Cut* (1981) Claire Williams takes up some of these issues. Her study is an examination of working class life in a mining town that houses and services the workforce of two coal mines in central Queensland. Two research questions are addressed: firstly, what is the nature of the everyday work lives of male manual workers in the town; secondly, how is the experience of the wives of these men to be understood?

Williams devotes much attention to a consideration of men's work relations at the mines. Following Braverman's (1974) analysis of the capitalist labour process, this is an examination of how relations of control and domination are an integral feature of manual work in contemporary capitalist societies. There is also an investigation of how working class consciousness might arise, both as a result of the nature of work at the mine sites and also due to the penetration of capitalist domination outside work, into community life. In general, Williams concludes that male discontent over the bureaucratisation of control and supervision is not sufficient for the development of class consciousness (Williams 1981).

A matter of central interest within Marxist class analysis, taken up by Williams, concerns the manner in which consciousness is determined by class relations. The exact nature of the relationship has been open to considerable debate in Marxist literature. Is consciousness directly caused by class relations, for instance, or do relations of production somehow set limits within which forms of consciousness may vary? In *Class Consciousness in Australia*, Chamberlain (1983) addresses these kinds of questions.

Chamberlain identifies three theoretical arguments concerning the way 'ruling ideas' or 'dominant ideology' are transmitted and accepted throughout society. In the first approach, it is argued that ruling class ideas and beliefs come to be the ideas and beliefs of almost all in society; consensus on these beliefs is almost 100 per cent. This 'cultural supremacy' of the ruling class is attributed very largely to their manipulation of the mass media (Chamberlain 1983). This is so-called hegemonic theory. A weak version of hegemonic theory, 'quasi-hegemonic' theory, suggests a partial penetration of ruling ideas. Although the mass media do transmit the principles of the ruling culture, these typically contrast with the direct experiences and social contacts of people producing only conflicting and fragmentary social understandings. Against hegemonic and quasi-hegemonic theory, 'structural' theory argues that consciousness and social imagery arise mainly from the individual's structural position in society, his or her direct experiences and primary social contacts. The mass media do transmit a ruling culture, but this is selectively interpreted in light of the day-to-day experiences of subordinate class members (Chamberlain 1983).

Chamberlain tests each of these theories by examining the attitudes of a sample of Melbourne residents to such matters as the present economic order, Australian political institutions and trade unions and strikes. On the basis of the data collected, Chamberlain concludes that hegemonic and quasi-hegemonic theories are not empirically supported. Social imagery attitudes and beliefs derive less from ruling ideas presented in the mass media than they do from the personal experiences and direct social contacts between individuals living in a class-based society.

The literature considered in this section has dealt fairly consistently with questions of class, politics, consciousness and ideology. However, there has been no specific analysis of one of the central questions to have occupied neo-Marxist social theory in recent times, namely the nature of the class structure of contemporary capitalist society of which Australia is, of course, an example.[2] The empirical question which has given rise to this concern is increasing recognition of the complex nature of the existing class structure; particularly the emerging middle strata of professional, technical, managerial and supervisory workers who cannot be unambiguously assigned either to the bourgeoisie or the proletariat. As we saw earlier in the chapter, the emergence of some of these groups was envisaged by Marx.

One of the main contributors to the discussion of 'the new

middle class' is Erik Olin Wright, whose approach combines a Marxist analysis of class relations with survey research methodology. At the University of Wisconsin, Madison, Wright developed a survey instrument enabling the investigation of key aspects of the social relations of production, and thereby the description of the class structure of contemporary capitalist society. Comparative studies using questionnaires similar to that developed by Wright are currently underway in some fifteen countries, including Australia, Canada, England, New Zealand, Finland, Norway, Sweden, Denmark, West Germany, France, Portugal, Israel and Japan. The Australian work started at Flinders University in Adelaide several years ago, with the mapping of the class structure of metropolitan Adelaide. More recently, the Class Structure of Australia project, with participants from the University of Queensland, Griffith University and the University of New England, undertook a pilot study in Brisbane in 1984 and a national survey of 1,400 respondents in 1986.

The core element of the study and indeed of Wright's analysis concerns the conceptualisation of the class structure of late capitalist society and its subsequent operationalisation. Wright has conceptualised class relations in two ways. His initial approach centred around the notion of domination (the presence or absence of control in the work situation), while the more recent approach, which Wright (1985: 57) asserts restores 'traditional centrality' to the concept of class, focuses upon relations of exploitation.

In Wright's early analysis, the concern was with relations of control or lack of control in business enterprises, rather than their legal ownership. He identifies three dimensions of control in capitalist social relations of production and these define the classes of the capitalist mode of production. These dimensions are economic ownership or control over money capital and the flow of investments, control over the physical means of production, and control over labour power (Wright 1978).

The structural antagonism between workers and capitalists is the result of their polarisation on these three dimensions. Capitalists control the flow of money capital, the physical means of production and labour power. Workers are excluded from control on each of these dimensions. However, while control or lack of control on these three dimensions represents an abstract theoretical 'ideal', the world is somewhat more complicated. In the first place, capitalist societies never contain only capitalist social relations, and in the capitalist mode of production other forms are often present. The most typical is simple commodity production, a vestige associated with the transition to capitalism from feudalism. The class associated with simple commodity production is the *petit bourgeoisie.* These are small business owners, such as the owner of the corner shop, and self-employed tradespeople. They own their business but employ no workers. They control capital accumulation and investment and the physical means of production, but provide their own labour power (Wright 1978).

Secondly, in addition to the proletariat, bourgeoisie and *petit bourgeoisie,* other class locations become significant because in actual societies there is typically not a perfect correspondence on the three dimensions of the social relations of production. In other words, the presence or absence of control in one dimension is not necessarily matched by the presence or absence of control in the other two dimensions. This non-correspondence gives rise to what Wright has called 'contradictory class locations' – class locations that simultaneously share features of two pure classes.

Three contradictory class locations are found in capitalist societies today. A supervisory managerial location shares features with capitalists in that its members exert authority over workers and control the physical means of production. However, they lack real economic ownership and the power to allocate funds. A group of semi-autonomous employees, often professionals such as engineers and lawyers, control their own labour power and organisation of work but are employed wage labourers. Finally, there is a contradictory location of small employers who are simultaneously self-employed direct producers (in common with the *petit bourgeoisie*) and employers of wage labour (in common with capitalists) (Wright 1985). The class structure of capitalist societies can thus be illustrated in the class map shown in Figure 3.1.

Recently, Wright has admitted that a major problem with this conception of class is that it is based upon control or domination within production rather than the classical Marxist concept of exploitation. Consequently, he has reformulated his theory of class; in doing so, he has relied heavily on John Roemer's (1982) theory of exploitation, based on the unequal distribution of assets. Briefly, Wright argues that those participating in economic activities or production have different kinds of productive assets, which are a source of income.

In capitalist society, the major productive asset is productive property or the means of production. Capitalists own property and appropriate surplus value or generate profits through the wage labour relationship, as we have already seen. They thus directly exploit workers. However, there are also two other kinds of productive assets in capitalist societies which generate income and involve exploitative relationships. A second productive asset refers to the ability to control the technical processes of production possessed by managers and bureaucrats. Managers control and

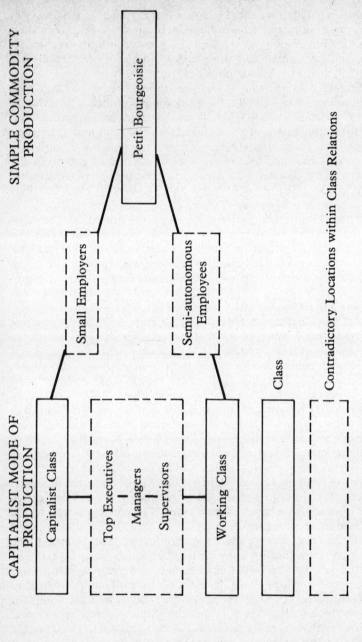

Figure 3.1 Basic Class Map of Capitalist Society

SIMPLE COMMODITY PRODUCTION

Petit Bourgeoisie

Small Employers

Semi-autonomous Employees

CAPITALIST MODE OF PRODUCTION

Capitalist Class

Top Executives
Managers
Supervisors

Working Class

Class

Contradictory Locations within Class Relations

Source: Wright 1985: 48

co-ordinate production and this is exemplifed by their position within the hierarchy of the enterprise. The control of organisational assets is unequally distributed and allows managers to appropriate part of the surplus generated in production activity. In a technical sense, therefore, the relationship is exploitative. The third kind of productive asset which generates income is skills or talents. These are seen most clearly when the possession of skills is associated with credentials (degrees, diplomas etc.). The operation of credentials limits the supply of a particular skill and employers consequently bid up the wages of owners of credentials. This increases the price of commodities produced with those skills so that they are higher than if produced by persons without credentials. As Wright notes, 'while the possessor of a credential is being paid a wage equal to the price of his or her marginal product, this price is above the price of the marginal product in the absence of credentials' (Wright 1985). The difference between the two prices illustrates the appropriation of surplus and the exploitation of unskilled and uncredentialled by the skilled and credentialled.

This analysis of Wright's is quite complex, and considering these three productive assets, a twelve-fold class schema characteristic of capitalist societies is produced. First, there are three classes of owners of the means of production: the bourgeoisie, small employers, and the *petit bourgeoisie*. They all own capital but vary regarding their ability to employ labour and the necessity to work the means of production themselves. The exploited non-owning group can be further differentiated into nine locations based on the ownership or non-ownership of organisational assets, the ability to control technical processes, and the possession of skills and credentials.

Wright's analysis, though clearly within the Marxist tradition, is quite different from the kind of generative class analysis proposed by Connell. The point of Wright's analysis is to locate individuals within particular class categories thereby producing 'maps' of class structure. This is achieved using a survey instrument which 'measures' aspects of the social relations of production. Connell's generative analysis, on the other hand, focuses attention on the processes of class formation and class action out of which classes emerged as significant historical forces. Generative analysis is concerned with elaborating the 'shape' of society as it becomes constituted by class processes. Although Wright, in common with Connell, stresses the primacy of class struggle (Wright 1978), for Marxist class analysis, his attention focuses on elaborating the class structure of capitalist societies, because this establishes the general limits within which processes of class formation may vary (Wright 1985).

Table 3.1 The Class Structure of Adelaide (1981) and Brisbane (1984) according to Wright's Contradictory Location Schema

	Adelaide (N = 439)		Brisbane (N = 304)	
	%	Weighted* %	%	Weighted* %
Bourgeoisie	2	1.4	1	0.5
Small Employer	5	5.4	6	5.3
Petit Bourgeoisie	4	3.8	3	2.1
Manager	18	17.2	8	7.0
Adviser Manager	4	4.2	20	16.2
Supervisor	14	13.8	13	15.0
Semi-autonomous Worker	12	13.0	10	7.3
Proletariat	42	41.2	38	46.4

*Weighted percentages are adjusted ones to be representative for capital cities
Source: Baxter *et al*. 1986

Table 3.2 The Class Structure of Adelaide (1981) and Brisbane (1984) According to Wright's Exploitation of Assets Schema

	Adelaide (N = 439)		Brisbane (N = 304)	
	%	Weighted* %	%	Weighted* %
Bourgeoisie	2	1.4	1	0.5
Small Employer	5	5.4	6	5.3
Petit Bourgeoisie	4	3.8	3	2.1
Expert Manager	6	5.2	3	1.2
Expert Supervisor	3	2.5	7	3.4
Expert Non-supervisor	3	3.0	4	1.9
Semi-credentialled Manager	6	5.5	2	0.9
Semi-credentialled Supervisor	1	1.3	11	5.4
Semi-credentialled Non-supervisor	4	4.4	7	4.0
Uncredentialled Manager	6	6.5	4	4.9
Uncredentialled Supervisor	14	14.2	16	22.4
Proletariat	47	46.8	37	47.7

*Weighted percentages are adjusted to be representative for capital cities
Source: Baxter *et al*. 1986

The second point to note in the consideration of Wright's analysis of the distribution of productive assets, particularly the treatment of skills and credentials, is that in this connection he is moving very close to a Weberian understanding of class as market capacity. The difference lies in the way Wright understands productive assets to be tied to exploitation and the appropriation of surplus; Weber's analysis does not consider these issues at all.

On the basis of Wright's analysis and data collected in the Brisbane pilot study and the Adelaide study, it is possible to compare maps of the class structure of these two Australian capital cities. Table 3.1 presents class maps based on Wright's first class model. This shows that the bourgeoisie are more common in Adelaide than Brisbane as are the *petit bourgeoisie* and managers. The proportion of people in the working class is greater in Brisbane than it is in Adelaide.

In Table 3.2 the class structure of Brisbane and Adelaide is presented, but this time it is based on Wright's exploitation of assets schema.

Once again a similar picture is presented. Bourgeoisie, managerial groups, and semi-autonomous workers tend to be more commonly represented in Adelaide than in Brisbane. Groups with a greater affinity to the proletariat, uncredentialled supervisors, semi-credentialled supervisors, semi-credentialled non-supervisors, seem to be found more commonly in Brisbane than they do in Adelaide. The reasons for these differences are presently under investigation, and an important objective of the larger study is to explore them further and provide an explanation of their occurrence.

Weberian Analyses
In contrast with the analyses of social class influenced by Marx, studies in the Weberian tradition are broadly of two kinds (Wild 1978). In the first place there are studies of class, status and party which focus on understanding the unequal distribution of social power in terms of relations between privileged and unprivileged groups in society. Work within this framework is linked very closely to the interpretation of Weber that we have previously outlined. Secondly, there are studies of stratification that Wild (1978) has identified as distributive. These treat stratification as 'the unequal distribution of such objective attributes as occupation, amounts of income, educational levels and skin colour' (Wild 1978: 22). Associated with the unequal distribution of such attributes is the differential distribution of social rewards and valued goods.

Wild's (1974) study is firmly within this former tradition. In it he is concerned with examining the relationships between class, status and party in the small community of Bradstow in New South Wales. Wild's understanding of the concepts class, status and party is very similar to that which we have already presented in our discussion of Weber. In considering the structure of power relations in Bradstow, the status order is particularly significant. Wild identifies six basic status groups whose members share common ways of life, forms of interaction and patterns of consumption, which can be hierarchically ranked according to honour or prestige (Wild 1981). Wild's analysis of the class system in Bradstow is market based. However, he identifies three dimensions of class situation revolving around property ownership, position as an employer or an employee, and as leisured or working (Wild 1981). He notes that while there is overlap of class and status relations the two are not coterminous: not all who are found in the top category of one hierarchy appear in the top category of the second.

In addition to class and status relations, Wild also considers the incidence of power in the public sphere. Political power in Bradstow, Wild asserts, is concentrated around the status order. Those with political influence are drawn from the upper hierarchies of the status system and act according to status-defined interests rather than class ones or the macro-level interests of party politics. The class system and the political system are reinforcing and supportive of the status hierarchy (Wild 1981).

In *Social Stratification in Australia*, Wild (1978) attempts the same type of enquiry at a national level, and further attempts to illustrate how race, gender and age stratification may all be understood in terms of the 'core phenomena' of class, status and party. In addition, he also outlines his understanding of the emergence of Australian capitalism, in keeping with the Weberian tradition. Although this bears similarities to Connell and Irving's (1980) interpretation, there are differences. For Connell and Irving the state is understood in terms of class relations, while for Wild the state and politics have a degree of separation or autonomy from economic or class relations (Wild 1978).

The class structure of Australia, Wild argues, is threefold. Market situations are differentiated by possession or lack of possession of income-generating property, educational qualifications and manual labour power. This yields a three-class structure of upper, middle, and lower or working class. In the upper class are property owners and entrepreneurs. The middle class comprises propertyless non-manual workers with educational and technical qualifications. They are in many ways similar to Wright's non-owning credentialled class locations. Like the upper class, the middle class is internally heterogeneous and is marked by differences of authority, lifestyle, prestige and values (1978). In the working class, Wild identifies propertyless manual workers who currently make up about 50 per cent of the workforce. Despite the relatively high wages of the Australian working class, and apparent similarities of lifestyle to the middle class, Wild notes that a collectivist solidarity based on shared work and home experiences (that is, factors pointing to a coincidence of class and status), produces a strong cleavage between manual and non-manual workers. This is reflected in a working class consciousness where working class members are aware of their oppositional interests to the upper and middle classes.

Wild's analysis of party examines the relationship between economic and political élites. Parties are explicitly concerned with acquiring power and influencing social action, while from major parties élites are formed. The four élites that Wild considers are the Australian government, trade unions, employer associations and the judiciary. The organisations comprising these élites are highly bureaucratised and members of the élite share similar social backgrounds. The union and business groups have economic interests while the political organsisations have political interests and objectives. It is important to note that Wild sees political dominance in Australia as based on a governing class rather than a ruling one which has political and not economic power. Class, status and party are the core elements to the social distribution of power. According to Wild they provide the basis for understanding all expressions of social inequality including those attributed to race, gender, age and other institutional factors.

Wild's approach shares some similarities with the generative analysis proposed by Connell. Both direct attention to the pattern of interaction or the relations between various groups, whether classes, status groups or parties. Although they would disagree about the nature of social relations which ought to be investigated, both share a belief that social relations are fundamental to explaining inequalities of power in society and thus ought to constitute the subject matter of sociological research.

Against this we may contrast studies which can be referred to as 'distributional' or 'categorical'. Such studies operate with a conception of social inequality as demonstrated by the unequal distribution of certain attributes. People can thus be ordered or categorised according to their relative possession of the attributes under consideration. Typically, this research addresses questions concerning the differential access of members of different groups to social rewards, for example: job opportunities, income, access to health, leisure and the political system.

Power, Privilege and Prestige (Daniel 1983) is an analysis from the distributional perspective. Based on previous research by Congalton (1953, 1962, 1963a, 1963b), it makes the assumption that the power and privilege that are vested in occupations are best indicated by the level of prestige that society accords them (Daniel 1983). By power Daniel means a command of resources and an ability to achieve goals even in spite of opposition. Her study involved asking different groups to rank a list of occupations on a scale of occupational prestige according to their perceptions of community evaluations of prestige. Daniel found that a major consensus about occupational prestige existed across the groups surveyed. The occupations that ranked highest in terms of prestige were professional ones, especially medicine and law. In addition to the professions Daniel was also interested in the prestige ranking of occupations with authority. Comparing the rankings for political occupations such as Cabinet minister, parliamentarian and mayor with occupations in private and public bureaucracies, she found consistently higher rankings for ministers than for parliamentarians. Department heads in the public service were ranked below the dominant professions, with Cabinet ministers being on a par with parliamentarians. In the private sector the managerial occupation that ranked most highly was that of managing director of a large organisation.

The high occupational prestige accorded the professions is an interesting finding. This group is one that is not considered in Connell's analysis of the ruling class and is identified by Wild as a middle class grouping. If Daniel is correct in asserting that prestige is the best indicator of occupational and therefore class power (Daniel 1983), then it is fairly obvious that Australians have a different perception of who holds power in society than is presented in the arguments of Connell and Wild. We can infer little from this discrepancy, however. Daniel's study is not explicitly to do with perceptions of a ruling or an upper class. We cannot conclude, therefore, that Australians see the professions in these terms. However, there is no doubt that the prestige accorded the professions does indicate that most people believe they are influential in some way. These results point to the desirability of investigations that reveal how perceptions of occupational prestige are tied to perceptions of class structure and class inequality, and also analyses of the 'objective' nature of class power that locate the professions within the class structure.

Broom and Jones' (1976) work *Opportunity and Attainment in Australia* is concerned with a similar question to that addressed by Daniel. Their research is within the status attainment tradition and follows closely such well-known studies as Blau and Duncan's *The*

American Occupational Structure (1967). Status attainment research is concerned with the processes by which individuals come
to fill particular occupations. Broom and Jones examine the
importance of social background, education and career structures
for the kinds of occupational positions that individuals eventually
fill and the amount of income that they receive for these occupations. The core of their analysis suggests that Australian society
can be divided into different social strata which can be defined in
terms of socio-economic status. Their measure of socio-economic
position is based on three scales, concerned with occupation,
education and income. By combining these scales they identify ten
major socio-economic strata in Australian society. Briefly, the
authors describe them as follows:

> The first stratum is consistently high status. Its members are
> predominantly in the higher income bracket, work in professional or
> managerial jobs and have experienced higher education ... The
> second stratum is similar to the first in that it consists entirely of
> tertiary educated men ... who come from a wider range of
> occupations and earn significantly lower incomes ... The next two
> strata (3 and 4) are termed old-middle classes because they contain
> occupations that require entrepreneurial skills rather than formal
> education ... but their average occupational status and income
> compare favourably with those in the first two strata ... Strata 5
> and 6 are difficult to interpret ... To some extent they are residual
> categories ... [which do not fit the dominant patterns of social
> differentiation] ... The middle mass strata 7 and 8 comprise skilled
> manual workers, lower white collar workers, less well-off farmers
> and managers and higher paid operatives ... The last two strata (9
> and 10) consist overwhelmingly of the semi-skilled and unskilled.
>
> (Broom and Jones 1976: 110–14)

Table 3.3 shows the proportions of their sample in each of these
strata.

These strata are essentially statistical groupings – that is,
distinct clusters of individuals with relatively similar occupation,
education, and income levels. Based upon their investigation of
father to son mobility within the sample in each of their ten strata,
Broom and Jones conclude that Australia is a stratified society with
patterns of inequality in 'occupational positions, skill and training,
income and other characteristics' (Broom and Jones 1976: 118). It
is not a class society, however, for although social inequality exists,
social and economic inequalities are not rigidly transmitted from
one generation to the next.

This analysis is extended in *The Inheritance of Inequality*
(Broom, Jones *et al.* 1980). Once again the purpose of this

Table 3.3 Australian Social Strata*

Stratum	% of Sample
1 Upper-middle Class A	7
2 Upper-middle Class B	4
3 Old-middle Class A	9
4 Old-middle Class B	12
5 Marginal A?	4
6 Marginal B?	7
7 Middle Class A	14
8 Middle Class B	19
9 Working Class A	11
10 Working Class B	13

Source: Broom and Jones 1976, Table T.1 and T.2 National Survey of 1,921 male
adults

research is to investigate the factors which influence the achievement of socio-economic position. The questions that concerned
the investigators included: what effects do social origins have on
opportunities for education and occupation? To what extent are
social inequalities transmitted across generations and what effect
does the education system have in terms of reproducing social
inequalities or enabling individual social mobility? (Broom, Jones
et al. 1980). As they note empirical research of the kind they
undertake informs debate on the extent of inequalities and how
these are transmitted over time and across families but it does not
typically examine how structured inequalities originally arise or
take the form they do. It is concerned with delineating 'the most
important factors influencing who gets what' (Broom, Jones *et al.*
1980: 7).

Our discussion to date has demonstrated both theoretical and
methodological differences in Marxist and Weberian analyses of
class and stratification. For Marxists empirical complexity is
ultimately or fundamentally explicable in terms of underlying
class relations. Weberian analyses of class usually revolve around
the (labour) market and recognise the significance of factors other
than class as bases of inequality. In general the differing theoretical
approaches have been matched by different research strategies.
Marxists have tended to prefer 'qualitative' methods, intensive
interviews and historical and documentary analyses. Researchers
within a Weberian framework have tended to rely upon survey
data and the use of multivariate statistical techniques. This
alignment of theory and method is not absolute. As the work of

Erik Wright in the United States and the Class Structure of Australia project indicate, some researchers within the Marxist tradition do not reject surveys as valuable data sources. Similarly, Wild's research in *Bradstow* and his arguments in *Social Stratification in Australia* indicate that not all Weberian sociologists are committed to survey research.

The appropriateness of different methodological approaches to the investigation of social class forms the subject of a debate that appeared in several issues of the journal *Search* in 1983. It began with an article by Kelley and McAllister (1983a) who 'compared' three 'measures' of class position as determinants of income, class identification and voting behaviour. Their class measures were: firstly, a blue collar/white collar occupational distinction; second, a status and educational hierarchy influenced by Blau and Duncan (1967) and Broom, Jones *et al.* (1980); third, a class measure incorporating 'conflict' aspects of Marxist theory that distinguished capitalists from workers and, following Dahrendorf (1959), separated supervisors from employees with no authority over other workers. Their data were collected in mass surveys in Australia, Britain and the United States and analysed using multivariate statistical techniques. Kelley and McAllister's argument was that comparison of the different measures would yield information as to which 'aspects of class' determine which class effects, and whether or not there are differences in these processes in Australia, the United Kingdom and the United States. In general their findings are similar for the three countries. Class identification is better explained by the blue collar/white collar measure than the others. Blue collar workers more consistently identify as working class, white collar workers as middle class. This measure also works well predicting voting behaviour, with white collar workers less likely than blue collar workers to vote Labor in Australia. The conflict measure also predicts votes consistently, with capitalists less likely than workers to vote for the ALP. Similar patterns are reported for the other countries.

For Kelley and McAllister, therefore, the three 'aspects of class' can each be objectively measured by way of surveys, as can 'class effects' such as class identification and voting behaviour, and then explained using appropriate statistical methods to determine the relationships between aspects of class and effects.

Connell (1983b), commenting on the article, takes Kelley and McAllister to task for three major reasons. In the first place he argues that the conceptual distinctions and history of the use of social class in sociology presented by Kelley and McAllister is incorrect. He also dismisses their claim that their work is the first attempt to combine the three aspects of class in one study. His major criticism, however, is reserved for their methodology. Quantitative mass surveys reduce class relations to sets of categories into which people are sorted according to their rankings on variables such as occupational status and level of education. The 'complex and contradictory aspects of people's lives' (Connell 1983b) which make up class relations must be forced to fit the *a priori* categories of the interview schedule.

The crux of Connell's argument is that class analysis should focus on social relations between groups, and that Kelley and McAllister reduce this via survey research to an analysis of the distribution of individual attributes. This denies the dynamic process by which relations of production structure and fill out social reality. Connell is, in other words, reiterating the need for generative historical analysis as opposed to quantitative categorical research. In reply to these points Kelley and McAllister (19183b) argue that the qualitative historical research strategies called for by Connell rely on impressionistic uncertain data from which researchers may only draw dubious conclusions. Survey research, on the other hand, which conforms to the requirements of objective science and class analysis is most clearly amenable to this kind of inquiry (Kelley and McAllister 1983b). Connell's argument is the exact opposite. Class analysis, by its very nature, cannot be undertaken using large structured surveys. The differences between approaches, although in this debate taking the form of arguments over method, reflect more basic differences. These include disagreements about the nature of the subject matter of sociology as a whole. Can human behaviour be explained scientifically and objectively in much the same way that the physical sciences deal with their subject matter? Are the research methods of physical sciences appropriate to sociology? How we answer these questions will determine the kinds of criteria we use to assess whether or not the knowledge generated by different sociological research methods is 'valid'.

The Class Structure of Australia

One might well wonder after this somewhat protracted discussion how we can best understand the class structure of Australian society. It will be clear, we think, that there is not one universal understanding. However, it is time now to try to draw the threads together and, by way of conclusion, provide a provisional statement of the class structure of Australian society as we see it, informed by the theoretical considerations we have discussed, yet mindful of the complexity of the empirical situation.

There are, it is clear, two conflicting theoretical positions. The first, derived from the work of Karl Marx, is based ultimately on notions of production and the concept of exploitation defined in terms of the creation of surplus value, while the second, drawing upon Max Weber, sees market capacity as the determinant of class situation and class situation as but one of several bases for the structure of society. To some degree cross-cutting these theoretical divisions are methodological questions which have to do with strategies of enquiry. One view would have it that class, however defined, is a lived historical process, an understanding of which can most adequately be obtained through intensive qualitative studies of relatively small contained communities or by broad historical analyses. The other view would assert that class, again however defined, can be captured through large-scale quantitative sample surveys of national populations. As we have seen, it is not possible to neatly connect methodological and theoretical positions. Marxist analyses are small-scale qualitative, historical and large-scale quantitative, as are those stemming from a Weberian perspective.

Where do we stand? Our view would be that the existing class structure is embedded in a historical process, but having said that we would also assert that it is possible to obtain an understanding of that structure by the employment of large-scale surveys. Historical analyses provide a comprehensive account of the emergence of social groups and the underlying conditions for social change. Quantitative surveys provide a systematic understanding of the relationships between key variables in contemporary analyses of the nature and significance of social class. In other words, we see considerable value in an integration of historical analyses and quantitative methods. In terms, next, of our theoretical stance we would want to assert that whatever theoretical position is adopted it must take account of existing and changing empirical reality.

As our concern is with class and stratification, the place to start is with the workforce. We need to know something about its size, scope and segmentation for these are the empirical considerations which will inform the model we develop.

First, to the issue of size; the Australian workforce involves nearly 41 per cent of the total population. Australia's population is approximately 15,500,000 persons. Of these approximately 6,262,000 are in the workforce, around one-third of whom, or 2,028,757, are in the public sector, employed by federal, state and local governments. Well over half of those in the public sector would be in relatively unskilled and routine clerical and manual jobs. A minority would have some supervisory responsibilities. The private sector, comprising 4,233,022 persons, makes up the

Table 3.4 Employment Sectors of the Australian Workforce

	%
Australian Public Service	3.2
Other Australian government	5.0
State governments	20.8
Northern Territory government	0.3
Total government sector	32.4
Total private sector	67.6
Total Workforce	6,261,600

Source: Australian Bureau of Statistics 1983

Table 3.5 Changes in Proportion of Workforce in Industrial Sectors over Time

Industrial Sector	% of Workforce	
	1971	1981
Primary (extraction industries)	10	7
Secondary (manufacturing and construction)	31	23
Tertiary (tangible economic services)	30	43
Quarternary (information processing)	29	27

Source: Australian Bureau of Statistics 1984

remaining two-thirds of the workforce (Table 3.4). Within the private sector, over the past decade or so, there has been a substantial movement of labour from manufacturing and construction to service industries. Changes that have taken place in the proportion of the private sector workforce in the four industry sectors between 1971 and 1981 are shown in Table 3.5. Primary industry has gone down from 10 to 7 per cent; secondary industry, which of course includes manufacturing, from 31 to 23 per cent; tertiary industry (tangible economic services) has risen from 30 to 43 per cent; and in the quartenary sector, the information processing one, the figures have remained relatively stable over the period.

The workforce can also be considered, of course, in terms of its occupational structure. Table 3.6 presents the eight major occupational categories used by the Australian Bureau of Statistics to categorise the Australian workforce, together with the proportions in each category. Upper white collar workers, the first two categories, make up about a fifth of the workforce; lower white collar workers, the next two categories, make up a little more than a quarter; and manual workers the bulk of the remainder. A changing pattern of occupations can also be observed over time. Within the last decade there has been a substantial increase in professional, technical and related workers and a corresponding decrease in farmers, miners, quarrymen, tradesmen, production and process workers and labourers; an increase in service workers of a variety of kinds has also taken place.

The changing structure of the Australian workforce, as revealed in this brief account, should strike a theoretical chord in those who have followed our earlier discussion. The growth of the upper white collar workforce, particularly among managerial/ professional and technocratic groups, has its parallels in the Marxist hypothesis about the growth of the middle class. These are the people who contemporary Marxist theorists such as Wright are attempting to locate within the class structure; they are also people who, in Weberian terms, are in an advantaged market situation over manual workers. Clearly, the changing structure of the workforce, identified in the above discussion, has been anticipated in the theoretical writings of both Marx and Weber, as considered earlier in the chapter.

The theoretical underpinnings of the model we are proposing revolve around several notions. We argue that the development of monopoly capitalism associated with the growth of state authority, as exemplified by the emergence of the welfare state, has had at least two observable consequences. The first has been the emergence of a class distinct from the bourgeoisie. While this class

Table 3.6 Occupational Structure of the Australian Workforce

	%
Professional, Technical and Related Workers	15
Administrative, Executive and Managerial	6
Clerical	18
Sales	9
Farmers, Fishermen, Timber-getters, etc.	7
Transport and Communication	5
Tradesmen, Production, Process Workers and Labourers, Miners	29
Service, Sports and Recreation Workers	10
Total Workforce	6,261,600

Source: Australian Bureau of Statistics 1983

lacks formal legal ownership of the means of production, it is typically able to control or exert considerable influence on the flow of money capital, the physical means of production and labour power. This group results from increasing complexity in the capitalist labour process as demonstrated by needs for management, supervision and the application of scientific and technical knowledge to capitalist production. The individuals comprising it share a number of other characteristics: high incomes, secure employment and advantageous working conditions. In other words, their privileged market situation, reflected in their possession of skills and services, is matched by a variety of material and non-material rewards. The next notion which underpins the model argues that there is an historically maintained cultural division between mental and manual labour. In simple terms blue and white collar workers behave differently in social and political life. While this is not sufficient to locate them objectively in different classes, it does mean that the manual/non-manual distinction is a significant cleavage within the working class.

The model we are proposing, therefore, consists of four classes. We make a fundamental distinction between owners and non owners of the means of production. The first class is a bourgeoisie, which owns the means of production and employs labour. In addition to business people this includes professionals in private practice who employ others. These are owners in the classical Marxist sense and in post-industrial capitalism are a very small group. The second class is that of higher managers and professionals, all of whom are wage and salary earners. It comprises individuals who are directly involved in decisions about budgetary matters in both the private and public sector. A significant segment of this group controls, manages and exercises policy making control over the activities of private business and industry. An equally significant segment carries out the same activities in the public sector. In addition, the class comprises those designated as 'professional' who are employed in both the private and public sector. Two important characteristics most analysts agree professionals possess qualify them for their position in this class. The first is autonomy in professiona activity. Although employed, professionals set their own standards, determine in important ways their conditions of work and the rules under which that work should be undertaken. The second characteristic is the power they are able to exert in the relationships that they establish with clients, patients or the consumers of the service the provide, manifested in the existence of professional associations and their control of accreditation practices.

The third class is a *petit bourgeoisie* which resembles closely

Wright's class of the same name. Finally, we come to the working class. This comprises white and blue collar employees with little control over the kind of work that they do or the way that they do it. The work of blue collar employees is often physically demanding, dirty and at time dangerous. By contrast, white collar work is frequently just as dull and routine but the level of physical exertion is less; the likelihood of individuals being physically at risk is also less and job security is often greater. Within the working class then, a major division exists between white collar workers, primarily in clerical and sales work, and blue collar employees. This division is reflected in differences in work relations and conditions, attitudes and lifestyles. The blue collar/white collar distinction demonstrates how aspects of status relationships may be superimposed on class relationships. The manual fraction of the working class is further split by divisions of skill. This four-class model: bourgeoisie, professional and managerial class, *petit bourgeoisie* and working class, contrasts with Erik Wright's two models of class structure employed in the Class Study of Australia project, and their predecessors and the simple Working Class/Ruling Class version of Connell, or the three-class, upper middle class, lower middle class, working class of the neo-Weberians. The class structure of Australia, as defined by the four class model, is presented in Table 3.7.

As can be seen, the bourgeoisie, owners or capitalists, comprise a little under 6 per cent of the workforce. The professional managerial class comprise a further 17 per cent, while the *petit bourgeoisie*, the class of largely small shopkeepers and independent tradesmen, are around 10 per cent. The working class make up the remaining two-thirds of the workforce although the blue collar fraction of this class is twice as large as the white collar fraction.

We would not assert that this model is superior to those described earlier. We believe that the issue of which model

Table 3.7 The Four-Class Model of Australian Society

Class Designation	%
Bourgeoisie	5.8
Professional/Managerial Class	17.1
Petit Bourgeoisie	9.8
Working Class: White Collar Fraction	24.6
Working class: Blue Collar Fraction	42.7

Source: Australian Bureau of Statistics 1983

provides for the most comprehensive understanding of the class structure is importantly an empirical one. In our view, there are two important empirical questions which any model must address. The first concerns the changing structure of the labour force. The growth in public sector employment, the growth of so-called non-productive groups and the growth of the new middle class, are all empirical issues to which any conceptual model must be sensitive. Secondly, there is the matter of explanation and prediction. Importantly, classes shape social and political life. While few Marxists these days would insist that a simple causal connection exists between the nature of the class structure and the rest of social life, a profound and complex relationship does exist. A critical issue has to do with identifying the model which best provides for an understanding of the nature and patterning of social and political life. Clearly this is an empirical question of some import and one which carefully designed empirical studies can help elucidate. Obfuscation and ungrounded theorising will throw little light on these topics which are among the most intractable in the social sciences.

Notes

1. This is not an uncontentious argument. There has recently been much criticism of both Marxist and Weberian class analysis by feminist theorists for their neglect of other forms of inequality and oppression, such as that due to gender. See, for instance, Williams (this volume), Game and Pringle (1983), Cass (1978) and Barrett (1980) for a discussion of class and gender relations.
2. Connell (1977) and Connell and Irving (1980) would probably argue that their analyses are concerned with this question. In their view class structure cannot be conceived of as a set of social categories; rather, it emerges out of historical processes.

References

Australian Bureau of Statistics (1983) *Cross Classified Characteristics of Persons and Dwellings*. Canberra: Commonwealth Government Printer.
Australian Bureau of Statistics (1984) *Year Book Australia*. Canberra: Commonwealth Government Printer.
Barrett, M. (1980) *Women's Oppression Today*. London: Verso.
Baxter, J. *et al.* (1986) '*The Class Structure of Australia*', paper presented at the Annual Conference of the Sociological Association of Australia and New Zealand. Armidale, NSW: University of New England.

Berry, M. (1984) 'The Political Economy of Australian Urbanisation', *Progress in Planning* 22: 1–83.

Blau, P.M. and Duncan, O.D. (1967) *The American Occupational Structure*. New York: Wiley.

Bottomore, T. (1966) *Classes in Modern Society*. London: Allen & Unwin.

Braverman, H. (1974) *Labor and Monopoly Capital*. New York: Monthly Review Press.

Broom, L. and Jones, F.L. (1976) *Opportunity and Attainment*. Canberra: Australian National University Press.

———, Jones, F.L., McDonnell, P. and Williams, T. (1980) *The Inheritance of Inequality*. London: Routledge & Kegan Paul.

Cass, B. (1978) 'Women's Place in the Class Structure', in Wheelwright, E. and Buckley, K. (eds) *Political Economy of Australian Capitalism*, Vol. 3. Sydney: ANZ Book Co.

Chamberlain, C. (1983) *Class Consciousness in Australia*. Sydney: Allen & Unwin.

Clegg, S., Boreham, P. and Dow, G. (1986) *Class, Politics and the Economy*. London: Routledge & Kegan Paul.

Congalton, A.A. (1953) 'Social Grading of Occupations in New Zealand', *British Journal of Sociology* 4: 45–59.

———(1962) *Social Standing of Occupations in Sydney*. Sydney: School of Sociology, University of New South Wales.

———(1963a) *Occupational Status in Australia*. Sydney: University of New South Wales.

———(1963b) *Nurses' Evaluation of Occupational Status and Other Studies*, Research Reports in Nursing, No. 3. Sydney: New South Wales College of Nursing.

Connell, R.W. (1977) *Ruling Class, Ruling Culture*. Melbourne: Cambridge University Press.

———(1983a) 'Logic and Politics in Theories of Class', in R.W. Connell *Which Way is Up?* Sydney: Allen & Unwin.

———(1983b) 'Social Class in Australia' *Search* 14: 247–48.

———and Irving, T.H. (1980) *Class Structure in Australian History*. Melbourne: Longman Cheshire.

Crompton, R. and Gubbay, J. (1977) *Economy and Class Structure*. London: Macmillan.

Dahrendorf, R. (1959) *Class and Class Conflict in Industrial Society*. Stanford: Stanford University Press.

Daniel, A. (1983) *Power, Privilege and Prestige: Occupations in Australia*. Melbourne: Longman Cheshire.

Edel, M. (1981) 'Capitalism, Accumulation and the Explanation of Urban Phenomena', in M. Dear, and A. Scott (eds) *Urbanisation and Urban Planning in Capitalist Society*. New York: Methuen.

Game, A. and Pringle, R. (1983) *Gender at Work*. Sydney: Allen & Unwin.

Giddens, A. (1971) *Capitalism and Modern Social Theory*. Cambridge: Cambridge University Press.

———(1981). *The Class Structure of the Advanced Societies*, Second Edition. London: Hutchinson.

————and Held, D. (1982) *Classes, Power and Conflict*. London: Macmillan.

Goldthorpe, J. (1983) 'Women and Class Analysis: In Defence of the Conventional View', *Sociology* 17: 465–88.

————(1984) 'Women and Class Analysis: A Reply to the Replies', *Sociology* 18: 491–99.

Hall, S. (1977) 'The "Political" and the "Economic" in Marx's Theory of Classes' in A. Hunt (ed.) *Class and Class Structure*. London: Lawrence & Wishart.

Kelley, J. and McAllister, I. (1983a) 'Social Class in Australia', *Search* 14: 93–95.

————and McAllister, I. (1983b) 'Modern Sociology and the Analysis of Class', *Search* 14: 249–52.

Marx, K. (1969a) Excerpts from *The Class Struggles in France, 1848 to 1850* in L.S. Feuer (ed.) *Marx and Engels: Basic Writings on Politics and Philosophy*. London: Fontana.

————(1969b). Excerpts from *The Eighteenth Brumaire of Louis Bonaparte* in L.S. Feuer (ed.) *Marx and Engels: Basic Writings on Politics and Philosophy*. London: Fontana.

————(1973) *Grundrisse*. Harmondsworth: Penguin.

————(1976a) *Capital, Vol. 1*. Harmondsworth: Penguin.

————(1976b) 'The Poverty of Philosophy' in K. Marx and F. Engels, *Selected Works*, Vol. III. London: Lawrence & Wishart.

————and Engels, F. (1955) *Manifesto of the Communist Party*. Moscow: Foreign Languages Publishing House.

Nicolaus, M. (1967) 'Proletariat and Middle Class in Marx: Hegelian Choreography and the Capitalist Dialectic', *Studies on the Left* 7: 22–49.

————(1968). 'The Unknown Marx', *New Left Review* 48: 41–61.

Ossowski, S. (1963). *Class Structure in the Social Consciousness*. London: Routledge & Kegan Paul.

Parkin, F. (1972) *Class Inequality and Political Order*. Frogmore, St Albans: Granada.

————(1979) *Marxism and Class Theory: A Bourgeois Critique*. London: Tavistock.

Roemer, J. (1982) *A General Theory of Exploitation and Class*. Cambridge, Massachusetts: Harvard University Press.

Turner, B. (1981) *For Weber*. Boston: Routledge & Kegan Paul.

Weber, M. (1964) *The Theory of Social and Economic Organisation*. New York: Free Press.

————(1971) 'Class, Status, Party', in H.H. Gerth and C.W. Mills (eds) *From Max Weber*. London: Routledge & Kegan Paul.

————(1982a) 'Status Groups and Classes' in A. Giddens and D. Held (eds) *Classes, Power and Conflict*. London: Macmillan.

————(1982b) 'The Distribution of Power: Class, Status, Party', in A. Giddens and D. Held (eds) *Classes, Power and Conflict*. London: Macmillan.

Western, J.S. (1983) *Social Inequality in Australian Society*. Melbourne: Macmillian.

Wild, R.A. (1974) *Bradstow: A Study of Status, Class and Power in a Small Australian Town*. Sydney: Angus & Robertson.
——(1978) *Social Stratification in Australia*. Sydney: Allen & Unwin.
——(1981) *Australian Community Studies and Beyond*. Sydney: Allen & Unwin.
Williams, C. (1981). *Open Cut*. Sydney: Allen & Unwin.
Wright, E.O. (1978). *Class, Crisis and the State*. London: New Left Books.
——(1985). *Classes*. London: New Left Books.

Chapter Four

Patriarchy and Gender: Theory and Methods

Claire Williams

In 1975 Margaret Power delineated the sex segregation of occupations, one of the main characteristics of the employment structure for women. In occupations that were disproportionately female 82 per cent of women were employed, and 77 per cent of men were working in occupations that were disproportionately male. Conversely, while 19 per cent of the male workforce was in occupations predominantly female, only 13 per cent of women workers were employed in disproportionately male occupations (Power 1975: 26). One-third of women were concentrated in three areas – clerical, sales and office employment – e.g. stenographer and typist (Power 1975: 28). Such a division is a characteristic feature of the employment structure which has been maintained throughout the century. Power was pessimistic about the possibilities of this situation diminishing because of the way in which male-dominated occupations became women's occupations once a large number of women entered them; men no longer entered the occupation or left it (Power 1975: 31). One reason for the preoccupation with the process of sex segregation in paid employment is that, without its recognition and substantial modification, women workers are unlikely to obtain economic equality with men. It is one of the reasons why women workers earn on average only 75 per cent of the wage of average male workers (Lewis 1982: 406) and why the attainment of equal pay affected so few women. Women tend to be clustered in positions which pay less than men's jobs, usually in less powerful industries. In the professions, women predominate in those with lower status and salaries, such as teaching, social work, the therapies, and in what is called the semi-professions, such as nursing.

Since the move in the late 1960s for greater equality between the

Table 4.1 Occupational Segregation, May 1985

Major Occupational Group	Females Number	Female % of Occupational Group
Professional, Technical	459,600	44.7
Administrative, Executive and managerial	76,000	16.6
Clerical	893,000	72.6
Sales	326,800	53.9
Farmers, Fishers, Timber-getters	107,400	24.3
Miners, Quarry Persons	*	*
Transport and Communications	44,800	13.8
Trades Persons, Production Process Workers and Labourers	225,000	12.1
Service, Sport and Recreation	415,100	64.2
Total	2,548,500	38.4

*Subject to sampling variability too high for most practical users
Source: 'Women at Work, Facts and Figures', Women's Bureau, Department of Employment and Industrial Relations, 1986

genders, one might expect to be able to report that the sex segregation of occupations is breaking down. However Power's original pessimism is confirmed. A study by the Women's Bureau in the Victorian Department of Employment and Industrial Relations shows women still concentrated in a narrow range of occupational groups, with 64 per cent of female employees concentrated in three major occupational groups: clerical, sales and service. While 18 per cent of female employees were in professional and technical occupations, 38 per cent of these were teachers and 28.5 per cent were nurses (Women's Bureau 1986).

Another economist predicts that 'unfortunately a continuation of past trends will mean that even by the year 2001 segregation by sex will be nearly as widespread and systematic as it is today' (Lewis 1982: 418). Ironically, job segregation is breaking down faster for men than for women (Equal Employment Opportunity Bureau 1982: 24).

While a small proportion of women has entered non-traditional occupations, Lucas' (1986) South Australian study of forty-three such women showed this to be a very isolating experience, and 79 per cent of the women were either harassed or discriminated against by male co-workers in the workplace, who intensified masculine practices in an attempt to repel such women's entry. The personal costs for individual women of attempting to break down sex segregation are high indeed.

While women are now entering tertiary education in vastly increased numbers (from one-quarter of university students to almost a half) (Anderson and Vervoorn 1983: 48), the pattern of sex segregation persists here as well. Women tend to select courses which reflect traditional definitions of femininity including nurturance and service to others. Women dominate in Humanities, Music, the Social and Behavioural Sciences (in areas such as Psychology and Social Work) and Education. They have made their greatest gains in Medicine, Paramedical areas, Education, Veterinary Science, Law and Humanities (Anderson and Vervoorn 1983: 54). Of these, perhaps Law and Veterinary Science represent a marked break with traditional definitions of femininity. Women have been slow to enter Natural Sciences (an increase of 15 per cent) and women comprise only 5 per cent of Engineering faculties and areas representing technology (Anderson and Vervoorn 1983: 51, 54). However, while 45 per cent of Bachelor degree graduates are women, only 29 per cent enrol in higher degrees (Anderson and Vervoorn 1983: 48) and their representation among university teachers is very low (Cass *et al.* 1983). A similar pattern persists in the higher levels of the public service. In 1982 women made up only 2 per cent of the Second Division of the Commonwealth Public Service (Equal Employment Opportunity Bureau 1982: 24).

A 1984 study of women in management in the private sector concluded that women managers in Australian business appear to be concentrated in the lower levels, particularly the junior ranks; that they receive less remuneration than their male counterparts at all levels of management; that they are employed mainly in service-oriented areas rather than mainstream management; and that they are not being given the same access to training and promotion opportunities as men managers (Still 1986: 36). In a related study of the advertising industry, Still found more women managers and directors than in the rest of private industry. However in this industry, which is more hospitable to women, and where one would expect them to have a more visible profile, women managers exist at the periphery of management and occupy the role and position of a 'marginal executive' (Still 1985: 18).

Women's subordination clearly persists because it is the result of social structures and processes which are integral to the kind of society in which we live. This subordination is so fundamental to the structure of society that it even pervades the analytical tools we use to describe society, the discipline of sociology itself. Until the

1960s, as part of the general invisibility of women in all disciplines studied at university, women were simply omitted from serious consideration in the main areas of sociology (Oakley 1974, Spender 1983). Few serious studies of women workers existed and women appeared fully only in studies of 'Marriage and the Family' where the comparable error of excluding men occurred. Since that time, feminist-inspired sociologists have elaborated feminist theories, both by writing women into sociology, and by providing an analysis which points to women's subordination as a central aspect of inequality in society.

This chapter will consider the contribution of three main kinds of feminist theories, radical feminist, Marxist feminist and socialist feminist, and contrast the strengths and shortcomings of these theories. It will then examine the way these theories have been used to understand Australian society. A further contribution to sociology has come from feminist-inspired writers on the methodology of sociology; these provide a challenge to well-entrenched, masculine, research strategies. Finally, two of the theories developed in the first part of the chapter are exemplified with Australian empirical data. The first, socialist feminist theory, is used to analyse the setting of open-cut mining, and the second, a radical feminist perspective, is used to examine unique features of flight attending as an occupation for women.

Feminist Theories

From the inception of feminist theoretical writings in the 1960s, a fundamental conflict of perspective has existed between radical feminists and Marxist feminists. The radical feminist, Adrienne Rich, first coined the term 'patriarchy' to refer to the universal oppression of women.

> Patriarchy is the power of the fathers: a familial-social, ideological, political system in which men – by force, direct pressure, or through ritual, tradition, law and language, customs, etiquette, education and the division of labor, determine what part women shall or shall not play, and in which the female is everywhere subsumed under the male ... Under patriarchy, I may live in *purdah* or drive a truck.
> (Eisenstein 1984: 5)

Shulamith Firestone in *The Dialectic of Sex* (1972) is perhaps the best known exemplar of radical feminist thinking. Firestone and other radical feminists hold that gender oppression (the oppression of women by men) is the oldest and most profound form of social inequality, predating and underlying all other forms, including that of race and class. Firestone argues that the Marxist analysis of the class division in society is not radical enough because it does not relate the structure of the economic class system to its origins in the sexual class system (Firestone 1972: 43). She believes that Freud grasped the crucial problem of modern life: sexuality. Freud, when referring to the Oedipal complex, describes power in the patriarchal family where women and children are dependent on the father (Firestone 1972: 48). She makes a somewhat crude cultural dichotomy between men and women, seeing men as essentially intellectual and creative whereas women are preoccupied with love: 'Women live for love and men' (1972: 121). She sees two basic cultural divisions: the male technological mode and the female aesthetic mode (1972: 165).

Firestone analyses romanticism and the part it plays in reinforcing sex class. Eroticism is part of romanticism. The distinguishing characteristic of women's exploitation as a class is sexual. For each woman her sexuality becomes synonymous with her individuality. Men characterise women physically as walking embodiments of breasts, legs or bottoms, singly or in combination. As a result, women come to value themselves in this way. This sex privatisation causes women to become preoccupied with their worthiness as sex objects while blinding them to their sexploitation as a class (1972: 142). If such characteristics are the only things valued, why trouble to develop real character? As Firestone put it, it is therefore far easier to light up the room with a smile until that day when the 'chick' graduates to 'old bag' and finds that her smile is no longer 'inimitable' (1972: 143). The kind of face that is typified as the sex object ideal does not allow for growth, flux and decay. Firestone wonders whether such a face expresses negative as well as positive emotions or 'does it falsely imitate the very different beauty of an inanimate object like wood trying to be metal? (1972: 147).

For all their shortcomings, radical feminists located gender as a main form of oppression in its own right, a subordination whose dynamic lies in sexuality, reproduction and culture. Their analysis remains useful where the sexual dimension is paramount, for example, in areas such as rape.

The Marxist feminists present a separate yet parallel tradition which attempts to situate gender inequality in a materialist analysis. Landes (1977–78) epitomises how a Marxist feminist analyses the Family. Domestic labour reproduces the fundamental class relations of capitalism in that the sexual division of labour allows the workers' creative capacity to be transformed into a commodity to be bought and sold and thus estranged from the worker. The wife plays a part in rejuvenating the male worker so he is ready for work on Monday morning. The working class family is pervaded by commodity relationships. Enjoyment and leisure in the home occur through commodities such as TV, computer games, videos and stereo equipment. Here Landes is only concerned with materialist, often property, aspects of sexuality and family life.

Another Marxist feminist, Vogel, regards the reproduction of labour power as the way those who provide labour in society are maintained and replaced (Vogel 1983: 140). Marx argued that the reproduction of labour power involving the housing, feeding and health care of workers, is essential for the continuation of capitalist societies, and an understanding of the mechanism by which this reproduction is achieved is crucial to the adequate analysis of capitalism (Abercrombie *et al.* 1984: 178). In most societies, it is in families where this takes place. But it can occur in other ways, such as the provision of barracks and single men's quarters at work-places; migrants can also provide an additional source of labour. While direct producers can be maintained in other ways, it is women who are crucial in the generational replacement of workers. For this there must be a sex division of labour of a minimal kind. For the dominant class there is a contradiction between the long-term needs of generational replacement of the labour force and the short-term needs for labour. The individual capitalist cares little about the reproduction of individual members of the working class, even though capitalism will need labour in the future. The dominant class has taken advantage of relationships between men and women that are based on sexuality and kinship (Vogel 1983: 146). Pregnancy and lactation entail a decline in the mother's capacity to work. The biological father or the father of the child-bearing woman will usually make sure the woman is provided for when she bears and cares for small children. Vogel introduces working class men into the analysis by regarding them as important in ensuring the means of subsistence are provided to the child-bearing woman (1983: 146). For Vogel, herein lies the source of the historical division of labour according to sex, that assigns women and men different roles with respect to necessary and surplus labour (1983: 146). Necessary labour refers to that amount of labour which creates a value equal to the daily requirements of the means of subsistence. For example, the first four hours of an eight-hour day equals the cost of the means of subsistence and reproduction of labour power; the extra four hours of labour will not be paid to the worker and is referred to as 'surplus labour' (Jalee 1977: 27). As noted above, Vogel claims the ruling class encourages male supremacy to keep the amount of necessary labour at just the level sufficient to reproduce their class, but not large enough to cut into the surplus appropriated by the ruling class themselves:

'Any attempt by women to appropriate to themselves more than is required for their subsistence is an indirect demand for part of the surplus appropriated by the ruling class. Thus male authority over women is supported and even enforced by the ruling class. On the other hand any attempt by men to evade their "responsibilities" for the support of women is also resisted.'

(Quick, quoted in Vogel 1983: 147)

Vogel is not interested in the advantages of this male supremacy for men themselves because, in the terms of her analysis, the ultimate benefactor is the dominant class (1983: 147). According to her, women have a greater responsibility for the ongoing tasks associated with necessary labour and especially for work connected with children; men correspondingly have greater responsibility for the provision of the material means of subsistence, a responsibility that is accompanied by their disproportionately greater involvement in the performance of surplus labour (Vogel 1983: 146).

For Vogel, the ruling class mobilises all members of the subordinate class, including women, into production. But this seems at odds with the empirical reality of the latest revolution in the means of production under capitalism, namely microelectronics and other new technologies which, by their nature, decrease the demand for labour. Micro-electronics are displacing labour particularly in women-dominated areas by as much as 30 per cent (Jones 1982, Werneke 1983).

Central to capitalism is the notion of short-term profit. Such a perspective, however, is at odds with the long-term reality of reproducing generations of working class people for future capitalist production. Vogel's focus on the concept 'reproduction of labour power' which is closely related to biological reproduction, over-emphasises the extent to which capitalist economic interests ever seriously took account of the long-term interests of capitalist society. Even if one could accept Vogel's assumption that the capitalist class was concerned with long-term generational reproduction, why would they leave this vital function so precariously located in the subsistence activities of the working class family? The short answer to this question is that the provision of the next generation of labourers is of little concern to the capitalist class.

Ultimately, what is wrong with Vogel's analysis is best characterised by Elshtain, who points out how easily Marxist feminists like Vogel dispense with the world of the private and lose the world of emotions through the use of terms such as 'the reproduction of labour power' (Elshtain 1982: 138).

One's fear and love for children are drained of their meaning, their emotional significance, when they are recast exclusively as relations between 'reproducers' and 'future labor power'.

(Elshtain 1982: 138)

This critique draws us back to the original strengths of radical feminist analysis and the refusal of radical feminists to be co-opted by a theory as powerful as Marxism. It is this very dilemma which led to the creation of socialist feminist analysis. While Marxist feminist writing is preoccupied with the capitalist mode of production, socialist feminism aims to focus on the system of subordination of women, which increasingly and loosely has come to be referred to as 'patriarchy', and the relationship of this subordination to the capitalist mode of production.

As Eisenstein points out (1979: 16), the study of women's oppression must deal with both sexual and economic material conditions if we are to understand oppression rather than merely understand economic exploitation. At the same time patriarchy should not be understood as merely biological. She argues that capitalism and patriarchy are neither autonomous nor identical systems. They are in their present form mutually dependent (1979: 21). This assumes that the patriarchal structure will change its form in response to the essential nature of capitalism. An example of this would be the way the family changed under capitalism. Production was no longer based on the family as it had been in the non-capitalist period, but men still retained their dominance. At the same time, capitalism incorporated patriarchal forms into its structure. For example, labour recruitment reflected aspects of the gender division of labour.

Within a similar frame of reference, Hartmann developed a socialist feminist analysis through a concept of patriarchal capitalism (1981: 18). Her concept of patriarchy rests upon two notions, one of hierarchy and the other of male dominance. She defines patriarchy as a set of social relations between men which has a material base i.e, it depends on men owning and organising the economy. Even though the class society is hierarchical, there is sufficient interdependence and solidarity among men to enable them to dominate women (Hartmann 1981: 14). In the hierarchy of patriarchy all men, whatever their rank in the patriarchy, are bought off or rendered less oppositional by being able to control at least some women (Hartmann 1981: 15).

While Hartmann at times does discuss interdependence, her analysis is firmly subsumed under what rapidly came to be termed 'dual systems' theory. There is an assumption here that there are

two separate systems of subordination with separate central determinants, a class system and a patriarchal or gender system.
However, dual systems theory has been criticised on a number of
grounds. Hartmann's definition of patriarchy tends to conceive of
women's subordination in terms of individual men and collectivities of men dominating women. However, the way the system is
structured, with women primarily responsible for child-rearing, is
more important than the wilful actions of individual men.
Hartmann's most important contribution lies in her critique of
Marxist categories such as class which she describes as 'sex blind'.
A concept like 'class' does not explain why particular people fill
particular places and why women are concentrated in working
class positions. It gives no clues as to why women are subordinate
to *men* inside and outside the family and why it is not the other way
around (Hartmann 1981: 10). Such a contribution has great import
for empirical research (Crompton and Jones 1984).

Probably the most challenging criticism to Eisenstein and
Hartmann's theoretical accounts has emerged among writers such
as Barrett (1980) and Beechey (1979) who have objected to the
concept 'patriarchy'. They do not like the way 'patriarchy' refers to
the universal subordination of women across all historical periods.
They think it should be specifically defined within particular time
periods, such as capitalism or feudalism. Instead, according to this
view, there would be specific accounts of patriarchal capitalism or
patriarchal feudalism or patriarchal socialism, and they give
primacy to the mode of production such as capitalism or feudalism
to determine the time period.

Eisenstein in turn has responded to such criticisms. In an
account published in 1981 she explicitly emphasises the universal
character of 'patriarchy'. She claims that there is a continuity to
patriarchal history because women have been subordinated in all
time periods and this has no parallel in economic history. At the
same time, her use of the term is also historical. Patriarchy changes
historically but particular elements of it are maintained over time
even if they are specifically redefined (Eisenstein 1981: 22). She
goes on to consider what feudal patriarchy and capitalist patriarchy
looked like. Here Eisenstein is giving primacy to patriarchy and
adapting the economic mode to it, because while economic systems
change, patriarchy has been continuous, women being subordinated under each mode of production. The feudal patriarchal
family was more public in a practical sense and in the ideas which
surrounded it (Eisenstein 1981: 25). The family only became a very
private sphere after the rise of capitalism. As mentioned earlier, in
pre-capitalist economic systems, production was located in the
family. One of the main effects of capitalism was to separate the

family from the economy and the public world. The state became more fully developed and passed legislation which made it appear that the division between public and private life was based on natural sex differences, with the public sphere representing the male and the private sphere representing the female. Thus the state formalised rule by men (Eisenstein 1981: 25).

In my view, Barrett's almost complete dismissal of the term patriarchy is unfortunate. I would argue for the utility of this concept because alternative concepts such as 'gender' are no less problematic. Both concepts are necessary for adequate empirical analysis and the term 'gender' does not carry with it the political and power connotations which is implicit in 'patriarchy'. 'Gender' is, if anything, more a-historical than the latter. In addition, Bernard points out that the term is more allied with a psychological approach, with the emphasis on individual differences (Bernard 1982: 35).

Feminist Sociological Research in Australia

We shall now briefly examine how Australian feminist sociologists have been inspired or otherwise by the theories discussed above. In the Australian context both Eisenstein's and Hartmann's formulations have been taken up as points of departure in at least two empirical works. I used Eisenstein's theoretical perspectives in *Open Cut. The Working Class in an Australian Mining Town* (1981). More recently, in *Women, Social Welfare and the State* (1983), Baldock writes:

> Throughout this book we maintain that capitalism and patriarchy are mutual reinforcements in the production of public policies which affect the lives of women in Australia.
>
> (Baldock 1983: 20)

Women, Social Welfare and the State is concerned with the way public policies within political parties, government, administration and the judiciary reinforce, challenge or transform some elements of women's unequal access to economic security and social autonomy.

Baldock's own position is inspired partly by Eisenstein and Hartmann, but is also indebted to others. The division of labour is perceived as an historical phenomenon and product of the dialectical relation between capitalism and patriarchy. Baldock assumes that public policies need to be seen as furthering the ends of the mutual accommodation of patriarchy and capitalism (1983: 21).

Men have historically acted as gate-keepers to the paid employ-ment of women. Baldock reviews the impact of the 1907 Higgins Harvester Judgment which legitimated and enshrined in law existing practices of sex segregation for at least 60 years. The living wage was applied to all male workers. There was general agree-ment that women's wages should be not less than 50 per cent but not more than 54 per cent of the male basic wage. It was falsely assumed that women had no dependants (1983: 34).

Baldock reviews the process by which sex segregation became firmly established in most state and federal awards. In addition, the original notion of the living wage for men and their families was not challenged until 1974 when a minimum wage for men and women was adopted (1983: 40). In 1974 there was intervention by women's rights groups in the arbitration procedures.

Baldock traces the events surrounding the National Maternity Leave Case in 1978–79. At the end of 1978 the ACTU mounted a test case for maternity leave in federal awards. The final decision, handed down in 1979, comprised a provision for fifty-two weeks unpaid leave with six weeks' compulsory leave prior to confine-ment, to be available only after a twelve-month eligibility period. While re-employment was to be guaranteed this could be at a lower pay rate (Baldock 1983: 44). When examining these gains, she notes that this increased access to paid labour but it also reinforced women's ideological identification with mothering (1983: 45).

In her closing remarks Baldock builds on the theoretical position set out previously. In its necessity to maintain its produc-tive forces capitalism has itself freed women from the chains of domesticity. But at the same time what are in effect patriarchal forces continue to lend strong ideological support for the mainten-ance of the family and the unpaid domestic labour behind it (1983: 51–52).

In another seminal contribution, Cass (1983) uses the imagery of class and feminism rather than capitalism and patriarchy to set out important social debates in Australian history about the living wage and child endowment. She details the class context of these debates. Employers and political/judicial élites, if they advocated child endowment, did so as a way of legitimating wage restraint. During the Great Depression of the 1930s with unemployment at 33 per cent, working class families and the organised labour movement came to view the possibilities of child endowment as regular sustenance for the families of the unemployed (Cass 1983: 75). The feminist contribution to these debates regarded child endowment as a just recognition of the rights of women and children to an income separate from the concept of the male living wage. From this standpoint child endowment was a recognition of the economic contribution made by women's non-market contribution of motherhood and domestic labour (1983: 63).

In one of the most important recent sociological accounts of gender relations in Australia, *Gender at Work*, (1982), Game and Pringle use what might be called a unitary or unifying theoretical position on the relationship of patriarchy to capitalism. They break with what they call the more sophisticated functional accounts, which assume that the sexual division of labour is something taken over by capitalism and used to its benefit. Thus they are clearly differentiating their analysis from dual systems theory which posits two autonomous but interdependent systems, one economic, the other gender-based. They are claiming that gender is one of the central defining features of the economic class system. In their view, the sexual division of labour takes highly specific forms under capitalism.

They avoid many of the problems associated with the term patriarchy by using the term gender. By gender relations they mean the social relations between men and women. These include the construction of masculinity and femininity and questions of identity and sexuality (Game and Pringle 1982: 15). Their aim is to explore the relationships between gender, the labour process and technological change. In their view the two sets of relations class and gender in the context of the implementation of new technology mediate, overlap and sometimes contradict each other. Their account can be described as unitary because they regard gender as built in at the level of the production/consumption division and in the way in which the labour process is organised. They assert that they need to look at the economic in relation to the sexual and the symbolic (1982: 23). Thus they are drawing together the strengths of both the radical feminist and Marxist feminist analyses set out earlier. The Marxist feminists were preoccupied with the economic, and the radical feminists' strength lay in their powerful exposures of patriarchy operating at the sexual and the symbolic level. At first sight this appears to solve the problems which caused Eisenstein and Hartmann to create dual systems theory which combines the strengths of an economic materialist focus (Marxist feminist) with those of an analysis which stresses the sexual and symbolic (radical feminist).

Game and Pringle reiterate their main theoretical proposition that the gender sexual division of labour is a central feature of capitalism even more decisively by asserting that the sexual division of labour is not some remnant from the past that is gradually being eliminated; rather it is a structural feature of modern capitalism (1982: 19). They go as far as to say that they reject the possibility of a 'non-patriarchal' capitalism (1982: 23).

They assemble five impressive case studies of industries and a discussion of domestic labour. These are informed by the theoretical propositions set out above. Very briefly, I will outline one of the case studies – the introduction of technical change in the white goods industry (refrigerators, washing machines, dryers etc.) in Adelaide.

Migrant workers made up 70 per cent of production workers in 1978, and in 1974 women were estimated to make up 60 per cent of the workforce in production areas (1982: 26). They note that the work was organised around a sexual division of labour which was based on a series of polarities broadly equated with masculinity and femininity. These are skilled/unskilled; heavy/light; dangerous/less dangerous; dirty/clean; interesting/boring; mobile/immobile (1982: 28). The first of each of these pairs is held to be appropriate for men, the second is seen as appropriately female.

With automation in this industry, overall there has been a narrowing of skills. Work has become less heavy, less dangerous, more boring and less mobile. In fact it has actually taken on features which are closer to past stereotyped definitions of women's work. However this has not meant that it has become more available to women. On the contrary, a new definition of the sexual division of labour has emerged. The division of labour has been reproduced along new lines with most jobs going to men. Women have been concentrated in fewer jobs than hitherto, in the remaining labour-intensive areas which are likely to be automated in the future (1982: 35).

Game and Pringle do not explain the processes which are involved. The changes have been accomplished in the first instance by management, who wanted to turn the press shop at Kelvinator into a male area (1982: 40). They are also supported by tradesmen who 'want to hang on to these jobs', 'their incumbents remain[ing] the most highly organised and relatively privileged section of whitegoods workers' (1982: 35). This also seems to be the case where management either was reacting to patriarchal power in male workers or choosing to use this as a legitimation to construct an all-male line. Game and Pringle need to delineate more clearly those processes through which the realignment of the sexual division of labour is accomplished. Why is it in management's interests to have all-male lines? On the other hand it is quite a different sociological process at work if management is reacting to working class men who initiate patriarchal class action at the shop floor in the form of collective pressure, at the expense of other sections of the working class, namely women. Game and Pringle's research suggests that both managers and workers are influenced by patriarchal ideology about the relationship of gender to nature. They share similar views that distinctions between the type of tasks men and women can do at the workplace are 'natural'.

> In one case when women were being moved off a line, the explanation management gave for the all-male workforce was that women wouldn't want to work closely with men.
>
> (Game and Pringle 1982: 38)

Despite their deceptively simple theoretical assertion that the gender sexual division of labour is a central structural feature of capitalism, Game and Pringle themselves fall into an almost classic dual systems mode of discussion in the chapter on the computer industry, 'Toys for the boys: Sexuality and the Computer'. Here, they bring to bear, in effect, a radical feminist perspective to explain apparent elements of overt sexuality in these workplaces. Echoing radical feminists or socialist feminists, they write that an economic analysis does not take account of gender; they are concerned with the symbolic. In workplaces in the computer industry 'blue movies' are projected on to the video screens together with computer printouts of naked women. According to their interpretation, technology and sexual domination are synonymous.

In another example in the white goods industry they note that dirty and dangerous work is done by both men and women migrants. They comment that the sexual division of labour intersects with a division by ethnicity. Here they tacitly accept that another hierarchy is in operation, an 'ethnic' one, and some acknowledgement of this is necessary to explain who fills which positions in the labour process. Their analysis on this point remains undeveloped. It is clear from this example that other sets of relations do intersect crucially with gender relations at the workplace and a unitary analysis has little to offer when faced with this social complexity.

Game and Pringle's assertion that the sexual division of labour is as central to capitalism as wage labour and surplus value is unconvincing. To paraphrase Vogel, but in another context, their empirical evidence is consistent with a position that gender is *historically* central to capitalism, but it is *not* consistent with a position that the sexual division of labour is *theoretically* central to capitalism. Patriarchal divisions predate capitalism.

There is no doubt that Game and Pringle's contribution to Australian sociology is impressive. Too much theorising has been conducted in studies of gender without recourse to any empirical grounding whatsoever, either of a contemporary or a historical kind. The data they present is extremely rich. In addition, the book is replete with much middle range, grounded theorising, which is of great value.

Feminist Methods

One of the main ways that sociologists study people is to use a scientific frame of reference and to use techniques such as surveys, interviews and statistical analysis. Such research is based on a number of scientific values: the verification principle or the search for evidence, and a belief in objectivity (facts and values) can, it is argued, be separated. Values, it is suggested, are only permitted expression at the stage of choosing the subject to research; otherwise they are regarded as contaminating. Many feminists have opposed this view of what constitutes a scientific (positivist) approach, because the separation of facts and values in mainstream sociology and social science has produced 'facts' which are male-biased and which have helped perpetuate the invisibility of women in 'legitimate' intellectual discourse and pursuits. These so-called 'facts' are based, it is argued, on assumptions which remain unquestioned. A different set of assumptions – in effect values – is required to point out that the facts are biased. This disillusion with positivistic approaches has led feminist researchers to explore other ways of studying people. Accordingly, there is an interest in what is called humanistic sociology and an attraction toward research techniques such as life histories, participant observation and historical approaches. Thus the first two concerns of this section are the reworking in new, feminist directions of 'humanistic' methods.

A third concern in methods' writings is partly a response to the obvious contradiction when decidedly committed feminist research takes its place beside 'objective', apparently uncommitted, yet clearly male-biased research. In the face of the inescapability of problems of bias, many feminist researchers stress the central importance of two accounts of research: the research act or process itself, and the version of social reality that it represents. However, at the same time, we can isolate a fourth preoccupation among other feminists who are seeking an accommodation with quantitative methods. Because feminist methods arise from a social change movement – the women's movement – feminist researchers are likely to be concerned with issues of exploitation and oppression.

Consequently there are two more concerns: a responsibility that those who are being researched are not treated as objects, and that research should play some part in social change. These themes will be explored more fully.

Shulamit Reinharz has used the term 'experiential' analysis for an approach which resembles existential sociology. The importance of the natural setting is paramount and the researcher is urged to avoid *a priori* categorising or ideas (or theories) worked out prior to entry to the field being studied. According to this view no research instruments are to be used which do not reproduce the subjects' categories of thought and action (Reinharz 1983: 178). The samples should be small, with the principal investigator fully participating in interviewing, taping interviews, transcribing and gathering up what is already 'there'.

Other feminists such as Stanley and Wise share the opposition to *a priori* theorising (derived from theoretical writings). For them, theory should be pragmatic, practical and everyday. Conceptual frameworks would derive from the particular facets of everyday relationships, experiences and behaviours (Stanley and Wise 1983b: 47). They claim that feminist *a priori* theorising is ultimately based on assumptions of false consciousness and continues the historical process of downgrading women's accounts of their lives (1983b: 69).

For these feminists, their position moves beyond methodologies in naturalistic settings which rely on empathy, and they embrace, rather uncritically, ethnomethodology (a sociological theory of how people obtain and use social meanings, ideas, values and feelings to make their actions understandable and acceptable to others). In their view, researchers in other traditions present doctored accounts of reality (1983b: 155). Such researchers write about the experiences of others as though they were directly available to them; they describe this as fictitious sympathy (1983b: 166). For Stanley and Wise, the researchers' construction is a central part of the final account, and the researcher should be much more concerned with presenting his/her understanding of what is going on. Social events and behaviours can only be interpreted and constructed by the person who is describing their experiences of them (1983b: 170). Thus research for Stanley and Wise comes down to feminists as researchers reproducing and analysing their own experiences of sexism. Such a research act would consist of an incident where a woman as researcher can choose to pass or not as a feminist. She can challenge the expression of sexism involved in opening doors for other people, for instance, and thus behave inappropriately as a deviant (1983b: 134) and, in this, 'do feminism'.

Such an exploration of reactions to feminism's different reality, they claim, will tell us a great deal about the reaction of men to women.

However this perspective is inadequate because it restricts feminist research to the same micro-sociological cul-de-sac in which ethnomethodology became trapped through its inability or unwillingness to link itself to macro discourses.

Moreover, Stanley and Wise, like experiential feminist researchers, fail to make explicit the assumptions on which their methodology is based. For example, the rejection of theory is not applied to ethnomethodology itself as a substantial body of theory. Both writers implicitly base their concern with the subordination of women on feminist theory, which is clearly influencing the perspective they are using, but this remains unacknowledged. In addition, one of the main criticisms which is made of studies using an experiential methodology is that by concentrating on people's commonsense accounts of their own experiences, such studies are in danger of merely reproducing commonsense thought, which is replete with forgotten 'theories' of the past. Commonsense thought contains a patriarchal component and experiential methodology has come under attack for having a hidden bias (Huber 1973, Lichtman 1970). For this reason, experiential methodology is often most effectively used when it is explicitly combined with theories from other traditions, such as feminism or Marxism. The importance of the experiential emphasis lies in the focus on women's own accounts of their personal, lived experiences.

A second important theme of feminist methodological writings is their anti-positivist stance. Matthews accused feminists of merely putting on new blinders by using a feminist theoretical framework which analysed society in terms of the concept of patriarchy. In her reply to Matthews, Zillah Eisenstein (1982) puts a powerful case against positivist social science which has harboured a patriarchal view of reality in the name of objectivity. For Eisenstein there is no value-free (objective) science just as there is no fact-free ideology. Feminist analysis, like scientific analysis, reflects the systematic knowledge of the material world. However feminism accounts for gender differences and does not reify them as scientific research has done by ignoring the structural differences between men and women (Eisenstein 1982: 36). Analysis which is explicitly feminist has a different view of science and works within a framework influenced by the sociology of knowledge, and in so doing is explicit about its biases.

While many feminist researchers embrace an experiential perspective, a different position is taken by those who embrace *a priori* feminist theorising, usually of a Marxist and critical kind. Such approaches are exemplified by Acker, Barry and Esseveld (1983). They explicitly discuss the importance of social structure and are concerned with the relationship between changes in the structural situation of women and changes in consciousness. The subjects of their study were wives and mothers who were attempting to move into the labour market. While they use many of the methods which have a great deal in common with those discussed above, they are also committed to theories of social change and are not content to merely describe social reality (Acker, Barry and Esseveld 1983: 424). Moreover, their aim of adequate reconstruction or faithful depiction of the social world is within the frame of reference of the phenomenologist, Schutz, rather than the positivist aim of prediction (Acker *et al.* 1983: 431).

Their actual methods include unstructured interviews, allowing the definition of consciousness as emergent knowledge to come out of the discussion. Written material was shown to the women who were written about. Life histories in the women's own words were used to typify particular patterns of change. The aim of the reconstruction was to reveal the underlying social relations that eventuate in the daily lives they were studying. To them this relationship between such underlying social relations and daily life lies at the heart of a sociology for women (1983: 431).

One of the feminist answers to the problem raised by issues of objectivity is to include an account of the research process with one of reconstructed reality as central parts of the final research report. In Stanley and Wise's words, all research necessarily comes to us through the central involvement of researchers, who necessarily interpret and construct what is going on. There is no other way to be involved either in research or life (Stanley and Wise 1983a: 196). Such a strategy is not entirely new (Plummer 1983) but here it receives a new emphasis. For Reinharz (1983) predispositions are only biases if they are not acknowledged or explored (1983: 175).

Graham (1983) criticises the growing tendency for feminist researchers to see quantitative research as representing the male style of knowing, while qualitative research is seen to operate within a different paradigm, representing a female style of knowing. She points out that this has the potential to reinforce the tendency to analyse women and men's lives separately. She recommends that rather than building a methodological ghetto for women we need to design research strategies that take account of their complex and overlapping inter-relationships with the public and private domains (1983: 136). The thrust of her argument consists of a searching feminist critique of the survey method which she characterises in Elshtain's terms of eclipsing the self-understanding of the female subject. She concludes with a call that the survey method should not be employed uncritically to obscure women's self-understanding (1983: 146).

At least one commentator, Toby Epstein Jayaratne, advocates the combination of qualitative and quantitative methods because of the limitations of both. Such a position does have unexplicated problems, as Bryman (1984) points out. Jayaratne advocates the use of quantitative methods because some methods in qualitative research do not permit generalisation. This is a serious oversight, because generalised statements are important both for advising policy-makers of public opinion and deciding on strategies to bring about change in public opinion itself. Moreover, she believes that feminists must develop quantitative literacy. In her view, there is an objective aura about traditional research which makes it convincing and influential. Thus, findings which are often products of poor methodology and sexist bias are interpreted by the public as fact. Feminists need to monitor closely and publicise the problems of such seemingly objective research (Jayaratne 1983: 158).

Many feminists involved in research have been concerned that they should not follow a tendency, implicit in the research act as it is presently constituted within a hierarchical division of labour, to transform those researched into objects of scrutiny and manipulation. Women researchers have all experienced the objectification of women in society. Thus there is a conscious aim among feminist researchers to transform the subject/researcher relationship into a non-hierarchical, non-authoritarian, non-manipulative relation. Oakley, in her account of the research for her book *Becoming a Mother*, found great conflict between these goals and what she came to regard as a purely exploitative attitude implicit in textbook advice about interviewing (Oakley 1981: 41). An attitude of refusing to answer questions or offer any kind of personal feedback was not even helpful in terms of traditional aims of promoting rapport, let alone in not treating people as objects. She offers a revised approach: 'no intimacy without reciprocity', which is particularly suitable for longitudinal, in-depth interviewing.

Acker also describes a new ethic to create conditions in which the object of research enters into the process as an active subject. Shulamit Reinharz (1983) describes this as subject participation. However Acker *et al.* warn that the high levels of trust which develop in such relationships also lead to ethical dangers. The researcher's goal is to gather information; thus the danger always exists of manipulating friendships to that end. Given that the power differences between researcher and researched cannot be completely eliminated, attempting to create a more equal relationship can, paradoxically, become exploitative. They try to overcome the distance between researchers and researched by showing the written material to the women in the study, especially with those with whom they had the most interviews, and who had identified themselves as consciously trying to change.

The above account of research is helpful because it is not overtly idealised and discusses real problems that are actually faced daily in the field. For example, they discuss their reluctance to share their interpretations with those they expected would be upset by them. There was potential conflict between the feminist frame of reference and the women's interpretations of their own lives. Their solution to this conflict was not to include such women as active participants in the analysis of the research. And they note that the problem of whether or not to confront groups or individuals with interpretations of their lives which are radically different from their own is an ethical question faced by anyone accepting critical social research. This is less of a problem for experiential research-ers who merely reproduce the subject's commonsense accounts, but it becomes an acute problem for a researcher using critical and feminist *a priori* theories as part of a final explanation.

Their final word on this moral problem is an acceptance of the dilemmas: researchers can maintain an awareness of when and why they were not able to make the research process a true dialogue. This position gives legitimacy to the subjectivity of the other as well as to the researcher. They conclude that it is impossible to create a research process that completely erases the contradictions in the relationship between researcher and researched.

Finally, feminist researchers want their research to be actively used to change women's lives in less oppressive directions. How-ever this goal is not achieved simply, or without problems. Initially Acker and her team set out principles of feminist research which include the goal to contribute to women's liberation through producing knowledge that can be used by women themselves. However they later write that perhaps the best we can do is to guard against our research being used against women, although that also may be difficult (Acker, Barry and Esseveld 1983: 198).

A recent study by Connell and others, *Making the Difference* (1982) conforms to many of the criteria set out in the preceding discussion. The research team use a critical theoretical perspective. They make use of an experiential technique called the limited life history, and reconstructed accounts of the life histories were discussed with the subjects. The thrust of the study is toward social change.

While I find many of the arguments set out above compelling on an emotional and intellectual level, I would sound a note of caution. In my own recent research, I continue to feel the need to deploy a more positivistic frame of reference alongside humanist methods such as life histories, and in this respect I agree with much of what Jayaratne (1983) writes. It is my aim to research macro social processes, and ultimately it is very difficult to use qualitative methods satisfactorily, and still complete research which handles large numbers of people and which is in a mode readily understood and used by other groups in society who are interested in reform – women, trade unions and government, for instance. Persuading other people of the authenticity of research is important and one of the definitions of methodology is to convince others that one's knowledge is correct (Bulmer 1977: 4). I have chosen triangulation or the mixing of methods, and while this is not without considerable problems, it is important to understand each method on its own terms (Silverman 1985: 21).

Reservations aside, the revival and reworking in new directions of experiential methods is long overdue. It should become a more common practice that reconstructions of reality include an account of the research process itself. In this way the false claim to objectivity can be transcended. More attempts should be made to include the subjects of research in the research process as active participants.

Empirical Analysis

Open Cut
In this section some of the theoretical ideas developed earlier will be used to illuminate the analysis of Australian empirical data, in the first instance taking material from my book *Open Cut. The Working Class in an Australian Mining Town*. Eisenstein's conception of capitalism and patriarchy as interdependent hierarchies, will be utilised to analyse the relationship of paid work to the family in the setting of open cut coal mining in central Queensland in the mid-1970s.

This study consists of a survey of about 500 coalminers from two mines. As well as the work study, it also comprises a field study and interviews with fifty married couples.

Men's participation in paid production is a central class experience for them, but it is also part of their gender identity, part of the social construction of masculinity. Definitions of masculinity enter into the way work is personally experienced as a life-long commitment and responsibility. An occupation is the basis of a man's adult life. Tolson (1977) identifies the deep structure of masculinity: having a job, physical strength, everyday routines such as getting out of the house, personal habits such as smoking and drinking, and intimate physical experiences such as sex (1977: 56). Tolson further argues that men go to work with an ambivalent emotional structure – a subservience to authority and a compulsive need for recognition. Yet under capitalism these are only partially confirmed, and in many respects denied. Masculine identity is precariously reaffirmed through the provider role and through the presence of an idealised image of home-centred leisure based on the private domestic sphere (Tolson 1977: 65–66).

For the majority of men in this Queensland study, home life was a relief and a haven from the monotony and dissatisfaction of work.

> You can relax – get your mind on other things off the job. Glad to get away from it. Screaming machinery. Accident. One bloke nearly went through a laminated windscreen. I was practically run over by a Euclid [truck].

It was men who had low levels of job control who felt the need for release from the strain of their jobs and they sought this in home-centred leisure. They talked about relief, strain, tension, pressure and sought in their home life a compensation from such circumstances.

The men with the most patriarchal orientation, men who believed men should make most decisions in the home, far outnumbered other men in regarding the home as a respite from stress and a free place where one relaxed. A very patriarchal man may suffer the rigours of the hostile work environment but he compensates for this and survives by controlling his domestic environment so that it remains a place where he can relax, uninhibited by autonomous demands from his wife.

Such men did seek relief by talking over their work problems with their wives. It is not interaction they seek, but rather women's taken-for-granted labour, the wife's undemanding and non-interfering presence, which allows for compensation. Some men, however, did not consider the home environment as a compensation area, because they did not control it.

The foregoing provides some support for the hypothesis that patriarchy in day-to-day life in the working class family provides a safety valve to alleviate the full impact of capitalist social relations.

In the setting of open cut coal mining, patriarchy plays a crucial role in facilitating instrumental rationality or the domination of people and their social relations by technical relations (Connerton 1980). Because of the embargo on jobs for women, the latter are forced into extreme sex roles reminiscent of the 1950s. This particular form of the family was called matriduxy by Adler (1966) and it facilitates the relentless regimens of shift-work and overtime which enable the machines to be worked continuously, human rhythms being completely subordinated to those of the machine. Men either work the seven-day roster (four days off a month) or the five-day roster. Both shifts involve night shift, followed by afternoon shift, followed by day shift or, alternatively, a small number of men work permanent day shift. It is very difficult to be rostered on permanent day shift. Some men worked fifteen hours of overtime per week.

There were wives who had adapted their lives to that of the machines and the men who maintained them. One woman said, 'I jump into bed with him. I sleep in the day.' It is difficult for women to have paid jobs, even if available, when men are working such long and irregular hours. This inability to have wages of their own reduces women's power in marriage because it is difficult for the woman to bring resources of her own to the marriage. In *Open Cut*, women found themselves doing men's domestic labour, including aspects of fathering, and again this is reminiscent of the matriduxy structure of the Australian family of the 1950s.

The above empirical cameo highlights the interdependence of patriarchy and capitalism. In the same study, there are instances of the autonomous nature of the two hierarchies. Chapter 7 of *Open Cut*, 'Aspects of Working Class Marriage', describes the working out of a key patriarchal institution, which is often strongly affected by its location in a capitalist mode of production. But this analysis shows that many features of women's subordination within marriage lie within the social relations of marriage itself, and these originate and are perpetuated by the time-honoured feature of patriarchy.

Industrial Behaviour of Flight Attendants

The second empirical illustration of the theoretical perspectives set out at the beginning of this chapter comes from an analysis of the industrial behaviour of flight attendants. Here a radical feminist perspective will be deployed to analyse a focal patriarchal feature of a service occupation. The study of flight attendants was carried out in 1981 and 1983, and consists of a survey of over 1,000 domestic flight attendants, and interviews with management, union executives and flight attendants.

An extreme form of gender definition – ascription – was woven into the very fabric of the occupation in the height, weight and age requirements. The first advertisement to recruit 'hostesses' was placed in a Queensland newspaper in 1937 and was headed 'Must retire at 35' (McRobbie 1980: 17). A class aspect was added to this: a middle class image of the demure young lady and, in the 1960s, advertising agencies shifted to a much more explicit sexual presentation of the 'hostess' as a sex symbol. This coincided with the flight attendant becoming a crucial part of the public relations function of the airline. In this period, there is an aspect to the presentation of the flight attendant as a service worker, with airline executives engaged in selling women's sexuality, while male passengers consumed this in a vicarious form. In the 1983 interviews, a senior male Ansett executive confirmed this interpretation when he spontaneously recalled: 'You [male passengers] would get a kick if a hostess grinned at you. It was as if she had spent the night with you.'

Even now the women flight attendants in their presentation to the public, their training and supervision, are a highly visible distillation of middle class notions of femininity. They symbolise *woman*. They are expected to enact two leading conceptions of womanhood: the loving wife and mother (serving food, tending to the needs of others), and the glamorous 'career woman' (dressed to be seen in contact with strange men, professional and controlled in manner very far from home) (Hochschild 1983: 175).

While elements from the patriarchal configuration have been modified in some ways, they continue to be living issues in the presentation of the flight attendant, and those around which industrial conflict between flight attendants and management occurs. Age continues to loom large as a point of dispute. The airline companies from the beginning instituted an age limit, and it has only been gradually lifted upward through feminist-inspired industrial action – resulting in a retirement age of fifty-five – which was negotiated in 1984–85. In the 1981 survey, 40 per cent of the sample was 25 or younger; 40 per cent aged 26–30; 13 per cent, 31–35, 2 per cent, 36–40 and 1 per cent over 40. The overt sexual connotation built into the specification of this occupation is clear from the way older women have been regarded as the illegitimate bearers of nurturant service. Part of the cultural definition of femininity is in terms of mothering, with all the caring, nurturing and servicing work that this implies. This latter aspect of femininity has patently not been one of the defining features of the nurturant service in aircraft. Feminist analysis in general has not paid as much attention to the question of age, but ageism is an integral feature of patriarchy, as pointed out by Firestone (1972: 143). For men, sexual value is defined more in terms of personality, intelligence and earning power than physical appearance. Women, however, must rest their case largely on their bodies (Bell 1970: 78). Their ability to attain status in other than physical ways and translate that status into sexual attractiveness is severely limited by culture. As a woman approaches middle age, she begins to notice a change in the way people treat her. This is reflected in the growing indifference of others toward her looks and her sexuality. The few studies available suggest that older women are one of the lowest prestige groups in society (Bell 1970: 78).

The companies tend to regard the 'older' flight attendant as a problem. This was not true of a minority of management executives interviewed. One management figure referred to the 'senior girls' as 'the most gracious, kindest women I have ever met. I saw the same in United Airlines [the American airline] – [such a flight attendant] is exemplary in her approach to people.' Another said that they were quite good if they looked after themselves. However, the majority response from both airline managements was: 'The older flight attendant is at odds with the public image of an appropriate flight attendant. They present an insoluble problem because the companies are dealing with someone very frustrated. The older they become the more detached they are from the organisation.' This view of the unintegrated older flight attendant is not borne out by the results of the 1981 survey. Those flight attendants over the age of 36 expressed high levels of loyalty to the companies – 61 per cent – and were only surpassed in this by the very young flight attendants of 19–20. The flight attendant group who expressed least loyalty to the companies were in the age group 26–30.

In other industries, older workers who are the most experienced are not usually referred to in this condescending way. However, most other jobs do not contain a covert sex object component and in terms of the historical gender definition of the occupation, the older flight attendant is a 'failed' sex object. Young flight attendants are by definition successful sex objects, and they were capable of expressing a similar aversion to the older flight attendant through an acceptance of the sexual component of the patriarchal ideology which has historically surrounded the occupation. During interviews, one very attractive young flight attendant described older flight attendants as 'flying fossils'. She went on to say: 'They should get all the old biddies out of flying as they have been flying too long and are too old for the job. There is nothing worse than having a grandmother serve you tea and coffee.' This comment indicates the profound association between sexuality and service work on Australian domestic aircraft. While middle-aged women and older women are some of the main people who serve tea and coffee in the society – even in airport cafeterias – and are indeed symbols of this kind of service in television biscuit commercials, they are not legitimate service workers serving male passengers on aircraft.

One of the most noticeable features of the flight attendant airline

culture is the way the attendants are referred to by management –
and refer to themselves – as 'girls'. Bell has theorised that the term
'girl' is an indirect way of communicating age limitation (1970:
79–80). She presents evidence from employment agencies using
the word 'girl' in advertisements, that the term means 'under 30' or
'under 35'. In her view, the use of the term 'girl' for women and
'boy' for blacks, indicates that the category under discussion is not
considered capable of full adulthood. She adds that blacks and
women are acceptable and even likeable when very old, but
somehow both are anachronistic as mature adults (Bell 1970: 80).
Male flight attendants are also referred to as 'the boys', a term
often used for blacks and adult working class male workers.
Hochschild (1983) found that many women flight attendants on the
American Delta airline, while they referred to themselves as 'the
girls', were opposed to the use of the term in principle because of
its connotation of not being allowed to age. Women in their thirties
were occasionally called 'granny' and when called 'girl' by passengers, it often denoted disrespect (Hochschild 1983: 180–81).

While the women themselves have spearheaded the agitation to
end the ageism based on sexism, the introduction of male flight
attendants into the domestic airlines in the early 1980s renders the
implicit ageism more problematic. It is more difficult to suggest
that men should end their working lives prematurely. The presence of the male flight stewards historically in Qantas had
provided such a contrast, and as a result, Qantas women flight
hostesses were permitted to choose retirement at thirty-five or at a
more normal retirement age (although even then they were
offered more favourable retirement at thirty-five to encourage
them to leave).

A radical feminist point of departure was favoured to analyse
data on age and the women flight attendant because a Marxist
feminist analysis would not have adequately analysed the patriarchal structure and ideology operating in this instance. A
Marxist feminist analysis stresses the capitalist dimension, which
in this instance is less important than the patriarchal one. The
importance of the patriarchal aspect can be seen in the way
patriarchal excesses such as ageism, which specifically related to
women flight attendants, have been dismantled by trade union
action (particularly the 1975 strike) (Williams 1988). Despite Sir
Reginald Ansett's opposition to older women flight attendants on
his aircraft, this ultimately made little difference to the economic
viability of the capitalist organisation. It is not even clear that
Ansett would sell more air tickets if it were able to have all blonde,
single women flight attendants, under 30, because the dismantling
of the more patriarchal aspects has coincided with an increase in

women passengers and this is itself part of the result of anti-
patriarchal struggles in other sectors of the society.

The two empirical examples reveal the way a theory such as
Eisenstein's enables us to consider the autonomy of the hierarchies
of capitalism and patriarchy, but also how they can be integrally
inter-related, as structures and ideologies.

Conclusion

This chapter began by showing how processes which have long
been associated with the subordination of women, such as sex
segregation of occupations, remain and continue to maintain the
pattern of inequality between the genders. The feminist theory
which currently exists and which attempts to explain such enduring features of the social structure is still in an embryonic state.
The three main theories which might account for these inequalities
were examined. Radical feminist theory introduced the term
'patriarchy', defined as men's power over women through a
familial-social, ideological and political system. Radical feminists
regarded sexuality, reproduction and culture as the mainsprings of
women's subordination. By contrast, Marxist feminists located
gender inequality within the basic tenets of Marxism, accepting
the conceptual framework of the modes of production and the
materialist determination of relations in society, including gender
relations. According to this, women are crucial to the generational
replacement of workers. However, a third analysis, socialist feminism, finds the latter theories limited and seriously flawed and tries
to combine the strengths of each by focusing on both sexual and
economic dimensions of women's subordination.

A number of Australian studies take aspects of these theories as
points of departure. Baldock's (1983) historical examination of
public policies in relation to women, argues that the aims of the
capitalist economy are satisfied even if the work of women, i.e. the
maintenance of productive forces (labour power) and the maintenance of the social relations of reproduction are not always mutually
supportive. Game and Pringle's *Gender at Work* (1982) examines a
number of case studies and is based on the theoretical premiss that
gender is a central feature of the way work continues to be
organised in capitalism. In the white goods industry when new
technology removed a number of jobs, the characteristics of men
and women's work were conveniently redefined to allow men to
take possession of most of the remaining jobs even though they

conformed more closely to the previous definitions of women's work. The case study material is compatible with their theoretical position, which remains somewhat underdeveloped.

Just as feminist theories are required to define women as legitimate actors in society and to explain subordination, so distinctively feminist methods have emerged to adequately give voice to women's personal, lived experiences. Feminist methods are often based on a questioning of the scientific basis of male-biased research which rendered women invisible for so long in social science research. This has paralleled a rediscovery and reworking in new directions of experiential or humanist methods, including unstructured interviews and life histories. At the same time, others warn of the dangers of building a methodological ghetto for women and recommend judicious and critical use of surveys, and the combination of qualitative and quantitative methods.

The final concern of the chapter was to show how one of the theoretical perspectives delineated earlier, socialist feminist analysis, could be deployed fruitfully in actual empirical situations to analyse data. Eisenstein's socialist feminist analysis was used in the context of open cut coal mining to emphasise the interdependence of patriarchy and capitalism. The ambivalent evaluation placed on the older flight attendant in the airline industry reveals the explanatory force of 'patriarchy' in its own right in a situation where few specifically capitalist features were operating to explain this outcome for women. In this case patriarchal features over-bore capitalist ones.

Feminist theory developed initially in a context where relatively little systematic empirical research had been completed. This was unfortunate, because the best sociology reveals a dynamic inter-play between theory and processes discovered and illuminated by the theory in the empirical world. Theory ultimately must be useful to the empirical researcher. If there is no relationship between theory and empirical reality then, in my view, such theory has a dubious status because it is often devised using observations from the empirical world where these remain unacknowledged. At the same time, research without a feminist theory of some kind merely repeats the serious error of sociological researchers in the first half of this century who rendered women intellectually invisible and who ignored gender subordination, thus providing a seriously inaccurate account of social reality. The contributions feminist thinkers are now making to methodological writings could indicate that feminist research will give greater attention and greater weight to a more humanist kind of sociology.

References

Abercrombie, N., Hill, S., Turner B.S. (1984) *Dictionary of Sociology*. Harmondworth: Penguin.

Acker, J., Barry, K. and Esseveld, J. (1983) 'Objectivity and Truth: Problems in doing Feminist Research', *Women's Studies International Forum* 6 (4): 423–35.

Adler, D.L. (1966) 'The Contemporary Australian Family' in *Human Relations* 19 (3), August: 265–82.

Anderson, D.S., Vervoorn, A.E. (1983) *Access to Privilege: Patterns of Participation in Australian Post-Secondary Education*. Canberra: ANU Press.

Baldock, C.V. (1983) 'Public Policies and the Paid Work of Women' in C.V. Baldock and B. Cass (eds) *Women, Social Welfare and the State*. Sydney: Allen & Unwin.

Barrett, M. *et al.* (1979) 'Representational and Cultural Production' in M. Barrett *et al.* (eds) *Ideology and Cultural Production*. London: Croom Helm.

———(1980) *Women's Oppression Today*. London: Verso.

———(1984) 'Rethinking Women's Oppression: A Reply to Brenner and Ramas', *New Left Review* 146, July–August: 123–28.

Beechey, V. (1979). 'On Patriarchy', *Feminist Review* 3: 66–82.

Bell, I.P. (1970) 'The Double Standard', *Trans-Action* November–December: 75–80.

Bernard, J. (1973) 'My Four Revolutions: An Autobiographical History of the ASA', in J. Huber (ed.) *Changing Women in a Changing Society*. Chicago: University of Chicago Press.

———(1982) 'Comment on Matthews', *The American Sociologist* 17: 35–36.

Bowles, G. and Klein, R.D. (1983) *Theories of Women's Studies*. London: Routledge & Kegan Paul.

Brenner, J. and Ramas, M. (1984) 'Rethinking Women's Oppression', *New Left Review* 144, March–April: 33–71.

Bryman, A. (1984) 'The Debate about Quantitative and Qualitative Research: A Question of Method or Epistemology?' *British Journal of Sociology*, XXXV (1), March: 75–92.

Bulmer, M. (ed.) (1977) *Sociological Research Methods, An Introduction*. London: Macmillan.

Burton, C. (1985) *Subordination, Feminism and Social Theory*. Sydney: Allen & Unwin.

Cass, B. (1983) 'Redistribution to Children and to Mothers: A History of Child Endowment and Family Allowances', in C.V. Baldock and B. Cass (eds) *Women, Welfare and the State*. Sydney: Allen & Unwin.

Cicourel, A.V. (1981) 'Notes on the Integration of Micro- and Macro-Levels of Analysis', in K. Knorr-Cetina and A.V. Cicourel (eds) *Advances in Social Theory and Methodology. Towards an Integration of Micro and Macro Sociologies*. London: Routledge & Kegan Paul.

Connell, R.W., Ashenden, D.J., Kessler, S. and Dowsett, G.W. (1982)

Making the Difference. Schools, Families and Social Division. Sydney: Allen & Unwin.

Connerton, P. (1980) *The Tragedy of Enlightenment, An Essay on the Frankfurt School.* Cambridge: Cambridge University Press.

Court, D. (1983) 'The Centrality of Patriarchy', *Arena*, 65: 162–71.

Crompton, R. and Jones, G. (1984) *White-Collar Proletariat. Deskilling and Gender in Clerical Work.* London: Macmillan.

Eisenstein, Z. (ed.) (1979) *Capitalist Patriarchy and the Case for Socialist Feminism.* New York: Monthly Review Press.

———(1981) *The Radical Future of Liberal Feminism.* New York and London: Longman.

———(1982) 'Comment on Matthews', *The American Sociologist* 17: 36.

Elshtain, J.B. (1982) 'Feminist Discourse and its Discontents: Language, Power and Meaning' in N.A. Keohane *et al. Feminist Theory. A Critique of Ideology.* Sussex: Harvester.

Equal Employment Opportunity Bureau (1982) 'Selection and Development of Women in Senior Positions in the Australian Public Service' Canberra: Australian Public Service Board.

Firestone, S. (1972) *The Dialectic of Sex.* London: Paladin.

Game, A. and Pringle, R. (1982) *Gender at Work.* Sydney: Allen & Unwin.

Giddens, A. (1976) *New Rules of the Sociological Method.* London: Hutchinson.

Graham, H. (1983) 'Do Her Answers Fit His Questions? Women and the Survey Method' in E. Gamarnikow *et al.* (eds) *The Public and the Private.* London: Heinemann.

Hartmann, H. (1981). 'The Unhappy Marriage of Marxism and Feminism: Towards a More Progressive Union' in L. Sargent (ed.) *The Unhappy Marriage of Marxism and Feminism.* London: Pluto.

Hochschild, A.R. (1983) *The Managed Heart, Commercialization of Human Feeling.* Berkeley: University of California Press.

Huber, J. (1973) 'Symbolic Interaction as a Pragmatic Perspective: The Bias of Emergent Theory, *American Sociological Review* 38: 274–84.

Jalee, P. (1977) *How Capitalism Works.* New York and London: Monthly Review Press.

Jayaratne, T.E. (1983) 'The Value of Quantitative Methodology for Feminist Research' in G. Bowles and R.D. Klein (eds) *Theories of Women's Studies.* London: Routledge & Kegan Paul.

Jones, B. (1982) *Sleepers Wake!* Melbourne: Oxford University Press.

Kelly-Gadol, J. (1976) 'The Social Relations of the Sexes, Methodological Implications of Women's History', *Signs* 1 (4).

Landes, J.B. (1977–78) 'Women, Labor and Family Life: A Theoretical Perspective', *Science and Society* XLI (4), Winter.

Lewis, D.E. (1982) 'The Measurement of the Occupational and Industrial Segregation of Women', *Journal of Industrial Relations* 24, September: 406–23.

Lichtman, R. (1970) 'Symbolic Interactionism and Social Reality: Some Marxist Queries', *Berkeley Journal of Sociology* XV.

Lucas, J. (1986) 'Work and Domestic Experiences of Women in Non-

Traditional Occupations', Unpublished Honours Thesis, Sociology Discipline, Flinders University, Bedford Park, SA.

Matthews, S.H. (1982) 'Rethinking Sociology through a Feminist Perspective', *The American Sociologist* 17, February: 29–35.

McRobbie, MA. (1980) 'A Subjective Study of Air Hostessing in Australia', BEd. Thesis, Department of Social Science, Coburg.

Oakley, A. (1974) 'The Invisible Woman: Sexism in Sociology' in A. Oakley *The Sociology of Housework*. Oxford: Martin Robertson.

———(1981) 'Interviewing Women: A Contradiction in Terms' in H. Roberts (ed.) *Doing Feminist Research*. London: Routledge & Kegan Paul.

Plummer, K. (1983) *Documents of Life: An Introduction to the Problems and Literature of a Humanistic Method*. London: Allen & Unwin.

Power, M. (1975) 'The Making of a Woman's Occupation', *Hecate* 1 (3), July: 25–34.

Reinharz, S. (1983) 'Experiential Analysis: A Contribution to Feminist Research' in G. Bowles and RD. Klein *Theories of Women's Studies*. London: Routledge & Kegan Paul.

Shroyer, T. (1970) 'Towards a Critical Theory for Advanced Industrial Society' in H.P. Dreitzel (ed.) *Recent Sociology* 2. London: Macmillan.

Silverman, D. (1985) *Qualitative Methodology and Sociology, Describing the Social World*. Aldershot: Gower.

Smith, D.E. (1979) 'A Sociology for Women' in J.A. Sherman and E.T. Beck (eds) *The Prism of Sex. Essays in the Sociology of Knowledge*. Wisconsin: University of Wisconsin Press.

Spender, D. (ed.) (1983) *Men's Studies Modified*. Pergamon: Oxford.

Stanley, L. and Wise, S. (1983a) 'Back into the Personal or Our Attempt to construct Feminist Research' in G. Bowles and R.D. Klein *Theories of Women's Studies*. London: Routledge & Kegan Paul.

———(1983b) *Breaking Out. Feminist Consciousness and Feminist Research*. London: Routledge & Kegan Paul.

Still, L.V. (1985) 'Women Managers in the Advertising Industry: An Exploratory Study', *Women in Management Series, Paper No. 3*. Kingswood, NSW: School of Business, Nepean College of Advanced Education.

———(1986) 'Women in Management: The Case of Australian Business', *Human Resource Management Australia* February: 32–37.

Tolson, A. (1977) *The Limits of Masculinity*. London: Tavistock.

Vogel, L. (1983) *Marxism and the Oppression of Women. Toward a Unitary Theory*. London: Pluto.

Werneke, D. (1983) *Microelectronics and Office Jobs: The Impact of the Chip on Women's Employment*. Geneva: International Labour Office.

Williams, C.R. (1981) *Open Cut. The Working Class in an Australian Mining Town*. Sydney: Allen & Unwin.

———'Domestic Flight Attendants in Australia: A Quasi-occupational Community?', *Journal of Industrial Relations* September: 237–51.

———(1988) *Blue, White and Pink Collar Workers in Australia. Telecom Technicians, Flight Attendants and Bank Employees*. Sydney: Allen & Unwin.

Women's Bureau (1986) 'Women at Work, Facts and Figures' Canberra: Department of Employment and Industrial Relations.

Young, I. (1981) 'Beyond the Unhappy Marriage: A Critique of the Dual Systems Theory' in L. Sargent (ed.) *The Unhappy Marriage of Marxism and Feminism. A Debate on Class and Patriarchy.* London: Pluto.

Chapter Five

Ideology and Coherence in the Australian Legal Order

Roman Tomasic

The legal system and legal order were of considerable interest to classical sociologists such as Max Weber and Emile Durkheim, amongst others. Whilst sociologists have tended in more recent years to turn to other aspects of social life, the legal order remains a central aspect of any overall study of society. Indeed, over the last two decades there has been an international revival of interest in the sociology of law, in view of the renewed recognition of the place occupied by law and legal institutions in society (see further Tomasic 1985). It is evident that the sociological study of law can contribute greatly to the enrichment of sociology itself (Hopkins 1978). This is especially true in Australia, a society which seems to be increasingly turning to law and legal institutions to deal with complex socio-economic problems and the allocation of rights and benefits. This seems to be part of a broader process of the legalisation of various social processes. This is in turn partly attributable to the authority or ideological utility of the processes of law as instruments of the modern state, and the decline of alternative mechanisms such as religion and traditional authority as bases for social organisation.

Part of the appeal of law and legal institutions as bases for public and private power lies in broad acceptance of what might be regarded as a sociologically naïve stereotype of law. Thus, for example, law is frequently perceived to be a rational, coherent and efficient instrument or mechanism for social action. This is quite misleading, especially when social behaviour in legal institutions is scrutinised. Close observation of these structures quickly reveals that legal institutions such as courts, administrative and regulatory agencies, the legal professions and the legislatures are extremely diverse and fragmented entities, despite their appearance of coherence or composure. This raises a central theme of this chapter, namely, the manner in which the legal system and the legal order are able to maintain the appearance of unity despite the abundant evidence of their decay, fragmentation and disintegration. This is of course a central concern of all sociology: the problem of order or the manner in which society is able to maintain and reproduce its organic appearance of coherence, what sociologists used to call the question of social control (E.A. Ross 1901).

The appearance of a coherent and authoritative set of legal institutions is also based upon popular misconceptions concerning the nature of law itself as well as of the nature of the power and impact of legal institutions. Thus, for example, law and legal doctrine are frequently perceived to compromise a 'gapless' or complete set of rational and consistent principles which can be applied to deal with social problems as they arise. Whilst lawyers and judges have sought to foster this perception ·with a view to preserving the authority and legitimacy of law, it should be realised that this picture is highly misleading. Law and legal institutions actually comprise a complex array of competing or inconsistent principles and practices. In fact, it would be sociologically unrealistic to expect anything else than this in practice, but the positivistic view of law as a set of hard and fast principles and practices has considerable ideological force. Nevertheless, as we shall see, negotiation and bargaining rather than strict adherence to legal rules or procedures are at the core of the legal system, constituting the lubricating mechanisms which help to sustain or mobilise the otherwise rigid formalities of the legal order.

Also, the power and impact of legal institutions are most apparent in some respects if they are seen to comprise streamlined systems of authority in which ultimate legal control rests, respectively, with appeal courts in the case of the judicial system; with Parliament in the case of all law-making authorities and with the heads of administrative and regulatory agencies in the case of administrative or enforcement structures. This highly formalised view certainly makes the authority of these processes of adjudication, law-making, and enforcement easier for the community to accept, although it is far from being the complete picture of the nature of the legal process. For example, the formalistic view of the court system in Australia would see the High Court as the most important court. However this is true in only a very narrow sense, namely that it can lay down principles which bind courts below it in the court structure. On the other hand, in terms of its impact upon the community, the High Court is really quite marginal to the lives of the vast majority of individuals and groups. It handles only several hundred cases in any one year, whilst courts at the so-called bottom of the judicial hierarchy, such as Magistrates' or local courts, and intermediate courts such as District or County courts actually process hundreds of thousands of cases in any one year, usually without any reference to principles laid down by the High Court. This seems to suggest that the legal pyramid, which places the High Court at the apex and local Magistrates' courts at the base, needs to be inverted to emphasise the sociological significance of these lower courts. As a matter of practice, we have a two-tiered system of courts in which the higher ones serve mainly to preserve the myth of adversary justice according to which parties are represented by opposing legal counsel and in which considerable legal procedural formality exists. In contrast, the lower courts are much less obviously concerned with reproducing the adversary myth or ideology. As the British sociologist of law, Doreen McBarnet (1981), has shown, the social function of the lower courts is simply to convict offenders and not in each case to provide opportunity for extensive argument and procedural niceties. McBarnet and many others have shown that contrary to the adversarial myth of the rule of law whereby court proceedings constitute an equal fight between two opposing sides, very few defendants in lower courts are actually found to be innocent by the

Table 5.1 Penalties handed down by New South Wales, Magistrates' Courts, 1978–82
(Column Percentages)

Penalty	1978	1979	1980	1981	1982
Not Guilty	3.9	4.3	4.8	4.6	4.9
Withdrawn/Dismissed	15.3	15.5	14.6	13.6	12.4
Recognisance with/ without fine/probation	10.0	10.5	12.2	12.3	11.8
Fine	52.4	50.7	53.4	55.9	56.5
Community Service	–	–	0.1	0.7	1.3
Periodic Detention	0.3	0.5	0.6	0.6	0.8
Imprisonment	5.6	5.1	5.1	5.1	5.0
Other	12.5	13.4	9.2	7.1	7.3
Total	100.0	100.0	100.0	100.0	100.0

Source: New South Wales Bureau of Crime Statistics and Research, *Court Statistics, 1982*, Sydney, New South Wales Government Printer, 1983, p. 11

courts. Such high conviction rates are incompatible with the expectation of an equally balanced fight, in which one might anticipate much lower conviction rates. Thus for example, as Table 5.1 shows, less than 5 per cent of people appearing before New South Wales lower courts are found to be not guilty, with, in 1982, over 75 per cent being sentenced in some way.

The lack of a real adversary system in the judicial process is also evident to some degree in the higher criminal courts. In New South Wales higher criminal courts in 1982, for example, only 7.4 per cent of offenders were acquitted as such, and 71.2 per cent did not even bother to contest the case against them, simply pleading guilty (New South Wales Bureau of Crime Statistics and Research 1983: 55–56). The high conviction rates in Australian Magistrates' courts are by no means a recent phenomenon, as Table 5.2 illustrates.

Lest it be thought that these kinds of trends are only to be found in criminal cases, it should be noted that the lower courts also process vast numbers of non-criminal or civil cases, and once again the pattern emerges of decisions being found in favour of those bringing the proceedings. Thus for example, in debt collection cases, very few of the summonses issued actually lead to a trial. For example, the Poverty Commission found that in 1974, of the 93,210 debt recovery summonses issued in South Australia, only

Table 5.2 Convictions for Offences charged before Australian Magistrates' Courts per 100,000 Population, Aged 10 years and Over, 1900–76*

	All Offences charged	Offences against the Person	Offences against Property	Offences against Good Order	All Petty Offences	Total Convictions
1900	5,728	165	302	2,232	1,797	4,496
1910	5,353	104	243	2,545	1,372	4,164
1929	4,529	85	293	1,445	1,709	3,532
1930	4,869	68	368	1,337	2,184	3,956
1940	5,343	52	388	1,361	2,836	4,638
1950	6,571	77	343	2,304	2,956	5,680
1960	10,010	89	694	2,111	6,139	9,083
1970	10,756	130	965	1,397	6,592	9,084
1976	11,474	150	934	1,315	7,192	9,591

* *Source*: Mukherjee 1981: 164–72 (figures have been rounded off to nearest whole number)

1,316 (or 1.4 per cent) led to a trial, whilst 36,895 (or 38.5 per cent) were decided in favour of the plaintiff in view of the failure of the defendant to appear in court. In the remaining cases the debt was acknowledged by the defendant (Kelly 1977: 35). In New South Wales in 1977 over 210,000 civil actions were commenced in courts of Petty Sessions with a view to recovering payments of debt or making monetary claims. Some 95 per cent proceeded simply without going to trial (Collins 1979: Foreword). This emphasises the conclusion which numerous studies have revealed, namely, that the lower civil courts are to a large extent merely debt collection agencies, rather than places where the full paraphernalia of the ideology of adversary justice is revealed or applied. (See further, Caplovitz 1983, Jacob 1969, Rock 1973 and Willis 1980.)

In addition to the above patterns of the 'law in action', one should point to the fact that the legal process is tending to become increasingly routinised in its handling of legal problems. Wherever possible, the courts, administrative agencies and law-makers have sought to divert complex and contentious matters to other, often less formal agencies, so as not to upset the smooth flow in the handling of legal matters. Thus, for example, courts have increasingly sought to divert disputes to less formalised mechanisms such as mediation centres, arbitration, conciliation and counselling. Similarly, law-makers have tended to refer more complex issues to Committees of Inquiry, Royal Commissions and Law Reform bodies, often with a view to defusing potentially explosive socio-legal issues.

Finally, administrative disputes have increasingly been referred to the array of new administrative tribunals and new institutions such as the Ombudsman, which have emerged over the last few decades. All of these actions are examples of the routinisation of legal decision-making which has taken place in this century. This in part reflects the considerable increase in the workloads of judicial, administrative, and legislative agencies and the need in some way to control their caseloads. As our state and society relies increasingly upon these kinds of legal institutions to perform basic social tasks, it will be inevitable that there will be occasions when these legal institutions will be unable to provide solutions to the problems brought to them – without entirely disrupting these institutions, so that alternative avenues need to be found into which more complex matters can be channelled. This is in part also attributable to the fact that our society cannot afford to deliver the rights and procedural guarantees which the ideal of the rule of law evokes. Thus, we increasingly hear of calls for the introduction of less expensive and time-consuming legal machinery to deal with disputes and the allocation of rights and benefits. Similarly, we increasingly hear that the availability of legal mechanisms to ensure that legal rights are provided to all who need them – such as through legal aid – should be curtailed in some way, because of the damage which such wider access to the legal process is causing to the justice system itself, such as through greater delays and longer cases and trials (see e.g. Yeldham 1984).

It is not only the poor who are thus being diverted from the judicial process, as business itself has been calling for less costly and time-consuming mechanisms for dealing with commercial disputes, such as by resort to arbitration. It is interesting to note that business has always been reluctant to resort to the formal legal process in dealing with disputes with other businesses. As a number of studies have shown since Macaulay's (1963) landmark research into this area, businessmen and corporations tend to prefer to resort to less formal mechanisms such as black-listing and the termination of business relationships as a means of achieving social control and order in the market-place (see further Macaulay 1977, Kurczewski and Frieske 1977). Moreover, other research into litigants has shown that it is extremely rare for large corporations or organisations to seek to deal with their disputes through court action. These entities tend mainly to initiate litigation against individuals or small entities, using courts largely as collection agencies. Moreover, it is the 'repeat player', or that type of litigant who is frequently involved in court action (and these are largely organisations), who is most successful in litigation and so able to structure the judicial process to suit the needs of 'repeat players' as opposed to the 'one-shotter'. This is achieved by being able to gain strategic advantages through the making of critical decisions such as the informal settlement (rather than the adjudication) of a case which might otherwise produce a ruling which may have adverse consequences to the 'repeat player'. On the other hand, 'repeat players' are in a much better position to select cases to pursue to the judgment stage with a view to producing new principles conducive to their organisational interests (see further Galanter 1974, 1975). Although there has been a large increase in the number of court cases involving individuals, in areas such as family law and industrial and motor vehicle accidents, there has not been an increase in the number of business disputes handled by the courts, despite the considerable degree of economic growth this century. This is an intriguing phenomenon in some ways. The American legal historian, Lawrence Friedman, has sought to explain this as follows:

> For whatever reasons, courts in Western industrial societies do not seem well suited to resolving certain kinds of disputes. They thus

fall far short of the ideal of 'justice for all', if by justice we mean a cheap, fair, effective tribunal close at hand ... Note that we are talking here mainly about private disputes. We are not talking about great constitutional cases, environmental disputes or major labor cases. We are talking about ordinary bread-and-butter cases, disputes between neighbours, family squabbles, small personal injury cases ... We are talking about most business disputes ... The courts are stiff, formal and expensive. Ordinary people do not like to use them, or they find them too costly or too remote. There are good reasons, too for business to avoid litigation.

(Friedman 1983: 21)

Although both law and sociology seek to be applicable to all aspects of society, the formalistic model of law falls far short of being so widely applicable. Formal legal institutions are severely limited in being able to meet the ideological claims made by their proponents. This stresses the need to distinguish between the form and content of law and legal institutions, as their actual meaning and impact will often be quite different from what the rhetoric of the rule of law might suggest.

Ideology and Legal Process

The above discussion suggests a basic contradiction or conflict of purposes or rationales within the legal system. Another way to put this is to see the legal system as operating at a number of different levels, each of which are at first sight incompatible, even though on closer scrutiny they are mutually sustaining. Thus, at one level the legal system can be seen as a powerful repository of symbols and ideological mechanisms – such as the rule of law and the notion of adversary justice – which sustain the legitimacy and authority of the modern state. At this more formal level law and legal institutions seek to set parameters for legitimate social, political or economic action. The Australian federal Constitution is one of the best illustrations of the attempt to structure social change by the imposition of an inflexible legal form, as Sol Encel (1979), a sociologist, has shown. The same point has been made by Geoffrey Sawer (1967: 208), a lawyer, when he observes that 'constitutionally speaking, Australia is a frozen continent'. In other words, laws such as the federal Constitution serve to define the parameters of social change. This is not to say that law is a sufficiently powerful mechanism to prevent change taking place at all, for it is far from being this, but it frequently has sufficient legitimate authority to structure the nature of change and to direct it along some often quite convoluted or even irrational pathways. However, laws such as the Constitution do not have this influence merely because of their formal content, but because such laws have reflected broader structural features of the social fabric, even though these may be less evident today than when the laws were enacted.

It should be said that whilst law is often perceived to be a tradition-bound and conservative social institution, it is not always a static one, despite the frequent claims of law reformers to this effect. To some extent law and legal institutions do reflect changes taking place in the broader social and economic base of society, although there may not always be a directly evident causal link. As law and legal institutions have developed their own values and culture, it frequently appears that the legal system seems to be acting autonomously from dominant social, economic and political structures in society. This in part serves to enhance the authority of the legal system and is consistent with the ideological claims made for it – in relation to the rule of law, for example. As there is in fact considerable diversity and even fragmentation in the Australian legal system, partly due to the existence of a federal system of government, ideological factors play a very important part in maintaining the appearance of unity and coherence in the legal system. We need therefore to ask how the legal system actually achieves order and coherence within the wider social context as well as to look at the ideological and other means by which the legal system gives the impression of coherence. These two questions are actually but two sides of the same one as it would be quite misleading to give the impression that the law and legal institutions are in some way isolated from, or independent of, the society in which they exist. Those who assume that the law is somehow apart from society often expect that the law and legal institutions will be used as instruments to change society or for purposes of social engineering. This strategy is highly problematic, and has been described as the instrumentalist fallacy, as law is in fact deeply embedded in social structures in which change is sought (see further Gusfield 1963, Massell 1968, Burman and Harrell-Bond 1979). It has even been suggested that if the measure of law's importance in society is its effectiveness as an instrument, then clearly law is not very important (Griffith 1979). However, law is important for many other reasons including its symbolic, ideological, legitimating and social ordering functions.

One way of exploring the apparent conflict between the pretensions of law and legal institutions and their actual significance is to focus upon a series of legal processes which are at the heart of what the legal system actually constitutes. The process metaphor is valuable as it serves to focus our attention upon the manner in which legal rhetoric and discourse is a product of social interaction, of negotiation and bargaining and the transformations which take place in the course of the processing of matters within legal institutions. The process metaphor has been increasingly relied upon in ethnographic and similar approaches to legal institutions to provide a more realistic understanding of these than is available from formal legal statements as to their roles or purposes. However, this is not to suggest that the latter, more doctrinal view be abandoned entirely – only that it be assessed critically – as traditional or formal legal rhetoric often serves as the legitimating ideology which holds these disparate legal processes together. Moreover, legal ideology, perhaps like all ideology (see Carlton 1977: 20–21), is more than a mere veneer upon a somewhat chaotic legal order or process: it actually influences that process to some extent. This is illustrated by the fact that at various times courts and legal institutions feel genuinely constrained by their own rhetoric – we might even say they become captives of that ideology – and so may act in ways which seem to run contrary to what one might predict, given the close relationship between the state and legal processes. In other words, ideologies such as the rule of law and the doctrine of precedent have even been used in such a way as to induce the courts to reach decisions which seem to be ones which judges themselves might not prefer. Ideological artefacts such as the rule of law can therefore serve to give the legal process a relative degree of autonomy from other state institutions. This reflects a broader contradiction which the executive arm of government has increasingly sought to neutralise by removing disputes out of the realm of traditional judicial processes and diverting them into tribunals and informal forums which are more readily controllable by governmental agencies. What is also notable about legal ideologies is that these tend to be reified in the legal process by legal functionaries such as lawyers, police officers and judges. It is this concretisation of legal ideologies (at least in the minds of their proponents) which gives them their potency. Thus, far from our moving into a period when ideology will be at end, it seems that, if anything, law has become an increasingly powerful ideological system which is relied upon both to discipline society and to distribute symbolic and substantive goods (see further Hunt 1985, Hirst 1979, Sugarman 1983, Sumner 1979).

Finally, it can be noted that a common stereotype of the legal process gives the impression that its principal purposes are related directly to the maintenance of social control in society. Whilst to some extent it is true to say that some aspects of the legal process are so directed, it would not be correct to conclude that social control is as important a function as many believe. Only a very small part of the infrastructure of the legal process is directed to purposes of this kind. The vast bulk of the personnel, structures and rules which comprise the process are concerned with a diversity of other goals, including the legitimation of resource allocation and decision-making structures, the maintenance and protection of property relations, and the production and reproduction of ideological mechanisms such as the rule of law. It should also be realised that much of the legal process is also directed at sustaining itself and its structures and therefore seeking to avoid their collapse or fragmentation. To this extent it is therefore locked in, in a somewhat inward-looking way, to its own myths and rhetoric, and as such, is ill-equipped to be an effective instrument of social control.

Specific social control activities, therefore, do not figure largely in the overall concerns of the legal system. These concerns might be described as being of a 'civil law' kind, covering such things as legal problems relating to contractual disputes and arrangements, compensation claims, the protection of property, commercial law, revenue law and so on. Areas of public law such as constitutional and administrative law are also far removed from the narrow social control model of law. All this suggests that the study of the legal process needs to take issue with long-cherished stereotypes of it. One means of doing this is to emphasise the manner in which ideologies and legal processes inter-relate.

Legal Processes and the Legal System

It is perhaps appropriate that we now turn to look more closely at some of the legal processes which constitute the legal system. As has been suggested above the legal system is of course only part of a wider social system. Society, like the legal system, is far from being an organic whole or totality, for as Alain Touraine has argued:

> ... it is divided against itself; each of its orientations is the object of opposing attempts at appropriation ... [despite] ... illusions of social integration.
>
> (Touraine 1977: 10)

Niklaus Luhmann has likewise pointed to the problem of integration or homogeneity which confronts society in general and the legal system in particular. Discussing the legal profession in the Federal Republic of Germany, for example, Luhmann observed:

... the profession as a whole is composed of heterogeneous elements, as far as values, interests, and attitudes are concerned, and is only differentiated within itself with regard to typical roles. These conditions are not very favourable for the internal coherence of the profession, let alone its efficiency as a political factor in society.

(Luhmann 1976: 103).

These kinds of observations have now been empirically supported by research on the legal professions in a number of countries, including Australia, as we will see later. For the moment, however, it is sufficient to note that diversity in the legal profession is a reflection of both diversity in the processes of the legal system itself as well as in the client base which lawyers serve. Broadly speaking, it could be argued that there are at least three main sets of processes within the Australian legal system, namely, law-making, the implementation of law and its interpretation.

The Law-making Process

Firstly, we have what we might call the law-making processes, those which involve the legislature, the courts and administrative officials engaged in formulating regulations or delegated legislation. Whilst many, more conservative, judges reject the view that they are engaged in law-making when they decide a case, it would be fair to say that this apparent judicial reticence is a reflection of the ideology of the separation of powers (between judicial, legislative and executive authority) as well as of the traditional common law view that judges merely *find* the law rather than *making* it for the first time. This narrow view of law-making is far from being an accurate reflection of what is widely recognised by judges as a reality of law-making in the court process. It might also be argued that law-making also takes place at a less formal level in the form of the customs and rules formulated or evolved by private groups or association such as business associations and sporting groups. Often the laws or norms developed by these less formal mechanisms have much greater significance for the lives of individuals than do the formal rules made by state agencies like the courts and Parliament. However, it would divert us too much from our primary concerns to look more closely at these informal law-making mechanisms in society. If for no other reason than their restricted authority or legitimacy in comparison with the rules produced by more formal structures, we can for the time being leave aside further consideration of these nevertheless important informal structures.

In many respects judicial law-making can be more difficult to overturn than legislative law-making. For example, to overturn a new ruling of the High Court, it could require at least seven Acts of Parliament, one from each state and one from the federal Parliament. Having said this, however, it should be stressed that the vast bulk of official law-making activity takes place at the parliamentary rather than at the judicial level. Moreover, few judicial opinions actually constitute a real innovation, in the sense of laying down a new code of conduct, as most decisions are written to apply only to the very narrow set of factual circumstances in that case. One reason for this is the reluctance of judges to lay down new broad general principles which may well constrain their future decision-making and so prevent them from reaching a decision which they might see as being the most just (see further Aubert 1983: 77–97). Sometimes, however, parliaments may be deadlocked or unable to act unilaterally or with sufficient authority in proposing a new law and so may turn to the courts for assistance. The so-called Tasmanian Dams Case is an instance of this situation. Here, the federal government went to the High Court in an effort to clarify its powers in relation to the preservation of a world heritage area in south-west Tasmania which would have been threatened by the proposed damming of the Franklin River by the Tasmanian government's Hydro-Electricity Authority. The High Court's decision in this case, although close, can be seen as a law-making one, because in addition to upholding federal government regulations regarding work on the Franklin Dam site, the court established new principles regarding the relative powers of state and federal parliaments. However, constitutional cases such as this comprise only a tiny proportion of the High Court's workload, and by no means provide the only illustration of its law-making activity.

Parliaments, however, make the vast bulk of our laws, as courts are poorly equipped to formulate broad sets of rules seeking to cover the whole of a particular area of law. The twentieth century in particular has seen a vast increase in legislative law-making, with the rise of what might be called the bureaucratic state and the consequent extension of law into many more sectors of society. The law-making activity of all Australian legislatures seems to have increased greatly over the last eighty years, as Table 5.3 illustrates.

The volume of delegated legislation or regulation made by statutory authorities and government departments has also increased over recent decades as Table 5.4 illustrates.

Whilst a variety of reform conclusions can be drawn from figures such as those in Tables 5.3 and 5.4, it is apparent that the cumulative effect of this growth is to emphasise the extent to which we have come to rely upon legislatures and their attendant

Table 5.3 Average Yearly Number of Statutes passed by
various Australian Parliaments, 1901–79*

Years	Commonwealth Statutes per year	New South Wales Statutes per year	Victorian Statutes per year
1901–09	21.2	52.5	58.5
1910–19	38.6	48.6	80.0
1920–29	44.3	48.8	81.0
1930–39	73.0	52.8	86.6
1940–49	74.4	47.9	72.9
1950–59	92.4	51.5	115.5
1960–69	118.2	66.9	132.5
1970–79	168.4	94.8**	143.75***

  Source: Tomasic 1979: 11
 **Average Figure for years 1970–75
***Average Figure for years 1970–79

Table 5.4 Comparison of the Volume of Regulations made in
Australia during the 1960s and 1970s

Period	Federal	NSW	Vic.	Qld	SA	WA	Tas.	NT	Total
10 years to 1969	1,963	1,557	2,190	3,179	924	184	2,433	–	12,420
10 years to 1979	3,017	3,511	4,072	4,494	1,697	274	3,030	36	20,131
Increase, second period on first	+54%	+125%	+86%	+41%	+84%	+49%	+25%	–	+62%

Source: Conferation of Australian Industry, *Government Regulation in Australia*,
       1980, p. 51

bureaucratic regulation-making structures.

Whilst some have argued that the bulk of this kind of law-making activity constitutes a 'mountain of minutiae', rather than being major turning points (Chambliss 1979: 149), it can nevertheless be argued that its sheer bulk does more to characterise the nature of the legal order in Australia than do the occasional attempts to strike out in a new direction with a 'significant' legislative innovation. To put it another way, the legal order seems to be structured more by what Hurst has called a process of 'drift' than by a conscious 'direction' in law-making activity. The unwieldy growth of social welfare and taxing legislation seems to provide some of the best illustrations of the extent to which law-making seems to have become the creature of the bureaucratic state. Attempts to rationalise it by resort to law reform commissions seems only to further entrench this bureaucratisation of law-making as only those proposed law reforms which seem either to serve the broad interests of bureaucracy, or at least do not threaten these, ever seem to be implemented (see further Tomasic and Bottomley 1984).

We have noted that bureaucratic concerns play an important part in shaping the legislative product. However, this is far from being the only source of input into the law-making process. Economic interests and considerations also frequently play an important part. This, of course, was long ago recognised by Weber when he observed that '... economic interests are among the strongest factors influencing the creation of law' (1954: 32). This has been most clearly the case in respect of the making of the Australian federal Constitution, as Encel (1979) has well illustrated. Seeing the Constitution as a social document, Encel argues that its framers sought to preserve the array of local economic interests which were dominant in the latter decades of the nineteenth century Australian colonies, rather than allowing the new national government to gain economic hegemony. The dominance of economic consideration is also evident in the evolution of Australian land legislation from the selection acts of the 1850s aimed at breaking the economic dominance of the squatters (Baker 1979) to the introduction of strata title legislation in New South Wales in the early 1960s aimed at facilitating the greatest use of capital by developers concerned about the economic insecurities inherent in the pre-existing system of ownership of home units (Kondos 1979). The continuing debate over formulating appropriate land rights legislation is also largely based upon economic considerations arising out of the conflicting claims of mining industry and other lobbies (see e.g. Keon-Cohen 1979). It has been well documented that laws regarding such fields as broadcasting, trade practices and companies and securities regulation have been heavily influenced by the interests of economic forces (see e.g. Armstrong 1979, Hopkins 1979, Sutton and Wild 1979, Hart 1979). However, this is not to suggest that economic interests have always had their way. One obvious reason for this is of course that they are far from being monolithic, so that the government may be swayed by pressures from small rather than big business, as

Hopkins (1979: 207) has shown in respect to the 1977 amendments to the Trade Practices Act regarding price discrimination rules. On the other hand, as Hopkins has also shown, at other times other pressures, such as those coming from the electorate or from consumers, may entirely outweigh the pressures emanating from business groups. In seeking to explain the intricacies of law-making processes one therefore needs to be wary of single cause or structural explanations, as O'Malley (1979) has argued, and to realise that different explanatory theories may be required to deal with different periods of time or types of law-making.

The Implementation Process

A second set of legal processes found in the Australian legal system deal with the implementation of legal rules which have been produced by law-making institutions. The impact and effectiveness of law does of course depend upon the processes of implementation which have been established both in the legal system and, more importantly, in society at large. This is not, however, to suggest that law and legal institutions are quite separate from society, for as we have seen, legal processes are embedded within broader social processes, so that there is considerable interaction and interdependence between them. This has frequently been overlooked by enthusiastic social reformers who have seen law as a powerful instrument for purposes of social engineering. Such reformers have frequently been disappointed when seeking to use law in this way, especially where the proposed change runs counter to deeply entrenched social values, such as in relation to alcohol consumption (Gusfield 1963), religious belief (Massell 1968) and drink-driving behaviour (Ross 1981). It is no wonder, therefore, that implementation can be the most agonising and frustrating feature of the legal process. This is because it is usually a far more complex process than that of creating the law in the first place. However, the simplicity of the latter process should not be taken for granted because many of the difficulties which may be experienced in seeking to implement a new law may be traced back to problems which were insufficiently thought out or resolved during the law-making stage. Frequently, therefore, the implementation process tends to involve a variety of games or strategies of opposition by those who were unsuccessful in having their views taken into account during the law-making stage. It is not surprising, therefore, that Bardach (1977) has characterised the post-law-making process as 'the implementation game'. Another aspect of the implementation process worth noting is that sometimes a law is not intended to be carried out at all, and that its passage or enactment merely represents a symbolic victory, whilst the real gains are received by those who are able to avoid or undermine its implementation. Edelman (1964, 1977) has characterised this situation as one of the symbolic use of politics, involving 'words that succeed and policies that fail'.

A fine recent illustration of the symbolic aspects of law-making as seen from the implementation process is provided by some advice given by Prime Minister Hawke to Queensland Premier Bjelke-Petersen as to how the latter could save face in dealing with some crippling anti-union legislation passed in Queensland in 1985. Hawke observed:

> ... I mean you can have legislation on the statute book which is not implemented ... so the matter is capable of resolution without the actual repeal of the legislation ...
> (*Sydney Morning Herald* 18 April 1985, p. 1)

In other words, this leading law-maker was suggesting that this particular piece of legislation might be retained on the statute books as a symbolic statement of the Queensland government's desired position, but for practical purposes, it should simply not be implemented. Such a situation is probably quite common, although few politicians are prepared to be so frank about it.

Thus we often find that an agency is set up to enforce or apply a policy, but it may be given very few resources to fulfil its function. Alternatively the agency may be subject to ministerial discretion to intervene and prevent it from doing anything, such as commencing protracted and expensive court proceedings. Bardach's (1977) study of the implementation process is a catalogue of such strategies. So, the mere passage of a piece of legislation, such as that dealing with affirmative action, privacy, environmental control or corporate regulation may merely constitute a symbolic reassurance to some elements in the community that these issues are important. In practice, the legislation may be so vague and difficult to implement that it does little to control the areas of social life to which it may be directed. It has become quite commonplace in the sociology of law, therefore, to point to the so-called 'gap' between the 'law in the books' and the 'law in action'. What is perhaps more interesting is to explain why this gap exists and what purpose it serves (see further Nelken 1981).

Despite the fact that a vast bulk of legal sociological research has been directed to documenting the impact, effectiveness or implementation of law, the theoretical understanding of this process is far from being satisfactory. We tend to have limited sets of hypotheses about segments of this process, but very few broader attempts to theorise about the relationship between law and social change (see, however, Friedman 1975, Chambliss 1979, S.D. Ross 1982, Evan 1965, Podgorecki 1974). Much of this literature has focused attention upon the limits of law as an instrument of social change (e.g. Allott, 1980, Packer 1968). In Australia, for example, we have seen a series of studies on the limits of drink-driving legislation, of drug laws, of juvenile delinquency legislation and of family law (see e.g. Robinson 1979, Hiller and Hancock 1979, Ozdowski 1979, Tomasic 1977a, 1977b). In a recent study of the Australian Family Law Act, for example, Ziegert (1984) has argued that the implementation of some of the more radical objectives of this legislation, seeking to escape from the fault concept in dealing with marital breakdown, have been severely limited by the somewhat legalistic constraints which the involvement of lawyers and their legal culture brings with it, such as the appropriate role of the judge. This stresses the fact that implementation takes place in a sub-cultural context and that the impact or effectiveness of a law will depend upon the support and enthusiasm for it by those whose task it is to implement it, such as lawyers and law enforcement officers.

This raises a theoretical issue which has been described as that of the mobilisation of law. Unless a law can be effectively used it will lie dormant, or at best be of only symbolic significance. Mobilisation can take place in two broad kinds of ways. Firstly, we can have what has been described as the 'reactive' mobilisation of law, merely responding to a complaint about the breach of a law. This is by far the most common manner in which a law is implemented. Secondly, we can have what is known as the 'proactive' mobilisation of law, or the deliberate and premeditated attempt to seek out those who have breached a rule. As proactive mobilisation is a far more labour-intensive and time-consuming method of seeking to implement law, it tends to be resorted to much less frequently than is the reactive kind. A good illustration of proactive mobilisation is a police blitz campaign against drink-driving based upon random breath-testing. This can be contrasted with a reactive approach to the same problem, which sees law being mobilised only once a suspicion of drink-driving behaviour has been raised, such as through erratic driving conduct or as a result of blood tests following an accident. Police morale tends to sag as a result of proactive policing, as this is both more time-consuming and less likely to produce results. Thus in the proactive area of random breath-testing, for example, a New South Wales Parliamentary Committee of Inquiry was told by a highway patrol officer that police morale here was low because of the 'soul-destroying nature of random breath-testing – it's a very repetitive job ... saying the same lines to motorists hundreds of times a week ...

And out of the thousands of tests, well under 1 per cent of motorists are charged' (*Sydney Morning Herald* 30 January 1985, p. 3). Moreover, as the deterrent effect of proactive policing of this kind is often doubtful (see e.g. H.L. Ross 1981), it is difficult to sustain this kind of policing without incurring significant economic and psychological costs.

By contrast, reactive policing does at least allow enforcement authorities to satisfy bureaucratic performance criteria by more easily producing a reasonable number of breaches. Unfortunately, reactive policing tends to lead to a focus upon trivial offences while proactive policing finds it much more difficult to meet simple performance criteria due to the fact that it tends to emphasise much more complex offences, or vast numbers of cases being scrutinised to reveal the existence of an offence. Thus, we see a reactive prosecution of drug users, rather than a proactive prosecution of the more difficult-to-discover drug-traffickers. Some of the best illustrations of the complexities of the proactive mobilisation of law have arisen in recent years in Australia from the areas of corporate crime and tax avoidance and evasion. These kinds of offences are extremely difficult to detect and prosecute, even though there is little debate as to their seriousness. Nevertheless, the number of successful prosecutions of such offences have been very few indeed, as the work of the Costigan Commission and that of the various special prosecutors appointed to deal with tax avoidance illustrates. For example, in his 1984 Annual Report, Special Prosecutor R.V. Gyles QC reported to the federal government that he had initiated twenty-eight court actions against promoters of tax avoidance schemes, but completed only one matter despite a staff of over 160 officers (Gyles 1984: 11–13). Special Prosecutor Gyles provided an insight into why proactive enforcement is so difficult when he observed that:

> Up to 30 June more than 500 search warrants had been executed by members of this office. In the year under review other documents have been forthcoming from sources such as the Australian Taxation Office, the Costigan Royal Commission, and the various Corporate Affairs Commissions. Approximately 1,000 persons have been interviewed, and over 4,000 statements and records of interview have been obtained. A number of other persons have been contacted but declined to be interviewed at all. In the main, those declining to be interviewed at all were principals who were or are likely to be charged. The task of analysing the documents obtained and the information obtained from interviews, and then carrying out the necessary follow-up enquiries, has been extremely time consuming, even with the assistance of the computer system ... I indicated in my last Report that I had chosen in the first place to

concentrate investigations on some identified large scale promoters, even though this necessarily involved a substantial commitment of resources to a small number of targets and a relatively long lead time before a brief could be prepared to deal adequately with the target.

(Gyles 1984: 3)

He went on to argue that it was necessary to abandon the procedural niceties usually followed when a decision to prosecute such offences was made, if the whole effort was not to be a waste of time. Gyles noted therefore that in complex fraud cases:

A prima-facie case may be established upon materials falling short of strictly admissible evidence long before compilation of the final brief of evidence to be presented at the committal proceedings. Indeed further evidence may be produced during the course of the committal proceedings, or between committal and trial. If the compilation of a full brief is awaited before the decision to charge is taken, the risk of the suspect absconding is greatly increased, and the inevitable delays in the court process lead to stale cases being brought, with all the attendant injustice to both prosecution and defence. While the decision to charge should never be made lightly, in my view there is a strong public interest in laying charges, where otherwise appropriate, as soon as the prosecution is in possession of material of appropriate credibility which establishes a prima-facie case.

(Gyles 1984: 4)

As evident from this quote, one of the problems often seen with proactive enforcement is that it undermines the usual procedural guarantees and leads to criticisms of the emergence of a police state. It is interesting to note that Gyles' successor as Director of Public Prosecutions, Ian Temby QC, has quite predictably called for greater powers and increased staffing. There are clearly major limits, therefore, to the proactive mobilisation of law arising out of available resources and the degree of public toleration of official interference in private lives. This suggests that the proactive mobilisation of law will remain far less common as a technique for implementing law than the reactive method, despite the fact that the latter is really only effective against minor offences. All of this does not bode well for the implementation of those laws which encounter any real resistance in society, especially where such resistance comes from more powerful and established sectors. Moreover, it also highlights the fact that despite the rhetoric of equal treatment under the law for all, the problems of implementing or mobilising law against some individuals and groups will be such that the impact of law will vary considerably across society.

For example, it is much more difficult to investigate and prove complex commercial fraud than it is to deal with minor and more visible public order type offences, such as assault and disorderly conduct, so that it is inevitable that enforcement activity will be directed against the latter. Similarly, it is much more difficult to deal with complex and sophisticated tax avoidance schemes than it is to deal with minor breaches of taxing statutes, such as the failure to furnish a tax return on time, so that the latter type of conduct will bear the brunt of enforcement practice, despite its relatively lesser significance.

The Interpretation Process

A third set of legal processes which we need to consider involve the interpretation of rules produced by law-making authorities. As the sociologist Talcott Parsons (1980) has pointed out, the interpretation function is probably the most important one of the legal system (1980: 65). This is because the very effectiveness and impact of rules is dependent upon the meanings attributed to them. Interpretation takes place at several levels. Firstly, and most obviously, there is the judicial level, especially in apellate courts. Interpretations which are made of rules at this level are a critical factor in their legitimation and authority, so that one could argue that appeal courts such as the High Court, largely serve to legitimate laws made by the federal Parliament, even though there may be some time lag, so that the High Court may actually be out of step with the government of the day. So, the interpretation of rules also serves an important political function at this level, as has long been recognised in the role of the United States Supreme Court (see e.g. Dahl 1978, Casper 1978, Adamany 1978, Choper 1980, Hodder-Williams 1980, Shapiro 1967, also see Griffith 1977).

At a second level, interpretation is much more pervasive, as it is an activity undertaken by a whole range of legal functionaries, including the police officer on patrol, the regulatory inspector investigating compliance with health and safety regulations, and lawyers giving advice to their clients, as well as by citizens faced with the problem of determining whether rules, such as those regarding the availability of social security benefits, apply to them. Although we tend to emphasise the first or 'top down' view of interpretation, the second, or 'bottom up' approach is really of much greater significance for the day-to-day operation of legal processes. The fact that so many rules are actually negotiated, and so either avoided in part or even wholly, does not negate the significance of interpretation, as negotiation needs to be broadly seen as part of the process of giving meaning to rules.

The 'top-down' and 'bottom-up' nature of interpretations given to rules will vary considerably, therefore, depending upon the position of the interpreter. This suggests that the meaning attributed to the same rules may well vary depending on the object or purpose of the interpreter. Judges, as we have seen, often seek to interpret general principles as narrowly as possible, to give themselves the greatest degree of freedom of movement in subsequent cases. In the bureaucratic context, rules will often receive quite different interpretations depending on both the position of the interpreter within the bureaucracy and also on that of the bureaucracy or agency in relation to the degree of support received from outside. Thus, rules may be interpreted far more formally at the head office of an agency than at the local or regional one. Similarly, the policeman on patrol, the regulatory inspector or the official at the front desk of the agency will usually interpret rules much more informally or resort to their discretion as to whether to apply a rule or not, than would the official higher up in each respective agency (see e.g. Lipsky 1980, Kaufman 1960). These variations in the interpretation of rules appear throughout the legal process and have their most publicised illustrations in the discrepancies which frequently appear in the decisions handed down by different judges under the same piece of legislation. Sentencing disparities have long been of concern to law reformers but these seem to be an inevitable aspect of the problems of interpretation, and disparities in interpretation arise in all contexts where laws are applied in society by individuals. All this variability in meaning also derives from what might be called the open-textured or porous nature of rules, which illustrates the fact that meanings are made in a process of application, rather than being fixed or pre-determined. This once again emphasises the problem of coherence facing the legal system and its processes. Thus, for example, the official at the peak of an agency will tend to interpret rules fairly strictly in terms of structuring and controlling the discretionary behaviour of lower level officials. In contrast, as one descends the bureaucratic ladder, the interpretation of rules is seen as a production process with considerable room for the use of discretion and choice. The work of the mythical policeman on the beat, for example, would be impossible if every apparent breach of a rule led to an inevitable apprehension of the suspected offender. In practice, a decision has to be made as to which rules to enforce, and hence which to give legal meaning and effect, as it is simply impossible to act meaningfully in response to all rule violations, due to limits upon enforcement resources. This is also a consequence of the fact that there is always an element of ambiguity as to whether the particular constellation of facts observed in a case fall precisely within the ambit of a rule (see further e.g. Weaver 1977, Black 1980).

The meanings attributed to a rule will also be influenced by the level of insecurity which the interpreter of that rule within a bureaucratic agency may experience. Thus agencies which are new and which enjoy considerable support from outside constituencies (such as consumer groups in the case of a consumer protection agency) will be likely to interpret rules far more strictly than would an agency which is isolated or which is being attacked from all sides. Thus the old Australian Broadcasting Control Board was very reluctant to adopt a strong legalistic approach with broadcasters, as it was constantly afraid of ministerial interference as a result of lobbying from broadcasters who might be threatened by the agency. Eventually, the Board had to be replaced, as it became an embarrassment in that it seems to have become 'captured' by the industry (Armstrong 1979). It has been replaced by a body far more ready to interpret its powers broadly in view of the fact that its active constituency is perceived to be wider than that of the industry alone. In other words pressures from consumer groups have provided the Tribunal with a wider social base of support and hence greater freedom in its interpretation of broadcasting legislation. The actual social context in which the process of interpretation takes place is therefore likely to be extremely important in determining the meanings to be given to rules. It goes without saying that this is in marked contrast to the popular conception of rules as being fixed and inflexible. They are only such if the context requires that this be so. Thus, for example, where the context of the interpretation of a rule is such that there is considerable time and legal talent brought to bear to elucidate its meaning, it is remarkable how an otherwise straightforward rule suddenly gains added complexity. Magistrates may, for example, assume that the meaning of a rule may be quite simple, especially where the case is not contested. However, as soon as there is an opportunity for legal argument, as occurs in higher courts, or when senior barristers descend into lower courts to argue cases, the interpretation of rules becomes far more problematic, as their ambiguities are exposed and as the complexities of the facts to which the rules are to be applied are revealed.

Whilst the existence of the High Court of Australia as the ultimate court of appeal in many matters, as well as the major single authority on the interpretation of law, is often said to facilitate greater uniformity, this claim is more ideological than completely accurate. This is so for a variety of reasons. Firstly, the High Court has not laid down an interpretation on more than a relatively few areas, and even where it has clearly done so, this will not be communicated to all interpreters of the law. There is also the problem of determining which, if any, principle has been established in a High Court case, as up to seven judgments may be given: that is, one by each judge. Furthermore, even where a High Court principle is well established an interpreter may seek to avoid it by some legalistic means, or to distinguish that decision as being based upon quite different circumstances or, even to ignore the High Court decision entirely in the knowledge that interpretation is unlikely to be challenged.

The processes of interpretation, therefore, seem to be characterised by considerable diversity and conflicting approaches, in spite of the legal theory that certainty in the meaning of law is a basic principle. Once again, then, we see that the legal process is an extremely loose array of practices which seem only to be tolerated in view of the over-arching ideologies which proclaim the existence of fixed, certain and uniform patterns of interpretation. Yet, despite the critical importance of the interpretation process, sociologists have devoted very little attention to it, certainly in comparison with the processes of law-making and law-implementation. This is unfortunate as it is clear that all three are closely related in that together they comprise much of what we might call the legal process. Moreover, each can only be adequately understood by reference to the other, as none stands alone. Together they do, however, emphasise the problems of integration and coherence which underly the entire legal system.

Structure and Organisation in the Legal System

So far, we have emphasised the importance of ideological concerns within the legal system as well as some of the key processes through which ideologies are generated and through which the tasks of the legal system are performed in Australia. Taking a somewhat different approach to these issues, it is useful to focus upon some of the principal actors who constitute the social structure and organisation of the legal system. These include such groups as lawyers; third party dispute-handlers such as judges and magistrates; administrators who may seek to apply rules; as well as consumers of legal services from the wider community, such as litigants and clients. The roles which each of these sets of actors performs tell us a great deal about the operations of the legal system, as may already be evident from our discussion of legal processes. Let us therefore look briefly at some of these.

Lawyers and Lawyering

One of the principal misconceptions about the legal profession is that it is a unified and coherent group. Although professional associations, legal education and judicial rhetoric often seem to foster this myth or misconception for their own quite different reasons, it is quite clear that many lawyers often have very little in common with other lawyers, particularly in terms of the legal work which they do and the client interests which they serve. It is thus evident that there are wide gulfs between different groups of lawyers and that there is relatively little mobility between these groups. These gulfs are enduring features of the social organisation of the profession which are sustained by rigid status differences between practitioners doing different types of legal work, as well as by the types of clients served by different lawyers. These two factors, type of legal work and type of clientele, probably do more to differentiate and distance lawyers from each other than any other factors, as a number of empirical studies in Australia (Tomasic 1983, Hetherton 1981) and in the United States (Heinz and Laumann 1982) have amply attested. In a study of New South Wales lawyers it was found, for example, that the prestige attached to various types of legal work varied greatly, with areas such as taxation, equity, superior court civil litigation, commercial and constitutional law work, ranking the highest in prestige, whilst the least prestigious work included fields like general legal aid work, family law, tenancy law, petty sessions litigation and acting for unions and applicants in workers' compensation cases (Tomasic and Bullard 1978: 38). These differences were obviously related to the social status of the respective clients served in relation to each type of legal work. Work undertaken for corporate organisational clients clearly had the greatest prestige, whilst that undertaken for individuals, particularly poorer clients who rarely sought the use of legal services, tended to have the least prestige. Based upon various measures of the kinds of legal work performed by lawyers, it has been possible to isolate a number of discrete types of lawyers. Four distinct types emerged from the New South Wales study referred to above. These were respectively, property lawyers, commercial lawyers, litigation lawyers and generalist lawyers (Tomasic 1983: 456). There were significant client-related differences between each of these four main lawyer types. For example, commercial lawyers devoted between five and nine times more time to serving major corporate clients than did the other lawyer types, but other lawyers devoted three to six times more to small business clients than did commercial lawyers. Also. while commercial lawyers reported seeing an average of only one individual person as client per week, other lawyers saw between nine and seventeen such clients during the same period (Tomasic 1982: 460; see also Tomasic 1981a).

These differences seem to have the effect of fragmenting the profession quite considerably. The question therefore arises as to how exactly it is able to preserve the impression of coherence and purpose. One answer is to be found in the ideological mechanisms developed within the profession, or what might otherwise be described as the legal culture of lawyers. Although there are a number of subcultural values or orientations found within different sectors of the profession, it seems evident that there is at least an over-arching set of values and predispositions amongst lawyers which serves to set them apart from the wider community and in fact to paper over the gulfs between them arising out of work and client-related differences (see further Tomasic and Bullard, 1978). Attitudinal data from lawyers suggests that it is the value of 'cynical realism', which is shared by the vast bulk of lawyers. This is to be contrasted with the often-espoused ideal of service, and instead, suggests that lawyers are primarily concerned with advancing their own narrow economic interests, rather than broader social justice concerns. What is doubly remarkable about the widespread nature of this predisposition within the profession is that the larger community seems to be all too well aware of this lawyer orientation (Tomasic 1983: 464–70).

At a different level, it could be argued that another mechanism bonds together an otherwise fragmented profession. This is the broader role which Cain (1983: 111–12) has pointed to in a small-scale study of London solicitors. Cain argues that lawyers can be seen, in Gramscian terms, as 'conceptive ideologists' of the bourgeoisie, in that they are concerned to constitute the form of legal relations in capitalist society. With this in mind, they serve a critical function of translating client problems into acceptable legal categories and then retranslate these for clients once an outcome has been achieved. Cain concludes:

> ... it has been argued that lawyers' characteristic and specific practice is *translation* into a discourse which they both use and create. It was shown that translation work is undertaken even for impecunious clients. However ... research has shown that lawyers do this work most and best for the *haute bourgeoisie* and the state which represents it. It is also appropriate therefore, to theorise lawyers as organic intellectuals of the bourgeois class.
>
> (1983: 129)

It is this over-arching ideological role, therefore, which further counteracts the divisions in the social base of the profession and gives it the appearance of coherence. However, it should be realised that there are limits upon the extent to which lawyers can go in pursuit of ideological goals, such as the rule of law, in the interests of their clients. For example, although the rule of law ideology is to be implemented through the ideal of adversary proceedings, the profession has placed severe constraints upon overly zealous advocacy in defence of a client, particularly where this might threaten the legitimacy or integrity of the judicial process. This was highlighted, for example, in a 1984 decision of the New South Wales Court of Appeal against a barrister who had over a long period provided an extremely vigorous defence of his clients, but who in so doing had been overly zealous in his abuse of magistrates whom he saw as likely to decide against his clients. The court ordered that the barrister was guilty of professional misconduct. (*The Prothonotary v. Costello*, 13 December 1984, unreported). This kind of decision seems to suggest that the role of lawyers as 'conceptive ideologists' is not free of constraints imposed by the need to preserve the broader ideological framework within which lawyers work.

In another study, Cain (1976) has argued that the legal ideology of English judges and barristers is clear-cut. She suggests that this has four components, which she describes as reification of law, reverence regarding objects constituted by reification, righteousness and rectitude. She suggests that the effect of this ideology is that these lawyers necessarily remain out of touch with the wider concerns of the population, or as she puts it: '. . . Maintenance of the unity of legal thought is contingent upon their being impervious to the day to day rationalities of other sections of the population . . .' (1976: 246). As Sexton and Maher (1982) have also put it in relation to Australian lawyers, techniques such as these are essential to the preservation of the mystique with which lawyers are held. Moreover, they serve to neutralise the tendencies toward disintegration which are so much a part of the social organisation of the legal profession in Australian society. These tendencies are only slightly less pronounced in that other arm of the legal profession, the judiciary, to which we can now, more briefly, turn.

Judicial and Other Third Party Dispute-Processors

The legal system has, as we have seen, evolved an ideology of legalism which is maintained and reproduced by a rigid hierarchy of centres of legitimate authority in relation to rule-making and dispute resolution activity. McBarnet has referred to this as the two tiers of justice (1981: 123). Put another way, we might say that on the one hand there is the more formal top-down approach (as illustrated by judicial decision-making in the higher courts) and, on the other hand, there is the more informal bottom-up approach (as illustrated by tribunals, lower courts and non-judicial dispute-processes such as mediators, conciliators and arbitrators). In other words, looking at the dispute-handling process, it could be argued that it tends to become increasingly formal and legalistic as one ascends the legal hierarchy. This is not to suggest that no informalities are allowed to creep in at this level, but that these would be quite uncharacteristic there. By contrast, from the 'bottom-up' point of view, dispute-handling seems to be embedded in a sea of informality and the further one moves from the peaks of the judicial system, the less formality is evident. Once again, this is not to suggest that non-judicial dispute processing cannot be quite formal, for in some circumstances, such as in respect to sporting disputes involving substantial sums, formalism does seem to have a habit of creeping in. However, this is again far from being characteristic of non-judicial dispute-handling. What is clear however, as Galanter (1983: 132) has observed, is that the legal system and law exist in the shadow of informal decision-making and bargaining, so that far from formality being the most characteristic type of dispute-processing, informality tends to prevail. This would again suggest that the traditional lawyer's pyramid, which sets the superior courts at the apex of the system and the informal or less formal dispute-handlers at the base, be inverted. As argued earlier, the apex receives the priority it does for ideological and not for substantive reasons, as the impact of the base-level dispute-handlers upon the processing of disputes in society at large tends to be of greatest significance, even though lawyers have tended largely to ignore this bottom-up perspective. One reason for this has been suggested by Black and Baumgartner, who argue that settlement roles can be distinguished by reference to their degree of authoritative intervention (1983: 87). Thus, these students of the dispute process point out that the least authoritative type of settlement role is that of the friendly peacemaker. This is followed, in terms of increasing authoritativeness, by the mediator, arbitrator, judge and repressive peacemaker respectively. No doubt we could include further types along this continuum. Black and Baumgartner also point out that the dispute process draws upon supporters for the principal disputants. They suggest that these support roles can be found in a continuum of the degree of partisan intervention in support of a disputant. Thus, these support roles range from informers, at the least partisan end, through advisers, advocates and allies to surrogates, at the most partisan end of the continuum (1983: 87). How it is that particular settlement and support roles are drawn upon by disputants would depend greatly upon the local legal culture, the social proximity of disputants (or what Black has elsewhere called their 'relational distance'), their respective resources, and the technological complexity of the society in which the dispute takes place (see further Felstiner 1974).

Despite the vast range of variables at play in the resort to dispute-processing mechanisms (see further Fitzgerald 1983), prevailing ideologies seem to have had a considerable bearing upon the manner in which disputes are channelled in society. For example, the prevailing ideology of legalism in Australian society has even had a major influence upon reformers who have argued that one of the most effective means of redressing inequities in bargaining endowments is to make available lawyers and legal sevices. Thus, 'legal needs' have tended to be seen in terms of the need for the services of lawyers so as to enable disputants to contest claims in the usual judicialised forums. Almost a decade was to pass in Australia before the limitation of this strategy, and its roots in the ideology of legalistic advocacy were to become apparent (see e.g. Sackville 1978). It is interesting to note that in more recent years the revolt against judicial formalism has been largely led by the judiciary itself, as judges and court administrators have advocated greater resort to mediation and bargaining as illustrated in the emergence of Community Justice Centres (see further Tomasic 1982), and in the use of pre-trial or pre-hearing conferences. This has been motivated by the hope of reducing court caseloads and delays, and has to a large extent been a product of the over-selling of the ideology of legalism. This is further illustrated by the frequent attacks by judges upon the recent greater availability of legal aid, which has apparently induced many more disputes to be legalised and litigated than would previously have been the case (Yeldham 1984).

Associated with this kind of criticism is the fact that the ideology of legalism can become a destabilising element in society if it is made available too widely by the state. It is for this reason that many of the more aggressive legal aid strategies, such as test cases and class actions, have tended to be frowned upon by governments and other power centres in society, such as by business leaders threatened by the spectre of class action upon behalf of disgruntled consumers. Whatever the real explanation for these ideological shifts in the official rhetoric associated with various dispute processes and alternatives, it seems to be true that the judicial process is, as Weber pointed out, an amalgam of formally and substantively rational approaches. It is for this reason, as Pound (1922) has observed, that over a number of decades we seem to have witnessed periodic lurchings from formalistic to informal approaches to dispute processing. This instability seems to be embedded in the uneasy balance which legal ideology seems to comprise, for by themselves, neither formalism nor informalism are very satisfactory bases for legitimate and authoritative dispute-processing. This is because a too-formalistic legal system may be seen as inflexible and rigid, whilst a too-informal system may be seen as erratic and arbitrary.

Individual Litigants and Consumers of Legal Services

The roles of litigants and consumers of legal services within the legal system are very much influenced, if not entirely determined, by the bargaining endowments enjoyed by them. Such endowments range from the availability of legal information and legal professional assistance, the familiarity which a litigant may have with the particular legal problem area, and the resources, whether financial, psychological or social, which might be available to citizens to pursue legal action to their best advantage. Information in itself is insufficient to allow individual litigants and consumers of legal services to redress the strategic disadvantages or inequalities in power which they tend to encounter in the legal process. One of the assumptions of the legal services movement has been that inequalities in access to legal services can be redressed by providing information about the availability of such services and to enable such services to be evaluated. On the face of it, this is a deceptively simple solution to the problem of solving legal needs. However, on closer scrutiny, it has become apparent that legal information is in itself insufficient to redress inequalities, as it is the manner in which such information is organised and applied which is critical. Thus, for example, it has been shown by Mayhew and Reiss (1969) that property ownership is an important lever by virtue of which information is channelled. Consequently, those who have frequent occasion to be involved in property transactions tend to be much more likely to seek the services of lawyers and so to become familiar with how best to use such services. So, legal contacts, and the availability of legal information, are heavily influenced by property ownership. As wealthier sectors of society are more likely to have recurrent property transactions, they are more likely than poorer sectors to obtain and maintain access to legal services (see further, Tomasic 1978: 59–65).

Related to the property ownership dimension of the social organisation of legal contacts is the fact that 'repeat players' or recurrent users of legal services enjoy further advantages over those who only intermittently seek to use legal services or to gain access to the legal system. Repeat players, as we have seen, are far more likely to be able to structure the legal process to their advantage and so to succeed than are the so-called 'one shotters' (Galanter 1974). As organisations are much more likely to be 'repeat players', they enjoy further resource advantages over the 'one shotter', who is most likely to be an individual. Repeat player organisations are therefore usually far more likely to be effective mobilisers of law, whether reactively or proactively, than is the individual consumer of legal services, unless the latter either has the economic resources to engage the services of a repeat player such as a lawyer, or else the access to networks which are powerful enough to create an alternative organisational structure, such as a consumer group. It is evident that it is quite rare for large organisations to take legal action in the courts against each other, as in cases such as this the costs of such litigation may be seen as excessive. Disputes between large organisations tend therefore to be dealt with informally rather than formally, although there will always be the occasional exception. In view of this somewhat stark picture, it is not surprising that many researchers have concluded that there is little or no access to law available to the vast majority of consumers with comparatively minor grievances, even though collectively these might constitute a major problem (Nader 1980). It is clear therefore that we need to look closely at ideologies which sponsor such notions as 'justice for all' or 'due process', as these notions can only be taken as far as existing structural barriers to access allow, and as far as available bargaining endowments permit.

Conclusions: Legal Change and the Problem of Order

The legal system, like society itself, is in a continuous process of change, despite its appearance of being tradition-bound or even stagnating. Although legal reasoning rests upon the static doctrine of precedent which assumes that contemporary cases can be matched to earlier ones, this matching is invariably a very rough one because the extent to which change is occurring in society is such that one can never find exact parallels between earlier and current cases. Having said this, we need to ask why it is that law reform receives the governmental support that it does in the form of extensive funding for law reform agencies. There is a paradox here, for it is soon apparent that law reform has very little to do with legal change in any serious sense. Although law reform commissions sometimes bring about change, this is in fact very rarely the case. It can be argued that law reform agencies are more accurately seen as ideological mechanisms which serve to legitimise the law by creating the impression that legal power is being updated and made more responsive to the needs of the population at large. Put simply, law reform is frequently more mythical than real, and this can be better appreciated if it is realised that law reform agencies are actually extensions of governmental bureaucracies, despite the occasional forays which they may make into what has curiously been called community law reform, based upon reform proposals received from the wider community. In fact, more often than not, the vast bulk of law reform activity seems to be generated by problems of a political or bureaucratic nature which are simply too hard or too complex for politicians or bureaucrats to handle. The law reform agency, like many a Royal Commission of Inquiry (See Tomasic 1981b), serves the convenient function of giving the impression that problems are being dealt with. In other words, in the vast majority of cases, when controversial matters are referred to law reform agencies, we could argue that there is overwhelming evidence to suggest that the impact of the agency is symbolic rather than substantive. This is not to say that sometimes 'rather technical' or 'lawyer's law' matters referred to such reform agencies do not lead to changes, but these are far removed from the popular conception of the nature of law reform activity. Ironically, some of the most significant law reform initiatives have not come from the work of the law reform commissions, but from the enthusiasm of a particular minister or bureaucracy determined to see their ideas enacted. This suggests that the kinds of matters sent to law reform commissions tend to be those about which there is no consensus or clear-cut position, although it might be seen to require some action. All of this explains why some sociologists have come to see law reform as a problematic activity (see further Tomasic and Bottomley 1984, Arthurs 1984).

This chapter has sought to cover a considerable amount of ground as the legal system impacts upon all sectors of society or upon all aspects of social life. Having such broad or wider-ranging applications it should not be surprising if we come across discontinuities or conflicting rationales at the margins of the legal system. What is significant, however, is that the problem of coherence does not strike only at the margins or peripheries of legal institutions, but is also to be found at its core and is reflected too in the processes and structures which constitute the legal system as we know it. This, as we saw, raises serious problems, as it threatens the legitimacy of the system because its authority is based upon its adoption of a rational and consistent approach to the tasks which are required of it. However, the legal process is far from being as consistent and formally rational as many might expect. Inevitably, inconsistencies, gaps and formally irrational approaches appear. This is because it is simply not possible for the system to deliver the kind of mechanistic uniformity in approach which might be expected, due to the vast array of problems brought to it.

Where attempts are made to streamline the legal system through law reform, these strategies need to be seen as part of a broader attempt to preserve the integrity and legitimacy of legal structures. They do little more than repair the damage to the legal system by failures of legal ideologies to be able to fulfil the claims which their proponents make for them. In any event, it is clear that sociologists need to direct their attention to the interaction between diverse legal behaviours and legal ideology, for both serve to make the legal system work. Legal behaviours and legal processes inevitably reflect diversity and inconsistency, as this flexibility is essential if the processes of law are to be able to operate. However, as this incoherence may cause immense damage to the authority of law and legal institutions, an array of legal ideologies has been developed with a view to preserving the appearance of coherence. The strength of law as an instituion is very much based upon this capacity to integrate under this ideological appearance much that is diverse and often contradictory. Legal ideology therefore must be seen as that vital social glue which holds the legal order intact, so that threats to dominant legal ideologies are threats to the very existence of the legal order itself.

References

Adamany, D. (1978) 'Legitimacy, Realigning Elections, and the Supreme Court' in S. Goldman and A. Sarat (1978) *American Court Systems; Readings in Judicial Process and Behaviour*. San Francisco: W.H. Freeman and Co.

Allott, A. (1980) *The Limits of Law*. London: Butterworth.

Armstrong, M. (1979) 'The Broadcasting and Television Act, 1948–1976: A Case Study of the Australian Control Board' in R. Tomasic (ed.) *Legislation and Society in Australia*. Sydney: Allen & Unwin.

Arthurs, H. (Chairman) (1984) *Law and Learning*. Ottowa: Social Sciences and Humanities Research Council of Canada.

Aubert, V. (1983) *In Search of Law: Sociological Approaches to Law*. Oxford: Martin Robertson.

Baker, D.W.A. (1979) 'The Origins of Robertson's Land Acts' in R. Tomasic (ed.) *Legislation and Society in Australia*. Sydney: Allen & Unwin.

Bardach, E. (1977) *The Implementation Game: What Happens After a Bill Becomes Law.* Cambridge: MIT Press.

Black, D. (1980) *The Manners and Customs of the Police.* New York: Academic Press.

———— and M.P. Baumgartner (1983) 'Toward a Theory of the Third Party' in K.O. Boyum and L. Mather (eds) *Empirical Theories About Courts.* New York: Longman.

Bottoms, A.E. and McClean, J.D. (1976) *Defendants in the Criminal Process.* London: Routledge & Kegan Paul.

Boyum, K.O. and Mather, L. (eds.) (1983) *Empirical Theories About Courts.* New York: Longman.

Buckle, S.R. and Buckle, L.G. (1977) *Bargaining for Justice: Case Disposition and Reform in the Criminal Courts.* New York: Praeger.

Burman, S.B. and Harrell-Bond, B.E. (eds.) (1979) *The Imposition of Law.* New York: Academic Press.

Cain, M. (1976) 'Necessarily Out of Touch: Thoughts on the Social Organisation of the Bar' in P. Carlen (ed.) *The Sociology of Law.* Keele: University of Keele, Sociological Review Monograph 23.

————(1983) 'The General Practice Lawyer and the Client: Towards a Radical Conception' in R. Dingwall and P. Lewis (ed.) *The Sociology of the Professions.* London: Macmillan.

Caplovitz, D. (1983) *Consumers in Trouble: A Study of Debtors in Default.* New York: Free Press.

Carlen, P. (1976) *Magistrates' Justice.* London: Martin Robertson.

Carlton, E. (1977) *Ideology and Social Order.* London: Routledge & Kegan Paul.

Casper, J.D. (1978) 'The Supreme Court and National Policy Making' in S. Goldman and A. Sarat (1978) *American Court Systems: Readings in Judicial Process and Behaviour.* San Francisco: W.H. Freeman and Co.

Chambliss, W.J. (1979) 'On Law-making', *British Journal of Law and Society* 6 (2): 149–71.

Choper, J.H. (1980) *Judicial Review and the National Political Process: A Functional Reconsideration of the Role of the Supreme Court.* Chicago: Chicago University Press.

Church, T.D. *et al.* (1978) *Justice Delayed: The Pace of Litigation in Urban Trial Courts.* Williamsburg: National Centre for State Courts.

Collins, D.A. (1979) *Guidebook to Civil Claims' Practice in New South Wales.* Sydney: CCH Publishers.

Dahl, R.A. (1978). 'The Supreme Court's Role in National Policy Making' in Goldman and Sarat (1978).

Edelman, M. (1964) *The Symbolic Uses of Politics.* Urbana: University of Illinois Press.

————(1977) *Political Language: Words that Succeed and Policies That Fail.* New York: Academic Press.

Einsenstein, J. and Jacob, H. (1977) *Felony Justice: An Organizational Analysis of Criminal Courts.* Boston: Little, Brown & Co.

Encel, S. (1979) 'The Social Impact of the Australian Constitution' in R.

Tomasic (ed.) *Legislation and Society in Australia*. Sydney: Allen & Unwin.

Evan, W. (1965) 'Law as an Instrument of Social Change', in A. Gouldner and S.M. Miller (eds) *Applied Sociology*. New York: Free Press.

Feeley, M.M. (1979) *The Process is the Punishment*. New York: Russell Sage Foundation.

Felstiner, W.L.F. (1974) 'Influences of Social Organization on Dispute Processing, *Law and Society Review* 9: 63–94.

Fine, B. (1984) *Democracy and the Rule of Law: Liberal Ideals and Marxist Critiques*. London: Pluto Press.

Fitzgerald, J. (1983) 'Grievances, Disputes and Outcomes: A Comparison of Australia and the United States', *Law in Context* 1: 15–45.

Fleming, R.B. (1982) *Punishment Before Trial: An Organization Perspective of Felony Bail Processes*. New York: Longman.

Friedman, L.M. (1975) *The Legal System: A Social Science Perspective*. New York: Russell Sage Foundation.

———(1983) 'Courts Over Time: A Survey of Theories and Research' in K.O. Boyum and L. Mather (eds) *Empirical Theories About Courts*. New York: Longman.

——— and R.V. Percival (1976) 'A Tale of Two Courts: Litigation in Alameda and San Benito Counties', *Law and Society Review* 10 (1): 267–301.

Friedman, L.M. and Percival, R.V. (1981) *The Roots of Justice: Crime and Punishment in Alameda County, California, 1870–1910*. Chapel Hill: University of North Carolina Press.

Galanter, M. (1974) 'Why the Haves Come Out Ahead: Speculations on the Limits of Legal Change', *Law and Society Review* 9: 95–160.

———(1975) 'Afterword: Explaining Litigation', *Law and Society Review* 9: 347–68.

———(1983) 'The Radiating Effects of Courts' in K.O. Boyum and L. Mather (eds) *Empirical Theories About Courts*. New York: Longman.

Goldman, S. and Sarat, A. (eds.) (1978) *American Court Systems: Readings in Judicial Process and Behaviour*. San Francisco: W.H. Freeman and Co.

Grabosky, P. (1977) *Sydney in Ferment: Crime, Dissent and Official Reaction 1788 to 1973*. Canberra: ANU Press.

Griffith, J. (1979) 'Is Law Important?' *New York University Law Review* 54: 339–74.

Griffith, J.A.G. (1977) *The Politics of the Judiciary*. Manchester: Manchester University Press.

Grossman, J.B. *et al.* (1981) 'Measuring the Pace of Civil Litigation in Federal and State Trial Courts', *Judicature* 65 (2): 86–113.

Gusfield, J.R. (1963) *Symbolic Crusade: Status Politics and the American Temperance Movement*. Urbana: University of Illinois Press.

Gyles, R.V. (1984) *Report to the Attorney General for the Year Ended 30 June 1984 by R.V. Gyles QC, Special Prosecutor*. Canberra: AGPS.

Hart, G. (1979) 'Some Aspects of Government Regulation of the Capital Markets: An Assessment of the Securities Industry Acts' in R. Tomasic (ed.) *Legislation and Society in Australia*. Sydney: Allen & Unwin.

Heinz, J.P. and Laumann, E.O. (1982) *Chicago Lawyers: The Social Structure of the Bar*. New York: Russell Sage Foundation and American Bar Foundation.

Hetherton, M. (1981) *Victoria's Lawyers: The Second Report of a Research Project on Lawyers in the Community*. Melbourne: Victoria Law Foundation.

Heumann, M. (1977) *Plea Bargaining: The Experiences of Prosecutors, Judges and Defense Attorneys*. Chicago: Chicago University Press.

Hiller, A.E. and Hancock, L. (1979) 'Juvenile Delinquency Legislation and the Processing of Juveniles in Victoria' in R. Tomasic (ed.) *Legislation and Society in Australia*. Sydney: Allen & Unwin.

Hirst, P. (1979) *On Law and Ideology*. Atlantic Highlands. NJ: Humanities Press.

Hodder-Williams, R. (1980) *The Politics of the US Supreme Court*. London: Allen & Unwin.

Hopkins, A. (1978) 'The Uses of Law to Sociology', *Australian and New Zealand Journal of Sociology* 14 (3): 266–73.

———(1979) 'The Evolution of Trade Practices Legislation in Australia' in R. Tomasic (ed.) *Legislation and Society in Australia*. Sydney: Allen & Unwin.

Hunt, A. (1985) 'The Ideology of Law: Advances and Problems in Recent Applications of the Concept of Ideology to the Analysis of Law', *Law and Society Review* 19: 11–37.

Jacob, H. (1969) *Debtors in Court*. Chicago: Rand McNally.

Kagan, R.A. Cartwright, B. Friedman, L.M. and Wheeler, S. (1978) 'The Business of State Supreme Courts', *Michigan Law Review* 76 (6): 961–1,005.

Kaufman, H. (1960). *The Forest Ranger: A Study in Administrative Behaviour*. Baltimore: Johns Hopkins Press.

Kelly, D. St L. (1977) *Debt Recovery in Australia*. Canberra: AGPS.

Keon-Cohen, B. (1979) 'Aboriginal Land Rights in Australia: Beyond the Legislative Limits?' in R. Tomasic (ed.) *Legislation and Society in Australia*. Sydney: Allen & Unwin.

Kondas, A. (1979) 'The Hidden Faces of Power: A Sociological Analysis of Housing Legislation in Australia', in R. Tomasic (ed.) *Legislation and Society in Australia*. Sydney: Allen & Unwin.

Kurczewski, J. and Frieske, K. (1977) 'Some Problems in the Legal Regulation of the Activities of Economic Institutions', *Law and Society Review* 11 (3): 489–505.

La Trobe University (1980) *Guilty, Your Worship: A Study of Victoria's Magistrates' Courts*. Melbourne: Department of Legal Studies, La Trobe University.

Lipsky, M. (1980) *Street-Level Bureaucracy: Dilemmas of the Individual in Public Services*. New York: Russell Sage Foundation.

Luhmann, N. (1976) 'The Legal Profession: Comments on the Situation in the Federal Republic of Germany' in D.N. MacCormick (ed.) *Lawyers in Their Social Setting*. Edinburgh: W. Green & Son.

Macaulay, S. (1963) 'Non-Contractual Relations in Business', *American Sociological Review* 28: 55–60.

———(1977) 'Elegant Models, Empirical Pictures and the Complexities of Contract', *Law and Society Review* 11 (3): 507–28.

Mather, L.M. (1979) *Plea Bargaining or Trial?: The Process of Criminal Case Disposition.* Lexington, Mass.: Lexington Books.

Massell, G.J. (1968) 'Law as an Instrument of Revolutionary Change in a Traditional Milieu: The Case of Soviet Central Asia', *Law and Society Review* 2 (2): 179–228.

Mayhew, L. and Reiss, A.J. (1969) 'The Social Organization of Legal Contacts', *American Sociological Review* 34 (3): 309–13.

McBarnet, D.J. (1981) *Conviction: Law, the State and the Construction of Justice.* London: Macmillan.

Mukherjee, S.K. (1981) *Crime Trends in Twentieth-Century Australia.* Sydney: Allen & Unwin.

Nader, L. (1980) *No Access to Law; Alternatives to the American Judicial System.* New York: Academic Press.

Nelken, D. (1981) 'The Gap Problem in the Sociology of Law: A Theoretical Review', *Windsor Yearbook of Access to Justice* 1: 35–61.

New South Wales Bureau of Crime Statistics and Research (1983) *Court Statistics 1982.* Sydney: New South Wales Bureau of Crime Statistics and Research.

O'Malley, P. (1979) 'Theories of Structure Versus Causal Determination: Accounting for Legislative Change in Capitalist Societies' in R. Tomasic (ed.) *Legislation and Society in Australia.* Sydney: Allen & Unwin.

Ozdowski, S.A. (1979) 'The Family Law Act 1975 and The Family: A Study in Knowledge and Attitudes' in R. Tomasic (ed.) *Legislation and Society in Australia.* Sydney: Allen & Unwin.

Packer, H.L. (1968) *The Limits of the Criminal Sanction.* Stanford: Stanford University Press.

Parsons, T. (1980) 'The Law and Social Control' in W.M. Evan (ed.) *The Sociology of Law: A Socio-Structural Perspective.* New York: Free Press.

Podgorecki, A. (1974) *Law and Society.* London: Routledge & Kegan Paul.

Pound, R. (1922) *An Introduction to the Philosophy of Law.* New Haven: Yale University Press.

Robinson, C. (1979) 'Drink-Driving: Social and Legal Considerations' in R. Tomasic (ed.) *Legislation and Society in Australia.* Sydney: Allen & Unwin.

Rock, P. (1973) *Making People Pay.* London: Routledge & Kegan Paul.

Ross, E.A. (1901–70) *Social Control.* New York: Johnson Reprint Corporation.

Ross, H.L. (1981) *Deterring the Drinking Driver: Legal Policy and Social Control.* Lexington, Mass.: Lexington Books.

Ross, S.D. (1982) *Politics of Law Reform.* Melbourne: Penguin Books.

Sackville, R. (1978) 'Lawyers, Law Reform and Legal Institutions – Some

Reflections' in R. Tomasic (ed.) *Understanding Lawyers*. Sydney: Allen & Unwin.

Sawer, G. (1967) *Australian Federalism in the Courts*. Melbourne: Melbourne University Press.

Sexton, M. and Maher, L. (1982) *The Legal Mystique: The Role of Lawyers in Australian Society*. Sydney: Angus & Robertson.

Shapiro, M. (1964) *Law and Politics in the Supreme Court*. London: Free Press of Glencoe.

Simon, W.H. (1978) 'The Ideology of Advocacy: Procedural Justice and Professional Ethics', *Wisconsin Law Review* 1978 (1): 29–144.

Sugarman, D. (Ed.) (1983) *Legality, Ideology and the State*. London: Academic Press.

Sumner, C. (1979) *Reading Ideologies*. London: Academic Press.

Sutton, A. and Wild, R., (1979) 'Companies, the Law and the Professions: A Sociological View of Australian Companies Legislation', in R. Tomasic (ed.) *Legislation and Society in Australia*. Sydney: Allen & Unwin.

Tomasic, R. (1977a) *Deterrence and the Drinking Driver*. Sydney: Law Foundation of New South Wales.

———(1977b) *Drugs, Alcohol and Community Control*. Sydney: Law Foundation of New South Wales.

———(1978) *Lawyers and the Community*. Sydney: Allen & Unwin.

———(ed.) (1979) *Legislation and Society in Australia*. Sydney: Allen & Unwin.

———(1981a) 'Criminal Lawyers and their Clients', *ANZJ Criminology* 14: 147–55.

———(1981b) 'The Politics of Implementing Drug Law Reform in Australia', *Australian Crime Prevention Council Forum* 4(1): 69–80.

———(1982) 'Mediation as an Alternative to Adjudication: Rhetoric and Reality in the Neighborhood Justice Movement' in R. Tomasic and M.M. Feeley (eds) *Neighborhood Justice*. New York: Longman.

———(1983) 'Social Organization Amongst Australian Lawyers', *ANZJ Sociology* 19(3): 447–75.

———(1985) *The Sociology of Law*. London: Sage.

———and S. Bottomley (1984) 'Editorial: Law Reform and Social Change', *Legal Service Bulletin* 9(6): 251–52.

———and C. Bullard (1978) *Lawyers and their Work in New South Wales*. Sydney: Law Foundation of New South Wales.

———and C. Bullard (1979) 'Lawyers and Legal Culture in Australia', *International Journal of the Sociology of Law* 7: 417–32.

Touraine, A. (1977) *The Self-Production of Society*. Chicago: University of Chicago Press.

Weaver, S. (1977) *Decision to Prosecute: Organization and Public Policy in the Antitrust Division*. Cambridge: MIT Press.

Weber, M. (1954) *On Law in Economy and Society*. Cambridge: Harvard University Press.

Willis, J. (1980) 'The Regulation of Debt Collection Practices' in A.J. Duggan and L.W. Darvall (eds) *Consumer Protection: Law and Theory*.

Yeldham, D.A. (1984) 'Delays in Criminal Trials', Paper presented to

Criminal Law Committee, Sydney University Law Graduates Association, 13 March 1984, Sydney Law School.

Ziegert, K.A. (1984) 'The Limits of Family Law: A Socio-Legal Assessment', *Legal Service Bulletin* 9(6): 257–63.

Chapter Six

Immigration and Ethnicity

James Jupp

'Ethnicity' is a slippery sociological concept, located as it is within the broader areas of culture and ideology, both notoriously hard to define and to operationalise in concrete situations. Broadly, ethnicity implies both individual and collective characteristics which change over time and situation (De Vos and Romanucci-Ross 1982). The individual is brought up within a community and culture, normally with a geographical base, though not necessarily so. This community has developed an ideology, or view of the world, which is based on the past collective experience of the community as interpreted by various 'culture-bearers' such as priests or teachers. The community may define its boundary very carefully, excluding those who marry out or change religion or lose the relevant language. Such rigidly-defining communities in Australia include Jews and Greeks. Thus there may be many of Jewish or Greek origin who are not regarded as part of the ethnic community by its cultural definers. They may, however, see themselves or be seen by others, as still belonging. Such a dilemma was faced most acutely by German Jews under Hitler. They had become Germanised but were defined out of the 'German race' by the Nuremburg laws. Thus a central problem in applying the concept of ethnicity in concrete situations is that it may be communally determined, individually determined or determined by those of a different ethnicity. In Australia such problems have always surrounded the official definition of an Aborigine, and will also undoubtedly arise around the new question on ethnicity in the 1986 Census (Australian Bureau of Statistics 1984).

Difficulty in applying the concept of ethnicity becomes particularly acute in immigrant situations when people sharing various cultural, linguistic or religious traits are placed in an environment dominated by those of another ethnicity. Most immigrant societies, and particularly Australia, have favoured assimilation, that is the abandoning of original ethnicity for that of the host community. This may, as with earlier public policy towards Aborigines of mixed descent, involve consistent coercion. More generally, assimilationism is simply an expectation of the host community, which cannot conceive of people leaving their homeland without leaving its culture behind. Alternative cultures may be seen as a threat to national cohesion, because nationality is based on a series of myths which others cannot share. Gallipoli does not mean the same to an Anglo-Australian RSL member as it means to a Turkish immigrant. Ned Kelly, Henry Lawson or William Lane cannot appeal to a Chinese Australian, as they were all in their various ways white racists. Assimilationism which regards other cultures as a threat or as permanently incompatible with the host culture, may be termed conservative assimilationism. It aims at preserving the rights and privileges of those who settled first. The White Australia policy was a prime example of such an attitude, forcing the exclusion or expulsion of those, who, because physically different, were assumed to be culturally unassimilable. The White Australia policy is normally associated with the Immigration Restriction Act of 1901, which imposed a dictation test on intending immigrants and had the effect of keeping out Asians and Pacific Islanders. Other legislation, often at the state level, provided that Chinese could not engage in mining without permission; that they should not be naturalised, and could not vote or own property unless they were; that Pacific Islanders could be deported; that 'aboriginal natives of Asia, Africa and the Pacific Islands' could not be naturalised; that Islanders were restricted to unskilled trades; and that goods must be stamped if made by non-European labour. Most of this legislation was passed between 1880 and 1920, although some earlier Acts were passed as early as the 1850s. The immigration restrictions reduced the numbers born in Asia to below 25,000 in the inter-war period and the numbers from the Pacific to less than 3,000 (Willard 1974, Palfreeman 1967).

What the Canadian professor John Porter has called the charter group (in this case Anglo-Australians) determined the national culture and required the submersion of all other cultures through assimilation (Porter 1975). In concrete terms this has meant the disappearance of languages (including British languages such as Irish or Gaelic), of distinctive dress (as for the Chinese), of separate educational systems (as for German Lutherans but not Irish Catholics), and of all loyalties to any homeland except the British Isles (as with Germans in 1914 and Italians in 1940).

Conservative assimilationism is easy to discern in Australian history and social thought. Until 1972, it largely determined immigration and ethnic policy. What might be termed 'rational assimilationism' and 'radical assimilationism' are more sophisticated. Rational assimilationism simply argues that in a new society the culture of the original homeland has no utility. As Professor Chipman puts it: 'How absurd it is that ... we should define our future in terms of a myriad of cultures of other times and places' (Chipman 1980). This assumes, of course, that Australian culture is free from the influences of other times and places, which is questionable. Apart from its varied British inheritance, it is increasingly influenced from the United States through the media. Nevertheless, much public policy has been shaped since 1972 by the belief that varied ethnicities are a transitory phenomenon of the immigrant phase and will disappear in the second generation. Radical assimilationism, which is mainly Marxist in inspiration, shares in the Marxist belief that ethnicity is ideological and mystifying, and must be replaced by class consciousness. Those immigrants who are in the industrial workforce are being misled by their compatriots in the upwardly mobile classes, who use ethnicity to gain access to power and who are used by the ruling class to integrate immigrants into the class structure (De Lepervanche 1980).

Assimilationism is an ideology, as is multiculturalism. They both posit arguments about the nature of society and desirable directions for it to follow. As most public policy is made within an ideological framework, the dominance of one view or another is crucial. A society which develops as a result of assimilation would ideally be very cohesive, because it is based on common values, attitudes and culture. One which develops from multiculturalism would be expected to be liberal, because it is based on tolerance for differing cultures and the denial of the superiority of one culture over all others. However, assimilation and ethnic diversity are also sociological 'facts', in the sense that members of ethnic groups do adapt to the host society over time, but to a society which contains within it many functioning subcultures based on ethnicity, class, generations or levels of education. The argument here centres around the extent and rapidity of assimilation to the dominant culture in the first and subsequent generations. Ethnicity may be seen as primordial, bred through the generations and therefore changing slowly, or situational, changing its form to accommodate to new situations. In plural societies (for example in Asia) ethnic variety continues indefinitely and ethnic boundaries are strictly maintained. In modern immigrant societies, where minority cultures do not have a firm geographical base, boundaries become very ragged (for example through intermarriage) and ethnic differences may disappear quite quickly. The rate of disappearance may depend on factors within the immigrant community. Those which have brought a strong sense of boundary maintenance may preserve their identity over several generations. Different communities may variously define their 'core values'. Poles or Ukrainians stress language maintenance, Greeks and Jews stress in-marriage, Chinese and Italians the family structure, and Irish and Lebanese religious denomination.

Immigrant groups in Australia are best understood as expressing distinctive ethnicities which are changing under the pressure of a dominant culture, which is itself changing under the influence of the media, of immigration, urbanisation and higher levels of education. The attempts to define Australian culture in terms of mateship, Ned Kelly, Phar Lap or Squizzy Taylor, are almost as certainly doomed to failure as the preservation of minor European languages and folkways. They have the advantage of media endorsement but are unrelated to the lifestyle and experience of most Australians of whatever origins.

There are three basic models of ethnic relations which have been discussed in relation to all societies containing ethnic minorities. These are the plural society model of Furnivall (1939) in which ethnic communities remain distinct and have limited relationships; the melting pot model in which a variety of cultures merge and create a new distinctive ethnicity (in this case American); and the ethnic mobilisation model of Glazer and Moynihan (1970) which argues that ethnicity is an organised resource which is based on lingering ethnic cultures but which recreates such cultures as minority interests in a liberal democratic society. Others have stressed that ethnicity must be understood within a general context of social structure and inequality. According to this view ethnic communities are internally structured along lines common to the broader society, while ethnic communities in general may reflect social stratification in the sense that members of some ethnic groups are privileged, while members of others are disadvantaged. In this view ethnic mobilisation is most meaningful when it improves the life chances of people from ethnic communities, rather than when it attempts to preserve homeland cultures (which are changing in the homeland itself).

Most of these views (except perhaps Furnivall's, which is mainly relevant to rural societies) emphasise that ethnic cultures are always in a state of flux. Conservative ethnicists, who want to preserve what they see as the basic character of their community, usually fight a losing battle in a modern, urban society like Australia. Quite large communities have completely disappeared in Australia, including the Gaelic-speaking population of the mid-nineteenth century. Most others, including the Jews, who have been present since 1788, faced constant erosion prevented only by

new immigrations. Rural communities, such as the Germans of
South Australia or the Italians of north Queensland, preserved
some distinctive characteristics for upwards of a century (Borrie
1954). Others, like the Danes or the Swiss simply vanished. The
'lesson of history' is that Australia has been a very homogenising
society. But that does not mean that ethnic variety will disappear
this century. Its numerical base is very substantial and official
policy no longer condemns it.

The Australian Situation

Australians between 1900 and 1950 frequently congratulated
themselves on being 99 per cent British, which was never strictly
true but became part of the national myth. They were certainly 99
per cent white, the residue being made up of Aborigines and dying
fragments of Chinese and Pacific Islanders left over from the days
before White Australia. Although Catholics of Irish descent had
considerable political influence, they too were declining in what
was overwhelmingly a nominally Protestant society. Irish immigration virtually ended in the early 1890s, while English and
Scottish immigration continued. Part of the national myth was that
in keeping out unassimilable minorities Australia would avoid the
racial strife evident in the United States. Despite continued
oppression of Aborigines and occasional riots such as that in
Kalgoorlie in 1934, this was indeed achieved. The myth of White
Australia was egalitarian and democratic, in the sense of arguing
that such conflicts were undesirable, that inequality based on
ethnic difference should be avoided (except for Aboriginals who
were a 'dying race') and that the happiest society was one in which
most citizens were very much like one another. These attitudes
were consensual and the attraction of non-British immigrants after
1947 was thus a major departure undertaken at some political risk,
but with great skill. It had to be argued (and was) that European
immigrants were fully assimilable, that they would become New
Australians as a preliminary to becoming full Australians, and that
their children would be indistinguishable from others. All forms of
ethnicity, other than the predominant Anglo-Australian forged
from varied British origins in the previous century, were
anathema.

Over thirty years of mass migration these attitudes began to
break down, although they are still widely held. Part of the official
welcome for East European refugees included the staging of dances
and festivals which, unknown to their Australian sponsors, were
often the external facade to a determined ethnic assertion. Mass

unassisted arrivals from southern Europe in the 1960s finally sank the notion of the rapid disappearance of distinctive ethnicity, and official rejection of assimilationism came after 1972. Australia is now officially a multicultural society in which all ethnic origins are equally valid and in which public funds are allocated (in rather small quantities) to 'maintain' non-British cultures, languages and religions. Australians who like eating, drinking, watching television and following sport can now do so in hundreds of ways which were unavailable to their parents. Ethnicity is celebrated, where it was feared and condemned. To almost everyone's surprise this has been accomplished without the social upheaval evident in other pluralist societies, including Britain itself.

Among reasons for this relative success have been the continuing economic expansion of Australia during the period of major immigration and the planned and controlled character of such migration. Until the 1970s United Kingdom citizens were virtually free to enter Australia under any circumstances, although a majority received assisted passages which were allocated on the basis of needed skills. All other immigrants, plus the British after 1972, had to be approved by an Australian immigration officer at the point of departure. While there have always been illegal immigrants, these arrived on nothing like the scale common in the United States, because of Australia's isolation. Immigration agreements were contracted with most major source countries, while refugees were also processed by Australian officials. The experience of rigid control built up under the White Australia policy since 1900 was sustained by later experience in the processing of refugees and the assistance of British and European migrants. Despite undoubted mistakes and miscalculations, Australia had one of the most tightly-controlled immigrant entries of any major receiver. Ever since the first introduction of assisted passages in 1831 the country had been colonised by equating economic demand for labour with the supply of immigrants and this continued to be the case for 150 years. The parallel is not with the United States or Britain but with Canada, which has had equal success in absorbing immigrants from a variety of sources through strict control. Australia also departed from the European practice of attracting 'guest workers' who were not expected to settle. While many Europeans have, in fact, returned home, this was not the intention of the Australian government, which placed considerable emphasis on permanent settlement, naturalisation and family reunion. Having committed itself to such settlement from a variety of ethnic sources, government was inevitably forced towards official multiculturalism and the abandoning of assimilationism.

Whatever the inter-relationship between ethnic groups and the degree of assimilation, a major concern in Australia as elsewhere has been the avoidance of structured inequality based on ethnicity. This is most common in 'racial' situations, when ethnic characteristics are presumed for those of different appearance, however far they may be removed from immigrant origins. The most obvious victims of such classification are the Aborigines, who are not immigrants at all. As with Black Americans, they have faced consistent and official discrimination and coercion, based on assumptions of their collective inferiority. Chinese and Melanesians suffered similar discrimination in the late nineteenth century, being barred from particular occupations by law and union rules. The general effect of such structured inequality is to produce anti-social behaviour among those being persecuted, which simply confirms the prejudice of the dominant community. No recent immigrant groups seem to have experienced this cycle of deprivation. While there have been high levels of mental instability and violence among some East European refugees (many of them now elderly) most immigrant groups show a very low level of anti-social behaviour compared with Anglo-Australians and New Zealanders (Francis 1981). More subtle forms of structural inequality have, however, not been absent. Southern Europeans have often been stereotyped as manual unskilled workers. Many East European refugees failed to gain recognition for their qualifications and were directed to manual work by immigration officials, from which most of them never escaped. The professions, and especially medicine, have been very reluctant to accept non-British qualifications and experience. There is a very long tradition in Australia of regarding all immigrants as needing to start at the bottom and of categorising races and ethnic groups in terms of inferiority or superiority. While few immigrants are as disadvantaged as single parents or the disabled (most of whom are native-born), the Henderson Report on poverty and the work of the late Jean Martin suggested that some, mainly southern European, groups were being locked into a situation of disadvantage (Martin 1978). The existence of 'migrant jobs' has also been commented on by Bob Birrell (Birrell and Birrell 1981).

Whatever their experience of discrimination (if any) members of non-English-speaking ethnic groups face many personal and collective choices which need not worry most of the native-born. These include the erosion of language, religion and customs and, most importantly, of paternal authority. Generational conflict in immigrant families has not been intensively studied in Australia, but it undoubtedly exists. One attempted solution, adopted by Irish Catholics in the last century, has been to sustain separate school systems, which now exist up to secondary level for Jews and Greeks and are planned for Muslims. As these all have a religious basis they are acceptable to public authorities used to the dual state/church system. However, most NES immigrants are too poor to support such systems. Separate media and language classes exist widely. Those of NES background are confronted with a tension between succeeding in Australian society and at the same time retaining their ethnicity. Many, perhaps most, do so by living in two worlds, which is often easier than Anglo-Australians assume, but more difficult for the second and later generations. Many immigrants, such as Jews, Greek Egyptians, Anglo-Indians or Overseas Chinese, have always done this. Thus ethnic relations are best understood in Australia in terms of compromise and partial assimilation, rather than as involving conflict between distinct entities with strictly-defined boundaries.

The Immigrant Communities

Immigrants normally have differing life chances in Australia, related to their homeland background, their competence in English and general educational level, their concentration in particular localities and industries and the extent to which they were rigorously selected for admission. In general those of English-speaking background (which includes many Asians, though predominantly from Britain) tend towards the upper end of the social and occupational scale, while those of NES background tend towards industrial employment. However this can be too simple a picture (see Table 6.1). Using as one measure of social composition the occupational classes of the Census, we might distinguish between those national groups which are predominantly 'working class' (in having a very low proportion in the middle class occupations), those which are close to the national average (with 36 per cent in professional, administrative and clerical classes) and those which are distinctly 'middle class'. In this respect the major NES communities fall within the 'working class' category, with some, like the Turks, the Yugoslavs and the Vietnamese having very small middle classes indeed. All the southern European groups which arrived most strongly in the 1960s and 1970s fall within this area, as do the largely refugee Poles, and Ukrainians and the Finns. From this we may generalise that those who came without public assistance or as refugees are those most likely to be found in the industrial classes. This does not mean that there are not substantial Italian or Greek middle classes, but rather that the 'typical' immigrant from these communities is in manual work on a

Table 6.1 Class Background of Migrant Groups in Australia, 1981 by Total Numbers from the Birthplace and Percentage of their Workforce in Professional, Administrative or Clerical Occupations[1]

'Working Class'

Cyprus	23,332	17.3%	Finland	9,507	25.5%
Malta	57,001	15.5%	Poland	59,441	24.8%
Spain	15,153	15.8%	Ukraine	10,941	16.2%
Greece	146,625	12.2%	Italy	275,883	14.7%
Lebanon	49,623	12.7%	Turkey	24,314	9.1%
Vietnam	41,097	9.2%	Yugoslavia	149,335	10.2%
Total	862,252				

'Average' (All-Australia = 36%; Australian-born = 38.1%)

Austria	22,805	33.9%	Czechoslovakia	16,152	39.5%
Baltic	22,945	38.4%	France	13,335	34.6%
Germany	110,758	34.8%	Hungary	27,987	35.9%
Holland	96,044	32.8%	New Zealand	176,713	38%
UK/Eire	1,132,601	38.9%	USSR	16,954	31.2%
Total	1,636,294 (NES 326,980)				

'Middle Class'

Canada	17,690	53.5%	India	41,657	54.6%
Israel	6,147	46.7%	Japan	8,060	56.6%
Malaysia	31,598	66%	Philippines	15,431	53.6%
South Africa	26,965	56.8%	Singapore	11,990	58.8%
Sri Lanka	16,966	60.4%	USA	32,620	61.3%
China	25,883	40.2%	Indonesia	12,463	43.5%
PNG	18,695	44.7%	Egypt	30,645	42.6%
Total	296,810			2,797,356	(87.9% of overseas-born)

Source: DIEA, *Profile 81*, AGPS, 1984 (for various origins)

[1] Division into classes is based upon ABS occupation codes 0, 1, and 2. If 0–29% of the migrant group were in the above categories, then they were classified working class; if 30–40% then average, and if 41% or more, then middle class.

weekly wage. This does not, of course, mean that the same is true of the second generation born in Australia.

At the core of the 'socially average' immigrants are the British, whose occupational structure only varies from the Australian-born in having rather less working in agriculture. To that extent the belief that the British assimilate best has been true, although it can be argued that those chosen as immigrants were already very close to the Australian norm before they departed. New Zealanders, too, are socially almost identical to the Australian-born on this measure. Immigrants from northern and central Europe are also very close to the norm, with refugees from the Baltic states, Hungary and Czechoslovakia being more middle class than those from Poland or the Ukraine. Those born in the USSR also had a strong middle class, but many of these were Jewish, and the ethnic Russian population is so old that many are no longer in the workforce at all.

Middle class immigrant communities are drawn overwhelmingly from Asia and from English-speaking societies such as the United States, Canada or South Africa. The Egypt-born population represents those Greeks and other non-Arabs leaving in response to Nasser's Egyptian nationalism. Egyptian Greeks and other Christians form, a significant middle class element in southern European communities, especially in Sydney. It is quite remarkable that the ending of the White Australia policy has led not to an influx of peasants but of professionals and white collar workers. This is enhanced in some communities (such as Malaysians) by the large number of students included, and in others (especially Filipinos) by an excess of women, who tend to be found in clerical and professional employment. It is difficult to generalise about middle class communities in terms of language, as many Asians are drawn from small minorities in their homelands among which English was a mother tongue. There is here a very marked contrast between the social situation of most free Asian immigrants and the refugee Vietnamese (Viviani 1984). Only the Vietnamese currently conform to the prejudiced belief that Asians are poor and unskilled. Thus prejudice against Asians in Australia is more likely to be confined to 'pathological reactions' against those of different appearance, than is the case in Britain or was previously the case in nineteenth-century Australia. On most observable social dimensions Asians are markedly 'superior' to the average Australian. There is reason to suppose from school and university results that this will continue into the second generation, including the currently impoverished Indo-Chinese.

Residential concentration is related to occupation and it is not surprising to find many southern Europeans concentrated in industrial suburbs while many Asians are scattered throughout the residential areas of the major cities. In general we can say that the more concentrated a community is in industry, the more it will be concentrated residentially. This is reinforced by the social desirability of living in suburbs where many services are provided by those familiar with community languages. For those not subscribing to the 'mainstream' Christian denominations there are also good reasons for congregating near appropriate places of worship, and it is noteworthy that the highly middle class Jewish populations tend to be more concentrated geographically than other similar ones. Geographical concentration of ethnic minorities has always been deplored by Anglo-Australians and public statements have regularly opposed the creation of 'ghettos'. There has been much confusion on this issue, partly because the term 'ghetto' is defined in different ways. In its original Jewish sense of a neighbourhood to which members of one ethnic minority were strictly confined, ghettos have never existed in Australia, except for Aborigines directed to missions by public agencies. In the common American sense of a poor urban neighbourhood dominated by a particular minority, Australian cities have never had them. Even such allegedly Irish strongholds as North Melbourne always contained immigrants from a variety of British origins. There is no state or federal electorate which contains an absolute majority of Catholics, let alone of any one birthplace group, a situation quite different from that, for example, in Boston. There is only one federal electorate (Bonython) in which the overseas-born have formed a majority in recent years, and they are drawn overwhelmingly from Britain under the resettlement schemes of the Playford Liberal South Australian government. Outside a few rural settlements there have never been one-nation minority ghettos in Australia other than an occasional street, nor are there any today.

What have been created by post-war immigration are 'ethnic areas', in which substantial populations are of overseas birth or NES origin. In such areas, usually dominated by southern Europeans, there is a mixing of origin. There is always a significant proportion of Anglo-Australians and they may control local municipal power even when in a numerical minority. In Melbourne in 1976 there were twenty-three municipalities in which more than 20 per cent were born in NES countries (with the highest proportions in inner-city Brunswick, Collingwood, Fitzroy and Richmond), thirteen in Sydney (highest in Botany, Marrickville, Sydney and the more middle class Waverley), and in Adelaide, six (highest in inner-city Hindmarsh and Thebarton). All of these had higher NES proportions than Wollongong, which is often described as an immigrant city. The major birthplace groups in such areas were almost invariably Italian, Greek and Yugoslav.

Census figures for birthplace suggest that there are clearly-defined areas of some major cities in which southern Europeans have concentrated and that these are close to the city centre in 'traditional' working class and ALP areas. However, this finding must be modified by taking into account the second generation and also acknowledging that the trend amongst the overseas-born is to move outwards into peripheral suburbs at least as fast as the Australian-born majority. In selected electoral subdivisions of Melbourne in 1982 voters distinguished by 'non-Anglo names' made up 28 per cent in Carlton North, 29.6 per cent in Richmond and 44 per cent in Brunswick, all in inner suburbs. But they made up 43 per cent of voters in Deer Park and 70.7 per cent in St Albans, both on the far western fringes. In Carlton and Brunswick, such voters were predominantly Italian, and in Richmond Greek. But in the outer suburbs there were major elements not only from these two countries but also from Malta and Yugoslavia. These were newly-built areas which were quite prosperous in the 1960s but became subject to increasing youth unemployment in the late 1970s. The second generation living in such areas often find themselves trapped in a social environment which is very limiting, with a lack of facilities, entertainment or employment. They may not be markedly 'ethnic' but are paying for the rundown of the industries which attracted their parents to Australia twenty years ago. Industrial restructuring may leave outer suburbs short of manufacturing jobs, a process which had already affected many inner suburbs by the early 1970s. But alternative jobs in offices or services may be less available on the outer working class fringes than closer to the city centre.

Causes of Immigrant Disadvantage

Immigrants, like women, are fashionably treated as a potentially disadvantaged group in Australian society. But, like women, immigrants are very numerous and varied and cannot be meaningfully treated as a category with common experiences, problems, attitudes or characteristics. Also like women, they may expect to meet some basic prejudices heavily ingrained in Australian culture. But these prejudices are often very mild and have no noticeable effect on life chances. Indeed, the now very attenuated 'colonial cringe' in some professions may work to the advantage of the largest single group of immigrants, those from the British Isles and other English-speaking societies. British academics or doctors are very well entrenched in some of the most prestigious and well-paid positions in Australian society. A glance at *Who's Who* will suggest that immigrants from some other European societies have also done very well. However, in some pursuits, such as politics and agriculture, the Australian-born are disproportionately represented, as they are in the social élites of the major metropolitan centres (Jupp 1984).

To understand the social position of immigrants it is necessary to break down the two large categories of immigrants (21 per cent of the population) and non-British origin (at most 25 per cent) into meaningful component parts. In terms of prejudice Australians have normally placed the English speakers in the most favoured position, northern Europeans next, southern Europeans lower, Asians lower still and Aborigines last of all. While scientific surveys of such attitudes do not extend back beyond the 1940s it seems reasonable to suppose that this general grading is deeply embedded in Australian culture, particularly as it is very similar to attitudes found in other British-derived societies and in Britain itself (Goot 1985). As has been argued, such a scale of prejudice is at variance with the realities of the Australian ethnic and immigrant population. Asians are much better educated and work in positions with higher prestige than do native-born or British Australians. Whether this fact is sufficiently well known to change popular attitudes is an interesting question. Whether reinforced prejudice against southern Europeans, who are heavily concentrated in industrial jobs and suburbs, will operate against their better educated and more mobile children is even more important. For at present it is possible to argue with considerable evidence that southern European immigrant workers hold jobs for which their lower levels of education qualify them. This will not be true of the second generation, who will resent any categorisation as inferior. Such resentment will probably create an 'ethnic pride' movement which will raise the salience of ethnicity even after reinforcement from the homelands is over, a trend parallel to that which raised the consciousness of Australian Catholics after Irish immigration had ended.

The most disadvantaged immigrants are those who are located in groups against which Australians are traditionally prejudiced: who have an inadequate command of English; who are in declining manufacturing industries; who are ageing or disabled; who live in inadequately serviced suburbs; or who are women. Further disadvantage may be suffered by recent arrivals, who are often quite young, unable to understand English, settling in poorer suburbs and seeking unskilled employment. In concrete terms concentrations of the disadvantaged are to be found in those from Yugoslavia, Turkey, Lebanon, Vietnam, Poland, Ukraine, Greece or Italy (see Table 6.2). Industrial workers most at risk are in clothing, textiles and footwear (mostly women), motor manufacture (mostly men) and in some unattractive occupations such as meat work or cleaning. In agriculture, there are growing threats to predominantly southern European small farmers in irrigation crops and sugar. The residential areas in which such ethnic disadvantage is most marked are the western suburbs of Sydney and Melbourne (particularly Fairfield and Broadmeadows) and some inner-city public housing estates with high concentrations of Turks or Vietnamese. Most disadvantaged 'ethnics' no longer live in inner-city 'ghettos', many of which have been taken over and gentrified by Anglo-Australians. However, there are still a few core 'ghetto' areas such as Marrickville in New South Wales or Richmond in Victoria. The rundown of manufacturing presents a special threat to second generation 'ethnics' such as Maltese, living in suburbs where there are few alternative forms of employment available, or in industrial cities such as Wollongong or Geelong.

These actual or potential disadvantages are related to ethnicity in the sense that certain nationalities have concentrated in particular areas and industries which are no longer as buoyant as when immigration was at its height. The peculiar age structure of some ethnic groups, especially those from Eastern Europe, has made them exceptionally susceptible to the problems of ageing. Multicultural or ethnic-specific services can ameliorate such problems but not solve them. Thus it is increasingly essential that services for the aged become more sensitive to the psychological needs of non-English-speakers. Industrial retraining must cope with workers whose English is very inadequate, many of them quite young recent arrivals. Trade unions have a major responsibility which until very recently they were reluctant to acknowledge. Local councils in areas of high ethnicity must be more responsive to the ethnic dimension of their work, in the appointment of relevantly qualified social workers, in ethnic-specific child care provision and in such vexed areas as planning permission for mosques or ethnic clubs. Public authorities, as major employers, must ensure that their employment policies give adequate scope to those immigrants or people from various ethnic groups unable to find jobs in declining private industries. School systems must adapt to the needs of children whose parents do not normally speak English and whose own job prospects are very uncertain. That all these problems would arise should have been obvious twenty years ago, when southern European immigration was at its height. They were, however, overlooked in conditions of full employment by authorities which were dominated by Anglo-Australians.

Much debate around ethnicity has concentrated on cultural and educational, rather than strictly economic, issues. Economic problems are, of course, shared by all in similar circumstances, although the above argument suggests that certain groups of ethnic

Table 6.2 Some Measures of Immigrant Disadvantage in Australia, 1981 Census

High Elderly Component (mean age over 50; all-Australian mean is 41.9 years)
(Estonia 60.4)   (Lithuania 60.3)   Ukraine 58.9   Latvia   56.9
(Bulgaria 56.4)   USSR   54.1   Poland   53.6   Hungary 52.1
Romania 51.2
Total Number from these Birthplaces = 145,807

Low Years of Education (under 9 years – all-Australian mean is 10.8 yrs)
(Cocos   3.1)   Portugal   6.7   Turkey   7.2   (Kampuchea 7.2)
Greece   7.5   (Syria   7.5)   Italy   7.8   Cyprus   8.1
(Laos   8.3)   Yugoslavia 8.3   Lebanon 8.4   Uruguay   8.4
(Iraq   8.4)   (Albania   8.5)   Spain   8.7   Ukraine   8.9
(Bulgaria 8.9)
Total Number from these Birthplaces = 735,192

Low English Capacity (below 70 on a scale 1–100; all-Australian mean is 96.6)
(Cocos 23.3)   (Kampuchea 40.5)   (Laos   40.6)   Vietnam   46.8
(Timor 50)   Portugal   50   (Syria   52.3)   (Korea   55.5)
Turkey 57.8   (Bulgaria   58.9)   Greece   61.3   (Colombia 61.2)
China   61.7   Chile   63.9   Uruguay 64.4   Cyprus   64.5
Spain   65   Argentina   66.1   (Taiwan   66.5)   (Ecuador   66.7)
Italy   67.9   Japan   68.4   Lebanon 68.7
Total Number from these Birthplaces = 680,013

High Unemployment (Larger Groups only) (All-Australia level was 5.8%)
Vietnam 20.8%   Lebanon 13.5%   USSR 13%   Turkey 12.2%
New Zealand   10.2%
Total Number from these Birthplaces = 308,701

Low Family Income (Below $15,000; all-Australian mean was $16,490)
By birthplace of 'head of household'; includes one-person households (in dollars)
(Timor   4,277)   (Bangladesh   4,900)   (Syria   8,222)
(Vanuatu   8,333)   (Kampuchea   8,821)   (New Caledonia 9,000)
(Laos   9,750)   (Cocos   10,100)   Ukraine   11,221
(Lithuania 11,644)   (Iraq   11,907)   Lebanon   11,945
(Taiwan   12,000)   USSR   13,000   Argentina   13,366
Latvia   13,552   Turkey   13,748   Vietnam   13,886
Malta   14,113   Italy   14,188   Greece   14,257
(Iran   14,335)   Cyprus   14,374   Portugal   14,376
Yugoslavia 14,743   Poland   14,929
Total Number from these Birthplaces = 918,458

Low Income of Employed (incl. Part-Time) (Below $10,000; all-Australian mean was $11,930 (in dollars)
(Samoa   4,500)   (Nauru   4,833)   (Taiwan   6,250)
(Venezuela   7,000)   (Colombia   8,000)   (Cocos   8,500)
(Albania   8,500)   (Thailand   8,500)   (Iraq   8,886)
(Cook Islands 9,000)   (Laos   9,000)   (Ecuador   9,250)
(Kampuchea   9,285   Turkey   9,303   Lebanon   9,365

| Portugal | 9,484 | (New Caledonia | 9,500) | Greece | 9,657 |

Argentina   9,725

Total Number from these Birthplaces — 263,855

Occupational Status (On the ANU Status Score of 0–100 a level of under 25; the all-Australian mean is 36)

(Laos	13.2)	(Kampuchea	14.1)	(Bangladesh	15.2)	(Colombia	15.9)
(Cook Isl.	16.7)	Portugal	17.6	Turkey	19.5	(Thailand	19.7)
(N. Caledonia	19.9)	Uruguay	20.9	(Ecuador	20.7)	(Albania	21)
Ukraine	21	(Tonga	21.7)	(Syria	21.9)	Yugoslavia	21.3
Vietnam	22.9	Greece	23.3	(Lithuania	23.6)	Argentina	24.2
Malta	24.7	Lebanon	24.6	Spain	24.9	Cyprus	24.9

Total Number from these Birthplaces = 576,192

Note: All references are to birthplace. Figures in brackets are drawn from a population of less than 8,000 and a 1% sample and may be unreliable.

Sources: *Profile 81*; Department of Immigration, Canberra, 1984; 1981 Census 1% User Sample

immigrants bear a greater burden than the average. Minority cultural expression may not have any obvious economic utility and for that reason, and because of the long-dominant ideology of assimilation, it may prove harder to justify to the public and to government agencies. Nevertheless, after the Galbally Report of 1978 and the consequent establishment of the Special Broadcasting Service, governments of both parties have become committed to cultural diversity beyond the strictly pragmatic necessity of communicating with immigrants in a language they can understand (Galbally 1978). It is the cultural aspect of ethnic policy which has attracted most criticism in recent years, especially from conservatives associated with *Quadrant*, who fear its consequences for social cohesion. Such public debate as there has been centres around language maintenance, cultural (including religious) diversity, separate schooling and the ethnic media (Smolicz 1979). From the earliest times it was accepted in Australia that non-Anglicans had the right to practice their religion. But between the ending of state aid to education in the 1880s and the adoption of official multiculturalism in the 1970s, it was not accepted that cultural forms and languages derived from elsewhere than Britain had legitimacy or should receive public support and subsidy.

Ethnicity, in the sense of cultural manifestations not shared by the majority community, has advantages and disadvantages. Those unable to function in English have very limited opportunities to enter the middle classes. They may be successful in business or in the provision of services or religious leadership to members of their own ethnic group. But the normal penalty for failing to master English is to remain in the manual working class and to suffer the insecurities which increase for members of that class with technical change. Political influence is very limited for those incompetent in the language and procedures of politics. The receipt of social service entitlement is restricted by lack of information. It was towards these disadvantages that the Galbally Report of 1978 directed its main thrust. The teaching of English to adult migrants has not been a success and both the translating and the community language teaching professions have been treated by authorities as peripheral. One hopeful sign has been the relative increase in those examined in 'community languages' rather than in French or Latin. But this has been achieved in an education system which has been drifting away from the teaching of any languages. There is at least a stratum of bilinguals in public policy areas, which was not the case when refugees began arriving in the late 1940s. However, some communities with small middle classes, such as the Turks, are still severely disadvantaged.

Ethnicity is disadvantageous if it creates prejudice in the host community such that the life chances of people of the different ethnic groups are restricted. This has clearly happened in Britain, but there is much less evidence of it being true of Australia. There is little doubt that many second generation people from the various new groups are passing through the higher education system into the professional and middle classes, a process previously followed by Jews and Irish Catholics. Asian students, many of whom will seek to remain in Australia, are very over-represented in some universities and professional courses and in the top levels of examination results. So far there is no serious challenge to the political and social élites, which are overwhelmingly Anglo-Australian. But change is coming, and will prove interesting when it does. Already in Queensland the descendants of German, Scandinavian and Italian migrants are well represented in the ruling National Party, as are descendants of German settlers in South Australian Liberalism. There is no doubt that closure against immigrants and the non-British is deeply ingrained in Australian attitudes. Yet the evidence that Australia is a 'racist society' rests heavily upon the Aboriginal experience and the history of White Australia. It seems highly probable that the middle classes and élites of a future Australia will derive from a variety of origins, as is true of the United States. As the industrial working class continues to decline, the children of immigrants will need to seek even more actively for alternatives to the occupations of their parents. There is a danger, already apparent in some areas, that some immigrant groups in manufacturing employment face escalating disadvantages. Public policy provision may need to be directed more centrally towards particular groups at risk, such as unemployed new arrivals, laid-off elderly workers, and geographical 'ethnic areas' of multiple disadvantage.

The advantages of distinctive ethnicity are not so immediately apparent and it is part of mainstream Anglo-Australian culture to deny them. Most important is the maintenance of community in a mass society. Australia is a peculiarly urbanised society, with an intellectual life dominated by the mass media and strong tendencies towards atomisation and homogenisation. Cultural life is strongly determined by the media, by mass marketing and consumption and by mass entertainment and sport. The 'typical' Australian lives in a middle suburb of a very large city, watches more than a dozen hours a week of commercial television, is buying a home almost identical to those for many miles around, is not actively interested in politics or religion, and spends a substantial part of the family income on motoring and gambling. In a liberal, pluralist and prosperous society, many are free to break out of these very uniform routines. Ethnicity provides one such route by sustaining networks, alternative forms of entertainment, more active religious and organisational involvement, and orientations towards societies other than Australia. While many NES immigrants have been excessively and even pathologically lonely, many others live within a warm environment of relationships which may be less alienating and atomising than the normal Australian nuclear family. Critics may see this as trying to sustain the village and neighbourhood life which has largely died out in urban Australia. But much of what passes for Australian culture still looks back with nostalgia to a world of neighbourliness and close-knit community which many ethnic groups have not yet lost.

Conclusions

One in five Australians was born overseas and one in four ultimately derives from somewhere other than the British Isles. There can be few generalisations which apply to all of them, except perhaps that they are likely to be less attached to many of the symbols and myths which appeal to the native-born of Anglo-Australian descent. The core of the overseas-born is still provided by the British and within that core by the English who have made up nearly 80 per cent of post-war British migrants. Many others come from such English-speaking societies as New Zealand,

America or Canada. But even if immigrants are divided into native speakers of English and the non-English-speaking there are still great contrasts, for example between the relatively impoverished Turks or Portuguese, and the well-educated and affluent Malaysians and Japanese. Sociological analysis and public policy both need to be sensitive to these differences as well as to the generational differences which can often produce lawyers and doctors from the families of peasants and shopkeepers.

Those migrants and people from communities most at risk are found in several overlapping categories. These include factory workers in industries which are running down, such as clothing, textiles and footwear; where employment is uncertain, as in steel or motor manufacture; women workers in unskilled manufacturing and services; those with low levels of education and low levels of English skill; newly-arrived refugees; those living in cities and suburbs experiencing high unemployment; the elderly who cannot improve their skills or their English. There is no ethnic group which has consistently suffered from damaging discrimination comparable with that experienced by Aborigines. Prejudice against Asians ignores their superior skills and education and is rarely based on job competition. As Australia does not permit uncontrolled immigration from Asia or the Pacific it is unlikely to experience a large influx of unskilled people of lower education and different appearance. Thus models of racial discrimination drawn from the United States or the United Kingdom or from Australia's past, are largely irrelevant. What is relevant is that areas of deprivation among immigrants should be identified and dealt with, and that the free exercise of different cultural patterns should be permitted and encouraged.

References

Australian Bureau of Statistics (1984) *The Measurement of Ethnicity in the Australian Census of Population and Housing.* Canberra: ABS.

Birrell, R. and Birrell, T. (1981) *An Issue of People.* Melbourne: Longman Cheshire.

Borrie, W.D. (1954) *Italians and Germans in Australia.* Melbourne: Melbourne University Press.

Chipman, L. (1980) 'The Menace of Multiculturalism', *Quadrant* 24 (10): 3–6.

De Lepervanche, M. (1980) 'From Race to Ethnicity', *ANZ Journal of Sociology* 16(1): 24–37.

Department of Immigration and Ethnic Affairs (1986) *Don't Settle for Less: Report of the Committee for Stage One of the Review of Migrant and Multicultural Programs and Services.* Canberra: AGPS.

De Vos, G. and Romanucci-Ross, L. (eds.) (1982) *Ethnic Identity: Cultural Continuities and Change*. Chicago: University of Chicago Press.

Francis, R.D. (1981) *Migrant Crime in Australia*. St Lucia: University of Queensland Press.

Furnivall, J.S. (1939) *Netherlands India*. Cambridge: Cambridge University Press.

Galbally, F. (Chair) (1978) *Migrant Services and Programs*. Canberra: AGPS.

Glazer, N. and Moynihan, P. (1970) *Beyond the Melting Pot*. Cambridge, Mass.: MIT Press.

Goot, M. (1985) 'Public Opinion and the Public Opinion Polls' in A. Markus and M.C. Ricklefs (eds) *Surrender Australia?* Allen & Unwin, Sydney.

Jupp, J. (ed.) (1984) *Ethnic Politics in Australia*. Sydney: Allen & Unwin.

Martin, J. (1978) *The Migrant Presence*. Sydney: Allen & Unwin.

Palfreeman, A.C. (1967) *The Administration of the White Australia Policy*. Melbourne: Melbourne University Press.

Porter, J. (1975) *The Vertical Mosaic*. Toronto: University of Toronto Press.

Smolicz, J.J. (1979) *Culture and Education in a Plural Society*. Canberra: Curriculum Development Centre.

Viviani, N. (1984) *The Long Journey*. Melbourne: Melbourne University Press.

Willard, M. (1974) *History of the White Australia Policy to 1920*. Melbourne: Melbourne University Press.

Chapter Seven

Aborigines and Islanders in Australian Society

Ian Keen

This chapter examines the historical changes experienced by Aborigines and Islanders in Australian society. Key factors in this history have been the development of the British industrial economy in relation to the British colonies, the related development of the Australian economy and its society, and the nature of Aboriginal economic and social life.

The Aboriginal and Islander population forms about 1 per cent of the Australian one. Recent surveys (Smith 1980, 1981 Census) put the Aboriginal population at about 160,000 compared with a total population of about 16 million.

It is important to stress the heterogeneity of the Aboriginal and Islander population, which maintains a wide variety of lifestyles, beliefs and degrees of integration with the wider society. It is important also to stress the great difference between Aboriginal and non-Aboriginal cultures. Many of those Aboriginal people whom many non-Aborigines do not recognise as Aborigines, but label 'half-castes', as against 'real' 'full-blood' Aborigines, maintain a strong sense of cultural distinctiveness and of Aboriginal identity. Recent anthropological accounts of the ways of life of Aboriginal people of southern Australia (i.e. those areas most densely settled by Europeans) show that they have distinctively Aboriginal cultures, demonstrated, for example, in modes of speech, kin relationships and family organisation and socialisation of the young.

The chapter begins with a discussion of the development of British and Australian capitalism.

The Development of British and Australian Capitalism

The capitalist economy began to develop in late eighteenth-century Britain (Wolf 1982). Following a Marxist analysis, the capitalist economy can be understood to involve a division of society into *classes*, the most fundamental of which are the working class which sells its labour in return for the necessities of life, and the class of those who own and control the means of production – machines and other capital equipment, land, factories etc. This simple model, which fits early capitalism well enough, is complicated by the emergence of managerial and executive classes, the existence of independent smallholders and so on.

These features of the social organisation of capitalist societies (some shared with other types of industrial society) contrast strongly with Aboriginal social organisation; but there are many other important contrasting features. For example, the *organisation* is typical of industrial society: it is a clearly-defined body with a specialised function (e.g. government, mining, education, religion, health care, sport), and with an internal structure of control, usually hierarchical in form, and sometimes involving a *bureaucracy*. The nation state could be regarded as the most inclusive of these organisations. Another characteristic is the existence of highly-specialised governmental, judicial, military, police and educational structures.

Certain conditions led to the emergence of industrialisation of production and capitalism in England (Hobsbawm 1969), which had no land-holding peasantry. Rather, there was a system of large land-owners, tenant farmers and landless agricultural labourers. Technology was sufficiently developed for it to be relatively cheap to adapt to the mechanisation of production. Entrepreneurs were induced to industrialise production because of the existence of a large and growing domestic market, especially for food and textiles, so that flour-milling, brewing and cotton production were at the forefront of industrialisation.

The export market was expanded through war and colonisation, through which England captured the former export markets of other European nations, and created new ones, making it profitable for its entrepreneurs to industrialise. Crucially, the British government was willing to subordinate foreign policy to economic ends, gaining a virtual monopoly of sea power. Thus, certain colonies were established as markets for British goods, as well as sources of raw materials to feed industry. As the British capitalist economy developed, however, Britain's capacity to feed its population through its own agricultural production decreased, so that the colonies supplied this need to an increasing extent. As well, it became more profitable to invest labour in the colonies than at home. As England became less able to compete effectively with other industrial nations, especially Germany and the United States, it relied on colonial expansion to supply an export market.

Settler Capitalism

The Australian economy and society developed, in relation to British capitalism, in a way that was to radically affect the lives of Aboriginals and Islanders. The features of Australian economy and society which it held in common with certain other European colonies – Argentina, Uruguay, Chile and also New Zealand – have been labelled by Denoon (1983) 'settler capitalism'. In common with these colonies Australia began as a military garrison outpost of a European empire. The indigenous population was of hunters and gatherers, of such a nature that they could not be exploited in order to support a population of conquering settlers; rather, the new civilisation was introduced as an enclave, absorbing some of the indigenous people, but destroying and replacing the existing economic system. (In some of these colonies, but not Australia, the colonisers did encounter agricultural communities, after a period of consolidation.) As the colonisers fanned out into the hinterland of the garrison outpost they found plenty of land but little labour, and pastoralism dominated production. The administration centred at the entrepôt registered titles and protected the property of the new landowners within the frontier, who consolidated control over land, labour and income from herds. On the frontier, individuals relied on fighting skills to appropriate land, defeat the indigenous population and survive.

The colony of New South Wales, established in 1788 primarily as a gaol, was at first dependent on England for supplies, but as Drakakis-Smith (1981) points out, a major goal of the early colonial administration in Australia was self-sufficiency in agriculture put into practice by encouraging small-scale ex-convict (emancipist) farming. At the same time the military/bureaucratic élite obtained large grants of land to which they constantly added by buying out indebted farmers, so creating a class of wage labourers. The principal source of labour during this period, however, was that of assigned convicts; Aboriginal labour was rarely used except in the earliest years for harvesting, and 'bush work' such as tracking and searching for water (Drakakis-Smith 1981: 38). Migration to Australia, both free and involuntary, was fostered by the large numbers of men demobilised for the Army at the end of the Napoleonic wars. Between 1821–33 more than

22,000 convicts were transported to Australia, with a further 27,000 between 1833–41. Unemployment in Britain accelerated the pace of migration (Drakakis-Smith 1981: 39).

From the 1820s the colony became a supplier of primary products to feed British industry and the home market. The discovery of productive land led to the importation of labour and capital, and entrepreneurs were attracted by prospects of high profits. The main area of highly-productive land was in the southeast corner of the continent, discovered and colonised by Europeans from the 1820s for the production of wool for export. Wool production was fostered by the reduction of the duty on Australian wool in 1820 by comparison with the rate on German wool, and the demand for the Australian product gradually increased up to the 1920s (Sinclair 1976). Large numbers of convicts were assigned to pastoral capitalists, the assisted migrants forming the agricultural labour force (Drakakis-Smith 1981: 39).

From the 1820s to the 1920s there was an associated increase in production for local consumption. Between 1815–1914, Australia, like the other colonies described by Denoon, took advantage of new production, transport and market opportunities to achieve a high level of prosperity and expansion, both demographic and territorial. With improvements in ocean transport such as refrigeration, a large potential market developed for Australian food products, so that after the 1850s there were something of a switch from wool to meat (mutton and beef) and to wheat production. Australian production thus moved slowly toward diversification. The discovery of gold had the effect of attracting migrants, increasing the population (including many Chinese), and expanding the local market for goods and services, and in turn attracting more labour, stimulating immigration. After the 1920s, economic growth in Australia came to be based mainly on manufacturing development, so that the economy bore a stronger resemblance to other industrial nations.

In Australia and similar colonies, hunter-gatherer populations suffered a very different fate from agricultural communities: they were displaced and destroyed, whereas agricultural communities often entered into *cash crop* production, converting part of their agricultural production to crops suitable for sale through the colonising power, and subject to its taxation. They became peasants, at least for a generation or two, then migrant labourers, agricultural labourers or plantation workers (see Wolf 1982). Aboriginal economies, however, were not converted to the requirements of capitalism. In large areas of Australia, where European settlement was most dense or intensive, it was largely destroyed. There were no products of value to the colonisers, nor could the production system be converted to cash crops.

Because a hunting-gathering economy is land-intensive, it was not possible to sustain the indigenous economy in order to provide a pool of migrant labour, as occurred, for example, in central and southern Africa. A hunting and gathering mode of subsistence requires large tracts of land with a varied ecology, in order to provide an adequate diet all the year round, and to give groups access to alternative areas in case of food shortage. Furthermore, hunter-gatherers and agriculturalists tend to compete for water as well as land; and introduced animals change the ecology and often displace the indigenous fauna.

Thus the course of development of Aboriginal-white relations was partly conditioned by the fact that Australia was a continent of hunting-gathering-fishing economies in temperate to sub-tropical environments. As van den Berghe (1981) points out, Europeans, with their deep-plough agriculture, were better adapted to such regions as North America, the southern tip of South America, southern Africa and temperate and sub-tropical Australia. In these regions the colonisers could adapt their agricultural practices to local conditions, and did not face problems with tropical diseases. Conversely however, the indigenous populations were prey to introduced diseases – even the common cold had devastating effects. The relatively sparse distribution of the Aboriginal population allowed the colonisers to swamp them, and their egalitarian and small-scale organisation, together with their less effective military technology, made it difficult for the Aborigines to put up an effective resistance to invasion in the long term. However, accounts which tell of the total destruction of Aboriginal culture and society are distorted. Even where many groups were destroyed or decimated, and a population of mixed descent grew, this has maintained a distinctive, and separate, culture and identity.

The degree of cultural continuity is greatest among Aborigines living in regions most remote from European settlement. The next section sketches some aspects of Aboriginal culture and social life as it was in the nineteenth century, and as it continues to varying degrees.

Aboriginal and Islander Economy and Society

A sketch of the pattern of Aboriginal social life as it was presumably lived before European colonisation will also help us to understand the way in which the position of Aborigines in Australian society developed. Necessarily this sketch is based on ethnographic descriptions made after substantial white colonisation. It is phrased here in the past tense, but the modes of life of many Aboriginal people display a high degree of continuity with the pre-colonial past, more or less modified with the adoption of items of European technology, and institutions such as community councils, as well as participation in the money economy.

Australia was populated by peoples with an intricate mode of life, bound through a dense network of inter-relations throughout the continent, and linking to the island of New Guinea, as well as to the Celebes via Macassan traders. Moreover, anthropological studies of Aboriginal social life increasingly reveal a great variation in social arrangements – not due to differences in relations with non-Aborigines, but to continuations of past variability.

Population and Subsistence
The conventional estimate of the size of the Aboriginal population at the end of the eighteenth century, made by the anthropologist Radcliffe-Brown (1930), is about 300,000. Some demographers now think that this estimate is conservative, and that a figure of 500,000 or even higher is more reasonable (Smith 1980). The population would have fluctuated due to disease, climatic variation and changes in the size of the land mass with the rise and fall of the sea level, as well as other factors. Current archaeological evidence suggests that Australia has had a human population for at least 40,000 years (White and O'Connell 1982). There is no direct evidence, of course, that the population of this time was ancestral to the present Aboriginal population, although it does seem likely. The Aboriginal population was distributed most densely along the coasts and islands, with densities of the order of one person per square kilometre. In the very arid regions, densities were probably as low as one person per hundred square kilometres. This pattern was correlated in part with the rainfall (Birdsell 1953, see also Jones and Bowdler 1980).

Aboriginals, as we have mentioned, were hunters, gatherers and fishers, using a technology of stone, wood, fibre, bone and skin. There was a marked division of labour, with women predominantly gathering vegetable foods and shellfish, hunting small game, and fishing, while men mainly hunted larger game and fished. The sexes co-operated in large-scale drives for game and fish. Food processing was often elaborate, and involved leaching out toxins (e.g. from cycad palm nuts); drying and storing meat; winnowing and grinding seeds; and cooking in earth ovens. Recent studies of hunting and gathering show that even in arid areas people only needed to work for an average of four to five hours per day to obtain a very adequate diet (Sahlins 1974, McCarthy and

MacArthur 1960, Altman 1984, Lee 1968). The stereotype of the poor hunter-gatherer scratching a bare existence from the desert is largely false.

Archaeologists and anthropologists now tend to stress the land-management aspects of hunting and gathering, through selective burning-off to stimulate regrowth and attract game, by replanting yam tops to ensure the next year's supply, and by the prohibition of hunting certain species during certain seasons to ensure reproduction. From this perspective the distinction between hunting-gathering and horticulture is less clear-cut. Nevertheless, the development of horticulture which occurred in the New Guinea highlands 10,000 years ago (White and O'Connell 1982: 173) did not diffuse into Australia, although the Torres Strait Islanders practised both kinds of subsistence economy.

Settlement

Another common stereotype is of Aborigines wandering randomly over the landscape. In fact, the degree of sedentism varied. Some coastal communities were and are quite sedentary, moving only a few kilometres between seasons (Meehan 1977). In more arid regions the search for water necessitated movement over much larger areas, but within known and owned land (Gould 1969, Tonkinson 1978).

People lived in groups of relatives. The modal size community was the 'band' of between twenty and fifty people, but where nomadism was necessary, at certain seasons the band would split up into smaller units, and aggregate into groups of several hundreds at others to exploit localised resources and to hold major ceremonies. Recent studies show that Arnhem Land people now, on outstations and settlement-townships, live in households consisting of a nuclear family, or a single adult or a group of bachelors. The members of a household have a common shelter (Wet season house, wind-break etc.) and hearth. Households group to form household clusters within which food is distributed, although work teams often crosscut household clusters (Altman 1984). People tend to choose to live near or with close siblings, a brother-in-law or sister-in-law, a parent, or a son or daughter-in-law. It is common for a son-in-law to live with his wife's parents in the early years of marriage to provide hunting services and gifts.

A Universe of Kin

Kin relations were not confined to the band. Aboriginal people traced kin relationships to a far wider network than do people of European cultures, and extended *fictive* kin relations to strangers in order to incorporate them into the social universe. (The use of the term 'aunt' for a parent's friend is an example of fictive kinship.) Some kin relationships entailed specific rights and obligations; for example it was very general for a brother and sister to have to avoid all social interaction, at least after early childhood and until old age; and a man had to avoid contact with the woman who was, or would be, his wife's mother. Brothers-in-law commonly had the duty to help each other with gifts, or support in disputes.

In many Aboriginal societies marriages were arranged through a system of 'promised' marriage; that is by contracts, sometimes arranged even before the birth of the potential wife, in which rights in a woman as a wife, and in her children, were transferred in return for gifts and services over a long period. In such systems spouses had to be in a particular kin relation, usually some kind of cousin, although in some societies marriage with a close cousin was forbidden. The degree of *polygyny* varied (polygyny is the marriage of one man to more than one woman at the same time); in some societies an older man might acquire twenty wives or more (e.g. the Tiwi of Melville and Bathurst Islands; see Hart and Pilling 1960), whereas in others, such as Western Desert groups, polygyny was rare.

Age and gender were other important bases of social organisation. In general, older people were accorded authority and respect as holders of knowledge, especially religious and magical knowledge, although this does not mean that all older people were revered or regarded as wise. Economic production, child-rearing and the organisation of religious practices were organised along gender lines; but the degree to which men as a category were politically dominant seems to have varied: in some societies men had sole access to secret religious knowledge and were highly polygynous, in others women also had their secret religious life and polygyny was less common, reflecting a greater degree of autonomy (Hamilton 1981a).

Social Units

I have discussed variation between Aboriginal 'societies', but a measure of caution is needed here, for there were probably few if any clearly-bounded Aboriginal 'societies'. Older, or more general sources describe the structure of Aboriginal society in terms of a hierarchy of more inclusive units: *families, clans, bands* or *hordes,* and *tribes.* This model is misleading. The 'tribe' notion implies the existence of discrete territorial groups, each having a common language and an internal political organisation under the control of 'elders'. Recent discussions of this topic suggest that the model is by no means universally valid (Peterson 1976, Sutton 1978,

Merlan 1981), based as it is implicitly on the concept of the nation state. Rather, Aboriginal social life was (and is) organised in terms of overlapping social categories and networks. These are too complex to discuss in any detail here, but some features can be described.

Bands were somewhat open in membership, with a core of more or less permanent members and a periphery of more transient ones. The most inclusive social category was in many areas based on a language or dialect – it is this category that has become known as the 'tribe'. Language was commonly connected with territory, so that in being affiliated to a language through one or both parents a person was also related to land. (A person could be affiliated to a language even if he or she did not speak it; it was a matter of identity.) But in many regions such as north-east Arnhem Land or Cape York Peninsula, speakers of one language or dialect were dispersed, and several discrete areas were associated with the same language or dialect. Furthermore, many people were bi- or poly-lingual, some identifying with more than one language or dialect. Finally, the language group was probably nowhere a distinct political unit, although in some areas it was a land-holding unit.

Land was held or 'owned' in many regions by a group based on *descent*, often through the male line (*patrilineal descent*, and sometimes through males and females (*cognatic* or *ambilineal descent*). These land-holding units, some of which are referred to as *clans* by anthropologists, held areas of land focused on clusters of sacred sites associated with spirit beings regarded as ancestors of the group, with rights in related ceremonies and sacred objects. But land-holding units were not autonomous, for their members were often dispersed by marriage and other ties among several bands, with each often united with others affiliated to the same spirit beings and rituals. Moreover, close relatives of members of a land-holding unit often had a say in its affairs concerning such affairs as religious ceremonies and land management.

For the purposes of the organisation of marriage and religious practices a local population was often divided into categories of other kinds. These included *moieties*, in which the population was divided into two named halves on the basis either of descent or generation, as well as more complex systems of *phratries*, *sections*, *sub-sections* and *semi-moieties* (see Elkin 1954, R.M. and C.H. Berndt 1981, Maddock 1981, Shapiro 1979). There was a great deal of variation among Aboriginal social systems, in which variants of these and other modes of organisation were put together in different configurations. The general picture is not one of discrete, localised societies, but of a continuous but ever-changing network, with, as it were, localised clusterings and overlapping patterns.

Religion and Government

It is appropriate to place Aboriginal religion and government together, for the government of Aboriginal social life was, in many regions, organised through religious belief and practice. There were probably no *specialised* governmental structures – no legislatures, judiciaries nor bureaucracies with general powers to control aspects of most social activities of a population within a defined territory, although some older sources do describe 'councils' and 'courts' of elders in some areas (R.M. and C.H. Berndt 1981: 348). Aboriginal government – by which I mean the control of social activities – was more diffuse. We could generalise, I think, by saying that those people with an interest in the matter at hand had a measure of control, and kin relations were of particular importance. Hence each different activity and occasion – a hunt, a ceremony, a dispute, fights, a marriage etc. – involved a somewhat different network of people. Some individuals within any network had more authority than others by virtue of their age, religious status and gender. Certain people managed to build up a high level of status through fighting ability, skilful or fortunate marriages and the acquisition of religious knowledge, and were consequently at the focus of a network of influence. Such people, predominantly men, had more influence and power than others, but they did not hold chiefly office, nor were their positions hereditary.

Social activities were subject to rules or laws founded in religious belief. Laws and conventions governing marriage, kin relations, exchange of goods and ceremonies, land tenure and religious practice itself were legitimised through the belief that ancestral spirit beings laid them down long ago. Present practice 'followed' these activities. Because such laws were not regarded as having been instituted by people, nor as changeable, they were enforced by members of the community at large, especially those with a particular interest and rights in the matter, as well as those with authority, rather than by a specialised body of law-enforcement agents. Thus those who dealt with a breach of the religious law were those with rights in, and control of, religious practice; and those who dealt with an offence against the person were that person (if still alive) and his or her close relatives.

Belief in a creative period, usually referred to in English as the Dreamtime, was pervasive. In this period, ancestral spirit beings, conceived of as having the attributes at once of humans and other species and phenomena (such as Water, Sores, Hollow Log, Rock), lived and travelled, leaving traces of their activities in the land and waters; instituting ceremonies and sacred objects, customs, laws and languages; and creating the forerunners of present groups as well as the powers to ensure their reproduction. Present religious practice was believed to re-enact Dreamtime events, and to make available to living people the powers of the spirit beings.

Politics came into play in the form of competition for the control of sacred objects and ceremony, and hence for authority, the control of land, and, indirectly, for the control of marriage-bestowals in some regions.

A corollary of this world view is the belief that human beings can avail themselves of these powers, and control natural processes to some extent through ritual action. In this way, beliefs in sorcery, love magic, healing powers, rain-making and foretelling the future were within one general conceptual framework. Belief in sorcery is widely reported to have been an element in interpersonal relationships. Other people were commonly blamed for causing sickness and death through ritual action on faeces or other bodily products, by singing over an image or pointing the bone. Belief in access to the power of spirit beings is the obverse of this – recreating the image and actions of the being gave access to the being's powers, to be utilised in love, reproduction or fighting or counteracting the effects of sorcery. (For general accounts of Aboriginal religion and belief see R.M. and C.H. Berndt 1981, Maddock 1981; for beliefs in sorcery and healing see Reid 1983).

Co-operation in religious practices such as major revelatory ceremonies often brought hundreds of people together from a wide region, and thus forged and reinforced wide-ranging social links. 'Trade' relations also created wide networks. Interpersonal relations between kin were marked by obligations to make and receive gifts of food, and objects such as tools, weapons, sacred objects and clothing. Through these hand-to-hand exchanges, goods travelled many hundreds or even thousands of miles along sometimes quite well marked 'trade routes' (McCarthy 1939). Some items of exchange, such as *pituri*, native tobacco, involved groups of people travelling many hundreds of miles to acquire the substance, after which they distributed it through exchange and barter in markets (Watson 1983).

Torres Strait Islanders

The way of life of the Torres Strait Islanders was rather different from that of the mainland Aborigines. (The following is based on Beckett 1972, and Moore 1978.) They lived in a variety of island environments, including small volcanic islands with dense vegetation, low sandbanks, large low-lying swampy islands, and large high rocky islands with good water and vegetation on the lower parts. There were in the eighteenth century perhaps 3 to 4,000 Islanders living in thirteen or fourteen communities.

The Islander economy emphasised to different degrees hunting, gathering, fishing and horticulture. In the eastern islands the emphasis was on gardening, in which the main crops were coconuts and yams. In the western islands, some of which were rather infertile, people depended more on hunting, gathering and fishing, gaining vegetable foods through trade. People of the islands off the coast of Cape York made gardens only when hunting, gathering and fishing failed to supply enough food.

The Islander communities were up to 1,000 strong, often much smaller, and the larger ones were composed of smaller settlements. There were no formal leaders: rather the leader of the religious cult associated with head-hunting had the greatest authority. As with Aboriginal communities, disputes were settled by the interested parties, with leaders playing a mediating role. Named groups held defined tracts of land, but garden land and some other key resources were individually owned, or owned by groups of relatives, and daughters were given land as dowry. Some communities, such as the people of Badu and Mabuiag, were rather nomadic between islands, whereas others, such as the Saibai people, were sedentary.

The Islander communities were related to one another, and to Cape York Peninsula Aborigines as well as the people of Papua New Guinea, through trade and warfare, carried out by means of large, double outrigger canoes, and among defined trading partners. Trade was in canoe hulls, bows and arrows, drums, feathers and pigments from New Guinea; wood, pigments, spears and spear-throwers from the Australian mainland; and vegetable foods, marine products, harpoons, shells and human heads from among the islands.

The religion was centred on the increase of resources through ritual, head-hunting and war. People believed that they could obtain power through ritual, and from sacred objects which represented the head-hunting hero, and also from human heads of an ancestor or a war victim.

The European Colonisation of Australia

Features of Aboriginal and Islander social and economic life summarised in the previous section go some way to explain the nature and results of the European colonisation of Australia.

Some of the major effects on Aborigines of European coloni-sation of Australia are simply stated: the population was decimated by disease and homicide, totally destroyed in some regions and displaced in many areas. In the regions of Australia most densely settled by whites and others, the Aboriginal population was transformed through miscegenation. The Aboriginal population as a whole declined from some half a million to about 67,000 in the mid-1930s. It has now recovered, as mentioned, to about 160,000 (1981 Census). Aborigines were swamped by the sheer size of the invading groups, overcome by superior military technology and organisation, and were prey to introduced infectious diseases.

Historians now stress the degree of resistance which Aborigines mounted against invasion of their lands, often characterising the conflict as guerilla warfare. Conflict arose basically over access to land, exacerbated by differences in property laws, patterns of obligation and other cultural differences. Colonisers appropriated lands and key water sources; their stock transformed the ecology. Historians point to the 'brutalisation' of the convicts as contribut-ing to conflict, and to the imbalance of the sex ratio of the colony as leading to conflict over women, with thirty-eight males to every female among the settlers in the 1840s (Broome 1982: 38). Aborigines treated stock as they treated wild species – as common resources, in conflict with European ideas of private property. Initial conflicts escalated into patterns of killing and retributive massacres.

In the early decades of the colonies Aborigines were able to mount a more effective resistance against the settlers armed with muzzle-loading weapons, than they could when faster breech-loading weapons were introduced. However, the small scale of Aboriginal social organisation and the absence of specialised armies limited the degree to which Aborigines could combine effectively for military action. Furthermore, they were commonly divided into numerous local networks, divided by enduring en-mities. The formation in the 1850s of the Native Police Force in New South Wales and Queensland, which exploited enmities among Aboriginal groups, and the introduction from the 1870s of breech-loading rifles, turned the tables decisively in favour of the Europeans.

The most drastic example of the destruction of Aboriginal people and their social life was that of Tasmania (Ryan 1981), where the majority of the population was killed by force of arms and disease, and, by 1831, the remnants rounded up, finally to die without issue on Flinders Island. The present Aboriginal population of the island is descended from Aborigine women and the white sealers of Cape Barren Islands.

Within 'settled' Australia, Aborigines were forced into a dependent role, living on the fringes of white society. The population of Aborigines of full descent declined rapidly – in New South Wales from about 3,000 in 1826 to about 1,000 by 1930 and 130 in 1965, according to colonial and state estimates (Smith 1980: 99). The population of Aborigines of mixed descent, on the other hand, grew from 2,400 in 1882 to 23,000 by 1966. The Aboriginal population as a whole in New South Wales is estimated to have fallen from about 48,000 in 1788 to about 7,400 by 1901, and to have recovered to 28,500 by 1971 (Smith 180: 101, cf. Butlin 1983).

Economic Relations

The role of the Aborigines in the developing Australian economy was at first largely casual and marginal. We have seen that Aboriginal and Islander economies were not incorporated into capitalism, as with cash-cropping and migrant labour. However, recent studies show that Aboriginals and Islanders often played a crucial role in the development of the Australian economy, and that continuity to some degree of a hunting-gathering-fishing economic base was important in the pattern of exploitation of Aboriginal and Islander labour.

In the south-east, Aborigines were employed as trackers, timber-cutters, drovers, domestics, shepherds, station hands, shearers and so on. For example, during the 1840s, the Ngarrindjeri of the Murray Lakes worked seasonally in the whaling industry, and as shepherds; in the 1890s they were employed seasonally as sickle reapers, until replaced by mechanical harvesters (Jenkin 1979). In Victoria, cheap Aboriginal labour was in demand in the 1850s when white labour was in short supply. Others managed to survive on seasonal and short-term employment, trading fish and skins, and begging, until rounded up onto reserves (Christie 1979). Men on Aboriginal reserves worked as part-time labourers or seasonal workers on pastoral properties. About a quarter of Victoria's Aboriginal population lived on reserves by the 1860s, with the remainder living as fringe-dwellers or rural labourers (Broome 1982: 85). On the whole, Aboriginal people worked to fulfil short-term economic goals (Broome 1982: 66).

As long as convict labour was available, Aboriginal participation in the capitalist economy was limited. However, Morris (1983), criticises images of Aborigines as wholly unprepared culturally to come to terms with Western society, as well as beliefs that Aboriginal culture simply collapsed passively under the impact of British colonisation (1983: 500). The Dhan-gadi of the MacLeay River initially resisted pastoral incursions by systematically spearing cattle, but were defeated during 1856–58 after the introduction of the Native Police; their population was reduced to about one-sixth of its former size (1983: 504). The dominance of beef production which was not labour intensive, in the 1850s and 1860s, an activity for which employers preferred white labour, meant that little Aboriginal labour was required until the economy diversified towards the end of the century.

Cheap Aboriginal labour was an essential component of the cattle industry for a hundred years or more (Stevens 1974). Aborigines in the cattle industry were often laid off in the off-season without sufficient remuneration to tide them over, and so fell back on hunting and gathering. In this way the costs of labour were drastically reduced. They were reduced also through the provision of only basic shelter, the non-provision of education, health and other services, and, of course, by the very low or nonexistent money wages. Brutality and sexual exploitation were commonplace, and master-servant relations were enforced by punitive legislation in, for example, Western Australia and Queensland.

In Queensland, the majority of squatters supported a policy of exclusion. Aboriginal settlements established after the 1897 Aboriginals' Protection and Restriction of the Sale of Opium Act were formed to protect Aborigines from abuses in employment, such as in the pearling industry, in part to remove Aborigines from stations, and in part to provide pools of cheap labour. In Western Australia, the rapid pastoral expansion (sheep and cattle) led to a great demand for Aboriginal labour, which provided the main source of shepherds, shearers, stock-riders and fencers in the districts north of the Murchison river. Remuneration was in the form of rations, clothing and tobacco. Aboriginal workers in Western Australia were virtually enslaved by the legislation of the 1880s which provided for the imprisonment of employees who absconded, for up to three months' hard labour and for flogging (Rowley 1970).

In the post-World War II period of consolidation and capitalisation beef prices rose, money wages for Aborigines became more equitable, and capital equipment increased. In 1968, Aborigines were included in the Cattle Station Industry Award of the Northern Territory, the Federal Pastoral Award and the Queensland Award. The increased cost of Aboriginal labour, together with increased capitalisation and lower demand for labour in general, led employers to lay off Aborigines in favour of whites.

Beckett (1977) has described the role of Torres Strait Islanders in the pearling industry in terms of 'internal colonialism' (Hartwig 1978, Wolpe 1975). Islanders worked from the 1870s as divers in these industries for very low wages, and had to supplement their earnings with seafood and garden produce.

In some industries, albeit marginal ones, Aborigines formed more equitable and mutually beneficial relations with entrepreneurs. Two examples are: the Kuku-Nyungkul people of the Annan River, north of Cairns, with the tin miners (Anderson 1983); and groups of Aborigines in the Alligator Rivers region of the Northern Territory with white buffalo hunter 'bosses', in which labour was exchanged for resources such as tobacco and food (Keen 1982, Levitus 1982).

Although there are some early examples of Aboriginal communities succeeding in indepedent economic enterprises recorded in the literature (Broome 1982: 72–73, 78 ff.), these seem invariably to have been under the direction of a white organiser, a mission superintendent in the case of the Coranderrk community (Barwick 1972), or an independent such as Don McLeod (Biskup 1973). These enterprises seem to have been opposed and undermined both by land-owners and the authorities. Numbers of individuals or small family units, however, have operated as independent farmers, prospectors and hunters, as well as contract workers (Broome 1982), and Torres Strait Islanders purchased luggers to become independent pearlers (Beckett 1977). More recently, Aborigines have formed pop music groups (e.g. 'No Fixed Address'), have acquired and run cattle stations, and formed contracting companies servicing mining towns.

The lives of Aborigines were least affected in regions least subject to intensive European economic exploitation, such as Arnhem Land and parts of Cape York Peninsula. In these regions missions and government settlements were the means of controlling the Aboriginal people, and Aboriginal economic and social life continued with varying degrees of disruption and interference. Many settlements have been seen as being established specifically as sources of cheap labour, in effect subsidised by mission and government funding, as well as subsistence products of settlement farms (Rowley 1971, Morris 1983). Most set out to inculcate the work ethic, and teach Aborigines skills associated with agricultural production and related technologies, as well as Christianity.

The Development of Policy

European interpretations of the vast differences between nascent industrial society and hunter-gatherer social life guided public policies in relation to Aborigines. The seventeenth and eighteenth-century philosophers and legal theorists did not regard hunters and gatherers as fully human – but as 'savage' (which meant 'wild') people, close to animals. Philosophers interested in the origin of private property assumed that fully-developed property rights were individual rather than communal, and were necessarily related to the development of agriculture; hence they attributed no property rights in land to the hunting and gathering 'stage of development'. Furthermore, fully-developed property rights were believed to be necessary for the existence of government. For example, Hobbes wrote that the 'savage' peoples of America had no government except that of small families:

> It is a consequent to this condition that there be no Proprietary, no Dominion, no *Mine* and *Thine* distinct; but only that to every man that he can get; and for so long as he can keep it.
>
> (1968 [1651]: 188)

John Locke argued that rights in land follow from cultivating the soil; hunters and gatherers let the land lie 'waste' and so have no property, and hence no government.

The rights of colonising nations in international law were related to these notions (Bennett 1978). For example, in his *Commentaries on the Laws of England* (1765), Blackstone distinguished two types of colony: conquered or ceded territory, and settled or occupied territory. The lands of peoples recognised as having systems of law and government were deemed to be colonised by conquest or cession, but lands inhabited by peoples who did not cultivate the land, and who were not recognised as having systems of law and government, were deemed to be colonised by settlement or occupation. In the first type of colony the indigenous systems of law were taken to be binding on the indigenous inhabitants until revoked by the Crown; in the second case, indigenous peoples came immediately under English law (in the case of English colonies), and indigenous law went unrecognised.

The British recognised American Indian property rights and made treaties with the Indians, despite the fact that many were hunters and gatherers, probably in order to form alliances with the Indians against other colonial powers, as well as for other reasons (Bennett 1978). In New Zealand the British negotiated the Treaty of Waitangi with the agricultural Maoris. In Australia, however, it gradually became established in law that Australia was a 'settled' colony, and not a conquered or ceded territory.

There was little in the way of coherent government policy in relation to Aborigines in the first half-century of the Australian colonies. One of the duties of a colonising power was seen to be to protect indigenous peoples, who were accorded the legal status of children – as 'wards' of the colonising 'guardians'. So it was that colonial governments, prompted by humanitarian pressure groups, also sought to segregate and protect Aborigines, regarded by many as a 'child race', from the effects of colonisation, and to 'civilise' them.

After early attempts at 'protection', the first comprehensive legislation in relation to Aborigines did not appear until the end of the nineteenth century. Aborigines were treated somewhat in the same way as the destitute. Those in absolute want were given rations, and labour colonies and farms were set up to provide training for the urban unemployed. Similarly, reserves were set aside for Aborigines, and missions encouraged to Christianise them and to inculcate the work ethic.

Legislation in relation to Aborigines was both protective and restrictive: it tended to segregate Aborigines from non-Aborigines, set up protective structures and restrict their rights and freedoms. For example, the Queensland Aboriginals' Protection and the Restriction of the Sale of Opium Act of 1897, which became a model for legislation in the other states, empowered the government to force Aborigines on to reserves and keep them there. For the next fifty years, they were steadily removed to reserves. The Minister was empowered, through police protectors and reserve superintendents, to control movement on to and from reserves, to enter employment contracts on the behalf of Aborigines, to hold their funds, control their spending and have legal custody of their children. Regulations prohibited alcohol and certain customary practices and provided penalties for breaches of discipline and insubordination. 'Half-castes' could seek exemption from the Act. Queensland Acts in relation to Aborigines and Torres Strait Islanders remained restrictive, although to a decreasing degree with periodic amendments, until their replacement in 1985 with the Community Services legislation.

People of mixed Aboriginal descent were picked out for special treatment from the late nineteenth century. For example, legislation in Victoria in 1886 removed 'half-castes' under thirty-four years from reserves on the grounds that they should earn a living and merge into the general community, but many of these people became fringe-dwellers, and the legislation was revoked. Later legislation (1915) provided for the rounding up of 'half-caste' youths into homes. In the Northern Territory many children with non-Aboriginal fathers were removed from their mothers to be raised in homes in Darwin and southern cities. In this way the normal processes of cultural transmission through the socialisation of the young were interrupted (Broome 1982: 82–84).

After 1949 the Australian economy rapidly expanded to become more complex structurally, and there was a rising standard of living. Welfare policies, increasingly centralised in the federal sphere, changed direction after 1940. The concern became to provide support for a variety of 'disadvantaged' categories, such as Aborigines. 'Cradle to the grave' social security was introduced, including old age pensions, invalid pensions, maternity allowances and veterans' pensions, financed by universal taxation (Butlin *et al.* 1982). Access to such benefits, and to education, was made universal.

From the 1940s Aborigines were increasingly incorporated into Australian society through the extension of such benefits to them, and through a policy of assimilation, adopted by a Native Welfare Conference of all the states, called by the Minister, Hasluck, in 1951. When fully articulated, the policy extended the same rights and privileges to Aborigines that other Australians enjoyed, but at the same time expected that they would eventually 'attain the same manner of living as other Australians and . . . live as members of a single Australian community'. This policy paralleled a similar policy in relation to migrants. The specific needs of Aborigines as a disadvantaged minority were catered for at the federal level after the 1967 Referendum, which amended the Census to include Aborigines, and gave the federal government the power to legislate in respect of Aborigines. A Department of Aboriginal Affairs was established and an advisory committee set up, including the anthropologist W.E.H. Stanner and H.C. Coombs, a leading economist.

The Whitlam government subsequently introduced a federal policy of 'self-management'. This policy was manifested in the Aboriginal Land Rights (Northern Territory) Bill (enacted in a revised form by the Fraser government in 1976), which followed a decade of strikes and protests on the part of Aborigines and their non-Aboriginal supporters. Other legislation and policies encouraged a degree of local autonomy on the part of Aboriginal communities, particularly in the Northern Territory, such as the formation and incorporation of Aboriginal Community Councils (with the concomitant phasing out of the supervisory role of missionaries), and the provision of grants for the purchase of land for Aboriginal groups by the Aboriginal Land Fund Commission, as well as for the setting up of 'outstations' and so on.

The 1976 Aboriginal Land Rights (Northern Territory) Act gave Northern Territory Aborigines freehold title over reserve lands, and the right to claim title to vacant Crown land, and lands held by or on behalf of, Aborigines. Land Rights Acts have also been introduced by Labor administrations in New South Wales and South Australia. Reserve lands in Queensland have been vested in Aboriginal Councils, not on a freehold basis but as deeds of grant in trust. Land rights legislation has been under discussion in Victoria and Western Australia, where it has been vigorously opposed, particularly by mining interests (see Maddock 1983 for a general account of such legislation).

The last decade has seen a burgeoning of independent Aboriginal organisations. Support organisations for Aborigines and Torres Strait Islanders have a long history, and include the Federal Council for the Advancement of Aborigines and Torres Strait Islanders, founded in 1958, mainly by Europeans and the One People for Australia League. More recently, many independent schools, Aboriginal legal services and Aboriginal health services have been formed, as well as independent Land Councils.

The fundamental issue is that of separateness and autonomy. A frequently-expressed view is that all Australians should have the same rights and opportunities. Such a view does not acknowledge Aboriginal cultural and social distinctiveness, and ignores the long history of racial intolerance and past acquisition of lands from its Aboriginal 'owners'. Indeed, many non-Aborigines fear such distinctiveness, labelling it as akin to 'apartheid'. Many Aborigines on the other hand, express a strong desire to have control of their own affairs, both at the local and the federal level, and to maintain their own particular lifestyles, while at the same time participating in the Australian community as a whole.

A Heterogeneous Category

The varying conditions and distinct histories of different parts of Australia have given rise to an extremely varied range of Aboriginal styles of life, and with varying degrees of continuity with the pre-colonial past.

We have seen that the Aboriginal population is about 160,000, compared with a total population of nearly 16 million (1981 Census). But the size of the Aboriginal population, as well as the proportion of Aboriginal/non-Aboriginal population varies greatly from state to state. Table 7.1 shows figures from the 1981 Census.

Table 7.1 Aboriginal and Islander Population, 1981 Census

	NSW	Vic.	Qld	SA	WA	Tas.	NT	ACT	Australia
Aboriginal and Islander population (to the nearest hundred)	35,400	6,000	45,000	9,800	31,400	2,700	29,000	800	160,000
Aboriginal population as % of total	0.7	0.1	2.0	0.7	2.4	0.7	23.6	0.2	1.1

Source: Australia Bureau of Statistics

The majority of Aboriginal people living in the northern half of Australia are of full descent, while the majority of Aboriginal people in southern Australia are of mixed descent. They live in a wide variety of social conditions: in settlements and missions with Aboriginal councils, at outstations on Aboriginal land and reserves, in cattle station communities, at town camps and town reserves, in fringe camps on the margins of towns and cities, in households and communities in country towns and cities, as well as in hostels and homes. There is space here only to select from the great range of research findings now available. The following contrasts settlement with urban life.

Settlements
Many Aboriginal people live on settlements of several hundred to over 1,000 people, located on Aboriginal reserves, and in the Northern Territory, South Australia and New South Wales, on Aboriginal land under land rights legislation. Some Aborigines live on Aboriginal Land Trust lands, and in states with land rights legislation, on Aboriginal land, including former missions and government settlements as well as in independent camps. Such communities were established, mostly after 1900, as missions or government settlements, with the purpose of protecting Aborigines from the worst effects of contact with whites, Chinese and others, to instill Christianity and the value of 'work', and to train people in agriculture and other activities associated with 'civilised' social life.

The inhabitants of such settlements in the Northern Territory are typically affiliated to land surrounding, or fairly close to, the settlement. In Queensland, however, it was government policy to remove Aboriginal people from their own areas to distant settlements, with the consequence of separating people from the territorial basis of their systems of religious law, and mixing up people of quite different cultures. People were removed to certain settlements such as Palm Island as punishment for infringement of regulations and other offences.

Settlements were administered mainly by mission authorities, backed by the state, in the form of small subsidies, and by access to police power, backed by the courts. In effect, where Aborigines were not forced on to reserves and settlements, they were induced there by the provision of rations of flour, tea, sugar and tobacco in return for work in the gardens, workshops etc. The degree to which the missionaries intervened in Aboriginal religious life, marriage systems, and socialisation of children varied greatly. In some cases, dormitory systems were introduced, removing children from the care of their parents and other relatives, and communal feeding was instituted; in others the dormitory system and communal feeding were short-lived. In some communities, Aboriginal religious ceremonies were vigorously discouraged (Trigger 1985), in others tolerated (McKenzie 1976) or continued clandestinely (Broome 1982). During the last two decades the administration of most settlements has gradually passed to Aboriginal councils working with white advisers and community workers, or with or under a white manager, as in Queensland.

Life in such communities is routinised, dominated by a daily round of work in gardens, on housing and town maintenance and servicing and weekend church attendance. Adults in some communities, such as Doomadgee (Trigger 1985), were and are employed in the cattle industry and as domestics; in others employment has been wholly internal. In the Northern Territory, the passing of community control to Aboriginal councils has resulted in an increased stress on traditional activities.

Since the granting of a 'training allowance' of less than the normal wage, then 'award' wages on settlements, and the extension of access to transfer payments (widow's pension, supporting mother's benefit, old age pension, disability pension, unemployment benefit), wages and social security payments have been the main sources of income, supplemented by sources such as the sale of art and craft work. Transfer payments have the advantage of regularity and reliability, while other sources are more sporadic and uncertain, particularly with the seasonality of pastoral employment.

A notable recent feature of settlement in the Northern Territory and to some extent in Queensland has been the 'outstation' or 'homeland centre' movement. With increasing access to cars, four-wheel drive vehicles and boats, people are increasingly choosing to move out of the large settlements to establish centres on their traditional lands where they can re-establish or reinforce traditional modes of social control, religious practices etc. Hunting, gathering and fishing become dominant in the economy of these communities, and religious life more vigorous (Altman 1982, Coombs 1974).

Cities

Australia ranks as one of the three most urbanised societies in the world, with about 60 per cent of the population living in cities. The rural population as a whole has been declining since World War II. The Aboriginal population, however, is predominantly rural, with only 15 per cent living in major urban areas (1971), although there is a high rate of migration into the cities. Many Aborigines of 'southern' Australia live as small minorities in predominantly white towns or capital cities, often as quite recent migrants from country areas. But the proportion of those in urban populations is very small, ranging from 0.05 per cent in Canberra to 0.38 per cent in Perth, less than 0.2 per cent overall (Altman and Niewenhuysen 1979: 145).

The economic status of Aborigines in the cities is depressed. In general, a smaller proportion of Aboriginal people hold semi-skilled, skilled and managerial positions than non-Aborigines, and a higher proportion holds unskilled positions in domestic work, services and manual work. Unemployment is higher than in the non-Aboriginal population, and consequently incomes are lower, with 55–76 per cent of Brisbane, Adelaide and Perth Aboriginal people below the poverty line, or 'rather poor' (100–120% poverty line) (Western 1983).

Aboriginal Cultural Continuity and Identity

Some writers have attributed the distinct identity of Aboriginal people of southern Australia to their economically disadvantaged position and to racist attitudes. However, recent anthropological and socio-linguistic research, as well as the writings of Aboriginal people (e.g. Gilbert 1977), show that Aboriginal people of mixed descent maintain a culture distinct from that of white Australians not only because of their relative poverty (Sansom 1982, Sansom *et al.* in press). The dimensions of cultural continuity and distinctiveness include: a more extensive network of kin relations than among white Australians, with people recognising and remembering relationships at a degree of remove far beyond that of White Australian kinship, and incorporating non-kin as fictive kin. Moreover, obligations to support relatives tend to be stronger in Aboriginal social life, taking precedence where there is a conflict with other obligations or interests, such as work or education. These obligations are evidenced in patterns of visiting and living in extended family households.

Socialisation practices among Ipswich Aboriginal people (Eckerman 1977) have some similarities with those described for a remote North Australian community (Hamilton 1981b), with an emphasis on the freedom of children, especially males, from adult control until puberty. Indigenous languages are maintained to a greater degree than formerly realised, being used in specific contexts where privacy is desired. Furthermore, Aboriginal English has a rather distinctive pattern of use; for example Aboriginal people of southern Queensland tend to avoid the use of direct questions, and etiquette does not demand that a person answer a question put to them, as white etiquette does (Eades 1981).

Not only are particular social practices distinct among mixed descent Aboriginal people, but many maintain a distinct Aboriginal *identity* – but this is a complex matter (Jordan 1985). So far I have taken the term 'Aboriginal' as unproblematic. The term has been used in this chapter to mean a person descended from an indigenous inhabitant of Australia. According to Commonwealth guidelines, an Aborigine is a person descended from an Aboriginal, who identifies as an Aborigine, and who is recognised by his or her community as an Aborigine. But there is no very clear-cut or cohesive category of 'Aborigines', either defined within the Aboriginal population, or from outside it.

Many white people reserve the term for Aboriginal people of full descent, but it is important to realise that the term has a different basis, when used in this way, from its use by an Aboriginal person.

Dimensions of Disadvantage

Aborigines and Islanders are economically and socially disadvantaged in terms of standards applied within the community in general. The degree of disadvantage can be measured along several dimensions, such as health status, education and economic status. (For more detailed studies see Altman and Niewenhuysen 1979, Gale 1972, 1982, and Western 1983.)

Economic Status

To generalise, a far lower proportion of Aboriginal people is employed in skilled occupation than Australians as a whole (about one-third of the norm according to Altman and Niewenhuysen 1979; about one-fifth according to Western 1983), especially as administrative, executive and managerial workers, and a lower proportion of Aborigines is employed in clerical work. A far higher proportion works in rural industries (nearly four times the average proportion of males, according to Altman and Niewenhuysen 1979), and a higher proportion of Aborigines is employed in unskilled and semi-skilled occupations compared with the norm, with eight times as many unemployed compared with the population as a whole.

Health

Aboriginal health is very much worse than that of the non-Aboriginal population of Australia, though it is improving. We have seen how introduced diseases had a profound effect on the Aboriginal population; just as significant have been changes in environmental conditions, and new habits of diet. Practices of hygiene and waste disposal suitable for a semi-nomadic life are not well adapted to life on permanent settlements, nor has the provision of services such as water supply been adequate. Poor physical-environmental conditions account for a high incidence of intestinal infections such as gastro-enteritis, intestinal parasites such as hookworm and skin diseases such as scabies. The adoption of a diet of white flour, sugar, tea, and often alcohol, in place of a varied and nutritious diet of wild foods, has led to malnutrition, diabetes, dental caries and alcoholism, and resultant low resistance to infection (Hetzel 1980).

The infant mortality rate (IMR) is a good indicator of the general health of mothers as well as infants. The IMR of the Aboriginal population of full descent in the Northern Territory for 1965–67 was 143 per 1,000 live births, compared with a figure of 21 for Australia as a whole (Hetzel 1980). By 1981 the rate had fallen to about 30.3 per thousand, as against 10.2 for the whole of Australia (Thomson 1983). The life expectancy of Aboriginal females at birth, however, is 49, and of males 55 (National Aboriginal Conference), an improvement of nine years over the last two decades (Hetzel 1980). Most early childhood deaths are due to respiratory and/or intestinal infections and malnutrition, a pattern typical of Third World countries.

Social factors influence health; there is a greater incidence of infectious disease on Queensland settlements to which people were moved from many different areas (Trigger *et al.* 1983), and such communities are riven by alcoholism and violence (Wilson 1983).

Education
Aboriginal involvement in schooling indicates a disadvantaged position also, although it, too, is improving. In general a higher proportion of Aboriginal children fails to attend school than non-Aboriginal children – 7 per cent in the 1976 Census as against 0.7 per cent of the non-Aboriginal population; those who do attend school start school later, and leave at an earlier age; a very much smaller proportion gains higher education – 0.1 per cent of Aborigines were enrolled for a higher degree in 1980 as against 2.0 per cent of non-Aborigines (Department of Aboriginal Affairs) and the drop-out rate is high. However, enrolments at the University of Queensland, for example, have dramatically increased, aided by the institution of an Aboriginal enclave program and the instituting of special entrance requirements. Government spending on Aboriginal education has been high since the 1960s, with the setting up of special programs such as bilingual ones, provision for Aboriginal teacher aides, appointment of advisory committees and funding of research into Aboriginal education. Several communities have recently instituted independent Aboriginal and Islander schools and pre-schools.

Conclusion

The last two centuries have seen great changes not only in the structure of Australian society as a whole, but also in the relationship of Aborigines and Torres Strait Islanders to it. In the early part of the colonial period there was a virtual war of conquest, in which the Aborigines and Islander population was decimated through fighting and disease over most of the continent. Behind the frontier, many Aborigines and Islanders participated in the rural economy as cheap labour and sometimes independently. Their crucial role in the development of the wider economy is seldom acknowledged by economic historians. At the end of the first century of white settlement, around the time of Federation, Aborigines and Islanders were increasingly segregated, institutionalised and 'protected'. They became legal children, wards of the state.

The decline in the size of the Aboriginal and Islander population led to the belief that it would not survive. But when from the 1940s, the recovery of the population became apparent, the people were expected, as migrants were, to assimilate into the white population. However, since the reforming Whitlam government it has become increasingly apparent that Aborigines and Islanders will remain culturally distinct to varying degrees, to an extent recognised in the official policy of multiculturalism.

During the last two decades Aborigines and Islanders have become more vocal in Australian political life, and more effective in developing political organisations, using legislation such as the Land Rights Acts and establishing their own community services and support groups. At the same time, the wave of public support apparent during the late 1960s and early 1970s has retreated, as the opposition to land rights expressed in the present suggests. It is clear that Aborigines and Islanders have values, interests, and enduring cultures generally different from those of the white majority. The fact is that Australia is a plural society, and the differences, as well as the resulting conflicts, will endure.

Acknowledgements

I would like to thank Pat Mullins for advice on 'settler capitalism' and Australian social policy, and David Trigger for comments on the manuscript.

References

Altman, J. (1982) 'Maningrida Outstations: A Preliminary Economic Overview' in E. Young and E.K. Fisk (eds.) *Small Rural Communities. The Aboriginal Component of the Australian Economy*, Vol. 3. Canberra: Development Studies Centre.

——(1984) 'Hunter-Gatherer Subsistence Production in Arnhem Land: The Original Affluence Hypothesis Re-examined', *Mankind* 14 (3): 179–90.

—— and Niewenhuysen, J. (1979) *The Economic Status of Australian Aborigines*. Cambridge: Cambridge University Press.

Anderson, J.C. (1983) 'Aborigines and Tin Mining in North Queensland: A Case Study in the Anthropology of Contact History', *Mankind* 13 (6): 473–98.

Barwick, D. (1972) 'Coranderrk and Cumeroogunga: Pioneers and Policy' in T.S. Epstein and D.H. Penny (eds) *Opportunity and Response*. London: C. Hurst and Co.

Beckett, J. (1972) 'The Torres Strait Islanders' in D. Walker (ed.) *Bridge and Barrier*. Canberra: Australian National University Press.

——(1977) 'The Torres Strait Islanders and the Pearling Industry: A Case of Internal Colonialism', *Aboriginal History*, 1, Canberra.

Bennett, G. (1978) *Aboriginal Rights in International Law*, Occasional Paper No. 37 of the Royal Anthropological Institute of Great Britain and Ireland.

Berndt, R.M. and C.H. Berndt (1981) *The World of the First Australians* (Revised Edition). Sydney: Lansdowne Press.

Birdsell, J. (1953) 'Some Environmental and Cultural Factors influencing the Structuring of Australian Aboriginal Populations', *American Naturalist* 87: 171–207.

Biskup, P. (1973) *Not Slaves, not Citizens: The Aboriginal Problem in Western Australia 1898–1954*. St Lucia: University of Queensland Press.

Blackstone, J. (1765) *Commentaries on the Laws of England*. Oxford: Clarendon Press.

Broome, R. (1982) *Aboriginal Australians: Black Response to White Dominance 1788–1980*. Sydney: Allen & Unwin.

Butlin, N.G., Barnard, A. and Pincus, J.J. (1982) *Government and Capitalism*. Sydney: Allen & Unwin.

———(1983) *Our Original Aggression*. Sydney: Allen & Unwin.

Christie, M.F. (1979) *Aborigines in Colonial Victoria 1835–86*. Sydney: Sydney University Press.

Coombs, H.C. (1974) 'Decentralization Trends among Aboriginal Communities', *Search* 5: 135–43.

Denoon, D. (1983) *Settler Capitalism: the Dynamics of Dependent Development in the Southern Hemisphere*. Oxford: Clarendon Press.

Department of Aboriginal Affairs, *Newsletter* 10.

Drakakis-Smith, D. (1981) 'Aboriginal Underdevelopment in Australia', *Antipode: a Radical Journal of Geography* 13 (1): 35–44.

Eades, D. (1981) 'That's Our Way of Talking': Aborigines in South-east Queensland', *Social Alternatives* 2 (2): 11–15.

Eckermann, A.K. (1977) 'Group Organization and Identity within an Urban Aboriginal Community' in R.M. Berndt (ed.) *Aborigines and Change: Australia in the 70s*. Canberra: Australian Institute of Aboriginal Studies.

Elkin, A.F. (1954) *The Australian Aborigines: How to Understand Them*. Sydney: Angus & Robertson.

Gale, F. (1972) *Urban Aborigines*. Canberra: Australian National University Press.

——— and J. Wundersitz (1982) *Adelaide Aborigines: A Case Study of Urban Life 1977–1981*. Canberra: Development Studies Centre, Australian National University Press.

Gilbert, K. (1977) *Living Black: Blacks Talk to Kevin Gilbert*. Ringwood, Victoria: Penguin Books.

Gould, R. (1969) *Yiwara: Foragers of the Australian Desert*. New York: Charles Scribner and Sons.

Hamilton, A. (1981a) 'A Complex Strategical Situation: Gender and Power in Aboriginal Australia' in N. Grieve and P. Grimshaw (eds) *Australian Women: Feminist Perspectives*. Melbourne: Oxford University Press.

———(1981b) *Nature and Nurture: Aboriginal Child-rearing in North-*

Central Arnhem Land. Canberra: Australian Institute of Aboriginal Studies.

Hart, C.W.M. and Pilling, A.R. (1960) *The Tiwi of North Australia.* New York: Henry Holt and Co.

Hartwig, M.C. (1978) 'The Theory of Internal Colonialism – the Australian Case' in E.L. Wheelwright and K. Buckley (eds) *Essays in the Political Economy of Australian Capitalism.* Sydney: Australian and New Zealand Book Co.

Hetzel, B.S. (1980) *Health and Australian Society.* Ringwood, Victoria: Penguin.

Hobbes, T. (1968) *Leviathan.* Harmondsworth: Penguin.

Hobsbawm, E. (1969) *Industry and Empire,* Pelican Economic History of Britain, Vol. 3. Harmondsworth: Penguin Books.

Hookey, J. (1984) 'Settlement and Sovereignty' in P. Hanks and B. Keon-Cohen (eds) *Aborigines and the Law.* Sydney: Allen & Unwin.

Jenkin, G. (1979) *Conquest of the Ngarrindjeri: The Story of the Lower Murray Lakes Tribes.* Adelaide: Rigby.

Jones, R. and Bowler J. (1980) 'Struggle for the Savanna: Northern Australia In Ecological and Prehistoric Perspective' in R. Jones (ed.) *Northern Australia: Options and Implications.* Canberra: Research School of Pacific Studies, Australian National University.

Keen, I. (1982) 'The Alligator Rivers Aborigines: Retrospect and Prospect' in R. Jones (ed.) *Northern Australia: Options and Implications.* Canberra: Research School of Pacific Studies, Australian National University.

Lee, R.B. (1968) 'What Hunters do for a Living, or, How to Make Out on Scarce Resources' in R.B. Lee and I. DeVore (eds) *Man and Hunter.* Chicago: Aldine.

Levitus, R. (1982) 'Everybody Bin All Day Work', Unpublished manuscript.

McCarthy, F.D. (1939) '"Trade" in Aboriginal Australia and Trade Relationships with Torres Strait, New Guinea and Malaya', *Oceania* 9: 405, 10: 80.

——— and M. MacArthur (1960) 'The Food Quest and the Time Factor in Aboriginal Economic Life', in C.P. Mountford (ed.) *Records of the Australian-American Scientific Expedition to Arnhem Land,* Vol. 2: Anthropology and Nutrition. Melbourne: Melbourne University Press.

McKenzie, M. (1976) *Mission to Arnhem Land.* Adelaide: Rigby.

Maddock, K. (1981) *The Australian Aborigines: A Portrait of their Society,* revised edition. Ringwood, Victoria: Penguin Books.

———(1983) *Your Land is Our Land: Aboriginal Land Rights.* Ringwood, Victoria: Penguin.

Meehan, B. (1977) 'Hunters by the Seashore', *Journal of Human Evolution* 6 (4).

Merlan, F. (1981) 'Land, Language and Social Identity in Aboriginal Australia', *Mankind* 13 (2).

Moore, D. (1978) *Islanders and Aborigines at Cape York: An Ethnographic Reconstruction Based on the 1848–1850 'Rattlesnake Journals' of O.W.*

Brierly and Information he obtained from Barbara Thomson. Canberra: Australian Institute of Aboriginal Studies.

Morris, B. (1983) 'From Underemployment to Unemployment: The Changing Role of Aborigines in a Rural Economy', *Mankind* 13 (6).

National Aboriginal Conference (nd) *Background Paper: Aboriginal Health.*

Peterson, N. (1976) Introduction, in *Tribes and Boundaries in Australia.* Canberra: Australian Institute of Aboriginal Studies.

Radcliffe-Brown, A.R. (1930) 'Former Numbers and Distribution of the Australian Aborigines', *Australian Yearbook* 23: 687–96.

Reid, J. (1983) *Sorcerers and Healing Spirits.* Canberra: Australian National University Press.

Rowley, C.D. (1970) *The Destruction of Aboriginal Society.* Canberra: Australian National University Press.

———(1971) *Outcasts in White Australia: Aboriginal Policy and Practice,* Vol. II. Canberra: Australian National University Press.

Ryan, L. (1981) *The Aboriginal Tasmanians.* St Lucia: Queensland University Press.

Sahlins, M. (1974) *Stone Age Economics.* London: Tavistock.

Sansom, B. (1982) 'The Aboriginal Commonality' in R.M. Berndt (ed.) *Sites, Rights and Resource Development.* Canberra: Academy of the Social Sciences in Australia.

———Baines, P. and Birdsall, C. (forthcoming) *Will and Worth: Family and Social Identity among Nyungars in Western Australia.*

Shapiro, W. (1979) *Social Organization in Aboriginal Australia.* Canberra: Australian National University Press.

Sinclair, W.A. (1976) *The Process of Economic Development in Australia.* Melbourne: Longman Cheshire.

Smith, L.R. (1980) *The Aboriginal Population of Australia.* Canberra: Australian National University Press.

Stevens, F. (1974) *Aborigines in the Northern Territory Cattle Industry.* Canberra: Australian National University Press.

Sutton, P. (1978) 'Wik: Aboriginal Society, Territory and Language at Cape Keerweer, Cape York Peninsula, Australia', Unpublished PhD dissertation, University of Queensland.

Thomson, N. (1983) .Aboriginal Infant Mortality', *Australian Aboriginal Studies* 1: 10–15.

Tonkinson, R. (1978) *The Mardudjara Aborigines: Living the Dream in Australia's Desert.* New York: Holt, Rinehart & Winston.

Trigger, D. (1985) 'Doomadgee: A Study of Power Relations and Social Action in a North Australian Aboriginal Settlement, Unpublished PhD thesis, Department of Anthropology, University of Queensland.

———, Anderson, C., Lincoln, R.A. and Maitlis, C.E. (1983) 'Mortality Rates in 14 Queensland Aboriginal Reserve Communities: Association with 10 Socio-economic Variables', *Medical Journal of Australia* 1: 361–65.

van den Berghe, P. (1981) *The Ethnic Phenomenon.* New York: Elsevier.

Watson, P. (1983) *This Precious Foliage,* Oceania Monograph No. 26.

212   *Part I: Basic Structures and Concepts*

Western, J. (1983) *Social Inequality in Australian Society*. Melbourne: Macmillan.

White, J.P. and O'Connell, J.F. (1982) *A Prehistory of Australia, New Guinea, and Sahul*. Sydney: Academic Press.

Wilson, P. (1983) *Black Death, White Hands*. St Lucia: University of Queensland Press.

Wolpe, H. (1975) 'The Theory of Internal Colonialism: The South African Case' in I. Oxaal, T. Barnett and D. Booth (eds) *Beyond the Sociology of Development*. London: Routledge & Kegan Paul.

Wolf, E. (1982) *Europe and the People Without History*. Berkeley: University of California Press.

Part II
Socially Patterned Behaviours

Chapter Eight

Education and the Social Order

Don S. Anderson

Ever since the dawn of civilization, class inequality has existed. . . .
Where education is concerned . . . an attempt is made to make the
children of the poor to think themselvès inferior to the children of
the rich.

Bertrand Russell, *Education and the Social Order*

Of the 16 million people inhabiting Australia almost one-fifth are
children enrolled in pre-school, primary school and secondary
school. Another 1.1 million are students enrolled in courses of
post-secondary education, mostly part-time. Within these two
main sectors of formal education – schools and post-school – there
are structural divisions which provide a convenient vantage point
for the study of education and society and, in this chapter, we shall
be using these to explore three questions from the sociology of
schooling:

First, to what extent does schooling and post-secondary education function as an agent for reproduction of the existing social
structure?

Secondly, to what extent is schooling or post-secondary education an agent of social mobility, assisting bright children from
humble origins to attain positions in the labour force of prestige,
power and material wealth? (This question, on the face of it,
implies an opposite role for schooling to that of the first question.)

Thirdly, are those schools or those sections of post-secondary
education which serve particular sub-groups in the broader community, agents for the role socialisation of children and students,
providing them with beliefs and dispositions which will make them
good functioning members of particular subcultures?

There are divisions between political regions associated with
Australia's federal system, with separate systems of public schooling in each of the eight states or territories. Such is the homogen-

eity of Australian society that there is little variation in structures, practices or outcomes across these systems. There are, however, divisions of considerable social significance within the school systems and within post-secondary education. There is age-related segregation of students into primary and secondary schools, some streaming between certain schools according to academic prowess, and some separation of the sexes. The division which is of greatest sociological interest is that between public and private schools. Almost three-quarters of all school students are in public schools which are the responsibility of the various state education departments; about one-fifth are in Roman Catholic schools (nearly all in so-called systemic schools which are organised and generally co-ordinated by state Catholic education offices); with the remaining 7 per cent of students in other non-government schools, most of which are associated with religious denominations. These last are subject to no overall co-ordination except the somewhat light requirements of accountability now required because of the extent to which their costs are subsidised from the public purse, most receiving more than half of their recurrent expenditure needs from federal and state governments.

Australia's dual public/private schooling systems have their roots in the beginning of European colonisation of the continent two hundred years ago. The First Fleet brought not only British civil and military authority, but also spiritual authority in the form of representatives of the Church of England. The latter regarded itself as the custodian of morals and manners as well as of the religious welfare of the first white residents and, among other things, soon took initiatives in providing schooling for the young. This monopoly over faith and morals was, before long, challenged by representatives of the Churches of Rome and Scotland, who claimed responsibility for the not inconsiderable numbers of Scots and Irish whose transgressions had earned them deportation to New South Wales. Denominational squabbling eventually stimulated intervention by secular authority concerning the provision of schooling, especially because the schooling of large sections of the population was being neglected. Thus the dual system of Australian education emerged from a conflict between church and state.

It took almost a hundred years after the first settlement however, before the pattern with which we are now familiar became established. And by that time social class as well as religion had become a factor associated with division between different sets of schools. In the period 1870–1900, the six colonial administrations, which were strung out along the southern and eastern coastline, had become exasperated with acrimonious interdenominational bickering, and, emboldened by post-Darwinian religious scepticism and, inspired by newly-emerging democratic sentiments, they enacted legislation which, in one form or another, required that they provide education which was compulsory, free and secular. State aid to church schooling ended, for the time being.

The division was cemented by an historic directive of the Roman Catholic bishops in 1879 that Catholic parents must send their children to Catholic schools. This caused parishes to attempt to provide a comprehensive and separate system of education for all Catholic children. Until the 1960s the burden of supporting these schools fell on the parishes, on the religious teachers and on parents By the mid-twentieth century around 70 per cent of children of Catholic parents were attending Catholic schools, far higher than in other countries where the average is 20 per cent. Following the end of state aid, the Protestant churches, too, continued to sponsor schools, but their funding came almost entirely from fees and herein lay the beginning of Anglican and non-conformist church schools which, as we shall see, are now noted more for their social distinctiveness than their Christian ethos.

In the following discussion the terms public, Catholic and other private will be used to distinguish the three main classes of school. The terms originate from administrative practice and refer to the categories into which the government places schools for the purposes of funding. For sociological purposes a more useful classification would distinguish academically selective schools, whether public or private, and, within the private sector, schools which serve the aspiring socially élite sector of society would be distinguished from schools whose chief purpose is cultural maintenance, religious or ethnic. The data are, however, generally not available for these and the conventional classifications must serve our analytic purposes.

Post-secondary or tertiary education (the terms are used synonymously in Australia) is, like Ancient Gaul, in three parts, namely: technical and further education (TAFE); colleges of advanced education (CAEs); and universities. The latter two, collectively, are known as higher education.

TAFE has a long history in Australia, going back well into the nineteenth century; and the apprenticeship system, for which TAFE contributes the education component, and in which there are almost as many apprentices as there are students in universities, has a history as ancient as that of universities. Unlike higher education, which is now fully funded by the federal government, TAFE remains principally a state-funded and administered enter-

prise linked closely to government through state education departments or, in some states, separate departments of technical education. Since 1973 the Commonwealth government has developed a
commitment to TAFE, and presently provides state governments
with 'topping-up' grants amounting to about 25 per cent of total
costs, the greater part being for capital. As well as technical and
trade training, including apprenticeships, TAFE embraces some
professional and para-professional courses, and an alternative
route to the Higher School Certificate (secondary Year 12) for
students who have left school. It also provides a vast range of
'hobby' courses. Even without the last category the number of
enrolments in TAFE is around 800,000, more than double that in
higher education, although most are part-time. The route into
TAFE is quite different from that into higher education. Students
are typically recruited two or three years before the completion of
secondary school. They are predominantly from public schools,
and from non-academic streams. Socially, recruits to TAFE are
much more representative of the community at large than are
students who enter higher education.

Compared with a very substantial research literature on the
sociology of higher education in Australia, particularly studies
concerning social mobility, there is a dearth of information on
TAFE, reflecting a degree of narcissism among scholars, nearly all
of whom, of course, are themselves graduates of universities or
CAEs.

Colleges of advanced education were established in the 1960s in
order to provide education and training of an equal intellectual
standard to university but of a more applied and directly vocational
nature. The system comprised some new institutions created in
that period of expansion, several high-level technological institutions of long standing and, by 1974, all former state education
departments' teachers' colleges. By the late 1970s there were more
than seventy CAEs; the number has since diminished due to
amalgamations forced by federal governments convinced that
these would lead to economies of scale. CAEs exist under Acts of
state parliaments and are co-ordinated by state statutory authorities, although by far the greatest part of their income is now
provided by the federal government, which took over the states'
share of higher education funding in 1974. One of the features
which distinguishes them from universities is the requirement for
external approval of new courses, and the accreditation of standards in all courses. Colleges award diplomas and degrees, generally for three years full-time, or equivalent part-time, courses.
They overlap with universities in many professional areas, for
example, teaching, engineering, architecture, management and

some commercial studies. Colleges have tended to be more innovative than universities in developing new courses; those colleges with courses of teacher education, however, have had the greatest difficulty in adapting to the recent and drastic downturn in the demand for school teachers. The numbers of students in colleges more than doubled during the 1970s and throughout this decade the gap between college and university enrolments was narrowed. Of the 186,000 students in 1984, just under half were studying full-time, 36 per cent part-time and 15 per cent external, i.e. off-campus, and with the aid of various techniques of so-called distance learning. Post-graduate research training is not extensive and research programs are expected to be of an applied nature.

The route into CAEs requires, for most students, satisfactory completion of Year 12 secondary school. There are also provisions for the entry of older people who may not have completed the normal entry tests which are required of school leavers. CAEs draw their students mainly from the middle and upper positions of the social order. The bias in representation is by no means as great as that in universities, although some recent evidence from studies by Linke *et al.* (1985) suggests that the gap is closing.

All but one of Australia's nineteen 'official' universities[1] are established under an Act of state parliament, the exception being the Australian National University, founded in 1946 by the Commonwealth government, initially as a non-teaching research institution. Although in some states universities are nominally subject to state level co-ordination, all enjoy virtual institutional autonomy. As well as providing professional courses (of four to six years' duration) in fields such as engineering, law, medicine, teaching and agricultural science, universities offer three-year pass courses in arts and science and four-year honours courses. They also, of course, have a large program of graduate studies and extensive involvement in both basic and applied research. In 1984 there were some 173,000 students; 61 per cent of them were studying full-time on-campus, 29 per cent part-time on campus and 9 per cent were enrolled externally.

The normal route into university is via Year 12 of secondary school including a satisfactory level of attainment in the Higher School Certificate examinations or their equivalent. The standard required, which is generally higher than that for a CAE, is not an absolute or criterion-referenced level in the various approved subjects, but rather is a sufficiently high position in the rank order of all candidates. Successful applications to popular faculties such as law require the candidate being in the top 10 per cent of all candidates or in the top 1 or 2 per cent in the case of medicine. Thus access to university courses (and to many CAE courses) is determined by success in a competition against peers, rather than by reaching a satisfactory level of attainment, which is determined independently of the number of candidates and the number of places available. The average social origins of school leavers entering full-time university studies is even more biased than that of CAE students, with professional and managerial families being over-represented and a disproportionately high number coming from private schools. Older entrants, for whom there are modified entry requirements, and part-time students, are a little more representative of the population in terms of social origin.

The social bias in higher education is no new thing. From the very beginnings of higher education in Australia there have been tensions between the élite and democratic viewpoints of the purposes of universities – whether they existed to prepare the young of the established classes for their roles as leaders, or to provide opportunities for bright children of more humble origin; whether to consolidate the established social order or to help create a more open one. With respect to curriculum the argument was over high culture or more utilitarian knowledge. Generally the advocates of a meritocracy were those who favoured a more practical curriculum.

In the 1840s lead-up to the University of Sydney (established 1852) it seemed to liberals like Henry Parkes that an oligarchic faction led by William Charles Wentworth was engaged in creating an exclusive upper class and conservative institution (Macmillan 1963). Despite protestations by the protagonists, that the University opened a path 'to the poor men to the highest position which the country could afford him', and that scholarships afforded 'encouragement to candidates of whatever degree', Parkes complained that the proposed curriculum was not useful and that the students were privileged. In his paper *The Empire*, he asserted '. . . . the whole matter wears an air of aristocratical predilection which with public money ought not to be indulged'. The distrust surrounding the Wentworth group and the design for the new University of Sydney led it to be regarded as a last bastion of privilege in a society which was just beginning to develop democratic political institutions. Some fifteen years after its establishment we find a university reform group determined to open 'the doors of the university to the intellect of the whole country'. More than a hundred years later, these sentiments were echoed in statements by the Whitlam Labor government which was determined to facilitate the participation of bright working class children. To this end in 1974 tuition fees were abolished and means-tested grants were introduced.

There is a confusion in policy thinking about the effects of interventions which are made by government in order to equalise educational opportunity. The confusion, which as we shall see later, has its parallel in sociological theory, is due to confusion between individual or group as the unit of analysis. When a government sets out to equalise the opportunity to participate in higher education, as the Whitlam government did in 1974, the unit is the group – the objective is to increase opportunities for working class children, or girls, or Aborigines or migrants. The unit of application however, is the individual, who receives the benefit. It is not the group, but a certain number of individuals, albeit deserving, who then benefit from the public expenditure which is invested in universities and colleges of advanced education. The system remains as unfair as it was before intervention because those who do not participate, whatever their social classification, miss out on a substantial private good which is financed by the general taxpayer. The working class, or the female sex or ethnic communities only benefit on the somewhat dubious assumption that those members whose participation is facilitated will use their professional qualifications for the particular benefit of their group. We shall return to this question when examining the socialising effects of higher education.

Reproduction or Social Mobility

Survey evidence of students' backgrounds became available for the first time after World War II. Since then there has been a wealth of data on the social origins of students for particular institutions. The unequal mix of students in higher education appears to have persisted over at least a thirty or forty-year period. This is despite all the economic and social changes which have taken place in Australia during that time, despite the expansion of education which has been at a rate well beyond population increase, and despite the implementation by government of policies committed to the ideology of equality and individual merit. For a sociologist the question of interest is why there is this seeming stability and particularly why the social bias appears to be so refractory to intervention by reformist government. This leads to the seeking of an explanation from the perspective of the reproduction theorists who take the pessimistic view that education serves to reproduce an unequal society; this is in contrast to the mobility theorists, who more optimistically see education as a ladder enabling poor but bright and motivated children to rise, or even as an instrument for reducing differences in wealth, status and power. We shall return to these theories shortly; first it is necessary to note some practical problems which are encountered when we ask if there has been a change in the social mix.

Making comparisons over time between even simple measures such as participation rates for different social classes is a tricky methodological enterprise. For one thing, occupational group, which is the most commonly-used operational indicator of social class position, does not remain static in a population even over a relatively short period. For example, during the 20-year period 1963–83, when the Australian labour force increased by about 30 per cent, participation in occupations classed as professional and para-professional increased by 100 per cent, whereas blue collar occupations increased by only 12 per cent. Rather than making comparisons of participation rates for occupational groups at different times, it is preferable, in estimating change, to keep the denominator constant by comparing equal fractions of social order, for example, the top third ranked on occupational status.

Participation rates can also be defined in a variety of ways, and there is sometimes an unconscious tendency for analysts to choose a measure which suits their preferred hypotheses. Suppose, for example, in 1970 the upper half of the social order had a participation rate of 50 per cent and the lower half had a rate of 10 per cent, and that by 1980 these rates had increased to 70 per cent and 20 per cent respectively. Has the system become more or less equal? The answer depends on how the question is framed. In terms of absolute difference the upper half gained 20 per cent, the lower half only 10 per cent, so the system is less equal. If, however, the question is how much each group changed relative to its initial rate, the answer is that there is greater equality, because the upper group increased by 40 per cent, whereas the lower one increased by 100 per cent. The question might be put, however, in terms of the increase relative to the maximum possible increase. Looked at this way the answer is a decline in equality, since the upper half increases by 40 per cent (20 on 50) compared with the lower's 11.1 per cent (10 on 90).

A useful coefficient, which takes the maximum (or minimum) possible change into account, was developed by Benini early in this century and recently discovered and used by Jones (1985) in cross-national studies of social mobility. A more complex model would employ a non-linear conversion in order to represent the accelerating difficulty of improving participation as the maximum rate is approached.

Of equal importance in exploring change is the need for a model of the processes which correspond to theoretical expectations – in the present case a model of what would be expected if the mobility theory holds, and one if reproduction holds.

Following expansion of the higher education system, or intervention to promote enrolment by poor students, it would be expected by mobility theorists that those less well-placed in the social order would gain ground relative to those from well-positioned families. As additional places are provided it is assumed that these will be taken up, in disproportionately large numbers, by bright but under-represented young people from families who constitute a reservoir of ability. Additionally, the removal of financial barriers in the form of the abolition of fees or the provision of grants targeted at the poor will also promote such participation. This is the upward social mobility model of Halsey *et al.* (1980) and of Martin Trow (1981); it is also the meritocratic view satirised by Michael Young in *The Rise of the Meritocracy* (1961).

According to the mobility view, the intellectual and motivational limits to participation are not dissimilar across the social order. With expansion, therefore, the rate of increase in participation by the upper groups declines as they approach saturation. At the same time, participation of the lower groups accelerates. Halsey has suggested that as higher education expands, participation for diferent sections of the social order may be portrayed by a series of overlapping 5-curves. Early in the process participation is mainly from the top group. Its rate increases slowly at first, then accelerates, and finally flattens out as the point is approached when intellectual and motivational potential is exhausted. Subsequently participation by the next group may be expected to follow a similar pattern, and later still by the lowest group which will accelerate when higher education becomes a mass system. (the terms 'élite' and 'mass' have been used by Trow to characterise different historical phases of the development of higher education.)

As we have seen, meritocracy or upward social mobility of the bright young was the view of the founding fathers of the University of Sydney; it was the belief of Daniel Bell (1973), who stated that under a meritocracy 'high scoring individuals, no matter where they are in society, should be brought to the top in order to make the best of their talents'; and it was the expectation of the Whitlam government that, when fees were abolished and grants introduced, enrolment by able students from poor families would be facilitated.

A contrasting view is that expansion or intervention will be ineffective in changing the social balance because those already well-placed will use their advantages – for example, wealth used to

Table 8.1 Participation Rates (%) in Higher Education for
Top, Middle and Lowest SES Levels (Australian
School Leavers)

| | Year enrolled in Higher Education | | | |
	1960[a] (n = 13,632)	1972[a] (n = 19,209)	1970–80[b] (n = 2,985)	1983–84[b] (n = 2,489)
Top	23.4	27.4	32.2	34.3
Middle	11.4	20.7	18.3	14.4
Lowest	6.7	12.0	12.8	10.1
All Groups	13.4	19.9	21.5	19.9

[a] Data obtained from Radford (1962) and Radford and Wilkes (1975)
[b] Data made available by Trevor Williams, Australian Council for Educational
Research, from Williams *et al., Youth in Transition Longitudinal Survey* (1980,
1981)

buy private education, or 'cultural capital'–to counter any discrimination in favour of the poor. Some interesting evidence has
emerged recently from separate studies by West (1985) at Monash,
and Dunn (1982) at Melbourne, which showed that first-year
undergraduates from private schools underperformed in their
university studies relative to their HSC score when compared with
public school students. One possible explanation is that private
schools are successful in providing their students with an advantage in the competition for high entry marks, but that this
advantage does not persist under conditions of university study,
where intellectual ability is of greater significance.

This 'no-change' model is what would be predicted by the
reproductionist school of education sociology. Bowles and Gintis
(1976) assert that meritocracy is an ideology serving to justify
existing inequalities: 'Beneath the facade of meritocracy lies the
reality of an education system geared towards the reproduction of
economic relations.' Bourdieu (1977) adds to this a mechanism for
reproduction. It is possession of cultural capital which, he says,
determines achievement in school and access to successive stages of
the education ladder. School, even if it may not discriminate in any
deliberate fashion, does not give everybody an equal chance,
because it is those already endowed with cultural capital who can
benefit from education. According to this view, removal of cost
barriers would not be a sufficient condition for equalising participation; a much more fundamental change involving the redistribution of cultural capital would be required. The social mobility
and reproductionist models of the change in the social balance of

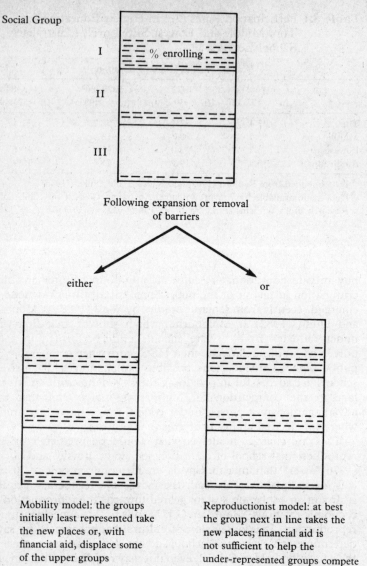

Figure 8.1 Mobility and Reproductionist Views of the Effect of Expansion or Removal of Barriers on the Participation Rate in Higher Education of the Top, Middle and Lowest Thirds of the Social Order

higher education following expansion or intervention are portrayed in Figure 8.1.

In order to test these alternative theoretical viewpoints, some
data have been reworked from studies of school leavers undertaken
since 1960 by the Australian Council for Educational Research.
Participation rates in higher education (universities, CAEs or
equivalent) for the top, middle and lowest thirds of the social order
(based on father's occupation ranked according to the ANU scale)
may be seen in Table 8.1. They represent young people who
enrolled immediately after school in 1960 or 1972, and by age 19 in
1979–80 or 1983–84.

There appears to have been a shift towards greater equality
during a period of overall expansion between 1960 and 1972, due
to the middle group advancing relative to the top and bottom. By
1979–80 however, after a period of only slight expansion, equality
declined as participation by the top third increased and participation of the lower two-thirds declined. This trend away from
equality became even more marked and, by 1983–84, the system
had become as unequal as it had been in 1960. (For details of the
analysis, using Benini coefficients, see Anderson 1986.)

In social science (perhaps all sciences) one must be wary of
generalisations based on one sample, or derived from one method.
It is of interest, therefore, that Jones (1986) has concluded, from an
analysis of the National Social Science Survey (NSSS) sample, and
using a log linear modelling method, that there 'is a social
regression in the most recent period, in that the chances of persons
from relatively advantaged backgrounds getting into higher education were better in the period after 1974 than in the three earlier
decades'. And, using an entirely different method (inferring social
position from post-codes) Linke *et al.* (1985) concluded, from a
study of applications and enrolments in the South Australian
metropolitan area 1974–84, that the overwhelming impression
from these results is one of little change in the socio-economic
profile of students commencing higher education over the past
decade, despite substantial changes during this period in total
population participation rates. The universities, traditionally regarded as strongly élitist, have become less so, and the colleges,
once regarded because of their vocational emphasis as a means for
egalitarian influence have instead become more élitist, with the net
result being virtually no change across the system as a whole.

Somewhat similar results were found when some Swedish data
(from a monograph by Kim (1983)), for the period 1957–77 were
analysed: expansion of participation in university (from 6 to 10 per
cent) was not accompanied by any equalisation between social

groups (Anderson 1986). In neither the Swedish nor the Australian case is there any indication of the S-curve suggested by mobility theorists whereby the groups lowest in the social order catch up as the system expands. Perhaps twenty or thirty years is too short a period for the process of upward social mobility to become apparent. Data from another survey spanning sixty years (Aitkin 1977) reveals that substantial differences in participation by members of the top, middle and lowest thirds of the social order persist over this period (Figure 8.2). For those born in the 1920s and 1930s the system appears to have become less equal than it was for those born in earlier decades. By the time those born in the 1940s and 1950s were enrolling, the overall participation rates were much higher than earlier, and the system had become more equal

Figure 8.2 Participation of Top, Middle and Lowest Thirds of the Social Order: Australians entering Higher Education at Any Age

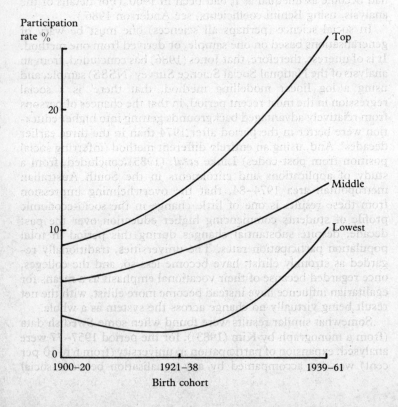

by dint of the lowest third having advanced. This gain is, however, relative to the middle SES group; at the same time the top third has also accelerated. Once again there is little indication of the S-curve pattern, and little apparent support for the mobility theory.

Apparently, even when the system expands substantially, as it did in this period, a disproportionate number of families which are well-placed in the social order are able to use their advantage (private schools, good home environment for studying, and so on) to secure additional places for their children. The advance of the lowest third relative to the middle, might be attributed to interventionist strategies, some of which had equality objectives. Means-tested grants, which generally became available in the post-World War II years, would have encouraged participation by students from the lower third; furthermore the massive recruitment of teacher trainees during the late 1950s and 1960s as state education departments, desperate to recruit teachers for the burgeoning school population caused by the post-war 'baby boom' and the upsurge in demand for education, provided valuable awards which enticed into higher education many thousands of young people from previously under-represented groups: lower SES, country residents, females.

None of these studies which have been briefly reviewed – four Australian and one Swedish – lend much support to social mobility theories. All suggest that the relative over-participation of those from the top of the social order, and the under-representation of those from the bottom, remain fairly constant over periods up to sixty years. Slight shifts to greater equality during the middle years appear to have been temporary. On the face of it this analysis scores nine out of ten points for the reproductionists, one out of ten for the mobility theorists. But, as we pointed out initially, it is easy to slip unwittingly from the group as a unit of analysis to the individual. At a group or macro-level, social structure seems almost invariant over substantial periods of time. The so-called class organisation of society is characterised by power and influence, prestige, income, education and lifestyle, and, from the beginning of European occupation of Australia, a hierarchical structure, ordered on these inter-related attributes of individuals, has been evident. A more equal society would occur only as the variation in these attributes diminished. At the individual level however, the structure provides the opportunity to move, and clearly many do, witness the not insignificant proportion from the lowest third who make it through higher education into the professions. It is not easy for them because, in a competition for places, they are up against families already well placed in the social order, who use their advantage to retain their position and to advance the life chances of their children. When positive discrimination is introduced in the form, for example, of means tested grants or admission quotas for the disadvantaged, those who are well placed will redouble their efforts to stay ahead. Nevertheless some bright children from poor families do advance through the education system – not all of them, and by no means in proportion of numbers – and for these, there is upward occupational mobility. Saha (1983), who has worked on reconciling reproductionist and mobility theories, cites the early twentieth-century sociologist, Pitirim Sorokin, who commented on the apparent anomaly thus:

> ... the open doors of a mobile society offer a great chance for the majority of leaders and ambitious persons to rise. Instead of becoming leaders of a revolution they are turned into protectors of social order.

Socialisation

A reproduction theorist is inclined to reject, or at least to ignore, socialisation as a process in education. Rather, following Bourdieu, schooling is viewed as a mechanism for sorting, advancing and promoting those children who possess the 'cultural capital' bestowed on them by family and class. There is evidence however, that schools do actively change individual students, not simply by adding to their store of knowledge and intellectual skills, but also by inculcating in them what are loosely referred to as attitudes, these attitudes being consistent with the social roles which the students will subsequently enter. This perspective is not inconsistent with schools also being agents of reproduction or social mobility. It does, however, imply a functionalist viewpoint, and this is the subject of some scholarly criticism (for example, by Olesen and Whittaker 1970), because it diminishes the role of an individual as an actor making choices and constructing his or her own reality.

Socialisation and role theory are closely connected. Here we shall use 'role' in the sense defined by Biddle (1979): 'those behaviors characteristic of one or more persons in context'; and socialisation to mean those environmentally-induced beliefs, preferences, skills, norms and dispositions which are characteristic of a particular social system and the possession of which facilitates an individual's participation in that system. In the case of occupations, socialisation is like Procrustes with his bed, lopping off superfluous members, stretching others, until the recruit fits the role. As with reproduction, we will illustrate the connection of schooling with socialisation by reviewing some recent work, firstly on private schooling and secondly, on higher education.

As we have seen, private schools in Australia are generally used by parents who regard public schools as not providing the particular religious, educational, cultural emphases they desire for their children. The formal objectives of traditional private schools may be expressed in terms of transmitting the Christian faith, or, in the case of non-Catholic private schools, educating students in a Christian ethos. Scholastic excellence and character development also feature prominently in the official objectives of private schools. Many recently established private schools are also concerned with the cultural maintenance of particular religious sects or ethnic groups. Institutions, of course, serve unofficial or unstated purposes and schools are no exception. The hidden agenda of a significant proportion of private schools may be inferred from the social profile of the families which use them. Partridge (1968), in analysing the social functions of non-Catholic private schools, concluded that 'motives connected with social exclusiveness are amongst the strongest forces that have sustained them'. He went on to observe that it is a little odd that it should be the churches that maintain institutions which gratify ambitions of social pride and exclusiveness. Similar conclusions concerning the functioning of non-Catholic private schools have been reached by Martin (1957), who saw them performing 'the task of preparing the child to take his place among the highest status members of the society by teaching him their customs, imbuing him with their values, and providing him with friends and contacts within this section of society'. Encel (1970) makes similar observations after an analysis in which he concludes that the most distinctive contribution of the education system to inequality is 'through the medium of private schools which help to create and perpetuate class, religious and economic divisions'.

The socialisation outcomes which might be expected from such analyses of the social functions of private schools would include conservative political values, career ambitions in the more prestigious occupations and, in accord with official objectives, religious beliefs and behaviour.

According to evidence from numerous surveys, people who have attended non-Catholic private schools are, on average, disposed to conservative political preferences. Former Catholic school students, however, are not greatly dissimilar from former public school students in this respect. For example, self-identification with the political right is shown, in the most recent survey (National Social Science Survey (NSSS) Anderson, forthcoming) to be more characteristic of former non-Catholic private school students, over 40 per cent of whom identify themselves as Right of Centre (rather than Centre or to the Left), whereas under 30 per cent of former Catholic and public school students make this identification. Earlier studies of party preference reached similar conclusions. Analysis of the Aitkin (1982) data set shows that identification with the political Right was even slightly higher than it is now for non-Catholic school students (44 per cent), identical for public school students (28 per cent), but higher than now for Catholic school students (41 per cent). Voting preferences followed a similar pattern – support for the ALP was public, 38 per cent; Catholic, 40 per cent; and other private, 19 per cent.

A study of university students who were in Australian universities in the mid-1960s (Anderson *et al.* 1982) produced associations between type of school and voting preference which were not dissimilar to the above figures. In 1984 a follow-up of the same sample revealed that relative political preferences had changed very little although there had been a shift of over 20 per cent to ALP in the intervening years.

The same survey of university students showed that students who had attended non-Catholic private schools were more likely to choose a career in law or medicine than in the less prestigious professions, that they expected to earn higher incomes, and, consistent with this, that they were more likely to have rated financial rewards as having been important when they made their career decisions. These results are probably best interpreted as 'knowing the ropes' rather than being due to any differences of selfishness or altruistic disposition between the school types. Survey evidence generally shows only slight differences between types of school with respect to such motives. The NSSS shows, for instance, that on the question of paying more taxes so as to improve the quality of social services, agreement was expressed by 78 per cent from public schools, 85 per cent from Catholic schools and 75 per cent from non-Catholic private schools.

Not unexpectedly, people who have attended Catholic schools report more frequent church attendance and greater strength of belief in God than students who have attended public schools. It may be of surprise to some, however, to learn that there is not much difference between public school students and non-Catholic private school students in these respects. In a major study of religion in Australia, *The Faith of Australians*, Hans Mol (1985) concluded that Catholic schools make a significant conribution to the religious development of their students. The problem with this conclusion, as with all of the associations which have been presented so far in this section, is that there is no effective control for other possible influences. The inference that Catholic school, or any other type of school, is somehow the cause of particular attitudes may be flawed because of unknown conditions which are the source of both choice of a particular school and of certain beliefs. The obvious possibility in the case of religion is that the underlying influence is family, and that religious families both send their children to church schools and inculcate religious beliefs. The evidence is conflicting. Mol, for instance, found that 80 per cent of his respondents who had attended parochial schools and who had parents who were regular church attenders, had no doubts about the existence of God. The proportions were lower – around 60–70 per cent – among Catholics, who had either no parochial education or non-church-attending parents. Unfortunately the numbers involved in Mol's study are so few that differences of this magnitude could simply be due to chance fluctuation.

Table 8.2 Political Preferences of Graduates x School Type: Percentage of Former Public, Catholic and Other Private Students preferring ALP, Liberal-National and Other Parties, 1984

	ALP	Lib.-Nat.	Other
Public	59	29	12
Catholic	49	38	13
Private	41	48	11

Source: Professions in Australia Project

In the matter of church attendance, Aitkin's political science surveys of 1969 and 1979 reveal that Catholics are considerably more frequent attenders than non-Catholics, whether or not they had attended Catholic schools. And those who had attended Catholic schools were somewhat more frequent than Catholics who had attended public schools. This certainly points to a family effect, but leaves open the question of the possibility of an additional contribution from school. Further evidence is provided by re-analysis of an interesting survey of school students in Victoria which was conducted by Poole (1983). In connection with students choosing a job, she asked about the importance of a variety of motives such as usefulness to the community, status, wages, security, interest and independence. Among these considerations was 'serving God'. Assuming that those students who gave this last item a high rating would have some religious commitment, 'serving God' can be used as an indication of religious purpose.

Not unexpectely, large proportions of students at Catholic schools rated 'serving God' as important in connection with choosing a job – 59 per cent of the 14-year-olds and 44 per cent of the 17-year-olds. Next, however, were not the students from other private schools, which also have avowedly religious objectives, but public technical schools (which recruit from a lower SES population than high schools), where 41 per cent of the 14-year-olds and 40 per cent of the 17-year-olds averred that 'serving God' was an important consideration when it came to choosing a career. In this respect other private schools were much more like public high schools, both having substantially fewer students with this particular religious motivation (30 per cent and 12 per cent in high schools, 23 per cent and 24 per cent in other private schools).

Thus we have the odd result that the officially Christian Catholic schools and the officially secular public technical schools are the ones where students appear to be most religious; and officially Christian other private schools and the officially secular public high schools are the least religious. The evidence points to family rather than school as the source of the career motive 'serving God', but it does not, of course, rule out a school influence.

The Anderson *et al.* 1982 study is the only one which attempts a rigorous statistical control of variables which might explain the connection between type of school and the socialisation outcomes which we have been considering – political, career and religion. Using regression methods to control for family, social and religious background, it was concluded that, once account is taken of family background, especially father's and mother's denomination and attendance, the statistically significant connection of school with religious feeling vanishes. The same conclsusion applies to social conservatism, which appears also to be an outcome of family. As with religious feeling, the connections with Catholic school would appear to arise because family (in particular mother's church attendance) is behind both school and values.

This conclusion is in line with the findings of Greeley (1960) and his associates in the United States and with the data of Mol in Australia (although Mol inteprets his data as if there is a Catholic school effect). Of course, we cannot conclude that school has no effect, but simply that this study and others like it have been unable to find evidence of one. At different times, with different measures, or with different samples, it is possible that connections between school and religious behaviour will be found and will remain even when allowance is made for family religion. (That of course would not prove that schools were having an effect since it always remaisns possible that there is some other influence at work but not represented in the analysis, such an influence being responsible for both school type and the apparent school effects.) Anderson *et al.* 1982 also show that the non-Catholic private school appears to influence political and career attitudes net of back-ground effects. Thus, private school remains related to political conservatism after allowance is made for effects from the father's occupation and income. Similarly, private school seems to enhance inclination to choose medicine rather than teaching, to have regard for financial rewards in making a career choice, to expect a high income in ten years' time, and to regard having been to a private school as important for career advancement.

In these respects experience at non-Catholic private schools appears to be producing and reinforcing in students values and beliefs which are not inconsistent with the position in the social order which they will attain by virtue of their family. To the extent that it is possible to generalise from the evidence from this one study, school not only advances these students who possess 'cultural capital', it also helps provide it.

Finally we turn to the socialising effects of higher education. Here we shall rely entirely on Anderson *et al.* 1982, which has the advantage of being both longitudinal and of encompassing a national sample of undergraduates, although regrettably it includes universities only, and not CAEs. The study hypothesises that there are two socialising agencies which affect students. One is the official or approved university culture which, in addition to the impartation of knowledge and skills, sets out to develop certain attitudes to knowledge, to methods of enquiry and, according to some authorities, particular liberal beliefs (Anderson and Western 1967). The other socialising agent is the professional culture for which students are preparing and which is influential through curriculum, associations with staff, journals, meetings and family connections. As undergraduate training proceeds, there is an increasing specialisation of curriculum and social life is restricted pretty much to other individuals with similar career destinies. Thus the peer group reinforces socialisation in those beliefs and dispositions associated with particular professions.

The study reached the interesting conclusion that dual socialisation occurs in most faculty groups. All students acquired values which are traditionally associated with the university experience: they became more liberal on political, social and economic issues; less dogmatic in their attitudes to knowledge; less pragmatic in problem-solving; less cynical and more interested in intellectual pursuits and high culture. There were differences between faculties and, while all changed in the same direction, the relative differences remained. Thus, for example, the engineering students stayed the most dogmatic, teachers the most disposed to intellectual interests, and the law and medical students the most politically conservative (the latter being, of course, consistent with the social background of the students and the greater likelihood of their having attended non-Catholic private schools).

At the same time, professional socialisation occurred in engineering, law and medicine, as students progressively acquired beliefs and dispositions which are characteristics of the culture of the profession for which they were preparing. In medicine students' initial idealism which students portrayed declined, and was replaced by a view that the interests of the practitioner and of the profession had to be given considerable weight in relation to client and public interest. This found expression in quite strongly held views by senior students in favour of fees for service, minimum government regulation and professional solidarity against criticism. Law and engineering students similarly came to accept their respective professional perspectives on community issues, believing for instance that in disputes with clients, and in defining the public interest, the final arbiter should be the profession itself.

Dual socialistion, by university and by profession, appears to have taken these students in contradictory directions: the university experience towards a more critical and less self-centred perspective on society, the professional influence to a strongly self-interested position. Although there is no way of testing the relative strengths of two such disparate influences, it was very clear that students' primary reference group became the profession. By the end of their training, the majority believed that professional education would be better were it conducted in a specialised professional institute rather than a multi-purpose university. The strength of both university and profession-centred attitudes which students developed, as they progressed through their training, appears not to have been connected with social origins. There was no evidence, for example, that students from working class backgrounds intended, any more than other students, to use their skills to help more disadvantaged sections of society. This does not mean that such a motive does not exist, but simply that this study found no evidence for it. Group identification is likely to be stronger where the group is more socially coherent, as is the case of Aborigines, or other ethnic subcultures.

Teachers were different. Whereas university socialisation

occurs in a similar fashion to that for engineering, law and medicine, there was little evidence of professional socialisation in the case of student teachers, all of whom were destined for secondary schools. This is accounted for by the lesser amount of specifically professional training which they received in their first two or three years of teacher education compared with the professional content in other faculties. Furthermore, the professional culture of teaching is less well defined than in other professions; indeed there are conflicting views about the nature and purposes of teaching which are not paralleled in enginering, law or medicine. There was some evidence that the socialisation of the teacher trainees was actually counter-productive from the perspective of common practices in schools. Whereas, for example, practising teachers approve a somewhat authoritarian demeanour, student teachers, who came into training with initial attitudes not dissimilar to those of practising teachers, moved by final year to more liberal and child-centred positions. Subsequent follow-up of this sample has revealed that those who have remained in the profession have changed their beliefs and behaviours to bring them into closer conformity with the dominant professional culture.

School and higher education, as well as imparting intellectual knowledge and skills, also socialise students in those norms, preferences, dispositions and beliefs which will facilitate participation in the particular subcultures, social and vocational, in which they as graduates are destined to become fully-functioning members. The precise contribution of experiences at school and university, as distinct from influences from family or other agencies outside education, remain unclear. As both social class and religious denomination are associated with particular sorts of schools, connections between school and belief may not be causal. Nevertheless, there is agreement among sociologists who have studied the question, supported with evidence from studies which attempt to control outside variables, that private schools considered as a group assist in developing conservative values. And at university level there is evidence that the experience is responsible for students acquiring, on the one hand, liberal and intellectual attitudes, and on the other, highly profession-centred perspectives about the ways in which professional services should be delivered.

At the same time as it is socialising them, the education system advances the life chances of those individuals who are able to make the correct professional choices. For bright children from poor families this facilitates upward social mobility. Private schools and higher education, as Encel asserts, make a distinctive contribution to inequality. But their contribution is to help sustain a society that is already unequal, rather than to create it. In this sense they are agents in the reproduction of a stratified social order.

Note

1. In the year between the first draft of this paper and final proof reading, two new universities have been established: a private institution, the Bond University, at the Gold Coast in Queensland, and the Curtin University of Technology in Perth, formed when the government of Western Australia renamed the Western Australian Institute of Technology. The federal government has announced that the Bond University will not receive funding and that the CUT will continue to be funded as a CAE. Other local initiatives have led to the establishment of university colleges in Darwin and the western suburbs of Sydney, each of which is almost certain to end up as an independent university.

References

Aitkin, Don (1982) *Stability and Change in Australian Politics*. Canberra: Australian National University Press.
Anderson, D.S. (1986) 'Changes in the Social Mix of Higher Education: Some Cross-Country Comparisons'. Canberra: Working Papers in Sociology, Department of Sociology, RSSS, Australian National University.
———(forthcoming) 'Values, Religious Commitment, Social Class and the Choice of Private School in Australia' in J. Kelley and C. Bean, *What Australians Think*. Sydney: Allen & Unwin.
———(forthcoming) 'The Influence of Public and Private Schools on Religious and Social Attitudes' in Jonathon Kelley and Clive Bean (eds) *Society and Politics in Australia*. Melbourne: Allen & Unwin.
———, Carpenter, P.G. Western, J.S. and Williams T.H. (1982) *Professional Socialisation in Training and Work*. Canberra: Working Papers in Sociology, Department of Sociology, RSSS, Australian National University.
——— and Western, J.S. (1967) *An Inventory to Measure Students' Attitudes*. Brisbane: University of Queensland Press.
Bell, Daniel (1973) *The Coming of Post-Industrial Society*. New York: Basic Books.
Biddle, B.J. (1979) *Role Theory: Expectations, Identities, and Behaviors*. New York: Academic Press.
Bourdieu, P. (1977) 'Cultural Reproduction and Social Reproduction' in J. Karabel and A.H. Halsey (eds), *Power and Ideology in Education*. New York: Oxford University Press.

Bowles, S. and Gintis, H. (1976) *Schooling in Capitalist America*. New York: Basic Books.

Dunn, T. (1982) 'Bias in HSC Examination Results', *The Australian Journal of Education* 26: 190–203.

Encel, S. (1970) 'Education and Society' in A.F. Davies and S. Encel (eds) *Australian Society: A Sociological Introduction*, Second Edition. Melbourne: Cheshire.

Greeley, Andrew M. and Rossi Peter H. (1966) *The Education of Catholic Americans*. Chicago: Aldine.

Halsey, A.H., Heath, A.F. and Ridge, J.M. (1980) *Origins and Destinations: Family, Class and Education in Modern Britain*. Oxford: Clarendon Press.

Jones, F.L. (1985) 'New and (Very) Old Mobility Ratios', *Social Forces* 63 (3).

———(1986) 'Access to Australian Higher Education', Seminar Paper. Canberra: Department of Sociology, RSSS, Australian National University.

Kim, Lillemor (1983) *At valja eller valjas*. Stockholm: Stockholm UHA.

Linke, R.D., Oertel, L.M. and Kelsey, N.J.M. (1985) 'Participation and Equity in Higher Education: A Preliminary Report on the Socioeconomic Profile of Higher Education Students in South Australia, 1974–1984', *Australian Bulletin of Labour* 11 (3): 131–32.

Macmillan, David S. (1963) 'The University of Sydney – The Pattern and the Public Reaction, 1850–1870', *The Australian University* 1 (1): 27–30.

Martin, Jean I. (1957) 'Marriage, the Family and Class' in A.P. Elkin (ed.) *Marriage and the Family in Australia*. Sydney: Angus & Robertson.

Mol, Hans (1985) *The Faith of Australians*. Sydney: Allen & Unwin.

Olesen, V. and Whittaker E.W. (1970) 'Critical Notes on Sociological Studies of Professional Socialization' in J.A. Jackson (ed.) *Professions and Professionalization*. Cambridge: Canbridge University Press.

Partridge, P.H. (1968) *Society, Schools and Progress in Australia*. London: Pergamon.

Poole, Millicent E. (1983) *Youth: Expectations and Transition*. London: Routledge & Kegan Paul.

Radford, W.C. and Wilkes, R.E. (1975) *School Leavers in Australia 1971–1972*. Melbourne: ACER.

Saha, L.J. (1983) 'Social Mobility or Social Reproduction? Paradigms in the Sociology of Education', *Educational Research for National Development: Policy, Planning and Politics*, Collected Papers from National Conference, Canberra.

Trow, Martin (1981) 'Comparative Perspectives on Access' in Oliver Fulton (ed.) *Access to Higher Education*. Surrey, UK: The Society for Research into Higher Education.

West, L.H.T. (1985) 'Differential Prediction of First Year University Performance for Students from Different Social Backgrounds', *Australian Journal of Education* 29: 175–87.

Williams, Trevor, Clancy, Jeff, Batten, Margaret and Girling-Butcher,

Sue (1980) *School, Work and Career: 17-Year-Olds in Australia.* Melbourne: ACER.

—— Batten, Margaret, Girling-Butcher, Sue and Clancy, Jeff (1981) *School and Work in Prospect: 14-Year-Olds in Australia.* Melbourne: ACER.

Young, Michael (1961) *The Rise of Meritocracy, 1870–2033.* Harmondsworth: Penguin Books.

Chapter Nine

Work and Technological Change in Australia

Stephen Hill

Precisely two hundred years ago, in 1785, the first Boulton and Watt condensing steam engine was installed in a textile factory at Pappelwick in Nottinghamshire, England (Derry and Williams 1960: 562). A year later, in August 1786, the King of England decreed an 'Order in Council' that New South Wales be established as Britain's new penal colony (Corbett 1973: 2). With the proximity of these two historic events, the birth of contemporary Australian society directly coincided with the technological start of the Industrial Revolution. But, by design, and by geographic distance from the centres of industrialisation, Australia was formed not as a participant, but as an outcropping of early industrialisation. Fashioned as it was from the marginal elements of an industrially strained British society, Australia's marginality to international productive life has characterised its history ever since. The product is a nation crouched in mendicant cringe to the technological fashion leaders of international capitalism.

Why this is so is not merely a result of the convict labour ward in which the nation was born and nurtured. Rather, it is a product of how it engaged in the key dynamic of progress in the international industrialising world, i.e. the harnessing and application of technical knowledge. In this enterprise, Australia's colonialist posture throughout the nineteenth century fundamentally flawed the subsequent development of the nation: its economy was based on successful primary product service to Britain; its sparce technical knowledge resources were developed from manpower crumbs dropped from Britain's industrial table; its models of science and ideologies of training emanated from Britain's imperialism.

Consequently, whilst the nation alternately basked in Britain's reflected imperialist glory, or rested languidly in the shadow of its own primary products, Australia stood still while the rest of the world industrialised. By the time the vulnerability of this complacency, along with the enforced isolation caused by World War II, permeated national consciousness, the leading edge of industrialisation had moved into an immediate dependence on new scientific discovery. For Australia to suddenly, belatedly, seek to enter the modern industrial age at that time was like seeking to board a jet airliner shortly after take-off. The shape of employment in Australia today, and its dependence on foreign control, is a direct result.

What this chapter does is to trace how this present situation in Australia has been fashioned from the link between the nation's colonial history and what drives international capitalism – technical knowledge. The argument therefore moves from the historic moment where, at the same time, the technical base for the industrial factory system was established in Britain *and* the colony of New South Wales was decreed. It moves into the present via an analysis of the necessarily deskilling consequence of technical change under capitalism, and Australia's inherited dependence on the new centres of capitalist development. The chapter therefore seeks to present *a way of understanding the relationship between employment and technology* in its historic context, rather than a detailed analysis of new high technologies, or labour market movements, or unemployment effects. Perfectly adequate analyses of these issues, at the time of writing this chapter, are presented elsewhere.

Colonialism as Cause of Marginalisation in Australian Technology

Industrialisation and Control of Technical Knowledge
What has become clear about industrial development, particularly over the last few years, is that it has progressed since the late eighteenth century as a series of overlays of inventive activity on the social/economic technical infrastructure that existed before. The industrial revolution took off on the basis of inventions in steam-power, textile manufacture and iron, and within a factory organisation system. The mid-nineteenth century economic recovery was stimulated by the development of *mobile* steam-power (railways) and steel and machine tools, and it created a

whole new infrastructure of economic opportunity for late nineteenth century development. The world economy crawled out of the 1890s Depression via the whole new infrastructure for production and distribution offered by inventions related to centralised electricity generation and the development of the chemicals industry. Finally, recovery from the 1929–33 Depression was directly related to inventions that developed the obsolescence-oriented automated factory, and allowed the development of synthetics, petro-chemicals and electronics and fuelled the 'waste' economy that emerged from World War II.[1]

Each new revitalisation of the economy depended on the structure and skills that had been developed earlier. Whilst there is debate over the direct attribution of long waves of economic recovery and decline to invention *per se* rather than other factors (van Duijn 1980, Low 1984: 355–73, Freeman 1985: 47–67), there is strong support from the work of people such as Schumpeter (1939), Mensch (1979) and Freeman (Freeman *et al.* 1982) (in particular) that new economic infrastructures *did* depend on technical innovations that 'swarmed' or 'bunched' together prior to economic take-off. This has been particularly the case where the innovations relate to core 'motive machinery', as Mandel argues,[2] which allowed the efficient *use* of developing energy sources, and thus *powered* the growth and spin-offs from a new wave of economic expansion.

The development of the main industrial economies therefore *progressed* through a layering of technical developments and abilities on those previously laid down. In this way, manufacturing *emerged* out of a previously agriculture-based infrastructure in a series of stages, and the industrial world's service sector emerged out of this. (This was not so in Australia, but I'll return to this shortly.)

The nation which led the industrial economy changed over time, for the fortunes of industrial nations were transformed as they let go or took hold of the leading edge of technical invention and application. In the nineteenth century, bemused by both empire and industrial leadership, Britain's 'machine men' remained complacent about the continuation of their international leadership, until the Great Exhibition of 1851 suddenly shocked them into recognising the evolving power of the USA. A resulting Commission sent from Britain in 1853 to inspect the American system came back applauding the extraordinary advances they had seen in the 'manufacturing principle', i.e.

the production in large numbers of standardised articles on a basis of repetition in factories characterised by ample workshop room and 'admirable system', designed to assist the progress of materials through the various stages of production.

(Burn 1930–33: 292–311)

From there on the USA surged ahead, particularly via important inventions in machine tools that were basic to standardisation and therefore mass production. Meanwhile, the British remained faithful to their dominance in iron technology and steampower. So, whilst they made some basic inventions in machine tools, and in the new steel-based technologies, electrical engineering and chemicals, the British rate of expansion slowed as British industry failed to participate in the new technologies that transformed the world economy at the end of the nineteenth century (Barraclough 1967: 50–51). Wedded to steam technology, indeed in love with the sheer aesthetics of its machines, Britain failed to notice the vast expansionary power that was offered by the emerging electricity base in industry, particularly heavy industry (Hill 1985: 36). Thus, by 1886, the USA had passed Britain as the largest steel producer, a major contribution to Britain's over-production and recession; by 1900, Germany, too, was a larger steel producer than Britain (Barraclough 1967). As for core industry, the overall economic impact on Britain was to create a major slide in its world economic dominance: in 1850, it contributed 40 per cent of the world's economic output, but this fell to only 20 per cent by 1900, and continued to slide – to 14 per cent in 1914, thence 4 per cent by 1963 (Jones 1984: 12).

A modern-day example of this same process can be seen in the emergence of Japan as a major power in the new high technologies. As at 1985, the USA is still, by far, the world leader in the international balance of payments for technology (receiving 68.2 per cent of the world's payments for new technology, and paying out only 15.6 per cent). But, as Table 9.1 shows, Japan is rapidly increasing its grasp on the world technology market: its *receipts* grew by 173 per cent in the eight years from 1972 to 1980, and payments dropped by 24 per cent (OECD 1984: Table 6: 27). What appears the most significant about the Japanese growth is that the national strategy is selective, concentrating knowledge control on to *core components in key technologies*, so the present balance of technological payments under-represents the future control of world markets that Japan is likely to enjoy. In machine tools, for example, although Japan controls only about 9 per cent of patents, the nation controls about *25 per cent* of those patents that relate to 'controlling devices', the core of the new wave of machine tool development (Preston 1985: Figure 2). The nation that controls the core applications of leading edge technology,

Table 9.1 Technological Balance of Payments in Selected OECD Countries (in millions at 1975 Prices and % of total)

Country[1]	1972			1980			% Change in Receipts	% Change in Payments
	Receipts	Payments	Balance	Receipts	Payments	Balance		
United States	3,470 (71.0)	368 (10.6)	3,102	4,905 (68.2)	584 (15.6)	4,321	+41.3	+58.7
Japan	173 (3.5)	934 (26.8)	−761	473 (6.5)	711 (19.0)	−238	+173.4	−23.9
Germany	272 (5.5)	634 (18.0)	−362	303 (4.2)	723 (19.2)	−420	+11.4	−14.0
France	303 (6.1)	462 (13.1)	−159	487 (6.7)	583 (15.4)	−96	+60.7	+38.7
United Kingdom	556 (11.2)	504 (14.2)	−52	583 (12.3)	469 (12.3)	−114	+4.9	−6.9
Italy	81 (1.6)	474 (13.3)	−393	165 (2.3)	468 (12.3)	−303	+103.7	−1.3
Austria	12 (0.2)	64 (1.8)	−52	17 (0.2)	80 (2.1)	−63	+41.7	−25.0
Finland[3]	19 (0.4)	38 (1.1)	−19	263 (3.6)	118 (3.1)	−145	+1,284.2	+210.0
Total	4,888 (100.0)	3,478 (100.0)	1,408 (100.0%)	7,196 (100.0)	3,737 (100.0)	3,460 (100%)		
Australia[2]	(1976) (9.2) (approx. 0.1)	(1976) 69.5 (approx. 2.0)	−60.3	(1981/2) 17.4 (approx. 0.2)	(1981/2) 126.0 (approx. 3.2)	−109.2	+89.1	+82.2

Sources:

[1] OECD (1984)

[2] ABS (1984b) Australian statistics are not available for the same periods as in the other OECD data. The figures for 1976 and 1981 are therefore presented separately for some comparison, and percentage of OECD payments is only approximate

[3] Finland's growth in technology balance of payments is proportionately extremely high. However, the percentage figures primarily reflect a low base in 1972 of payments and receipts

does, as industrial history demonstrates, control its own international economic position.

Australia's Colonial Dependence and Industrial Technology Development

Through this whole development of technology at the leading edge of industrial change, however, Australia sat complacently in the background watching it all go past, and borrowing from Britain's ideology well after Britain had started to slide into world manufacturing obscurity. In keeping with its colonial status and its servicing of British interests, Australia very early established the foreign-trade philosophy of 'tonnage-out'/'technology-in', and developed a tonnage-oriented technical-economic base for national development. Indeed, the resulting lack of development of a manufacturing base was a direct result of conscious imperialist strategy: in 1822–23, Commissioner Bigge, in his Reports to the British House of Commons, specifically discouraged colonial manufacture of goods which could be imported from Britain on the premiss that 'only agricultural labour was likely to reform convicts' (Corbett 1973: 6) – an ideology that only thinly disguised the vested interests of Britain's emerging bourgeoisie.[3]

Thus, Sydney's 'first mechanical engineer of substance', John Dickson, who had learnt his trade directly from James Watt, brought the colony's first steam-engine with him to Australia in 1813. But whilst this did stimulate the development of *basic* diversification in the local economy, and a basic ship-building industry (the only transport link between colonies), it did not stimulate the development of an industrial sector as Boulton and Watt's engine had in Britain twenty-eight years earlier. Local markets were very small, and Dickson, like the rest of the free settlers in the colony had their heads turned towards open plains and exports rather than indoor machine systems (*New South Wales Statistical Register 1901*: 146). Even towards the end of the steam era, by 1901, when the separate Australian colonies federated, and after the post-gold rush manufacturing surge, *41 per cent* of all Australian factories used *only* manual labour and had no power-driven machines (*New South Wales Statistical Register 1938–39*: 445).

Even as Britain's use of Australia as a gaol for its more marginal and intractable elements subsided, Australia's colonial status had a major impact on the development of industrialisation. In 1860, across New South Wales, manufacturing works covered fairly basic needs of a colony that was so remote from Britain, i.e. a small number of food and provisions manufacturing establishments, a large percentage of other provisions and household goods still being imported; a major concentration on the production of agricultural machinery (38 per cent of all factories); and ship-building and repair, the lifeline of the colony. The dominance of agricultural machinery manufacture remained right through the nineteenth century, accounting for 70 per cent of industrial establishments by 1876.

Basic engineering factories grew up in association with agricultural machinery production and railways: by 1876, 158 factories were operating as iron and tin works; iron, brass and copper foundries; lead works; machinists'; engineers'; and type foundries, compared with 119, nine years earlier. Moreover, the manufacturing economy was starting to diversify as it moved into the 1880s. On the one hand the colony was now large enough to allow an adequate consumer market; for example, the number of coach and wagon manufacturers had doubled over the seven years preceding 1875. On the other hand, sophisticated surgical and scientific instruments started to be manufactured by one firm in 1873 (the number of such establishments rising to seven by the turn of the century) (*New South Wales Statistical Registers 1860, 1861, 1863, 1867, 1876, 1895, 1901*). But whilst these changes reflected the development of both basic and sophisticated technical skills as well as a local consumer demand, the economy still remained wedded to agriculture and to providing services to a relatively wealthy, largely urbanised population.[4]

This lack of development of an industrial technology base had a multiplier effect. Namely, when major core technologies were imported – like those used for railways and, later, electricity – their impact, whilst dramatic, was nowhere near as deep as in the USA and Europe. The developing heavy industrial base simply was not there for them to bed into, and stimulate.

The former core technology, railways, was introduced into Australia from 1852, not long after their European application, when B.H. Babbage arrived to build the first steam-powered railway in the colony of South Australia, from Adelaide to Port Adelaide (Buchanan 1982). From there on, the rail system expanded very rapidly across all states, particularly in the post-gold rush period from 1870 to 1890 (from 1,030 to 10,394 miles of track across the Australian continent).[5] But it developed an inter-connected industrial base (as it did in America),[6] less than it provided a means of getting crops to seaports, imports from one colony to the next, and people between the isolated crities. The enormous boom in this period was based on primary production and urban construction, not on railways-led manufacturing.

The later core technology, electricity, appeared to have an immediate effect on manufacturing industry when it started to disseminate into industry at the turn of the twentieth century. In New South Wales in 1893, for example, before electricity, 96 per cent of all installed energy-producing machinery (by horsepower) was powered by steam, and the rest by gas and water; by 1895, this percentage had dropped to 93 per cent, remaining stable until 1901 when electricity generation first started to be introduced. At that time, nearly 10 per cent of the energy used in the 'heat, light and power' industry was still produced by *water* power. Just five years later however, in 1906, electricity was a rising force, and steam power accounted for 84 per cent of machinery power (dropping to 81 per cent three years later); there had been a growth in the percentage of power generated from *electricity generating stations* from 11 per cent in 1901 to 32 per cent, which then continued to rise to 53 per cent by the start of World War II. But, most importantly, directly coinciding with the five-year growth in electricity application there had been a growth in the total installed energy capacity for industry of 270 per cent. The effects on manufacturing industry were immediate. In 1901, 41 per cent of all establishments used *only* manual labour and no power-driven machinery; by 1906, this had fallen to 35 per cent – (thence 29 per cent in 1911, and finally, 5 per cent in 1939). Between 1901 and 1906 there was a 50 per cent increase in the number of manufacturing factories, accompanied by a 64 per cent increase in employment in secondary industry (*New South Wales Statistical Registers 1892, 1895, 1904, 1938–39*).

Thus, the early twentieth century take-off in manufacturing industry was facilitated by centralised electricity production. *But*, without the prior industrial development, and without the orientation to *use* heavy industry, take-off in manufacturing followed its earlier light industrial path into wider diversification for consumers rather than heavy industry development. The contrast to what was happening in Germany and the USA was enormous. Both had been strongly expanding and concentrating in the heavy industry base that Australia was lacking. Krupps, the steel manufacturer in Germany, employed 16,000 people by 1873, rising through the early twentieth century, with the advent of electricity, to 70,000 in 1914, a pattern of growth and concentration that was similarly reflected in France's Schneider-Creusot, Britain's Vickers Armstrong, and the American Carnegie corporations (Barraclough 1967: 51). The labour force at Krupps in 1901 exceeded the total manufacturing labour force of New South Wales. Meanwhile Australia was importing steel, trade that accounted for 5 per cent of total imports in 1901, and these were imports across enormous distances from the USA and Europe. As an import, steel was only surpassed by machine tools and implements (13 per cent); textiles and dress materials (26 per cent); 'drinks, narcotics and stimulants' (11 per cent); and staple 'vegetable substances' (6 per cent) (Coghlan 1901: Table 93: 32), imports that as a pattern reveal an economy that was fundamentally dependent on European and American society for lifestyle, technology and heavy industry, the substance of the twentieth century economy. Australia was merely playing on the edge of the development of twentieth century industrialisation.

As a result, whilst Europe and the USA were vying with one another for industrial dominance, Australia was basking in the glory of its agricultural wealth, living off primary industry in cities that were largely oriented to services, not industrial development. Thus, as Barry Jones observed, Australia jumped across the development of a manufacturing *base* to become the first 'service-based' economy in the world. Unlike Britain, the USA and Western Europe, manufacturing was *never* dominant in the employment of the Australian labour force; instead, as Figure 9.1 shows, services replaced agriculture to become the largest employer towards the end of the nineteenth century, some thirty years before the manufacturing sector surpassed the agricultural sector occupations as the second largest employment source.[7]

The consequence is very important indeed. The relative predominance of primary and tertiary industries led to an economy based on relatively low-skilled enterprise. When the *international* economy *later* crossed from manufacturing to service sector dominance, this sector was linked into a highly developed technical infrastructure. This was not the case in Australia, where the predominant skill of the nineteenth century service industry was household management (domestic servants constituting 16 per cent of the entire 1891 non-primary producer labour force (*Official Yearbook of the Commonwealth of Australia 1924*: 938, *1911*: 1284–85).

Australia's Colonial Dependence and the Development of Technological Skill Resources

In parallel with the lack of development of manufacturing industry in colonial Australia, there was a very poor development of higher-level technological skills, such as those which would be necessary for the independence and take-off of any post-nineteenth century industries. Again, this was a direct product of Australia's colonial obedience to British (educational) ideology.

During the nineteenth century, Australia drew its population of engineers almost exclusively from Britain. From Angus Buchanan's analysis of the *Australian Dictionary of Biography*, 71 people could be classed as engineers in Australia during the period from 1788 to 1850, and all but 2 were immigrants from the British Isles; and of the 138 listed for the period between 1851 and 1890,

Figure 9.1 Change over Time in Occupations within the Australian Labour Force

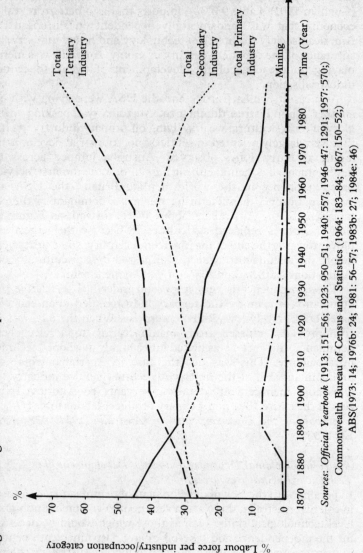

Sources: Official Yearbook (1913: 151–56; 1923: 950–51; 1940: 557; 1946–47: 1291; 1957: 570;)
Commonwealth Bureau of Census and Statistics (1964: 183–84; 1967: 150–52;)
ABS(1973: 14; 1976b: 24; 1981: 56–57; 1983b: 27; 1984c: 46)

whilst 6 per cent had emigrated from other major industrialising nations than Britain, i.e. the USA, Germany and France, still 80 per cent were British-born. Thus, as Buchanan concludes, 'for all practical purposes, Australian engineering was an extension of British engineering' (Buchanan 1982: 56). These results, being based on biographies, are indicative rather than comprehensive.

Some independence started to emerge as engineering opportunities appeared in the late nineteenth century and Australia started to organise engineering as a profession and train its own engineers. The Engineering Association of New South Wales was founded in 1870, and the Victorian Institute of Engineers in 1885; university courses began at the University of Melbourne in the 1860s and at the University of Sydney in the 1880s. Engineering education grew very slowly, however: by 1915 only 200 engineers were enrolled in university engineering courses in Australia (compared with nearly 1,000 doctors and 1,300 Arts students) (Brown 1949: 151) and the low level of concentration continued. As Brown concluded shortly after World War II (Brown 1949: 152):

> except for expansion brought about by its importance in time of war [engineering] education has plodded along at much the same level between the war periods of 1918 and 1939.

Meanwhile, across the Pacific in the USA over the same period, the number of professional engineers had escalated by a factor of *10* between 1890 and 1938 – from 25,000 to 250,000 people (Rochlin 1974: 150–51). Australia had established independence from importing British engineers, but engineering itself was not treated as a central concern to Australia's development.

Part of the reason clearly lies in the colonially-inspired industrial structure of the nation. More importantly however, was Australia's emulation of British educational practices at a time when the mother country was losing its grip on the technological edge of world industrial competition.

In Britain, 'technical education' was very slow to develop from its early origins in the Glasgow Mechanics Institute of 1804, due to a lack of official support and a general apathy on the part of the hard-nosed 'machine men' of industry to science and technical training. Universities, on the other hand, were intentionally unconnected to anything as base and practical as industry and commerce. They were largely theological in character and hostile to the new philosophies of science. Consequently, it was not until 1894 that *mechanical* science (engineering) was introduced at Cambridge.

Whilst technological education was accorded low prestige and was disconnected from higher education in nineteenth century Britain, this was not the case in Germany. Great prominence had been given there to technological education since the early days of industrialisation. It was also not the case in the USA, where technological faculties were given prominence at various universities from their establishment between 1850 and 1870; where, even by 1938 (when Britain had had some time to develop engineering education), the USA had *twice as many* full-time engineering *staff* in universities as Britain had *students*, and was spending five times per head of population the outlay of Britain on engineering education (Brown 1949: 143). The effect on Britain was to impoverish the knowledge base from which it could retain a grip on the leading edge of industrial development, as industrial leadership increasingly depended on the application of advanced scientific knowledge. Although Britain had, since the 1850s, made some very important industrial inventions relevant to late nineteenth century industrial transformation, the nation did not have the structure or engineering resources to apply them before their international competitors. This reinforced the decline from material greatness in 1885 to severe industrial shortcomings, revealed when World War I's conflict with Germany undermined British complacency (Brown 1949: 142).

The effect in Australia of *copying* British educational philosophy was equally disastrous, but the cost did not become apparent until a quarter of a century later, when World War II isolated the nation from its technological sources. When a *National Register* of professional engineers was developed towards the end of the War, it was discovered that 50 per cent of engineers had neither a university degree nor a technical college diploma (Brown 1949: 149). In educational terms they were literally getting by as if they were still in the early nineteenth century. Consequently, as Brown, Professor of Electrical Engineering at the New South Wales University of Technology (later, the University of New South Wales) concluded in 1945:

> As in England, we have failed to realise the importance of soundly trained men in industry, and have failed, therefore, to make full use of scientific developments. While America and continental countries have been training more and more engineers and industry has been making full use of their knowledge, we have stood at a standstill.
>
> (Brown 1949: 152)

The Marginalisation of Technological Invention

From the discussion and evidence so far it is hard to escape the conclusion that the poverty of Australia's industrial and technological skills can be directly attributed to national obeisance to Britain's imperialist intentions and ideologies. Thus, where technical invention occurred in Australia, it often died because the knowledge-base to adopt and bed it into industry simply did not exist. Shortly before World War II for example, one-third of the 4,000 or so engineers in Australia were employed in private industry; the rest were primarily working on government public works programmes (Moore 1939a: 259–62, 1939b: 331–34). Add to this the relatively small size of Australian markets, and distances from the main metropolises of the world, and local innovation faced very considerable difficulties: an arid industrial knowledge-base and efficient higher scale international competition, often resulting in Australian inventions either being bought out by international firms or just not ever quite making it into successful production.

It is not as though Australians have not proven themselves to be inventive. The nation's history is characterised by some quite extraordinary genius, often with a very particular national flavour to it – inventions that have an 'improvising-battler-against-the-environment' style about them. This was particularly demonstrated in the quite extensive inventiveness Australians such as John Ridley and James Morrow during the nineteenth century applied to agricultural machinery that would work in Australia's harsh climate.[8] An ideal type of the Australian inventor was John Robertson Duigan, who built the first successful Australian aeroplane in 1910. Working from a book on the principles of flight and a photograph of the Wright Brothers' plane, Duigan built a working aircraft in a makeshift corrugated iron lean-to on his property at Mia Mia, eighty miles from Melbourne. He had to improvise most of the components and many of the tools; the airframe was made from ash and red pine, with piano wire for stays; old steel bands from wool bales were used for sheet metal fittings. He only gave up flying his plane and dveloping it further when he ascended high enough for him to realise that he didn't know how to fly, and went off to flying school in Britain (Brogden 1960: 20–33).

Indeed, the takeover of Australian inventiveness can be seen in the early history of patenting in the colony of New South Wales. The system was established in 1854, following the first Patent Act, two years earlier. In 1855, 3 patents were registered, but this number grew steadily to 32 new registrations in 1870, 89 in 1880, and 203 by 1886. By 1887, 408 patents were registered in the colony, 78 per cent of which were registered by Australians, either from New South Wales or another Australian colony. At this stage, overseas interests started to impinge more heavily on the New South Wales patent system, so that by 1890, only 67 per cent of patents were registered by Australians, and by 1895, 62 per cent. This was the start of a trend that continued in parallel with overseas industrial development, the percentage dropping to 58 per cent in 1900, thence to 56 per cent in 1903.

This trend is but another example of the way that the intrusion of foreign interests into control of Australian technology coincided directly with the international late nineteenth century industrialising leap forward. To look further at the reflections in Australia, in 1893, for example, 17 patents were taken out in New South Wales related to the new industrial energy source, 'electricity and magnetism'; just two years later, the number had nearly doubled, shortly before the major revolutionising effects of electricity were introduced into the Australian economy. Furthermore, the patent records at this time also show the start of the shift in power over technical know-how from Britain to the USA as it commenced to take over international leadership of technological development. In 1887, 48 per cent of New South Wales patents registered to overseas interests were for British interests, and 19 per cent for American ones; by 1895 only 36 per cent of New South Wales patents were registered for British interests, whilst 25 per cent were registered for American. This trend continues up to the present day, so that in 1981–82 Australia paid 3.5 times as much for American based technical know-how as it did for British (*New South Wales Statistical Register 1893 1895 1901*, ABS 1984c: Table 18: 23).

The fact that it was not inventiveness that held Australia's technological development back, but the industrial system, is classically shown in attempts by Australian inventor/engineers to enter the automobile market. One of the very first successful automobiles in the world was developed by an Australian foundry apprentice from Melbourne, Herbert Austin. However, this was after he had returned from the colony to Britain in 1893, having been befriended by the car maker F.Y. Wolseley (Buchanan 1982: 55). Then, Colonel Harley Tarrant and Howard Lewis built a two-cylinder powered car in Melbourne in 1899; Felix Caldwell invented a four-wheel-drive power train in Adelaide in 1907; and William Wege designed a radical valveless petrol engine which he displayed at South Australia's first Automotive Show in 1920. But the Australian market was dominated by imported automobiles, particularly Henry Ford's T Model (Stubbs 1972: 1–29, Bloomfield 1978: 256). It was not until World War II had forced the establishment of a heavy industry base in Australia that it was

practicable to develop mass-produced locally manufactured automobiles. By that time American car manufacturers were firmly
entrenched in the Australian economy, so the Holden, 'Australia's
car', was designed by American engineers according to American
automotive thinking, and produced for American profit.

Technical invention in Australia thus tended to be an improvis-
ing response to the nation's distance from the technology centres of
the world, and often involved considerable ingenuity. Not only,
however, was it alienated from industrial enterprise because of
industry's skills-deficient base, but it was also alienated from the
development of scientific research in the country. The hand of
British imperialism had been laid on that enterprise, too.

The Marginalisation of Scientific Research

The Australian scientific research system was fashioned towards
improving agricultural and pastoral productivity; it has never been
linked into the development of manufacturing activity. This
orientation is directly in line with the imperialist models that
informed its inception and growth. Sagasti and Guenero observe
the process whereby imperial science was used as a means of
controlling peripheral colonialist economic development for the
advantage of the imperial metropolises: science was a means by
which 'dependent economies were manipulated to increase
colonial integration through world markets and in which the
extension of knowledge, through education, remains dependent on
the metropolis' (Sagasti and Guenero 1982). As Roy MacLeod
continues, referring specifically to Australia, as a result, the
objectives and programmes of research were 'determined by the
interests of the imperial power' (Macleod 1982).

In keeping with a colonialist model, Australia's research effort,
oriented largely towards agriculture, was primarily government-
funded. Very little effort was put into promoting technology for
industry (whilst in the late nineteenth to early twentieth century,
the American and German governments provided extensive patronage for industry (Briggs 1974: 95–97). Thus, when the Council
for Scientific Research (CSIR) was established in 1926 to promote
Australian science and its application, it was based on the British
research model as a centrally-funded organisation, was oriented
towards agriculture (but not agricultural technology), and, following British research ideology, emphasised freedom of scientists
from government control. The fierce defence of scientific freedom
by CSIR's founding Chairman, Sir David Rivett, set the organisation on its path towards scientific excellence, but disconnection
from application. The Commonwealth Scientific and Industrial
Research Organisation (CSIRO), as it has now become, holds the

centre stage in Australia's present scientific effort, but whilst having made some important contributions to agricultural productivity, through such things as improved seed varieties, it has done little for agricultural technology, minerals exploitation technology, or manufacturing industry.

Australia's knowledge-generating capacity in the 1980s has been fashioned from its colonial seeds, the explicit belief in research freedom, and the associated expectation that undirected research excellence *per se* would one day spin off into positive economic growth. Moreover, until the recent establishment of Sirotech as a commercialising arm of CSIRO, and the development of science and technology 'parks' in several Australian states, it assumed that the bridge between knowledge creation in government, and application in industry, is an easy one to cross. No such assumptions have ever characterised the research systems of any of the major industrial nations of the twentieth century – the USA, Germany and Japan particularly. These nations primarily conduct their research and development (R & D) in industry, where it is embedded in a framework of expectations that emphasise commercial development relevance rather than research excellence.[9] As Figure 9.2 shows, over 77 per cent of research and development expenditure in Australia is in government or higher education institutions, i.e. remote from industrial demand and application. In this sense, Australia is more similar to agriculture-based development countries than it is to the industrialised First World.

When, under enforced isolation, the nation finally did realise that an integrated and heavy industry base had to be developed, government aimed the development of manufacturing industry primarily at replacing products that were imported. With a poorly-connected science base, and the need for a relatively uncompetitive production system (marketing for small internal markets), little appropriate research and development was either available or required (Johnston 1983: 10). The technologies could be imported. Furthermore, from the lowered stance which resulted from crouching behind high trade barriers there was little incentive to *develop* the capacity to compete, whether in terms of price or quality, for export markets. Consequently, whilst the USA, Germany, Japan and the rest of the industrial world put massive investment into new technology for the post-War leading edge high technology industries – petro-chemicals, synthetics and electronics – Australian research concentrated on isolated scientific excellence; and managers, government officials and politicians became increasingly confirmed in a generally conservative attitude to the need for new ideas and products.

Australia's relative deficit in knowledge resources, compared

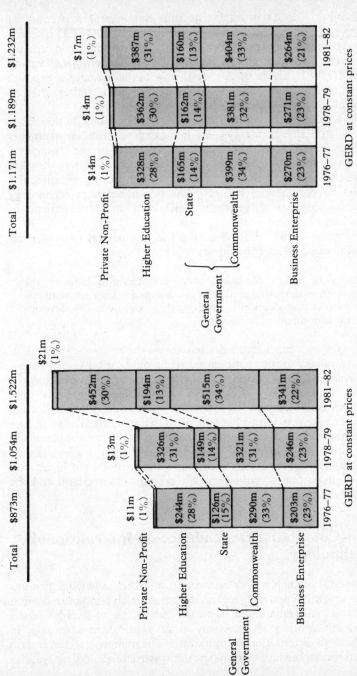

Figure 9.2 Gross Expenditure on Research and Experimental Development (GERD) carried out in Australia 1976–77, 1978–79 1981–82 by Sector at Current and Constant (average 1979–80) Prices   *Source:* ABS, 1984b

with other OECD countries, is thus not merely a product of relative size of expenditures (1.05 per cent of total OECD research and development expenditure in 1981, versus 46.33 per cent for the USA. 17.04 per cent for Japan, and 9.87 per cent for Germany (OECD 1981: Table 3: 20). It is also fundamentally a product of its orientation towards a colonialist past rather than a technologically-competitive future.

As a result, although commercialised innovations do flow from the Australian science system, including scientific instruments such as atomic absorption spectrophotometry, or the 'Interscan' airport system and 'Sinrock' for buying nuclear waste, they are more the exception than the rule, and often have great difficulty achieving commercial success. The occasional high technology success obscures a generally low level of development of technology.

Johnston (1985: 104) observing the commercial fruit of Australian science thus concludes:

> under the present conditions of the manufacturing industry, the research system irrespective of its deservedly high international reputation, can contribute relatively little to the effective development of technology in Australia.

This is shown most forcefully in data on the relative contribution of Australians to international scientific publication versus patented knowledge. As Table 9.2 shows, Australia ranks ninth in the world in frequency of scientific publication, but owns only 0.65 per cent of the world's patented knowledge. The publication rate per patent is somewhat similar to that of Canada, also an heir of British colonialism. From a comparison of the ratio of patents in the USA per year to the number of publishing *authors*, again, Australia fares very badly, with a ratio one-tenth that of Japan, and one-sixth to one-seventh that of Germany, Switzerland and the USA (Hurst 1985).

Neo-Colonialist Dependence on International Technology

The result of such a poor connection between knowledge generation, inventive activity, technological skills and industrialisation is that as Australia embarks on the last couple of decades of the twentieth century its economy is at a major disadvantage in relation to international capitalism. The nation has never laid down the succeeding technological infrastructures and capabilities

Table 9.2 Patents owned by Country (Absolute Figures and as Percentage of Patents owned Overseas, 1979)

Country	Patents owned by Country			Ranking of Countries according to Number of Publishing Scientists		
	Number	World Total	Rank Position – Patent Ownership	Number of International Publications	Infra Rank	Number of Publications per Patent
Unites States	47,636	37.39	1	108,780	1	2.18
Germany FR	28,189	18.58	2	16,408	4	0.58
Japan	16,101	10.61	3	14,265	6	0.88
France	10,458	6.89	4	15,102	5	1.45
United Kingdom	9,315	6.14	5	25,005	2	2.68
Switzerland	8,745	5.76	6			
Netherlands	4,861	3.20	7			
Italy	4,635	3.05	8	4,691	10	1.01
Sweden	4,035	1.66	9			
Soviet Union	2,406	1.59	10	24,418	3	1.01
Canada	1,806	1.19	11	11,907	7	6.59
Austria	1,542	1.02	12			
Belgium	1,376	0.91	13			
Germany DDR	1,193	0.79	14			
Hungary	1,067	0.70	15			
Australia	982	0.65	16	5,341	9	5.44
India	46	0.03	38	6,000	8	149.56

Sources: D.J. Frame *et al.* (1977) 'The Distribution of World Science', *Social Studies in Science* I, and World International Property Organisation, 1980

Table 9.3 Imports and Exports 1969–82

Year	Category	High Technology Components*		Food and Live Animals Chiefly for Food		Crude Materials, Inedible (except fuels)		Total
		$	% of Total	$	% of Total	$	% of Total	$ of Total
1969–70	Exports	479,955	11.61	1,234,516	29.35	1,296,159	33.76	3,009,630
	Imports	2,219,439	4.62	139,851	0.11	247,245	0.18	2,606,535
			57.18		3.69		6.37	
1971–72	Exports	—		1,728,440	35.32	1,339,585	27.33	3,068,025
	Imports	—		159,791	0.09	218,694	0.16	378,475
					3.99		5.46	
1973–74	Exports	—		2,179,310	31.52	2,220,973	31.12	4,400,283
	Imports	—		236,728	0.11	414,951	0.19	651,679
					3.89		6.81	
1975–76	Exports	1,299,444	13.85	3,089,860	32.98	2,578,356	27.52	6,967,660
	Imports	4,890,111	3.75	274,811	0.09	387,381	0.15	5,552,303
			59.84		3.33		4.70	
1977–78	Exports	1,741,314	14.19	3,670,728	29.92	3,266,404	26.44	8,678,446
	Imports	6,550,022	3.96	531,270	0.14	476,954	0.15	7,558,246
			58.65		4.76		4.27	
1979–80	Exports	1,765,908	9.36	6,300,422	33.39	5,569,288	29.51	13,635,618
	Imports	9,731,417	5.51	655,203	0.10	698,605	0.13	11,085,225
			60.00		4.04		4.31	
1980–81	Exports	2,116,131	11.03	6,129,622	31.96	5,761,390	30.04	14,007,143
	Imports	11,855,424	5.60	654,819	0.11	763,728	0.13	13,273,971
			63.51		3.45		4.03	

1981–82	Exports	2,218,700	11.33	5,802,813	29.63	5,822,362	29.73	13,843,875
	Imports	14,769,413	6.66	732,152	0.13	769,483	0.13	16,261,048
			64.18		3.10		3.34	

* This category includes:
Petroleum, petroleum products and related materials
Organic chemicals
Inorganic chemicals
Medicinal and pharmaceutical products
Explosives and pyrotechnic products
Artifical resins and plastic materials, and cellulose esters and ethers
Chemical materials and products (not elsewhere stated)
Machinery and transport equipment
Professional, scientific and controlling instruments and apparatus (not elsewhere stated)
Photographic apparatus, equipment and supplies and optical goods not elsewhere stated, watches and clocks

Source:
[1] Data for 1969–70, 1975–76 to 1978–79 is taken from ABS 1980b
[2] Data for 1970–71 to 1974–75 is taken from ABS 1976a
[3] Data for 1979–81 to 1981–82 is taken from ABS 1983

Figure 9.3 Ratio of Imports/Exports per Selected Trade Category, 1969–70 to 1981–82

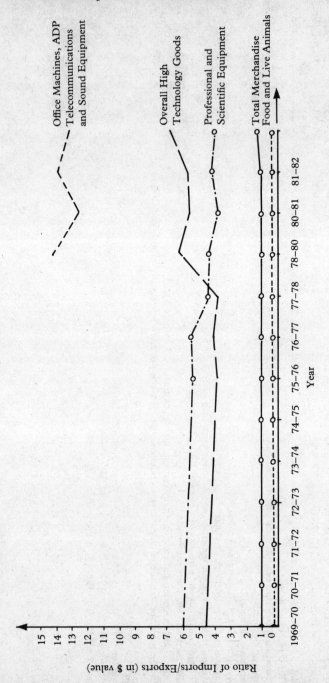

that are pre-conditions for the successful development and rapid application of high technologies today. The nation is therefore fundamentally dependent upon new technologies supplied from elsewhere, and also dependent on the neo-colonialising influences of the latest technological fashion leaders.

The comparative position of Australia is revealed very clearly in the recent calculation by the OECD of relative technological dependence of OECD countries, assessed as a ratio of the nation's technological payments to research and development expenditures of business enterprise. Of the 15 OECD nations, Australia is the *fourth most dependent*, being surpassed in technological dependency only by Portugal, Spain and Finland (OECD 1981: Table 8: 29). Australian companies pay to the USA alone 26 times the amount for technical know-how that is paid to other Australian interests (OECD 1984: Table 18: 23). Furthermore, as an economic presence in the world market, Australia is still back in its colonial history as a primary producer, 74 per cent of the nation's exports being of relatively unprocessed agricultural and mineral products.[10] Low technology exports therefore pay for the nation's high technology dependence, in much the same way that sheep and gold paid for the imported lifestyle of nineteenth century Australia. As Table 9.3 shows, those trade goods which embody a high technology component constituted 64 per cent of Australia's *imports* in 1981–82 (compared with 11 per cent of exports), having steadily risen as a percentage of imports since the start of the 1970s. Meanwhile, an approximately equivalent percentage of *export* earnings (59 per cent) was provided by food and live animals, and 'crude [inedible] materials' alone – both being trade sectors that embody a minimal knowledge or technology component in the commodities. However, perhaps the most useful indicator of the balance of overseas technological contribution against Australian technological capacity is shown in Figure 9.3 where the *ratio* of imports to exports per trade category is graphed. Here there is a consistent very high import dependence on high technology goods, (13 to 1), particularly in the area of office machines, automatic data processing, sound and telecommunications equipment – the technology most directly relevant to growth in the service sector labour force.[11] The negative effect on Australia's trade balance in technology-based products is demonstrated in the continuous downward trend shown in Figures 9.4a and 9.4b.

The most insidious impact of Australia's colonially-inspired technology deficit is not, however, just on the nation's trade balances. It is more in the position of *double jeopardy* that has followed from not being in charge of technological change ourselves. Australia's position is *jeopardised* on the one hand because

Table 9.4 Research, Technology Purchases and Foreign Control by Industry Sector

ASIC CODE	Description	Total R & D Expenditure	R & D Intensity (Enterprises)[1]	Technical Know-how Payments ($,000) — Total Payments	Payments within Australia	Total Payments Overseas	% Overseas Payments Made to Related Enterprises	% Foreign Control (Value Added)[2]	Value added as % Total Manufacturing	Value added per Firm ($m)	Turnover ($m)	R & D Turnover	Technical Know-how Turnover	Total Knowledge Expenditure/ Turnover
Manufacturing														
21	Total food beverages & tobacco	13,124	2.9	14,864	n.a.[3]	n.a.	n.a.	31.5	19.1	1.73	18,507.0	0.071	0.080	0.151
23–24	Total textiles, clothing & footwear	785	0.4	1,398	0	1,398	86.0	28.7	7.0	0.83	5,064.5	0.015	0.030	0.045
25	Total wood, wood products & furniture	1,719	0.2	1,201	0	1,201	93.5	7.8	5.4	0.41	3,981.8	0.043	} 0.011	} 0.078
26	Total paper, paper products, printing & publishing	5,255	0.3					15.6	9.9	1.05	6,484.5	0.067		
2753	Synthetics, resins & rubber	2,646	14.5	n.a.	n.a.	n.a.	n.a.	93.8				0.081	n.a.	
2654–2755	Organic, inorganic industrial chemicals	22,046	14.3	n.a.	n.a.	n.a.	n.a.	81.3	1.0	4.69	1,058.7	0.250	n.a.	
2763	Pharmaceutical & veterinary	13,528	20.0	9,547	n.a.	n.a.	n.a.	74.5	n.a.	n.a.	n.a.	n.a.	n.a.	n.a.
(27–2763) 27	Total chemical petroleum & coal products	53,114	12.4	36,316	405	35,911	82.9	75.2	9.1	3.68	916.8	1.475	1.041	2.516
28	Total non-metallic mineral products	4,826	1.4	5,577	0	5,577	87.8	18.1	5.0	0.91	3,704.6	0.130	0.150	0.280
29	Total basic metal	27,359	4.5	7,603	n.a.	n.a.	n.a.	47.3	8.0	4.56	9,431.4	0.290	0.082	0.371
31	Total fabricated metal products	6,729	1.1	3,277	244	3,032	19.7	14.7	8.5	0.62	6,424.1	0.105	0.051	0.151
32	Total transport equipment	31,933	2.3	10,835	134	10,701	63.9	51.6	10.6	2.53	8,040.8	0.397	0.135	0.532

ASIC	Industry												
334	Total photographic professional & scientific equipment	5,083	4.5)	11,476)	190)	11,476)	77.0	51.9	1.0	0.86	611.2	0.832) 0.831)	1.060
3351–3352	Radio & TV receivers, audio equipment & electronic equipment	26,786	13.5)	n.a.)	n.a.)	n.a.	n.a.	3351: 70.1 60.1 3352: 44.1	1.86	2.02	1,175.7	2.278) 0.831)	n.a.
335	Total appliances & electrical equipment	37,208	9.6)						6.2	1.70	4,472.3		
336	Total industrial machinery & equipment	14,654	4.0	3,215	29	3,187	62.5	30.2	5.0	0.69	3,501.6	0.418	0.092	0.510
33	Total other machinery & equipment	56,945	5.6	14,881	219	14,662	80.7	39.1	12.1	1.01	8,585.0	0.663	0.173	0.836
34	Total miscellaneous machinery	7,326	1.6	3,253	n.a.	n.a.	n.a.	30.3	5.1	0.72	3,972.4	0.184	0.082	0.266
C.	Total Manufacturing	209,116	1.9	99,204	2,193	97,010	74.08	34.6	100.00	1.12	82,320.6	0.254	0.120	0.374

Mining and Other Industries

F.	Wholesale & Retail Trade	11,912	0.1	13,076	96	12,980	95.35						
B,D–F, G–I,	Mining & Other, n.e.c.	119,479	n.a.	14,304	200	14,095	65.12						
B,D–I,	Total Mining & Other Industry	131,391	n.a.	27,380	305	27,075	79.62						
	Total All Industries[4]	340,507	0.2	126,584	2,499	124,085	75.28						

[1] Number of enterprises that carried out R&D expressed as a percentage of the total number of enterprises in the industry

[2] 'Foreign control' includes direct foreign control, joint control, naturalised and networking categories

[3] Not available

[4] This category excludes ASOC Division A

Sources:

ABS *Foreign Ownership and Control of the Manufacturing Industry, Australia, 1982–83*, Canberra: ABS Catalogue No. 5322.0 (1985), Table 5

ABS *Research and Experimental Development, Business Enterprises, Australia, 1981–82*, Canberra: ABS Catalogue No.8109.0 (1984), Tables 3 and 17

Figure 9.4a Trade in Technology-based Products (Australia)

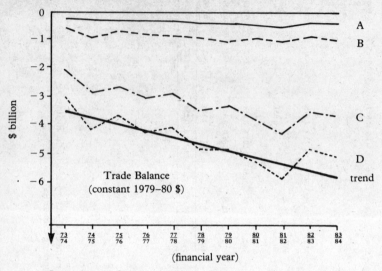

Legend
A = Instruments: div.87,88 of SITC rev.2
B = Chemicals: div.51,52,53,54,58,59 as above
C = Machinery: div.71,72,74,75,76,77 as above
D = Total 'Technology Based Products', i.e. A + B + C

Figure 9.4b Trade Deficit per capita (constant 1979–80 $)

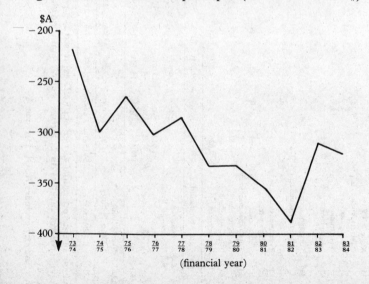

Source: Healy 1985

, in the leading edge industries, the nation must continue to import both the technologies and products as well as pay for the royalty privileges of using foreign technologies in Australia. These costs can only continue to increase.[12] The national position is *doubly jeopardised* because it also sold out its *ability to compete* on the international technology markets. This happened through the way that foreign interests were able to gain control of the leading edge of knowledge-*generating* resources in the country.

The story of how this happened is a direct sequel to the technological marginality inherited from the nation's colonial history. To follow the nation's post-war import substitution and industrialisation strategy meant inviting in foreign control as down-payment on imported capital and technology. The nation simply did not have the technological capacity to jump into a major new industrial infrastructure. The effect was strongest in the development of the minerals industry, where very heavy machinery was required to exploit massive potential export wealth. Foreign ownership increased steadily from after World War II to cover 57.8 per cent of the industry during the 1970s, along with very high levels of concentration.[13] Foreign control also significantly penetrated the manufacturing sector, reaching most deeply into the heart of industry where the demand for sophisticated technology is the highest. Therefore, whereas the overall level of foreign control in Australian manufacturing industry stood at 34.6 per cent by 1981, as Table 9.4 shows, the level of control in the very high technology sectors was radically higher: 93.8 per cent in the 'synthetic resins and rubber' sector, 81.3 per cent in the 'organic and inorganic chemicals' sector, 74.5 per cent in the pharmaceuticals sector, and 70.1 per cent in the 'radio, TV and electronic equipment' sector (ABS 1976c: Table 5).

To establish the importance of this observation, and to explore its consequences for the direction that modern international capital is likely to take Australia, we need, as before, to look back to where industrialisation began as an international force, for it is here that the basic principles were laid down. In this exploration, we therefore return to the point in history where Karl Marx first saw the importance of the shift in the *concept* of labour that had accompanied the advent of industrial capitalism and its technological system. As an aside, to set this exploration in the context of what was happening in Australia, it should be noted that at the time Marx was writing about the mainstream of British industrial repression, 57,000 of the most marginal elements of this emerging industrial society had been shipped to Australia to create its colonial servicing of the very process that Marx observed.

What Marx saw was that labour had become chained to the

Figure 9.5 Research Intensity in Manufacturing Industry by Foreign Control

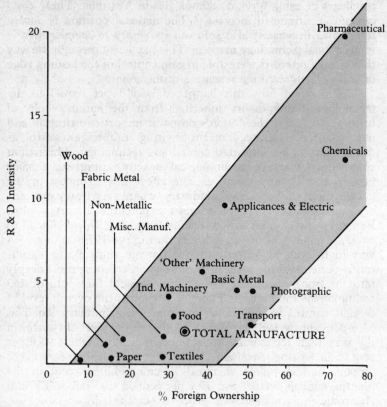

Figure 9.6 Research and Development vs Technological Know-how

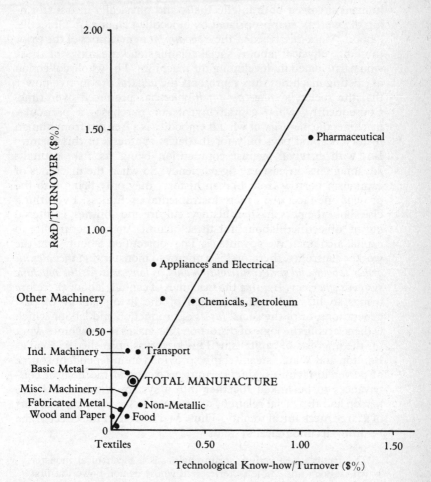

technological system, chained in slavery to the class that controlled this system. 'Living labour', he wrote, that sensual activity of humans involved both intellectually and physically in transforming the world, 'is appropriated by objectified labour.'[14] 'Objective labour', Marx described as the *embodiment* in machines of the prior thinking, physical labour, social relations and meanings of those who participated in developing the machines. The whole collection of existing machines thus represents the general productive power that the society's *collective intelligence* has produced over time. Consequently, when capital invents or purchases a particular machine, the majority of what it embodies is a free gift from human history. Capital pays only for the latest synthesis of this history. But with survival against competition being its risk, capital's advantage lies in cost-saving efficiency. So when the machines of capitalism borrow from human history, they only bring into the present one facet of it: mere instrumental usefulness. Everything else about the person, their history, culture and abilities, is filtered out of 'objectified labour' for these qualities do not contribute to capital's competitive advantage. The 'objectified labour' that the worker confronts, therefore, is a one-eyed monster that *includes his or her labour and skill cosntribution only as long as it fits the machine system's efficiency*. In *using* the machines of capital, labour therefore brings to life a distorted version of the living labour of past generations, or of the social *forces* of production and labour which is then serving the logic of distortion that makes the machines work for the interests of capitalism. This logic was unleashed as soon as Boulton and Watt's steam-engine provided an independent source of power to factories, thus permitting chains of mechanical contrivances to be linked together into a system within which the person and the social relations of production were merely one part of a large mechanical totality. Thus, Marx wrote of the effect of the resulting technological systems:

> The factor's 'self-acting' steam engine, is a mechanical monster whose body fills whole factories, and whose demon power, at first veiled under the slow and measured motion of his giant limbs, at length breaks out into the fast and furious whirl of his countless working organs.

and

> the labourer becomes a mere appendage in an already existing material condition of production.
>
> (Marx 1974: 360–61, 364)

The new material conditions of labour that Marx observed did not reflect merely a shift in conditions of employment, for the new machine systems represented a co-optation of the social *forces* of production. Thus industrial capitalism was predicated on a shift in the culture of those who sold their labour to capital's new system-masters. Andre Ure, himself an apologist for the emerging system, observed this when he extolled the industrial virtuosity of Arkwright in dragging the new breed of servants into abiding by the rhythm of machines, and then lamented:

> The main difficulty is in training human beings to renounce their desultory habits of work, and to identify themselves with the unvarying regularity of the complex automation [so that] it is found nearly impossible to convert persons past the age of puberty, whether drawn from rural or from handicraft occupations, into useful factory hands.
>
> (Ure 1835: 91)

If the skills of the person best suit the interests of capital accumulation when they align in a productive system with machine capacities, it follows from the system's logic that human skills, which are costly and inefficient, should be mechanically replaced. Thus, a centralised source of power, such as was provided by the steam-engine, allowed the machine system to develop; this in turn allowed the incorporation of labour skills within the system; and the *instrumental* skill of the person is drawn off from the entire praxis of labour, these being the full joining of intellect and physical labour used by capital until this partial component of human capacity itself can be replaced. As Marx observed in his *Grundrisse*: as the system moves towards its final automation,

> The production process has ceased to be a labour process in the sense of a process dominated by labour as its governing units. Labour appears, rather, merely as a conscious organ, scattered among the individual living workers at numerous points of the mechanical system; subsumed under the total process of the machinery itself, as itself only a link of the system, whose unity exists not in the living workers, but rather in the living (active) machinery ... The increase of the productive force of labour and the greatest possible negation of necessary labour is the necessary tendency of capital ... *The transformation of the means of labour into machinery is the realization of this tendency.*
>
> (Marx 1973a: 693)

Thus, it is a basic principle of industrial capitalism to use new instrumental knowledge to replace those parts of a technical *system* that are the least efficient. The cultural principles of '*progress*' and *new knowledge creation* ensure that new knowledge will continuously appear, and therefore that competition on the grounds of efficiency is perpetual. Thus the *dynamic* of industrial capital is that of subjugating the person to the instrumental knowledge products of their own social and cultural history. When the 'person' is no longer needed, their instrumental skill will be; when their skill can be incorporated into the machine system (and improved upon), it will be; and labour (potentially) will disappear entirely. As the joke about Telecom has it, the new automatic telephone exchanges will be run by a person and a dog: the dog to guard the machines, and the person to feed the dog. This is the *dynamic* of capitalism, yet it must end in conflict with a society where purchasing power is isolated in the hands of a small élite group – *unless* there is a radical redistribution of wealth.

This principle, though the framework for early capital accumulation, was glimpsed only dimly throughout the nineteenth century. It leapt forward to shower a massive bounty on to capital progress when perceived directly. This occurred when the engineers who had been tinkering around in the engine room of factories turned their attention to the people-part of their systems. Thus, around the turn of the twentieth century what was called 'Scientific Management' or 'Taylorism' (after the original investigator) was born. Again, for comparison, it should be noted that at this time, 41 per cent of Australian factories still did not have a centralised motive power source.

Taylorism broke down the labour process into its component elements, and reconstituted them into the most efficient sequence of human actions either modelled on a machine, or directly in service of a machine system. Thought, conception or plan were separated from execution of labour; the human labourer was alienated from his or her own praxis, and controlled by management's time-and-motion study formulae. As Braverman asserts, this dissolution of the unity between conception and execution in work was a critical contribution towards the progressive deskilling of labour under late capitalism (Braverman 1974).

Under these conditions of 'engineering the person', it was in the controllers' interests to reduce the initiative, creativeness and autonomy of those who laboured. Taylorists argued that humans, thus alienated from their own human qualities, were happier, because they, too, would come to value their own efficiency and the higher wages it would yield. Gilbreth, one of Taylor's key followers, therefore asserted (Gilbreth 19: 122):

> The speed boss . . . does not drive the men at all. He is their servant . . . [and simply determines] . . . the correct speed at which the man can work day after day, year after year, and continuously improve in health.

The workers knew, however, that the consequences of selling their ownership of 'conception' to management meant:

> There was never a moment of leisure or opportunity to turn my head ... The men have no rest except for fifteen minutes at lunchtime and can go to the toilet only when substitutes are ready to relieve them.
>
> (Crudin 1931)

There was no time for thought or reflection by the worker, because this did not maximise 'system efficiency'.

Taylorism dissipated over time as a form of worker control to be replaced by more subtle forms of control embodied in pseudo-assertions of humanness in the application of theories of human relations and industrial democracy (Boreham and Dow 1980: 14–15) – pseudo because 'human' needs were referred to only as long as they did not interfere with instrumental efficiency and productivity. But, the system-principle of Taylorism remained, i.e. the separation of conception from execution. As Braverman (1974: 87) claims:

> If Taylorism does not exist as a separate school today, that is because, apart from the bad odor of the name, it is no longer the property of a faction, since its fundamental teachings have become the bedrock of all work design.

To see the consequence of this in another way, human thought skill is a valuable commodity that management must possess to ensure system-survival in the intensely competitive corporate environment of the twentieth century. As I demonstrated in the first part of this chapter, the evolution of industrial capitalism has been directly associated with the increasing co-optation of new thought and knowledge directly into the hands of management. So, the human alienation that Taylor's concept represented has been institutionalised into organisation structures, and into a value to be applauded in the leading edge corporations of late capitalism. As a result, adjusting instrumental skills of the person to the system's efficient operation, and minimising levels of skill by skill incorporation into machine systems, is the norm of industrial capitalism. To the extent that upgrading' of skills is visible, it is counter to this basic principle of capitalism, and is either a temporary hiccup in a path towards skill replacement, or is a smoke-screen that obscures the job replacement that is going on behind it.

This can be demonstrated by examining a criterion case – what is happening in employment related to the use of computers in Australia. This is a criterion case because of all modern areas of employment, this is generally regarded as the wave of the future. It is a form of employment that tends to be regarded very positively by virtue of its proximity to computer brain power and pristine air-conditioned office space – which, of course, is required by the machine rather than being a work condition for the employee.

First, if computer employment is the leading edge of an employment wave, then its amplitude is very much smaller than many would predict. Indeed, in Australia, the Electronic Data Processing (EDP) industry displaced more jobs than it created in the early 1970s, shortly before the Fraser government stopped the collection of survey statistics.[15] Indeed, with industrial capacity relatively static over this time, most new manufacturing investment has been in rationalisation, so computerisation has enhanced the propping up of an ailing 'waste economy' through job displacement (Hill 1985).

This observation runs counter to the assertion often heard from apologists for the benefits of an 'information society', that computer-based technologies will *expand* employment opportunities as other core technologies did in the past. The evidence runs against such a position and instead suggests that computer technology is not a core technology with the same employment infrastructure developing potentials as those such as railways and electricity which have regenerated industrial economies in the past. At least its similarity is limited only to the very early stages of the diffusion of computerisation throughout the international economy. The *difference* is that computer technology's main point of economic penetration lies in the savings in labour costs it can yield through labour replacement – across *all* manufacturing and service sectors, that in any way depend on, or deal with, information flows. In other words, new sorts of industry will be (and have been) developed, but the multiplier effect is not merely replacement of older similar industries; rather, it is to affect labour levels throughout the entire economy. The basic *economic* structure that is so affected was laid downs through, and following, World War II – a 'waste' or obsolescence-oriented economy. Having reached its saturation level, this industrial base is not expanding at its previous rate, so rates of profit can only be sustained through continuous labour displacement and plant rationalisation. Data presented in Figure 9.7 on capital expenditure by Australian industry through the 1970s supports this position. Whilst there has been a continuous rise in expenditure on plant and capital equipment, there has been a declining rate of on new industrial construction, i.e. plant is not being expanded, but displaced (Hill 1985).

The pattern of 'rationalising expenditures' is also reflected in other OECD countries (Productivity Promotion Council of 1980: Australia 51–534).

Figure 9.7 Investment in Plant/Equipment and Building Cons-truction (Australia, 1974–75 Prices)

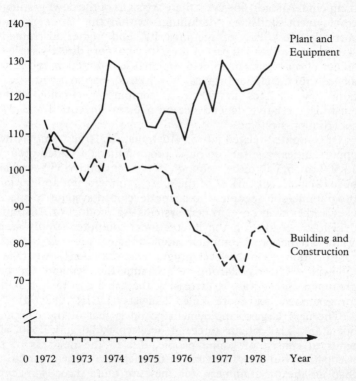

Source: ABS, 1980a

Consequently, as well-supported projections for the USA demonstrate also for Australia (due to international penetration into Australia's technology economy), there may be relatively high growth in high technology employment areas (such as for computer analysts). And the contribution of these areas to the overall employment scene is quite small; for example, whilst there is likely to be an 85 per cent increase in high technology jobs in the USA between now and 1995, these will only constitute 6 per cent of overall employment (Kutscher 1984). In other words, in spite of the information-processing emphasis of the evolving economy, high technology employment is the prerogative of a small employment élite. Already however, there are signs of the downgrading of employment skills (or 'deskilling') within this élite, or, more correctly, deskilling of the majority, and higher instrumental skilling of a very small part of the élite who more directly serve the ability of management to plan, rationalise production and generally control the labour process. This transformation is a product of both key changes in the core computer technologies, and Australia's relative dependence on overseas invention and computerisation strategies.

Of computer-related jobs in Australia, the largest employment opportunities exist for computer programmers, a skilled group of 13,500 to 16,500, mostly young (75 per cent under 35 years) and male (80 per cent). Most of these programmers are 'applications' programmers, or people who adapt developed systems to specific uses, rather than develop new systems – a product of Australia's dependent posture in the international computer supply scene. With international computerisation moving towards increased routinisation of lower-level programmer functions, Australia is following. This is starting to cut into the demand for programmers, or at least is increasing the gap between less skilled 'programmers' and more skilled 'analysts' (DEIR 1982: 74).

The next largest employment group is that of the computer operators. This labour force, of between 6,000 and 7,500, also tends to consist of young people, due to the newness of the occupation, but they suffer rather harsher employment conditions than do the programmers, for they are quite directly machine servants. The job involves relatively low levels of skill, constant shift work, limited promotion prospects and early retirement: the majority of the labour force is, needless to say, female. Computer operators are disappearing, however, as much of the demand for computers has moved since the 1970s towards mini-computers, which can be operated directly by users with little or no training. Meanwhile, with technological advances in mainframe computers, the demand for operators is diminishing, because of the increased ability of such computers to perform their own operating functions. In other words, the occupation of computer operator is coincident only with the early development of computer systems, and the employees' skills are already being incorporated into the technology. For those left in the business there is some movement upwards from operating to programming, but with the change in programming towards an élite 'analyst' group, and the upgrading of entry requirements, the number of operators who become programmers is now diminishing (DEIR 1982: 116).

Finally, there is the small group of 1,500 to 2,000 computer technicians. Nine-tenths of this workforce is male and relatively young (under 40 years), but, as with the other two categories of computer employment, the occupation is undergoing rapid transformation due to technological change. There are *short-term* prospects for relatively skilled employment in servicing *older* EDP equipment. But, as with computer programmers, the longer-term demand is for an élite cadre of highly-skilled technicians who are capable of dealing with both hardware *and* software (DEIR 1982: 159). Those with older-order skills will fall into obsolescence.

From this evidence it is clear that movement in computer-based employment in Australia is towards a widely-separated set of skills – towards the small élite 'analyst-specialist' group on the one hand, and the relatively large group of relatively unskilled keyboard operators on the other: male analysts, female keyboard operators; full-time highly-paid career analysts, casual poorly-paid early-retiring keyboard operators. And the *range* of skills and employment possibilities in between is disappearing. Both groups have skill levels, as Braverman would describe them, that are 'adequate to the needs of capital', but no more (Braverman 1974: 447).

These data are counter to the 'upgrading' thesis that could be expected to apply to computer-related employment, if nowhere else. For such a thesis would posit not only skill development, but also more interesting, varied and less alienative work, greater security, and some sense of career (Dunkerly 1980: 164–66). The counter 'deskilling' thesis is shown to be even more persuasive when we look more closely at the computer-producing centres from which the ripples of change emanate that directly impinge on Australia, i.e. at the various 'Silicon Valleys' of the USA. As a recent report on high technology industry in the Boston area demonstrated, in spite of the EDP industry's positive, progressive image, working conditions are poor for employees. None of the companies in the high tech consortium, 'the High Technology Council', was unionised, and working conditions were often tense and tedious, with risk of exposure to hundreds of toxic chemicals, whilst 60 per cent of the employees were paid below the national

average wage. Furthermore, the enterprises are operating so close
to the leading edge of technological change that they have to be
capable of adjusting very quickly or they go out of business. The
result is the need to build 'flexibility' into employment practices
lest outmoded skills make the business uncompetitive. Put more
realistically, this means that management *have* to be able to hire
and fire as *they* choose (Massachusetts High Technology Council
1984).

Computer employment is the criterion case of what deskilling
means in the 1980s. It is both a model for emerging employment
sectors and, through its products, a direct influence. It is the sector
where the trend towards marriage between knowledge-generation
and production is closest. In Australia our neo-colonialist dependency on the industry moguls in Japan and the USA is inescapable.
And what deskilling means in this context is not an overall
downgrading of skills *per se*, but *precise alignment between labour
skill levels and their minimum instrumental adequacy for capital*.
Hence a very small highly-skilled group is required to apply
management *conception* to system design, but a large gap is tending
to appear between this élite and the skill levels required to use the
computers – by those who are totally dependent on software and
system design created elsewhere, by those who *execute*. If skills are
required, they must be available as a *commodity resource* to be
bought and sold at will, because with the speed of change in the
market-place (particularly now, with vast investments in computer
research – $(US)2,000 million being spent on fifth generation
computers alone – the *person* must be dispensable.

General Trends in Australian Employment

Changes in the general structure of work in Australia over the last
twenty years demonstrate the replacement of many occupations by
technologies that can do the same work. Technological change is
removing former skills from occupations generally: book-keepers,
accountants and insurance managers are being replaced by computer systems; spray-painters and welders by Unimate robot arms;
designers, drafts-persons and boiler-makers by CAD/CAM
(Computer-Aided Design/Computer-Aided Manufacturer) systems; warehouse workers and clerks by automated stacking and
delivery systems; and so on. Much of the skill replaced was
instrumental, but some of it was not. For these are *human* skills
that are being replaced – the direct engagement of the person in
craft and design. Like the skills of cooper and coach-maker, from
early capitalism, these will never return.

Counter to this, there is some evidence in aggregate statistical data that with the recent development of Australia's information sector there has been growth in *skilled* employment. On closer inspection, however, these data have to be treated with some caution. What labour force figures collected by the Australian Bureau of Statistics (ABS) show is a shift from blue collar to white collar jobs. This is, however, the product of two interacting trends, the first being that of de-industrialisation which has resulted in Australia's uncompetitive international standing, and the second being the demand for low-skill, mainly part-time white collar jobs in the growing service sector. Associated with this, the fastest *rates* of growth during the 1970s were for *system-managers*: jobs for professional white collar workers increased by 7.5 per cent per annum, and for skilled white collar workers by 3.0 per cent (Tertiary Education Commission 1979). Meanwhile however, the mechanical and craft skills of labour were disappearing: while craftsperson and technician occupations were increasing in numbers of employees by 11.5 per cent from 1961 to 1966, and from 8.1 per cent to 1971, from there on the absolute numbers have been *dropping* by 2.5 per cent annum into the 1980s. Thus, with the overall labour force expanding steadily over this time by 48.9 per cent, the percentage of the labour force represented by skilled blue collar workers in all sectors has dropped from 27.5 per cent in 1961 to 18.3 per cent in 1981.[16] However, while the loss of manufacturing skills is permanent, the 1970s rise of the professional white collar class is not. The 1970s was a time of concentration on the introduction of computers into the service sector, particularly after the impact of mini-computers in the middle of the decade. It was also a time when the socially erosive effects of burgeoning unemployment created the demand for community/professional personnel to pick up the pieces. In other words, the 1970s reflected the early transitory effects of computer introduction into the economy. It represents a hiccup in the progress towards the deskilling progress that capitalism, intrinsically, must follow. In Australia, the nation is at a fairly early stage along the path towards computerisation (DEIR 1982: 74), so the longer-term occupation transformations are not yet clear. But, in the USA, the trends provide significant signals of what can be expected to occur within Australia.

In the USA, the Bureau of Labour Statistics has an excellent track record of predictive accuracy. Ron Kutscher, presenting their most recent predictions to an Australian audience, showed that within the next 10 years, only 15 to 20 per cent of the top 20 employing occupations will need an education beyond high school, while only teaching and nursing will need tertiary degrees. As

Keith Windschuttle observes of Kutscher's data (Windschuttle 1984: 12), major growth will be in the unskilled areas of the service sector in the lowest-paid jobs – part-time, casual, un-unionised, contract jobs with no career paths – jobs which reflect late twentieth century capitalism's view of the person as an 'instrumental skill commodity'. What is particularly disturbing is what the labour market statistics present about the social malaise of the future. Holding apart the élite, skilled 'alphas' and the unskilled, alienated 'proles', is the fast-developing security business: 'The United States expects demand for private detectives to be up by 100 per cent; guards up by 83 per cent; correction officials and jailers up by 48 per cent; legal assistants by 163 per cent; and judges up by 34 per cent' (Windschuttle 1984).

The strains of deskilling on society are evident in these figures. Furthermore, however, as the evidence also suggests, as skills in the workplace became progressively stripped of their human *in*efficiency, the quality of 'humanness' itself and the satisfaction of *human* needs is also excluded: as the above evidence shows, conditions of work are therefore changing towards less secure, less well-paid jobs. As is already evident in Australia, in the first instance, less secure and deskilled employment is associated with the female labour force. But this is likely to be only at the start. As Table 9.5 and Figure 9.8 show, part-time employment for females has risen from 26 per cent to 46 per cent of the female labour force since 1970; but also, significantly, although the percentages are much lower, the rate of part-time employment for males has almost *doubled* in this period. In other words, the effect cannot merely be attributed to the large number of married females able to accept part-time employment who re-entered the labour force in the 1970s; rather it reflects a change in the structure of work.[17]

A second trend emerging is towards increasing centralisation of the labour force, both within larger corporate conglomerates and within the cities. The latest statistics on industry concentration in Australia demonstrate that the largest two hundred firms control 47 per cent of the industrial labour force and 58 per cent of manufacturing turnover. Both figures have been increasing steadily since the 1960s (employment from 42 per cent in 1968–69; and turnover from 52 per cent in 1968–69) (ABS 1985b: 1). Moreover, continuing with computer-related employment as a criterion case of future trends, 80 to 90 per cent of all the computer-related jobs described earlier were in capital cities.

However, in terms of transformation of the social relations of production, what is potentially of even more importance in the

Table 9.5 Part-time Employed as a Proportion of Total Employed in each Gender Category

Part-time Employed Year by Category (August)	1970	1972	1974	1976	1978	1980	1982	1984
Males, Part-time as percentage of overall male employment	3.20	3.31	3.49	4.42	1.38	5.24	6.00	6.11
Cumulative percentage change:		3.4	9.1	38.1	68.1	63.75	87.5	90.9
Females, Part-time as percentage of overall female employment	26.14	26.56	29.15	33.35	34.87	35.77	36.18	36.83
Cumulative percentage change:		1.6	11.5	27.6	33.4	36.8	38.4	74.3
Persons, Part-time as percentage of overall employment	10.51	10.86	12.18	14.39	15.94	16.36	17.08	17.76
Cumulative percentage change:		3.3	15.9	36.9	51.7	55.7	62.5	68.98

Source: ABS, 1985a

future is the effect of present-day technological change, with its deskilling, casualising, centralising tendencies, on overall organisational structures and rewards within industry and commerce. All the above observations are merely different manifestations of change in the nature of labour, as the instrumental component of human capability is stripped off from the rest of labour praxis and labourer humanness, and *used* for the benefit of capital. As such, all the technology and labour force trends demonstrate an observation that 'critical school' sociologists[18] made some time ago about a key dynamic of late capitalism. That is, the alienation of 'instrumental action' (practical, controlling, powerful) from human 'communicative action' (comprehension, communication between speaking and acting subjects who, without domination, understand through shared symbols). Along with this alienation and capitalism's consequent appropriation of instrumental action (aided and abetted by Taylorism), came the perception of the

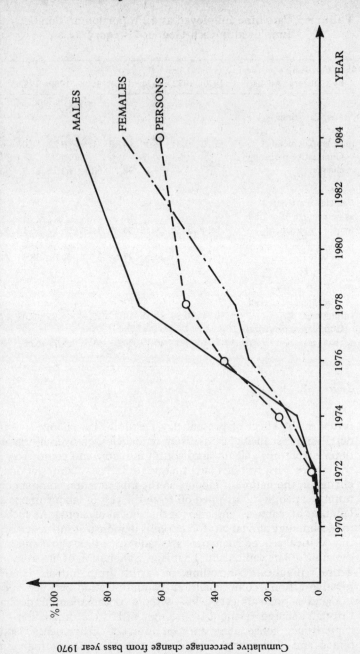

Figure 9.8 Change in Part-time Employed as a Percentage of Total Employed in each Gender Category

person – at all levels in the labour process, including management – as the 'skill commodity' referred to earlier. Thus, to extend the trend to its logical conclusion, organisations of the future will be populated by 'skill-commodities' rather than thinking, acting, comprehending subjects; their lines of interaction will be instrumental, and technologically mediated, via computerised systems and data access. In other words, the trend of late capitalism is towards 'deskilling' the human communicative component out of the '*instrumental information flow system*', as productive organisation could well come to be called.

That this is already happening is demonstrated most vividly in the casualising of work and the destruction of connections between the life goals and career structures of people and their organisation, as well as in the elimination of middle-management structures – in banking, insurance and retailing, particularly. The instrumentalising system decrees that these orientations are no longer relevant in the face of the need to develop organisations based on 'skill-commodities'.

However, there is a very real, but as yet unrecognised danger, in this path. Like all cultures and sub-cultures, the culture and meaning system of an organisation is *made* in the actions of participants producing *together*. Instrumentalising the human elements of interaction marginalises the person and his or her commitment. The ultimate effect on organisational climate, personal commitments, and the organisation's capacity to respond creatively to a turbulent social and physical environment could thus in the future be severely impeded.

Thus capitalism's appropriation of instrumental action is but a more sophisticated version of the dynamic relationship between it and the technological change that has persisted since the Industrial Revolution. But now, the ultimate contradiction could be confronting us. For capitalism's appropriation of instrumental action has within it the seeds of late capitalism's own destruction through its inability to respond to the turbulent, fast-changing environment this dynamic itself has created.

Conclusions

When Frank Gilbreth, Taylor's disciple, talked of skill he said:

> Training means merely enabling him to carry out the directions of his work schedule. Once he can do this, his training is over, whatever his age.
>
> (Gilbreth 1974: 447)

For Gilbreth there still was a 'skilled person', delimited as a person to their specific instrumental physical properties, but still a person who, once trained, had a slot securely allocated within the machine system. Capitalism has now moved on. The 'commodity' quality of personal skill is now baldly exposed.

Under the conditions of late capitalism, the (ideal) person is no more than the instrumental skill level and breadth required to feed a specific element of the machine system. As a commodity, the movement of the labour force towards greater hiring and firing 'flexibility' and career-less, non-unionised, casual forms of employment – no matter how technically 'skilled' the description of the occupation might be – is the aim. Communicative action, understanding, personal un-power-oriented interaction play little part in the 1980s system. The fundamental dynamic created by technical knowledge as the powerhouse of capital accumulation has unerringly headed towards this point since Pappelwick 1785, to where the person is seen as *no* more than a disposable instrumental skill commodity (even in management 'conception' roles). Australia's dependence on neo-colonial knowledge-masters is a direct result of Australia's marginality to Britain's industrialisation at the same time as the nation was colonially linked into it. The pauperisation of Australia's industrial technology resources that resulted laid the basis for the 'double marginality' that ensured, where the nation was not only co-opted into knowledge dependency on foreign powers, but so too were the nation's knowledge-generating resources through which escape could have been possible. In this context of external control the 'knowledge masters' are more likely to draw future 'conception' and system-control skill unto themselves, and leave Australia to 'execute' our part in the international economy and division of labour.

The result could well be a return to the basic economy of a resource-providing colony – that of a mine and a farm for the rest of the world. Only now, compared with the more languid wealthy days of the late nineteenth century in Australia, the labour process has been indelibly transformed. Perhaps what is most important about this transformation is the distance that control has moved away from the labour process itself, yielding a prevading sense of 'heteronomy' as Ivan Illich dubs the antonym of autonomy (Illich 1976), a sense of powerlessness in the face of external controls, a 'technological heteronomy' that creates a culture of spectators who are enchanted with the fruits of a technological world, but who fear the very incomprehensibility that is a product of not being involved in the essence of its creation. As Robert Pirsig observed in his now classic book, *Zen and the Art of Motor-Cycle Maintenance*:

All this technology has somehow made you a stranger in your own land. Its very shape and appearance and mysteriousness say, 'Get out!' ... What you see is the NO TRESPASSING, KEEP OUT signs and not anything serving people but little people, like ants, serving these strange, incomprehensible shapes. And you think, even if I were a part of this, even if I were not a stranger, I would be just another ant serving the shapes.

(Pirsig 1974: 24–25)

To address such a future requires a double-edged strategy within Australia's development, for we need *both* to grasp an initiative in the international technology race, *and* to humanise labour.

Given its late start into the international technological structure and the vast expenditures overseas on new generation technologies, Australia will never be able to compete directly across all forms of modern technological development. The nation has, however, a well-developed science base, though this has only recently started to become connected into Australia's industrial structure. We need to capitalise on this potential strength, and foster the development of closer industry/research integration. The nation needs to focus this effort not on broad-brush competition, but onto specific areas where Australia can develop an advantage within particular niches in the international economy. Given the international connectedness of the national economy, we can only hope to find a unique position of strength within the international scene, and bargain our way out from there. To strengthen this general bargaining position it is critical, in addition, to develop an adequate new technology knowledge capability, within government, education, research and industry, particularly within Australian-based concerns, so that we can take at least some command over the choices or technology that Australia accepts in the future. There are choices, but the ignorant or the bemused cannot recognise them. Unless we as a nation develop a general ability to know and internalise new technologies, the economy will remain perpetually dependent on changes injected into it by the overseas fashion houses of new technology development. These interests are far more likely to see Australia primarily through the eyes of commercial exploitability rather than in terms of what Australians might want from their future. If the nation remains dependent on the changes that emanate from outside, as our colonial history demonstrates, it runs a very real danger of increasingly being a mere implementer of others' designs rather than a conceptualiser of our own path.

It is from such a position of relative strength, rather than dependent weakness, that the nation can determine the human shape of labour it might wish to foster. International economic pressures are such that we cannot avoid having to compete, and increasingly, the terms of this competition are technologically determined. But success in this competition does not necessarily guarantee a more human face on the body of labour in this country – because competition could be fought on the terms set by international interests, i.e. paying primary attention to instrumental efficiency in the international arena rather than anything else.

In addition, a new *consciousness* is necessary. It is one that stresses not only international competitive advantage, but also the direction of technological change towards more fulfilling labour. This implies both closer involvement of unions in the design, acceptance, and application of new technologies, as well as the integration into technology design parameters of the goal of human fulfilment as well as competitive advantage. To make this happen requires the involvement of all Australians in every aspect of their participation within education, research, politics, and the Australian labour force. For whilst we sit back, and with all-too-frequently seen Australian apathy, remain spectators in a world changing around us, and outside our control, we will remain glued to the designs made for us within the board-rooms and foreign affairs policies of controlling international interests. Not only that, but, given a general disquiet within the labour movement worldwide, about the pauperisation of work, taking a leading role in the development of human technologies could well provide the edge in international technology change that Australia so desperately needs.

Without this dual strategy – of international competitiveness and labour enrichment – the future of Australia looks bleak, for it promises a perpetual dependency on international interests, a continued process of deskilling and labour pauperisation, and a further visiting upon our future of the technological sins of the past inherited from our colonial history. Australians need not be 'ants serving the shapes', nor 'strangers in our own land'. But to avoid this each of us needs to *act* to determine our own future.

Acknowledgement

I would particularly like to thank Mr V.V. Krishna, who was my Research Assistant, for developing the data for this chapter. With both a creative flair for searching out obscure but fascinating statistics and trends, and a competent interest in the task, Krishna's assistance was invaluable.

Notes

1. This view of economic history as a series of long cycles or waves is drawn from a theory of long waves of economic change named after an early protagonist, Nikolai Kondratiev. For a discussion of the development and use of this theory see Hill (1985a) and Windschuttle (1985).
2. These were transitions from handicraft-made or manufacture-made steam engines, to machine-made steam engines, to electric and combustion engines, to the generalised control of machines and their power usage by electronic apparatus. This argument is presented in Mandel (1975).
3. The usefulness of Australia's colonies to Britain's nineteenth-century bourgeoisie is demonstrated in import statistics for the colony of NSW over the later part of the nineteenth century. Between 1860 and 1870, 69 to 70 per cent of *all* imports into NSW, excepting those from other Australian colonies, came from the United Kingdom. The percentage rose to nearly 80 per cent by 1880, but then proceeded to fall steadily through the 1880s and 1890s, to 61 per cent by 1901. The figures reflect the United Kingdom's declining influence as a centre of international manufacturing as the nineteenth century closed, and the twentieth opened up. (The above data is taken from the *New South Wales Statistical Register* (1901: 146).)
4. Barry Jones, quoting A. Maddison, asserts that in the period from 1870 to 1890 Australia had the highest per capital income in the world. See Barry Jones (1984: 56). Also, the percentage of the Australian population living in the capital cities was increasing by 5–6 per cent every 20 years, from 24.7 per cent in 1860, to 29.8 per cent in 1880, to 35.3 per cent in 1900: see Coghlan (1901: Table 2: 1 and Table 14: 5).
5. The railway mileage open for traffic across Australia increased from 243 miles in 1861, 1,030 miles in 1871, 4,192 miles in 1881, 10,394 miles in 1891–92, to 13,497 miles by 1900–01: see Coghlan (1901: Table 51: 18).
6. Walter Rostow comments on the nineteenth century impact of railways in the United States as 'the leading growth sector in American growth from 1840s to the 1880s. Closely linked to the emergence of the steel industry after the Civil War, the railroads were surely connected in one way or another with immigration, with population increase, internal population movement, and almost everything else that mattered in the American economy' (Rostow 1975: 725).
7. Barry Jones comes to the same conclusion, but identifies the time of crossover to services somewhat earlier in the nineteenth century. I

have been unable to replicate Jones' data from the original statistical sources. Figure 9.1 demonstrates the results when reasonably safe assumptions are applied to colonial, Census and ABS data on the labour force. The sources of these data are identified with the figure. (For Barry Jones' analysis see Jones (1984: 55).)

8. Buchanan, R.A. (1982: 55). Of the patents registered in NSW towards the end of the nineteenth century, in 1895, for example, 50 (6.4 per cent) were for agricultural implements and methods alone. See *New South Wales Statistical Register* (1895: 744). As a result, Australia's main technological export item in the early twentieth century was agricultural machinery, being the principal export, worth 31,847 to Argentina in 1906 (*Official Yearbook 1901–1907*: 508).

9. In Australia only 23.5 per cent of R&D is performed in the business sector; by way of contrast, in the United States 71 per cent, in West Germany 69.2 per cent, and Japan 60.7 per cent, respectively, is performed in the business sector. The Australian figure (for 1981–83) is taken from ABS (1984b: 5); the United States figure (for 1981) is taken from Barfield (1982: 130); the Japanese figure (for 1981) is taken from Statistics Bureau, Prime Minister's Office (1984); and for West Germany, the figure (for 1979) is taken from the OECD (1981).

10. Three-quarters of these exports are completely unprocessed materials (ABS 1984a).

11. The one apparent exception to the high technology component in imports is that of 'miscellaneous manufactured items'. The ratio of imports to exports is high (in data used to construct Table 9.3) at nearly 10 to 1. However, this category of goods is primarily of apparel, handbags, furniture, etc., imported largely from cheap labour nations. Of the high technology goods, the ratio for scientific equipment has fallen since the 1970s: this could well reflect the preponderance of knowledge contribution in Australia *within* scientific enterprise rather than in industry-related technology enterprise.

12. The conclusion follows simply from projecting trends. Payment costs for all forms of technical know-how have steadily increased since the late 1970's – from $69.5 million in 1976–77, $108.6 million in 1978–79 to $126.6 million in 1981–82, across all industries. Over this time, the ratio of payment to receipts has remained around 7 to 1 (ABS 1984c: 21).

13. In the mining sector, foreign ownership rose to 27.3 per cent in 1963, to 57.8 per cent in 1974–75 (Crough 1980). Since that time, the level of foreign ownership appears to have plateaued; see ABS (1984d). Foreign ownership of food processing, the other industry where foreign control gets close to the heart of Australia's main exports, is lower (at 31.5 per cent), and has also remained fairly stable since the early 1970s. Here, less sophisticated technologies were required. See ABS (1976c, 1985c).

14. This quote is taken from Marx, K. (1973b: 15) *Grundrisse*, in D. McLennan, *Marx's Grundrisse*, St Albans, Herts: Paladin. The whole section, entitled: 'The Labour Process and Alienation in Machinery

and Science' (from *Grundrisse*, pp. 583–92), is an elaboration of the idea. It is worth noting that Marx carried this idea a great deal further in analysing the psychic illness that resulted from humankind being alienated from its own means of production under capitalism. The term 'objectification', as it was used by Marx, meant man's natural means of projecting himself through his productive activity on to nature – *in* the objects of his creation; 'objectification' allowed the possibility of man contemplating himself in a world of his own making. But, under capitalism, what was objectified, what it was that stood *for* man's relationship to nature, was the machine or 'fixed capital' that the worker confronted in the factory. What was objectified was under the private control of the capitalists. So the world of humankind's collective making, the whole productive power of humankind's progress, was alienated from the worker in each moment when he or she intervened in nature through labour. Labour which is thus 'estranged' from what Marx termed humankind's 'species being' in turn 'estranges man from his own body, from nature as it exists outside him from his spiritual essence (*Wesen*), his *human* essence', creating a deep human existential sickness. (For Marx's description of this effect, see Marx (1975).)

15. From September 1968 to March 1973, employment in the Electronic Data Processing industry grew by 68.9 per cent, or 12.1 per cent annually. But whilst 3,080 jobs were created in 1972–73 (mainly for specialists in software development), 3,266 jobs were replaced. This number represented 2.7 times the number of jobs replaced in 1968; see Department of Labour and National Services (1968, 1974).

16. Craftsperson and technician figures were obtained from aggregation of labour force figures for occupational groups. My category includes all blue collar occupations with a substantial craft or technical skill component, e.g. toolmakers, electricians, compositors, millers and spinners. Sources used were, Commonwealth Bureau of Census and Statistics (1964: 175–76, 184; 1967: 139, 151) and ABS (1973: 144–48; 1976b: 33–34; 1981: 60–67).

17. For a variety of reasons there has been a very large increase in the number of married females entering the workforce over the last 25 years. This group, in general, has been more willing to accept part-time work. This, in August 1984, of all females between 25 and 54 years who were employed part-time, over 86 per cent were married. This compares with 57 per cent for females between 25 and 34 years employed full-time, and 74 per cent for females between 35 and 54 years employed full-time (ABS 1985a).

18. For example, the top 8 companies in the petroleum and coal products sector control 89 per cent of industry turnover; in the synthetic resins and rubber sector the equivalent percentage is 66 per cent; in the photographic, professional and scientific sector, 59 per cent; in the radio, TV receivers and audio equipment sector, 84 per cent; and the top 4 motor vehicle companies control 84 per cent of turnover (ABS 1985b: 39, 41, 43, 57, 61).

References

Australian Bureau of Statistics (1973) *Labour Report No. 58.* Canberra: ABS.

——(1976a) *Overseas Trade 1974–75*, Cat. No. 5410.0. Canberra: ABS.

——(1976b) *Census of Population and Housing 1976*, Cat. No. 2426.0. Canberra: ABS.

——(1976c) *Foreign Ownership and Control of the Manufacturing Industry, Australia 1972–73*, Cat. No. 5322.0. Canberra: ABS.

——(1980a) *New Capital Expenditure by Private Enterprise in Australia*, reproduced from Productivity Promotion Council of Australia (1980) *People and Technology in the 80s.* Melbourne: PPCA.

——(1980b) *Overseas Trade 1978–79*, Cat. No. 5410.0. Canberra: ABS.

——(1981) *Census of Population and Housing 1981*, Cat. No. 2452. Canberra: ABS.

——(1983a) *Overseas Trade 1981–82*, Cat No. 5410. Canberra: ABS.

——(1983b) *Labour Statistics, Australia 1982*, Cat. No. 610.0. Canberra: ABS.

——(1984a) *Foreign Trade, Australia 1982–83*, Cat. No. 5410.1. Canberra: ABS.

——(1984b) *Research and Experimental Development All Sector Summary, Australia 1981–82*, Cat. No. 81120.0. Canberra: ABS.

——(1984c) *Research and Experimental Development, Business Enterprises, Australia 1981–82*, Cat. No. 8104.0. Canberra: ABS.

——(1984d) *Foreign Ownership and Control of the Mining Industry, Australia 1982–83*, Cat. No. 5317.0. Canberra: ABS.

——(1984e) *Labour Statistics, Australia 1983*, Cat. No. 610.0. Canberra: ABS.

——(1985a) *The Labour Force, Australia August 1984* (and previous years), Cat. No. 6203.0. Canberra: ABS.

——(1985b) *Census of Manufacturing Establishments and Electricity and Gas Establishments, Industry Concentration Statistics, Australia 1982–83*, Cat. No. 8307.0. Canberra: ABS.

——(1985c) *Foreign Ownership and Control of the Manufacturing Industry, Australia 1982–83*, Cat. No. 5322.0. Canberra: ABS.

Barraclough, G. (1967) *An Introduction to Contemporary History.* Harmondsworth, UK: Pelican.

Barfield, C.E. (1982) *Science Policy From Ford to Reagan – Continuity and Change.* Washington: American Enterprise Institute for Public Policy.

Bloomfield, G. (1978). *The World Automotive Industry.* North Pomfret: David Charles.

Boreham, P. and Dow, G. (1980) The Labour Process and Capitalist Crisis in P. Boreham and G. Dow (eds) *Work and Inequality – Vol. 1, Workers, Economic Crisis and the State.* Melbourne: Macmillan.

Braverman, H. (1974) *Labour and Monopoly Capital – the Degradation of Work in the Twentieth Century.* New York: Monthly Review Press.

Briggs, A. (1974) 'Technology and Economic Development in Scientific American', *Scientific Technology and Social Change.* San Francisco: W.H. Freeman.

Brogden, S. (1960) *The History of Australian Aviation*. Melbourne: Hawthorne Press.

Brown, H.J. (1949) 'Trends in Higher Technological Education and Development in New South Wales', *Journal, Institution of Engineers, Australia* 21 (9): 151.

Buchanan, R.A. (1982) 'Engineers in Australia 1788-1890. A Preliminary Analysis', *Journal, Institution of Engineers, General Engineering Transactions* 54.

Burn, D.G. (1930–33). 'The Genesis of American Engineering Competition 1850–1870', *Economic History* 2: 292–311.

Coghlan, T.A. (1901) *Statistics, Six States of Australia and New South Wales 1861–1900*. Sydney: William Applegate Gullick, Government Printer.

Commonwealth Bureau of Census and Statistics (1964) *Labour Report No. 51*. Canberra: Commonwealth Bureau of Census and Statistics.

——(1967) *Labour Report No. 53*. Canberra: Commonwealth Bureau of Census and Statistics.

Corbett, A.H. (1973) *The Institution of Engineers, Australia – A History of the First Fifty years, 1919–1969*. Sydney: The Institution of Engineers, Australia, with Angus & Robertson.

Crough, G. (1980) 'The Political Economy of the Mineral Industry' in G. Crough *et al.* (eds) *Australia and World Capitalism*. Melbourne: Penguin.

Crudin, R.L. (1931) 'The End of the Ford Myth', *International Pamphlets No. 24*, quoted in Giadin Siegfrid (1975) *Mechanisation Takes Command – a Contribution to Anonymous History*. New York: W.W. Norton.

Department of Employment and Industrial Relations (1976) *Employment in EDP – 1973*. Employment and Technology Series No. 17. Melbourne: AGPS.

——(1982) *Employment Prospects by Industry and Occupation*. Canberra: AGPS, July.

Department of Labour and National Service (1968). *Employment in Electronic Data Processing*. Employment and Technology Series No. 1. Melbourne: AGPS.

——(1969) *Employment in EDP* Employment and Technology Series No. 4. Melbourne: AGPS.

Derry, T.K. and Williams, T.L. (1960) *A Short History of Technology*. Oxford: Clarendon.

Dunkerly, D. (1980) 'Technological Change and Work: Upgrading or Deskilling' in P. Boreham and G. Dow (eds) *Work and Inequality, Vol. 2 Ideology and Control in the Capitalist Labour Process*. Melbourne: Macmillan.

Frame, D.J. *et al.* (1977) 'The Distribution of World Science', *Social Studies in Science* 1.

Freeman, C. (1985) 'Technological Change and the New Economic Context' in S. Hill and R. Johnston (eds) *Future Tense? Technology in Australia*. Brisbane: Queensland University Press.

——*et al.* (1982) *Unemployment and Technology Innovation*. Greenwood Press.

Gilbreth, F.B. (1912) *Primer for Scientific Management*. New York: D. Van Nostrand, quoted in Giadin Siegfrid (1975), *Mechanisation Takes Command – A Contribution to Anonymous History*. New York: W.W. Norton.

———(1974) Quoted in H. Braverman (1974) *Labour and Monopoly Capital – The Degradation of Work in the Twentieth Century*. New York: Monthly Review Press.

Healy, M. (1985) Department of Science, Canberra: Data presented to ASEAN S&T Policy Training Seminar, Centre for Technology and Social Change, University of Wollongong, April.

———(1985) 'Technology and Society' in S. Hill and R. Johnston (eds) *Future Tense? Technology in Australia*. Brisbane: Queensland University Press.

Hill, S. and Johnston, R. (eds) (1985) 'Technology and Society', *Future Tense? Technology in Australia*. Brisbane: Queensland University Press.

Hurst, N.W. (1985) 'Indicators for Science and Technology Policy Formulation and Monitoring', paper presented to the ASEAN/COST High Level Consultative Meeting on S&T Policy Training, Canberra, March 1985. Department of Science, Figure 7, Patents and Publishing Scientists, Selected OECD Nations.

Illich, I. (1976) *Medical Nemesis: The Expropriation of Health*. New York: Random House.

Johnston, R. (1983) 'The Critical Barriers to More Effective Results', paper delivered to the ANU Public Affairs Conference, Science Research in Australia: Who Benefits?, 23–24 June, Department of HPS, University of Wollongong (mimeo).

———(1985) 'The Control of Technological Change in Australia' in S. Hill and R. Johnston (eds) *Future Tense? Technology in Australia*. Brisbane: Queensland University Press.

Jones, B. (1984) *Sleepers, Wake! Technology and the Future of Work*. Melbourne: Oxford University Press.

Kutscher, R.E. (1984) 'Changing Employment Structure of the United States – Factors Contributing to These Changes', paper presented to the US-Australia Joint Seminar, The Future Impact of Technology on Work and Education, Monash University, September.

Low, W. (1984) 'Discoveries, Innovations and Business Cycles', *Technological Forecasting and Social Change* 26 (4): 355–73.

MacLeod, R. (1982) 'On Visiting the 'Moving Metropolis': Reflections of the Architecture of Imperial Science', *Historical Records of Australian Science* 5 (3): 1–16.

Mandel, E. (1975) *Late Capitalism*. London: New Left Books.

Marx, K. (1973a) *Grundrisse: Foundations of the Critique of Podlitical Economy*. Harmondsworth: Penguin.

———(1973b) Quoted in D. McLellan (1973) *Marx's Grundrisse*. St Albans, Herts: Paladin.

———(1974) *Capital, Volume I*. Moscow: Progress Publishers.

———(1975) 'Economic and Philosophic Manuscripts' in C. Lucio, *Karl Marx – Early Writings*. Harmondsworth, UK: Penguin.

Massachusetts High Technology Council (1984) *Massachusetts High Technology: The Promise and the Reality*. Barten.

Mensch, G. (1979) *Stalemate in Technology*. New York: Ballinger.

Moore, J.R. (1939a) 'Survey of the Engineering Profession – Tabulated Results and Statistics', Journal, Institution of Engineers 11 (7): 259–62.

———(1939b) 'Survey of the Engineering Profession – Tabulated Results and Statistics. *Journal, Institution of Engisneers* 11 (9): 331–34.

New South Wales Statistical Registers (1860): 167.

———(1861): 190.

———(1863): 111–112.

———(1867): Table 74.

———(1876): 188–89.

———(1892): 483.

———(1893 and previous years): 608–09.

———(1895 and previous years): 606–07, 618–19, 625–29, 744–54.

———(1901 and previous years): 146, 263, 626–29.

———(1904): 234–35, 426.

———(1938–39): 445.

Official Yearbook of the Commonwealth of Australia 1901–1907, No. 1.

———*1911*, Vol. III.

———*1913*, No. 6.

———*1923*, No. 16.

———*1924*, No. 17, Vol. III.

———*1940*, No. 33.

———*1957*, No. 43.

Organization for Economic and Community Development (1981) *OECD Economic Surveys*.

———Group of National Experts on Science and Technology Indicators (1984) *Science and Technology Indicators*, Working Paper No. 2. *Indicators of the Technological Position and Performance in OECD Countries During the Seventies*. OECD, DSTI/SPR/84, 43, Scale E, Table 6: 27.

Pirsig, R.M. (1974) *Zen and the Art of Motorcycle Maintenance: An Inquiry into Values*. London: The Bodley Head.

Preston, D.H. (1985) 'Strategic Use of Patent Information', Technology Information Branch, Australian Patents Office, Canberra (mimeo).

Productivity Promotion Council of Australia (1980) *People and Technology in the 80s*. Melbourne: PPCA.

Rochlin, G.I. (1974) 'The Technological Imperative – Introduction, in Scientific American', *Scientific Technology and Social Change*. San Francisco: W.H. Freeman.

Rostow, W.W. (1975) 'Kondratieff, Schumpeter, and Kuznets: Trend Periods Revisited', *Journal of Economic History* 35: 725.

Sagasti, F. and Guenero, M. (1982) Quoted in R. MacLeod (1982) "On Visiting the 'Moving Metropolis'": Reflections of the Architecture of Imperial Science', *Historical Records of Australian Science* 5 (3): 5.

Schumpeter, J.A. (1939) *Business Cycles*, 2 vols. New York: McGraw-Hill.

Statistics Bureau, Prime Minister's Office (1984) *The Statistical Handbook of Japan, 1983.*

Stubbs, P. (1972). *The Australian Motor Industry, a Study in Protection and Growth.* Institute of Applied Economic and Social Research, Monograph No. 5, University of Melbourne.

Tertiary Education Commission (1979) *Employment Trends by Occupation and Skill 1971–78.* Canberra.

Ure, A. (1835) *The Philosophy of Manufacturers.* London: Charles Knight, reprinted in T.P. Hughes (ed.) (1964) *The Development of Western Technology since 1500.* New York: Macmillan.

van Duijn, J.J. (1983) *The Long Waves in Economic Life.* London: Allen & Unwin.

Windschuttle, K. (1984) 'High Tech and Jobs', *Australian Society* 3 (5): 12.

———(1985) 'Technology and Unemployment' in S. Hill and R. Johnston, (eds) *Future Tense? Technology in Australia.* Brisbane: Queensland University Press.

World Intellectual Property Organisation (1980) *Industrial Property Statistics 1979.* World Intellectual Property Organisation, IP.STAT/1979/A, Publication A, Geneva.

Chapter Ten

Health and the Australian Population

Jake M. Najman

Health involves both a social process and a physical reality. Health in this sense is a state of mind which allows people who may have significant disabilities to continue functioning relatively normally or which totally restricts those whose physiological status appears normal. In so far as illness represents a deviation from a subjective state of normal functioning, its physical manifestations are filtered through societally derived perceptions of physical normality. Whether we consider health behaviours advocated by those who would prevent our becoming ill (for example both Galen and Hippocrates suggested what we would now label as lifestyle modification as a means of maintaining health), or the interactions that individuals have with representatives of the health system, health and illness involve social processes which need to be understood. Consequently, it is not surprising that the involvement of sociologists in the study of health, illness and the health care system has a long history.

This chapter begins with a short review of the development of medical sociology to the present time. It considers the contributions of sociologists who have studied health and illness both in Australia and overseas. Following this, it continues with a social epidemiological analysis of the health of Australians. This analysis comprises an overview of patterns of illness and death, and an assessment of the association between these disease outcomes and the characteristics of groups who differ in their religious beliefs and practices, racial composition, socio-economic and marital status.

Early Developments

Sociology has, from its beginning, demonstrated a concern for those factors which threaten the health of groups living in various societies. Engels (1845) in describing Manchester in 'The Condition of the Working Class in England', focused upon the filth, squalor and, implicitly, the impact of industrialisation and urban living on the health of the people.

When the American Social Science Association was created in 1865 it included reference in its aims to the health consequences of poverty (Lazarsfeld and Reitz 1975: 1). While much was written in the intervening years (see for example, Durkheim's *Suicide* 1912), the beginning of the mid-1950s is when major developments in the field of medical sociology occurred.

In 1954, Simmons, a sociologist, and Wolff, a neurologist, published an introductory medical sociology text – the first. It pointed to those aspects of society and social interaction which were of relevance to health and health care delivery. The text suggested that much illness was stress-induced. This orientation underlines a body of current research. Koos (1954) at the same time described class differences in health and health-related behaviour in Regionville, and his work stimulated two major continuing debates in the literature. The first concerns the impact of social and economic inequality on health. The second involves the identification of the social factors which influence those who have symptoms to seek medical and other help for them.

In 1957, Merton and his group (Merton, Reeder and Kendall 1957) published a series of reports of medical student socialisation. These continue to guide current thinking on the education and training of medical practitioners, nurses, dentists and other health workers.

Two papers reviewing the field of medical sociology appeared in 1957, both predicting a rapid growth in the field (Freeman and Reeder 1957, Strauss 1957). In his review, Strauss was able to find 110 Americans whose work was primarily in the field of medical sociology, the majority of whom were employed by universities in teaching medical and nursing students or who were working in government health departments or hospitals.

By the early 1960s a number of medical sociology readers had appeared (Jaco 1958, Apple 1960, Freeman, Levine and Reeder 1963) as had major studies of such topics as patients' perceptions of their doctor and the doctor-patient relationship (Freidson 1961), medical student culture (Becker *et al.* 1961) and life in a hospital ward (Coser 1962). At about the same time Irving Goffman described the perceptions and experiences of both staff and patients in psychiatric institutions (Goffman 1961). Research into the societal basis and definition of mental illness has a long history in sciology (see, e.g. Faris and Dunham 1939; Hollingshead and Redlich 1958) and allied to the contributions of some medical psychiatrists (Laing 1961, Szasz 1970, Cooper 1970) has transformed psychiatric institutions and psychiatric care. Since the early 1960s there has been a rapid growth in the field of medical sociology. The medical sociology section of the American Sociological Association subsequently grew to become (and remains) its largest section (in 1986 it had 961 members, an increase of 15 per cent over the previous year – ASA Footnotes, March 1986: 20).

This review of early developments is provided to emphasise two points. Firstly, it suggests that sociologists have had, and continue to have, a significant impact on developments in the health care field, though they are rarely directly involved in the delivery of health services.

Secondly, the subject matter with which sociologists deal in their studies of health and illness is extraordinarily varied. In this report of (predominantly) the Australian literature, it is not possible to discuss this full range of topics, and only some are included. This chapter emphasises one of the key area of medical sociological research, namely the environments and behaviours which produce health and illness.

The Most Common Illness

One might begin a sociological analysis of the health of society by asking whether health care is provided, as one might presume, to those who are ill. This question raises three issues of interest to medical sociologists. Firstly, it would seem important to know if some groups in Australian society (say the poor or aged) fail to obtain medical or other care when they are ill. Secondly, it may be the case that some groups receiving health care may not require such care. These persons might be using medical care services in circumstances where previously a priest or family member would have been consulted. Thirdly, it may be that some health care fails to benefit the patient or the benefit is less than alternative (non-medical) care could have provided. These issues are addressed in Table 10.1.

The *Australian Health Survey* (1986) sampled 18,000 private dwellings between February 1983 and January 1984. Of the 1983 Australian population of 15,166,900, it was estimated that 10,767,000 persons (71 per cent) took some action related to their health and that 9,446,200 persons (62 per cent) experienced an

Table 10.1 Illness Conditions Experienced in the Two Weeks Prior to Interview

Respiratory System (mainly colds, flu, asthma)	2,781,700	18.3
Digestive System (mainly dental, stomach, constipation)	1,707,300	11.3
Circulatory System (mainly hypertension, heart disease)	1,562,400	10.3
Headache (ill-defined, unspecified or trivial causes)	1,543,800	10.2
Musculo-skeletal System (mainly arthritis, back trouble)	1,451,099	9.6
Skin and Subcutaneous Tissue (mainly eczema, dermatitis, rash)	1,392,200	9.2
Nervous System, Sense Organs (mainly migraine, eye diseases)	770,100	5.1
Injuries	595,200	3.9
Mental Disorders (mainly nerves, tension, depression)	554,700	3.7

Source: Australian Health Survey 1986: 47

'illness condition' *in the two weeks prior* to interview. Some 18 per cent of the population consulted a doctor in this two-week period though a smaller proportion sought help from (in order of frequency) a chemist, chiropractor, physiotherapist, optician and district nurse. As Table 10.1 indicates, respiratory conditions were experienced by 18.3 per cent of the population, while problems with digestion, blood pressure, heart and headaches were also common. A substantial minority of the population reported problems of living (ill-defined headaches, mental disorders and insomnia). In this same two weeks, 33 per cent of the population used pain relievers, 25 per cent used vitamins and minerals and 12 per cent used skin ointments and creams.

A similar type of survey undertaken in 1975 in Gosford-Wyong and Illawarra found that 53 per cent of the former population and 35 per cent of the latter had a chronic illness (Shiraev and Armstrong 1978). Sample surveys in Canberra (Hennessy, Bruen and Cullen 1973), and Melbourne (Krupinski and Stoller 1971) have suggested that about 20 per cent of the Australian population has some symptoms of mental illness at any chosen time, principally feelings of anxiety and/or depression.

These findings would seem to suggest that illness or the experience of symptoms is not only common, but in a statistical sense, normal in society. Further, the majority of people who report that they have symptoms also report attending to these symptoms either by taking medications for them, discussing them with friends and relatives and, less frequently, seeking the help of a doctor or other health care provider. It is important to note that many of these illnesses are not curable (e.g. colds, emotional problems) nor may the condition benefit from the care provided, but such care nevertheless demands substantial medical resources. It is also pertinent to observe that for most illness conditions the majority of those experiencing the relevant symptoms do not appear to suffer serious consequences, despite their failure to obtain medical care.

The Most Common Causes of Hospital Admission

Hospital admission and length of stay data provide another approach to measuring the health of people in the community. Such data are available only on a state by state basis. According to them, the major reasons for hospital admission are, for males: accidents, poisoning and violence, then diseases of the digestive system, principally chronic liver diseases and ulcers, and diseases of the circulatory system, principally heart disease and strokes. For females the most common cause of hospital admission is pregnancy and childbirth followed by diseases of the genito-urinary system (*Social Indicators* 1984: 87). However, if we consider the length of hospital stay as a relevant factor in determining the importance of a particular condition, then mental disorders (male average stay 91.8 days, females 100.9 days) must also be added to the conditions which are a major source of morbidity in Australian society (with accidents, poisonings, violence, males average a stay of 7.1 days, and females 13.7 days). Perhaps a better estimate of the importance of a condition could be derived by multiplying the number of people admitted for a condition by their length of stay, but such data are not generally available.

As we will note in the sections which follow, the illnesses which lead to death or hospital admission are (partly) a consequence of lifestyle and of the interaction of people with their environments.

Changing Patterns of Mortality

While Australian morbidity data has only recently become available, mortality data has long been used as an indicator of national health. Such analyses of mortality data can be divided into three important and distinct historical phases: that period prior to the availability of modern (antibiotic) medicines, say to 1940; the period from 1941 to about 1970, and the period 1971–85.

In the late nineteenth century and until the 1940s, the major causes of death in Britain (Powles 1973, McKeown 1976), the United States (McKinlay and McKinlay 1977) and Australia (Gordon 1976) were the infectious diseases, principally respiratory conditions like pneumonia and influenza. Gastric infections, tuberculosis and diptheria were also major causes of death. The first effective treatments for these conditions became available in the mid-1940s and early 1950s. Figure 10.1 illustrates this point for gastric infections in males (in 1908–10 the major cause of death) in their first year of life, but similar figures could be produced for adults and children and respiratory conditions, diptheria, whooping cough and many other causes of death (see Gordon 1976, and McKinlay and McKinlay 1977). Note that the decline in mortality began well before effective remedies became available and appeared to continue apparently unaltered by medications which subsequently appeared. However, as both Gordon and McKinlay and McKinlay point out, some other conditions such as tuberculosis and whooping cough had an acceleration in their mortality decline once the new therapies became available. These patterns may have implications for health care planning at the present time. The major decline in mortality occurred prior to the availability of effective medical treatments. The mortality decline probably occurred as a result of improved sanitation, hygiene and the nutritional status of the population. Thus changes in personal lifestyle (diet) and in the physical environment had the major impact of reducing death rates. Once remedies became available then the decline in mortality for some of the infectious diseases accelerated. Thus, largely as a result of the improved nutritional status and hygiene experienced by the population, and partly as a result of the new medications, infectious diseases were reduced to a minor factor in Australia's death rates (with the notable exception of Aboriginal mortality rates).

The second period (1941–71) was associated with the development of a wide range of treatments for infectious diseases, and the introduction of numerous medications which could be used to alter mood (the psychotropic drugs) and which led to the technological transformation of medical care with the widespread introduction of body scanning, foetal monitoring and organ replacement surgery. In this period the major causes of death were heart disease, cancer, strokes and accidents, that is, conditions which were, in the main, chronic and incurable. During this period a variety of

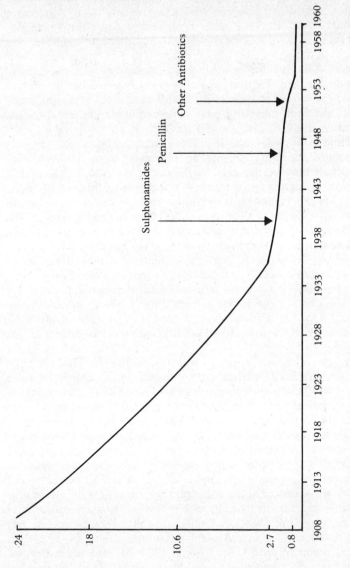

Figure 10.1 Male Deaths from 'Gastro' in First year of Life per 1,000 Liver Births*

secular trends (e.g. changes in the extended family, increased mobility) and the availability of seemingly effective mood-modifying medications led to medical practitioners supplementing (and sometimes supplanting) the family as a source of emotional support. That is to say, the kind of help doctors were expected to provide changed. Further, as Powles (1973) points out, this was a period (1960–70) of increasing health care costs at a time when Australian adult mortality rates remained at similar levels (*Social Indicators* 1984: 62, Heyde and Ring 1984: 7).

While it is true that the 1960s was a period of relatively unchanged mortality despite an increased input in health resources, it may be the case that some of the new therapies and procedures significantly improved the quality of life of many whose life expectancy remained unaltered. However, such a benefit is not self-evident in all instances (see Najman and Levine 1981), and one consequence of this dissonance between increasing health costs and unchanged mortality rates was the increasing demand for evaluation – that is, for new treatments and procedures to be scientifically assessed and their benefits judged against their costs. Assessment of effectiveness remains a consideration in the delivery of health care services at the present time. While the precise figure remains a matter of speculation, it is not yet possible to refute the suggestion that the majority of medical care services delivered lack demonstrable benefit.

The third period of interest was around the late 1960s and the early part of the 1970s when a major decline in adult mortality rates began. In Queensland between 1969–72 and 1979–81, mortality rates from heart disease declined by 26 per cent (Figure 10.2), from stroke by 35 per cent, from accidents by 24 per cent, and from pneumonia by 52 per cent. While overall mortality rates have declined in this period by 22 per cent, cancer mortality rates have increased by 7 per cent. Lung cancer remains the major cause of cancer death (cigarette smoking is the major relevant behavioural factor), while cancer of the colon and rectum is next in importance (possibly attributable to diet), with breast and stomach cancer next (Heyde and Ring 1984). A similar overall mortality decline has been noted in Western Australia (Holman 1986: 14–15), then United States (*Health United States* 1985: 11) and Great Britain, where the decline appears to have selectively benefited non-manual workers more than those in manual occupations (Marmot and McDowall, 1986: 274). The decline is particularly evident for coronary heart disease and stroke. It appears to comprise a reduction in the incidence of these diseases rather than improved survival following hospital admission, suggesting that the decline is a result of changed lifestyle and better control of high blood

Figure 10.2: Trends in Queensland Mortality 1952–81.
(percentage in brackets is the change between 1969–72 and 1979–81)*

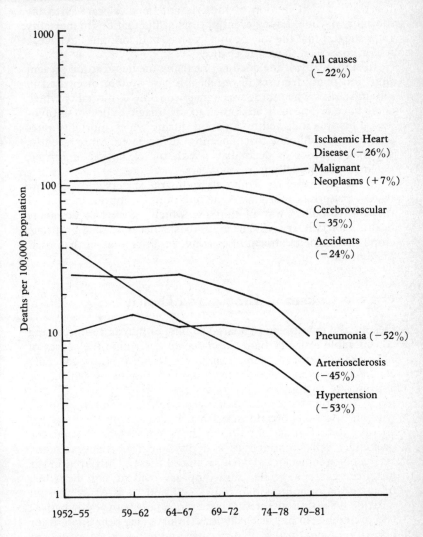

Source: Heyde and Ring 1984

pressure (Siskind *et al.* 1987, Holman 1986: 14). While both these explanations go some way to explaining the mortality decline, it is not clear whether other factors should also be considered or what the relative contribution of lifestyle and medical care is to the mortality decline. In any event, the major fluctuations in mortality rates suggest that the way people live has, and continues to have, a major impact on their 'life chances'.

In sum, many of the doctors practising medicine at the present time and many features of our health care system originated in circumstances when there was a major decline in mortality which some have erroneously attributed to the 'magic bullet' of antibiotics. This was followed by a period during which mortality rates altered little, while the cost of health care increased. More recently, the major causes of death have, with the exception of cancer, declined substantially in recent years.

In the context of contemporary industrial society and a chronic disease pattern of mortality some question the appropriateness of the 'magic bullet' way of thinking which appears to dominate health care delivery. Such an approach places an inappropriate emphasis on the treatment of existing conditions rather than their prevention.

On the Causes of Illness and Death

Despite the investment of a large volume of human resources and considerable research funds intended to determine the causes of illness, it is clear that much remains to be learnt. It is now generally acknowledged that there are few major conditions for which it is appropriate to think in terms of a single dominant cause. This is not to deny that some illnesses are a consequence of human contact with an infectious organism, or that injuries involve a release of energy. Rather it is to point to the need to look beyond the proximate cell abnormalities and physiological changes to the events or circumstances which produced these. Thus even in the instance where a single cause appears evident e.g. hepatitis, tuberculosis or injury following a collision, it is likely that an individual's nutritional status (infections), peer network (hepatitis) and preference in physical activities (injury) may bear upon his or her consequent health. Nutritional status, peer network and preference in physical activities are likely, in turn, to be dependent upon a range of factors.

If we then examine the major causes of illness and death we find that they are associated with many posited causes. Thus heart disease rates have been causally associated with diet, the smoking

Figure 10.3 Range of Structural Factors found to influence Smoking

(i)			General Model		
Social Structure	→ Health Behaviour	→ Biological Characteristics	→ Physiological Changes or Pathology	→ Illness or Death

(ii)			Specific Example		
Poverty Gender Age Social Networks	→ Smoking	→ Biological Characteristics	→ Physiological Changes or Pathology	→ Heart Disease, Lung Cancer

of cigarettes and, more generally, an individual's country of origin (Richard 1985). Lung cancer has been linked closely to cigarette consumption but also to some types of work environment (such as mining). Lung cancer also occurs more frequently in urban than rural areas. Thus it is appropriate to think of much illness as multi-causal, with sociologists generally choosing to emphasise the structural basis of illness (i.e. causes which a consequence of the manner in which society is organised or functions) while others may focus upon more immediate causes (e.g. cell abnormalities, cholesterol levels). Figure 10.3 presents a simplified, schematic view of this multi-causal approach, which identifies a range of structural factors which have been found to influence smoking. It acknowledges that there are likely to be some people who are biologically more susceptible to illness than others, though not a great deal appears to be known about them. Finally, one is able to observe higher rates of pathology and illness in those who engage in less healthy behaviours. This figure is simplified and does not consider a range of other factors which may also be important in determining one's 'life chances', such as one's gender, social class and decisions about when to seek medical care. The causes of the major illnesses can be considered under four headings.

Biology/Heredity
Various epidemiological studies have unequivocally demonstrated the importance of a hereditary component to some of the major illnesses. Thus a good predictor of whether an individual will become a diabetic is evidence that one or other of his/her parents had diabetes (Mann 1975: 743). Much the same evidence is available for breast cancer (Gordon 1976: 379), and it has been

reasonably well established that some mental illnesses (e.g. schizophrenia) may be biologically determined (see Fieve *et al.* 1975:
125–215 for a number of relevant papers).

Some have acknowledged the evidence that illnesses may occur
more commonly in relatives of those who have already manifested
the same condition, but they point out that behaviour patterns are
also similar in these families. It could consequently be argued that
evidence of higher rates of similar conditions within families could
be evidence both for the biological approach as well as the
sociological and environmental. Simply put, parents who smoke
more often have children who smoke, with both parents and
children being more likely to manifest smoking-related health
conditions. In the cases mentioned above (diabetes, breast cancer,
schizophrenia), this latter possibility has been assessed and dismissed either by statistically controlling for environmental factors or
by assessing the magnitude of the overall effect relative to the
known magnitude of environmental effect. Nevertheless, for each
condition, evidence of higher rates within families is, of itself, not
sufficient to demonstrate the importance of biological or environmental etiology.

Adequacy of Medical Services/Quality of Care
The ready availability of high-quality health services would seem
an important prerequisite for the health of a nation, or the groups
who live in it. For a variety of reasons it is, however, difficult to
know what the specific contribution of health services is to health.

Firstly, people differ in their definition of such services. Some
refer to basic hospital services, others include private medical
services, some add specialist care and investigative services, while
yet others might include a broad range of community health
services and preventive facilities. Secondly, it is not unambiguously clear (Donabedian 1980) what distinguishes good and
less adequate health services. Thus more services might be less
desirable if these additional facilities entail a risk to health or life,
with little apparent benefit. The well-known instance of the
decline in mortality which resulted from the Los Angeles doctors'
strike emphasised this point (James 1979, Roemer 1979). Thirdly,
it is likely to be the case that there is an optimum level of health
(medical care) services beyond which further services produce few
or no benefits (at substantial cost).

Despite these qualifications, it is likely to be the case that the
health of people is not adequately addressed by health services
which are below a certain level. Thus, persons living in Australia's
rural areas may receive less prompt care for their injuries or other
life-threatening conditions (e.g. heart attacks), or they may receive

less ready access to specialist care and investigations. Whether such an explanation will account for the health differences of the groups considered in the following section remains to be considered.

Lifestyle

The impact of lifestyle on health will be considered in detail in the sections which follow. There has been a great deal recently written about the impact of various lifestyle variables on health (see Syme 1986 for one recent review). Catchlove (1984) has gone so far as to argue that 'lifestyle' is now viewed as the pathogen of the 1980s.

Aside from the data which implicates cigarette use, excessive alcohol consumption, diet, stress and numerous other variables in the etiology of many illnesses, lifestyle variables implicitly acknowledge the possibility (unlike biological variables) of intervention and change.

Two cautions should be considered in discussions of the impact of lifestyle on health. Firstly, there may be a tendency to 'oversell' the importance of lifestyle, to falsely attribute some health conditions to it, or to exaggerate its overall impact. Secondly, there may be a simplistic acceptance of lifestyle variables at face value, and a tendency to focus all change efforts on the individual smoker or drinker, rather than deal with the process that leads an individual to behave in a way which is damaging to his or her own health. This is tantamount to assuming the individual deliberately chooses to risk his own life or health. Such an assumption tells us as much about the observer as it does about the observation. It is in error in so far as it fails to deal with the relevant data (what is it about being unemployed, for example, that induces smoking?), and misleading in so far as it limits efforts to change health behaviour to those which focus on the individual.

Social Structure

Society is patterned and organised in ways which suggest that people in similar positions in the social system come to be there through similar experiences. Thus the poor usually come from an environment where poverty is a common experience.

Similarly, health-related behaviours are, in part, derived from a common set of previous experiences. Thus we know that the unemployed are more likely to smoke cigarettes (Najman *et al.* 1983), and that excessive alcohol consumption is evident with some groups of Aboriginals.

The key problem is accounting for the patterns of behaviour associated with group membership. If smoking is a response to poverty and excessive alcohol consumption to the dispossession of

Aboriginals and the disruption of their culture, then it follows that efforts to change behaviour must address the underlying structurally-based determinants of this behaviour.

In the section which follows we consider four key social structural variables and the extent to which they are associated with health-related behaviours and consequent illness and death.

Social Structure and Health

Religious Affiliation
There have now been many published studies of the health of members of minority religious groups in the United States, particularly Seventh Day Adventists (SDAs) and Mormons. Members of such groups have a lifestyle which places great emphasis upon family and friendship networks, and they rarely smoke cigarettes or drink alcohol. They also limit their intake of stimulants such as coffee or tea and tend to eat little meat and fish.

It is interesting to note that the health of members of such minority religious groups appears to be much better than others of comparable socio-economic status living in the same communities. Thus SDAs have rates of cancer which are only 71 per cent of the rates of comparable others (Wynder *et al.* 1959), while for the other major causes of death (coronary heart disease, stroke, traffic accidents) their death rates are only about half that of a comparable non-SDA population (Lemon *et al.* 1964, Lemon and Walden 1966, Lemon and Kuzma 1969, Phillips 1975). These major health advantages of members of minority religious groups have been also found, at a more general level in society, when comparing those who attend church more and less frequently. The more frequent church-attenders in one early study had half the rate of heart disease and pulmonary emphysema and only a quarter the rate of suicide (Comstock and Partridge 1972).

The intriguing question, as yet only partly answered, concerns the explanation of these observed associations between religion and health. Religious group membership encompasses not only many characteristic behaviours (including diet, activity levels and the seeking of medical care) but also a particular type of response to emotional and physical stress situations. It would clearly be useful to know what aspects of religious group membership contribute substantially to reduced morbidity and mortality. Fortunately there are Australian studies which go some way to identifying the key variables involved.

Armstrong and his colleagues, in a series of studies, have examined the diets and blood pressure levels of SDAs, Mormons and others (controls). In an early study (1977), Armstrong found that 418 Western Australian SDAs had lower blood pressures than 290 residents of Narrogin, a country town 187 km from Perth (Armstrong *et al.* 1977). Subsequent studies tested the hypothesis that a diet which excluded meat accounted for the lower blood pressures of SDAs. In one such study SDAs (who did not eat meat) were compared with Mormons, who shared many of the types of religious and other circumstances of SDAs, but who did eat meat. The data showed that SDAs had lower systolic and diastolic blood pressure levels (Rouse *et al.* 1983a). In a further comparison staff volunteers at Royal Perth Hospital were allocated to one of three groups; a control group and two groups which were alternatively allocated to a meat and a meat-free diet. Both experimental groups during the period they were exposed to a vegetarian diet showed a decline in blood pressure, and an increase in systolic and diastolic blood pressure when they returned to a meat diet (Rouse *et al.* 1983b). Other researchers in Sydney have confirmed the lower blood pressure levels of SDAs and have also noted lower plasma cholesterol levels and a substantially smaller rate of mental and emotional problems (Webster and Rawson 1979).

While the above evidence points to a specific aspect of diet and its health consequences, much remains to be determined. The impact of stronger social networks or bonds characteristic of minority religious groups has not yet been assessed. While reduced cigarette and alcohol intake are likely to confer health benefits, the reduced use of other stimulants (coffee, tea, mood-modifying drugs) may also have health consequences. The example of the health benefits of minority religious group membership emphasises three features of the association between health and the social and environmental causes of illness. Firstly, the social and environmental circumstances of individuals and groups may have a major impact not only on their health but also on their life expectancy. Secondly, we are dealing with a number of inter-related social and environmental variables whose individual or aggregate impact is only in the process of being determined. Thirdly, those with a health advantage frequently appear to have better 'all-round' health, with reduced death rates from most causes of death and often lesser rates of psychological and emotional problems.

Race
The sociological perspective is distinguished, in part, by an emphasis on the extent to which human behaviour and 'life chances' (both qualitatively and quantitatively) are a consequence

of a group's position in the social structure. Structural factors are important in explaining human circumstances for a number of reasons. At its simplest level, people in the same position in the social structure are exposed to a similar socialisation process. However, one must also seek to understand how a current process of socialisation comes to be established, particularly in the context of rapid social change and a clash of cultural values. This directs attention to broader social processes and the exercise of power by dominant groups to maintain their supremacy. It is only by assessing Aboriginal culture and health from this historical and political perspective that we may account for the present health circumstances of Aboriginals in Australian society.

Prior to European colonisation, the bulk of Aboriginals lived a semi-nomadic existence stopping at different temporary campsites in a defined geographic area.[1] Aborigines were tied to their land and dependent upon it for survival. Generally, social organisation comprised relatively small clans or bands (estimates vary but are generally between 10 and 200 persons) who shared a language and customs. Population estimates of Aborigines in 1788 are the subject of some debate. Original estimates were of about 300,000 Aborigines in about 500–600 tribes, with distinct dialects or language but Butlin (1983) argues that there were up to five times that number.

Laws and mores were largely administered by the older men who enforced a code of rigid rules. Of particular relevance was a belief in the supernatural and a fear of events beyond the familiar. Thus disease might be interpreted as a consequence of sorcery, as a result of an offence one might have given to another person. European notions of infectious agents and of hygiene and sanitation were (and in some cases still are) foreign (see Reid 1982 for a discussion of various Aboriginal conceptions of health).

Aboriginal laws prescribed and proscribed the content and nature of relationships between relatives and placed an obligation on individuals to share their resources. There was an emphasis on formalised reciprocity, of sharing with others according to set rules. It could be argued that this emphasis on reciprocity was a consequence of living in a subsistence economy where the survival of individuals and groups was dependent upon receiving 'gifts' at times when food was in short supply.

Keen (1987) and others (Reynolds 1972, Rowley 1978, Stevens 1981) have traced the history of early contact between the white European settlers and Aborigines in Australia. Determining features of this contact were massive numbers of deaths attributable to contact with common European infectious agents, an imperialist/capitalist ideology which demanded the exploitation of land for economic reasons, and a popular stereotype of Aborigines as a debased and primitive people. This was a time when undiluted ethnocentrism ruled popular thinking. British values and culture were held to be necessary, and others, particularly those of persons of non-European origin (e.g. Chinese, Australian Aborigines) were treated with derision, and disparaged. Consistent with this approach there were claims that:

> Moral laws they [Aborigines] have none; their festive dances and corroborees are of the most lewd and disgusting character, their songs, rites and ceremonies utterly revolting and fiendish ... [if we] ask the question as to the possibility of chastity among their women the idea becomes preposterous.
>
> (Comment of a pastoralist quoted in Stevens 1980)

while the *Bulletin* of 1887 suggested that:

> Christianity was never intended for Black-Fellows. Its higher doctrines they are incapable of understanding ... [they are] spineless creatures with all the savagery taken out of them.
>
> (Quoted in Stevens 1980)

In the above context it is not surprising that those Aboriginals who survived the infectious diseases which were perhaps deliberately introduced (Butlin 1983), were systematically exterminated, either by being shot or by consuming poisoned food which might have been left for them. There were many recorded instances of atrocities, including the almost total destruction of the Aboriginal population of Tasmania and the murder of infants (see Stevens 1980, Keen 1987).

Of particular relevance to the present circumstances of Aborigines were laws passed which denied normal rights and freedoms to Black Australians. Most states passed Aboriginal Protection Acts, purportedly to protect the 'natives'. These had a two-edged intent, to protect but also to control the Aboriginal people. In Queensland, for example, Aboriginal settlements were established in 1897 and Aborigines were required to live on these. They were often located aways from traditional lands, where traditional foods might not be available. Superintendents of these reserves had great control of movement and behaviour. They could, for example, beat young children (and adults) for trying to escape. In Western Australia, Aborigines who absconded from work (i.e. quit) could be flogged and jailed (Keen 1987). They were rarely paid in money for their work. A major employer in the Northern Territory stated he was 'opposed to the payment of wages to natives ... money seems to be the root of all evil'.

The more recent period of White-Aboriginal contact is perhaps best characterised as a series of attempts to redress and undo the past, at least by some groups and governments. Many of these efforts have been a consequence of studies showing extraordinarily high rates of Aboriginal morbidity and mortality. Thus, blindness amongst Aborigines has been of epidemic proportions (Taylor 1980) while the prevalence rate of ear infections amongst Aborigines is amongst the highest recorded for any group in the world (Moran 1979). Not only do Aborigines manifest high rates of diseases which are more generally common in a developing country, but they also appear to have developed high rates of heart disease, hypertension and diabetes (Bastian 1979), diseases usually associated with affluent, developed societies.

Recent data shows that Aboriginal infant death rates are between two and five times the white Australian rates (Table 10.2), that the life expectancy of male Aboriginals at birth is about 50 years in rural New South Wales and 56 years in Western Australia (compared with 74 years for all male West Australians). Comparable data for females is 55 years, 63 years and 79 years (Hicks 1985). Thomson (1985) in a review of Aboriginal mortality rates, suggests they are between two and four times those of non-Aboriginals 'and up to 7 times those for postneonatal deaths' (p. 547). Of perhaps greater concern, however, was his suggestion of a 'marked worsening of Aboriginal adult mortality, in country regions of New South Wales at least' (p. 48).

Thus it is worth noting that the Aboriginal population in Australia manifests many of the same health problems experienced by American Indians and Canadian Eskimos. Many Aboriginal groups have reacted to their physical, cultural and social dislocation by adopting unhealthy 'white' patterns of behaviour, often without the limits and controls that European culture provides.

Are the high morbidity and mortality rates experienced by Aborigines a consequence of inadequacies in health care delivery? Without discussing this possibility in its entirety, it is unlikely that more health services of the type provided to other Australians will significantly improve Aboriginal health.

In one interesting study of the impact of modern medical care on the health of an Aboriginal group, Navajo Indians living in poverty were provided with sophisticated medical services including doctors, drugs, vaccines, diagnostic equipment and surgery. Their morbidity and mortality levels were then monitored over a five-year period. There was no evidence that this medical care had a significant impact on infection levels or upon the mortality rate (Science 1972: 25). Another experiment in three villages in rural Guatemala produced similar results. One village was monitored (the control village), a second received dietary supplements but no additional medical care, while a third received comprehensive medical care, immunisation and some help with sanitary services. While there was some evidence of reduced morbidity in both the treatment and nutritional supplements villages, the improved diet seemed to have the greater impact. On some measures, the health of those in the treatment village remained very poor (Scrimshaw *et al.* 1969). Thomson (1985)[2] has suggested that the improvement of diet and the social and physical environment represent minimal prerequisites to better Aboriginal health, and that more medical care is perhaps best conceptualised as fine tuning once major improvements have occurred.

Table 10.2 Aboriginal Stillbirth, Neonatal, Perinatal, Postnatal and Infant Mortality (Data for Qld, SA, WA, NT, Relative Risk of Death, Aborigines Compared with Australian Population)

	1979	1983
Stillbirths	2.7	2.6
Neonatal mortality	1.9	1.7
Perinatal mortality	2.4	2.2
Post-neonatal mortality	4.5	5.1
Infant mortality	2.8	3.2

Source: Report of the Director General of Health 1983–84: 244

The cumulative impact of these studies is to question the likely reduction of Aboriginal health problems by providing more of the types of any medical services already available to the white community. These studies re-emphasise the point we have already noted, that health is dependent upon a variety of social and environmental factors. A recent New Zealand study (Smith *et al.* 1985) has emphasised this point by noting that New Zealand Maoris who had converted to the Mormon religion and adopted a set of behaviours and circumstances which differed from their non-Mormon Maori counterparts, had substantially lower(ed) mortality rates. In the context of Australian Aborigines, the key social and environmental factors include:

- a history of cultural dislocation and ideological deprecation which limits Aborigines adopting either traditional or white lifestyles;

- a history of political oppression which has limited Aboriginal participation in the dominant political processes;
- a consequent high level of cigarette use, alcohol consumption, poor diet and other adverse lifestyle characteristics;
- health services which are generally limited to treating acute illnesses, with little attention to the circumstances which generate these conditions.

Social Class

While the existence of social and economic inequalities has fuelled intense debates and, on occasion, rapid change, it is the consequences of such inequalities which are of major concern in this section. Koos in a 1954 study of 514 families living in a small town in New York state, described class differences in morbidity. This study was extensively quoted in subsequent writing and its importance is evidenced by its re-publication thirteen years after it originally appeared. Koos divided his sample into three groups, Class 1 comprising business and professional persons, Class 2, skilled and semi-skilled workers, and Class 3 labourers and itinerant workers. Koos' major findings were that Class 3 persons:

- were less 'sensitive' to symptoms and, compared with Class 1, reported they would be less likely to seek medical care for the same symptoms;
- were found to have a higher rate of disabling illnesses;
- were less likely to have received medical care for their reported illnesses;
- more often sought non-medical (e.g. chiropractor) help for their illnesses;
- were much less likely to report having a family doctor;
- were more likely to be dissatisfied with the medical care they had received;
- more frequently consulted a pharmacist for their health problems;
- generally did not have family dentists and when they went to a dentist were likely to go for an extraction, while Class 1 persons more often went for preventive care and dental repairs.

Studies in a number of countries have confirmed some of Koos' findings, but not others. It appears clear that there are substantial class inequalities in adult (Antonovsky 1967) and infant (Antonovsky and Bernstein 1977) mortality, with lower class groups having higher mortality rates. Some have raised methodological objections to these findings and argued that they fail to address the possibility that persons who are ill are downwardly mobile – that is, they become lower class following an illness which limits their capacity to work. While this process undoubtedly does contribute to the association between class and mortality, there are two sources of evidence which suggest that this process is not a major factor. Firstly, the data consistently show that the wives of lower class men (presumably not ill themselves), have as high a mortality disadvantage as their partners (Registrar General 1971).

Secondly, a British study of 529,936 men followed up from 1971, apparently of good health at interview, produced the pattern in Table 10.3 In the first year of follow-up (occupational class recorded at the time the men joined the study in 1971) the expected pattern was not evident, but over a number of years the usual pattern emerged, providing convincing evidence that the association between social class and mortality in Britain was not a statistical artefact.

Koos' finding of an association between morbidity, health care seeking and social class have not, however, been universally confirmed and it may be that these findings reflect upon the sample chosen or an earlier period of time in a different health system. This suggestion is supported by Canadian research which showed that, after the introduction of a 'free' health care system, lower class Canadians substantially increased their use of medical care services (Beck 1973). Further, Kunitz *et al.* (1975) were able to resurvey the original Regionville using some of Koos' original questions, and found that class differences on some items had diminished and that the perceptions of the classes were now more alike than they had been previously.

These overseas studies are helpful in directing our attention to the likely situation in Australia, but our unique (convict) origins, recent major migrant settlement and strong egalitarian façade point to the need for Australian data.

A discussion of class differences in Australia has appeared elsewhere (Western, this volume). While there is considerable inequality in incomes and acquired wealth as well as occupational prestige (Congalton 1969), it is difficult to know whether these

Table 10.3 Mortality of Men aged 15–64 by Social Class (Standardised Mortality Ratios)

	1971–72	1973	1974–75
Class I	105	89	60
Class II–IV	86	91	92
Class V	111	110	124

Source: Registrar General 1971

inequalities in Australia exist to a greater or lesser extent than in other comparable countries (*Statistics on the Distribution of Income and Wealth in Australia* 1981). Irrespective of how Australia compares with other countries, there is evidence of considerable poverty. Using the Henderson[3] poverty levels it is estimated that over 9 per cent of Australians are living in poverty, this being concentrated in such groups as the unemployed and sole parents (*Report on Poverty Measurement* 1981). What, then, is the impact of social class on morbidity and mortality in Australia?

There have been relatively few Australian studies of morbidity (illness) and social class. Data from three of these, the Australian Health Survey (Broadhead 1985), Brisbane (Najman *et al.* 1979) and Gosford-Wyong/Illawarra (Shiraev and Armstrong 1978) show that there are few consistent or strong associations when occupational type is the relevant criterion of social class. However, when income differences are used, and these arranged to reflect those below, at, or above the Henderson poverty line then both males and females below it experience higher rates of recent illness, more chronic conditions and higher rates of mental and emotional problems (Broadhead 1985: 95).

The association between income level, as an indicator of socio-economic position and morbidity in the Australian Health Survey is confirmation of an earlier Gosford-Wyong/Illawarra study, which found that those below the poverty line reported more illness conditions, more emotional symptoms, poorer subjective perceptions of their own health and fewer visits to a dentist (Table 10.4). This study also suggested that the wealthier groups in the community more often go to a doctor when they feel ill.

Australian occupational mortality data have only recently become available, but they have been consistent in confirming the inverse association between social class and mortality, whether Census-based occupational criteria are used (Taylor *et al.* 1983) or occupational status (McMichael 1985) or whether the analysis is based on individual or area data (Siskind *et al.* 1987). Thus Brisbane data (Table 10.5) show that those living in the lowest status areas have, overall, mortality rates which are about 35 per cent higher than those experienced by persons living in the highest status areas. The trend appears consistent for the major causes of death, though it is relevant to note that lung cancer rates for women do not follow the general pattern. This inconsistency may change as more lower class women become smokers. Similarly breast cancer rates, accident rates (females only) and suicide rates did not manifest the general trend in the Brisbane study.

In sum, social class and Australian morbidity and mortality rates are related in a way which is similar to the findings of a number of overseas studies which have been discussed.

Table 10.4 Income Levels by Morbidity and Health Care Use in Gosford-Wyong

	Poverty line or below	Little above* poverty line	Twice poverty line income or more
Percentage with illness condition	65	55	56
Percentage emotionally disturbed	32	25	19
Percentage reporting their health as poor	11	5	2
Percentage dentist visit in preceding year	25	40	52

* 120 per cent–150 per cent poverty line
Source: adapted from Shiraev and Armstrong 1978

Table 10.5 Standardised Mortality Ratios by Socio-economic Position in 1976 in Brisbane

	Stratum/Class				
	I	II	III	IV	V
Coronary Heart Disease (M)	88	90	110	107	107**
Stroke (M)	78	90	120	96	123**
Lung Cancer (M)	79	99	122	99	104**
Lung Cancer (F)	115	62	126	79	121
Breast Cancer (F)	96	85	91	122	107
Motor Vehicle Accidents (M)	76	93	89	124	121**
Accidents-not MVA (M)	68	87	98	112	145**
Accidents-not MVA (F)	71	82	104	142	108
Suicide (M)	82	87	107	122	107
Chronic Obstructive Airways Disease (M)	87	92	96	101	131**

*Where data for males and females are similar, only male rates have been reported;
Class 1 is highest, Class V is lowest, adapted from Siskind *et al.* (1987)
**Chi squared p < 0.05

Marital Status

Marital status represents another social structural characteristic with health implications. Durkheim (1912) found that single people had higher suicide rates, and he interpreted this as demonstrating the importance of an individual's social networks and ties to the broader social system. More recent research has suggested

Table 10.6 Marital Status and Cause-specific Mortality, Age-standardised Mortality Rate (per 10,000), Australia 1965–67

		Single	Married	Widowed	Divorced
Infectious diseases	Males	1.35	0.41	0.95	1.30
	Females	0.50	0.24	0.36	0.25
Cancer of digestive organs	Males	5.73	4.54	7.40	5.50
	Females	5.02	3.52	5.79	3.41
Lung cancer	Males	4.18	3.66	4.92	6.54
	Females	0.50	0.52	0.71	0.80
Breast cancer	Females	3.09	2.11	2.62	2.17
Stroke	Males	12.56	8.22	19.00	10.81
	Females	16.48	8.43	19.20	9.01
Ischaemic heart disease	Males	39.48	30.16	55.05	39.57
	Females	25.52	14.96	31.57	18.34
Motor vehicle accidents	Males	6.06	2.70	3.59	6.58
	Females	1.74	0.97	2.95	2.29
Accidents	Males	5.82	2.07	4.02	6.75
	Females	2.65	0.97	2.83	3.07
Suicide	Males	3.48	1.40	5.87	7.16
	Females	1.32	0.92	2.66	4.49

Source: Adapted from Najman 1978

that many other disease conditions are influenced by marital status. Table 10.6 illustrates some of the typical findings of this research. It shows that for all the causes of death listed, married males and females have lower age-adjusted mortality rates. Thus, whether one is considering the infectious diseases, cancer of the lung or digestive organs, stroke or heart disease or the violent causes of death, widowed and divorced persons die at higher rates. Further, in some instances the magnitude of advantage of married persons is such that they have a death rate half that or less of those who are not married.

While the data appears relatively clear (see Kobrin and Hendershot 1977 for an American example), it is susceptible to various interpretations. Some would suggest that unhealthy single persons are less likely to marry. According to this view married persons are healthier because of a selection process. Another interpretation is that social bonds and strong social ties serve to protect or buffer the impact of stress on health. Yet another view is that much health-related behaviour (e.g. smoking, excessive alcohol consumption) occurs in a family context and that single people behave in a less healthy way because they are less subject to the moderating influence of family members.

At the present time we are unable to confidently choose between the above possibilities, though some comment on their plausibility is possible. Selection factors undoubtedly contribute to the observed differences in health, but they appear unlikely to account for the poor health of widowed persons (what type of selection could produce these differences?). Strong social networks appear to offer some health benefits, particularly in respect to emotional and psychological problems, but it is not apparent that they protect individuals from the range of causes of death identified in Table 10.6. Finally, it does appear that non-married persons behave in a less healthy manner (Wilsnack *et al.* 1984, Layne and Whitehead 1985). These behavioural differences may contribute to their poorer life expectancy.

Discussion

There have been a number of major changes in patterns of morbidity and mortality since the beginning of the twentieth century. These serve to emphasise the impact of the social and physical environment on health.

Much of what constitutes 'illness' in contemporary Australian society comprises either minor and self-limiting infections (respiratory and digestive system conditions) or 'problems of living' (headaches, nervous and mental disorders) both of which are unlikely to benefit materially from medical care. Hospital admissions also appear to be a consequence of some social and environmental processes (e.g. pregnancy and childbirth, accidents, mental illnesses), through in some instances the factors involved are poorly understood.

However, the most compelling illustration of the impact of Australian social organisation on health is provided by changes to, and contemporary patterns of, mortality. Thus the major decline in mortality in the twentieth century is, as we have noted, largely a consequence of the manipulation and engineering of the human environment. It has, however, led to a pattern of mortality largely involving the chronic diseases. These appear to have their causes in the lifestyle of individuals and the social structures which generate these lifestyles.

The patterns of morbidity and mortality considered in the previous sections showed:

- the major health advantage of members of some minority religious sects in Australia;
- the major health disadvantage of Aborigines in Australian society;
- the existence of some morbidity and mortality differences, with those in the lowest economic or status stratum of Australian society having the worst health;
- the apparent health advantage of married persons.

In each of the above instances we observe major health differentials which need to be understood. The factors leading to such health inequalities have been introduced, but these may now be reconsidered in the context of the available data.

An Artefact of the Data
It could be argued that the observed differences are a consequence of either the manner in which the data has been collected or interpreted. Thus, specifically in relation to 'class' differences, it has been suggested that:

- the poor are under-enumerated at the Census, thus producing an inflated mortality rate (deaths being correctly recorded but the population from which these deaths came being underestimated – Wise *et al.* 1985);
- the definition of 'classes' has changed over time. Thus in Britain the lowest class accounted for 20 per cent of births in 1931 and only 6 per cent of births in 1970–72. Consequently the high (infant) mortality rates experienced by the lowest class apply to only a small group in contemporary society (Illsley 1983);
- there is a process of selection where the least 'fit' in a social and physical sense are downwardly mobile, while those most fit are upwardly mobile. It consequently follows that class differences remain the same over time, but that they apply to a shifting group in the population. Thus, it is suggested the 'sick' become lower class (Alderson 1972: 246), as a consequence of their incapacity;
- Other coding inaccuracies or inconsistences associated with deriving rates from data obtained from different sources (Census, death certificates) produce the misleading observation of class differences (Alderson 1972: 247).

While it is not possible to consider all the above in detail, it is unlikely that their cumulative impact is to be totally misleading. Thus the problems noted with the data do not generally apply to the racial, religious or marital status differences and their cumulative impact, as estimated in studies which have controlled these sources of error (Alderson 1972, Fox and Goldblatt 1982) has been modest.

Biology/Heredity
It appears extraordinarily unlikely that hereditary differences between religious, racial, class and marital status groups, account for the observed variations in morbidity and mortality. Certainly the causal impact of such biological variations has not been seriously argued, though some might suggest that Aboriginal groups have lowered resistance to some infections or that their capacity to metabolise alcohol may be reduced. Regardless of the validity of these claims, it is relevant to recall that the infectious diseases were eliminated largely as a result of environmental control and thus this should again be possible in the context of Aboriginals in Australia. Further, regardless of Aboriginals' tolerance of alcohol, the real issue is that their life circumstances apparently lead some of them to consume excessive amounts. It is these circumstances rather than biologically-determined metabolic processes that warrant attention.

Adequacy of Medical Services
In the absence of Australian data on the distribution of medical services, it is possible only to offer some informed speculation about their likely contribution to observed inequalities in morbidity and mortality.

As the majority of Aborigines live in relatively isolated areas, it may be that their poor health is partly attributable to the health care they fail to receive. Thus high rates of death from accidents and injuries, or coronary heart disease, might partly reflect delays in receiving care associated with their physical remoteness. Also, more systematic care might lead to better control of high blood pressure, diabetes and a range of other potentially fatal conditions. However, as we have noted, the underlying social environmental processes produce extraordinarily high rates of illness for the Aboriginal population, and without attention to these, more medical care would only be palliative, not remedial.

The inadequacy of care possibility does not appear a sustainable explanation of the health inequalities for two further reasons. Firstly, major inequalities in health and mortality have been, and continue to be, found in circumstances where individuals appear to be receiving equally good care (Baird and Wyper 1941, Wise *et al.* 1985). Secondly, in the instance of religious, class and marital status variations in mortality, there is little reason to anticipate major differences in the quality of care that is received. ·

Evidence of inequalities in health and mortality might be used to justify some additional, specifically-targeted health initiatives, but the inequalities are unlikely to be reduced by improving access to traditional types of health services.

Lifestyle

There can now be no doubt that some of the variations in morbidity and mortality are a consequence of lifestyle differences. Those who belong to some minority religious sects have a healthier lifestyle and consequently a considerably reduced level of morbidity, mortality and longer life expectancy.

Data from the United Kingdom have also clearly shown that as smoking patterns change, so cardiovascular and lung cancer mortality differentials also change (Marmot and McDowall 1986: 275–76). The major and potentially modifiable aspects of lifestyle which are worthy of attention are:

- cigarette consumption;
- inappropriate alcohol consumption and related behaviours;
- diet with insufficient fibre and excess salt and cholesterol;
- inability to deal unaided with day-to-day stresses;

Social structure

Lifestyle variations are not randomly distributed within society. Rather they are systematically patterned, with members of religious sects, upper class persons, European Australians and possibly married persons manifesting systematic advantages.

While the existence of societally patterned lifestyle variations can be identified, it is somewhat more difficult to explain their origins and changes. Richard (1985) has compared various nations' cardiovascular mortality rates. He has found that persons in countries who share a similar genetic background have vastly different rates of coronary heart disease mortality rates (rates in New Zealand, Australia and the United Kingdom were more than twice those of Switzerland, Portugal, Spain and France). Also we know that women have begun smoking at higher levels, and that their rates of respiratory (lung) cancer have consequently increased (Ireland and Lawson 1980, Holman *et al.* 1986). However, it is unclear why women (or lower class men) have adopted health damaging lifestyles in recent years. Nevertheless the very existence of a class pattern, or one associated with religion or race, suggests that membership of these groups in society is causally important, and must be further investigated.

Policy Implications

If health and illness are, as this chapter argues, substantially influenced by the social and physical environment, then presumably health care delivery systems may be assessed in terms of the extent to which they deal both with the immediate manifestations of, and the factors that produce, illness. While this chapter is not specifically concerned with the effectiveness or appropriateness of medical treatment, such care appears to be the main activity of the current Australian health care system.

If, as we suggest, types of social structure produce identifiable health consequences, then these should also be the focus of therapeutic efforts. Jenkins (1977) has pointed out that those areas experiencing natural disasters are frequently the subject of emergency aid, yet in situations where large numbers of persons become ill or die as a consequence of their social and environmental circumstances, little is done. Presumably in situations which are chronically 'disastrous', that status quo is accepted.

Others have already noted that the solution to these disastrous states of poor health may be outside what has traditionally been defined as the health care sector (see Gray 1982: 369, Egbuono and Starfield 1982: 555). It was this perception of health as dependent upon political and structural changes which motivated Virchow to join the 1948 Berlin working class revolt (Navarro 1976). Similarly, one of the fathers of the discipline of sociology, Georg Simmel, noted in 1897 that structural solutions were needed to solve problems created by the social structure (see Casparis and Higgins, 1968–69).

Of course it is somewhat easier to call for change than to identify specific changes, and their intended and possibly unintended consequences. Unfortunately when one deals with the details of possible structural changes, they frequently represent 'a shot in the dark' (Scrivens and Holland 1983: 104). There appears to be a need for more innovative social experiments to test the impact of proposed structural changes.

The consistent finding that, in Britain, the impact of inequality on perinatal and infant mortality becomes greater after birth and though the first year of life (Antonovsky and Bernstein 1977) should be assessed in Australia. The lack of a health data base must be remedied before we are likely to understand the parameters of the health problems we face. As a first step it would appear appropriate to expand health promotion and disease prevention efforts directed at specific 'at risk' behaviours. If poverty, unemployment and racial injustice lead to unhealthy lifestyles, then programs which diminish such inequalities should be expanded on a trial basis, possibly through the income redistributive mechanisms of the taxation system.

Conclusion

Health and illness are fundamentally a consequence of the way societies are organised and function. Health is substantially influenced by the political, economic and cultural processes which prevail in any society. It follows from these observations that continued attention must be paid to racial, economic and other inequalities and their reduction as a necessary step in the improvement of health of minority groups in Australia. At the same time it is clearly appropriate that a redirection of health effort take place, with a greater emphasis on specific health promotion and disease prevention programs.

Notes

1 Many discussions of traditional Aboriginal society and its early contact with European culture are available: see, for instance, Rowley 1972, Franklin 1976.
2 Personal communication.
3 Using criteria which emphasise the minimum needs of people for food, housing and clothing.

References

Alderson, M.R. (1972) 'Some Sources of Error in British Occupational Mortality Data', *British Journal of Industrial Medicine* 29, 245–54.
Antonovsky, A. (1967) 'Social Class, Life Expectancy and Overall Mortality', *Milbank Memorial Fund Quarterly* 45: 31–75.
——— and Bernstein, J. (1977) 'Social Class and Infant Mortality', *Soc. Sci. Med.* 11: 453–70.
Apple, D. (ed.) (1960) *'Sociological Studies of Health and Sickness.* New York: McGraw-Hill.
Armstrong, B. *et al.* (1977) 'Blood Pressure in Seventh-Day Adventist Vegetarians', *American Journal of Epidemiology* 105 (5): 444–49.

Australian Bureau of Statistics (1986) *Australian Health Survey 1983*, No. 4311.0. AGPS: Canberra.

———(1986) *Household Expenditure Survey, Australia*, No. 6530.0. AGPS: Canberra.

Baird, D. and Wyper, J.F.B. (1941) 'High Stillbirth and Neonatal Mortalities', *Lancet* 2: 657–59.

Bastian, P. (1979) 'Coronary Heart Disease in Tribal Aborigines – the West Kimberley Survey', *ANZJ Med.* 9: 284–92.

Beck, R.G. (1973) 'Economic Class and Access to Physician Services under Public Medical Care Insurance', *Int. J. Health Services* 3 (3): 341–55.

Becker, H.S. *et al.* (1961) *Boys in White*. Chicago: University of Chicago Press.

Broadhead, P. (1985) 'Social Status and Morbidity in Australia', *Community Health Studies* 9 (2): 87–98.

Butlin, N.G. (1983) *Our Original Aggression*. Sydney: Allen & Unwin.

Casparis, J. and Higgins, A.C. (1968–69) 'Georg Simmel on Social Medicine', *Social Forces* 47: 330–34.

Catchlove, B. (1984) 'Community Demands for Health Services' in M. Tatchell (ed.) *Perspectives on Health Policy*. Canberra: Health Economics Research Unit, ANU.

Comstock, G.W. and Partridge, K.B. (1972) 'Church Attendance and Health', *J. Chron. Dis.* 25: 665–72.

Congalton, A.A. (1969) *Status and Prestige in Australia*. Cheshire: Melbourne.

Cooper, D. (1970) *Psychiatry and Antipsychiatry*. St Albans, Herts.: Paladin.

Coser, R.L. (1962) *Life in the Ward*. East Lansing: Michigan State University.

Donabedian, A. (1980) *The Definition of Quality and Approaches to its Assessment*. Ann Arbor, Michigan: Health Administration Press.

Durkheim, E. (1912) *Le Suicide*, originally published in Paris, various translations available, including that by J.A. Spaulding, and G. Simpson (1952), *Suicide*. London: Routledge & Kegan Paul.

Egbuono, L. and Starfield, B. (1982) 'Child Health and Social Status', *Pediatrics* 69 (5): 550–57.

Engels, F. (1845) 'The Condition of the Working-Class in England' reprinted in *Karl Marx and Frederick Engels, Collected Works*, Vol. 4. London: Lawrence & Wishart.

Faris, R.E.L. and Dunham, H.W. (1939) *Mental Disorders in Urban Areas*. London: Phoenix Books.

Fieve, R.R. *et al.* (eds) (1975) *Genetic Research in Psychiatry*. Baltimore: Johns Hopkins University Press.

Fox, A.J. and Goldblatt, P.O. (1982) *Longitudinal Study*, Series LN No. 1. London: HMSO.

Franklin, M.A. (1976) *Black and White Australians*. Melbourne: Heinemann.

Freeman, H.E. and Reeder, L.G. (1957) 'Medical Sociology: A Review of the Literature', *American Sociological Review* 22 (1): 73–81.

————, Levine, S. and Reeder, L.G. (eds) (1963) *Handbook of Medical Sociology*. Englewood Cliffs: Prentice-Hall.

Freidson, E. (1961) *Patients' Views of Medical Practice*. New York: Sage.

Goffman, E. (1961) *Asylums*. Harmondsworth: Penguin.

Gordon, D. (1976) *Health, Sickness* and *Society*. St Lucia: University of Queensland Press.

Gray, A.M. (1982) 'Inequalities in Health. The Black Report: A Summary and Comment', *International Journal of Health Services* 12 (3): 349–80.

US Department of Health and Human Services *Health United States*. (1985) Hyattsville DHHS Pub. No. (PHS): 86–1,232.

Hennessy, B.L., Bruen, W.J. and Cullen, J. (1973) 'The Canberra Mental Health Surveys: Preliminary Results', *MJA*. 1: 721–28.

Heyde, V. and Ring, I. (1984) *Cancer Mortality in Queensland: Trends 1952–1981: Comparisons with Australia 1979–81*. Queensland Department of Health, Brisbane.

Hicks, D.G. (1985) *Aboriginal Mortality Rates in Western Australia 1983*. Perth: Health Department of Western Australia.

Hollingshead, A.B. and Redlich, F.C. (1958) *Social Class and Mental Illness*. New York: Wiley.

Holman, C.D.J. *et al.* (ed.) (1986) *Our State of Health. An Overview of Health and Illness in Western Australia in the 1980s*. Perth: Health Department of Western Australia.

Illsley, R. (1983) 'Social Aspects of Pregnancy Outcome' in S.L. Barron, and A.M. Thomson (eds) *Obstetrical Epidemiology*. London: Academic Press.

Ireland, A.W. and Lawson, J.S. (1980) 'The Changing Face of Death', *Medical Journal of Australia* 14 June: 587–90.

Jaco, E.G. (ed.) (1958) *Patients, Physicians and Illness*. New York: Free Press.

James, J.J. (1979) 'Impact of the Medical Malpractice Slowdown in Los Angeles County: January 1976', *American Journal of Public Health* 69 (5): 437–43.

Jenkins, C.D. *et al.* (1977) 'Zones of Excess Mortality in Massachusetts', *NEJM* 296 (23): 1,354–56.

Keen, I. (1987) 'Aborigines and Islanders in Australian Society' in J.S. Western and J.M. Najman (eds), this volume.

Kobrin, F.E. and Hendershot, G.E. (1977) 'Do Family Ties reduce Mortality? Evidence from the United States, 1966–1968', *Journal of Marriage and the Family* November: 737–45.

Koos, E.L. (1954) *The Health of Regionville*. New York: Columbia University Press.

Krupinski, J. and Stoller, A. (1971) *The Health of a Metropolis*, Melbourne: Heinemann.

Kunitz, S.J. *et al.* (1975) 'Changing Health Care Opinions in Regionville, 1946–1973', *Medical Care* XIII (7): 549–61.

Laing, R.D. (1961) *The Self and Others*. London: Tavistock.

Layne, N. and Whitehead, P.C. (1985) 'Employment, Marital Status and Alcohol Consumption in Young Canadian Men', *Journal Studies in Alcohol* 46 (6): 538–40.

Lazarsfeld, P.F. and Reitz, J.G. (1975) *An Introduction to Applied Sociology.* New York: Elsevier.

Lemon, F.R. *et al.* (1964) 'Cancer of the Lung and Mouth in Seventh-Day Adventists', *Cancer* 17: 490.

—— and Kuzma, J.W. (1969) 'A Biologic Cost of Smoking', *Arch. Environ. Health* 18: 950–55.

—— and Walden, R.T. (1966) 'Death from Respiratory System Disease among Seventh-Day Adventist Men', *JAMA*, 198: 137–46.

Mc Dermott, W., Deuschle, K.W. and Bornett, C.R. (1972) 'Health Care Experiment at Many Farms', *Science* 175: 23–31.

McKeown, T. (1976) *The Role of Medicine: Dream, Mirage or Nemesis.* London: Nuffield Provincial Hospitals Trust.

McKinlay, J.B. and McKinlay, S. (1977) 'The Questionable Contribution of Medical Measures to the Decline of Mortality in the United States in the Twentieth Century', *Milbank Memorial Fund Quarterly* Summer: 405–28.

McMichael, A. (1985) 'Social Class (as estimated by Occupational Prestige) and Mortality in Australian Males in the 1970s', *Community Health Studies* 9 (3): 220–30.

Mann, W.N. (ed.) (1975) *Conybeare's Textbook of Medicine*, Sixteenth Edition. Edinburgh: Churchill Livingstone.

Marmot, M.G. and McDowall, M.E. (1986) 'Mortality Decline and Widening Social Inequalities', *Lancet* 2 August: 274–76.

Merton, R.K. Reader, G.G. and Kendall, P.L. (eds) (1957) *The Student Physician.* Cambridge Mass.: Harvard University Press.

Moran, D.J. *et al.* (1979) 'Ear Disease in Rural Australia', *MJA* 2: 210–12.

Najman, J.M. (1978) *A Social Epidemiology of Australia, using Mortality Data: 1965–67*, PhD Thesis, University of New South Wales.

——*et al.* (1979) 'Patterns of Morbidity, Health Care Utilisation and Socio-economic Status in Brisbane', *ANZJS* 15 (3): 55–63.

——Levine, S. (1981) 'Evaluating the Impact of Medical Care and Technologies on the Quality of Life: A Review and Critique', *Soc. Sci. Med.* 15F: 107–15.

——*et al.* (1983) 'Employment, Unemployment and the Health of Pregnant Women', Joint Issue of *Social Alternatives, Impact and New Doctor* 9–12 Sept.–Oct.

Navarro, V. (1976) 'The Underdevelopment of Health of Working America: Causes, Consequences and Possible Solutions', *AJPH* 66: 538–47.

Phillips, R.L. (1975) 'Role of Lifestyle and Dietary Habits in Risk of Cancer among Seventh-Day Adventists', *Cancer Research* 35: 3,513–22.

Powles, J. (1973) 'On the Limitations of Modern Medicine', *Science, Medicine and Man* 1: 1–30.

Registrar General (1971) *Decennial Supplement England and Wales 1961: Occupational Mortality Tables.* London: HMSO.

Reid, J. (ed.) (1982) *Body, Land and Spirit.* St Lucia: University of Queensland Press.

Report of the Director General of Health 1983–84 (1984). Canberra: AGPS.

Social Welfare Policy Secretariat, *Report on Poverty Measurement* (1981) Canberra: AGPS.

Reynolds, H. (ed.) (1972) *Aborigines and Settlers*. Melbourne: Cassell.

Richard, J.L. (1985) 'The Epidemiology of Coronary Heart Disease: A Review', *Effective Health Care* 2 (5): 197–209.

Roemer, M.I. (1979) 'Comment on Los Angeles Study of Physician Malpractice Slowdown', *AJPH* 69 (8): 826–27.

Rouse, I.L. *et al.* (1983a) 'The Relationship of Blood Pressure to Diet and Lifestyle in Two Religious Populations', *Journal of Hypertension* 1: 65–71.

———(1983b) 'Blood-pressure-lowering Effect of a Vegetarian Diet: Controlled Trial in Normotensive Subjects', *Lancet* 1: 5–10.

Rowley, C.D. (1972) *The Destruction of Aboriginal Society*. Melbourne: Pelican.

———(1978) *A Matter of Justice* Canberra: ANU Press.

Scrimshaw, N.S. *et al.* (1969) 'Nutrition and Infection field Study in Guatamalan Villages, 1959–64, *Arch. Environ. Health* 18: 51–62.

Scrivens, E. and Holland, W.W. (1983) 'Inequalities in Health in Britain. A Critique of the Report of a Research Working Party', *Effective Health Care* 1, (2): 97–109.

Shiraev, N. and Armstrong, M. (eds) (1978) *Health Care Survey of Gosford-Wyong and Illawarra 1975*. Sydney: Health Commission of New South Wales.

Simmons, L.W. and Wolff, H.G. (1954) *Social Science in Medicine*. New York: Sage.

Siskind, V. *et al.* (1987a) 'Socio-economic Status and Mortality: A Brisbane Area Analysis' forthcoming in *Community Health Studies*.

———(1987b) 'Trends in Coronary Heart Disease in Queensland 1971–80: An Interpretation', (submitted).

Smith, A.H. *et al.* (1985) 'Mortality among New Zealand Maori and non-Maori Mormons', *Int. J. Epid.* 14 (2): 265–71.

Social Indicators (1984) Canberra: Australian Bureau of Statistics.

Statistics on the Distribution of Income and Wealth in Australia (1981) Canberra: Department of Social Security, Research Paper No. 14.

Stevens, F. (1980) *The Politics of Prejudice*. Sydney: Alternative Publishing Co-op.

———(1981) *Black Australia*. Sydney: Alternative Publishing Co-op.

Strauss, R. (1957) 'The Nature and Status of Medical Sociology', *American Sociological Review* 22 (2): 200–04.

Syme, S.L. (1986) 'Social Determinants of Health and Disease' in J.M. Last (ed.) *Maxy-Roseman Public Health and Preventive Medicine*, Twelfth Edition. Norwalk, Conn. Appleton-Century-Crofts.

Szasz, T.S. (1970) *The Manufacture of Madness*. New York: Harper & Row.

Taylor, H.R. (1980) 'Prevalence and Causes of Blindness in Australian Aborigines', *MJA* 1: 71–76.

Taylor, R. *et al.* (1983) *Occupation and Mortality in Australian Working Age Males, 1975–77*. Melbourne: Health Commission of Victoria and Department of Social and Preventive Medicine. Monash University:

Thomson, N. (1985) 'Review of Available Aboriginal Mortality Data, 1980–82', *MJA* 143, 28 October, Special Supplement, 546–49.

Webster, I.W. and Rawson, G.K. (1979) 'Health Status of Seventh-Day Adventists', *MJA* 1: 417–20.

Wilsnack, R.W. *et al.* (1984) 'Women's Drinking and Drinking Problems: Patterns from a 1981 National Survey', *AJPH* 74 (11): 1,231–38.

Wise, P.H. *et al.* (1985) 'Racial and Socio-economic Disparities in Childhood Mortality in Boston', *NEJM* 313: 360–66.

Wynder, E.L. *et al.* (1959) 'Cancer and Coronary Artery Disease among Seventh-Day Adventists', *Cancer* 12: 1,016–28.

Chapter Eleven

Political Behaviour

David Kemp

In discussing the extent to which society constrains or conditions political behaviour, a number of general propositions should be kept in mind.

First, most political behaviour is organised behaviour, and organisation implies that leaders have a significant role in developing patterns of mass behaviour. Leaders are, by definition, takers of decisions, sources of purpose and direction, and this in turn implies choice and the potential for different decisions with different effects. Even such apparently individualistic acts as voting, marching or letter-writing on close inspection often turn out to be responses to varieties of leadership.

Second, to identify a role for leaders is to point to an aspect of political systems where social structure may constrain but rarely removes the possibility of choice. Leaders often find themselves behaving in similar ways to their predecessors in the same organisation or to their colleagues in other systems. It is the existence of these constraints that provides the opportunities for a sociology of politics, but just how constrained leaders may be is a matter for continuing theoretical analysis and investigation through research. Leaders can be thought of as continually testing their environments for sources of support and resources with which to pursue their causes.

Third, individual people may act politically outside frameworks of leadership and authority, and more rarely, may act as part of a crowd or other aggregate without apparent leadership. Within any society there will also be people who remain wholly or largely outside the main institutionalised political processes, and this behaviour too invites explanation, especially in a society where political participation in some form is seen as a good.

Simplistic theories which suggest that political behaviour is determined by some one feature of social systems must be set aside.

Most of the key analytical features of social systems can produce variations in patterns of political behaviour. The most important ones include: institutional rules and norms; values, beliefs, culture; the character and use made of basic social relationships, such as authority, exchange, persuasion or coercion; identifications with social categories of class, race, sex, religion, residence, nationality; differential access to values, resources (power and influence).

There are also environmental variations which may be important as they interact with society. These include the physical characteristics of the territory occupied by the society (its size, strategic characteristics, isolation), changes in technology, the global context, the incidence of diseases and so forth.

Political Behaviours Requiring Explanation

Much of the writing on the social patterning of political behaviour has focused on voting behaviour and related matters such as party identification (which may be readily researched through available electoral and Census data and with survey techniques). There are, of course, many kinds of political behaviour, important in their consequences, which require explanation if we are to gain a comprehensive understanding of politics and the way in which it is patterned by other features of society (for example, Barnes, Kaase *et al.* 1979).

We also need to be conscious of the fact that much political behaviour is directed towards making, and acting on, collective decisions. Collective decisions are an important feature of the political process: that is, certain key decisions are taken by procedures which aggregate individual decisions, principally voting procedures of one kind or another. Political decision-making is not only by individuals, but by electorates, by parliaments, by conventions and conferences, and collective decisions may have a relation to the values of the individual participants which may be quite complex (Arrow 1951, Olson 1965, MacKay 1980). If we are to understand the impact of features of society on political and policy outcomes, our framework of explanation must include reference to the procedures – the norms or rules – by which individual decisions are aggregated to a collective one, for these procedures are not neutral in their impact and indeed may be central to understanding the relationship between causes of individual behaviour, such as values, goals, and interests, and collective decisions and their resultant effects (Laver 1983).

With this warning in mind, in this chapter we will largely be concerned with the behaviour of individuals – leaders and followers – conceived as purposeful decision-takers. The study of behaviour from this perspective necessarily must include a study of the purposes which direct behaviour, recognising that there may nevertheless be slippage between purposes and behaviour.

The main types of behaviour on which we will focus in this context include the following:

Leadership Behaviour
- The prevalence of leadership in political activity, and activities directed to leadership maintenance, largely regardless of the stated purposes of this activity;
- Participation in leadership; access to leadership roles;
- Different styles of leadership in governmental, party and other institutional roles;
- Variations in the ideological behaviour of leaders; the different appeals for support articulated by leaders; phenomena such as ideological conflict and the pursuit of 'the middle ground'; factionalism; the establishment of new parties, interest groups and other organisations; protest activity;
- Variation in policy behaviour between leaders, i.e. in the authoritative decisions made by different leaders.

Follower-ship Behaviour
- The nature and bases of loyalty to leaders; awareness and perception of leaders.
- Partisanship.
- Making collective decisions; choosing and changing leaders – voting and vote-changing.
- Forming and changing opinions.
- Levels of participation in political processes; the increase in political participation in Australia.

Apolitical Behaviour
- Apathy towards system politics.

There are clearly-marked variations in the frequencies and content of different kinds of leadership and follower-ship behaviour between societies, within a given society, and over time. Leadership styles may vary from constitutional to revolutionary; from directive to consultative, from populist to élitist; from democratic to authoritarian. Leaders may be predominantly of one sex or more evenly balanced between the sexes; they may come from a wide range of backgrounds in society or from a few; they may seek to reflect widely-held social values or the ideology of a small group; leaders' appeals for support may be radical, conservative or liberal; they may seek an extensive role for the state or a restrictive one; they may emphasise values of freedom or equality or participation; they may be socially 'close' to or 'distant' from their opponents. Party organisations may be stable or subject to constant rearrangement; there may be many parties or few; parties may be unified or factious; voters may be loyally partisan or independent; they may participate as party members, voters, protesters or listeners, or they may ignore and withdraw from politics.

The issue of the nature of the autonomy possessed by leaders and followers bears on how we answer a number of questions which recur continually about politics: what are the chances that a new political party can establish itself as a long-term force? What chance of success can a specific appeal for support expect to achieve? What change in conditions can be expected to increase or diminish support for particular appeals? How is the remarkable stability in the party system in Australia to be explained? Can leadership of a certain style succeed in Australia? Is a more radical or a more conservative politics possible in Australia?

Features of Society which Pattern Political Behaviour

It is useful at the start of this inquiry to recognise that some features of Australian politics almost certainly arise from general features of human society, and hence constitute a core of politics common to all societies. Other features are likely to reflect particular ways in which Australian society differs from other societies. Both kinds of features provide components for major theories of political behaviour. A comprehensive understanding of political behaviour in Australia requires attention to both.

Reduction of Uncertainty

In all human societies the individual decision-takers live in conditions of uncertainty in relation to the achievement of their values. As between individual people, values differ (though within a society similarities will be evident), as does the extent to which individuals may achieve their values. Uncertainties arise from natural events, such as flood or fire, and from the decisions of others (within and outside the society). In the broadest sense, political behaviour can be thought of as behaviour designed to reduce uncertainty in value achievement by either influencing the decisions of others or achieving greater independence or autonomy from others (or some combination of the two). *Freedom* and *control* are thus dominant themes of political life (and of political ideologies) in all societies.

Since autonomy for one decision-taker is incompatible with control by another, and since all are engaged in the process of adjusting degrees of autonomy and control, some *conflict* is inevitable, regardless of the values being pursued. Only the hermit at one end of the spectrum and the omnipotent at the other can avoid this political process. Traditional and industrial societies, capitalist and socialist, all experience these tensions and associated conflicts in one form or another. Ideological themes of freedom and regulation have long been at the heart of political dispute in Australia, and while their form requires reference to specific features of Austalian culture, their centrality relates to deeper features of human society.

A further aspect of all human societies relevant to the nature of politics is the reliance on a relatively few basic social relationships to achieve autonomy and/or control. In their political aspects, these relations can be thought of as *basic mechanisms of social control* (Lindblom 1977). A list might usefully include authority, exchange, persuasion, physical coercion and the internalisation of social rules. The dominant political ideologies in Australia and elsewhere have much to say about the scope that should be accorded to each of these relations in society. Each mode of control has its own distinctive features and consequences. From an economic point of view, each entails costs. Societies vary in the scope allowed to each mechanism. Socialist societies tend to make more extensive use of authority; governments in Western mixed economies allow wider use of exchange. All societies use some combination of these mechanisms. Each possesses its own distinctive relation to the problems of freedom and control and hence to the nature of the uncertainties which underpin the agenda of political disputation.

There is not space here to detail at any length the consequences of these mechanisms for political behaviour in Australia, but some summary points mays be made about two of the principal mechanisms: authority and exchange.

Authority.   Authority may be thought of as the basic relationship within all formal organisations, including government, business, trade union and voluntary organisations (Lindblom 1977: 17–18). Milgram has argued that by enabling organised coordinated activity for common purposes, authority confers survival capacity and that the potential to be a part of structures of obedience has become an ability of the human organism through evolutionary processes (Milgram 1974: Chapter 10). A political mechanism authority involves acceptance of the opinions or decisions of another as binding, implicitly or explicitly, and hence acceptance of another as acting on one's behalf (Weber 1968: III, 946). Continuing (and partially successful) efforts are made to extend it to systems of laws, rules, regulations and adjudication. It is the basis of systems of property and it underlies the process by which identification with parties and other groupings influences behaviour. Authority is potentially a threat to individual autonomy. Conflicts can thus arise within authority structures and the maintenance and extension of such structures requires continuing resort to ideological appeals to justify their existence.[1] The absence of authority in government increases resistance to legal and institutional reform. Attitudes to authority are thus an important topic in the study of socialisation.

Exchange.   Exchange is the basic mechanism in markets. From a political perspective it is a mechanism for the exercise of mutual control through the exchange of benefits. By definition it improves the value position of each party to the exchange, and its widespread use in society is associated with long-term increases in value achievement. It also gives rise to its own characteristic uncertainties – for third parties; for those whose resources are insufficient to obtain what they want, and where alternative exchanges are few or non-existent (monopolistic situations) – thus stimulating political action to reduce market uncertainties. Much of Australian political behaviour reflects the direct and indirect consequences of the extensive use of exchange, from the effects of affluence to interest demands for regulation.

Leadership

Leadership is an important and ubiquitous form of political behaviour, closely linked to the use of authority. Leadership exists both inside and outside organisations. An important form of leadership outside organisation is the opinion leader, who becomes a point of reference or an authority for others (Lane and Sears 1964). The extent to which leadership is individual and that to which it is collective varies according to the ideology of the group. Its emergence is almost completely independent of group or party ideologies, though the norms which govern the conduct of leadership roles do vary among political parties and interest groups. The Liberal Party, for example, accords authority of wide scope to individual leaders and expects leaders to adopt decisive and directive styles. Labor Party ideology has generally defined a narrower role for leaders as facilitators of collective decisions and as the voices of group views. Leaders who breach these norms, as both Mr Whitlam and Mr Hawke did within the Labor Party, generate conflict.

A final feature of all human societies relevant to politics that will be mentioned here is that they are *systems for dealing with information.* This is implicit in the perspective that societies comprise individuals and authorities taking decisions. Each social relationship requires information and each handles information in different ways. The extended markets of modern societies transmit information through prices which represent in an aggregated form the valuations of market decision-takers. Authoritative interventions in market systems through price controls alter (and from an economic perspective, distort) this information and produce new patterns of market behaviour and political conflict. Authority systems are principally effective in transmitting information outwards. Because authority systems by definition imply centralised decision-making, information flowing to the centre of authority systems rapidly enters a bottleneck and must be filtered and reduced in order to be managed. Authority systems also tend to develop features resisting the central flow of information to defend the autonomy of individual participants, tending to develop features such as delegation, specialisation and checking systems to handle the information problems, as well as incremental decision processes. A great deal of policy behaviour and related institutional developments can be seen as flowing from this feature of authority systems, including the development of independent departments and tribunals, Cabinet, party and parliamentary committee systems, planning mechanisms to provide additional processing for information, and so forth. When central authorities act on inadequate information, dissatisfaction with their decisions is more likely, and political conflict may result.

Differences between Societies

Human societies can be seen as differing along a number of analytical dimensions, and variation between them on each dimension may produce variation in some aspect of political behaviour. Differences occur between constitutional systems and governing institutions, in the content of laws and other rules and how they are applied, in the content and distribution of values and beliefs, and in the relation between these and the ideologies of the dominant institutions. Societies differ in the rules applying to the way in which each basic social mechanism can be used: in the way in which authority is exercised in relation to property, in the activities which may be co-ordinated by exchange, in the rights to exercise persuasion. Societies differ in the way in which access to valued things is distributed (i.e. in the distribution of power) and hence in the capacity of individuals and institutional roles to produce given effects. And societies differ in the extent to which certain shared characteristics and social locations are viewed as important and become a basis for organisation. The task of the sociology of politics is to understand how much additional variation in political behaviour can be attributed to variations on each of these dimensions.

Stability in Australian Political Behaviour

Central features of Australian political behaviour have persisted for many decades; some have persisted since colonial times.

Constitutionalism
In an international perspective perhaps the most important persistence has been the willingness of leaders of powerful institutions, and of government in particular, to work within a stable, though evolving, constitutional framework. The transition from penal colony to free society, mass migrations, depressions, wars, industrial conflict and technological changes have all been handled by leaders within an agreed framework of governmental institutions, laws and regulations made under that framework. Leaders with revolutionary attitudes have been few, and their followings small. Constitutionalism is a way of life for leaders in almost all areas of Australian life.

Constitutionalism is a characteristic of the culture of politics in Australia which precedes the introduction of popular constitutions in the 1850s. The practice of constitutional reform to accommodate change had come to be gradually accepted in Britain after the American War of Independence, and was translated to Australia under British tutelage. With the exception of the Eureka incident, the transition to popular government was achieved within this tradition. Higley, Deacon and Smart (1979: 265) concluded that the preparedness of Australian institutional leaders to act

> within the framework of accepted and customary rules of public and private behaviour . . . is not a constitutional artefact. Rather it is the accumulated historical and contemporary experience of the national élite that its members are as a whole trust-worthy partners in the operation of these institutions that makes this self-serving, but still peaceful, behaviour possible.

Constitutionalism is one solution to the political problem of uncertainty in the achievement of values. It contributes predicta- bility and calculability to political processes. It is likely therefore only to be under threat when the urgency of achieving values of high priority overwhelms the virtues of procedural stability. In wars the constitutional system is self-adjusting – the defence power confers on government the enormous extension of authority required to defend the physical security of the society. In the constitutional crisis of 1975 fears of breakdown momentarily surfaced in the face of uncertainty over the constitutional solution to the impasse between the House of Representatives and the Senate.

A number of features of Australian society have been identified as supporting constitutionalism by diminishing the likelihood that extreme conflicts will overwhelm procedural agreement.

Firstly, as an advanced 'high mass-consumption' industrial society Australia falls into a class of countries which have all sustained competitive political regimes based on highly-inclusive rights of participation (Dahl 1971: 66). A number of cross-national studies have suggested that wealth and income in Australia are relatively evenly distributed in relation to other comparable coun- tries, but while such international comparisons are suggestive, methodological problems are substantial (Department of Social Security 1981). Inequalities and areas of relative poverty exist. These are significantly related, however, to life cycle events such as youth, sickness, marital breakdown and ageing (Australian Government Commission of Inquiry into Poverty, 1975: especi- ally Chapter 3) rather than indicating the kind of regional, ethnic or class inequalities which might provide a basis for severe political cleavage.

This leads to a further feature of Australian society which probably moderates conflict: cross-cutting social categories (Tru- man 1965, Lipset 1966, Dahl 1971: Chapter 7, Rae and Taylor 1970). While there are many characteristics associated in Australia with some form of value deprivation – whether income, property or status – these characteristics are rarely concentrated in collectivities which might be mobilised on a program to right them. Social class, religion, ethnicity, urban-rural residence, and of course sex characteristics, are only weakly associated. Those experiencing deprivation in relation to some values will often be able to achieve gratification in relation to others. Studies over the years have found Australia to be a society with an unusually high level of cross-cutting in its potential social 'cleavages', confirming it as a society with few opportunities for community-based conflicts (Clarke and Kornberg 1971).

One explanation for this feature of Australian society is its relatively open stratification system. Opportunities to attain higher levels of value gratification, especially in relation to income, education and status, appear to be relatively open across generations (Broom and Lancaster Jones 1976: 20, Broom, *et al.* 1980, Headey and O'Loughlin 1978, Aitkin 1982: Chapter 9). As a consequence there appears to be a continuing process of homogenisation within institutional centres of power with respect to these social characteristics over time. Catholics become leaders in institutions where leadership positions were formerly held by Protestants; migrants from central and southern Europe become leaders in institutions formerly Anglo-Saxon-led; relative income equality and the emergence of other bases of status such as education make discrimination on status grounds more difficult.

A significant activity for government in Australia has been to expand opportunities through income redistribution, an activity both driven and reinforced by a culture in which concern for disadvantage and support for equality of opportunity are entrenched. The open stratification system of Australia doubtless reflects and is reinforced by a culture strongly emphasising concepts of opportunity which removes from the 'agenda' of politics for the most part active support for the entrenchment of social privilege. (Australian politics is, by contrast, constantly dealing with demands for institutional privileges, as we will see.)

The most persistent cleavage line to find expression in Australian politics has been the rural-urban one. This cleavage alone has produced a continuing political force which recruits and develops programs for one side of the cleavage line only. An open stratification system can have relatively little impact on such a cleavage, existing in Australia for many decades, of a declining rural population. In this circumstance the rural-urban split tends to be intensified by other cleavages based on education and ethnicity (Kemp 1978: Chapter 8). In areas where rural population has increased and the homogenisation process is operating, the political tendency has been for the assimilation of political conflict into the broader national partisan competition.

In such a context Australia becomes a modern exemplar of Aristotle's dictum that a large middle class is conducive to stability. Australia's middle class is unusually large by international standards, and by subjective measures encompasses some 60 per cent or more of the population. Few Australians appear to think that class conflict is inevitable. Most do not see class mobility as difficult. Class labels are 'lightly worn' (Aitkin 1982: Chapters 8, 12).

Parties and Stability

A further reinforcement of constitutionalism in Australian political behaviour has been achieved by the emergence and workings of the party system. The domination of Australian politics for almost eight decades by two major political groupings can be argued to have moderated political conflict in Australia. Here the dynamics of organisational maintenance (including electoral success) have operated to reinforce the effects of culture and social structure.

Parties have an institutional interest in constitutionalism, because it is within the constitutional framework that they have a clear and undisputed place. The personal interests of party leaders in career success reinforce whatever interests they may have in specific programs to support constitutional policies. From the perspective of party leaders horrendous uncertainties multiply outside constitutional politics.

Australian parties have been successful in attracting loyalties. Some 90 per cent of Australian citizens associate themselves with one or other of the political parties. An aspect of this identification is that they see 'their' party as speaking for, or representing, them in the process of government. They participate in politics through their party, and in their view its existence gives them access to power. Stokes, for example (1963: 151–52) wrote that 'the public's perception of its influence on political leaders is part of what confers legitimacy on the decisions of leaders', and since political parties link citizens to leaders, 'parties and party systems have played an immensely important role in developing the public's control of leaders and conferring legitimacy on the regime'. An empirical conclusion from this is that those who do not see themselves as represented by political parties are more likely to be disaffected from the constitutional system. Historical support for this hypothesis is offered by the emergence of conservative para-military organisations supporting revolutionary action after the breakdown of conservative parties during the 1930s Depression in New South Wales. The emergence of an effective new political force, the United Australia Party, led by J.A. Lyons, saw the decline of these movements. The preparedness of groups with strong political positions without a clear party voice to engage in civil disobedience, such as certain environmental and right-to-life groups, also supports the hypothesis.

Inevitably a few large parties seeking to generate support in a society with a social structure such as Australia's develop bases of support which are quite diverse in social structural terms. While the major parties produce a *political* cleavage which reaches into every part of the country, this political division does not reflect a matching *social* division. In terms of the locations of the mass of their supporters in the social structure, and hence in the political interests that may be linked to those locations, the difference between the supporters of the Labor Party and the supporters of the Liberal/National Party coalition are of degree and emphasis only. (The electoral bases of support for the parties are dealt with in more detail below.)

Because there is no single interest emergent in the social structure which is large enough to confer political power by itself (unless it be the 'middle class'), under the conditions noted above the rhetoric of politics in Australia tends to be inclusive rather than exclusive. The efforts of party leaders to maintain their existing support and further extend their bases of support leads them to formulate appeals which necessarily extend beyond the interests of any one part of the social structure. Probably the effect of this over time is to further increase the similarities between the parties' bases of support. Indeed, it does appear to be the case that in social structural or categorical terms the parties' supporters became more similar in their characteristics during the 1970s. There is evidence that this process has been continuing for decades (Aitkin 1982: 304, Kemp 1978: 63ff).

The Stability of Parties

If Australia's parties contribute to the stability of the constitutional order, how can the stability of the parties themselves be explained? Since the Labor Party came into existence in the 1890s and the Liberal Party's ancestor of the same name in the first decade after Federation, Australian society has undergone great changes. The occupational structure of the workforce has become increasingly professionalised and white collar; manufacturing industries have developed and (since 1970) declined in terms of their share of the workforce; the rural population has diminished; the Catholic proportion has risen, as has the proportion with no religion; the proportion of the immigrant population born outside the United Kingdom has increased greatly; the size of the non-market sector (government administration, community services, health and education) has increased its claims on resources (public expenditure has risen from 20 per cent to 42 per cent of GDP, 1901–84) and continues to do so (see Butlin *et al.* 1982: 5 for early figures). Yet despite all these changes the party system has remained remarkably stable. The average proportions of the electorate supporting each of the main political forces has scarcely altered by more than a few percentage points on average across the decades. Short-term fortunes fluctuate and the political careers of individuals are made and ruined, but the party system in its broad outlines seems almost a permanent fixture (Aitkin 1982: 5).

The following are some of the main features of the Australian political framework and environment which have contributed to the stability of the party system despite social change.

Electoral Systems

Since parties tend to design electoral systems to suit themselves (Rokkan 1968), it is perhaps not surprising that electoral arrangements tend to buttress existing features of the party system. Single-member electorates with preferential voting do not impose quite the pressure for a two-party system that first-past-the-post or optional preference systems would. It has allowed the continued coexistence of the coalition partners, who can exchange preferences while making it difficult for smaller parties to impose damage. It is a system which offers some rewards for new groupings which split away from the existing parties, for they can damage the larger forces by the allocation of preferences, as the experience of both the Democratic Labor Party and the Australian Democrats has shown. These are negative incentives for fragmentation. By contrast, the Senate system of proportional representation has been kinder to minor parties and independents and has encouraged a degree of fragmentation around the fringes of the party system. Their institutional interest also induces these smaller parties to advocate proportional representation for lower chambers.

Spatial Distribution of Social Characteristics

Current voting systems enable existing parties to benefit from certain 'spatial' characteristics of Australian society: in particular, the rural-urban industrial division and long-standing social differences between suburbs, particularly in the older and larger cities of Sydney and Melbourne (Kemp 1978: Chapter 4, Aitkin 1982: Chapter 11, and, generally, Taylor and Johnson 1979).

One of the most important political effects of the socio-political structure of Sydney and Melbourne is the phenomenon of the 'safe seat'. This is a constituency in which a party has a majority exceedingly unlikely to disappear in the ordinary swings of the political pendulum. The vast majority of urban 'safe seats' in Australia are in Sydney and Melbourne. It is sometimes assumed that they are in areas where social class feeling is much higher than elsewhere, or in areas where there is an exceptionally high concentration of those social categories which tend to support one

Figure 11.1 Actual v. Expected labor Vote by Percentage
Non-manual in Workforce, Melbourne Electorates, 1983

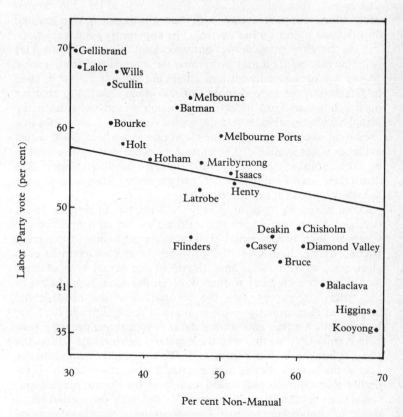

Source: Expected Labor vote based on survey data (Morgan Research, election
day survey, 5 March 1983)

party or the other. Neither of these explanations is completely
satisfactory and the first is misleading.

Figure 11.1 shows the percentage votes recorded for the Labor
Party in the 1983 House of Representatives election in the
Melbourne metropolitan electorates. It displays these votes according to the proportion of the electorate in non-manual occupations, as revealed in the 1981 Census. At first glance it seems to
confirm the view that occupational class and voting are strongly
related. For example, at the extreme Left of the figure, Labor in

Gellibrand received about 70 per cent of the vote, and some 70 per cent of the workforce in that electorate are other than non-manual. Yet we know from other kinds of research, such as survey research, that even in such safe seats as Gellibrand, not *all* those in manual occupations support Labor and not all those in non-manual occupations support other parties. The apparently simple relationship is, therefore, misleading, but we cannot tell from Figure 11.1 just how misleading it may be because we cannot learn from it what proportion of non-manuals and others *did* support Labor in 1983 in Gellibrand (or indeed in any of the other seats). For that we need a different kind of evidence, which would show both the actual occupational class and the actual vote of *each voter*, not just the broad overall figures for the electorate as a whole. Such direct evidence is not available. The closest we come to it is the evidence of public opinion surveys. Nevertheless, if sound sampling procedures have been used it is possible to generalise from such surveys to voters who were not interviewed.

Now when we look at survey evidence an intriguing result emerges. From surveys we can estimate the actual proportions of voters in each occupational class who support each of the main parties. If we then know the proportions of each class in each electorate, we can make an estimate of the actual vote that we would expect each party to record, given the occupational class of the voters (in survey data the occupation of the head of the household is commonly used, so there is some slippage here too between the Census and survey data). When the expected Labor vote is calculated in this way the expected proportions fall on the straight line marked in Figure 11.1. We can readily see that in the case of the 'safe' Labor seats the actual Labor vote recorded is far higher than the vote we would anticipate on the simple occupational class composition of the seats. In the 'safe' opposition seats, the actual Labor vote is much *lower* than the occupational composition of the voters would lead us to expect. This is a strong indication that some other factor is at work.

If we pursue the evidence of survey data we find that it is not that class voting is higher in the safe seats, but that all voters are much more likely to vote in the partisan direction of the dominant group. In 'safe' Labor seats, it is not so much that the Labor vote directly reflects the higher proportion of voters in manual occupations, it is that the Labor vote reflects the much higher likelihood that voters in non-manual occupations will also vote Labor. The converse is true for the safe Liberal seats. We can gain some further clues about why this should be so by looking closely at the *variation* in the Labor vote in electorates with similar occupational

Table 11.1 Occupations of Federal MPS (by Party)

Occupation	ALP 1971	ALP 1983	Lib. 1971	Lib. 1983	National 1971	National 1983	Other 1971	Other 1983
Teacher	5.8	10.5	–	1.7	–	–	12.5	16.7
Lecturer, Tutor (tertiary)	3.5	9.5	4.4	3.6	–	–	–	16.7
Union Official	20.9	10.5	–	–	–	–	–	16.7
Legal	9.3	5.7	19.1	32.1	–	4.8	12.5	–
Public Servant	9.3	8.6	–	1.8	–	4.8	12.5	–
Party Official	3.5	7.6	4.4	7.1	–	4.8	12.5	–
Medical Practitioner	5.7	5.7	–	1.8	–	–	12.5	–
Company Director/ Manager	2.3	–	13.2	12.5	–	9.5	–	–
Primary Producer	2.3	3.8	23.5	10.7	80.0	38.1	–	–
Accountant, Auditor, Secretary	5.8	4.8	4.4	7.1	–	9.5	–	–
Tradesman/Artisan	5.8	1.9	–	–	–	9.5	–	–
Clerical	5.8	–	2.9	–	–	–	–	–
Agents (inc. Auctioneers, Real Estate, Travel Agents)	1.2	–	7.3	–	4.0	–	–	–
Consultant	–	2.9	2.9	3.6	–	–	–	33.3
Retailer, Wholesaler	4.7	5.7	–	–	4.0	4.8	12.5	–
Member of State Parliament	–	2.9	–	3.6	–	9.5	–	–
Other	14.0	19.9	17.9	14.4	12.0	4.7	25.0	16.6
Members	86	105	68	56	25	21	8	6

Sources: Commonwealth Parliamentary Handbook, Seventeenth Edition, 1971, p. 459; *Parliamentary Handbook of the Commonwealth of Australia*, Twenty-second Edition, 1984, p. 194

distributions. Even at fairly low levels of non-manual voters there is a 10 per cent difference in Labor's vote between, say, Wills and Holt. In the middle of the occupational composition scale (around 50 per cent non-manual) there is almost a 20 per cent difference in the Labor vote between an outer metropolitan seat such as Flinders and the inner metropolitan seat of Melbourne. This shows that there are certainly other factors, probably a number of these, at work. One hypothesis, however, is that in the *traditional* Labor seats, where Labor voting is almost an *expected* partisan orientation, Labor does much better than in the newer areas where political tradition has pointed in the other direction. Both the homogeneity of the seat and the tradition of the area are factors which need to be brought into the explanation to actually account for the 'safe seat' phenomenon. An important relevant phenomenon may be a local partisan culture rather than a direct compositional effect of interests associated with individual social characteristics.

Leadership Recruitment

Each of the major parties has remained closely linked with the institutions associated with their foundation. The Labor Party continues to recruit leaders at both the parliamentary and organisational levels from the trade union movement; rural and urban business entrepreneurs and managers as political recruits overwhelmingly join the coalition. Nevertheless, even since 1971, some shifts in the occupational experience of the parties' parliamentary representatives can be observed (see Table 11.1). The most striking change, perhaps, on the Labor side is the growing proportion of parliamentarians with backgrounds in teaching. Teachers at all levels comprised 9.3 per cent of Labor MPs in 1971, and 20 per cent in 1983. Conversely, the number of trade union officials in Parliament declined in a mirror image of this change, from 20.9 per cent to 10.5 per cent of Labor parliamentarians. The proportions of these with trades and clerical backgrounds also seems to have declined markedly. Among Liberal MPs, those with legal backgrounds became more prominent, while rural businessmen (primary producers) declined in relative importance. The National Party seems also to have cast its recruiting net more widely, moving from an almost exclusive emphasis on primary producers towards, especially, a wider spread of business-related occupations. One straw in the wind, perhaps reflecting the growth of the parties' own bureaucracies and the growing number of roles for partisan supporters in ministerial officer positions, is the growing proportion in all parties of parliamentarians with previous employment as party officials. Labor continued to recruit significantly more recruits from the public sector than other parties – from education, statutory authorities and the public service directly. The organisational linkage between the Labor Party and the trade union movement through the concept of affiliated organisations remains a significant structural rigidity in the party system which undoubtedly limits the impact of the process of social homogenisation which is occurring at the level of electoral support.

Ideology

The ideological appeals of the major parties have remained remarkably stable throughout their history (Loveday *et al.* 1977: especially Chapter 9). There are two principal features of this aspect of political behaviour. Firstly, there is a significant overlap in the values emphasised by the parties (constitutionalism, democracy, nationalism, evolutionary change). Secondly, there have been long-standing differences of emphasis. The coalition parties have tended to emphasise general values of freedom, choice, achievement, independence, initiative, enterprise, leadership, teamwork, loyalty and moral standards and have overtly supported federalism and the traditional Westminster features of the Constitution: constitutional monarchy, the non-partisan public service and Cabinet government. The Labor Party has tended to emphasise values of equality, fairness, equity, solidarity, sharing, co-operativeness, collective decision-making, welfare and security and has been consistently more favourable to constitutional change towards a unitary Constitution. Labor leaders have used class rhetoric (but with diminishing frequency); coalition leaders have traditionally eschewed such rhetoric in favour of concepts of common interests or identified themselves with 'the middle class'. Labor has lauded the contribution of trade unions and been sceptical to critical of private enterprise. Coalition rhetoric has supported a limited role for government, Labor rhetoric the more extensive use of government authority to aid the underprivileged. The emphasis within the appeals of each of the parties has altered from leader to leader and time to time, but the broad consistencies are apparent. We will consider political behaviour resulting in inconsistencies between rhetoric and policy.

Changes in the social characteristics of supporters combined with stability of ideological appeal suggests a degree of independence between specific features of social structure and values and beliefs. It is known from research into party images that the ideological differences between the parties are perceived by citizens, and that these differences play a role in the evaluation of the parties (Aitkin 1982: Chapters 4, 19). There are also perceptions of differences in the group associations of the parties – their linkages to other institutions (particularly business and trade unions) and to social categories (farmers, workers, poor people, triers, etc.). These, too, form elements in the evaluation of the parties. It seems apparent that in the mobilisation of support these ideologies and associations are of central significance.

The terms of the ideological dispute between the parties reflect ideas developed principally in the eighteenth and nineteenth centuries, but drawing on older traditions. Conservative, liberal, socialist, utopian, Marxist and Christian thought all feed into Australian political debate.

More generally, a political debate focused on concepts of freedom and control expresses continuing tensions in human

society as decision-makers search for certainty in value achievement. Autonomy appeals to those who believe that their own
unregulated efforts can achieve what they are seeking; control
appeals to those who are conscious of their own weakness without
assistance. These tensions are always present – in pre-industrial,
industrial and post-industrial societies, and in capitalist and
socialist economies. Ideologies focused on such themes have great
lasting power, and elements can be traced back centuries into the
history of Western culture. Such ideologies also have considerable
ability to adapt to change at the detailed level of policy
prescription.

Nevertheless, because autonomy or control are rarely exclusive
strategies for any decision-taker, political ideologies focused on
one or the other are frequently driven into inconsistency as their
proponents attempt to retain stable support. The trade union
movement, while seeking the protection and support of the state
for itself and tight control over employers, nevertheless also seeks
the lightening of legislative restrictions on union activity, and a
laissez-faire stance from government where union power is adequate to force a decision in a dispute. Employers support freedom of
enterprise except when market uncertainties threaten the enterprise. Unionism exists to give greater certainty to the individual
worker, but he or she cannot ask for too high a degree of autonomy
from the union. In each ideology it is impossible to achieve
consistency, because the tensions between autonomy and control
for decision-takers are ever-present.

Party Identification

One of the strongest forces for stability in the party system is the
fact that parties themselves come to act as authorities on politics
for a large proportion of voters. This is the phenomenon of party
identification (Campbell *et al.* 1960, Budge *et al.* 1976, Aitkin
1982: Chapter 3). Voters' loyalties to political parties are of varying
strengths, but some 70 per cent of voters consider themselves 'very
strong' or 'fairly strong' supporters of one party of another.

These loyalties tend to stabilise the party system in several
ways:

- They inhibit short-term vote-changing, and do so with
  greater effect on supporters with stronger loyalties. This
  makes it difficult for 'flash' parties to emerge at any single
  election.
- They enable voters to reduce the amount of information
  they require in order to make electoral decisions. In so doing

they increase communications problems for new parties. The stronger the identification the higher the interest in politics but the less likely the supporter is to be swayed by 'the other side'.

- They increase the capacity of existing parties to act as interpreters of issues for loyalists. The existing parties thus 'educate' the public to view events through the eyes of party leaders, and over time tend to create standardised perspectives on issues. In this sense parties are probably significant forces in the reinforcement of culture as well as in the creation of opinion on specific issues. Parties, however, do not have a monopoly on opinion creation though the impact of their efforts can be seen from time to time on the attitudes of supporters where the main parties are polarised.
- They increase the capacity of existing parties to mobilise the active support of large numbers of people. This becomes important in taking full advantage of features of the electoral system, such as the manning of polling booths, helping infirm voters to the polls, canvassing for candidates, and so forth.

Inheritance

The long-term stabilisation effect of party identification is reinforced by the fact that party loyalties tend to be inherited. Party identification seems to be one of the most reliable cultural elements transmitted between generations (Kent Jennings and Niemi 1981: 48ff). Even in a changing society a pattern of loyalties laid down in

Table 11.2 Party Identification by Education, 1979

	Primary	Secondary	Tertiary*
Labor	52.7	43.6	37.0
Liberal	29.3	38.0	37.4
NCP	5.1	4.5	3.0
Australian Democrats	1.0	2.0	4.2
No Ident.	11.9	12.0	18.4
	100.0	100.0	100.0
N	294	985	695
Total %	14.9	49.9	35.2

*includes attended tech., university, completed university
Source: Macquarie *Australian Political Attitudes Survey*, 1979.

an earlier era has a certain persistence which tends to change only slowly (Aitkin 1982: 94).

The 'drag' effect of inherited party loyalties probably helps to explain why, in a relatively open stratification system, upward career mobility or educational mobility do not lead necessarily to the adoption of the traditional party loyalties of higher social status groups, but rather produce a homogenisation of political loyalties in these categories. Expanding access to higher education has been matched by increasing Labor identification among those with tertiary education. Current levels are shown in Table 11.2. Inherited identifications may be part of the explanation for this.

Formation
Because of the importance of party identifications in explaining voting behaviour and party stability there has been considerable interest in discovering the mechanisms by which such identifications are formed in the first place.

In inherited identifications the motivation is probably provided by the desire to be at one with parents and a family tradition.

Table 11.3 Voting Intention by Priorities 1983

	Freedom	Equality
Labor	45.7	61.6
Liberal	41.9	25.0
NCP	6.0	6.9
Australian Democrats	0.6	0.0
Other	1.5	1.7
No Answer	4.2	4.8
	100.0	100.0
N	633	287
Total %	68.8	26.4

Source: Australian Values Study (Roy Morgan Research Centre) 1983

Note: *Question:* Now, thinking about *freedom* and *equality*. Which *one* statement comes closer to your own opinion? Certainly freedom and equality are important. But if I were to make up my mind for one or the other, I would consider equality more important, that is, nobody is underprivileged and that social class differences are not so strong ... OR ... I find that freedom and equality are important. But if I were to make up my mind for one or the other, I would consider personal freedom more important, that is everyone can live in freedom and develop without hindrance.

Table 11.4 Voting Intention by Self-described Ideology, 1983

	Very Traditional	Somewhat Traditional	Middle of the Road	Somewhat Progressive	Very Progressive	Don't Know
Labor	31.7	39.0	49.4	64.8	61.3	30.0
Liberal	41.5	40.4	32.4	20.6	22.6	25.0
NCP	17.1	9.9	5.5	2.5	3.2	0.0
Australian Democrats	0.0	6.4	6.9	5.5	9.7	5.0
Other	0.0	0.0	0.6	0.5	0.0	5.0
No Answer	9.8	4.3	5.3	6.0	3.2	35.0
	100.0	100.0	100.0	100.0	100.0	100.0
N	41	141	510	199	31	20
Total %	4.4	15.0	54.1	21.1	3.3	2.1

Source: *Australian Values Study* (Roy Morgan Research Centre) 1983

Note: Question: Looking at the next *white* card. (PAUSE). How would you describe *your own* general viewpoint with regard to social issues and social trends in Australia? Just say the letter after it.

A. VERY TRADITIONAL B. SOMEWHAT TRADITIONAL
C. MIDDLE/OF THE ROAD D. SOMEWHAT PROGRESSIVE
E. VERY PROGRESSIVE F. DON'T KNOW

In new identifications the motivation may be equally a by-product of loyalty to a primary group which comes to act as an authority in relation to opinion: a group of friends, workmates, sporting acquaintances, church, etc. It is known that most small groups tend towards homogeneity of opinion and homogeneity in political opinion may be an aspect of this if political opinion is salient to the group. There may also, however, be a more direct linkage between a party's policies and appeals and the values and perceived interests of the individual voters (though these too will often be interpreted or understood through a group process). The interests of a social role, such as business manager, trade union leader, property owner, taxpayer, breadwinner, may be closely linked to a particular party's approach. A personal ideology or values may match more closely the ideology or values of one party than another. Personal needs in autonomy, harmony, sociability, opposition may seem to be gratified more by one party than the other. Table 11.3, for example, shows that a higher priority on equality than freedom is associated with Labor Party voting, and Table 11.4 that a self-perception of oneself as traditional in personal ideology is associated with Liberal and National voting intentions.

The positive appeal of one party may be less important than the negative evaluation of another (dislike of trade unions may incline a voter towards the Liberal Party; dislike of big business towards the Labor Party, for instance). The results of active participation in a political campaign to influence policy on an issue such as environmentalism, may be relevant in both voting and future identifications. Membership of a group believed by the voter to have been significantly advantaged by a particular party mays be central. Generally it seems theoretically likely that the perception that one party has the greater capacity to deal with a problem of deprivation in relation to values central to a personal belief system, will be an important source of identification. This perception will generally need to be sustained by the group context of the supporter.

Partisanship and Social Structure
It should not, therefore, be assumed that a political party will necessarily have a basis in a single aspect of the social structure. Indeed, a unique social basis is especially unlikely in the case of a few large parties in a relatively complex society. Tables 11.5–11.12 shows that this is so in Australia.

Several observations should be made about the patterns of party support which appear in these tables. Firstly, these patterns do not themselves 'explain' partisan behaviour. Explanation requires us to examine more closely the processes which have produced each

Table 11.5 Party Identification by Subjective Social Class,
1979

	Middle	Working
Labor	33.8	60.6
Liberal	44.6	21.7
NCP	4.4	3.5
Australian Democrats	3.0	2.7
No Ident.	14.5	11.5
	100.0	100.0
N	1,106	515
Total %	68.2	31.8

Table 11.6 Party Identification by Trade Union Membership,
1979

	Members	Non-Members
Labor	55.8	37.4
Liberal	25.1	41.0
NCP	1.8	4.9
Australian Democrats	3.8	2.3
No Ident.	13.4	14.4
	100.0	100.0
N	553	1,421
Total %	28.0	72.0

pattern. The simple statistics of each table take us only a short distance towards understanding the underlying processes producing partisanship. Secondly, these patterns are not immutable. They change over time, as the forces or processes which generate and sustain them strengthen or weaken. Thirdly, the longer-term prospects for a party cannot be predicted simply by extrapolating some trend in one or other of these social indicators. An ageing population, or a more professional workforce, do not necessarily favour the coalition parties, nor a larger immigrant percentage, nor an increase in union membership nor in higher education, the Labor party. The social meaning or significance of belonging to a category (such as working women) can change over time, and the behaviour of party leaders will also tend to adjust to maintain support.

Table 11.7 Party Identification by Birthplace, 1979

	Australia	UK, USA Canada, NZ	N. Europe	S. Europe	E. Europe	Asia
Labor	42.4	46.8	28.9	57.4	31.8	33.3
Liberal	37.1	32.4	48.9	25.4	43.2	36.1
NCP	4.9	0.5	2.2	0.0	0.0	2.8
Australian Democrats	2.6	2.3	4.4	4.3	0.0	2.8
No Ident.	13.0	18.0	15.6	12.8	25.0	25.0
	100.0	100.0	100.0	100.0	100.0	100.0
N	1,574	222	45	47	44.	36
Total %	80.0	11.3	2.3	2.4	2.2	1.8

Table 11.8 Party Identification by Religion, 1979

	C of E	Catholic	Uniting	Other Protestant	No Religion
Labor	39.3	49.1	37.2	24.3	52.3
Liberal	41.4	32.4	47.6	52.3	24.7
NCP	5.9	3.2	4.8	5.6	2.6
Australian Democrats	2.7	2.1	1.3	2.3	3.2
No Ident.	10.7	13.2	9.1	15.4	17.1
	100.0	100.0	100.0	100.0	100.0
N	488	438	231	214	497
Total %	26.1	23.4	12.4	11.5	26.6

Table 11.9 Party Identification by Age 1979

	18–21	22–29	30–35	36–45	46–55	56–65	66 +
Labor	46.1	49.4	41.0	36.8	42.0	42.0	40.6
Liberal	25.7	29.6	34.9	36.1	42.0	42.0	43.0
NCP	3.7	4.1	7.2	4.2	1.4	3.9	4.5
Australian Democrats	4.2	3.0	4.4	3.9	1.7	0.8	0.8
No Ident.	20.4	13.8	12.4	18.9	13.0	12.0	10.9
	100.0	100.0	100.0	100.0	100.0	100.0	100.0
N	191	362	249	285	355	259	266
Total %	9.7	18.4	12.7	14.5	18.0	13.2	13.5

Table 11.10 Party Identification by Sex, 1979

	Men	Women
Labor	45.6	39.8
Liberal	32.1	40.7
NCP	3.9	4.1
Australian Democrats	2.9	2.4
No Ident.	15.5	13.0
	100.0	100.0
N	941	1038
Total %	47.5	52.5

Table 11.11 Party Identification by Occupation, 1979

	Prof.	Semi-Prof.	Clerks-Office	Skilled	Semi-Skilled	Un-Skilled
Labor	25.5	31.8	39.4	62.5	52.0	51.5
Liberal	47.1	44.7	40.9	18.0	29.1	30.4
NCP	3.9	5.0	2.2	1.5	5.1	3.1
Australian Democrats	1.0	3.3	3.6	3.5	1.1	2.3
No Ident.	22.5	15.1	13.9	14.5	12.7	12.7
	100.0	100.0	100.0	100.0	100.0	100.0
N	102	443	411	200	275	260
Total %	6.0	26.2	24.3	11.8	16.3	15.4

Table 11.12 Party Identification by Income 1979

	Up to $3,000	$3,000–$7,500	$7,501–$10,000	$10,501–$13,500	$13,501–$16,500	$16,501–$19,000	Over $19,000
Labor	44.7	46.0	49.8	50.4	40.8	41.8	15.6
Liberal	35.2	34.6	33.2	29.9	35.7	38.2	58.3
NCP	4.6	3.0	2.2	3.1	6.7	1.8	5.2
Australian Democrats	1.7	2.5	3.2	4.3	3.8	1.8	2.1
No Ident.	13.8	13.9	11.5	12.2	13.4	14.5	18.8
	100.0	100.0	100.0	100.0	100.0	100.0	100.0
N	349	361	313	254	157	55	96
Total	23.4	24.2	21.0	17.1	10.5	3.7	6.0

The nature of the process which tends to produce a particular partisan disposition among those who belong to a social category varies according to the category. The process by which Catholicism came to be associated with Labor support is different from the process by which rejection of religious belief is associated with such support. The former relates to the historical association of economic status, union membership, Irish immigrants and the conflict over Home Rule with church membership. As the social status of Catholics has risen and the Irish issue faded, so there has been a marked weakening in the association between Catholicism and Labor voting (Kemp 1978: 192). The link between rejection of religious belief and Labor voting may well be associated with the impact of education and links between religious and social radicalism, having more to do with linkages between individual belief systems and party ideology rather than economic or social status. Linkages between youth and Labor voting may be an Australian expression of a phenomenon observed frequently overseas: the greater responsiveness of young people to new political circumstances because party identification has not yet stabilised. Between 1958–69 younger people had disproportionately favoured the coalition parties. During the 1970s there emerged a number of new political forces (environmentalism, consumerism, feminism), high youth unemployment and political leaders in the Labor Party personally attractive to young people. All these were probably important in creating an age bias towards Labor. Given the operation of 'inheritance' as a process in producing party identification, it is perhaps not surprising that a significant source of Labor's gains among young people during the 1970s came from those whose parents were not partisans of either of the major political forces (Aitkin 1982: 299).

Australia has seen only one political party with its principal base of support in organised religion (the Democratic Labor Party). The Country (later National) Party has had a base with both regional and industrial elements (being most firmly based in certain rural industries such as wheat, dairying and fruit-growing), but with an ideology in which anti-urbanism has been an important component. The Labor Party basis has been most explicitly among the blue collar working class, but also including Irish, small business, and Catholic elements. Table 11.8 shows that both in terms of absolute numbers, as well as in terms of strength of bias, Labor now gains more support from those without religious belief than it does from Catholics. The tension between these orientations has been a significant source of sectarian conflict within the Labor Party over the years. The Liberal party has appealed most strongly to enterprise managements, to Anglican and other

Protestant groupings, to larger rural producers, and the higher status conservative professions, as well as small business and socially conservative elements.

Of all these social categories the one which continues to have the strongest association with the direction of party loyalties is occupational class, but this association is not strong and has greatly weakened in recent decades (Kemp 1978). As Aitkin discovered in reviewing the results of three national surveys investigating attitudes to political parties in 1967, 1969 and 1979, over the twelve years: 'First, the set of social structural variables explained less in 1969 than in 1967, and in 1979 than in 1969. Second, there was a dramatic reduction, in particular, in the power of head of household's occupational grade. Third, all the "class" variables declined in power. Fourth, only one variable – religion – grew more important' (1982: 299). Kelley and McAllister (1985) concluded after a recent analysis that the status aspects of class are irrelevant to political preference; that the categorical white collar/blue collar distinction has a clear, though relatively small effect, and that government employment has again a distinct (though small) pro-Labor effect. They found political attitudes more important than class in accounting for partisanship (p. 10). 'In short, the need is to explain the poverty of social structural variables in accounting for partisanship ...' (Aitkin 1982: 302, also Rose 1974: 17). It is noteworthy that at the time of the most bitter political conflict of recent times, the constitutional crisis of 1975, the linkage between the major parties and occupational class bases had probably never been weaker (Kemp 1978: 67). The dynamics of politics lay elsewhere.

Partisanship and Culture

Edelman (1967) has emphasised the 'symbolic uses of politics' by party leaders, who in their efforts to maintain and extend their coalitions of support, communicate symbolically by language. It is the culture which provides the symbolic resources through which meaning is given to social reality and through which voters recognise their representatives – those who speak for them – in the political domain. Culture can be considered to provide a source of patterning for political behaviour which is to some extent independent of social structure, and which thus adds further to our ability to explain political behaviour. Tables 11.3 and 11.4 show linkages between voting intentions and various attitudinal and value positions.

Several observations can be made about the 'patterning' of political behaviour by culture. Firstly, as with social structure, there is a process which produces the associations such as those in

Table 11.3 that must be examined before we can claim to fully 'explain' partisan behaviour. For example, explaining why the Labor party is more strongly associated with the concept of equality invites both an historical enquiry, but also the kind of enquiry into fundamental strategies for achieving values already outlined. Why some people find certain values and beliefs attractive invites equiry into their institutional roles (and hence back into social structure) but also into personal belief systems and personality. Davies and Little, for example, have suggested that certain socialising experiences in the family, especially the experience of authority, create dispositions towards authority outside the family – oppositional or accepting which may come to be linked to political style and stance (Davies 1972: Chapter 11, also 1980, Little 1973). Maslow has posited a hierarchy of human needs, with non-material values gaining in marginal priority as material values are satisfied (Maslow 1954, see also R. Inglehart 1977, Kemp 1979).

Secondly, as with social structural linkages to partisanship, the culture/party relationship is not immutable, though the stability of leaders' ideological appeals suggests it is not readily altered in its core characteristics. Indeed, it is an objective of the leaders' efforts at communication to both reinforce but also to shift this association in their favour. Given the appeal of concepts of personal autonomy as a road to value achievement in Australian culture (as in other Western cultures) it is perhaps not surprising that extensive efforts have occurred over the years to redefine the term 'freedom' to cover egalitarian policies of income and wealth redistribution. Because of the role of parties in creating opinion, the recognition and understanding of a concept is itself likely to be influenced by the prominence of that concept in party debate. Stereotyped usages of concepts such as 'class' may well be in part a function of the way in which these concepts are generally employed by party leaders. Political parties may thus influence, and be influenced by, culture in a manner parallel to the impact they may have on social structure through their policies.

Where does 'culture' come from? An important issue for theory and research is to establish how the cultural meanings which affect politics are created, sustained and changed. This is difficult to establish empirically. One view, put by Connell (1977: 187) is that Australian culture is decisively influenced by the fact that production in Australia is largely organised by business enterprise based on private property ownership. This is seen as being evidenced by the tendency of socialisation in the 'whole social structure' to encourage a 'prudential respecting of (rather than an attitude of respect for) authority and private property'. Connell sees the *absence* of 'an oppositional working class culture' as evidence of the effectiveness of this social structure in producing a homogeneous culture. Yet while it is inherently plausible that private property tends to generate its own supporting ideology, Connell does not provide compelling evidence that it is the dominant or 'ruling' element in the social structure in the generation of culture.

Disentangling the cultural impact of a particular institution from the impact of others in a society and from specific historical experiences is, of course, a very complex matter. Each significant institution has its own ideology which it seeks to promote, and the dominant values and beliefs which must have some cultural impact. The trade union movement in Australia has long promoted values of collective action, solidarity, fairness, equality and an emphasis on material incentives. The Arbitration Commission has promoted values such as legalism and comparative wage justice. Public services have promoted values of technical expertise, partisan neutrality, the importance of administrative procedure, impersonality, equality of opportunity and personal security. Churches have been significant institutions promoting values of family life, faith, brotherhood and humanity. In our society the diversity of institutional authorities seems to require a broad initial perspective in understanding the processes of cultural generation and change. Private property is one feature of the organisation of authority which must certainly have a cultural impact. Whether that impact is 'good' or 'bad' is a matter of active debate between supporters of private enterprise and its opponents.

A feature of all societies in which there are a number of institutional interests – socialist or private enterprise – is a degree of institutional conflict. The rules which determine how this conflict is played out, and the opportunities for acquiring re-sosurces, power or influence in its course, seem likely to have an important influence on the development of culture. In Australia the existence of important individual and institutional freedoms doubtless tends to give this institutional conflict a reinforcing role in relation to the concept of freedom. Unlike the position in socialist societies, every institutional ideology has an extensive concept of freedom which is continually employed in public debate: freedom of enterprise, freedom of the press, academic freedom, freedom of association, the independence of the ju-diciary, the neutrality and anomymity of the public service, the secrecy of Cabinet and the privilege of Parliament. The cultural value placed on freedom clearly has much more extensive founda-tions in Australian society than simply the existence of a business enterprise system based on private property.

The Future of Party Identification

Whether parties can continue to recruit firm supporters depends logically on there being conditions or issues in which contrasting appeals can have partisan implications. Issues with the emotional intensity of the Vietnam War, associated with party polarisation, are rare. In the last decade the dominant themes of major party appeals have centred around the issue of which party can provide greater certainty and security to the mass of voters. The credibility of these appeals varies for each party from election to election, depending on the state of the economy and who has been in power. Such appeals seem unlikely to provide the basis for longer-term identifications. Over the same period factional differences have increased within the major parties and these differences 'signal' values associated with one party or the other.

In both the United Kingdom and the United States social change has been associated with a weakening of traditional party attachments. In Australia this has not occurred to a great extent. Although there has been a consistent third party vote for several decades it has been relatively minor. One explanation which has been given for this is compulsory voting – a rule which forces voters to consider the options and to seek a way of making a decision. Another is specific to Australian history – the circumstance has not arisen in which both the major political forces are seen to have failed to cope. In Australia the succession of governments has been at a pace in which the main opposition party has had time to seem rejuvenated and ready once more for power. The openings for third parties to recruit on the basis of wide disaffection have been narrow and few.

Political Strategies

Ultimately the stability of the Australian party system requires reference to the stabilising activities of the party leaders. Leaders have personal interests in adjusting the appeals of their parties to win sufficient support to gain office. Leaders of each party are constantly engaged in seeking to maintain and extend a value and interest coalition sufficient to confer political power. This involves them in continual efforts to communicate to both wide and narrow audiences of voters.

Communication behaviour is of such central importance that it is not surprising that the institutional structures associated with leadership communication have become increasingly elaborate as new knowledge and technology have expanded opportunities. A

century ago relations with newspaper proprietors were important
for communication through the printed press, but face-to-face
meetings and the use of personal agents were also key mechanisms.
The advent of electronic media, together with the development of
communications techniques in private enterprise and survey technology by market researchers, has led to the supplementation of
the old techniques by new possibilities which have been increasingly exploited.

The professionalisation of political communication during recent decades is indicated by the employment of professional
advertising agencies during election campaigns, and increasingly
between them; the use of professional opinion research organisations to monitor opinion and interpret the mood of the electorate
and its perception of issues; the appointment by the central offices
of the major parties of research directors whose task is to liaise with
the professional research companies and design research programs
and collate research data; the expanding numbers of staff employed
in the leaders' press offices and the appointment of communications directors with broader responsibilities; the establishment
(with public funds) of government information units or media
liaison units; and the increasing use of government advertising to
promote the policy achievements of the government of the day.
The capacity of governments to offer alternative employment to
journalists has also created a new path to influence over the media.
In recent times there has also been a growing amount of opinion
research undertaken by public service departments, the results of
which may assist with both policy development and the communication of policy. A principal role for communication rests with the
leaders themselves, and communication skills in the electronic
media appear to have become more important in the selection of
leaders.

Stability in Policy Behaviour

Despite ideological differences between the parties it has often
been observed that in office the policy behaviour of the leaders of
the two main political forces does not differ greatly. This observation depends very much for its validity on the observer's concept
of what constitutes a 'great' difference. The partisans of each
generally take the view that it *does* matter which party is in power.
Presumably the differences in policy performance, albeit marginal
from some ideological perspectives, are differences which tend to
matter to party supporters. Tufte (1978: 99) has shown that there

is a strong correlation between the size of the government sector's claim on national resources and the length of time that a country has had a social democratic government. At any time voters can compare the expected performance of the governing party with the expected performance of the opposition in a number of specific policy areas with little difficulty, and such comparisons frequently form a component of the parties' election research. More severe partisan polarisation occurs. In 1975 a substantial majority of Liberal identifiers appear to have believed that the Labor government would endanger the country, while an almost equally substantial body of Labor supporters believed that it would not.

While the position that it makes little difference which party is in power is a value judgement, it can more usefully be said that the policy behaviour of party leaders on both sides takes place within certain constraints. These include the leaders' beliefs in constitutionalism, in the need to facilitate the operation of most major institutions in society – especially the business enterprises producing employment and resources – and in the need to convince a sufficient number of voters that their party can continue to meet their values more satisfactorily than any alternative. Governments in their policy behaviour are thus constrained by the élite culture, by the nature of the political economy, and by the wider values and beliefs of the electorate, as they come to influence voters' evaluation of the government.

It is not necessary here to elaborate the constraints on Australian governments imposed by constitutional and other rules; these are detailed elsewhere. It behoves the political sociologist to be aware of the great importance of these rules in accounting for policy behaviour.

Political Economy as Constraint
The most important features of the political economy which act as constraints on all governments are:

- The reliance on relatively autonomous enterprise managements to invest funds and decide on production and distribution policy. These managements are either in government-owned statutory authorities (which include 19 out of the top 100 business undertakings in Australia in terms of revenue) or privately-owned and publicly-regulated enterprises.
- The co-ordination of these enterprises with each other and their adjustment to the values of individual consumers, principally through exchange processes operating in a market system based on prices for goods, labour and capital.

These two features together mean that management decisions are heavily dependent on government policy behaviour that facilitates planning at the enterprise level (including ensuring that costs of investment and employment are acceptable to managements). The efforts of managements in the market sector to secure their role success in conditions of market uncertainty conduces to efficient use of resources and hence economic growth, but also encourages political lobbying to reduce competition and control regulators. Enterprises in the market sector have generally resisted legislation against restrictive practices, but sought incentives and allowances, wage restraint and government subsidies, and regulation of market competition. The failure of government to produce managerial and entrepreneurial confidence leads to delays in investment, reduced employment and widespread failure in society to achieve values. Hence both Labor and coalition governments tend to seek policies which will be acceptable to enterprise managers. Enterprises in the non-market sector have become heavily reliant on protected monopolies, subsidisation of losses, retirement schemes and tenured employment to achieve this level of certainty. As a consequence, the extension of government's claims over resources and of the scope of the exercise of government authority has continued in Australia under governments of all political persuasions, though more rapidly under Labor governments (Butlin *et al.* 1982).

The basic process at work here was identified a 140 years ago by Alexis de Tocqueville in his analysis of American democracy:

> Democratic ages are times of experiment, and adventure. There are always a lot of men engaged in some difficult or new undertaking which they pursue apart, unencumbered by assistants. Such men will freely admit the general principle that the power of the state should not interfere in private affairs, but as an exception, each one of them wants the state to help in the special matter with which he is preoccupied, and he wants to lead the government on to take action in his domain, though he would like to restrict it in every other direction.
>
> As a multitude of people, all at the same moment, take this particular view about a great variety of different purposes, the sphere of the central government insensibly spreads in every direction, although every individual wants to restrict it.
>
> (de Tocqueville 1969: 672)

Culture as Constraint

Culture comes to impose constraints on government policy behaviour in several ways. First, policy which goes beyond the scope of authority conceded to government by citizens may lead to law-breaking and other forms of non-compliance, even active resistance. This may not stop governments from so acting, but it has the potential to greatly increase the costs of implementing the policy, especially in a society such as Australia where competitive elections occur. Examples of such resistance beyond the law have included some activities or actions of the anti-conscription movement, the anti-abortion movement and elements in the environmental movement. It also appears that a significant proportion of Australians believe it is 'wrong for governments under any circumstances to nationalise private business'. Historically such policies have led to emotional anti-government campaigns.

Governments acting within the scope of their authority still face cultural constraints on policy. A government seeking to increase its own certainty of continuance in office has an incentive to pursue policies which increase value achievement and avoid value deprivation. In economists' terms, there is pressure to achieve the Pareto optimum policy in which at least some are better off and none are worse off. The distribution of values across voters is therefore relevant in assessing the nature of the constraints on policy. The relationship of policy outcomes to value achievement is often a complex matter which is interpreted for voters by political parties, interests groups and the media. The difficulties of analysis mean that many voters judge a government's performance not by its policy actions but by their personal circumstances at election time. 'Good times' or 'bad times' themselves become for some voters the measure of government performance, regardless of the impact of government policies.

Satisfaction of values which are near-universal thus tends to become a central objective of a government which wishes to remain in power. These are generally values which increase the level of certainty and capacity to plan ahead of individual citizens: law and order at home, effective defence or peace abroad, income-earning, employment opportunities, protection against exploitation. Butler and Stokes call these 'valence issues' (Butler and Stokes 1969: 189). There are, in addition, many values held to by substantial majorities of Australians which a government fails to gratify at its peril. These include provision of security for the aged and sick. Opinion research throughout the 1970s indicated that a majority of Australians continued to feel such provision was inadequate, despite concern over the rising burden of taxation. While there is a minority of people who claim to be pleased to pay their taxes, taxation is perceived by most people as a largely unwelcome exercise of state power over them, and during the last decade or so there has been rising discontent over the level of taxation (Kemp 1980). Other positions which survey research indicates are those of a majority of Australians include the belief that government intervention in private life should be reduced; that government ownership of commercial enterprises should not be extended but, if anything, should be reduced; that greater regulation of trade unions is desirable; that women should have equal opportunities with men; that greater assistance should be provided to the family; and that Australian industries should be protected from unfair competition. A valuation is also placed on national symbols and institutions: the parliamentary system is accepted as on the whole having worked satisfactorily (though reforms are possible), the constitutional monarchy is supported by a majority of Australians, the present Australian flag attracts substantial support. Support for the Senate increased from 1969–79. There is wide and long-standing opposition to the transfer of further authority to the federal government, and support for more assistance to state governments (Aitkin 1982: 383 ff.). Change through gradual reform is generally supported.

In achieving their values Australians generally support strong leadership which can offer a sense of purpose and direction. They are sceptical that most political conflict is necessary (it threatens to undermine certainty), though they strongly support the system of competitive political parties. Leadership, however, must be in touch with the people and must not be arbitrary or overbearing. The most valued qualities – competence and integrity – are those most centrally related to the task of leaders in offering confidence and predictability for the future.

Within such a culture both major political forces are largely constrained to fairly conservative policies, though incremental change is possible. Partly as a consequence, both parties attract substantial support from people who view themselves as traditional or 'middle of the road' (Table 11.4).

In practice, the balance of forces and opportunities in Australian politics has produced several clear long-term trends in the allocation of power. The most significant of these are the growing centralisation of power in the federal government, the increasing claim of the government sector on national resources (measured by taxation revenue as a proportion of Gross Domestic Product), and the increasing level of regulation of private property and private enterprise management.

Levels of Participation

Australians participate extensively in politics, but at a distance. Some 95 per cent regularly cast a vote, and some 90 per cent see themselves as followers of one party or another. Only 6 per cent say they have no interest at all in politics, though another 23 per cent claim little interest. It is when we look at the variety of modes of participation which embody more sustained political activity that most Australians seem prepared to leave active political life to others. Most are generally watchful (60 per cent claim to follow politics a good deal on television) but a majority is cautious about talking politics (55 per cent say they do not talk politics much with other people). This is despite the fact that in 1979 some 68 per cent agreed that it did make a difference which party was in power in Canberra. Between interest, awareness and concern on the one hand, and sustained political activity on the other, there is a vast gulf. Most of those who are partisan loyalists and who believe that it matters which party governs do not themselves seek an active role in determining political outcomes. They rely largely on their vote to obtain the political outcomes they want.

Party loyalty is at the core of Australians' relations with politics. Knowledge about individual representatives is low (only 38 per cent could name their federal member and 47 per cent their state member), and even basic information about the political system is not universal (according to a recent survey by the Australian Electoral Office, only 60 per cent could accurately name the two chambers of the federal Parliament).

Only some 6 per cent of Australians subscribe to a political party. While most have signed a petition at some time (70 per cent), only 17 per cent have ever written to their state or federal MP or to a newspaper about a political matter, and only 12 per cent have ever taken part in a protest movement on a local or larger scale, or have demonstrated on an issue. Other forms of less conventional political action involve very few people indeed (Table 11.13).

The preparedness of most Australians to do their principal political duty (as they see it) of voting and listening to their political leaders but otherwise remaining apart from politics, is not because Australians are an apathetic people in a wider social sense. On the contrary, they lead socially active lives exhibiting a good deal of social concern. Most Australians belong to at least one organisation outside their family (Table 11.14), and even if churches, political parties and trade unions are excluded, some 48 per cent have membership in organisations such as school associations, business and professional associations, sporting clubs, and so on. Only some 27 per cent of Australians belong to no organisation at all.

A partial explanation for the extensive but distant involvement in politics of most Australians, despite its conceded importance, may be that most people believe they can make a greater

Table 11.13 Participation in Political Action

	% have done
Signing a petition	69.7
Joining a political party	9.0
Joining in boycotts	4.9
Attending lawful demonstrations	12.2
Joining unofficial strikes	5.2
Occupying buildings or factories	2.0
Damaging things, like breaking windows, removing road signs, etc.	1.1
Using personal violence, such as fighting with other demonstrators or the police	0.7
Going to jail for your beliefs	1.1

Source: Australian Values Study (Roy Morgan Research Centre) 1983

Question: I am now going to read out some different forms of political action that people can take. As I say each one, I'd like you to tell me whether you might do it, or would never, under any circumstances do it.

Table 11.14 Membership of Organisations, 1983

A charity concerned with the welfare of people	12.5
A church or religious organisation	25.9
An education or art group	13.0
A trade union	18.6
A political party or political group	4.2
An organisation concerned with human rights at home or abroad	3.0
A conservation, environmentalist or animal welfare group	3.4
Youth work (e.g. Scouts, Guides, youth club, etc.)	6.3
A consumer group	1.8
A professional association/society	12.9
A business association	8.4
A sporting group	26.3
A community service group	6.7
A hobby group	8.3
None of them	27.0

Source: Australian Values Study (Roy Morgan Research Centre) 1983.

Question: Looking at [this] card. Which if any of those do you belong to?

contribution to achieving the things which are important to them by other kinds of activity (Dahl 1984: 97–100). Since the value priorities governing behaviour are decided at the margin, the marginal value of non-political activity is seen to be greater than direct political action. This is supported by responses to a question asked in the 1983 Australian Values Study, which suggested that Australians believe the main methods for solving social questions lie outside politics and government. The two main paths to the solution of social questions are education and economic development (47–48 per cent), followed by new technology (39 per cent) and changes in human nature [behaviour?] (31 per cent). Among institutions, non-governmental organisations such as religious (27 per cent) and charitable organisations (23 per cent) together with visionary individuals (22 per cent) were seen as having a greater role to play than parliamentary politics, political parties and trade unions. While it is undoubtedly the case that politics impinges on the performance of all of these, most Australians opt for participation more directly in these areas than in organised politics.

The preference for involvement in social activity outside political parties may also be based on an appreciation that within the hierarchical structures of politics and government the authoritative decision-makers are inevitably few in number, and that significant influence requires the expenditure of considerable energy and the exercise of considerable skills. Historically it has been perceptions of threats from other political activists that has greatly increased the extent of mass participation in party politics. The membership of opposition parties tends to peak during periods in which dissatisfaction with the government of the day is growing.

During the 1970s interest in politics, measured by an indicator such as talking about politics with others and following politics by at least one medium, seems to have become more widespread in the electorate. This higher level of interest accompanied 'a more pessimistic and critical view of society and politics' (Aitkin 1982: 274). Criticisms were general in nature, but by 1979 economic problems had increased very greatly in importance in voters' minds and were clearly dominant among the problems they believed the government should do something about (p. 279). An important factor in increasing interest in politics during the 1970s appears to have been the politicisation of a larger proportion of women during that decade.

An explanation for participation relying on its marginal net costs is supported by evidence showing that participation tends to be greatest among those with the greatest direct benefits to gain and those whose marginal costs are least. Education is positively associated with both interest and participation, probably because the formal intellectual training provided by secondary and tertiary institutions facilitates the handling of complex information and tends to provide skills in analysis and argumentation. Education is also associated with the adoption of ideological labels such as 'Left' and 'Right' which, like party identification, simplify political analysis but require greater capacity to deal with abstractions (Kemp 1978: 323).

Political Apathy

In order to understand the phenomenon of political 'apathy' in Australia, it is illuminating to focus on that relatively small fraction of the electorate (6.2 per cent) who claim no interest at all in politics. A close look at the category of respondents with 'no interest' in politics in the 1979 National Survey is revealing. The validity of this category is attested by the fact that more than nine out of ten of them had never written to an MP nor a newspaper, nor taken part in a demonstration. None in this category (with a single exception) had any university education. Three out of four were women. They were not notably more dissatisfied with government and politics, though they were more likely to have no opinion. Low income, youthfulness and age were also associated with low interest. Political apathy is thus found among those who lack political resources – status, income, knowledge, analytical training – deficits markedly more likely to be found among women than men in Australia. The growing access to education by women appears, for example, to be a most important component of the increase in political interest among women which took place during the 1970s (Aitkin 1982: 281).

Political activism also increases among the leadership levels of the major economic and social institutions, where status (and power) increase the likelihood that political activity will be effective. Managers and administrators, and trade union officials, are more likely to participate in a range of ways than employees or ordinary members in these organisations.

A difficult question to answer is whether this pattern of participation is 'healthy' or 'satisfactory' for Australian democracy. One important non-trivial test is whether Australians obtain, through such a pattern of participation, a satisfactory level of value achievement. Cross-national comparisons of overall satisfaction with life indicators suggest that Australians rank relatively highly by such measures. Nevertheless, low levels of direct participation do tend to reduce the potential recruits for parliamentary office and narrow the choice of abilities and qualities among the people's representatives.

There is some evidence that a smaller proportion of Australians undertake direct political participation than do citizens of other countries. Party membership is much higher elsewhere – in New Zealand, for example – where the National Party has recruited up to 25 per cent of its voters as members (Levine 1979: 71).

The explanation for the lower level of direct participation in Australia seems to be in part the different rules under which Australian parties operate. Compulsory voting removes from parties the need to 'get out the vote'. Preselection procedures do not benefit candidates who recruit members (as they do in New Zealand). The geographic spread of the Australian population and the multiple levels of government reduce the sense of community and knowledge of the more remote levels. Knowledge of leaders, members and candidates appears to be markedly higher in the more 'intimate' political system of New Zealand (Bean 1984). Public funding may further reduce the reliance of party leaders on the support of a mass membership and further lower the incentives to recruit members, as does the notification of party labels on the ballot (doing away with the need for members to hand out how-to-vote cards). Participation is higher where parties have become significant elements in the functioning of community (as in some rural areas). In the Labor Party the dominance of decision-making in the organisation by trade union officials, combined with the legalistic character of Australian trade unions and their grass roots weakness, means that the party has low individual membership. It is hard to avoid the conclusion that institutional structures in Australia have tended to detach leaderships from those they are supposedly representing. The resort to legislation to require voting and to guarantee membership to unions has weakened the grass roots of Australian politics.

There is considerable evidence that most Australians are uneasy about this situation. Many, though probably not a majority, of them appear to feel 'left out' of politics. There is a very widespread belief that 'some of the people in government pay more attention to what the big interests want' (78 per cent) than they do to the principle of giving everyone a fair go (16 per cent) Almost as large a proportion believes that 'the people in government are too often interested in looking after themselves' (67 per cent) than they are in doing the right thing nearly all the time (28 per cent). By the end of the 1970s a substantial minority of people declared that they were 'not satisfied' with the 'state of government and politics in Australia' (43 per cent). Substantial majorities believed that both big business and trade unions had too much power in Australia (Aitkin 1982).

Changes in Australian Political Behaviour

Changes in the social environment continue to open the possibility of new uncertainties and new conflicts. The perceived capacity of the political economy to meet expectations is, as we have seen, inversely related to political interest. But solving economic problems is seen as the task of the political parties so participation does not appear to change much in the face of economic difficulties. Other problems of recent years have clearly produced new forms of mobilisation. The increasing impact of society on the natural environment, changes in knowledge and technology, and in cultural norms, have produced new patterns of conflict. The ideological disputes between feminists and right-to-life movements, for instance, have key cultural values at stake; environmentalism is confronted by specific interests – private and governmental – in contexts where often little compromise seems possible. In such areas more than in any others the commitment to constitutional procedures has been most challenged in recent times. The explanation of the direction of partisanship in relation to these issues doubtless must involve reference to sub-group membership and internalised values and norms.

A potential cleavage line will not become an actual line of conflict unless leaders conceptualise a consequent value deprivation. Macro-changes in social structure and culture may be intensifying certain lines of political cleavage in Australian society.

One such line of cleavage is that between the government sector and the private one. This is a cleavage between two broad categories of institutions with different modes of acquiring and distributing resources, and different conditions of employment. The conflict is once again based on conflicting institutional interests. It arises in part because the resources which enable public sector institutions to expand and provide secure employment are derived, for the most part, from private sector institutions or from people employed in them. It is also based on the fact that public sector institutions which are regulatory in character (many aspects of departments and tribunals) have institutional interests in the restriction of the operating autonomy of private sector ones. Private sector institutions have interests in maintaining their autonomy and in turn expanding control over the public sector. The issues between these sectors have been conceptualised in recent times in terms of levels of taxation, employment tenure, retirement provisions and regulation. Political conflict has occurred in a variety of forms, from advertisements by public sector unions defending the virtues of government programs, political disputation between government and private sectors in education, as well as in the long-standing critique by private enterprise of government spending, taxing and borrowing programs. What gives these conflicts a new dimension is the voting strength in elections of the employees and beneficiaries of the expanding public sector programs.

To some extent the party conflict has always had an element of private versus public sector within it, with the Liberal and National Parties most clearly associated with private sector interests and the Labor Party with government sector ones. This institutional cleavage line has generally been bridged, however, by an accepted role for government among both major political forces in providing a degree of security and assistance to weak but valued private interests. The expansion of the government sector during the 1970s and into the 1980s in Australia has sharpened the ideological conflict between proponents of 'bigger' and 'smaller' government. It is a conflict which continues to be restrained by the interests of voters as taxpayers in retaining substantial autonomy in allocating their own earnings.

A further factor restraining differences between the parties along this line of cleavage has been the growing policy (and hence political) influence of economists as a profession on both major party groupings. A key characteristic of economics as a discipline is that of all the social sciences it has historically been the one most specialised in the analysis of market relations, and its growing influence tends therefore to raise the salience for policy-makers of the market implications of policy options. This is so despite the diversity of judgement and values which otherwise exist among economists. The growing social and political role for economists is seen in a large number of institutional developments on the advisory side of government: the emergence of a significant analytical capacity in the Tariff Board during the 1960s and its subsequent transformation into the Industries Assistance Commission in 1973; the establishment of policy analysis units within government such as the Bureaux of Agricultural Economics, Industry Economics, Labour Market Research and the Social Welfare Policy Secretariat. Economists have played a major role in independent policy enquiries surrounding poverty, employment and technology, education, the financial system and the operation of public statutory authorities such as Telecom and Australia Post, and of the industrial relations system. In the 1970s the departmental strength of economists increased with the bifurcation of the Department of Finance from the Department of Treasury and the development of the Prime Minister's Department. Independent economic advisers were also employed as consultants by Prime Ministers and Treasurers during this period. When Labor came to power in 1983, the establishsment of an Economic Planning Advisory Council (which gave further policy access to independent economists and University economic research centres) was a centrepiece of its program.

The rise of the economics profession as a class to political influence has probably greatly increased awareness at the policy level of the conflicts involved in government versus private sector growth (often expressed in economic concepts of efficiency and costs). Not surprisingly, by 1980, market-oriented politicians acquired a label, 'the Dries', and this was applied to politicians in both major parties, though as a near-faction, 'Dries' were most evident in the traditional private sector party, the Liberals.

The social and political influence of economic thought can be viewed as a continuation of the trend in Western culture towards rationalisation identified by Weber. It is part of the 'information revolution' or 'knowledge revolution' supported by the technology of information processing which has become so prominent a feature of Western societies in the last two decades, and has led some theorists to speak of the emergence of 'the post-industrial' society.

The cleavage between public and private sectors at an institutional level and its continuing, indeed growing, relevance as a basis of political conflict confirms the importance of the institutional structures of society in understanding political behaviour. It is also linked, however, as the above discussion shows, to changes in the nature and allocation of political resources. In particular, it is linked to the growth in the size of the class of people with advanced training in social and technical knowledge (and in the institutions with which they are associated – the universities, colleges, training institutions and school systems). This knowledge class has greatly increased in recent decades the sheer quantum of social analysis which has become available to institutional leaders and individuals. While often contributing to the development of policies to resolve or at least compromise conflicts, this analysis has also served to sharpen awareness of conflicts of interests, and the analysts have themselves become a class associated with educational research and policy institutions, with interests in the expansion of the control and the development of the autonomy of these institutions.

Undoubtedly the development of this knowledge class has been a key element in the emergence during the last two decades of political lobby groups dealing with community development, consumer protection, conservation of the architectural and natural heritage, equal opportunity for women, Aboriginal affairs and other ethnic interests and social welfare. This is in addition to the rise of educational institutions as significant lobbies in their own right. The institutionalised generation of cultural change has become a key element in the moulding and remoulding of political behaviour across traditional social categories and in shifting the balance of power between the traditional institutional interests of Australian politics.

Conclusion

Not only is political behaviour patterned by society; society itself is in turn patterned and re-patterned by politics. The political process understood in its broadest sense is a central one for stability and change in society as a whole. Even in the narrower sense of the politics of governing a society, the political process has a profound effect on the nature of Australian society.

The process by which leaders in society's authority systems seek autonomy and claim control over others is possibly the main process by which concepts such as freedom, independence, security and certainty are reinforced. The continuing attempts to exert influence and to find justifications for new arrangements are likewise a principal force for cultural innovation. The political process works with, and reworks, culture as decision-takers at all levels attempt to achieve their values, through mobilising support.

The outcomes of politics – new arrangements between institutions, organisations and individuals expressed in new rules, agreements and laws – in their turn can significantly re-allocate the balance of political resources between the participants in the political process, opening yet further opportunities for change. In Australia the use of governmental authority by successful parties and interests to redistribute income; alter the terms of the industrial conflict; promote environmental improvement; diminish the impact of racist or sexist attitudes on employment practices; promote competition or strengthen the communications monopoly; support national culture or a host of other decisions, all remould in varying degrees features of Australian society which themselves will have causal impact. The chance to do so is indeed the major incentive for participating in the central political processes of Australian society.

Note

1. Hence Weber's famous hypothesis (*Economy and Society*, Vol. 1, p. 31, 1968) that domination which is legitimate is more stable than domin-

Part II: Socially Patterned Behaviours

ation which is not. The existence of conflict within authority structures was the principal concern of Ralf Dahrendorf in *Class and Class Conflict in Industrial Society* (1960).

References

Aitkin, D. (1982) *Stability and Change in Australian Politics*, Second Edition. Canberra: Australian National University Press.

Arrow, K. (1951) *Social Choice and Individual Values*. Cambridge, Mass.: Harvard University Press.

Australian Government Commission of Inquiry Into Poverty, (1975) *First Main Report*. Canberra: AGPS.

Australian Values Study Survey (1983). Roy Morgan Research Centre.

Barnard, Chester (1938) *The Functions of the Executive*. Cambridge, Mass.: Harvard University Press.

Barnes, S.H., Kaase, M. *et al.* (1979) *Political Action: Mass Participation in Five Western Democracies*. Beverly Hills: Sage Publications.

Bean. C. (1984) 'A Comparative Study of Electoral Behaviour in Australia and New Zealand', PhD Thesis, Australian National University.

Broom, L. and Lancaster Jones, F. (1976) *Opportunity and Attainment in Australia*. Canberra: Australian National University Press.

———, Jones, F., McDonnell, P. and Williams, T. (1980) *The Inheritance of Inequality*. London: Routledge & Kegan Paul.

Budge, I., Crewe, I. and Farlie, D. (1976) *Party Identification and Beyond*. New York: Wiley.

Butler, D. and Stokes, D. (1969) *Political Change in Britain*, New York: St Martins.

Butlin, N.G., Barnard, A. and Pincus, J.J. (1982) *Government and Capitalism: Public and Private Choice in Twentieth Century Australia*. Sydney: Allen & Unwin.

Campbell, A., Converse, P.E., Miller, W.E. and Stokes, D.E. (1960) *The American Voter*, New York: Wiley & Sons.

Clarke, H.D. and Kornberg, A. (1971) 'Social Cleavages and Democratic Performance', *Comparative Political Studies* 4: 349–60.

Coleman, J.S. (1980) 'Authority Systems', *Public Opinion Quarterly* 44: 143–63.

Connell, R.W. (1977) *Ruling Class, Ruling Culture*. New York: Cambridge University Press.

Dahl, R.A. (1971) *Polyarchy*. New Haven: Yale University Press.

———(1984) *Modern Political Analysis*, Fourth Edition. Englewood Cliffs, New Jersey: Prentice-Hall.

Dahrendorf, Ralf (1960) *Class and Class Conflict in Industrial Society*. Stanford: Stanford University Press.

Davies, A.F. (1972) 'Political Socialisation' in F.J. Hunt (ed.) *Socialisation in Australia*. Sydney: Angus & Robertson.

————(1980) *Skills, Outlooks and Passions*. Cambridge: Cambridge University Press.
Department of Social Security (1981) *Statistics on the Distribution of Income and Wealth in Australia*, Research Paper No. 14. Canberra: Research and Statistics Branch, Development Division.
Eckstein, H. and Gurr, T.R. (1975) *Patterns of Authority*. New York: Wiley.
Edelman, M. (1967) *The Symbolic Uses of Politics*. Urbana: University of Illinois Press.
Friedrich, C.J. (1982) *Tradition and Authority*. London: Macmillan.
Headey, B. and O'Loughlin, T. (1978) 'Transgenerational Structural Inequality: Social Fact or Fiction', *British Journal of Sociology* 29: 110–20.
Higley, J., Deacon, D. and Smart, D. (1979) *Elites in Australia*. London: Routledge & Kegan Paul.
Inglehart, R. (1977) *The Silent Revolution: Changing Values and Political Styles among Western Publics*. Princeton: Princeton University Press.
Kelley, J. and McAllister, I. (1985) 'Class and Party in Australia: Comparison with Britain and The USA' *The British Journal of Sociology* XXXVI (3): 383–419.
Kemp, D.A. (1978) *Society and Electoral Behaviour in Australia*. St Lucia: University of Queensland Press.
————(1979) 'The Australian Electorate', in H.R. Penniman (ed.) *The Australian National Elections of 1977*. Canberra: Australian National University Press.
————(1980) 'Taxation: The Politics of Change' in *The Politics of Taxation*. Canberra: Australian Institute of Political Science.
Kent Jennings, M. and Niemi, R.G. (1981) *Generations and Politics*. Princeton: Princeton University Press.
Lane, R. and Sears, D. (1964) *Public Opinion*. Englewood Cliffs, New Jersey: Prentice-Hall.
Laver, M. (1983) *Invitation to Politics* Oxford: Martin Robertson.
Levine, S. (1979) *The New Zealand Political System*. Sydney: Allen & Unwin.
Lindblom, C.E. (1977) *Politics and Markets*. New York: Basic Books.
Lipset, S.M. (1966) *Political Man*. London: Heinemann.
Little, G. (1973) *Politics and Personal Style*. Melbourne: Nelson.
Loveday, P., Martin, A.W. and Parker, R.S. (eds) (1977) *The Emergence of the Australian Party System*. Sydney: Hale & Iremonger.
MacKay, Alfred F. (1980) *Arrow's Theorem: The Paradox of Social Choice*. New Haven: Yale University Press.
Maslow, A.H. (1954) *Motivation and Personality*. New York: Harper.
Milgram, S. (1974) *Obedience to Authority*. London: Tavistock.
Olson, Mancur (1965) *The Logic of Collective Action*. Cambridge, Mass.: Harvard University Press.
Rae, D.W. and Taylor M. (1970) *The Analysis of Political Cleavages*. New Haven: Yale University Press.
Rokkan, S. (1968) 'Electoral Systems' in D. Sills (ed.) *International*

Encyclopedia of the Social Sciences, Vol. 5. New York: Free Press.

Rose, R. (1974) *Electoral Behavior: A Comparative Handbook*. New York: Free Press.

Stokes, D. (1963) 'Political Parties in the Normative Theory of Representation' in J.R. Pennock and J. W. Chapman (eds) (1968) *Representation: Nomos X*. New York: Atherton.

Taylor, P.J. and Johnson, R.J. (1979) *Geography of Elections*. Harmondsworth: Penguin.

Tocqueville, A. De (1969) *Democracy in America* (G. Lawrence, translator). New York: Doubleday-Anchor.

Truman, D.B. (1965) *The Governmental Process*. New York: Knopf.

Tufte, E.R. (1978) *Political Control of the Economy*. Princeton: Princeton University Press.

Weber, M. (1968) *Economy and Society*. G. Roth and C. Wittich (eds). Berkeley: University of California Press.

Chapter Twelve

Crime

John Braithwaite

Sociologists who study crime are interested generally in social structural variables – poverty, urbanisation, culture conflict and the impact of <u>one's position in the social structure on one's likelihood of either committing a crime or being the victim of one.</u> But the sociologist's interest does not begin with the causes or consequences of crime. It begins rather with understanding how things come to be defined as crimes in the first place. Why, for example, is rape within marriage not a crime in many societies?

This concern leads the sociologist to pose questions about whose interests are served by the law, and by the criminal justice system which enforces the law. In this introductory chapter, I will not attempt to address questions about the causes of crime. Rather, I will try to summarise what we know about the level of crime, and about what kinds of people are most likely to be victims of crime. Knowing these correlates of crime is the first step towards grasping the interests served by the criminal justice system and to understanding why police, court and prison systems are stable or expanding institutional domains in modern societies.

Before we go any further, however, we must address the critique that crime is an 'unscientific' construct which is inappropriate to sociology.

Is 'Crime' a Suitable Construct for Sociology?

Crime is defined here as behaviour which is proscribed and punishable by law. While punishable by law, it is not *necessarily* punished. It would be a perverse sociology which required punitive action by the state before behaviour could be classified as crime, since a prime sociological concern is with the question of the circumstances in which the state chooses to turn a blind eye to it.

Some, like Quinney (1975: 194), view the law as a tool of ruling class interests. Anatole France was an early exponent of this view, saying: 'The law in its majestic equality forbids the rich as well as the poor to sleep under bridges, to beg in the streets and to steal bread.'

We must make a crucial distinction here between the law in the books and the law in action – the law as it is written and the law as enforced in practice. We will see that while the law in the books is better designed for serving the interests of the working class than those of the ruling class, it is nevertheless true that the ruling class manage to influence the way the law is enforced in practice to make it better serve their interests.

There are, in fact, many more laws on the books in Australia which criminalise behaviour of, predominantly, members of the ruling class, than there are laws which oppress the poor. Peter Grabosky and I recently completed a study of ninety-six of the most significant business regulatory agencies in Australia (Grabosky and Braithwaite 1986). Most of these are responsible for a number of different statutes, each of which criminalise a variety of different kinds of ruling class behaviour, concerned with environmental protection, occupational health and safety, consumer protection, food standards, customs, tax, trade practices, labour law and a disparate array of other areas. The numbers of offences created in state criminal codes (traditional street crimes, for want of a better term) are tiny compared with the thousands of criminal offences created under these business regulatory statutes. Moreover, they tend to give much greater powers to business regulatory agencies to search without warrant, to compel suspects to answer incriminating questions, and the like, than are available to the police (Braithwaite and Grabosky 1985: 34–36, Grabosky and Braithwaite 1986: Chapter 14).

In this sense the law in the books is progressive, but the law in action is not. Most of the agencies in our study detected vast numbers of business offences every year, but almost never prosecuted them. In fact, a third of the agencies did not obtain a single conviction in the three years to 30 June 1984. The disjunction found in all capitalist democracies between tough laws against business and weak enforcement of them indicates a need to separate the instrumental and symbolic effects of legislation (Edelman 1964, Gusfield 1967, Carson 1975, O'Malley 1980, Hopkins and Parnell 1984) – the difference between what legislation is designed to achieve and what it is designed to be seen to achieve. Edelman is undoubtedly correct that unorganised and diffuse interests (such as consumers) tend to receive symbolic rewards (like legislation), while organised professional ones reap tangible rewards (like freedom in practice to do whatever they want). Thus, the clamourings of the powerless for legal protection are defused by enacting legislation which is rarely enforced.

Feminists make a similar point about laws to protect women and children from domestic violence largely perpetrated by men. Laws against rape, incest and other forms of domestic violence exist; the problem is in getting the police and the courts to enforce them. The law in the books is not fundamentally sexist; indeed almost all the offences criminalised in Australia (prostitution and abortion being notable exceptions) are predominantly perpetrated by men. Yet there are some very fundamental ways in which the law in action, by turning a blind eye to domestic violence (Scutt 1983), and by persecuting adolescent girls (but not adolescent boys) for sexual promiscuity (Hancock 1980, Hancock and Chesney-Lind 1985, Fielding 1977, Leaper 1974, Hiller and Hancock 1981), is sexist.

Putting aside business crime for the moment, and focusing solely on crime in the streets (murder, assault, rape, theft), we will see that in Australia the evidence suggests that the poor, and particularly the unemployed, are the most likely victims of these crimes. This, combined with the high proportion of laws which criminalise the behaviour of the ruling class, adds up to the conclusion that it is ludicrous to reject the law in the books of democratic capitalist societies as the basis for a definition of crime on the grounds that these laws reflect ruling class interests.

Hegemonic Policing

A second basis some would raise for rejecting crime as a sociological construct is that it is one which assumes consensus over issues which are in reality subject to great dissensus. In fact, however, a vast literature on public perceptions of crime demonstrates remarkable consensus on the relative seriousness of different crimes, with the exception of victimless crimes such as homosexuality and marijuana use (see the fifteen studies cited at Reference 43 in Braithwaite 1982, but note the methodological caveats of Miethe 1982 and Cullen *et al.* 1983). Even outside the capitalist democracies, it is doubtful whether there are or will ever be, substantial numbers of people who will believe that behaviours such as murder, rape and theft should not be punished.

These days it is rare for Marxist sociologists to characterise law as a tool of ruling class interests; it is seen rather as operating generally to maintain capitalism. The widespread acceptance of the law by the working class is seen as hegemonic: the use of force is based on the consent of the majority created by ideological domination.

O'Malley (1983: 52–72) has described what he regards as the

rise of hegemonic policing. The early police in New South Wales were widely hated by both the rural people and by the miners during the goldrush (Ward 1966). The rural police were controlled by the squatters and viewed as class traitors by the rural working class. O'Malley argues that the rule of law and therefore the stability of Australia's emerging capitalism was so threatened in the nineteenth century by this mistrust of the police that a solution had to be found. The solution was, he argues, the deliberate creation of a 'hegemonic police', a force identified as an agency of 'the community', supplying a broad range of services to secure social order and harmony. And so the ideology was born of a police which reacts to all serious complaints and investigates them without fear or favour, even when the complaints are against the ruling class. We have already seen that it was an ideology which was not always put into practice. Australian police forces have often thrown off the ideology of reaction to the complaints of citizens in favour of proactive political policing by special branches to persecute activists (e.g. White 1977), and 'verballing' (fabrication of confessions) to get difficult customers out of the way (e.g. Lucas Report 1977). As O'Malley concedes:

> Hence while the general strategy of police in Australia and similar states has been a 'soft' hegemonic strategy of peace-keeping, minimal and reactive enforcement, it would be absurd to suggest that repressive and coercive strategies are not also part of the police repertoire.
>
> (O'Malley 1983: 60)

The empirical evidence is consistent with O'Malley's analysis. While the historical record is one of nineteenth-century hatred of the police, in the twentieth century, survey research data show very high respect being accorded to the police by the community (Chappell and Wilson 1969, 1972, Milte and Weber 1977, Tomasic 1976: 105–06).

Possibly this public esteem has been threatened of late by police corruption scandals, particularly in New South Wales. The interesting question is whether this general community respect is 'hegemonic' – the working class being misled into identifying with ruling class interests – or whether most of the working class simply and accurately perceive the criminal justice system as something which on balance serves their interests more than it damages them. We will return to this question after we have assembled some facts about who suffers from criminal behaviour.

Figure 12.1 Convictions per 1,000 Population for Serious Acquisitive Crime, New South Wales, 1811–92

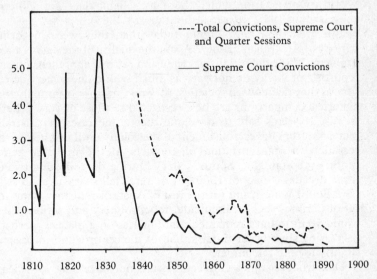

Source: Reprinted with permission from Grabosky 1977: 33; for data showing a similar trend for serious aggressive crime, see Grabosky 1977: 34

The Level of Crime Today and in Australian History

The mass media exaggeration notwithstanding, Australia is not a society with an unusually significant crime problem. Comparisons of crime rates between countries are notoriously difficult because of the existence of different definitions of offences and different counting rules between countries. However, when international comparisons are made (e.g Clifford and Harding 1985), there is no suggestion of anything other than a rather average crime rate compared with other OCED countries. The only international comparisons which cautious scholars make are based on homicide rates, where problems of definitional differences and variable non-reporting of crime are at their least (Archer and Gartner 1984: 35–58). Here Interpol statistics clearly show Australia with an average number of homicides per 100,000 population, compared with other OCED countries (with some, like the United Kingdom, being considerably lower, and some, like the United States, considerably higher), and a very much lower rate than most Third World countries from which there are reliable data (e.g. Clifford and Harding 1985: 47, see also Grabosky 1983).

But are crime rates higher today than they were in earlier periods of Australian history? Again the quality of the data is a real problem. While definitions of crime and rates of apprehension and reporting probably do not vary as much within one society across time as they do between societies, they do vary so substantially that historical comparisons are best restricted to those of very general trends. It seems safe to conclude that crime rates in Australia increased from the establishment of the colony until just before the cessation of transportation of convicts in the mid-nineteenth century (1840 in New South Wales). During the following two or three decades (to about 1860) crime rates fell sharply (at least in New South Wales), and for the rest of Australian history, rates for serious crimes such as homicide, rape, robbery and serious theft would seem to have remained more or less on a plateau, perhaps decreasing slightly for the first half of the century and increasing slightly for the remainder.

Data from the nineteenth century are, not surprisingly, the least adequate. The best we can do is rely on those concerning New South Wales Supreme Court Convictions (where serious crimes were tried) collected by Grabosky (1977: 31–36). Figure 12.1 shows such a sharp downward trend in the middle decades of the century that, however problematic the figures, the conclusion above seems safe enough. Much better data are available for the twentieth century thanks to the work of Mukherjee (1981), who concluded:

> Acts that are traditionally labelled as offences, that is, offences against the person, against property and against good order, have remained remarkably constant during the entire century. The analyses indicate that increases in the total volume of crime have been primarily because of increases in petty offences.
>
> (Mukherjee 1981: 61)

This conclusion seems unexceptional from the huge amount of data collected by Mukherjee. At the same time, however, his work demonstrates the questionable association between 'real crime rates' and those inferred from convictions in the courts. Mukherjee found that the crime rate was positively correlated with criminal justice resources. More police mean more arrests; indeed, he found that the number of offences charged per police officer has been fairly constant over the century. Yet the number of police officers

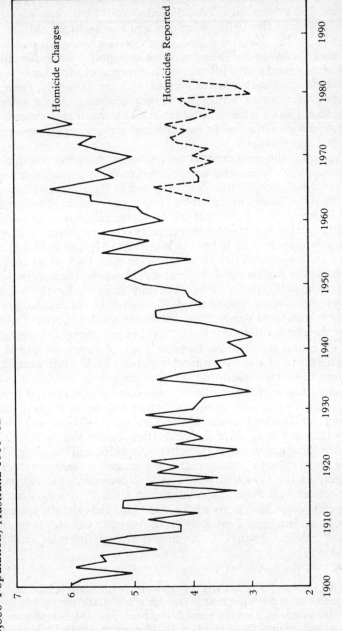

Figure 12.2 Charges for Homicides before Magistrates' Courts and Homicides reported to the Police per 100,000 Population, Australia 1900–82

Source: I wish to gratefully acknowledge the assistance of Satyanshu Mukherjee and Anita Scandia of the Australian Institute of Criminology, who supplied these data

per 100,000 population has varied considerably over the century, starting at a fairly high level, declining until 1930, then increasing steadily until the 1970s, when a sharp rise occurred (Mukherjee 1981: 35–39). He also found a very strong trade-off across the century between the number of arrests police make for minor offences ('good order' offences such as vagrancy, drunkenness and obscene language) and for serious offences. That is, when the police make more arrests for minor offences, serious offences decline. Thus it is highly problematic how much crime trends are the result of variations in real criminal activity versus changes in enforcement activity.

As with the international comparisons, the most sensible approach is to concentrate on the offence which provides the most meaningful comparative data in terms of high reportability and minimum changes in definition across time – homicide. The data in Figure 12.2 suggest that the homicide rate has varied within fairly narrow limits across this century. Data on homicide charges suggest a steady drop in rates to World War II, followed by a post-war increase which has taken homicide rates back to where they were at the beginning of the century. However, the superior data on homicides *reported*, which are only available for the last two decades, show no upward trend whatsoever. Homicide charges are higher than those reported partly because when different offenders are charged for the same homicide, they are counted separately.

Of course the mass media paint a very different picture of the modern era as one of unusual violence. Each adult generation seems to be convinced that the younger one constitutes a delinquent scourge such as has never been seen before. Thus, Australia has seen a succession of media-created folk devils (Cohen 1973), from the 'larrikins' of the 1890s (Grabosky 1977: 84–85), to the 'bodgies and widgies' of the 1950s (Braithwaite and Barker 1978), to the 'hooligan menace' (Windschuttle 1978) and the 'hippies' of the late 1960s, to 'punks' and 'bikie gangs' (actually a recurring theme) in the 1970s and 80s. The well-documented moral panics associated with these folk devils totally misrepresent the nature of juvenile delinquency. As Mukherjee (1985) has shown, systematically on data from 1964 to 1981, in Australia violence is an adult male problem relatively uncommon among juveniles (children under 17):

> Boys as a proportion of all male arrests for homicide have been fairly stable at under 5 per cent except for a few erratic jumps, and for serious assault a similar trend is observed. For both homicide and serious assault, the proportion of boys among arrested males has been much lower than their proportion in the total population.
>
> (Mukherjee 1985: 27)

Self-report studies in which adolescents are asked whether they have committed each of a variety of offences show that most Australian adolescents are delinquents in the sense that they have broken the law (Warner 1982, Braithwaite 1977: 26, Braithwaite and Law 1978, Braithwaite and Braithwaite 1978).

But mostly the delinquency is of a minor nature from which children desist if they are not stigmatised: it is just a part of growing up. Moral panics cause the minor delinquencies of a rather arbitrarily selected group of young people to be given a deeper social significance as exemplifying the malaise of modern society. Substantial public resources may then be allocated to stigmatising these young people – apprehending, punishing, 're-habilitating' and conducting psychological and sociological studies of them – thus confirming them in a deviant identity which makes it more difficult for them to engage in the normal process of growing out of their delinquency (Becker 1973, Schur 1973, West and Farrington 1977).

The Political Economy of Punishment

It is not strictly correct to say that the selection of juveniles for criminal justice system processing is 'rather arbitrary'. It is arbitrary in the sense that their law-breaking is often not very different from that of their peers whose deviance is ignored. But they are not selected because their offences threaten law and order so much as because their lifestyles are seen to threaten more fundamental societal values such as the work ethic, deference to authority and sexual restraint by unmarried girls.

Many sociologists have sought to understand the social functions of punishment as distinct from its crime control functions. Unfortunately, much Australian work has been informed by American theorising which relates to historical trends in punishment which are exactly the opposite to ours. While in the United States imprisonment rates have substantially and fairly consistently increased between the mid-nineteenth century and the present (Calahan 1979, Clifford and Harding 1985: 50), the pattern in Australia has been one of steep decline from the second half of the nineteenth century to 1920, followed by fairly constant rates from 1920 to the present (Figure 12.3). One explanation employed to explain this trend has been Andrew Scull's (1977) contention that 'decarceration' is a result of the fiscal crisis faced by modern capitalist states. In considerable measure the fiscal crisis is seen as a result of welfare expenditures crowding out investment in wealth-generating enterprises. At the same time the infrastructure of unemployment benefits and other welfare measures makes increasingly

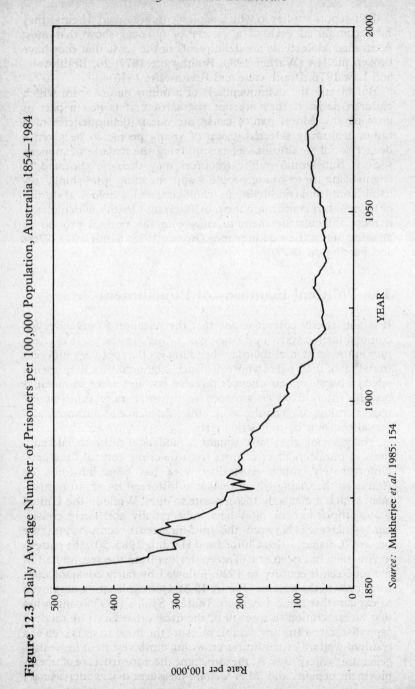

Figure 12.3 Daily Average Number of Prisoners per 100,000 Population, Australia 1854–1984

Source: Mukherjee *et al.* 1985: 154

possible the maintenance of offenders in the community. The fiscal crisis thus provides both the incentive to decarceration to cut prison expenditures, and the welfare expenditures largely responsible for the fiscal crisis make 'community corrections' feasible.

In fact, however, this theory has little appeal, because while Figure 12.3 shows a dramatic decline in imprisonment rates, all the decline occurred prior to 1920, before the reforms of the welfare state and 'the fiscal crisis of the state'. O'Malley (1983: 158–60) tries to rescue the theory by suggesting that while decarceration has not occurred in 'absolute' terms, it has occurred in 'relative' ones. He suggests from Grabosky's (1977) data that 'most of the decline in imprisonment rates in the early period can be put down to massive declines in serious criminal offending' (O'Malley 1983: 158). But as far as we can tell, this is wrong. Grabosky's (1977) data suggest that while 'the massive decline in serious criminal offending' occurred between 1830 and 1860, imprisonment rates did not begin to decline in New South Wales until at least 1880 (compare Figures 2.2 and 2.13 in Grabosky 1977). Further, O'Malley suggests that while the imprisonment rate may have been more or less on a plateau since 1920, 'rates for serious acquisitive crime trebled between 1920 and 1870'. As we have seen, Mukherjee's (1981) work lays to rest any suggestion of an explosion in serious crime between 1920 and 1970. While acquisitive crime did increase very substantially during this period, total serious crime did not. The massive increase in post-war criminal prosecutions was largely a result of what Mukherjee (1981) called 'petty offences', a great number of which were traffic offences.

Australia has seen an explosion of minor crime, or rather an explosion of social control of minor crimes which earlier in the century, when police were not so numerous, tended to be ignored. It is true that this expanded enforcement against minor crime has not bloated our prison populations. The extension of social control has occurred by increased use of fines, probation, community work and other non-custodial sanctions (Alder and Polk 1985). Though it is doubtful that a post-welfare state decarceration has occurred in either absolute or proportional terms, O'Malley's (1983: 161) ultimate conclusion that there has been 'a widening, refining and disguising of the entire control network' is correct.

While we must reject a Scullian interpretation of Australian decarceration, it certainly did occur prior to the advent of the welfare state and remains to be explained. It may be that the decline in imprisonment rates between the late nineteenth and early twentieth centuries corresponds with the demise of serious labour shortages and the concomitant destruction of the profitability of prison industry, just as the earlier demise of transportation had much to do with overcoming earlier crises of labour shortages in the colonies. More work is needed on this question. Additional research is also required on what seems to be some tendency, within the framework of an overall trend towards decarceration, for severe economic crises to be associated with heightened punitiveness of the criminal justice system (Grabosky 1984: 170, Braithwaite 1980: 195, 203–04, Jankovic 1977). Whether this suggests a greater need for the state to control crime when unemployment is high, a heightened demand for class domination during crises of capitalism (as Quinney 1977 would suggest), or simply a propensity to blame the victims of the crisis (the poor, Aborigines) for it, is worthy of examination.

Who Are the Criminals?

The answer to the question of which types of people in Australia engage in most serious crime is not difficult. They are predominantly respectable business people who breach the enormous array of laws regulating business described earlier in the chapter. I have argued at some length elsewhere that white collar offenders cause much greater injury to people (e.g. occupational health and safety offences) and much greater loss of property (e.g. company frauds) than street offenders (Braithwaite 1982: 742–45). Murder and assault are responsible for fewer deaths and injuries than violations of industrial health and safety laws by employers, and the sale of hazardous consumer products by manufacturers. Australian tax and company frauds have netted more than all the money stolen from Australian banks in a year.

One can establish that the number of offences and offenders against people and property is greater with white collar than with blue collar crime simply by taking a minor part of the white collar crime problem and showing the huge volume of offences involved. Surveys in New South Wales and Canberra have found 15 and 32 per cent respectively of petrol pumps to be giving short measure petrol to motorists (*Sunday Telegraph*, 3 February 1980; *Canberra Times*, 13 January 1981). Every one of the sales on these vast numbers of pumps involved weights and measures offences, or indeed fraud, should consumer affairs agencies choose to prosecute for this offence.

In 1982, the Victoria Department of Labour and Industry surveyed compliance with regulations concerning the guarding of power presses. Of 2,381 presses, 51 per cent did not comply with the requirements of the law (Department of Labour and Industry 1983: 20).

In 1983, the Queensland Department of Mines surveyed compliance with statutory standards for stone dusting in coal mine roadways to prevent the spread of explosions, and 35 per cent of the 1,095 dust samples failed to comply with the standard prescribed by the Coal Mining Act (Queensland Department of Mines 1983: 19).

A study of odometer fraud in Queensland found that over a third of vehicles randomly selected from used car lots had had their odometer turned back (Braithwaite 1978). The sample was not sufficient to assert with confidence that this kind of fraud occurred for a third of used cars sold in Queensland, but using a third as the best estimate available would imply about 70,000 odometer frauds in Queensland in the year of the study, compared with 81,181 offences of all types (including victimless crimes, but excluding public order offences) reported to the Queensland police that year. Moreover, in most odometer frauds, as in most other kinds of white collar crime, there is a conspiracy involving more than one individual offender plus a corporate offender.

If more evidence is needed, we can move from these small-time white collar crimes to the offences of transnational corporations – for example, to the fact that nineteen of the twenty largest American pharmaceutical transnationals have admitted to bribery of health and other government officials on a staggering scale (Braithwaite 1984: Chapter 2).

Putting aside white collar crimes (those involving the abuse of the power inherent in occupational roles), who commit most of the other kinds of common street crimes such as theft, robbery, rape and assault? There is a great deal of Australian evidence on this question. The offenders are disproportionately likely to be poor, unemployed and black. Of people in Australian prisons on 30 June 1984, 11 per cent were Aborigines or Torres Strait Islanders compared with 1 per cent in the total Australian population (see also South Australian Office of Crime Statistics 1984: 79, Clifford 1981: 18, Gorta and Hunter 1985, Duckworth *et al.* 1982, Mitchell Committee 1973: 202–04, Foley-Jones and Tandowski 1977: 1, Eggleston 1976: 15–16, Martin 1973, New South Wales Bureau of Crime Statistics and Research 1972a, New South Wales Department of Corrective Services 1974: 19, Biles 1973). One study of the juvenile justice system found that Aboriginal youngsters in South Australia over a five-year period appeared before a juvenile court or Children's Aid Panel at a rate of 440 per 1,000 youths (Sarri and Bradley 1980).

It is reasonable to suspect that much of this over-representation of Aborigines is due to racial and class bias in the criminal justice system (Eggleston 1976, Armstrong and Neumann 1976, Sanson-

Fisher 1978). One can accept that many of the 19.8 per cent of prisoners guilty of assault who are Aborigines are there because of all too great a willingness of police and magistrates to lock up participants in minor altercations when they happen to be black. But it is more difficult to explain away with racism the 6.4 per cent of homicide offenders who are Aborigines (Walker and Biles 1985: 66). Is our criminal justice system really so racist that when it comes to a matter of the gravity of homicide it can unjustly produce a six-fold over-representation of Aboriginal homicide offenders in our prisons? When Wilson (1982, 1985: 51) shows us that the homicide rate on Queensland Aboriginal reserves is ten times the rate for Australia as a whole, we can't seriously suggest that this is not a result of extraordinary rates of violence among Aboriginals themselves.

The second striking characteristic of offenders in Australia is unemployment (Institute of Criminology 1978, South Australian Office of Crime Statistics 1979, 1980a, 1984) and low socio-economic status generally (Barber 1973, New South Wales Bureau of Crime Statistics and Research 1974, Kraus 1975, Smith 1975, Dunstan and Roberts 1977, Braithwaite 1979, cf. Warner 1982).

Only 20 per cent of inmates of Australian prisons on 30 June, 1984 were employed (or self-employed) at the time they were arrested or charged (Walker and Biles 1985: 30). While there is such a disproportionate tendency for offenders to be unemployed, one of the puzzles of Australian criminology is that there is considerable ambiguity on whether or not there is a tendency for periods of high unemployment to be those when crime rates are high (Mukherjee 1981: 107–50, Institute of Criminology 1978).

At yet another level of analysis – the ecological – there is consistent evidence that areas of cities with high levels of unemployment or high concentrations of lower socio-economic status inhabitants experience higher crime rates (Dunstan and Roberts 1977, Vinson and Homel 1972, Kraus 1977). Indeed Braithwaite's (1979) work suggests that the combined effects of coming from a lower class family and living in a lower class area in increasing delinquency may be greater than the sum of their individual effects.

Possibly the strongest correlate of criminality in Australia, however, is gender (Biles 1977, Althuizen 1977, Challinger 1977). Less than 4 per cent of all people in Australian prisons on 30 June 1984 were females, and 5 per cent of homicide offenders were female (Walker and Biles 1985: 13, 60–61). If one takes self-report measures seriously as anything other than a doubtful measure of trivial offences, Australian self-report studies show by contrast fairly small sex differences in offending rates (Warner 1982,

Braithwaite 1977: 26). Following up on this latter evidence, some have suggested that women benefit from a 'chivalry' factor in enforcement and criminal sentencing (Krohn *et al.* 1983), but this has been hotly disputed in the literature (Scutt 1979, Hancock 1980). Any evidence of 'chivalry' in the criminal justice system is insufficient to explain there being twenty times as many male homicide offenders as female homicide offenders in Australian prisons. It would be ridiculous to suggest that nine out of ten female murderers who would have been convicted had they been men are let off!

Exaggerated assertions have been made about growing feminist consciousness in recent decades causing 'the rise of the new female criminal' (Adler 1975). While the proportion of property crime committed by females has increased since the mid-1960s, this is not true of crimes against the person (Mukherjee and Fitzgerald 1981), and much of the rise in the proportion of property crime perpetrated by females may be in 'traditional' female areas such as shoplifting (Alder 1985: 57).

Another very strong correlate of crime is youth (New South Wales Department of Corrective Services 1973, New South Wales Bureau of Crime Statistics and Research 1974). The group most strongly involved in serious crime are 18–25-year-old males. Only 23 per cent of inmates of Australian prisons are 35 and over, and, of course, many of these are in prison for offences they committed in their 20s (Walker and Biles 1985: 19).

With juveniles, a particularly strong association exists between poor school performance and delinquency (see 20 studies cited at fn. 57, p. 271, Braithwaite 1979, Warner 1982). This association has generated an increasingly influential reformist literature on reshaping education so that segregationist and other practices which label students as failures are rejected, and competition against other children is replaced by competition against the student's own past performance (Knight 1985, Conventry *et al.* 1984, Wilson and Braithwaite 1977, Marnier 1980). Crime rates are higher in the capital cities than in country areas (New South Wales Bureau of Crime Statistics and Research 1972b, 1974, Kraus 1973, Braithwaite and Biles 1979) and offenders are more likely to be unmarried than married (Martin *et al.* 1979, South Australian Office of Crime Statistics 1980b). This exhausts what we can say with confidence about correlates of crime in Australia.

Who are Victims of Crime?

Surprisingly, the answer to the question of who are the victims is very similar to who are the offenders. The primary source of data for exploring the characteristics of victims is a National Crime Survey of the criminal victimisation patterns of 18,694 citizens conducted by the Australian Bureau of Statistics in 1975 (Australians Bureau of Statistics 1979). Unfortunately, relevant results from the 1983 survey are not available at the time of writing this chapter.

In Najman's (1980: 266) study of homicide, he found a strong tendency for homicide victims to be in the lowest socio-economic group. In fact, age-standardised homicide victimisation rates per 10,000 population were nine times as high for those in the lowest socio-economic group compared with those in the highest. While the National Crime Survey of 1979 failed to show consistent associations between occupation, education and income and crime victimisation rates, there was a striking tendency for unemployed people to be more susceptible to victimisation (Braithwaite and Biles 1979). The strongest association was with assault, where the unemployed were more than twice as likely to report being a victim of assault than those in full-time jobs, and six times as likely to have been assaulted over the previous year than respondents not in the workforce or in part-time jobs. Unfortunately, there are no systematic data on the race of Australian victims of crime.

In aggregate, women are less likely to be victims of crime than men (Braithwaite and Biles 1984: 4, Wilson and Brown 1973, Congalton and Najman 1974), though women are more likely to be victims of rape, 'peeping', indecent exposure and nuisance telephone calls. That is, women are much more likely to be victims of sexual violence and sexual harassment, and men are disproportionately victims of other kinds of crime, including homicide (Najman 1980: 274, South Australian Office of Crime Statistics 1981b), vehicle theft, other theft, fraud, forgery, false pretences and assault (Braithwaite and Biles 1984: 4).

The National Crime Survey showed 20–24-year-olds to have the highest victimisation rates, with the aged (over 60) having the lowest rates (see also Wilson and Brown 1973, Congalton and Najman 1974, Najman 1980: 275). The survey also showed residents of state capital cities to be much more likely to be crime victims than people living outside the state capitals (Braithwaite and Biles 1980). Unmarried people have higher rates of victimisation than those who are married – for homicide data (Najman 1980: 275) and victim survey data (Braithwaite and Biles 1984: 6,

Congalton and Najman 1974). Extraordinarily high victimisation rates prevail for those who are separated or divorced.

In summary, it can be said that the characteristics of victims of crime in Australia are very similar to the characteristics of offenders (excluding white collar criminals): both groups are disproportionately unemployed, male, young, unmarried and residents of state capital cities. This mirrors almost perfectly the situation found in the United Kingdom (Gottfredson 1984) and the United States.

> To summarise, offenders involved in the types of crimes of interest here are disproportionately male, young, urban residents, black, of lower socio-economic status, unemployed (and not in school), and unmarried. In our brief review of victim characteristics ... it was seen that victims disproportionately share these characteristics.
>
> (Hindelang *et al.* 1978: 259)

The most credible explanation for this finding in light of other evidence is that people with victim/offender characteristics (young, male, unemployed, unmarried etc.) are more likely to spend their time in public space – in trains and buses rather than private cars; streets and parks rather than offices and homes; public bars rather than private clubs. Most crucially, they are more likely to spend time in public space in the evening, when crimes disproportionately occur. Sitting at home watching television in the evening, one is not likely to seize on an opportunity to commit a crime, have one's purse snatched, or be arrested for a crime one did not commit (Braithwaite and Biles 1984: 7).

Whose Interests does the Criminal Justice System Serve?

The British criminal justice system was used, through transportation, to serve the imperialist objective of quenching a thirst for crude labour power in Australia; the police may have been quite blatantly tools of the interests of the rural ruling class for a large part of the first century of Australian history; yet today, the commitment to administrative neutrality in the criminal justice system is strong and few scholars would contend that it is blatantly a tool of ruling class interests.

Indeed, as O'Malley (1983) suggests, the very fact that the police in the first half of the nineteenth century were proactive agents of the squattocracy threatened commitment of the working class and the bourgeoisie to law and order, and ultimately threatened the stability of emerging Australian capitalism. Thus, the police, and the criminal justice system generally, became a reactive, administratively neutral, servant of community demands for law and order.

This has left Australia with a criminal justice system which is remarkably stable, which can survive major corruption scandals, prison bashings and riots, even intermittent suspension of administrative neutrality so that the police can be used against striking unionists and 'political extremists'. It can survive all of these things while retaining a high degree of community respect and commanding support for an exponential increase in criminal justice system expenditure during the past twenty years (Mukherjee 1981: 31–38 and 99–105, Mukherjee *et al*. 1981: 16 and 27, Chan and Zdenkowski 1985: 61–71) which cannot be justified by any appeal to evidence that increased criminal justice expenditure actually reduces crime, or even that the serious crime problem is getting out of hand.

Ironically, the criminal justice system, having helped secure the stability of Australian social order by ceasing to be a tool of ruling class interests, now provides this country with a criminal law which runs against ruling class interests via a proliferation of business regulatory statutes which criminalise exploitative behaviour of capital. This situation could be expected to destabilise the criminal justice system were it not for the fact that the multitude of laws criminalising the behaviour of the ruling class are rarely or never enforced. Responsibility for enforcing the regulatory statutes is not generally with the police, but with specialist agencies with an ideology of negotiation rather than enforcement. For example, consumer protection laws are the responsibility of state consumer affairs bureaux which predominantly resolve complaints by conciliation between consumers and traders rather than enforcement. Any ruling class resentment at occasional enforcement of regulatory statutes is consequently not going to be directed at the police or the courts. 'Overzealous' enforcement of the Trade Practices Act destabilises the Trade Practices Commission, but not the criminal justice system.

The criminal justice system is stable and expanding in Australia precisely because it has something to offer all interests. The ruling class might be threatened by the law in the books, but the law in action not only does not threaten them, it unburdens them of enormous private security costs. Even though victim surveys clearly show that individual victimisations for offences such as burglary far exceed corporate victimisations, one remarkable study worthy of replication in Australia showed that in a police depart-

ment near Toronto, Canada, nearly two-thirds of complaints dealt
with by the police were from corporate victims, and only one-third
from individual victims (Hagan 1982). Moreover, the complaints
from corporate victims were more likely to lead to convictions, and
corporate victims expressed greater satisfaction at the assistance
they received from the criminal justice system compared with
individual victims. Even the post-Watergate explosion of public
concern about white collar crime has been captured by the
corporate sector, so that enforcement resources are being directed
towards white collar crimes where corporations are victims rather
than offenders (computer crime and embezzlement).

We have also seen, however, that the criminal justice system
potentially has much more to offer the working class because they
stand a greater risk than the ruling class of suffering the ultimate
loss from crime – their lives – be that loss the result of an
occupational safety offence or murder. The fear of bodily harm is
something which all members of the working class experience,
while only a fraction of 1 per cent of them suffer the horrors of our
prisons. With Aborigines, the balancing of sympathies may be
different, however. Among them, the minority are those adults
who have not at some stage been processed by the criminal justice
system. Aborigines, then, may be the only group in Australian
society, perhaps together with some motley youth subcultures, for
whom destabilising the criminal justice system has any collective
appeal. But in real political terms their views do not matter.

Beyond the ruling class and the working class, a third growing
force in an increasingly corporatist Australia is welfare recipients,
who are mostly retired; and, finally, women in the home are also
slowly becoming a more potent political force. Women and the
aged are curious cases. They do not exploit the criminal justice
system to cut their security costs in the way the ruling class do;
they do not confront the level of risk of loss of life or serious injury
from crime to which male workers and the unemployed are
exposed; yet their commitment to the criminal justice system has a
deeper emotional content.

Australian research confirms overseas findings that even though
women and the aged have lower objective risks of criminal
victimisation, their subjective fear of crime is higher than other
groups in society (Mugford 1984, Braithwaite, Biles and Whitrod
1982). With women, the explanation is undoubtedly that the
crimes to which they are disproportionately exposed – notably rape
– are unusually terrifying, in the way they compound prolonged
sexual degradation upon protracted physical violence. Some sections of the women's movement have been amongst the most
vocal advocates of repressive criminal justice solutions to social

problems. On the other hand, Broadhurst and Indermaur (1982: 288) found women to be less punitive than men in their suggestions as to what sentences different offences should attract. With the aged, the generally-posited explanation for high fear of crime in the face of low objective risk is that the aged are traumatised by the prospect of their physical incapacity to cope with crime – to stay on their feet, call for help, think quickly, flee, fight back.

In summary, what we have in Australia is a criminal justice system which can endure a great deal of scandal – be it police corruption or prison riots – without destabilisation, because of the enormous support it has from the ruling class, the working class, the welfare sector and women. So pervasive is this support that while there might be a fiscal crisis of the state, and while there might not be a problem of rising crime rates in Australia, the exponential growth in criminal justice expenditures endured by Australian taxpayers over the past two decades is likely to continue.

References

Adler, F. (1975) *Sisters in Crime: The Rise of the New Female Criminal.* New York: McGraw-Hill.
Alder, C. (1985) 'Theories of Female Delinquency' in A. Borowski and J.M. Murray (eds) *Juvenile Delinquency in Australia*. Sydney: Methuen.
——and Polk, K. (1985) 'Diversion Programmes' in A. Borowski and J.M. Murray (eds) *Juvenile Delinquency in Australia*. Sydney: Methuen.
Althuizen, F. (1977) 'Juvenile Offenders in South Australia' in P.R. Wilson (ed.) *Delinquency in Australia: A Critical Appraisal.* Brisbane: University of Queensland Press.
Archer, D. and Gartner, R. (1984) *Violence and Crime in Cross-National Perspective.* New Haven: Yale University Press.
Armstrong, S. and Neumann, E. (1976) 'Bail in New South Wales', *University of New South Wales Law Journal* 1: 298–326.
Australian Bureau of Statistics (1979) *General Social Survey: Crime Victims*, Catalogue No. 4105.0. Canberra: Australian Bureau of Statistics.
Barber, R. (1973) 'An Investigation into Rape and Attempted Rape Cases in Queensland', *Australian and New Zealand Journal of Criminology* 6: 214–30.
Becker, H.S. (1963) *Outsiders: Studies in the Sociology of Deviance.* Glencoe: Free Press.
Biles, D. (1973) 'Aborigines and Prisons: A South Australian Study', *Australian and New Zealand Journal of Criminology* 6: 246–50.
——(1977) 'Car Stealing in Australia' in P.R. Wilson (ed.) *Delinquency*

in Australia: A Critical Appraisal. Brisbane: University of Queensland Press.

Braithwaite, J. (1977) 'Australian Delinquency: Research and Practical Considerations' in P.R. Wilson (ed.) *Delinquency in Australia: A Critical Appraisal*. Brisbane: University of Queensland Press.

———(1978) 'An Exploratory Study of Used Car Fraud' in P.R. Wilson and J. Braithwaite (eds) *Two Faces of Deviance: Crimes of the Powerless and Powerful*. Brisbane: University of Queensland Press.

———(1979) *Inequality, Crime, and Public Policy*. London: Routledge & Kegan Paul.

———(1980) 'Political Economy of Punishment' in E.L. Wheelwright and K. Buckley (eds) *Essays in the Political Economy of Australian Capitalism*, Vol. IV. Sydney: ANZ Books.

———(1982) 'Challenging Just Deserts: Punishing White Collar Criminals', *Journal of Criminal Law and Criminology* 73: 723–63.

———(1984) *Corporate Crime in the Pharmaceutical Industry*. London: Routledge & Kegan Paul.

———and Barker, M. (1978) 'Bodgies and Widgies: Folk Devils of the Fifties' in P.R. Wilson and J. Braithwaite (eds) *Two Faces of Deviance: Crimes of the Powerless and Powerful*. Brisbane: University of Queensland Press.

———and Biles, D. (1979) 'On Being Unemployed and Being a Victim of Crime', *Australian Journal of Social Issues* 14: 192–200.

——— and ———(1984) 'Victims and Offenders: The Australian Experience' in R. Block (ed.) *Victimization and Fear of Crime: World Perspectives*. Washington, DC: United States Department of Justice.

———, ———and Whitrod, R. (1982) 'Fear of Crime in Australia' in H.J. Schneider (ed.) *The Victim in International Perspective*. Berlin and New York: Walter de Gruyter.

———and Braithwaite, V. (1978) 'An Exploratory Study of Delinquency and the Nature of Schooling', *Australian and New Zealand Journal of Sociology* 14: 25–332.

———and Grabosky, P. (1985) *Occupational Health and Safety Enforcement in Australia*. Canberra: Australian Institute of Criminology.

———and Law, H. (1978) 'The Structure of Self-Reported Delinquency', *Applied Psychological Measurement* 2: 221–37.

Broadhurst, R. and Indermaur, D. (1982) 'Crime Seriousness Ratings: The Relationship of Information Accuracy and General Attitudes in Western Australia', *Australian and New Zealand Journal of Criminology*, 15: 219–34.

Calahan, M. (1979) 'Trends in Incarceration in the United States since 1880', *Crime and Delinquency* 25: 9–41.

Carson, W.G. (1975) 'Symbolic and Instrumental Dimensions of Early Factory Legislation: A Case Study in the Social Origins of Criminal Law', in R. Hood (ed.) *Crime, Criminology and Public Policy*. Glencoe: Free Press.

Challinger, D. (1977) *Young Offenders*. Carlton: Victorian Association for the Care and Resettlement of Offenders.

Chan, J. and Zdenkowski, G. (1985) *Just Alternatives: Trends and Issues in Deinstitutionalization of Punishment*, Draft Working Paper. Australian Law Reform Commission, Sydney.

Chappell, D. and Wilson, P.R. (1969) *The Police and the Public in Australia and New Zealand*. Brisbane: University of Queensland Press.

———(1972) 'The Australian Police and Public Revisited', in D. Chappell and P.R. Wilson (eds) *The Australian Criminal Justice System*, First Edition. Sydney: Butterworths.

Clifford, W. (1981) *Aboriginal Criminological Research: A Workshop Report*. Canberra: Australian Institute of Criminology.

———and Harding, R.W. (1985) 'Criminal Justice Processes and Perspectives in a Changing World' in *Australian Discussion Papers for the Seventh United Nations Congress on the Prevention of Crime and Treatment of Offenders*. Canberra: Australian Institute of Criminology.

Cohen, S. (1973) *Folk Devils and Moral Panics*. St Albans: Paladin.

Congalton, A.A. and Najman, J.M. (1974) *Who Are the Victims?* Sydney: New South Wales Bureau of Crime Statistics and Research.

Coventry, G. (1984) *Skipping School: An Examination of Truancy in Victorian Secondary Schools*. Melbourne: Victorian Institute of Secondary Education.

———Cornish, G. and Cramer, B. (1984) *Student Perspectives on Truancy*. Melbourne: Victorian Institute of Secondary Education.

Cullen, F.T., Link, B.G., Travis, L.F. and Wozniak, J.F. (1983) *Consensus in Crime Revisited: Emprical Reality or Methodological Artifact?* Paper to Annual Meeting of American Society of Criminology, Denver, Colorado, USA.

Department of Labour and Industry, Victoria (1983) *Annual Report 1982*. Melbourne: Government Printer.

Duckworth, A.M.E., Foley-Jones, C.R., Lowe, P. and Maller, M. (1982) 'Imprisonment of Aborigines in North Western Australia', *Australian and New Zealand Journal of Criminology* 15: 26–46.

Dunstan, J.A.P. and Roberts, S.F. (1977) *Delinquency and Socioeconomic Status: An Ecological Analysis of Melbourne*. Melbourne: Caulfield Institute of Technology.

Edelman, M.J. (1964) *The Symbolic Uses of Politics*. Urbana: University of Illinois Press.

Eggleston, E. (1976) *Fear, Favour or Affection: Aborigines and the Criminal Law in Victoria, South Australia and Western Australia*. Canberra: Australian National University Press.

Fielding, J. (1977) 'Female Delinquency', in P.R. Wilson (ed.) *Delinquency in Australia: A Critical Appraisal*. Brisbane: University of Queensland Press.

Foley-Jones, C.R. and Tandowski, N.M. (1977) *Relevance of Correctional Programmes for Female Aboriginal Prisoners*. Western Australian Department of Corrections, Research and Information Series No. 16.

Gorta, A. and Hunter, R. (1985) 'Aborigines in New South Wales Prisons', *Australian and New Zealand Journal of Criminology* 18: 26–40.

Gottfredson, M.R. (1984) *Victims of Crime: The Dimensions of Risk*. London: Home Office Research and Planning Unit.

Grabosky, P.N. (1977) *Sydney in Ferment: Crime, Dissent and Official Reaction*. Canberra: Australian National University Press.

——(1983) 'How Violent is Australia?', *Australian Society* 1 July: 38–42.

——(1984) 'The Variability of Punishment' in D. Black (ed.) *Toward A General Theory of Social Control*, Vol. I: Fundamentals. Orlando, Florida: Academic Press.

——and Braithwaite, J. (1986) *Of Manners Gentle: Enforcement Strategies of Australian Business Regulatory Agencies*. Melbourne: Oxford University Press.

Gusfield, J. (1967) *Symbolic Crusade*. Urbana: University of Illinois Press.

Hagan, J. (1982) 'The Corporate Advantage: A Study of the Involvement of Corporate and Individual Victims is a Criminal Justice System', *Social Forces* 60: 993–1,022.

Hancock, L. (1980) 'The Myth that Females are Treated More Leniently Than Males in the Juvenile Justice System', *Australian and New Zealand Journal of Sociology* 16: 4–14.

——and Chesney-Lind, M. (1985) 'Juvenile Justice Legislation and Gender Discrimination' in A. Borowski and J.M. Murray *Juvenile Delinquency in Australia*. Sydney: Methuen.

Hiller, A.E. and Hancock, L. (1981) 'The Processing of Juveniles in Victoria' in S.K. Mukherjee and J. Scutt (eds) *Women and Crime*. Sydney: Allen & Unwin.

Hindelang, M.J., Gottfredson, M.R. and Garofalo, J. (1978) *Victims of Personal Crime: An Emprical Foundation for a Theory of Personal Victimization*. Cambridge, Mass.: Ballinger.

Hopkins, A. and Parnell, N. (1984) 'Why Coal Mine Safety Regulations in Australia are not Enforced', *International Journal of the Sociology of Law* 12: 179–84.

Institute of Criminology (1978) *Unemployment and Crime*. Sydney University Law School.

Jankovic, I. (1977) 'Labour Market and Imprisonment', *Crime and Social Justice* 8: 17–31.

Knight, T. (1985) 'Schools and Delinquency' in A. Borowski and J.M. Murray, *Juvenile Delinquency in Australia*. Sydney: Methuen.

Kraus, J. (1973) 'Urbanization Patterns of Juvenile Delinquency in New South Wales', *Australian Journal of Social Issues* 8: 227–33.

——(1975) 'Ecology of Juvenile Delinquency in Metropolitan Sydney', *Journal of Community Psychology* 3: 384–95.

——(1977) 'Some Aspects of Delinquency in Australia' in P.R. Wilson (ed.) *Delinquency in Australia: A Critical Appraisal*. Brisbane: University of Queensland Press.

Krohn, M., Curry, J.P. and Nelson-Kilger, S. (1983) 'Is Chivalry Dead?', *Criminology* 21: 417–37.

Leaper, P.M. (1974) *Children in Need of Care and Protection*. Melbourne: Department of Criminology, University of Melbourne.

Lucas Report (1977) *Report of the Committee of Inquiry into the Enforcement of Criminal Law in Queensland*. Brisbane: Queensland Government Printer.

Marnier, L. (1980) *The Affective Education Project.* Adelaide: Education Department of South Australia.

Martin, J., Rook, M.K. and Filton, P. (1979) *Trends in Prison Population in Victoria.* Melbourne: Department of Community and Welfare Services.

Martin, M.A. (1973) *Aborigines and the Criminal Justice System: A Review of the Literature.* Western Australian Department of Corrections, Research and Information Series No. 2.

Miethe, T.D. (1982) 'Public Consensus on Crime Seriousness: Normative Structure or Methodological Artifact?', *Criminology* 20: 515–26.

Milte, K. and Weber, T. (eds) (1977) *Police in Australia: Development, Functions, Procedures.* Sydney: Butterworths.

Mitchell Committee (1973) *Criminal Law and Penal Methods Reform Committee of South Australia, First Report: Sentencing and Corrections.* Adelaide: South Australian Government Printer.

Mugford, Stephen (1984) 'Fear of Crime – Rational or Not? A Discussion and Some Australian Data', *Australian and New Zealand Journal of Criminology* 17: 267–75.

Mukherjee, S.K. (1981) *Crime Trends in Twentieth-Century Australia.* Sydney: Allen & Unwin.

————(1985) 'Juvenile Delinquency: Dimensions of the Problem' in A. Borowski and J.M. Murray (eds) *Juvenile Delinquency in Australia.* Sydney: Methuen.

————and Fitzgerald, R.W. (1981) 'The Myth of Rising Female Crime' in S.K. Mukherjee and J.A. Scutt *Women and Crime.* Sydney: Allen & Unwin.

————, Jacobsen, E.N. and Walker, J.R. (1981) *Source Book of Australian Criminal and Social Statistics 1900–1980.* Canberra: Australian Institute of Criminology.

————, Walker, J.R. and Jacobsen, E.N. (1985) *Crime and Punishment in the Colonies.* Sydney: University of New South Wales Printing Unit.

Najman, J.M. (1980) 'Victims of Homicide: An Epidemiological Approach to Social Policy', *Australian and New Zealand Journal of Criminology* 13: 272–80.

New South Wales Bureau of Crime Statistics and Research (1972a) *Aborigines in Prison: Census 1971.* Sydney.

————(1972b) *Crime in Our Cities: A Comparative Report.* Sydney: Statistical Report 6.

————(1974) *A Thousand Prisoners.* Sydney: Statistical Report 3.

New South Wales Department of Corrective Services (1973) *NSW Prison Population 1973: A Statistical Report.* Sydney: Research and Statistics Publication No. 3.

————(1974) *Census of Prisoners 1974: Prisoners' Social Background.* Sydney: Research and Statistics Publication No. 12.

O'Malley, P. (1980) 'Theories of Structural Versus Causal Determination: Accounting for Legislative Change in Capitalist Societies' in R. Tomasic (ed.) *Legislation and Society in Australia.* Sydney: Allen & Unwin.

————(1983) *Law, Capitalism and Democracy.* Sydney: Allen & Unwin.

Queensland Department of Mines (1983) *Annual Report 1983*. Brisbane: Government Printer.

Quinncy, R. (1975) 'Crime Control in Capitalist Society' in I. Taylor, P. Walton and J. Young (eds) *Critical Criminology*. London: Routledge & Kegan Paul.

———(1977) *Class, State and Crime: On the Theory and Practice of Criminal Justice*. New York: Longman.

Sanson-Fisher, R.W. (1978) 'Aborigines and Crime Statistics: An Interaction Between Poverty and Detectors' *Australian and New Zealand Journal of Criminology* 11: 71–78.

Sarri, R. and Bradley, P.W. (1980) 'Juvenile Aid Panels: An Alternative to Juvenile Court Processing in South Australia', *Crime and Delinquency* 20: 42–62.

Schur, E.M. (1973) *Radical Non-Intervention: Rethinking the Delinquency Problem*. Englewood Cliffs: Prentice-Hall.

Scull, A. (1977) *Decarceration: Community Treatment and the Deviant: A Radical View*. Englewood Cliffs: Prentice-Hall.

Scutt, J. (1979) 'The Myth of the "Chivalry Factor" in Female Crime', *Australian Journal of Social Issues* 14: 3–20.

———(1983) *Even in the Best of Homes: Violence in the Family*. Ringwood: Penguin.

Smith, G. (1975) 'Leisure, Recreation and Delinquency' MA Thesis, Department of Anthropology and Sociology, University of Queensland.

South Australian Office of Crime Statistics (1979) *Crime and Justice in South Australia: Quarterly Report for the Period Ending 31 December 1978*. Adelaide: Attorney-General's Department.

———(1980a) *Robbery in South Australia*. Adelaide: Attorney-General's Department.

———(1980b) *Statistics from Courts of Summary Jurisdiction, Series II, No. 4*. Adelaide: Attorney-General's Department.

———(1984) *Crime and Justice in South Australia, 1 July–31 December 1982*. Adelaide: Attorney-General's Department.

Tomasic, R. (1976) *Law, Lawyers and the Community*. Sydney: Law Foundation of New South Wales.

Vinson, T. and Homel, R. (1972) *The Coincidence of Medical and Social Problems Throughout a Region*. Sydney: New South Wales Bureau of Crime Statistics and Research.

Ward, R. (1966) *The Australian Legend*. Melbourne: Oxford University Press.

Walker, J. and Biles, D. (1985) *'Australian Prisoners 1984: Results of the National Prisons Census – June 1984*. Canberra: Australian Institute of Criminology.

Warner, C. (1982) 'A Study of Self-Reported Crime of a Group of Male and Female High School Students', *Australian and New Zealand Journal of Criminology* 15: 255–72.

West, D.J. and Farrington, D.P. (1977) *The Delinquent Way of Life*. London: Heinemann.

White, J. (1977) *Special Branch Security Records: Initial Report*. Adelaide: Government Printer.

Wilson, P.R. (1982) *Black Death, White Hands*. Sydney: Allen & Unwin.
———(1985) 'Black Death, White Hands Revisited: The Case of Palm Island', *Australian and New Zealand Journal of Criminology* 18: 49–57.
———and Braithwaite, J. (1977) 'School, Truancy and Delinquency' in P.R. Wilson (ed.) *Delinquency in Australia: A Critical Appraisal*. Brisbane: University of Queensland Press.
———and Brown, J. (1973) *Crime and the Community*. Brisbane: University of Queensland Press.
Windschuttle, K. (1978) 'Granny Versus the Hooligans' in P.R. Wilson and J. Braithwaite (eds) *Two Faces of Deviance: Crimes of the Powerless and Powerful*. Brisbane: University of Queensland Press.

Chapter Thirteen
Leisure
David F. Ip

One of the main currents of change underway in the advanced industrial societies is the growth of leisure, and this deserves sociological attention. It is interesting to note that most of the work done on the subject of leisure has concentrated on either the study of recreational activities, which may be best characterised as what Coalter and Parry (1982: 1) termed a 'sociography' of leisure, or on the 'problem of leisure' where this is interpreted as a threat as well as a central challenge to social scientists, planners, politicians, moralists and others in the post-industrial era.

Sociologists have long been unhappy about the lack of unifying theory in leisure research. Parker complains that the sociographic studies are conceived primarily at the individual behavioural level and they are accounted for by only a mixture of psychological factors (1975: 94). Similarly, Mayhew opposed strongly their misplaced location of sociological enquiry (1980). It seems that the comments made by Berger as early as 1963 (p. 21) also reflect contemporary reality: 'Despite the fact that the "problem" of leisure is already a conventional phrase in the language of social sciences, the *problem* has hardly been formulated and the *concept* of leisure has only rarely been directly confronted.'

This does not necessarily mean that a theoretical framework for a sociology of leisure has not been attempted. The concern of Wilensky's analysis, the decline of the work ethic, clearly points to the central problem of sociology – the Durkheimian notion of the nature of social bond, i.e., whether or not concepts of work are being replaced by other values which 'integrate' people into society as the work ethic has been able to. Issues such as the changing basis of social solidarity, the 'pluralisation of social structures, the relative decline of the collective conscience and the concomitant strengthening of the cult of the individual as a moral value, and the problems of the anomic potentiality of much of modern leisure', according to Coalter and Parry (1982: 5) however, 'have all formed the agenda of an admittedly non-cumulative and diffuse leisure sociology'. To them, one effect of such 'recreational/leisure' studies has been a tendency towards a functionalist approach in which leisure is understood in terms of its positive functions within society, either at the individual or at the societal level.

What, then, can we do about the state of the sociology of leisure? Stedman-Jones argues that leisure cannot be seen in isolation; it must be situated within the broader social structure, particularly that of capitalism (Stedman-Jones 1977). Rojek (1985) further suggests that when sociology is dominated by forms of theory which deal with the extensive critical literature on power, knowledge and the mode of production, the theories of 'leisure without society' can be re-examined in the light of leisure relations and leisure forms, how they are produced and reproduced in the context of a historically specific system of power, and how they reflect the principles and the ideology of capitalist society.

This chapter is intended to explore the sociological concept of leisure with a set of parameters similar to those suggested by Stedman-Jones and Rojek. We would like to re-examine the nature of leisure and its connection to work, but in the context of capitalism. This chapter will then delineate further the practices and forms of leisure and their relationship to social control. In this context it is important to clarify the validity of the concept of leisure to assess its relevance for some specific groups, such as women in society. By looking at the Australian experiences of leisure as well as those overseas, we gain an understanding of its role and varying manifestations in the context of the historical development of capitalist society.

The Nature of Leisure

Through the organisation of the work process and the advent of the factory system, industrial capitalism brought with its emergence a prominent feature which was hitherto nonexistent in pre-industrial society: the forced separation between the place of work and the place for labour power reproduction – the home. The concept of leisure in its modern sense, according to many (Dumazedier 1974, Parker 1976, Burkart and Medlik 1981), simply did not exist until then. In other words, work was not considered as instrumental, as a means-to-end obligation for economic subsistence, until industrial capitalism came of age. Burns, for example, believes that work in pre-industrial society was basically 'part and parcel of everyday life and leisure was not a separate section of the day' (1974: 43). Quoting Varagnae, Dumazedier also describes work as having a natural rhythm, interrupted by breaks, by songs, by games and ceremonies. It tended to coincide with the pattern of the day, from sunrise to sunset, and there was no clear-cut division between it and rest (1974: 14).

The change in mental concept, that is, from an undistinguished conceptualisation of both work and rest, to a dichotomised distinction between the two, therefore came about only when wage labour was introduced to workers required to earning their livings. A recognition of the concept of this free time began to take shape. As Parker points out. 'It was only when work came to be done in a special place, at a special time and under special conditions that leisure came to be demanded as a right' (1976: 24). This is echoed by others as well: 'only when the place of earning one's living began to be separated from the place where one reared one's family, could the modern separation of work and leisure be valid' (Burkart and Medlik 1981: 4).

Within the household men, and increasingly women and children, were also being drawn into the labour force in order to secure a minimum level of economic subsistence. Industrialisation created not only the increasingly sharp separation of home and work, but also of production and consumption. Leisure became the time when commodities were purchased and consumed. Frith (1982) observes that by the end of the nineteenth century, there was a well-established market for consumer durables, and their consumption was made possible by new, binding arrangements of credit-hire-purchase. In his words, 'leisure meant certain commitments' (1982: 250).

All this meant that when industrial production was organised around the developing principles of rational work discipline, that is, when workers were subjected to the social organisation of the factory and to the technical requirements of machinery, work became a matter of routine and repetition, inflexible in its use of time and space. An equally rational leisure discipline also emerged. By the end of the nineteenth century, leisure was no longer an occasional event like a fair, a carnival or a harvest festival, but more a routine, a daily experience of 'non-work'.

The ideology which accompanied the growth of such 'free time' was that people worked in order to enjoy their leisure as they wished. The money they made was spent on the commodities they wanted to purchase. Marx argues that consumption and 'consumerism' are the major forms of domination and reification (1970: 72). In other words, while the Malthusians worried that if workers ever became affluent enough to enjoy 'idleness' they would never work again, we should really note that in practice, work and the experience of work remained the only justification for such idleness. During the great Depression of the 1930s, mass unemployment did not mean mass leisure, but rather, it made more urgent the need for a job. 'Free time' without a job meant only shame and boredom. And as Frith further suggests, 'post-war affluence rested not on idleness but overtime, as people worked harder and harder to buy the leisure goods they didn't have time to enjoy' (1982: 250).

Despite the fact that leisure is generally defined as 'time free from work and other obligations and it also encompasses activities which are characterised by a feeling of (comparative) freedom' (Parker 1976: 12; see also Dumazedier 1974: 2), the 'freedom' involved in these standard accounts of leisure is, in fact, deceptive. Leisure is a necessary component of industrial capitalism. It is the time when labour is replenished physically and culturally, a re-creation time, but it is also the time when people consume, when surplus value is realised. 'Free' time is not only structured by ideas, but also by material forces, by the availability of goods and resources, by the effects of the labour process on people's capacities and desires. The size of their pay packet determines what resources people have; work prospects and career possibilities limit the leisure risks they are prepared to take; work discipline and the organisation of workers mentally and physically on the job limit their leisure capacities. In short, leisure involves a tension between choice and constraint, and this tension is the expression of the general relationship between production and consumption.

Leisure is, on the one hand, a source of fun and freedom and pleasure (Kaplan 1975: 26), a necessary counter to alienating labour; but it must also be, on the other hand, constrained and controlled and made trivial so as not to interfere with the labour process. Historians acknowledge the fact that the implementation of the British Factory Acts which provided the free Saturday afternoon would have had as much to do with the support of the capitalists as the campaigns of the workers (Walvin 1978: 5,60). After all, happy workers were more efficient and amenable than those who were selling their labour power under the dull compulsion of necessity. And the expression 'weekend' is precisely what this tension between works and leisure is all about: Friday and Saturday nights are party times just because there's no work to go to the next morning. Leisure is not really free time at all, but an organisation of non-work that is determined by the relations of capitalist production.

Leisure as Social Control

How does capitalism permit the private existence of a sphere of autonomy and still reproduce a disciplined work force? How does

capitalism maintain the separation of work and play and simultaneously maintain a necessary link between the two? Not all forms
of leisure necessarily are conducive to good order. Drinking, for
example, has been a familiar issue not only in recent times but also
in history. And this emphasises the contradiction between the need
to organise or to control the workers' leisure (so that it does not
disrupt work time) and leisure's ideological importance as free
time (the time when workers experience themselves as free
labourers).

For some Marxist scholars, this is simply a question of leisure as
social control. If work in capitalist society is intrinsically meaning-
less, and there is the general acceptance that the character of labour
is basically instrumental, then the alienation experienced at work
will lead the worker to seek self-fulfilment in leisure. However, just
as the capitalist system shapes his working day, it also shapes his
leisure activities. Alienation also creates the passive consumer who
finds satisfaction in the consumption of the commodities produced
by the manufacturing and entertainment industries. To Gorz (in
Haralambos 1980: 236), the directive to consume 'numbs a
stunted, mass-produced humanity with satisfactions that leave the
basic satisfaction untouched, but still distract the mind from it'. In
a capitalist society, it is argued that workers are not only alienated
both from work and leisure, but are also controlled at work and at
leisure.

Marcuse (1972) takes a similar view. He claims that work is
'exhausting, stupefying, inhuman slavery' and leisure simply
involves 'modes of relaxation which soothe and prolong this
stupefaction' because it is based on and directed by 'false needs'
which in turn are created by the mass media controlled by the
establishment. Therefore, Aronowitz (see Coalter and Parry 1982:
7) says that because this private sphere is experienced as restrictive
and oppressive, leisure activities are displaced into forms of mass
consumption. The needs of industrial capitalism or 'late capitalism' for the regulation and synchronisation of production and
consumption, and the continuance of necessary labour discipline,
are thus achieved via the organisation of leisure. Far from being a
private domain, leisure in fact forms part of a 'universal sphere of
consumption'.

This perspective suggests that work itself, because it is dull,
routine and mindless, destroys the workers' ability to be free, and
to enjoy themselves in other meaningful ways. Commercial leisure
commodities, in turn, are designed to confirm their cultural
incapacities. The result is a denial of the concept of pleasure: that
is, the workers have no cultural purpose of their own, and cannot
experience anything else other than what is provided by the

all-powerful capitalists. Frith, quoting Marx in the *Grundrisse*, suggests that the capitalist needs consumers for his products, 'searching for means to spur workers on to consumption, to give his wares new charms, to inspire them with new needs by constant chatter, etc. It is precisely this side of the relation of capital and labour which is an essential civilising moment, and on which the power of capital rests' (Frith 1982: 264). In short, he argues that leisure commodities may have supported the power of the capitalists, but they also have their civilising moments. The argument that the workers are totally passive and therefore can be controlled both at work and leisure is too glib and simplistic.

Social Control of Leisure

There certainly is a difference between leisure as social control and the social control of leisure. In either case, the simplicity of social control cannot be automatically assumed. The 'control' of leisure is difficult – both the workers' ideological freedom as consumers and the different interests of commodity producers have made such control problematic.

Frith is correct in pointing out that regulation has always been more important than repression (except in brief experiments like Prohibition), and capitalist leisure has developed with a framework of licences and licensing authorities (1982: 254). Malcolmson's (1973) history of popular recreation in England between 1780 and 1850 documents the fall of traditional popular recreation and increasing intervention from the state. He notes that 'the most direct (and traditional) means to encourage labour discipline was through the application of state power, and this kind of control continued to be generally applauded' (Malcolmson 1973: 97).

The state's efforts were significant. Storch (1976) argues that the police force in England was developed primarily to patrol leisure, in applying the licensing laws. Frith (1982: 254) further argues that in the English industrial cities of the nineteenth century the working class was isolated in its own areas, and had its own activities. It was the police who had to supervise the pubs, the crowds and the street corners and to enforce regulations on drink and prostitution, gambling and performance. The emphasis was on surveillance rather than prevention; the policeman's duty was to prevent workers' leisure from becoming public disorder and public holidays from becoming political events. In Storch's view, the policeman was a 'domestic missionary', bringing middle class restraint and decency to working class lives. And this was also a symbol of nineteenth-century leisure: class divisions. Employers and their workers did not meet in their free time in the ways that the landed gentry and their tenants and labourers met at rural feasts and sports, or the aristocracy and lumpenproletariat met on the race track and around the boxing ring (Bailey 1978).

Fuller (1977) sees a similar picture in his study of the class bias of legislation on gambling in England, while Downes *et al.* (1976) as well as Walvin (1978) also record that various attempts were made to regulate and to prohibit alcohol consumption among the working class. The gist of such regulations was based mainly on moral grounds. Labelling activities such as drinking and gambling as unsuitable pastimes means that leisure in the nineteenth century was seen as a means to the end of self-improvement. Leisure was perceived by some as an educational institution, and rational recreation therefore should be encouraged as much as possible, directed at producing a more civilised, educated and profitable workforce (Best 1973, Basini 1975).

In other words, the regulation of unsuitable leisure goes with the promotion of suitable leisure – the 'rational recreation' of Victorian England is perhaps a forerunner of the industrial recreation movement. Goldman and Wilson's (1977) study of the industrial recreation movement beginning in the 1880s shows how scientific rationality was applied not only to work but to leisure as well. They point out that 'the industrial recreation movement was part of a general orientation to the phenomenon of leisure stimulated by three principle concerns: technical efficiency, control over the production process, and the maintenance of legitimacy. The industrial recreation programmes were designed to integrate structurally and ideologically the working man's leisure into the needs of corporate capital' (Goldman and Wilson 1977: 183).

Underlying these views is, of course, the Protestant work ethic: pleasure must be justified; leisure, too, should mean effort and self-discipline; and this does not only apply to labourers but to the middle class as well. The subordination of leisure to work has meant, at its simplest, the organisation of middle class social life around business needs, every activity being chosen for its career effects. But there is also an ideological distinction involved between improving experiences, embodied in certain forms of arts and sports, and 'wasteful' hedonism. By the end of the nineteenth century, the distinction between rational and irrational leisure was institutionally enforced: rational leisure was promoted in schools, municipal parks and libraries; irrational leisure was patrolled and regulated by police and directly or indirectly by policies on housing, education, health and the family. The systematic efforts by teachers, clergymen and journalists in the United Kingdom to apply to the working classes the moral principles embedded in public school games – discipline, effort, competition, team spirit, and good manners (Frith 1982: 255) – was a good example. From a reading of Foucault's work one might tend to agree that leisure relations are not entirely relations of freedom but relations of discipline, training, coding and control (Foucault 1977: 152–64). The municipalisation of recreation under Welfare Capitalism in the 1920s in America, in O'Connor's view (1973), is another example of such promotion and regulation of leisure, but he also notes that in this process, the socialisation costs of production have been gradually handed over to the state, eventually cumulating in its contemporary fiscal crisis (O'Connor 1973).

'Rational' recreation was basically a contradictory concept: leisure is, by definition, a contrast to work, duty and routine, involving a 'sapping of moral fibre'. But leisure is also, for the same reason, the setting for the non-routine experiences of love and art and ecstasy. The nineteenth-century problem had been how to combine the necessary discipline and relaxation, the necessary order and disorder. As the religious or moral control of leisure waned, commercial entrepreneurs emerged, churning out leisure goods with reference not only to their financial proceeds, but also to bringing leisure 'needs' into line with the goods that were available.

Commercial entrepreneurs were also concerned about the problem of order and routine. 'Irrational' leisure, i.e., spontaneity, drunkenness, disruption and the like, was liable to affect profit as well as people. As Frith points out, this is, however, a simple problem of form rather than content, and therefore, the characteristics of the production of leisure commodities has been the premium emphasis on the organisation of leisure by notions of professionalism and predictability, the latter notion being especially significant, being important in reducing commercial risk (Frith 1982: 256). Giving the paying customers what they want has always been the guiding principle of the commercial process, and secures an orderly and a mass audience.

The development of mass media and their bureaucratic control eventually further contributed to the 'refinement' of leisure in the twentieth century. The rise of the cinema, radio and television meant not just the standardisation of popular entertainment, but also the regulation of its spontaneous, disruptive and anarchical elements. In Frith's words, this was the 'translation of working class pleasures into middlebrow formulas' (1982: 257). To put it in another way, the older leisure occupations finally had to give way to the more ordered and disciplined recreations which the new

industrial society demanded, entertainments which were conso-
nant with the wider social and economic interests of contemporary
society.

Leisure in Australia

Research on leisure in Australia is sparse. Still, it would not be
difficult to see that the regulation of leisure, particularly that of
working class leisure activities, and the promotion of acceptable
rational leisure in Australian history, falls into a pattern similar to
that of the United Kingdom.

According to Connell and Irving (1978), it was not until the late
1930s that Australia systematically experienced the impacts of
industrialisation on everyday life. One of the major consequences
was shorter working hours. In 1856 the Eight Hour Movement
first won the building trades an eight-hour day in legislation
(Murphy 1896), but such practice was uneven. Lack suggests that
'at the beginning of the 1880s only a minority of urban working
men – including most building craftsmen, quarrymen and a few
groups in the metal trades – had won the eight hours' boon' (1978:
50). However, because of the relative openness of the early class
structure in Australian society, especially through the influence of
employers, formerly tradesmen, made shorter hours less a threat
than a goal aspired to by both workers and small capitalists.
Consequently, the eight-hour day or the forty-eight-hour week
gradually became a general feature of Australian working life in the
early 1900s (Cannon 1973).

The move to leisure coincided with the suburban development
of the 1880s. When industrial production was combined with a
high commitment to suburban home ownership, the ideology of
individualism, familism, private ownership and privacy was not
only cemented, but a peculiar pattern of leisure centred around the
home also emerged.

This is particularly true for the middle class. In his study of
middle class leisure in Victoria, Cannon (1973: 223) suggests that
in the late nineteenth century, it seemed that both husbands and
wives were spending more and more time in and around the home.
Wives, for example, were engaged in often hectic and ritualistic
rounds of social calls patterned after the British example. A
superior home life, education and surplus wealth seemed to be the
ideal for them. Their leisure outside the home and family, on the
other hand, consisted of activities that were more of a display to
cement their middle class consciousness rather than enjoyment.

Balls, garden parties and organised picnics were often constrained activities, designed to indicate hierarchical status.

The study of Footscray by Lack (1978), however, offers a different picture for the working class. The author believes that the home as the centre of leisure for this class was simply limited to games and reading. 'Home life must have been a round of never ending chores for wives, and with the best will in the world a large majority of working men would have had only two or three waking hours each weekday, to relax at home ...' (Lack 1978: 53). The pattern of working class leisure in nineteenth-century Victoria, in his view, was largely located in entertainment outside the home because of housing size, quality and location differences. Bottomley (1980) suggests that perhaps this is part of the reason why in Melbourne there was such a frequent mention of high commitment to sport and spectatorship in leisure time.

One can postulate that the social control of working class leisure in Australia has been more indirect than direct. On the one hand, there were numerous attempts on the part of the governments to regulate drinking, gambling and other social vices as documented by Dunstan (1968) and McMillen (1985), something strongly supported, and campaigned for, by moral reformers. Consequently, state intervention into working class leisure later supported the provision of a 'healthy' environment (Powell 1980) – for example, the provision of libraries and mechanical institutes by local governments. On the other hand, however, Bottomley (1980) suggests that the suburban ideal of home-centredness became more prominent in working class leisure, possibly through the principle of stratified diffusion (Wilmott and Young 1975). Perhaps there is really no need for any 'control' at all when mass leisure becomes home-centred.

There have been numerous studies which confirm that the 'general way of life' in Australia has been one of home-centred leisure (Oeser and Hammond 1954, Cleland and Stimson 1972, Pearson 1977). In the 1940s a survey in a town in New South Wales found that the five most popular pastimes were reading, radio listening, going to the pictures, watching football and gardening (Walker 1945). In 1956, a Gallup Poll carried out before the advent of television revealed that listening to the radio and reading accounted for 64 per cent of week-night time and 43 per cent of weekend time. Olley confirmed in 1964 that the average person (male) spent about three-quarters of his active leisure (non-working and non-sleeping time) in and around the home (1962: 4). Scott and U'Ren (1962) in study of a suburban housing estate, found similar patterns for working class residents.

More recently, Lansbury (1970) found that the middle class leisure pattern was based on family, home, car and garden. Findings from Cleland and Stimson's (1972) study on leisure pursuits in Adelaide, not surprisingly, emphasised a similar picture. Kalkett pointed out in 1975 that the backyard was 'far and away the most important venue for recreation, beside which pubs, clubs, the beaches and public parks pale into insignificance' (1975: 7). His estimate was that residents in Adelaide spent on the average about ten hours per week in the garden (Kalkett 1975). Extrapolating from this figure, Kemeny (1978) estimates that about $300 million in labour costs is expended by home-owners on garden maintenance each year. Such patterns of leisure remain even in the 1980s, as shown when Bottomley (1980) researched the work-leisure relationship of outer-suburban male workers in Melbourne.

In 1958, Meyersohn and Jackson correctly noted that 'if one were to rank leisure activities in terms of visibility, gardening would probably win out' (1958: 276). Judging from the data presented above, this remark seems to be just as appropriate as ever. In terms of time allocation, the most significant leisure activity is watching television. In 1963, according to a Gallup Poll, 7 our of 10 Australians watched television regularly, 3 in 10 watched almost every night, 4 in 10 watched 3 nights a week, and only 3 in 10 hardly ever saw it (Smith 1983: 30). Mansutti (1981) cites more recent information from the Federation of Australian TV Stations: 'Ninety-eight per cent of Australians live in TV homes. The TV set in those homes is on for an average of 30 hours and 21 minutes a week. Of those homes 79 per cent have both a colour TV set and a black and white one' (Goodluck and Goodluck 1981: 46). Television viewing time might constitute an even greater component of leisure time spent at home nowadays if we consider the statistics offered by the *Sydney Morning Herald* (29 March 1986: 7). It is reported that 50 per cent of homes in Australia now have a VCR (video cassette recorder) compared with only 11 per cent in 1982, despite the fact that sales of VCRs have decreased from 768,000 units in 1983–84 to 658,000 units in 1984–85. The average number of movies rented by a VCR household is suggested to be 1.4 a week. It is argued that in Sydney, the typical 'user profile' today is of a married couple, on lower incomes, over the age of thirty-five; and the success of many video outlets in Sydney's western suburbs and in low-income areas, tends to confirm this. It is therefore not surprising to find that the result of the Australian Department of Sport, Recreation and Tourism's Recreation Participation Survey of April–May

1985 shows that television-watching is at the top of the list of leisure activities in the age group 25–39 years (i.e., the child-bearing years) (Wearing 1986: 7).

Outside the home environment, Caldwell (1972) claims that three of the most frequently cited Australian leisure activities are sport, gambling and drinking. We have to note, however, according to Cleland and Stimson's (1972) study, that when respondents were asked an open-ended question, what their main spare-time activity was, it was found that sport received a higher rating than would have been expected from participation rates. Hallows (1970) also points out that the image of Australia as a nation of sportsmen is substantially incorrect. It is the total availability of sport which is unmatched anywhere else, and which makes it safe to assume that Australians spend more of their leisure time in the open air than any other people. In a more recent study of Queensland Telecom workers, Williams (1983: 232) finds that sport is the most favoured leisure activity after hobbies as a whole, but only among single people. Among the married, gardening is the preferred activity. Interestingly, the least approved leisure activity and the one which has the lowest priority is 'political activity'.

Both drinking and gambling, however, possibly play a larger role in Australia than in other Western countries, according to Taft and Walker (1958: 181). McGregor (1966: 131) claims that 'if one excludes sex and conversation, drinking is probably the most important social activity in Australia'. Smith (1983: 31) maintains that consumption of beer is also very high by world standards and has become an integral part of the mateship subculture. The significance of gambling is not to be underestimated, either. McGregor (1966: 142) found that the national estimated turnover for the year 1960–61 was twice as high as expenditure on social services, and three times as much as the defence bill. Caldwell (1972) indicates that Australians spend about $160 per head each year on legalised forms of gambling. This is certainly higher, he reports, than the United Kingdom ($30), New Zealand ($52) or the United States ($90). More recently, it was reported in the *Courier Mail* (16 August 1986: 1) that total gambling in Australia had jumped from more than $400 million in 1973 to almost $2,000 million in 1983. Moreover, Australians gambled between $650 and $850 a head each year; this was twice the English level and four times that at which Americans legally gambled. In terms of the amount of spare household cash gambled each year, figures have quadrupled between 1973 and 1983. Moreover, Australians gambled between $650 and $850 a head each year, twice what the English and four times what Americans legally gambled. In terms of the amount of spare household cash gambled each year, figures quadrupled between 1973 and 1983. In terms of percentages of personal consumption expenditure, Haig (1985: 74) agrees that Australia has the highest level of gambling expenditure per head of the advanced Western countries (Table 13.1). Arguably, the comparison is a little unfair because presumably much of this money is continually recycled; still, it should not distract us from the fact the 'Australians have always had a reputation as remarkable gamblers, and gambling has been, and still is an integral and romanticised part of Australian culture' (McMillen 1983).

In a more recent study on Australian gambling, Haig (1985: 72) further compares the gross and net expenditure on gambling with expenditure on elected items of personal consumption. According to his calculation, on the average, personal gambling accounts for about 15 per cent of expenditure on food. However, if only 75 per cent of people gamble (and they spend the same amount), then expenditure on this is about 20 per cent of their expenditure on food (Table 13.2).

The important point though, according to McMillen (1985), is that both drinking and gambling have been part of the attempt by the state to regulate and provide the population, especially the

Table 13.1 Net Expenditure on Gambling, Australia and Various Countries (% of Personal Consumption Expenditure)

	1960	1980
Australia	1.5	1.6
Britain	1.0 (a)	1.1
Greece	0.7 (b)	1.0
Finland	0.6	1.0
New Zealand	1.4	0.9
Sweden	0.7	0.9
Ireland	0.8	0.8
Spain	n.a.	0.7
Norway	0.5 (c)	0.6
Canada	n.a.	0.5
Netherlands	0.2 (d)	0.5
Italy	n.a.	0.4
Belgium	0.3	0.3
Average (excluding Spain)	0.6	0.8

(a) 1963   (b) 1970   (c) 1962   (d) 1961
Source: Haig, B. (1985) 'Expenditure on Legal Gambling' in G. Caldwell *et al.* (eds) *Gambling in Australia*, p. 74

Table 13.2 Net Expenditure on Gambling and Items of
Consumption per head, Australia, 1982–83

Gambling: Turnover	$580
Net Expenditure	146
Food	1,119
Tobacco	123
Private Education	360
All Consumption	$6,638

Source: Haig, B. (1985) 'Expenditure on Legal Gambling' in G. Caldwell, *et al.*
(eds) *Gambling in Australia*, p. 72

working class, with organised leisure. The regulation of both
drinking and gambling, in fact, is the provision of a dual structure
dominated by private enterprises, with the state supervising the
public conditions of existence of such activities so that they take
place in institutionalised facilities such as pubs, clubs, race courses
or casinos. While Bottomley (1980) argues that the government's
policy on urban development shapes the distinctive pattern of
Australian home-centredness leisure, McMillen takes the argument further to insist that the state's intervention into leisure
activities such as drinking and gambling, which are central aspects
of working class culture, is evidence of the imposition of bourgeois
rationality to define class boundaries and institutionalise new
forms of distinction. Privatised gambling, after all, simultaneously
expresses and symbolises the contradictions between the freedom
and constraint inherent in capitalist society. If gambling is the
source of self-indulged gratification and the expression of active
dissatisfaction with, and alienation from, such activities, they
therefore have to be brought under an accepted moral 'frame' in
which the visibility of working class gambling (read reckless
spending, speculative and impulsive practices) will not be an
affront to the 'respectable' morality of the bourgeoisie (the personal commitment to thrift, hard work and self-denial.

Gough Whitlam's policy speech (November 1972) summarised
the sentiment well: 'There is no greater social problem facing
Australia than the *good use* of leisure ... this may well be the
problem of the 1980s' (quoted in Goodluck and Goodluck 1981: 7).
The fear of uncontrolled or 'wasted' leisure was also expressed in a
1981 seminar on the creative or destructive use of future leisure
time in Australia:

We are beginning to awaken to the reality that the leisure crisis is
not simply a problem of increased free time which people are not

equipped to use, or a want of more recreational facilities ... We are beginning to feel the vibrations of a social disaster, a breakdown of social cohesion throughout the industrialised world such as has never been experienced before and is hard for us to imagine.

(Goodluck and Goodluck 1981: 7).

Morals aside, the regulation and control of leisure activities such as drinking and gambling do underline the broader macro-structural problem of the state – the legitimacy crisis and the problem of hegemony (Habermas 1973).

As the 'hand of the state' is becoming more visible and more diversified, the bureaucratic structure of the state apparatus has grown increasingly complicated, requiring an expanding state budget. The state has to finance itself through taxation and loans from capital markets, but it cannot do this in a way which interferes with the capital accumulation process or which jeopardises economic growth. Viewed from this perspective, rationalised gambling and drinking are perhaps necessarily profitable enterprises for government revenue and therefore also a means to overcome the fiscal crisis. In providing centralisation of facilities, extended opportunities for gambling, improved technologies and efficiency, (McMillen 1983), the contradictions between the dominant bourgeois ideology and that of the 'destructive' ideology of working class gambling can thus be resolved and hegemony restored.

Leisure and Control: The Case of Women

The argument so far is that leisure has been organised and controlled either directly or indirectly by applied regulations or policies, or through the promotion of particular goods and activities. The Marxist view is that the rationalisation of leisure essentially involves the imposition of the 'hegemonic discourse' of the ruling class or the state on the subordinate working class. The contradictions of leisure are thus the signs and arena of leisure struggle expressed on class lines and manifested in social control. Stedman-Jones (in Dixon 1981: 1) has grave reservations about this approach. He suggested that it is basically a 'cowboys and Indians' view of class struggle, and he did not see the necessity of over-politicising 'leisure' as an area of struggle and separating it from work. Frith (1982) has a more sympathetic view towards it but finds it eventually too gloomy and mechanical. He argues that leisure politics are more about situations than intentions; the capitalist control is not of ideas but of culture practice, and therefore it is still a one-sided account of leisure. Certainly there have been attempts at intervention and control, but they have not completely determined the shape of working class leisure. He insists that we need to look more closely into workers' own use of leisure, and their responses to these provisions.

Ultimately, according to McIntosh (1981), even a Marxist critique of leisure tends to overlook the very significant issue of women and leisure. She points out that patriarchy, as a critical dimension, is often ignored (1981: 103). Griffin (1981: 122) suggests, for example, that women are leisure for men, and vital to men's leisure:

> Firstly, women service men's leisure, in that it is only because of women's unpaid work in the home, and the primary childcare responsibilities, that men can go out for drinks with the lads, and have as much leisure time as they do. Secondly, women are an integral part of men's leisure, as 'escorts', whether paid or unpaid, or in relation to the myriad ways in which women must present and construct themselves for men, both materially and psychologically.

The fact is, therefore, that women themselves are constructed *as leisure* by men, and men's activities in work, existence and leisure practically determine the women's activities.

Hobson's (1981) research supports this view. She finds that one of the most obvious changes in the lives of women since their marriage is the lack of any 'leisure' or time they consider to be 'spare', when they could do what they want. Studies by Coles (1980), Cass (1978) and Bottomley (1980) in Australia reach a similar conclusion: in the home there is, strictly defined, very little leisure – at least, it seems, for married working mothers. Wilson (1980) suggests women's leisure appears to be home-centred and relatively passive. Much of it seems to be part of domestic labour, producing goods for use, to be consumed by the family.

If 'leisure' activities involve women outside the home, they are more likely to be the ones defined as acceptable by their husbands – such as bingo or socialising (gossiping) with friends, or they often taken place in a family group context (parties, nights out or trips). It is therefore not surprising to find that even the social participation in voluntary organisations in Australia between men and women manifests an unequivocal dividing line: men predominate in sporting, recreational and social groups, and women in religious, civic and service activities (Bryson and Thompson 1972: 175).

Williams (1983: 232) concludes that current leisure concepts are masculine-biased, but are also closely related to the way we conceive paid work, and intimately linked to consumerism. When our society is increasingly aligning consumption with leisure, consumerism is construed by women to be 'leisure'. To Wearing (1986: 13), it is thus understandable to find that many housewives considered shopping not only as a leisure activity, but as one of their most enjoyable.

When leisure values are necessarily based on consumption as well as paid income, it means that only those who have unimpeded access to open-ended incomes will be able to turn non-work time into leisure, for leisure derives its meaning from the relationships of production, and also contributes to the reproduction of those relationships. Therefore it is not surprising to observe that in Williams' (1983) study, despite the fact that there is potential for increased leisure, the 'work ethic' is still deeply entrenched.

Conclusion

The nature of leisure has conventionally been assumed to be identified with free time, choice, flexibility, spontaneity and self-determination (Parker 1981), and as social experience in which institutional constraints and obligations are minimised (Neulinger 1981: 21). While there is often a discharge of spontaneous and intense emotion, and an outburst of excitement in our leisure activities, we have argued that modern leisure is not synonymous with freedom, and our leisure activities are increasingly 'civilised' and restrained. This is because modern leisure obeys a historically specific economy of balances and restraints, with intense emotions being unleashed in an often controlled form which is defined as legitimate. In other words, behind our leisure activities, there is always a socially-produced effect of structural rules of pleasure and unpleasure, few of which can be divorced from their immediate economic and class context. Yet one also has to keep in mind that such regulation of leisure need not be a conspiracy or manipulation (though this certainly is encouraged); nor is it complete.

Ultimately, the study of leisure and popular recreation in our society cannot be seen in isolation. It must be situated within the work/wage-relation context where class expression and social control take place as complementary dimensions of the same social process. If leisure is about freedom, fun and consumption, it is also about regulation, power and production. If leisure is about struggle and needs, these struggles and needs are defined by capitalism. Maybe Frith (1982) is right: leisure does not challenge the system, it reflects and illuminates it. Nor is leisure about living outside the system; the final issue is how to live within it.

References

Bailey, P. (1978) *Leisure and Class in Victorian England.* London: Routledge & Kegan Paul.

Basini, A. (1975) 'Education for Leisure: A Sociological Analysis' in J.T. Howorth and M.A. Smith (eds) *Work and Leisure.* London: Lepus Books.

Berger, B. (1963) 'The Sociology of Leisure: Some Suggestions' in E.O Smith (ed.) *Work and Leisure.* New Haven: College and University Press.

Best, G. (1973) *Mid-Victorian Britain 1851–1875.* St Albans: Panther.

Bottomley, B. (1980) 'Work and Leisure in a Melbourne Suburb', Unpublished MA Thesis, Monash University, Melbourne.

Bryson, L. and Thompson, F. (1972) *An Australian Newtown.* Malmsbury: Kibble Books.

Burkart, A.J. and Medlik, S. (1981) *Tourism: Past, Present and Future.* London: Heinemann.

Burns, t. (1974) 'Leisure in Industrial Society', in M.A. Smith *et al.* (eds) *Leisure and Society in Britain.* London: Allen Lane.

Caldwell, G.T. (1972) 'Leisure Co-operatives: The Institutionalization of Gambling and the Growth of Large Leisure Organizations in New South Wales', Unpublished PhD Thesis, Australian National University, Canberra.

Cannon, M. (1973) *Life in the Cities.* Melbourne: Nelson.

Cass, B. (1978) 'Women's Place in the Class Structure' in E.L. Wheelwright and K. Buckley (eds) *Essays in the Political Economy of Australian Capitalism,* Vol. 3. Sydney: Australian and New Zealand Book Co.

Cleland and Stimson (1972) *A Survey of Entertainment Habits and Needs in Adelaide.* Adelaide: School of Social Sciences, Flinders University of South Australia.

Coalter, F. and Parry, N. (1982) *Leisure Sociology or the Sociology of Leisure?* London: Papers in Leisure Studies No. 4, the Polytechnic of North London.

Coles, L. (1980) 'Women and Leisure: A Critical Perspective' in D. Mercer and E. Hamilton-Smith (eds) *Recreation Planning and Social Change in Urban Australia.* Melbourne: Sorrett Publications.

Connell, R.W. and Irving, T. (1978) 'The Making of the Australian Industrial Bourgeoisie 1930–1975', *Intervention* 10 (11): 5–38.

Dixon, D. (1981) 'Gambling and the Law: The Street Betting Act, 1906 as an Attack on Working Class Culture' in A. Tomlinson (ed.) *Leisure and Social Control.* Brighton: Chelsea School of Human Movement, Brighton Polytechnic.

Downes, D.M., Davies, B.P., David, M. and Stone, P. (1976) *Gambling, Work and Leisure. A Study Across Three Areas.* London: Routledge & Kegan Paul.

Dumazedier, J. (1974) *Sociology of Leisure.* New York: Elsevier.

Dunstan, K. (1968) *Wowsers.* Melbourne: Cassell.

Foucault, M. (1977) *Discipline and Punishment.* Harmondsworth: Penguin.

Frith, S. (1982) *Sound Effects. Youth, Leisure and the Politics of Rock 'n' Roll*. New York: Pantheon Books.

Fuller, P. (1977) 'Gambling: A Secular "Religion" for the Obsessional Neurotic?' in J. Halliday and P. Fuller (eds) *The Psychology of Gambling*. Harmondsworth: Penguin.

Goldman, J. and Wilson, J. (1977) *The Rationalization of Leisure, Politics and Society*, Vol. 7.

Goodluck, P. and Goodluck, J. (eds) (1981) *The Future of Leisure in Australia*. Glenelg, SA: J. and P. Goodluck, Van Cle Foundation.

Griffin, C. (1981) 'Young Women and Leisure' in A. Tomlinson (ed.) *Leisure and Social Control*. Brighton: Chelsea School of Human Movement, Brighton Polytechnic.

Habermas, J. (1973) *Legitimation Crisis*. London: Heinemann Education Books.

Haig, B. (1985) 'Expenditure on Legal Gambling', in G. Caldwell *et al.* (eds) *Gambling in Australia*. Sydney: Croom Helm.

Hallows, J. (1970) *The Dreamtime Society*. Sydney: Collins.

Haralambos, M. with Heald, R.M. (1980) *Sociology: Themes and Perspectives*. Slough: University Tutorial Press.

Hobson, D. (1981) 'Young Women at Home and "Leisure"' in A. Tomlinson (ed.) *Leisure and Social Control*. Brighton: Chelsea School of Human Movement, Brighton Polytechnic.

Kalkett, I. (1975) 'Private Gardens, Private Worlds. The Need for Greater Consideration of the Residential Garden as a Venue for Recreational Activities', *Communications* 2 (1): 4–8.

Kaplan, M. (1975) *Leisure: Theory and Policy*. New York: Wiley & Sons.

Kemeny, J. (1978) 'Australia's Privatized Cities: Detached House Ownership and Urban Exploitation', Paper presented to Housing Problems and Policy Seminar, Centre for Urban Studies, Swinburne Institute of Technology.

Lack, J. (1978) 'Working Class Leisure', *Victorian Historical Journal* 1 (49): 49–65.

Lansbury, R. (1970) 'Leisure in New Suburbs', *Sociologiske Meddelelser*, 14: 79–92.

Malcolmson, R.W. (1973) *Popular Recreations in English Society 1700–1850*. Cambridge: Cambridge University Press.

Mansutti, E. (1981) 'Mass Media in Creative or Destructive Use of Free Time' in P. and J. Goodluck (eds) *The Future of Leisure in Australia*. Glenelg, SA: J. and P. Goodluck, Van Cle Foundation.

Marcuse, H. (1972) *One Dimensioned Man*. London: Abacus.

Marx, K. (1970) *A Contribution to the Critique of Political Economy*. Moscow: Progress Press.

Mayhew, B. (1980) 'Structuralism vs Individualism: Part I, Shadow Boxing in the Dark', *Social Forces* 59 (2), December: 335–75.

McGregor, C. (1966) *Profile of Australia*. Ringwood, Victoria: Penguin.

McIntosh, S. (1981) 'Leisure Studies and Women' in A. Tomlinson (ed.) *Leisure and Social Control*. Brighton: Chelsea School of Human Movement, Brighton Polytechnic.

McMillen, J. (1983) 'Loaded Dice: The Transformation of Gambling in

Queensland,' Unpublished Honours Thesis, Department of Sociology, University of Queensland.

———(1985) 'Gambling and the State: Queensland's Plunge on the Trifecta', Paper presented to SAANZ 85 Conference, University of Queensland, 30 August to 2 September.

Mercer, D.C. (1985) 'Australians' Time Use and Preferences: Some Recent Findings', *Australian and New Zealand Journal of Sociology* 21 (3) November: 371–94.

Meyersohn, R. and Jackson, R. (1958) 'Gardening in Suburbia' in W.M. Dorbinger (ed.) pp. 271–86.

Murphy, W.E. (1896) *History of the Eight Hour Movement*. Melbourne: Spectator Publishing.

Neulinger, J. (1981) *To Leisure: An Introduction*. Boston: Allyn & Bacon.

O'Connor, J. (1973) *The Fiscal Crisis of the State*. New York: St Martin's Press.

Oeser, O.A. and Hammond, S.B. (eds) (1954) *Social Structure and Personality in a City*. London: Routledge & Kegan Paul.

Olley, A.K. (1964) 'Leisure in Australia', *Hemisphere*, January: 2–7.

Parker, S. (1975) 'The Sociology of Leisure: Progress and Problems', *British Journal of Sociology* 26 (1): 91–101.

———(1976) *The Sociology of Leisure*. London: Allen & Unwin.

———(1981) 'Choice, Flexibility, Spontaneity and Self-determination in Leisure', *Social Forces* 60 (2), 323–31.

Pearson, K. (1977) 'Leisure in Australia' in D. Mercer (ed.) *Leisure and Recreation in Australia*. Melbourne: Sorrett Publications.

Powell, J. (1980) 'The Philistines and the Populace: Leisure and Recreation Before 1945', in D. Mercer, and E. Hamilton-Smith (eds) *Recreation Planning and Social Change in Urban Australia*. Melbourne: Sorrett Publications.

Rojek, R. (1985) *Capitalism and Leisure Theory*. London: Tavistock.

Scott, D. and U'Ren, R. (1962) *Leisure*. Melbourne: Cheshire.

——— and ———(1966) 'Leisure in the Suburbs', *Architecture in Australia* 54: 59–60.

Smith, J.E.M. (1983) 'Leisure Theory and Australian Public Policy', Unpublished MSPD Thesis, University of Queensland, Brisbane.

Stedman-Jones, G. (1977) 'Class Expression vs Social Control', *History Workshop–A Journal of Social History* 4, Autumn: 162–70.

Storch, R.D. (1976) 'The Policemen as Domestic Missionary', *Journal of Social History* 9.

Taft, R. and Walker, K. (1958) 'Australia' in A. Rose (ed.) *Institutions of Advanced Societies*. Minneapolis: University of Minnesota Press.

Walker, A. (1945) *Coaltown: A Social Survey of Cessnock, New South Wales*. Melbourne: Melbourne University Press.

Walvin, J. (1978) *Leisure and Society: 1830–1950*. London: Longman.

Walker, A. (1945) *Coaltown: A Social Survey of Cessnock, New South Wales*. Melbourne: Melbourne University Press.

Walvin, J. (1978) *Leisure and Society: 1830–1950*. London: Longman.

Wearing, B. (1986) 'All in a Day's Leisure: Gender and the Concept of Leisure', Paper presented at the Annual Conference of the Sociological

Association of Australia and New Zealand, University of New England, Armidale, New South Wales, 9–12 July.

Williams, C. (1983) 'The 'Work Ethic', Non-working and Leisure in an Age of Automation', *ANZJS* 19 (2): 216–37.

Wilmott, P. and Young M. (1975) *The Symmetrical Family*. Harmondsworth: Penguin.

Wilson, J. (1980) 'Sociology of Leisure', *Annual Review of Sociology* 6: 21–40.

Part III
Current Issues and Concerns

Chapter Fourteen
Family Change
Don Edgar

There seems no doubt that if we look at the family unit from a sociological and historical perspective, the second half of the twentieth century will mark a period of notable transformation. Indeed, since World War II, we have been living in the 'Age of Familism' (Canada 1983).

Partly because the family is such a fundamental social unit, arising as it does from mankind's basic sexuality, the long infancy period which requires extended nurturing and protection, and the greater control over the environment which social interaction confers, it is difficult to see how change in the family could ever take place if mankind is to survive. However, the social *form* which families take in different societies and over time reflects and creates variations and changes in the resources which form the basis of control, the nature of economic exchange, and the groups which have power over both resources and cultural meanings.

It is worth remembering that the word 'family' in its current meaning of close kin group, is fairly recent. Deriving from the Latin *famulus* (servant), and *familia* (household), it referred until the mid-seventeenth century to the entire 'household', including servants, or to the 'house' of a particular lineage. Williams (1976) suggests that the modern usage of family as a small kin group in a single house grew not so much from the bourgeois family of early capitalism but more from the new working class and lower middle class who were defined by wage labour. As he puts it (Williams 1976: 111):

Family or family and friends can represent the only immediately positive attachments in a large-scale and complex wage-earning society . . . it is a history worth remembering when we hear that 'the family, as an institution is breaking up', or that, in times gone by and still hopefully today, 'the family is the necessary foundation of all order and morality'.

Statistics Canada (Canada 1983: 231) sums up its review of divorce law and the family in similar vein:

... viewed across the sweep of history and different cultures, the family has had neither the form nor the functions of today's version. Rather, for many cultures and for much of history, the fundamental unit of sociation has been the household and not the standard nuclear family with its two parents and their immediate offspring. Nor has this household been formalized by the requirements of church and state as the family is today. Across time and across cultures, the household has had many or few members, has pivoted around the authority of a central female or male, and has been structured with greater or lesser importance determined either by marriage or by blood relations.

It is important to emphasise that 'the family' is sociologically prior to 'marriage' and its various connotations. As Wittich (1976) argued, drawing on the work of Malinowski (1944), Zelditch (1964) and others:

> The family is embedded in instinctive life resulting from the biological necessity of preservation of the species ... This binding force of the family has been intensified by ethical concepts and other controls ... and became a social institution called 'marriage'.

In this light then, it must be kept in mind that marriage, kinship structures, divorce, child-care and so on, are all social *mechanisms* by which certain goals and interests are achieved. They are not immutable or universal social forms at all, as should be manifestly clear from any scant knowledge of history or anthropology. We must therefore ask who or what produces these social mechanisms as they exist now in our society, and why they are changing, if they are.

Increased Personal Control

Although contraception has always been practised, the modern birth control pill is historically and socially significant because it is reliable and because it is controlled by women. Despite some criticism that scientists have put little effort into male contraception and that the pill has undesirable side-effects on women, the power of married women in society was markedly enhanced by the pill's advent in the 1960s. Children could no longer be imposed or accidental for those willing to take it, and men had to discuss the birth of children in a new light.

Some theorists in anthropology and sociology have argued that marriage as an institution cannot be 'explained' in terms other than the control of sexual reproduction. But sex can be had without marriage or children, children can be cared for without marriage, and economic production does not need the family unit. Lévi-Strauss (1969) saw marriage as having little to do with the sexual urge but much to do with the incest taboo and the sexual division of labour. However, Malinowski (1944) and Gough (1960) stressed the importance of the 'legitimacy principle' and 'legal paternity' as the basis for marriage, since only the exclusive sexual rights of marriage could establish the child's full birth status rights. Exceptions such as the Nuer and Nayar caste in India (where one of several 'visiting' husbands took responsibility for a child) or the high illegitimacy rates of the Caribbean have led others such as Zelditch (1964) to argue that marriage is a mechanism not for regulating sex or incest, but for ensuring that children born to the woman are recognised as the legal offspring of *both* parents. Since men could never guarantee or prove biological paternity, the need for a *social* father provides the basis for marriage (Wittich 1976). Weber (1930) saw the origin of legal marriage in the widespread custom among high status families of giving their daughters away in marriage only on the clear assurance that they and their children would have preferred status (Glendon 1977). Marriage thus became a status-conferring institution, with the 'legitimacy' principle (for wives as opposed to concubines, for offspring and for property transfer) only gradually becoming 'legality'.

In this light, social control over reproduction and social legitimation become central to explaining the forms that marriage and the family have taken. Shifts in the nature of property and the advance of sexual equality over status distinctions have changed their social basis. Enhanced personal control, and control in the hands of women are likely to lead to changes in marriage and the family, as has already been suggested. Children become important to couples for other than economic reasons, the most important consequence perhaps being that both partners invest more of themselves (emotionally and financially) in the few offspring they deliberately produce. A male-dominated, patriarchal family structure becomes less likely when the female has more control.

Shifts in Social Values

To explain change, we also need to ask how new definitions of what is acceptable or legitimate behaviour come to be socially respected. The central ethic of Western societies has long been that of individualism, expressed in various forms of Judaism, Christianity, the Enlightenment, the Protestant ethic and the spirit of modern capitalism. Yet strict normative expectations have been established in relation to legitimate male/female roles, husband/

wife duties and obligations, and the place of the family as the venue for private life within the public life of the community. In fact, the family has been manipulated and controlled as the most central mechanism of wider public control. For example, the state and the church have variously permitted certain freedoms and latitudes for behaviour within the bounds of family life, while circumscribing other behaviour such as sex outside marriage or too much reliance on the public purse for family support (Donzelot 1979).

However, individualism as a dominant value ethic has not been permitted to outweigh social obligations and rigid role prescriptions in which traditional authority is based on and reinforced by personal loyalty, obedience and custom. Weber (1930), Durkheim (1933) and others examined exhaustively the ways in which a more complex division of labour required more flexibility, interchangeability and delegation of authority, thus opening up vast new realms for the development of individual competence and decision-making; though the bureaucratic nature of this new 'rational-legal' authority (with its stress on clear rules, lines of command and co-ordination of functions) could become an 'iron cage' setting limits to man's freedom, creativity and personal responsibility. In man's new state of alienation from both the products of his own labour and from control of the means of administration and of war, the family unit inevitably became the one small sphere in which man (but not necessarily woman) could exercise control and individuality. Because some sense of efficacy and control is so important to human survival, it is not surprising that a strong defence of the 'sanctity of the home', of 'privacy', of the home as a 'haven in a heartless world', was mounted.

Marriage and the family have been the focus of what Collins (1983) describes as three forms of property rights – material property, sexual property and generational property (children) – which both the individual male and the state had every reason to protect and guard jealously. As the nature of each of these changes, so too will the balance of power and the nature of the family in relation to society as a whole.

The post-war years, with their rising affluence inevitably led to an increased emphasis on personal satisfaction and on individualism which has long been the central ethic of modern capitalism. Without documenting here the roots of individualism (Williams 1961, 1976; Glendon 1977, O'Neill 1973, Durkheim 1933), conditions in the second half of this century certainly conspired to produce a flourishing of self-exploration, anti-institutionalism, a rejection of authority and rigid role prescriptions, especially in the 1960s' 'flower power', student revolution, black rights and anti-Vietnam war movements.

The point here is that people came to expect marriage and the family to satisfy individual, not institutional needs.

> 'Companionate' marriage arises because we have been taught to seek individual satisfaction, as consumers, as persons, as cogs in the machine that binds family and work together. That machine pushes emotional well-being back into the privatised world of the home so it doesn't disrupt the efficiency of economic productivity at work. Marriage now is a means of personal exploration and self-fulfilment, not just a legitimation of sexual and property rights, so the emotional pressures on families are greater than ever before.
>
> (Edgar 1980: 8)

Such an insistence on the primacy of the individual – what Lasch (1979) calls 'the culture of narcissism' – is unlikely to be conducive to any social unit which by its very nature depends upon co-operation, compromise and at least partial subjugation of self. When it comes to family relationships, individualism is hardly a workable ethic (Edgar 1983). Although writers such as Laing (1965), Fromm (1974), Maslow (1962), Rogers (1951), Reich (1974), Castaneda (1968) and others have argued that one can only truly 'share' if one 'knows oneself', that message is rather complex and its achievement even more so. The mass media popularisation which 'co-opts' (Sinclair 1974) such 'counter-cultural' notions, leads many people to misunderstanding, mistakes and confusion in human relationships. And though one could argue that such ideas of 'freedom' characterise only the educated middle class which can afford to explore them, there seems no doubt that social values of this kind permeated widely in the 1960s and 1970s and had a marked effect on the way many people viewed themselves and their marriages. Writers such as Yankelovitch (1982) and Mitchell (1983) argue that the 'excesses' of that era are giving way to a new balance within the 'giving/getting compact' that constitutes every social transaction, including marriage. This, Yankelovitch calls an 'ethic of commitment', a growing concern for connectedness and room for creative co-operative expression. There is a hunger for deeper and more sustained personal relationships as well as a shift from purely material or instrumental values to what he calls the 'sacred/expressive' ones.

The Family as Maker

Lest any impression remain that the family is merely a passive and powerless unit buffeted by the winds of demographic, economic and social change, we need to be reminded that families are *active* units, constructing and reconstructing their environment to serve their *own* purposes as best they can.

Theories of reality construction (Douglas 1971, Edgar 1980, Bourdieu and Passeron 1977) are important in understanding both the structural place of the family in society and the way in which families 'socialise' children. For they view the family as 'the crucible of competence', the child as an active user of family resources rather than a passive recipient of parental socialisation. A powerful analysis of *familia faber* (the family as maker of the future) by Boulding (1983) serves as a salutary jolt to assumptions about change from within and without the family unit. She challenges the mental gymnastics of social theorists who, on the one hand, claim that industrialisation and modernisation bring richness, complexity and problem-solving maturity to families while, on the other hand, stressing the problems involved in adaptation that bring families to breaking point. As Boulding says, we have ignored 'the role of the families in creating new institutions at the community level, in producing new environments to live in'.

This concept of *familia faber* is also a useful antidote to views that stress individual statuses within (often almost in blindness to) the family. The status of women, the rights of children, the needs of youth cannot be addressed without considering family structures and processes. Feminists such as Eisenstein (1984) recognise this, but one wonders whether some of those making policy recommendations about women do. Boulding insists that the familial household must be a central unit of analysis, claiming that everyone lives in a household of some kind and defining it (Boulding 1983: 258) as comprising 'those persons living together over time (unspecified) who perform basic physical and psychosocial maintenance and development functions for one another'. Without such a perspective, 'we are blinded ... to some key dynamics of macrochange processes that are based at the microlevel of the household', for the family has never been as bounded or simple a reality as some describe it to be, and its members actively change their environments to suit their own purposes.

Boulding refers to the familial identities formed inside households, to the sub-cultures formed as households interact selectively with certain community structures, to the way 'continued commitment over time multiplies opportunities for extended-kin contact and for shared problem-solving in the community', to the way 'the family parliament' changes daily as it sifts the alternative realities outside so they 'fit' with familial goals and agendas. The family is, in this light, 'a workshop in which solutions to social problems can be tried out' and it is the activities of 'shaper families' which make communities (one might even say, societies) more liveable. She points to immigrant groups and to new arrivals in boom towns as exemplars of this constructive family role and claims superiority (because of wider networks and resources) for dual career families and 'whole-family involvement' in community activities. There are several messages here for policy-makers, service-providers and researchers which go beyond the scope of this chapter. But we should keep in mind that it is families which make marriage work, which deal with socially-produced problems, and which forge the new values and behaviours which become the core values of Australian culture and shape the behaviour of society.

Public versus Private Control

Simply because the family is seen as belonging to the realm of private activities as opposed to public affairs, does not mean that the state and other public agencies have no influence on it. What must be asked is how the family came to be private and in what senses it is really free to make its own choices to behave in its own way? Indeed, no society ever permits total freedom in the private sphere though each varies in the extent to which it allows the family (or some of its members) to commit violence and rape, to enforce labour, to deny food, education or decision-making power within or beyond family confines. Some writers suggest that the family has become the major means of social control, all services being directed to policing it, turning people inward and thus making it 'possible to avoid the real dangers of the family's autonomy while facilitating social regulation by referring the frustrations of individuals to the family, by attaching their dreams and ambitions to it' (Donzelot 1979: 233). The work of Boulding on *familia faber*, referred to earlier, is a useful balance to this view.

It is worth remembering that a legal marriage certificate issued by the state and, usually but less frequently of late, sanctioned by religion, is historically very recent. In Europe, until the Council of Trent (1562–63), private informal marriages had been on an equal footing with public formal ones, the latter having been important only for the wealthy who need 'legitimacy' to pass power and possessions on to acceptable successors via the marriage-property link (Finlay 1979, Harrison 1981, Glendon 1980). But that does not mean that marriage did not exist prior to 1563 or that family units were not regulated by social norms. It was a long and compromised power game that led to marriage being taken over first by the church and finally by the codification of state laws (Mount 1982).

As indicated earlier, marriage is a *social* mechanism for controlling sexual reproduction and the distribution of status and property. It is also a means for controlling (by structuring in a special way) the sexual division of labour. Mitchell (1971, 1974) insisted that the feminist critique must move beyond biological arguments to look at four main 'structures' which, via marriage and the family, had led to the oppression of women. These were women's roles in economic production; the reproduction of children (which many writers held to be the universal basis for the relegation of women to the private sphere); the regulation and control of sexuality (usually directed more at women than men); and the socialisation of children (which had come to be 'the social cult of maternity' replacing other economically productive work for women).

If one asks what laws, what forms of legal regulation there were in the Australia of the 1890s, 1920s, 1950s even, compared with those that now apply to women's employment, the reproduction of children, sexual behaviour and responsibility for the care of children, one can see starkly how much the state's control of family life has altered. Sex discrimination and human rights legislation, equal pay provisions, and the access of women to education and training opportunities, all confer new resources and individual power on women. New laws on illegitimacy, abortion, adoption, artificial insemination and other means of producing children alter the way in which marriage controls sexual reproduction. More liberal laws and social attitudes to sexual behaviour, prostitution, homosexuality and some removal of the male 'double standard' have left sex to individual choice not supposedly restricted, as previously, to sex within marriage. And new economic conditions have led to better (though still inadequate) public child-care provisions and a greater role for schools and other institutions in the socialisation of children.

Just as marriage through Roman times and through the Middle Ages was essentially a private matter only gradually regulated by church and state laws, we are now again experiencing, as Glendon (1977: 321) notes

> ... a dissociation between legality and legitimacy regarding marriage, its conduct and dissolution ... a shift in the posture of the State with respect to the family, a shift which is approached in magnitude only by that which occurred with the Reformation in most European countries, when the State acquired jurisdiction over matrimonial causes from the ecclesiastical authorities.

On the public-private dimension, therefore, it could be said that the state has progressively moved away from regulation of private choices within some areas of the family sphere, although it has at the same time taken control away from other areas and in particular away from the male so that women also gain the benefit of choice.

Writers such as Chester (1981) hold that the essence of modern life is 'optionality', the freedom to choose for one's self what is right, where to go and what to do. Though this will always be held within some form of social limit, we must recognise that many previous limits have been removed. This removal may bring benefits but also creates some confusion and strong opposition among those who prefer more absolutist moral standards upheld by legal sanctions. The reality is, of course, that modern society cannot operate within the sorts of community constraints and oppressive laws that once held sway (Durkheim 1933). Where once the individual was bound into the system to such an extent that thoughts of freedom or individualism were virtually impossible, now the system only regulates parts of our lives, such as those at school or at work.

In a book called *The Asymmetric Society,* Coleman (1982) argues that children are the last vestige of an earlier social structure in which responsibility for the person as a whole took priority over responsibility in a corporate sense for some activities of a person who was replaceable (Coleman 1982: 121–22):

> The family is the last institution to continue to contain strong elements of the earlier form of social organisation. Until recently, family law kept married women from full citizenship status, unable to make contracts on their own, and under the legal protection and authority of the husband. Slowly, family law has changed, recognizing the wife's rights, but it remains a legal entity different from any other in modern society, with traces of the old hierarchical social structure remaining within it.
>
> These traces remain principally at one point, in the authority of the parent over the child and the responsibility of the parent for the child's actions ... for as each of the other 'subjects' was freed each could come to exercise responsibility and authority over self, with the minimal state exercising only that authority necessary to maintain order ... But if a similar emancipation of children from the authority of their parents were to occur, then neither the state nor the child would be in a position to take over the responsibility. As a result, the 'emancipation of children' has proceeded much more slowly than any other emancipation.
>
> Nevertheless, it does proceed. It proceeds in part because the family is a legal anachronism, difficult to sustain in the midst of

other social organizations in which persons are transient and only the structure is permanent.

Family Trends in Australia

Australia, like most Western countries, experienced a unique period dating from the end of World War II to the 1970s. It has been called 'the age of familism' (Canada 1983) because the post-war years saw a confluence of factors which brought the family unit to centre stage. A marriage boom was followed by a baby boom, creating two generations whose experience of family life would be widely different from that of previous generations.

The 'rush to marriage' was of young couples born in the 1920s and 1930s who had lived through the Depression years and the War. They now faced their own 'family formation' years at a time of post-war relief and reconstruction optimism, a nearly total absence of unemployment, strong economic growth and rising affluence. The weight of social opinion, through the church, the mass media and the political system enjoined them to marry early, to have children early and to have more children than their own parents had had.

On the other hand, the children they produced – the 'baby boomers' – were to grow up enjoying the improved living standards their parents had achieved, being better-educated than their parents were, and coming to maturity in an era (the late 1960s) characterised by a worldwide revolution in cultural values. This 'counter-culture' challenged the validity of such institutions as the family, the corporate state, racism, the military-industrial complex and the overall subordination of individual desires to externally-imposed constraints. Having been nurtured in an age of familism they were to blossom in an age of individualism, epitomised, as already mentioned, in 'flower power', 'self-exploration', black rights, freedom marches, draft-dodging, anti-Vietnam protests and a general questioning of the apparent hypocrisy of their parents' generation in failing to live up to the values they had taught the new generation.

Thus, the 1970s period saw, in Australia as elsewhere, a great shift in family-related behaviour. Young people left home earlier, lived more in groups or in *de facto* relationships, and delayed both getting married and having children, thus setting the scene for very different family relationships.

Other factors of course played a significant part in this change. Declining economic fortunes, rising unemployment, the demand for further education, the sorry example of rising divorce among their parents' generation, all added to a sense of uncertainty and questioning about accepted family values and forms. So too did the enhanced control women had over their own lives, through better education, greater labour force participation, the contraceptive pill and the option of abortion, and the advance of the women's movement which accompanied their enhanced control.

So, in understanding the place of 'the family' in Australian society at present, it is crucial to differentiate. The post-war formers-of-new-families differ markedly from their 'baby boom' offspring who were considering family formation in the late 1960s and 70s. It is likely that their children too, entering young adulthood in the 1990s, will face very different circumstances in their choices of marriage and having children.

Nevertheless, a picture can be drawn of Australian family types and of these changes that suggests some future trends. Most of the detail must come from the 1981 Census, a very imperfect survey of Australia's population that will be much improved by the July 1986 one. Other sources of data are the 1982 ABS *Family Survey*, the Australian Institute of Family Studies' 1981–82 *Family Formation Survey* and other analyses by the Department of Immigration and Ethnic Affairs and the Australian Bureau of Statistics.

Living in Families or Not?

In 1981, of all (14,923,300) Australians, 77 per cent were living in some type of 'family' household. But these varied greatly in type, with only 28.6 per cent of all families being what is known as the 'typical', or 'traditional', 'nuclear' family comprising two parents plus dependent children. Another 5.2 per cent of all families were one-parent ones with non-adult offspring, 22.1 per cent were couples only, and 20.8 per cent were families with relatives in other combinations. The rest of the population lived in 'non-family' households, with 23.1 per cent living alone.

The major changes between 1976 and 1981 in the living arrangements of Australian people were an increase of 57 per cent in the numbers of one-parent families, compared with only a 11.7 per cent increase in two-parent households and a shift towards 'non-family' households – that is people living alone or in unrelated groups. Most of those living alone are aged 60 years and over, while three-quarters of those living in groups are aged between 15 and 34 years.

Several of the social trends noted in the introduction to this

Table 14.1 Australia: Changes in Family Types, 1966, 1976 and 1981 Census

Family Type	1966 %	1976 %	1981 %	% Change 1976–81	Change 1966–81
1. Single person alone	15.7	19.8	23.1 (1,113,134)	+ 32.1	+ 115.4
2. One-parent and dependants	3.4	3.8	5.2 (252,061)	+ 57.0	+ 128.0
3. Couple only	20.2	22.5	22.1 (1,063,317)	+ 11.3	+ 59.9
4. Couple and dependants	30.7	29.0	28.6 (1,378,502)	+ 11.7	+ 36.4
5. Head and other adults	5.9	4.7	4.6 (223,369)	+ 11.1	+ 13.7
6. Head and other adults and dependants	1.6	1.4	1.3 (65,130)	+ 6.7	+ 24.3
7. Couple and other adults	10.3	8.9	7.7 (369,896)	− 2.6	+ 8.6
8. Couple and dependants and adults	12.1	9.8	7.2	− 16.6	− 12.4
Number of families	3,288,734	4,251,282	4,813,443	+ 13.2	+ 46.3
Population	11,600,000	14,033,100	14,923,300	+ 7.5	+ 28.6
Average family size	3.53	3.30	3.10	− 6.1	− 12.2

chapter help explain why the structure of Australian living arrangements has changed.

Leaving Home Behaviour

The first step in new family formation is usually the establishment of some degree of adult independence from one's parents. As young people mature, they take on their own interests, grow in their capacity to look after themselves, start to earn their own income, and seek to 'separate', both physically and psychologically, from their parents.

Because girls have traditionally been less well-educated than boys, and not encouraged to enter the paid labour force with lifelong careers in mind, they have had to trade dependence on parents against dependence on a husband. But marriage has always been the main point of 'separation' for women, marking their entry into adult life in their own right. In Australia up to the 1970s the same was largely true for men as well. They stayed at 'home' until they got married, relying on parents for housing and household services even though earning their own income.

Changes in employment patterns and the need for higher education, however, meant a prolongation of that semi-dependent state. Adolescence has been extended into 'youth', lasting roughly from 15 to 25. The Australian Institute of Family Studies 1981 *Family Formation Survey* shows that in the decade from 1971 to 1981 the reasons for leaving home changed markedly. Whereas

Table 14.2 Reasons for First Leaving Home of Those who Left before Age 18 (% of Group)

Reasons for leaving	Period when first left	
	Early 1970s	Early 1980s
Conflict:		
Males	3.1	16.5
Females	16.4	20.5
Independence:		
Males	20.7	32.2
Females	13.8	31.0
Marriage:		
Males	2.2	1.7
Females	25.8	9.4
Vocational:		
Males	50.4	33.0
Females	32.7	26.3
Other:		
Males	18.5	16.5
Females	11.3	12.8

Source: Australian Institute of Family Studies, *Family Formation Study*, 1981

25.8 per cent of women and 2.2 per cent of men first left the parental home in order to marry in the 1970s, by the 1980s marriage was the reason for leaving for only 9 per cent of women and 1.7 per cent of men (Young 1984).

Instead of marriage, the main reasons for leaving home in the 1980s seem to be as follows (Edgar and Mass 1984: 32).

- seeking independence is more prevalent
- conflict with parents has increased dramatically for all groups
- vocational reasons, though still important, have reduced in proportion, reflecting the shrinking job opportunities for young people.

Yet a further change is that many young people now return to the parental home from time to time. The trend is to leave home earlier, particularly where there is conflict. Young people live in group households sharing the rent, or alone, or in fairly short-lived *de facto* relationships. Shortage of suitable accommodation is a major problem (Burke, Hancock and Newton 1984) but so too is the high youth unemployment rate.

Australian youth are therefore seeking independence, but, unable to maintain themselves financially, are thus falling back on parents for support. Further conflict results and the ritual of leaving home at marriage has been replaced for many by a sequence of shuttling to and from various unsatisfactory living circumstances.

Later Age at Marriage

Not surprisingly then, the average age at marriage has increased.

The timing of marriage is clearly affected by changing social conditions. In Australia, a shortage of males in the early years meant both delay and a high proportion never married. Marriages were postponed in the Depression years, reaching a low point in 1931. By 1942, when Australia was under threat, marriage hit its highest point. It then enjoyed a long run of popularity until the 1970s and has slumped ever since. Greater education levels for women and economic uncertainty seem to be the main reasons (McDonald 1983, Carmichael 1983).

These fluctuations are reflected in age at first marriage and in the proportions never married. Whereas in 1947 the median age at first marriage was 25.3 for males and 22.5 for females, by 1971 it had dropped to 23.8 for males and 21.2 for females and has increased since then to, in 1981, 24.4 for males and 22.1 for females. The proportion of people still never married by age 45–49 is a good indicator of those who will not marry during their lifetime. For women aged 45–49 there was a marked decline from 16.6 per cent never married in 1921 to only 4.1 per cent in 1981. For men, the decline has been from 19.7 per cent to 8.1 per cent. So marriage is still very popular, though delayed marriage is likely to lead to an increased number who choose to stay unmarried throughout their lifetime. Carmichael (1983) suggests this may be as high as 25 per cent for those born in the early 1960s.

De facto Unions

Of course those who do not marry now are less likely to stay celibate than their 'spinster' and 'bachelor' forebears. Living together is now more socially acceptable as part of the 'courtship' ritual and as an alternative to the stronger commitment which marriage implies. In 1982, the estimate was that some 69,000 females and 73,500 males aged 20–29 were living in *de facto* arrangements, with a higher likelihood for the young unemployed and those who were separated or divorced. Khoo's (1986) analysis of young people living in *de facto* relationships suggests a wide variety of reasons for doing so and an increasing trend across the population to have this experience prior to marriage, though not necessarily with the final marriage partner.

Table 14.3 Age at First Marriage and Percentage Never Married

	1947	1961	1971	1981
Median Age At First Marriage				
Males	25.3	24.3	23.4	24.4
Females	22.5	21.4	21.1	22.1
Percentage Never Married At Age 45–49				
Males	13.9	10.0	9.0	8.1
Females	12.6	7.4	4.9	4.1

Source: ABS *Social Indicators* No. 4, 1984, p. 30; Australian Institute of Family Studies *Annual Report*, 1982–83, p. 10–13

Child-bearing

It is now more likely that the desire to have children leads to marriage rather than the desire to establish an independent adult life through marriage. Improved contraception has also meant a reduction in the number of 'shotgun' marriages (from a high point of 23 per cent of all brides pregnant before marriage in 1963).

The place of children in society has changed dramatically. Whereas large numbers of offspring were essential when family households worked together as productive economic units, and when infant mortality was high, children have become net consumers rather than producers for the family. As children survived longer, people 'discovered' the importance of 'childhood' (Aries 1962, Shorter 1976). Theories of child development and research on family effects combined with the need for universal literacy and primary education to produce a greater 'investment' by parents, both financially and psychologically, in the fewer children they had. This investment has increased as the cost of children has grown.

Of older women living at the time of the 1911 Census, 40 per cent had had 9 or more births. Total fertility rates declined to a low level in the 1930s, then increased to reach a high point in the period 1956–60. It remained high until 1971, then declined, to bottom out at the lowest level ever recorded in 1980.

Two factors changed to produce the 'baby boom' years. Not only were more people marrying earlier and having a first child early in the marriage; they also increased the number of children they had during their lifetime. Social structures and values were geared to child-bearing and -rearing, and most women spent long periods of their life as full-time homemakers. Davis (1984) calls this the 'breadwinner family system', describing it not as 'typical' or 'normal' but as an 'aberration' that resulted from the separation of the home from the workplace and the man's sole control of economic productivity.

During the 1960s, married women began to re-enter and stay in the paid labour force, and to delay the first birth. While in 1960, 68 per cent had their first child before the end of the second year of marriage, for those married in the later 1970s, less than 35 per cent did so. Contraceptive control made planning family size more reliable and couples began to question the need for large families. Women became averse to child-bearing at ages beyond the mid-thirties and fertility rates are now below replacement level. The longer the delay in having a child, the more likely it is that fewer children will be born.

Teenage Pregnancies

At the same time as birth rates generally were rising so did the teenage birth rate, by 95 per cent between the 1940s and 1960s, continuing to increase to a peak in 1971. From then on among teenagers the rate declined by 50 per cent to 1982, more rapidly than any other age group under 40, from 55.2 per thousand to 27.4 (Siedlecki 1984: 21). Nevertheless, '85 per cent of all teenage conceptions and 59 per cent of teenage births occur outside marriage', a figure indicating widespread need for better sex education and family planning advice. Siedlecki argues that there is no room for complacency because the proportion of repeat abortions rose to 12.5 per cent by 1982, and the unemployed and socially disadvantaged seem to be over-represented among pregnant teenagers. Marriage is a declining option, the Supporting Parent Benefit 'allows a change of status from "dole bludger" to "supporting mother"' and a 1983 survey showed that 74 per cent of girls aged 18 were sexually active. Poverty and poor parenting are the undesirable social results of teenagers bearing children.

There is a complex interaction between control over reproduction, higher levels of education, increased workforce participation and the economic circumstances of women. Women can now plan both a career and a family, with fewer years out of the workforce and a larger proportion of the life-cycle being 'child-free'. With a two-year old costing $19.73 a week and a teenager costing $49.04 even in low-income families (Lovering 1983, updated to 1986 COL), it is not surprising that fertility levels have declined. The corollary is, of course, a completely different 'family' experience for children themselves, with fewer siblings, greater parental interest in 'successful' parenting and often more stress on children themselves. China's 'one child only' policy is having dramatic consequences there, but the effects of smaller family size in Australia are only now being properly researched.

Australian Institute of Family Studies' research shows that only 4 per cent of 18–34 years olds say they 'never' want to have a child, and though 22 per cent say they want four or more children, few will do so. They say they would delay having children until their marriage was 'established', jobs were secure, they had 'enough money' or until they had a house or home. Clearly 'motherhood' is no longer an all-consuming role and the value of children in people's lives is changing. We are seeing a return to the situation for women born early this century where 20 per cent remained childless, and can expect an increase in the 'couple only' family type. The consequences flow through into migration policy, the size of the labour force and care of the elderly as Australia's population ages.

Separation and Divorce

Decreased family size may be the most significant demographic change in recent Australian history, but increased divorce rates would rank second in importance. Whereas death of a spouse was once the most common cause of marital dissolution (18 per 1,000 married couples in 1961), by 1981 divorce almost matched death, with 12 marriages ending by divorce compared with 14 ending by death. In Australia, many marriages also used to 'end' through the desertion of one spouse rather than through divorce which until 1976 required 5 years' separation or proof of 'fault'.

Divorce rates increased post-war to 5 per 1,000 married persons, dropped to 2.8 in 1961, then rose steadily to 7.1 per 1,000 in 1971. With the new one-year separation, 'no-fault' provisions of the Family Law Act 1975, this figure jumped to 19.5 divorces per 1,000 married persons in 1976 when a total of 63,267 divorces took place. Of these, only 15.5 per cent were of marriages that had lasted less than 5 years, with 23.7 per cent being marriages of over 20 years' duration.

Divorce declined after the 1976 'peak', then stabilised at around 12 per 1,000 married persons, and has declined each year since 1984 to a low of 11.1 per thousand in 1985. But there has been a shift towards divorces within the first five years of marriage, suggesting greater social acceptability for a quick end to unsatisfactory marriages. The marked trend towards later marriage is likely to mean a continued decline in divorce rates, and the Australian Institute of Family Studies has revised its estimate of 40 per cent of marriages ending in divorce, to one of about 30 per cent for those who married in the mid-1970s (Carmichael and McDonald 1986).

Several factors led to the increased divorce rate. Because couples married earlier, had children earlier and had longer life expectancy, the quality of the marital relationship took on a new importance. Youthful marriages are particularly susceptible to breakdown and with the new value emphasis on personal happiness, autonomy and self-realisation, plus the enhanced capacity of women to earn an independent income, a 'divorce boom' was to be expected following the 'marriage boom' of the 1950s and 60s.

Women's Employment and Economic Independence

The economic dependence of wives on their husbands was a major underpinning of 'traditional' marriage. The movement of married women back into the paid labour force, especially in the late 1960s, is therefore another significant factor affecting the nature of family life in Australia today.

So, too, was the extension in 1973 of federal income assistance via the Supporting Mothers' Benefit to women who left their husbands. Though some states provided welfare support for such women, federal benefits had been restricted to deserted wives (Jones 1980). The change meant wives could now leave an unsatisfactory marriage and receive the SMB after a six-month qualifying period (to 1979, when it was removed. The benefit was extended to men, as a Supporting Parent Benefit, in 1977.) By December 1985, there were 172, 982 people receiving SPB, 94 per cent of whom were women and 6 per cent men. This number represents an increase of 484 per cent since 1975 and a federal Budget outlay in 1984–85 of close to one billion dollars. Though the maximum pension payable (if other income does not exceed $36) for a supporting parent with one child is only $130.10 per week, for many women this represents a regular income free from the need to rely on a husband's earnings in a marriage that is unsatisfactory.

The more important source of women's income however is their own employment. There have been massive increases in the proportions of married women employed. Whereas in 1954 only 13 per cent of married women with dependent children were in paid work, that figure rose to 29 per cent in 1966, 43 per cent in 1981 and is currently 47 per cent. Table 14.4 indicates the relationship between employment and stage of the life-cycle, with only 33 per cent working if they have children aged 0–4, compared with 55 per cent for those with school age or older children. It also reveals their preference for part-time work, given that women still bear the main burden of housework and child-care, regardless of whether both husband and wife work (Glezer 1984). Not only do men need re-educating but work structures themselves must be made more flexible to meet the needs of all workers with family responsibilities.

Recent research (Clemenger/Reark 1984) shows that of those married women who were working, 64 per cent were 'income-oriented' compared with 36 per cent who were 'career-oriented'.

Table 14.4 Labour Force Participation of Women in Married Couple and One-Parent Families, 1985 (according to Age of Youngest Child)

Age of Youngest child	Mothers in Married Couples Families			Mothers in One-Parent Families		
	Participation Rate	% Full-time	% Unemployed	Participation Rate	% Full-time	% Unemployed
0–4	33	36	9	33	55	22
5–9	59	42	9	28	51	14
10–14	62	49	6	41	64	11
15–20	59	54	3	51	66	*
Total	45	50	5	41	59	13

Source: ABS, 'Labour Force States and Other Characteristics of Families, Australia, July, 1985', Cat. No. 6334.0

Both figures are revealing. If over a third have career aspirations, there has been a marked shift in the values of Australian women, reinforced by better education, equal pay and affirmative action provisions, but stemming also from changed family patterns. But two-thirds of married women are working because they need the money, and that reflects another exigency of family life in Australia in the 1980s.

Family poverty

Family poverty is of growing concern, and two incomes (usually really one-and-a-bit) are increasingly necessary for survival. A married couple family can increase its income by 57 per cent if the second income earner works part-time, and by 82 per cent if full-time work is taken. The Henderson Poverty Inquiry (1975) found that the number of families in poverty would double if wives did not engage in paid work. The 1978–79 ABS Income Survey data show that there were 126,400 married couple families with dependent children receiving incomes less than $7,000 per annum, which was approximately the poverty line for a couple with two children. Without the income of wives with paid jobs, that number would have virtually doubled.

The most recent data on family incomes is the 1981–82 ABS *Income and Housing Survey*. The Australian Institute of Family Studies (1985) compared these figures with the parallel 1978–79 ABS survey and found there had been an increase in the intervening years of 54.4 per cent in the number of couples with children whose incomes were below the poverty line, and an increase of 38.6 per cent for one-parent families living on incomes below the poverty line. This meant that in 1981–82 there were 381,900 families, with over three-quarters of a million children living below the poverty line. Single people and childless couples were less likely to have below-poverty incomes.

Moreover, the 1982–83 recessions and increasing unemployment levels have most affected families with children. Unemployment levels for couples with children nearly doubled, to 17.3 per cent, between 1982 and 1983. In July 1983, 462,800 families had one or more family members unemployed and there were 182,200 families with no member at all employed. The median duration for husbands out of work incrased from 10 weeks in 1982 to 28.1 weeks in 1983. For one-parent families the median duration was 22.1 weeks for female heads and 40.1 weeks for male heads.

Children and Family Influences

Poverty, of course, has its worst effects on children because it deprives them of the resources necessary for the development of competence. Not only is housing quality and good nutrition affected, but neighbourhood quality may be poor (Burns and Homel 1983), and the home may be crowded and lacking in books, toys and privacy – all essential if learning is to proceed effectively.

Divorce is clearly traumatic for families but not always in ways people expect. Its poverty-producing impact is probably worse than the emotional trauma of family breakdown because the latter can be modified by sensible separation behaviour and conflict-reduction, whereas the split into two separate households must inevitably reduce income, living standards and have lasting effects on later life chances.

In its study of *The Economic Consequences of Marriage Break-down in Australia* (McDonald 1985), the Australian Institute of Family Studies found the incomes of women post-divorce fell by an average of $78 per week. These figures take into account the matrimonial property settlement and the payment and receipt of child maintenance and reflect the impact of time spent out of the labour force to rear children on the income-earning capacity of women. Movements for reform of both property division and maintenance collection under the Family Law Act are currently in train.

Several recent studies have examined the impact of divorce on children, and consistently find that reduced living standards are more significant than emotional adjustment problems. Dunlop and Burns (1984) found adolescents in divorced homes are not less well-adjusted than those in intact families, but where conflict exists in either family type, teenagers are badly affected. Smiley, Chamberlain and Dalgleish (1986) found the same was true for young children, though there are variations by age and sex. Ochiltree and Amato (1983, 1984, 1985) in a major study of how children view family life, found that conflict, whether between parents or between parents and child, is the major factor producing lower levels of self-esteem. Low income seems to affect reading comprehension, and the degree of independence and household help expected of children affects the level of everyday life skills. No significant effects were found for the employment of mothers, but the degree of interest shown by parents, especially fathers, in their children has important outcomes in terms of self-esteem and other forms of competence. In other words, family processes are import-ant, as are family income and other material resources, but these vary across all family types and people should avoid generalising or stereotyping families according to their type or composition. Many one-parent families cope extremely well, despite poverty, and not all stepfamilies are conflict-ridden or unhappy.

Ethnic variations

Added to the enormous variations in family size, type and process is the fact that Australia is one of the most multi-cultural nations in the world. One quarter of our population was born overseas and a further 20 per cent have at least one parent born overseas. Many of our schools contain over twenty different nationalities. Obviously the values of Vietnamese families will differ from those of Italians, Greeks or Turks. But so too, do the values of ethnic parents differ from those of their children, who grow up in 'two worlds' and gradually adapt to the dominant Australian culture. Storer *et al.* (1985) document the variation not only between but also within, ethnic groups, and Khoo (1985) and Callan (1980) show how some of these value differences affect behaviours such as choice of marriage partner, having children, sex role and behaviour, and life goals.

Table 14.5 Birthplace Composition of Post-War Australia: Population by Birthplace (%)

Place of Birth	1947	1954	1961	1966	1971	1976	1981
Australia	90.2	85.7	83.1	81.6	79.8	79.9	79.4
UK and Ireland	7.2	7.4	7.2	7.9	8.5	8.2	7.8
Italy	0.4	1.3	2.2	2.3	2.3	2.1	1.9
Greece	0.2	0.3	0.7	1.2	1.3	1.1	1.0
Yugoslavia	0.1	0.3	0.5	0.6	1.0	1.1	1.0
Germany	0.2	0.7	1.0	0.9	0.9	0.8	0.8
Netherlands	–	0.6	1.0	0.9	0.8	0.7	0.7
Other Europe	0.5	2.3	2.6	2.6	2.5	2.3	2.2
America	0.2	0.2	0.2	0.3	0.4	0.6	0.7
Aisa	0.3	0.6	0.8	0.9	1.3	1.8	2.5
Africa	0.1	0.2	0.3	0.4	0.5	0.5	0.6
New Zealand	0.6	0.5	0.4	0.5	0.6	0.7	1.2
Other	0.1	0.1	0.1	0.1	0.2	0.2	0.2
Total	100.0	100.0	100.0	100.0	100.0	100.0	100.0

Source: ABS 1980: unpublished 1981 Census information

Ageing Population

The problem of the ethnic aged (AIMA 1985) is just one aspect of the wider problems that will face an ageing Australian population. As the 'baby boom' ages and the 'lower birth' products of the 1970s enter their twenties, fewer people will be available to enter the labour force. Hugo (1985) predicts that this will continue the trend for married women to participate and may see an increase in the participation rate of older workers which could challenge current rules about retirement age. An ageing population combined with a decreasing workforce may mean further welfare expenditure (aged pensions already comprise 40 per cent of all social security payments), but not necessarily if early retirement decreases or if technological advantages improve productivity without rises in the numbers working.

Nevertheless, family patterns will certainly be affected by the ageing of our population. Since life expectancy for women is now 79.1 years and 6½ years less for men, widows will constitute most of the 'aged problem' (Borrie 1981). Though we now have more three-generation 'extended' families than ever before in our history, they do not often live in the same household, and care for the aged becomes more problematic when there are fewer offspring to support them. While most men will have wives to support them until they die, their widows will have no partners and fewer offspring to rely upon. Divorce and remarriage also affect extended family relationships. The independence ethos which affected attitudes to marriage, income earning and other sex role behaviours, has also affected those entering old age, and there is great resistance both to becoming dependent on 'family' and to being institutionalised (Day 1985, Kendig *et al.* 1984). We are likely to see new patterns of relationships between families and their aged members emerging as the century moves on.

'The family' is therefore a dynamic unit, not a passive one (Boulding 1983), actively seeking the most satisfactory ways of meeting the needs of its members. Changing social and economic circumstances produce change in family patterns, but families also actively resist or promote this by seeking to achieve their own goals. A recent *Age* poll (15 March, 1986) asked people to rank their source of greatest satisfaction in life. Family was ranked first by 70 per cent of those surveyed, with leisure time next at 10 per cent and friends, work, religion and possessions well below. Obviously family well-being and family change are central to any understanding of Australian society.

References

AIMA (1985) *Ageing in a Multicultural Society*. Melbourne: AIMA.

Alwin, D.F. (1984) 'Trends in Parental Socialization Values: Detroit, 1958–1983', *American Journal of Sociology* 90 (2): 359–82.

Aries, P. (1962) *Centuries of Childhood: A Social History of Family Life*. New York: Knopf.

Bernard, J.S. (1982). *The Future of Marriage*. New Haven: Yale University.

Borrie, W.D. (1981) 'Australia's Population Structure and Trends: Background Paper' in W.D. Borrie and M. Mansfield (eds) *Implications of Australian Population Trends*. Canberra: Academy of the Social Sciences in Australia, Australian National University.

Boulding, E. (1983) '*Familia Faber*: The Family as Maker of the Future', *Journal of Marriage and the Family*, May: 257–66.

Bourdieu, P. and Passeron, J.C. (1977) *Reproduction in Education, Society and Culture*. New York: Sage.

Brint, S. (1984) ' "New-Class" and Cumulative Trend Explanations of the Liberal Political Attitudes of Professionals', *American Journal of Sociology* 90 (1): 30–71.

Burke, T., Hancock, L. and Newton, P. (1984) *A Roof Over Their Heads: Housing Issues and Families in Australia*. Melbourne: Institute of Family Studies, Monograph No. 4.

Burns, A. and Homel, R. (1983) 'Neighbourhood Quality and Child Adjustment' in *Proceedings* VI. Melbourne: Australian Family Research Conference, IFS.

Callan, V. (1980) 'The Value and Cost of Children: Australian, Greek and Italian Couples in Sydney, Australia', *Journal of Cross-Cultural Psychology* 11, December: 482–97.

Canada (1983) *Divorce: Law and the Family in Canada*. Ottawa: Research and Analysis Division, Statistics Canada.

Carmichael, G. (1983) 'The Transition to Marriage: Trends in Age at First Marriage and Proportions Marrying in Australia' in *Proceedings* 1: 99–175. Melbourne: Australian Family Research Conference, IFS.

———and McDonald, P. (1986) 'The Rise and Fall (?) of Divorce in Australia 1968–1985', Australian Institute of Family Studies, unpublished paper.

Castaneda, C. (1968) *The Teachings of Don Juan: A Yaqui Way of Knowledge*. Berkeley: University of California Press.

Cherlin, A, and Walter, P. (1981) 'Trends in United States Men's and Women's Sex-role Attitudes: 1972–1978', *American Sociological Review* 46 (4): 453–60.

Chester, R. (1981) 'Divorce and its Consequences for Society', Conference proceedings, XIXth International CFR Seminar on Divorce and Remarriage, Leuven, Belgium.

Clemenger/Reark (1984) *Beyond the Stereotypes: Illuminating Perspectives on Australian Women*. Melbourne: Clemenger.

Coleman, J.S. (1982) *The Asymmetric Society*. New York: Syracuse University.

Collins, R. (ed.) (1983) *Social Theory 1983*. San Francisco: Jossey Bass.

Davis, K. (1984) 'Wives and Work: The Sex Role Revolution and its Consequences', *Population and Development Review* 10 (3), September: 397–417.

Day, A.T. (1985) *'We Can Manage': Expectations About Care and Variations of Family Support Among People 75 Years and Over*. Melbourne: Institute of Family Studies, Monograph No. 5.

Donzelot, J. (1979) *The Policing of Families*. New York: Pantheon Books.

Douglas, J.D. (1971) *American Social Order, Social Rules in a Pluralistic Society*. New York: Free Press.

Dunlop, R. and Burns, A. (1984) 'Adolescents and Divorce', Institute of Family Studies, unpublished manuscript.

Durkheim, E., translated by George Simpson (1963) *The Division of Labor in Society*. New York: Free Press of Glencoe.

Edgar, D.E. (1980) *Possible Directions for an Australian Family Policy*. Melbourne: Institute of Family Studies, Discussion Paper No. 1.

———(1983) 'Disposable Marriage', Opening address, First National Conference of the Australian Association of Marriage and Family Counsellors, unpublished paper. Melbourne: Institute of Family Studies,

———and Maas, F. (1984) 'Adolescent Competence, Leaving Home and Changing Family Patters', *Key Papers*, I: 355–426, XXth International CFR Seminar on Social Change and Family Policies, Institute of Family Studies Melbourne.

Eisenstein, H. (1984) *Contemporary Feminist Thought*. London: Unwin Paperbacks.

Finlay, H.A. (1979) *Family Law in Australia*. Sydney: Butterworths.

Fromm, E. (1974) *The Art of Loving*. New York: Harper & Row.

Glendon, Mary-Ann (1977) *State, Law and Family: Family Law in Transition in the United States and Western Europe*. New York: North Holland Publishing Co.

Glezer, H. (1984a) 'Changes in Marriage and Sex-role Attitudes Among Young Married Women: 1971–1981', *Family Formation, Structure, Values, Proceedings* 1, November 1983. Melbourne: Australian Family Research Conference, Institute of Family Studies.

———(1984b) 'Antecedents and Correlates of Marriage and Family Attitudes in Young Australian Men and Women', *Key Papers* I, XXth International CFR Seminar on Social Change and Family Policies, Institute of Family Studies. Melbourne.

Gough, E.K. (1960) 'Is the Family Universal? – The Nayar Case' in N.W. Bell and E.F. Vogel (eds) *A Modern Introduction to the Family*. New York: Free Press.

Harrison, M. (1981) *Informal Marriages*. Melbourne: Institute of Family Studies, Working Paper No. 1.

Heilbroner, R. (1980) *An Enquiry into the Human Prospect*. New York: Norton.

Hugo, G. (1985) 'Some Demographic Aspects of the Australian Workforce in the Early 1980s', *1981 Census Study*. Canberra: Department of Immigration and Ethnic Affairs, Population and Research Branch, Working Paper No. 10.

Institute of Family Studies. *Annual Report 1982–83*, Melbourne.
————(1985) *Families and Australia's Economic Fugure* and *Changing the Australian Taxation System*. Melbourne: Submissions to the Economic Planning Advisory Council, IFS.
————(1983c) *1982–83 Annual Report*. Melbourne: Institute of Family Studies.
Jones, M.A. (1980) *The Australian Welfare State*. Sydney: Allen & Unwin.
Kendig, H.L., Gibson, D., Rowland, D. and Hemer, J. (1983) *Health Welfare and Family in Later Life*. NSW Council on the Ageing.
Khoo, S.E. (1985) 'Family Formation and Ethnicity', Melbourne: Institute of Family Studies, Working Paper No. 9.
————(1986) 'Living Together'. Melbourne: Institute of Family Studies, Working Paper No. 10.
Laing, R.D. (1965) *The Divided Self*. Harmondsworth: Pelican Books.
Lasch, C. (1979) *The Culture of Narcissism: American Life in an Age of Diminishing Expectations*. New York: Norton.
Lévi-Strauss, C. (1969) *The Elementary Structures of Kinship*. London: Eyre & Spottiswoode.
Lovering, K. (1984) 'Cost of Children in Australia'. Melbourne: Institute of Family Studies, Working Paper No. 8.
McDonald, P. (1983) 'Can the Family Survive?' Melbourne: Institute of Family Studies, Discussion Paper No. 11.
————(1985) *The Economic Consequences of Marriage Breakdown in Australia, A Summary*. Melbourne: Institute of Family Studies.
————(ed.) (1986) *Settling up: Property and Income Distribution on Divorce in Australia*, compiled by the Australian Institute of Family Studies. Sydney: Prentice-Hall.
Maslow, A.H. (1968) *Towards a Psychology of Being*. New Jersey: Nostrum-Reinhold, Princeton.
Malinowski, B. (1973) *A Scientific Theory of Culture*. Chapel Hill: University of North Carolina Press.
Mitchell, A. (1983) *The Nine American Lifestyles*. New York: Warner Books.
Mitchell, J. (1971) *Woman's Estate*. New York: Vintage Books.
————(1974) *Psychoanalysis and Feminism*. New York: Pantheon Books.
Mount, F. (1982) *The Subversive Family, An Alternative History of Love and Marriage*. London: Unwin Paperbacks.
Ochiltree, G. & P. Amato (1983) 'Family Conflict and Child Competence', *Proceedings*, VI: 1–47. Australian Family Research Conference, Institute of Family Studies.
————(1984) 'The Child's Use of Family Resources', *Key Papers* I: 247–322. XXth International CFR Seminar on Social Change and Family Policies, Institute of Family Studies.
————(1985) *The Child's Eye View of Family Life*. Melbourne: Institute of Family Studies.
O'Neill, J. (ed.) (1973) *Modes of Individualism and Collectivism*. London: Heinemann.
Reich, W. (1974) *The Sexual Revolution: Toward a Self-Regulating Character Structure*. New York: Farrar, Straus & Giroux.

Rheinstein, M. (1972) *Marriage Stability, Divorce and the Law*. Chicago: The University of Chicago Press.

Rogers, C. (1951) *Client-centered Therapy*. Boston: Houghton-Mifflin.

Scanzoni, J. (1983) *Shaping Tomorrow's Family: Theory and Policy For the 21st Century*. California: Sage.

Sennett, R. (1976) *The Fall of Public Man*. Cambridge: Cambridge University Press.

Shorter, E. (1977) *The Making of the Modern Family*. London Fontana.

Siedlecki, S. (1984) 'Defusing a New Teenage Baby Boom', *Education News* 18 (12) 20–23.

Sinclair, J. (1974) 'Mass Media and Society: Critical Theory and Critical Research' in D.E. Edgar (ed.) *Social Change in Australia*. Melbourne: Cheshire.

Smiley, G., Chamberlain, E. and Dalgleish L. (1986) *Young Children in Divorce*. Melbourne: Australian Institute of Family Studies, unpublished manuscript.

Social Indicators No. 4 (1984). Canberra: Australian Bureau of Statistics.

Storer, D. (ed.) (1985) *Ethnic Family Values in Australia*. Australia: Prentice-Hall.

Weber, M., translated by Talcott Parsons (1930) *The Protestant Ethic and the Spirit of Capitalism*. New York: Charles Scribner's Sons.

Weitzman. L. (1981) *The Marriage Contract: Spouses, Lovers and the Law*. New York: The Free Press.

Williams, R. (1961) *The Long Revolution*. London: Chatto & Windus.

———(1976) *Keywords: A Vocabulary of Culture and Society*. London: Fontana.

Wittich, E. (1976) 'Getting Behind the Mystique of Social Institutions: Marriage'. Bundoora: La Trobe University, La Trobe Sociology papers, No. 31.

Yankelovich, D. (1982) *New Rules: Searching for Self-Fulfilment in a World Turned Upside-Down*. Toronto: Bantam Books.

Zelditch, M., Jr. (1964) 'Family, Marriage and Kinship' in R. Faris, *Handbook of Modern Sociology*: Chicago: Rand McNally.

General References

Australian Institute of Family Studies (1983) *Proceedings* I–VI. Melbourne: Australian Family Research Conference.

Bottomley, G. and de Lepervanche, M. (1984) *Ethnicity, Class and Gender in Australia*. Allen & Unwin.

Burns, A. & Goodnow, J. (1979) *Children and Families in Australia*. Allen & Unwin.

Coleman, J.S. and Husen, T. (1985) *Becoming Adult in a Changing Society*. Paris: OECD-CERI.

Department of Immigration and Ethnic Affairs (1985) *Australia's Population Trends and Prospects*. Canberra: DIEA.

Dreitzel, H.P. (1973) *Childhood and Socialization*. New York: Macmillan.

Edgar, D.E. (1980) *Introduction to Australian Society: A Sociological Perspective*. Australia: Prentice-Hall.

English, B.A. and King, R.J. (1983) *Families in Australia*. Sundey: Family Research Unit, University of New South Wales.

ISA-CFR (1984) *Key Papers* and *Discussant Papers* I–V, XXth International Committee on Family Research Seminar on Social Change and Family Policies, Institute of Family Studies, Melbourne.

Mol, H. (1985) *The Faith of Australians*. Allen & Unwin.

Mount, F. (1982) *The Subversive Family: An Alternative History of Love and Marriage*. London: Unwin Paperbacks.

Chapter Fifteen

Unemployment

Adam Jamrozik

Perceptions and Explanations of Unemployment

For some years now, unemployment has been a subject of public interest, evoking responses of concern, moral indignation and criticism of the government, the capitalist system, the trade unions and of the unemployed themselves. There have also been numerous explanations of the growth of unemployment, the perceived causes ranging from technological change and global recession to demographic trends – that is, a 'bulge' arising from high birth rates in the early post-war years, the entry of women into the labour market, and the suspicion of people's unwillingness to work.

Recent high levels of unemployment have spawned considerable research interest, evident in a great volume of literature on this subject available today. For example, a bibliography compiled by Encel and Garde (1984) lists 237 publications concerned with unemployment published in Australia from 1978 to 1983, over a range of disciplines: economics, sociology, psychology, geography, education, law, social welfare, social work, and a variety of interest groups.

Unemployment is commonly regarded as economically wasteful and socially undesirable. However, the expressed public concern and the volumes of research reports on this issue seem to demonstrate that the amount of interest and generated information about a social condition which is perceived to be a 'social problem' does not necessarily lead to a solution to it. This would suggest that either the condition is beyond the control of individuals, societies and governments, or the perceptions and explanations are flawed, inadequate or misdirected. It may also suggest that the condition is seen to be undesirable, but that the solution would disturb and threaten the established social order.

Clearly, a comprehensive analysis and explanation of unemployment is beyond the scope of one chapter in a book. The content of this chapter is therefore restricted to perceptions of unemployment in recent years, followed by an analysis of statistical data on unemployment in Australia from 1966 to 1984. It closes with some observations on the data and comments about the implications the observed trends in unemployment seem to have for the society and for social policy. The analysis is directed at the structure in which unemployment occurs, that is, at the labour market, and at the processes and changes that take place in that structure. The aim is to identify some of the forces which affect the operation of the labour market, such as the nature of the economic system, the policies of government and the global capitalist system of which Australia is a part.

The approach is thus based on the assumption that it is more fruitful to examine the terrain in which unemployment occurs rather than to seek causes in unemployed people themselves. While they are undoubtedly active social agents, in the relationship between the supply of labour and the demand for it, the latter is the component which might be altered. Unemployment results from changes in the labour market, these changes occurring by deliberate rational decisions of individual employers, and national and international forces (Jamrozik and Hoey 1981, 1982).

Unemployment in History and in Recent Times

Unemployment is not a 'new' phenomenon. It has been experienced in varied intensity throughout human history, not only during the Great Depression of the 1930s. According to Garraty (1978) it was already a problem in Ancient Greece, Rome and even Egypt. Garraty suggests that the pyramids of Egypt and the temples of Athens were 'job creation' programs devised by the authorities of the day for the purpose of employing surplus labour. In more recent history, unemployment was always greater in times of technological change. For example, the Industrial Revolution of the eighteenth and nineteenth centuries might have created employment but it also led to social disruption because it demanded behaviour from people which was unnatural to them – a problem similar to that experienced now in developing countries. The change of behaviour was forced upon people by severe sanctions such as dispossession from land and livelihood in, for example, Scotland, deportation or forced emigration of 'unemployables' to the colonies, and the introduction of workhouses in England. Many of these measures were based on the suspicion that some people were unemployable because they did not want to work. Thus the 'dole bludger syndrome' and measures to deal with it such as the 'Work Test' had their precursors in earlier times. That suspicion might have been attenuated during the Depression of the 1930s but it certainly came back with considerable force in the late 1960s when the growing numbers of unemployed were met at first with disbelief, because the Western world was still enjoying an economic boom.

In the conditions of post-war economic boom, unemployment was generally considered to be a thing of the past. There were, however, exceptions to the prevalent attitudes. For example, in 1965, Theobald predicted that full employment was not sustainable in this modern era because the productive capacity of the industrialised world was considerably greater than the capacity for the consumption of goods produced. He pointed out that

> Unemployment rates must therefore be expected to rise in the sixties. This unemployment will be concentrated among the unskilled, the older workers and the youngster entering the labour force; minority groups will also be hard hit. No considerable rate of economic growth will avoid this result.
>
> (Theobald 1965: 46)

Theobald went on to observe (1965: 57) that 'not only has the abundant economy ceased to absorb additional people, but it has now begun to reject some who had already entered it'. He thought that this problem was due not only to the growth in the productive capacity of modern industry but also to the changing occupational structure of employment, which called for new skills and for an overall more skilled labour force. He commented on this trend by saying

> Recent re-examination of the total unemployment picture has resulted in growing awareness of the nature and size of the problem. There is increasing evidence that those with low levels of skills and education will not only be unemployed but also permanently unemployable in coming years.
>
> (Theobald 1965: 70)

In his analysis of trends in the labour market, Theobald saw the emergence of three distinct groups in the industrialised countries: large numbers of totally unemployed, subsisting on government schemes designed merely to ensure their survival; the greatest proportion, working shorter hours, earning sufficient income for reasonable living; and a small group, earning high incomes and working long hours. He also foresaw a growing trend towards higher employment opportunities for women and correspondingly declining opportunities for men, which assumption, he argued, contained the potential for significant changes in the customary social roles of men and women (1965: 87–88).

Theobald's predictions are mentioned here not to demonstrate their validity or otherwise, although to a large extent they appear to have been correct. The significance of his analysis is in the focus on the trends observed in the labour market which, in his view, would produce inequalities in access to employment, with certain consequences for Western societies that would necessitate policy responses by governments. This comment is of particular relevance to the conditions in Australia, as the changes in the structure of the labour market have been clearly evident for some years and unemployment has now reached high proportions. However, the policies of successive governments, which sought to reduce the level of unemployment, have focused mainly on the unemployed rather than on the causes of unemployment in the labour market.

Although unemployment in Australia became an issue of public concern only in the 1970s, the signs of growing unemployment were already visible in the 1960s. The first identifiable group experiencing difficulties in finding employment consisted of young people, especially those with low educational qualifications, later identified as 'early school leavers'. For example, in 1969, the rate of unemployment for adult males was at the time calculated at 0.7 per cent and for adult females at 0.9 per cent, but the rates for junior males and junior females were 1.7 per cent and 2.3 per cent respectively, or approximately 2.5 times higher than for adults (Department of Labour and National Service 1970). Even then, the aggregate data tended to conceal the growing 'hard core' of unemployment among young people. Examination of records of state welfare agencies at the time showed that the rate of unemployment among some groups of young people was already as high as 30 per cent in 1966 (Jamrozik 1973: 32).

Unemployment in Australia has followed a trend similar to that experienced in other countries of the Western world. In some of these, notably the United States and Canada, the signs of growing unemployment, especially among young people, began to appear in the 1950s (Pankhurst 1981) and similar trends soon became evident elsewhere. During the 1970s, unemployment began to rise and spread to other age groups, and what at first was perceived as a temporary aberration gradually became acknowledged as a long-term endemic problem.

When the numbers of unemployed in Australia began to rise in the early 1970s, few voices expressed concern that Australia might be experiencing the onset of a trend with long-term implications.

Those who did express such concern were mainly from welfare organisations which had come into contact with the unemployed. The relatively small numbers of unemployed, concentrated almost exclusively among the low-skilled and less educated, were typically seen by the public in the early 1970s as 'inadequate' individuals with personal problems who might warrant attention from welfare workers and perhaps psychologists, but not as a serious social or economic issue.

Yet there were some people who even then noted that there was a relationship between growing unemployment and the changing structure of the labour market. For example, the Melbourne-based Brotherhood of St Laurence (1972: 1) warned that 'Australia has ... a growing pool of unemployed, unskilled and semi-skilled persons who are virtually unemployable because they lack qualifications and experience'. Looking to the future, the authors pointed out that although unemployment in Australia had been, until then, lower than in other countries of the West, the situation was rapidly changing and 'unless effective action is taken now ... Australia will also eventually experience unemployment levels of 4 per cent to 5 per cent' (!). The authors also noted (1972: 16) a growing discrepancy between an increasing pool of unskilled and semi-skilled unemployed on the one hand, and a growing pool of professional and skilled jobs on the other.

The first study of unemployment in Australia which attracted wide attention was that by Windschuttle (1979). The strong reaction the book evoked was due not so much to the author's demonstration of the extent of unemployment, as to the implications he had drawn from his analysis, and his assertion that Australian society and the government of the day seemed to show very little interest or concern at the social effects and personal hardships experienced by the unemployed. In the opening sentence of the book Windschuttle commented that 'Although unemployment has been at high levels in Australia since 1974, for a long time it proved difficult to get anyone to take the issue seriously.'

Windschuttle portrayed growing unemployment as an economic and social crisis affecting individuals and families. For the people affected, it meant a virtual exclusion from the mainstream of economic and social life. This, Windschuttle argued, could not fail to have a detrimental effect for the society as a whole because

Work and its absence emerge as the crucial elements in determining the general degree of social cohesion, the nature of ideology, the state of health, the condition of family life and the forms of social control.

(Windschuttle 1979: 4)

As to the causes of unemployment, Windschuttle identified these in the world-wide recession of the 1970s and technological innovations in the production process which had been instrumental in reducing the demand for labour. He saw the decline and probable failure of Australian manufacturing industries, and he predicted that unemployment would remain high until at least the 1990s. In his view, these were outcomes of the basic structural cause of unemployment, which was to be found in the cold rationality of the capitalist system itself. It was the inhumanity of that system that he criticised, by saying

> Capitalism is a system that defines humanity by work but denies work to a large number of people. Personal trauma and social malaise follow inevitably. Unemployment reveals this system as basically inhuman.

(Windschuttle 1979: 4)

Windschuttle's study was an attempt to highlight the social effects of certain trends in the labour market and explain these as predictable outcomes of a capitalist economy in times of technological innovation. The concern he expressed at the lack of interest by governments and the country in the hardships experienced by the unemployed was an inference that the majority of the population was not affected by unemployment, and that it was seen to be an individual, rather than a structural problem.

It was Windschuttle's perception and interpretation of the issues involved that made his study a significant contribution to a sociological analysis of unemployment. A similar theme was taken up by Sinfield (1981) in his analysis of unemployment in the United Kingdom. He pointed out that most studies of unemployment '...have largely overlooked the wider implications of unemployment and insecurity, and one consequence has been the failure to develop a systematic analysis of the sociology of unemployment' (Sinfield 1981: 123). He saw this neglect by sociologists as rather remarkable, considering that the central concern of sociology was with the nature and significance of the social division of labour and the structure of inequality in society.

This is not the place to discuss at length the extent to which Sinfield's criticism applies to studies of unemployment in Australia. It seems to be the case, however, that few sociological studies have examined the issue of unemployment from a structural perspective. Many studies have focused on the issue of 'social concern', and some have attempted to situate unemployment in a wider societal perspective (e.g. Sheehan 1980, Cass 1981). Most writers, however, have tended to focus on the personal hardships of the unemployed, but have failed to relate the issue to any theoretical framework. Some studies have followed the 'evil causes evil' theory, attempting to show a relationship between unemployment and smoking, alcohol intake, drug-taking or even suicide. To that extent, they have contributed to the public awareness of the social effects of unemployment but little to the explanation of its causes.

More generally, the majority of studies of unemployment in the 1970s and early 1980s were undertaken by economists, and it is in that discipline that explanations have been sought for its rise and continuation. It is true that economists have made considerable advances in demonstrating the extent and characteristics of unemployment but their explanations of its causes and relationships have been less impressive. Most economists have followed the orthodoxy of analysing unemployment as an issue of 'supply and demand'. This has led to various conjectures on suspected relationships between the level of unemployment and the level of wages, or the level of unemployment and the availability and level of welfare benefits.

There is no intention here to engage in a critique of the economists' work in this area. It needs to be acknowledged, however, that unemployment has been treated as an 'economic' rather than a social issue, and little relationship between the two perspectives is evident in the vast volume of research published in recent years. The 'economic' perspective has also been dominant in government policy and indeed in the community. One reason for this may be due to the perception of the rise of unemployment in the 1970s as a 'temporary' phenomenon. It is only more recently that the perceptions began to change, and it is now generally accepted that unemployment will not disappear in the foreseeable future. However, the quality of analyses has not necessarily improved. In fact, what seems to be of interest now, both in studies of unemployment and in the media is variations in the percentage of the unemployed in the labour force rather than the issue of its causes.

As a generalisation, the prevailing perceptions and explanations of unemployment may be grouped in three broad categories: unemployment as an outcome of the recession of the 1970s; unemployment as an outcome of technological innovation and a corresponding lessening demand for labour: and unemployment as an issue of social concern because of its effect on the unemployed and, in the long term, on society as a whole. Other orientations have blamed the capitalist system, or have manifested a deep-rooted belief or suspicion that the causes of unemployment lie in the nature and disposition of the unemployed themselves. The 'dole bludger syndrome' is not quite dead; it surfaces with regularity, not only in the public pronouncements of the moralists, but also indirectly in studies directed at the unemployed with the aim of discovering the reasons for their unemployment and how they feel about it.

Certainly, studies focused on the unemployed do not necessarily indicate a deliberate intention of researchers to search for causes of unemployment in the make-up of the unemployed persons. There is probably a 'practical' reason: the unemployed constitute an easily accessible 'captive audience'; it is relatively easy to interview them and also easier to 'count heads' than to investigate more complex, less easily quantifiable factors of the labour market structure. The outcome of this approach, however, leads predictably to remedial responses from policy-makers. These tend to seek to 'improve the employability' of the unemployed rather than to tackle the much more difficult task of job creation or at least the task of re-allocating resources in such a way that the level of available employment is shared with greater equity by the whole community.

The analysis of data on unemployment in the next section presents unemployment in the context of the changes in the structure of the labour market in Australia from 1966 to 1984. The aim of this approach is to demonstrate how these have affected the labour force, both quantitatively and qualitatively. As such, the analysis does not attempt to explain the rise of unemployment in terms of any general theory but it relates unemployment to a range of structural variables which together have produced not only certain rates of unemployment but also certain trends from which implications may be drawn for social policy.

The selection of the year 1966 as a benchmark has been made for a number of reasons. Firstly, it enables a comparison of data at two fairly distant points of time, thus indicating the magnitude of change that has taken place in the intervening years. Secondly, the Australian Bureau of Statistics has been collecting data on the labour force consistently since 1966, thus allowing comparison of data from a common base. The third reason is related to the comment made earlier, namely, that although unemployment became an issue of concern only in the mid-1970s, it was in the 1960s that the first signs of the problem began to appear.

Unemployment and its Dimensions

In common perceptions and interpretations, an unemployed person is a person without a paid job. However, unemployment statistics are compiled on various criteria that are not always consistent with one another and, consequently, can produce different results. The statistics can be used to demonstrate that there are more, or fewer, unemployed people than is generally believed to be the case.

In Australia, ever since unemployment became the subject of public concern, especially since the mid-1970s, there has been a variety of official statistics relating to it. For some years, the prevalent source of data was the Commonwealth Employment Service (CES) which recorded the numbers of people registered seeking employment. These numbers would be given either as true or seasonally-adjusted figures, and the politicians of the day would choose either and interpret them to support their arguments. The government would usually choose the lower figures, while the opposition would choose the higher. As unemployment levels continued to rise, the CES data were used less frequently and were later replaced by data from surveys of the labour force conducted by the Australian Bureau of Statistics (ABS), which tended generally to produce lower estimates than the data derived from the Commonwealth Employment Service. The reason for discarding the CES data was based on the argument that among people registered for employment were those who were employed at the time but who wanted to change jobs, the effect thus being an overstatement of the numbers really unemployed. However, the other reason for the usually lower figures from the ABS was the definition of unemployment used by it in its surveys. The ABS definition has consistently used narrow criteria which exclude some people who would be considered as unemployed if a broader definition were used.

The current definition used is:

Unemployed persons are those aged 15 years and over who were not employed during the survey week, and
  (a) had actively looked for full-time or part-time work at any time in the four weeks up to the end of the survey week and:
     (i) were available for work in the survey week or would have been available except for temporary illness (i.e. lasting for less than four weeks to the end of the survey week); or
     (ii) were waiting to start a new job within four weeks from the end of the survey week and would have

> started in the survey week if the job had been available then;
>
> or (b) were waiting to be called back to a full-time or part-time job from which they had been stood down without pay for less than four weeks up to the end of the survey week (including the whole of the survey week) for reasons other than bad weather or plant breakdown.
>
> (ABS Catalogue No. 6203.0, August 1984)

By definition, then, unemployed persons are 'all persons above the age of 15 years who during the reference period were neither in paid employment nor self-employment ..., were currently available for work ... and were actively seeking work during the reference period' (McMahon and Robinson 1984).

The ABS definition excludes persons who during the survey week had worked for one hour or more for pay, profit, commission or payment in kind, in a job or business; ... or worked for 15 hours or more without pay in a family business ... or were on leave or on strike, or on lockout ... or were employers or self-employed, but were not at work.

The labour force data are now collected an published monthly by the ABS. As was the case previously with the CES data, the results are usually interpreted in a variety of ways, not only by politicians but also by media commentators. To the general public this monthly ritual must be rather confusing and probably boring. The confusion is increased when the data for a given month are related to the figures from the previous month, previous quarter, previous year or even a decade. While the difficulty of establishing common uniform criteria has to be acknowledged, it is the politics of unemployment rather than the real unemployment situation that the public receives from the media. This is no different from any other issue where certain social conditions relating to such matters as health, crime, income or wealth are translated into quantified data.

The statistics on employment and unemployment presented in this chapter are all related to a common base. They have been extracted from the ABS labour force surveys, and the numbers of the recorded unemployed are actual numbers, not seasonally adjusted. The benchmark to show the trend in unemployment is, as mentioned, the year 1966 and all statistics there are for the month of August, except in Tables 15.6 and 15.7 which show the educational qualifications of employed persons which are collected by the ABS in February.

The trend in unemployment from 1966 to 1984 is shown in Table 15.1 and in graphic form in Figure 15.1. The data show a

Table 15.1 The Labour Force, Unemployment and Unemployment Benefits Paid, Australia, 1966–84

Year	Labour Force				Mean duration (weeks)	Unemployment benefits paid as at 30 June	Ratio of unemployed/ unemployment benefits paid
	Labour Force N('000)	Employed N('000)	Unemployed N('000)	%			
1966	4,902.2	4,823.6	78.6	1.6	3.0	19.5	4.03
1967	5,019.6	4,932.8	86.8	1.7	3.0	24.0	3.62
1968	5,136.6	5,055.5	81.1	1.6	8.9	21.3	3.81
1969	5,261.8	5,182.9	78.9	1.5	7.4	15.9	4.96
1970	5,473.8	5,395.6	78.2	1.4	7.3	13.0	6.02
1971	5,608.3	5,515.6	92.7	1.7	6.6	19.4	4.78
1972	5,753.9	5,609.9	144.0	2.5	9.7	41.6	3.46
1973	5,888.7	5,782.9	105.8	1.8	9.3	37.9	2.79
1974	5,996.1	5,885.2	140.9	2.4	6.5	32.0	4.40
1975	6,119.7	5,841.3	278.4	4.6	12.7	160.7	1.73
1976	6,190.6	5,897.9	292.7	4.7	17.5	188.4	1.55
1977	6,354.8	5,995.5	359.3	5.7	20.9	250.3	1.44
1978	6,365.3	5,969.6	395.7	6.2	26.2	286.1	1.38
1979	6,415.3	6,041.5	373.8	5.8	28.4	312.0	1.20
1980	6,639.0	6,246.7	392.3	5.9	32.1	311.2	1.26
1981	6,733.4	6,356.3	377.1	5.6	35.1	314.5	1.20
1982	6,806.0	6,347.5	458.5	6.7	32.8	390.7	1.17
1983	6,916.7	6,232.6	684.1	9.9	41.5	635.0	1.08
1984	7,066.9	6,462.3	604.6	8.6	45.5	584.5	1.03
Change ratio 1984–66	1.44	1.34	7.69	5.38	15.17	29.98	—

Source: Australian Bureau of Statistics, *The Labour Force, Australia, August*, Catalogue Nos. 6203.0 and 6204.0 (various years); Department of Social Security, *Annual Report 1983–84*

number of variables and the relationship between them. For example, in 1966 there were 4902.2 thousand persons (of both sexes) in the labour force and 4823.6 thousand of them were employed, leaving 78.6 thousand unemployed, or 1.6 per cent of the labour force. The average (mean) duration of unemployment per person was 3 weeks. At the same time, on 30 June of that year, 19.5 thousand persons were receiving unemployment benefits.

Figure 15.1 Unemployment in Australia, 1966–84: Number of Unemployed and Unemployment Benefits Recipients and Average (mean) Duration of Unemployment

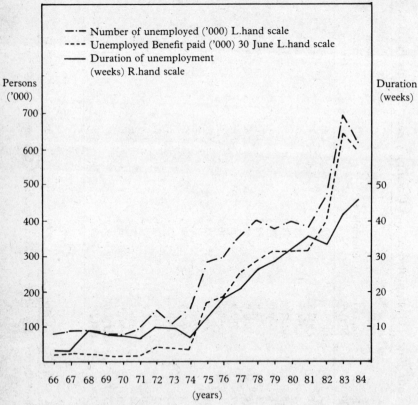

Source: Australian Bureau of Statistics: *The Labour Force, Australia, 1978*; Catalogue No. 6204.0; *The Labour Force, Australia, August 1984*; Catalogue No. 6203.0; Department of Social Security: *Annual Report 1983–84*

This means that fewer than 1 unemployed person in 4 was receiving unemployment benefits. Over the subsequent years, the number of unemployed had grown at a faster rate than the rate of growth in the labour force and that of employed persons, reaching a peak of 684.1 thousand unemployed in 1983, or 9.9 per cent of the labour force. What is important here is that by 1984 the mean duration of unemployment had risen to 45.5 weeks and the ratio between the unemployed and those receiving unemployment benefits had almost reached parity. (It needs to be noted here that unemployed married persons (mostly women) whose partners are employed and earn sufficient income are not entitled to unemployment benefits.)

It may be deduced from these trends that not only the extent but also the nature of unemployment has changed over the period. The lower numbers and the short-average duration of unemployment in the earlier years indicate a high level of 'frictional' unemployment, that is, unemployment related to people's changing jobs. Later, both the numbers of unemployed and average duration of unemployment have risen, indicating a growing 'structural' unemployment, that is, people who found themselves to be out of work had experienced a growing difficulty in finding it. The two important dimensions of unemployment that are relevant here are the *stock* and *flow* of unemployed people (Stuart 1984). A high stock of unemployed at any given time may represent a large number of short-term unemployed, or a large number of long-term unemployed. What the trend from 1966 to 1984 indicates, however, is an increasing stock and a decreasing flow, or a growth of what has been referred to as 'hard core' unemployment, meaning people who gradually become 'unemployable'. Thus the numbers alone of unemployed persons give only one dimension of unemployment but when the numbers are related to other variables a more adequate picture of the nature of unemployment is revealed.

The growth of 'hard core' unemployment becomes further evident when the rates and the duration of unemployment are related to the age of the unemployed (Table 15.2). It has been observed for some time that younger people, especially those in the age groups fifteen to nineteen years had high rates but relatively short duration of unemployment, indicating a high rate of flow in and out of work, or short periods of employment interspersed with spells of unemployment between jobs (Foster and Gregory 1982). The older the age group, however, he longer the periods of unemployment, although the rates would tend to be lower, thus indicating a growing trend towards unemployability. The difference between the mean and median average duration of unem-

Table 15.2 Unemployment Rates and Duration of Unemployment, Australia, August 1984

Age group (years)	Males		Females		People	
Unemployment rate (%)						
15–19	22.1		19.7		21.0	
20–24	14.3		10.3		12.5	
25–34	7.6		7.0		7.4	
35–44	5.0		5.6		5.3	
45–54	5.7		4.6		4.9	
55–59	5.4		★		6.6	
60–64	8.1		★			
All unemployed	8.7		8.3		8.6	
Duration of Unemployment (years)						
Age group (years)	Mean	Median	Mean	Median	Mean	Median
15–19	28.6	17.1	29.2	17.1	28.9	17.1
20–24	45.5	26.1	46.4	22.0	45.9	26.0
25–34	49.6	26.1	35.5	16.0	44.7	24.0
35–54	61.4	39.2	50.4	26.1	57.4	33.2
All unemployed (a)	48.6	27.0	40.1	21.0	45.5	26.0

Sources: Australian Bureau of Statistics, *The Labour Force, Australia, August 1984*, Catalogue No. 6203.0
(a) Includes people aged 55 years and over (not shown separately)
*Frequency too small for statistical influence

ployment, with the means being consistently higher, further indicate a growing 'harder' core within the 'hard' core.[1]

The averages, of course, conceal the variations among the unemployed. The unemployed recorded in August 1984 (Australian Bureau of Statistics, Catalogue No. 6203.0) for example, had durations of unemployment ranging from less than four weeks (15.1 per cent of the unemployed) to two years or longer (15.3 per cent). Thus for a substantial minority unemployment had become a way of life.

How can this growth of unemployment be explained? A comprehensive analysis is beyond the scope of this chapter. Viewed from the side of the *demand* for labour, a range of variables may be encountered, the sectors of industry and occupation being the most significant. Changes in the structure of industry would be expected to account for varied demand of labour with certain qualifications. As will be seen from the data below, changes in the structure of industry and occupations can be related to changes in the sex and age of persons employed or seeking work.

Table 15.3 Changes in Employment Between 1966–84

Industry/Occupation	Persons Employed 1966 N('000)	1966 %	1984 N('000)	1984 %	Change 1966–84 N('000)	Change 1966–84 %
Industries						
Community services	486.0	10.1	1,138.4	17.6	+652.4	+134.2
Finance, property and business services	294.4	6.1	619.3	9.6	+324.9	+110.4
Public service, communications, gas, electricity and water services	366.9	7.6	601.2	9.3	+234.3	+63.9
Mining	58.0	1.2	93.2	1.4	+35.2	+60.7
Recreation, personal and other services	287.0	5.9	420.0	6.5	+133.0	+46.3
Transport and storage	270.0	5.6	354.1	5.5	+84.1	+31.1
Wholesale and retail trade	993.5	20.6	1,271.4	19.7	+279.9	+28.0
Construction	406.0	8.4	423.2	6.5	+17.2	+4.2
Agriculture and related industries	429.6	8.9	400.2	6.2	−29.4	−6.8
Manufacturing	1,232.5	25.6	1,141.4	17.7	−91.1	−7.4
All industries	4,823.9	(100.0)	6,462.3	(100.0)	+1,638.4	+34.0
Occupations						
Professional, technical, etc.	472.8	9.8	1,105.7	15.7	+542.9	+114.9
Service, sport, recreation	395.7	8.2	650.1	10.1	+254.4	+64.3
Clerical	729.0	15.1	1,169.2	18.1	+440.2	+60.4
Sales	397.7	8.2	579.0	9.0	+181.3	+45.6
Administrative, executive, managerial	330.1	6.8	442.4	6.8	+112.3	+34.0
Transport and communications	302.5	6.3	324.2	5.0	+22.0	+7.3
Miners, trades, process work, etc.	1,731.3	35.9	1,836.4	28.4	+105.1	+6.1
Farmers, fishermen, timbergetters etc.	464.8	9.6	445.5	6.9	−19.3	−4.2
All occupations	4,823.9	(100.0)	6,462.3	(100.0)	+1,638.4	+34.0

Source: Australian Bureau of Statistics, *The Labour Force, Australia, 1978*, Catalogue No. 6204.0; *The Labour Force, Australia, August, 1984*, Catalogue No. 6203.0

To consider the sectors of industry and the occupational structure of employment first, between 1966 and 1984, the number of employed people rose by 1638.4 thousand, or by 34.0 per cent (Table 15.3). The sectors in industry and occupations have been ranked in Table 15.3 in an order to show those industries and occupations that have grown at a faster rate than the growth of total employment and those that have grown at a slower rate than the total. In terms relative to the total growth of employment, the industries and occupations may thus be referred to as either 'expanding' or 'shrinking', respectively (Jamrozik and Hoey 1982). In this perspective, the changes in the structure of the labour market give a clearer view of the dynamics of the market than isolated data. Certainly the comparison of data from two points of time separated by eighteen years does not directly explain the processes and variations that might have occurred in the intervening years, but the differences between the two years do clearly indicate the trends.

It can be ascertained from Table 15.3 that in August 1984, 44.4 per cent of all employed people were in the 'expanding' industries and the remainder (55.6 per cent) were in the 'shrinking' ones. However, in the occupational structure, a higher proportion (59.7 per cent) was employed in 'expanding' occupations. These different rates of change between industries and occupations indicate not only that certain industries have 'grown' or 'shrunk' but also that the occupational structure within them has changed. In industries, the fastest-growing has been the public sector, classified by the ABS as 'community services', and including health, welfare and education. Finance, property and business services came second, followed at a distance by public service, communications, and gas, water and electricity services, mining, and the composite sector of recreation, personal and other related services. The remaining industries registered a below-average growth, and in two of them employment actually decreased in absolute numbers (manufacturing, and agriculture and other primary industries).

On the occupational scale, by far the fastest-growing has been the composite category of 'professional, technical etc.' occupations, corresponding clearly to the growth of community services in which a large proportion of these occupations lie (Jamrozik and Hoey 1982, Jamrozik 1983, 1984). Five other occupational groups also recorded above-average growth, but at a slower rate. Of the shrinking occupations, only one group (farmers, fishermen, timbergetters, etc.) recorded a decrease in absolute numbers.

It is important to note in these data a distinct trend towards polarisation in the comparative rates of growth, especially evident

Table 15.4 Employment, August 1984

Industry/Occupation	People Employed			
	Men		Women	
	N('000)	%	N('000)	%
Industries				
Community services	410.7	10.2	727.7	29.7
Finance, property and business services	324.4	8.1	294.9	12.0
Public service, communication, gas, water and electricity services	447.9	11.2	153.2	6.3
Mining	84.8	2.1	8.4	0.3
Recreation, personnel and other services	194.7	4.8	225.4	9.2
Transport and storage	296.7	7.4	57.4	2.3
Wholesale and retail trade	721.6	18.0	549.8	22.4
Construction	380.1	9.5	43.1	1.8
Agriculture and related industries	303.3	7.6	96.9	4.0
Manufacturing	848.2	21.1	293.2	12.0
All industries	4,012.4	(100.0)	2,449.9	(100.0)
Occupations				
Professional, technical etc.	546.9	13.6	468.5	19.1
Service, sport, recreation	245.5	6.1	404.7	16.5
Clerical	323.8	8.1	845.5	34.5
Sales	265.8	6.6	313.2	12.8
Administrative, executive, managerial	375.2	9.4	67.2	2.7
Transport and communications	282.2	7.0	42.0	1.7
Miners, trade, process work etc.	1,622.7	40.4	213.7	8.7
Famers, fishermen, timbergetters	350.4	8.7	95.1	3.9
All occupations	4,012.4	(100.0)	2,449.9	(100.0)

Source: Australian Bureau of Statistics, *The Labour Force, Australia, August 1984*, Catalogue No. 6203.0

in the occupational structure. For example, the rate of growth in the professional group, if measured by percentages, has been 18.8 times faster than the rate for the category of manual workers (114.9/6.1 = 18.8).

The changes have also occurred between the rates of growth in the employment of men and that of women (Table 15.4). The comparison of data from Tables 15.3 and 15.4 will show that in 1984 the majority of women (57.5 per cent) was employed in the expanding industries while the majority of men (63.6 per cent) was employed in shrinking ones. Similar differences can be seen in the occupational structure, where an overwhelming majority of women (85.6 per cent) was employed in the expanding occupations with only a minority of men (43.8 per cent) engaged in these occupations. Changes in the structures of industry and occupations that have occurred between 1966 and 1984 have thus led to a division of labour between the sexes, referred to in some writings as the 'segmentation' of the labour market. The data also seem to indicate that Theobald's 1965 predictions about the trend towards increasing employment of women rather than men had some validity.

It needs to be noted, however, that the numbers of persons employed do not alone tell the whole story. Employment may mean full-time, or part-time or even casual employment, with a high proportion of women being employed on a part-time basis. In August 1984, 36.8 per cent of women were in part-time employment while only 6.1 per cent of men were so employed, and among married women part-time employment amounted to 45.6 per cent (Australian Bureau of Statistics, August 1984, Catalogue No. 6203.0.). Furthermore, different industrial sectors have varied degrees of 'dynamism', which often means instability of employment. Two such sectors – recreation, personal service, etc., and the wholesale and retail trade – fall into these categories, and both these sectors employ a significant proportion of women.

The links between the rates of unemployment and the trends in industries and occupations can be ascertained from the data in Table 15.5. The data indicate that in August 1984, of all recorded unemployed persons (604.6 thousand), 56.2 per cent had been previously employed in full-time work for at least two weeks in the two previous years. Of these, the rates of unemployment were, on the whole, lower among the unemployed who had been employed in the expanding industries and occupations. The exceptions were the industries in the recreation and personal services group, and in the occupations related to service industries, i.e., sales, and service, sport and recreation.

The most dramatic change in the structure of the labour market has occurred in the educational qualifications of employed people and, correspondingly, in the educational qualifications of unemployed ones. Constant statistics on this aspect have been collected by the ABS only since 1979, and the changes that have occurred between 1979 and 1984 are shown in Table 15.6. In that period of five years the number of people employed rose by 331 thousand, or 5.5 per cent. However, the number of employed people with post-school qualifications rose over the period by 557 thousand, or 14.8 per cent, and one-third of these were people with a degree or

Table 15.5 Previous Employment of Those Unemployed, August
1984

Industry/Occupation	Men N('000)	Rate %	Women N('000)	Rate %	People N('000)	Rate %
People who had worked full-time for two weeks in the last two years, in:						
Industries						
Community services	9.5	2.3	15.7	2.1	25.1	2.2
Finance, property and business services	11.0	3.3	6.4	2.1	17.4	2.7
Public service/other industries	20.7	4.4	7.1	4.4	27.9	3.9
Mining	★	★	★	★	★	
Recreation, personal and other services	19.1	8.9	14.3	6.0	33.4	7.4
Transport and storage	13.4	4.3	★	★	15.2	4.1
Wholesale and retail trade	48.9	6.3	26.8	4.6	75.7	5.6
Construction	40.0	9.5	★	★	41.5	8.9
Agriculture and related industries	19.3	6.0	★	★	21.6	5.1
Manufacturing	66.1	7.2	15.7	5.1	81.8	6.7
Occupations						
Professional, technical, etc.	9.6	1.7	9.9	2.1	19.5	1.9
Service, sport, recreation	20.0	7.5	18.8	4.4	38.8	5.6
Clerical	8.4	2.5	26.2	3.0	34.5	2.9
Sales	15.5	5.5	16.3	4.9	31.8	5.2
Managerial, security, administrative and others	8.0	2.1	★	★	10.1	2.2
Transport and communications	17.8	5.9	★	★	19.6	5.7
Miners, trades, process work, n.e.c.	144.0	8.2	14.6	6.4	158.6	7.9
Farmers, fishermen, timber-getters etc.	24.7	6.6	★	★	26.8	5.7
All previously employed as above	248.0	5.8	91.8	3.6	339.8	5.0
Looking for first job	47.5	—	46.0	—	93.5	—
Other	84.3	—	80.9	—	165.2	—
Stood down	★	—	★	—	6.1	—
All unemployed	381.5	8.7	223.1	8.3	604.6	8.6

Source: Australian Bureau of Statistics, *The Labour Force, Australia, August, 1984*, Catalogue No. 6203.0
Note: Unemployment rate = unemployed persons as percentage of people employed and people seeking work
★Frequency too small for statistical inference

Table 15.6 Educational Attainment of Employed People, February 1979 and 1984

| | Employed in 1979 and 1984 ('000) | | | | | | Change 1979–1984 ('000 and %) | | | | | |
| | Men | | Women | | People | | Men | | Women | | People | |
	1979	1984	1979	1984	1979	1984	N	%	N	%	N	%
With post-school qualifications												
Degree or equivalent	314	425	111	184	425	610	+111	+35.3	+73	+65.8	+185	+43.5
Trade, technical etc.	1,235	1,425	539	704	1,774	2,129	+190	+15.4	+165	+30.6	+355	+20.0
Total (a)	1,576	1,881	667	919	2,243	2,800	+305	+19.4	+252	+37.8	+557	+24.8
Without post-school qualifications												
Attended highest secondary level	442	454	253	333	695	788	+12	+2.7	+80	+31.6	+93	+13.4
Did not attend highest secondary level	1,846	1,619	1,173	1,062	3,019	2,680	−227	−12.3	−111	−9.5	−339	−11.2
Total (b)	2,295	2,081	1,430	1,399	3,725	3,481	−214	−9.3	−31	−2.2	−244	−6.6
All Employed (c)	3,900	4,000	2,135	2,366	6,035	6,366	+100	+2.6	+231	+10.8	+33	+5.5

(a) includes people with other post-school qualifications
(b) includes people who never attended school
(c) includes people 15–12 years still at school

Source: *Labour Force Education Attainment, Australia, February 1983*: ABS Catalogue No. 6235.0
      Labour Force Status and Educational Attainment, Australia, February 1984: ABS Catalogue No. 6235.0

Table 15.7 Unemployment and Educational Attainment, Feburary 1979 and 1984

	Men								Women							
	Unemployed N('000)		Rate %		Average Duration (Weeks) Mean		Median		Unemployed N('000)		Rate %		Average Duration (Weeks) Mean		Median	
Educational Attainment	1979	1984	1979	1984	1979	1984	1979	1984	1979	1984	1979	1984	1979	1984	1979	1984
With post-school qualifications																
Degree or equivalent	6.6	18.9	2.1	4.3	12.3	34.7	8.6	12.1	*	14.2	*	7.1	*	11.7	*	8.0
Trade, technical	45.4	96.7	3.5	6.4	26.1	35.3	12.2	21.1	41.4	71.1	7.1	9.2	21.6	26.6	7.3	9.0
Total (a)	53.4	118.6	3.3	5.9	24.0	35.3	11.5	19.1	50.3	88.5	7.0	8.8	21.0	25.0	7.6	9.1
Without post-school qualifications																
Attended highest secondary level	30.8	60.6	6.5	11.8	19.8	37.5	11.0	15.0	29.5	41.4	10.4	11.0	19.4	32.9	8.6	12.0
Did not attend highest level	145.7	238.5	7.3	12.8	39.3	54.4	18.4	39.1	131.2	156.1	10.1	12.8	27.8	45.9	10.8	18.1
Total (b)	177.4	301.6	7.2	12.7	36.1	51.2	16.6	32.1	160.7	198.0	10.1	12.4	26.3	43.3	10.2	16.1
All employed (c)	241.4	435.8	5.8	9.8	32.4	45.6	14.2	26.1	219.0	201.9	9.3	11.3	24.5	36.4	9.5	13.0

(a) includes people with other post-school qualifications
(b) includes people who never attended school
(c) includes people 15–20 years still at school

Source: Australian Bureau of Statistics, *Labour Force Status and Education Attainment, Australia, February 1983–1984*, Catalogue No. 5235.0

equivalent qualification; their numbers rose by 43.5 per cent.

By contrast, the numbers of employed persons without post-school qualifications fell over the same period by 244 thousand, or 6.6 per cent. The fall was a composite effect of an increase in employment of 93 thousand, or 13.4 per cent, among people who had attended the highest level of secondary school; with a large decrease of 339 thousand, or 11.2 per cent, in the employment of people who had left school early.

Educational qualifications thus appear to have become one of the most important factors in access to employment in the conditions of the changing demand for labour experienced in recent years and continuing today. They are reflected also in comparative unemployment rates as well as in the duration of unemployment of people with different educational qualifications (Table 15.7). On the whole, the higher a person's educational qualifications the lower the probability of his or her becoming unemployed; and if that person is unemployed, the duration of unemployment is likely to be, on average, considerably shorter than for a person without post-school qualifications.

In sum, over the past two decades a shift has occurred in the structure of the labour market, from primary and secondary industries to service ones. A significant factor in that shift has been the growth of employment in the public sector of community services and in the business and finance management industries. The new jobs in these expanding industries are 'white collar' ones, in professional and sub-professional categories, thus accounting for the growth in employment of people with post-school qualifications. At the other end of the scale there has been a decline in the demand for labour in industries employing manual labour. As a result, while there has been a growth of unemployment, the most affected persons have been those with low educational qualifications.

The changes in the structure of industries and occupations examined so far have resulted in quantitative as well as qualitative changes in the demand for labour, but they do not account fully for the rise of unemployment or for differential rates, especially those related to age groups. A clearer picture emerges when the changes in the demand for labour are compared with the supply of it over the same period.

As shown earlier (Table 15.1) between 1966 and 1984, the labour force (that is, people over 15 years in employment or seeking work) increased by 44 per cent, while employment increased by only 34 per cent, thus accounting for the rise in unemployment. The growth in the labour force resulted entirely from the growth of the population of employable age (15 years and

Table 15.8 Changes in Total Employment in Youth (15–19 Years) Employment, 1966–84

Industry (ranked in order of magnitude of change)	Changes in total employment 1966–84			Changes in youth employment 1966–84		
	1966 N('000)	1984 N('000)	Change %	1966 N('000)	1984 N('000)	Change %
Employment rising above the average for all industries						
Community services	486.0	1,138.4	+134.2	52.4	47.2	−9.9
Finance, property, business services	294.4	619.3	+110.4	66.9	53.7	−19.7
Public service, communication, gas, electricity, water	366.9	601.2	+63.9	55.4	32.0	−42.2
Mining	58.0	93.2	+60.7	*	4.7	*
Entertainment, recreation, etc.	287.0	420.0	+46.3	34.2	48.7	+42.4
All industries	4,823.9	6,462.3	+34.0	651.7	584.3	−10.3
Employment rising below the average for all industries						
Transport and storage	270.0	354.1	+31.1	18.6	12.5	−32.8
Wholesale and retail trade	993.5	1,271.4	+28.0	180.0	138.5	+32.4
Construction	406.0	423.2	+4.2	38.3	26.5	−30.8
Agriculture and related industries	429.6	400.2	−6.8	41.2	25.5	−38.1
Manufacturing	1,232.5	1,141.4	−7.4	160.6	95.0	−40.8

Source: Australian Bureau of Statistics, *The Labour Force Australia, 1978*, Catalogue No. 6204.0; *August 1984*, Catalogue No. 6203.0.

over), as the participation rates in the total labour force were the same in 1984 as in 1966 (59.9 per cent). There was a decrease in male participation rates from 84.0 per cent in 1966 to 75.7 per cent in 1984, and an increase in female participation rates from 36.8 per cent in 1966 to 44.6 per cent in 1984. However, the age structure changed over that period, resulting in a greater proportion of the population being in the age groups 20 to 44 years than was the case in 1966 (Australian Bureau of Statistics 1973, Reference No. 4.15; 1982, Catalogue No. 3201.0). The labour force in the same age groups had increased even further because of the increase in the female participation rates in that group (Australia Bureau of Statistics 1978, Catalogue No. 6204.0; 1983, Catalogue No. 6203.0). Analysis of the ABS labour force data would show that the majority of employed persons in that age group were in 1984 employed in those industries and occupations which had expanded since 1966 above the rate of growth in total employment. This would be expected as people in that age group would have educational and occupational qualifications most closely corresponding to the requirements of the expanding industries and occupations.

In comparison with the increase in the employment of people in the age group 20 to 44 years, there has been a massive departure from the labour force of men of older age, especially of those in the age group 60 years and over (Merrilees 1982), but starting from the age of 45 years. Young people who entered the labour market in the age group 15 to 19 years found increasing difficulty, first in finding employment and, second, in finding employment offering secure jobs and opportunities for advancement. As shown in Table 15.8, the numbers of employed young people had declined in comparison with 1966 in all sectors of industry except two: entertainment, recreation etc.; and wholesale and retail trade. Of all employed young people in that age group, almost a half (49.1 per cent) were employed in these two industrial sectors. Employment in these two sectors of industry has been notoriously unstable, and it offers negligible opportunities for advancement, with a high proportion of jobs being part-time. By contrast, the largest percentage decrease in young people's employment over the period (42.2 per cent) has occurred in the public sector, although employment there has grown over the same period by 63.9 per cent.

The cause of high rates of unemployment among young people may thus be seen not so much in the overall low demand for labour as in the changes in the occupational structure of certain industries which have become effectively closed to young people.

Unemployment Data and their Significance

The most evident trend in the data presented in the previous section is an almost uninterrupted growth of unemployment over the past two decades (see Table 15.1 and Figure 15.1). The significance of this trend lies in its two dimensions: the number of the unemployed, and the average duration of unemployment per person. The increase in both dimensions indicates, firstly, a declining increase in the demand for labour; and, secondly, a trend towards relative exclusion of certain sections of the population from the labour market. This means that an increasing proportion of the population now relies on public provisions for income support, with corresponding loss of social status and income, and a different lifestyle and life chances from those of the majority of the population.

The second trend indicates a transformation in the structure of industry and occupations. Some industries show above-average expansion, others a gradual decline either in relative or absolute terms. The industries in decline are those which have been employing manual labour, and, as a result, unemployment has been increasing at a faster rate among these. Among the expanding industries, the fastest-growing have been those which employ labour with post-school qualifications, professional, sub-professional, or technical. Employment in those industries is relatively stable and offers a career structure. The other industries in the expanding category do not offer such prospects and employment in them lacks stability or career prospects. As a result, many people employed in them experience intermittent periods of unemployment.

These divergent trends indicate a growing polarisation of the labour force: firstly, between the people who are employed and those who are not; and, secondly, among the employed, between those who have good jobs, good incomes and security of tenure, and those who have low-quality jobs, low incomes and no security of tenure but rather a sort of 'serial employment' and poor prospects of improvement. If these trends continue, they will predictably lead to an even greater polarisation of society that will become evident in two distinct lifestyles, distinct patterns of economic and social consumption, and distinct levels of social functioning.

The trends in Australia are similar to those observed in the other industrialised countries. High levels of unemployment have now become a feature of the Western economies in the capitalist system. On recent indications, there are 34 million unemployed people in the 24 countries which constitute the membership of the Organisation for Economic Co-operation and Development (OECD) and this amounts to 10 per cent of the labour force (Vertiainen 1984). Moreover, although there have been some signs of economic recovery in these countries, there are no signs of any amelioration in employment. On the contrary, in some countries, such as the United Kingdom, unemployment has continued to rise and there are now over 3 million unemployed in that country, or 13 per cent of the labour force.

While the recession of the 1970s had undoubtedly contributed to the rise of unemployment it is the technological innovation in the production process that poses the threat of unemployment for years to come. The recession might have, in fact, contributed to the acceleration in technological innovation, as firms and countries attempted to maintain or improve their competitiveness in the market. The advances in technology have also affected the organisation of production, increasing flexibility and more efficient utilisation of labour according to demand for product or service. From the point of view of economic efficiency, hence profitability, the effects may be positive, but for the labour force this means instability of employment, and unemployment.

It is this cold rationality with which the changes take place in the labour market that justifies the criticism of the capitalist system made by Windschuttle and others. It is now evident that a modern industrial economy can function efficiently but at the price of shedding the surplus labour into unemployment. This 'human residue' of technological innovation is tacitly and often overtly accepted as a somewhat unfortunate necessity. As Mayo (1980) has commented on the British scene, 'labour has been deskilled, disorganised, and shed altogether, as part of the rationalisation process'.

The issue of unemployment must therefore be seen in the context of the changes that have taken place in the structure of the labour market and the economy as a whole. Furthermore, the numbers of employed and unemployed alone give only a partial indication of changes in the structure. The qualitative aspects of employment are equally important and probably more significant in their implications for the future. For example, the flexibility in he organisation of production is reflected in the growth of part-time employment. In Australia in 1966, 9.8 per cent of employed persons work part-time; the proportion in 1984 was on average 18.2 per cent, and in some industries such as the retail trade, and recreation and personal services, part-time employment was 30.3 per cent and 37.8 per cent. Part-time employment does not necessarily mean that all people so employed would want to work full-time. On the contrary, the ABS surveys consistently indicate that a large majority who work part-time do so by choice, or by necessity caused by other obligations such as family responsibilities. It is appropriate to note here that women account for most part-time employment: the proportion of part-time employment among women in 1984 was 36.8 per cent, as against only 6.1 per cent among men.

Thus, in effect, apart from unemployment officially recorded as such, there is a certain amount of 'under-employment' in the labour force as well as 'hidden unemployment', that is, people who would like to be employed but do not actively seek employment either because they believe that no work is available for them, or because they cannot work and discharge other responsibilities at the same time (Stricker and Sheehan 1981).

Responses to Unemployment

Ever since unemployment became a subject of public concern, the measures taken to overcome the problem have been directed mainly at the unemployed. This approach is best illustrated by the methods adopted towards young people. Initially, acting on the belief that a significant cause of unemployment among young people was their unwillingness to work, the government adopted measures of control aimed to ensure that the life of the young unemployed remained uncomfortable and unpleasant. Work tests and associated procedures acquired the distinct characteristics of measures used during the operation of the Poor Law in nineteenth century England. The procedures were aimed at rooting out such suspected character traits as 'unwillingness to work', 'inappropriate attitude to work', 'undisciplined work behaviour' or 'lack of effort to find work'.

Government programs designed to deal with the unemployment problem achieved little result. The program aimed to 'improve the employability' of young people but did not increase the demand for labour. 'Improving employability' meant in practice, not improving young people's work skills but rather teaching them how to present themselves for job interviews and preparing them to accept any job that might be available. The purpose of these programs was thus to serve as a socialisation process, aimed to maintain young persons' 'work readiness' while at the same time lowering their ambitions about occupational prospects. For example, the initial aim of the Community Youth Support Scheme (CYSS) was to 'progressively accustom the young unemployed to being employed and to learning some of the discipline associated

with having a job' (Minister's *Press Release*, 21 October 1976).
When the CYSS guidelines were reviewed in 1982, the new
programs were to 'concentrate on providing training in work skills,
and would encourage work experience, community service work,
part-time, casual and temporary work for young people ...'
(Minister's *Press Release*, 27 January 1982 – Brown 1982).

These approaches to young people's unemployment were consistent with the prevailing opinions (still held now) that young
people's employability was low because of their inappropriate or
inadequate education, their attitude to work, and lack of experience. All these arguments may be valid, thus suggesting that young
people who leave school early are not adequately equipped to
compete successfully for employment with other age groups,
especially in the 'expanding' sectors of industry. When the changes
in employment in various industries (Table 15.2) are compared
with the position of young people (15 to 19 years) in these
industries, the loss of jobs by young people in the 'expanding
industries' is clearly evident. As shown in Table 15.2, there were
about 1,638.4 thousand more people employed in 1984 than in
1966, a rise of 34 per cent. Where has this increase occurred? The
industries which had expanded above the rate of 34 per cent
accounted for 1,379.8 thousand, or 84 per cent of total growth.
Over a half of the total increase in employment has occurred in
the public sector and public sector-related services: community
services, public service, gas, electricity and water services,
and communications. Community services alone accounted for
39.8 per cent of the total growth in employment. At the same time,
employment of young people (Table 15.8) decreased in all these
sectors of industry. Yet, it was here that many young people used
to begin their working life and future careers. 'Where have all
junior clerks gone?' one may ask.

The only two sectors of industry in which young people have
inreased in numbers are those in which employment is part-time,
casual, and generally unstable: wholesale and retail sales, recreation and personal services, etc. In fact, in 1984, close to a half of
employed young people were working in these two industries and a
significant proportion of them were working part-time while still
in school.

It is appropriate to note at this point that the Manpower and
Social Committee of the OECD in its report, *Review of Youth
Policies in Australia* (1984) commented at length on the necessity
for a range of measures to overcome what it saw as an 'economic
crisis' in the unemployment problem for young people in this
country. While emphasising the urgency of raising educational
attainment and occupation skills of young people, the Committee

also recommended 'selective initiatives and interventions to increase the youth share of overall employment growth', 'giving high priority to young people in the allocation of existing jobs', and 'introducing structural changes to increase overall employment'. Further, the Committee commented:

> In view of the size of public service employment and the marked decline in the share of that employment for teenagers, Australian authorities should evaluate the need for positive discrimination in favour of teenagers.
>
> (OECD 1984: 13)

It thus appears that irrespective of the 'future of work', which does not look very promising, societies and their governments may have to make choices about the allocation of work and its rewards as work becomes an increasingly scarce commodity. For the problem of unemployment to be solved, a profound reassessment of economic and social policies, as well as of theories and values on which such policies are formulated and implemented, would need to take place. The experience of the past decade suggests that such a reassessment is not likely to occur in the foreseeable future.

Notes

1 The mean is the sum of the duration of unemployment of all unemployed people, divided by the number of the unemployed, while the median is the mid-point of the duration of unemployment, indicating that one-half of the unemployed had the duration of unemployment longer than that number and the other half had a shorter duration. Thus, if the mean is greater than the median, this indicates that more than one-half of the unemployed had a duration of unemployment *below* the mean, while a smaller proportion had a duration of unemployment *above* the mean.

References

Anthony, P.D. (1972) *The Ideology of Work*. London: Tavistock.
Australian Bureau of Statistics (1973) *Estimated Age Distribution of the Population: Australian States and Territories, 1966 to 1971*, Reference No. 4.15. Canberra: ABS.
———(1978) *The Labour Force, Australia*, Catalogue No. 6204.0. Canberra: ABS.
———(1982) *Estimated Resident Population by Sex and Age: States and*

Territories of Australia, June 1971 to June 1981, Catalogue No. 3201.0. Canberra: ABS.

———(1984a) *The Labour Force, Australia, August*, Catalogue No. 6203.0. Canberra: ABS.

———(1984b) *The Labour Force and Educational Attainment, Australia, February*, Catalogue No. 6235.0. Canberra: ABS.

Brotherhood of St Laurence (1982) *Unemployment: The Facts and Effects*. Melbourne: Aldine Press.

Brown, N.A., Minister for Employment and Youth Affairs (1982) *News Release*, 27 January. Canberra: Parliament House.

Cass, B. (1981) *Unemployment and the Family: The Social Impact of the Restructuring of the Australian Labour Market*. Kensington: Social Welfare Research Centre, Reports and Proceedings No. 7, University of New South Wales.

Department of Labour and National Service (1970) *An Analysis of Full Employment in Australia*. Melbourne: Labour Market Studies No. 2.

Encel, D. and Garde, P. (1984) *Unemployment in Australia: An Annotated Bibliography, 1978–83*, Kensington: Social Welfare Research Centre, Reports and Proceedings No. 36, University of New South Wales.

Foster, W. and Gregory, R.G. (1982) 'The Contribution of Employment Separation to Teenage Unemployment', *The Economic Record* June: 118–33.

Garraty, J.A. (1978) *Unemployment in History: Economic Thought and Public Policy*. New York: Harper & Row.

Jamrozik, A. (1973) *The Delinquent and the Law: Trends and Patterns in Juvenile Delinquency, South Australia, 1954 to 1971*. Bedford Park: Flinders University of South Australia.

———(1983) 'The Economy, Social Inequalities and the Welfare State: Implications for Research' in J. Jarrah (ed.) *53rd ANZAAS Congress: SWRC Papers*. Kensington: Social Welfare Research Centre, Reports and Proceedings No. 31, University of New South Wales.

———(1984) 'The Labour Market, the Public Sector and the Class Structure' in R. Hooke (ed.) *54th ANZAAS Congress: SWRC Papers*. Kensington: Social Welfare Research Centre, Reports and Proceedings No. 47, University of New South Wales.

———and Hoey, M. (1981) *Workforce in Transition: Implications for Welfare*. Kensington: Social Welfare Research Centre, Reports and Proceedings No. 8, University of New South Wales.

———and———(1981) *Dynamic Labour Market or Work on the Wane? Trends in the Australian Labour Force 1966–1981*. Kensington: Social Welfare Research Centre, Reports and Proceedings No. 27, University of New South Wales.

Jones, B. (1982) *Sleepers, Wake! Technology and the Future of Work*. Melbourne: Oxford University Press.

Kumar, K. (1980) 'No Bright Prospects on the Horizon', *Social Policy* II (3), November–December: 45–47.

McMahon, P. and Robinson, C. (1984) 'Concepts, Definitions and Measures of Unemployment and the Labour Force: Are They Appropriate for Economic Policy Analysis in the 1980s?', *Working Paper No. 41*. Canberra: Bureau of Labour Market Research.

Mayo, M. (1980) 'A British Perspective', *Social Policy* II (3), November–December: 48–51.

Merrilees, W.J. (1982) 'The Mass Exodus of the Older Males from the Labour Force: An Exploratory Analysis', *Australian Bulletin of Labour* 8 (2), March: 81–94.

Mills, C.W. (1959, 1970) *The Sociological Imagination*. Harmondsworth: Penguin.

Organisation for Economic Co-operation and Development (1978) *Youth Unemployment*, Vols. 1 and 2. Paris: OECD.

——(1984) *Review of Youth Policies in Australia*, Report of the Manpower and Social Affairs Committee (MAS) 84 (20). Paris: OECD.

Pankhurst, K.V. (1981) 'The (Non-American) OECD Experience' in C.E. Baird, R.G. Gregory and F.H. Gruen (eds) *Youth Employment, Education and Training*. Canberra: Australian National University.

Sheehan, P. (1980) *Crisis in Abundance*. Melbourne: Penguin.

Showler, B. and Sinfield, A. (ed.) (1981) *The Workless State*. Oxford: Martin Robertson.

Sinfield, A. (1981) *What Unemployment Means*. Oxford: Martin Robertson.

Street, A.A., Minister for Employment and Industrial Relations (1976) *Press Release*, 21 October 1976. Canberra: Parliament House.

Stricker, P. and Sheehan, P. (1981) *Hidden Unemployment*. Melbourne: Institute of Applied Economic and Social Research.

Stuart, A. (1984) 'Changes in the Social Distribution of Unemployment Benefit Duration 1980–83', *Social Security Journal*, June: 19–34. Canberra: Department of Social Security.

Theobald, R. (1965) *Free Men and Free Markets*. New York: Anchor Books, Doubleday.

Vertiainen, H.J. (1984) *Initiatives for Employment Creation in Finland*. Paris: Organisation for Economic Co-operation and Development.

Windschuttle, K. (1979) *Unemployment: A Social and Political Analysis of the Economic Crisis in Australia*. Harmondsworth: Penguin.

——(1980) 'Unemployment and Class Conflict in Australia, 1978–79' in E.L. Wheelwright and K. Buckley (eds) *Essays in the Political Economy of Australian Capitalism*, Vol 4: 243–66. Sydney: Australian and New Zealand Book Co.

——(1981) 'Unemployment – No End in Sight', *The Australian Quarterly* 53(a), Winter: 167–76.

Chapter Sixteen

Welfare Issues of the Eighties

Lois Bryson

In its general English usage, the word welfare simply means well-being. It has been co-opted also to refer to a set of more specific institutions of the society which apparently promote basic physical and social well-being, such as income support and health services. Within this specific usage the term may be used to denote a broad range of state functions or may be more narrowly focused on assistance to individuals, or may refer to some variation of these extreme positions. To give examples, Sweden may be referred to as a welfare state, suggesting that the major social systems are organised to provide basic access to an acceptable quality of life for all citzens. At the other extreme individuals seek welfare assistance from a charitable organisation to tide them over an economic crisis.

When we consider how the term is used in Australia we find that it is not used in reference to all the population. Welfare commonly refers to the system of government and non-government assistance provided to those who, for a variety of reasons, are not able to provide for themselves. Thus we find a move in meaning of the word away from general well-being to an emphasis on a portion of the population only. Welfare is not about all citizens but about those who are poor or relatively poor. Perhaps even more curious is the fact that a certain negative evaluation is associated with the receipt of 'welfare'.

In this chapter I consider the way in which welfare is defined and the implications of this for our understanding of who gets what in the name of welfare, and who gets what under other labels. From such an analysis it becomes obvious that there is a bias involved which works to the detriment of those at the bottom of the socio-economic system.

The well-known British social theorist, Richard Titmuss, is concerned at the way in which welfare is generally defined in this narrow way. He suggests that this emphasis focuses only on the social welfare system, which was in fact aimed at those in poor economic circumstances. He proposed that a more useful and fairer way of defining the system was to see it as made up of three parts, social welfare, fiscal welfare and occupational welfare. Fiscal and occupational welfare benefits are typically directed to those who are better off.

In this chapter the Australian welfare system will be looked at within this tri-partite framework. It will be demonstrated that when approached in this way the commonly-held view that too many resources are being diverted to the poor through 'welfare' expenditure is not supportable.

Social welfare expenditure has in fact been rising in recent years as the number of unemployed has increased. It is a quite complex argument as to whether this expenditure should be construed in the circumstances, as a bad thing for the economy, but it is certainly possible to clearly assert that the rise in expenditure is largely the result rather than the cause of the current economic problems. As Hindricks *et al.* (1984–85) point out, the current economic crisis is one of the wage labour system, not of the welfare state. Additionally, as the tax debate has indicated, problems of the revenue foregone through fiscal and occupational welfare must be taken into account when considering who benefits from the 'welfare' support provided by governments.

Welfare: A Biased Term

Many critics who claim that welfare expenditure is too high advocate more government activity to support business activity, for example, for oil exploration, tariffs or small business. Thus at the same time as they want less government outlay for the welfare area they may recommend increased outlays for other groups, in effect welfare for the wealthier. It is significant, though, that public assistance to the wealthier is never actually called welfare. Deductible business losses, tariff protection, subsidies and infrastructural services such as the monetary and communications systems, that make business profitable for its few shareholders, transfer benefits to particular individuals and groups as much as does a rent rebate to a pensioner. Yet such government-provided benefits are not called welfare. This term is reserved for certain kinds of transfers and these, not coincidentally, are likely to have a stigmatising effect.

The selective use of terms clearly represents a great deal more than mere semantics. It reflects the way in which those who are powerful are able to so frame the debates that their advantages are rarely challenged. At the same time they avoid stigmatisation.

To illustrate the complexity and bias in the usage of the term welfare it is instructive to consider the 1985–86 federal Budget. The word *per se* does not seem to have been used in the Treasurer's speech (as reported in *The Age*, 21 August 1985: 14) but the sentiments expressed clearly indicate when the notion of welfare in the traditional sense is being invoked. The announcement of increases to social security benefits over and above indexation was prefaced with the statement that the Labor government had been increasing such benefits because it 'is irrevocably committed to justice and compassion for those in genuine need' – a statement that is clearly a descendant of the 'deserving poor', 'charity' lineage. When we come to transfers to farmers we have quite different terminology, the terminology of the business world – no charity here!

> The government is concerned about the economic difficulties faced by many of our primary producers, particularly in view of the extremely poor international commodity prices flowing from sub-sidised overprotection by our major competitors.
>
> (*The Age* 21 August 1984: 14)

The farmers, as no doubt did the less vocal beneficiaries, believed they received too little assistance by way of their rebate of the excise on diesel fuel, a subsidy which reduces the cost of locally-produced grain harvesters and a number of relief schemes for specific sub-groups. It is not the merit of the two cases that is in question here, but merely the way reality is being defined. Many farmers are clearly having a hard time making ends meet. Rural proverty has been estimated at somewhere between 15 and 20 per cent (Lawrence 1985: 18). Ostensibly, then, the state is intervening in both cases to provide the recipients with assistance to meet the basic cost of survival. Yet given the different phrasing which was used to announce the two initiatives, it is difficult to assess whether the groups have received equivalent treatment. Certainly the terminology casts pensioners and beneficiaries into a supplicant role, dependent on compassion, while farmers are still cast as part of the mainstream business world.

Another comparison from the Budget makes the point in a somewhat different way. An allocation of $30 million was announced for the America's Cup defence in 1987. As part of another item, it was announced that a portion of an $8 million grant provided for Aboriginal advancement programs is to be spent on renovations to a sports' club and gymnasium in an inner city area of Melbourne. Here we have two programs with a sporting focus.

The latter will be clearly recognisable as a welfare program, but what will the former be identified as? It is just as certainly a government transfer that will serve the interests of particular groups.

This excursion into Budget allocations highlights the issue of definition and the way in which different ones are employed in relation to different groups. This might not matter if we could be sure that the outcomes were the same but a look at the income distribution of those receiving traditional welfare support makes it clear that they are not.

Social Welfare

Thus the issue of how welfare is defined is of fundamental importance. Welfare is the term used to describe support given to those who are most economically disadvantaged and socially vulnerable. The term encompasses such supports as housing for the poor, hand-outs of food and clothing, public health services, social security payments, particularly those of a restricted nature such as those for supporting parents, unemployment and sickness benefits. The term is also used to cover interventive public services, those for young offenders, child protection, and a range of family support services. The concept welfare state can clearly be used to encompass universalistic services as well, though these fit somewhat less comfortably within the definition. These services include, for example, family allowances, age pensions, the general health care system and education. At times the total social system is called a welfare state, although this usage seems to be becoming more infrequent as greater emphasis on integrated economic management has developed. It can be suggested that we have reached a post-welfare state stage, a point that is taken up later.

In a recent publication by the Australian Bureau of Statistics, *Social Indicators* (1984: 302) the difficulty of achieving agreement on a definition of welfare was discussed. This partly explains why 1984 was the first time an ABS *Social Indicators* series included a separate chapter devoted to welfare. One might of course be for- given for assuming that the whole enterprise would be classified as welfare.

The welfare chapter of *Social Indicators* includes information provided by the states through a 'joint State and Commonwealth project concerned with the standardisation and improvement of social welfare statistics', called WELSTAT (ABS 1984: 302). In developing this system, welfare activities have been classified by the Australian Standard Activities Classification (ASWAC). Welfare is seen to be concerned with the following:

- financial assistance and support by either cash transfers or taxation concessions;
- direct provision of material needs essential for daily living;
- providing social support services and substitute care arrangements for individuals and families;
- ensuring the protection and safety of persons against excesses by themselves or others;
- improving the efficiency and effectiveness of the welfare service delivery system generally.

(ABS 1984: 302)

This new form of data collection will provide more and comparable information about these activities, and thus increase our understanding. However, the approach is a restricted one. The chapter looks almost exclusively at social security issues with some additional information on other traditionally-defined services, such as those for the aged and disabled. Thus it suffers from the same sort of problem already illustrated by the Treasurer's Budget speech. It focuses on what Titmuss (1985) called social welfare, but ignores the other two parts of his tri-partite system of welfare, fiscal and occupational welfare. Nonetheless, the definition potentially allows a much wider focus. 'Financial assistance and support by either cash transfers or taxation concessions' (see point three, above) could be interpreted to include transfers to the wealthier, especially if unintended concessions are included. In order to gain a broad understanding, it is crucial that we look in more detail at fiscal and occupational welfare. However, before doing this, it is instructive to consider in some detail the parameters of social or traditional welfare, as this essentially provides the basis for an overall assessment of the equity of the Australian welfare system.

Development of Income Security Provisions in Australia
Until quite recently the terms welfare and charity were inextricably linked. Only the most vulnerable were provided with any assistance and this was likely to be relatively haphazard and associated with good behaviour and being deserving. Dickey (1980), in his history of welfare in Australia after European settlement, divides the period up to the twentieth century into two.

In the first period, up to 1850, responsibility, such as it was, was taken by the governors of the colonies, with some additional provision by public societies. Whichever the auspices, the assistance was minimal at best. The second period takes us to the

Depression of the 1890s, the era of *laissez-faire* capitalism. This was the heyday of the charitable societies, often under religious auspices. Subsequently there was a significant challenge to the dominant class which, among other things resulted in the establishment of the Labor Party and, after Federation, the gradual development of income security measures. It has been these latter state provisions that have become the focus of most analyses of welfare in recent years. However we do well to remember the charity ancestry of the welfare state because attitudes are still strongly affected by the past. The Treasurer's Budget speech, in justifying increases to welfare payments in terms of 'compassion for those in genuine need' (*The Age* 21 August 1985: 14) demonstrates that the legacy of the traditional notion of charity still influences state approaches to the economic problems of its citizens. As well, non-government welfare organisations remain of key importance within the total system. Even though many have changed their mode of operation quite significantly, history remains an important force. Some church organisations, such as St Vincent de Paul and the Salvation Army, have maintained direct assistance to the poor, a point which underscores the continuity with the past.

The first national income security measures to be established were the age and invalid pensions; the Act was passed in 1908. For the aged it provided for a pension to be paid to men and women at the age of 65 years, the maximum rate being 26 pounds. When finances permitted, the age limit for women was to be lowered to 60, which was in fact instituted in 1910. Permanently incapacitated persons between the age of 60 and 65 were eligible for an invalid pension paid at the same rate. The pensions were subject to means test on both income and property (Kewley 1973: 74–5).

The next major development took place after World War I, with the establishment of a range of provisions for returned servicemen. Such provisions for returned servicemen and women and their dependants have been a major feature of the Australian system. Interestingly, these are often overlooked in discussions of welfare. This seems to be another example of the way all but the least powerful are able to escape from the stigmatising definition of welfare. Those who have been officially involved in a war can apparently accept state assistance on a different basis. The fact that men are essentially the beneficiaries is also no doubt relevant (Wheeler 1985).

It was not until the 1940s that the rest of the framework of the current system was developed. Historians of this period point to the fact that this was the time at which the welfare state became 'a support system for the middle class' (Roe 1975: 146). This view echoes similar judgements made in relation to other Western industrial societies. Abel-Smith (1958) came to such a conclusion when he analysed for Britain, 'Whose welfare state?'

In 1941 child endowment, which in 1976 became family allowance, was introduced. This initially provided a flat rate of five shillings per week for each child except the first, until the age of sixteen years. It was a universal payment and not taxable (Kewley 1973: 194). It remains untaxed today. An important feature of the payment was that it was, and still is, normally paid to the mother. It thus represents a transfer directly to women, as was the maternity allowance, or baby bonus as it was sometimes called. This was established in 1912 and was paid at the birth of each child with a view to defraying the expenses associated with the birth. It too was universal (Kewley 1973: 103). When it was abolished by the Fraser government in 1978, the reason given was that 'it had been superseded by the health care and family allowance arrangements' (Ferber 1980: 333).

The next major income support to be introduced was the widows' pension, in 1942. It recognised *de jure* and *de facto* widows and covered three categories. Class A widows were those who were responsible for at least one dependent child under 16 years; Class B were those over the age of 50 but without dependent children; and Class C widows were under 50 years of age, without dependent children, eligible for a pension for 26 weeks after the death of their partner, to allow for a period of rehabilitation. Widow was defined widely to include those who were divorced, had been deserted for over 6 months and women whose husbands were in a mental hospital or, later, in prison. With only minor variations these criteria hold today.

In 1944, unemployment, sickness and special benefits were introduced, and that completed the main structure of income security until 1973, when the Supporting Mothers' Benefit was introduced. This allowed payments to single mothers, who previously were inadequately covered by the special benefit. In 1977 this benefit was extended to fathers and became the Supporting Parent Benefit.

This very schematic outline of the Australian income maintenance system provides a basis for considering the extent to which the population is reliant on it. What we find is a quite dramatic increase in those in receipt of most pensions and benefits over the last fifteen years. In 1969, 9.6 per cent of the population were in receipt of these payments or were the children of recipients. By 1983 this figure had risen to over one-quarter of the population (26.5 per cent) or over 4 million people (ABS 1984: 314).

Three factors account for the major part of this increase. Firstly the high rate of unemployment from the mid-1970s which has not only affected the take-up rate of unemployment benefit (which in 1983 was 40 times the 1969 rate) but has also had an effect on the rate for other pensions and benefits as well (cf. Stricker and Sheehan 1981, Social Welfare Policy Secretariat 1984). Secondly, the introduction of the Supporting Parent Benefit, which was being paid to 140,000 recipients in 1983. Thirdly, a relaxation of the eligibility criteria for pensions and benefits. The increase in age pensioners has been affected most by this relaxation. The rate has almost doubled in the thirteen-year period. However, this increase has been contributed to by demographic changes as well. There has been an increase in the number and proportion of elderly people in the population. Age pensioners increased from 5.8 per cent of the population in 1969 to 9 per cent in 1983 (ABS 1984: 314).

Whereas the Whitlam government progressively abolished the means test for persons over 70, the trend with the Hawke government has been to again restrict eligibility. In an effort to stem the increasing cost of expenditure on age pensions, the Labor government reintroduced an income test for pensioners over the age of 70 years and in 1984, a much-publicised assets test.

Table 16.1 shows the proportion of the population receiving the different kinds of payment and illustrates the very dramatic increase since 1969. It is noteworthy, though, that most of the changes had occurred by 1977. Table 16.2 sets out the cost of these programs as a percentage of Gross National Product. Again the

Table 16.1 Pensioners and Beneficiaries (% of Population)

At 30 June	Age Pensioners	Invalid Pensioners	Unemployment Benefit Recipients	Widows, Pensioners and Supporting Parent Beneficiaries
1969	5.8	1.0	0.1	0.6
1974	7.5	1.1	0.2	1.0
1977	8.5	1.4	1.8	1.3
1978	8.8	1.4	2.0	1.4
1979	8.9	1.5	2.1	1.5
1980	9.0	1.6	2.1	1.6
1981	9.2	1.5	2.1	1.8
1982	9.0	1.4	2.6	1.9
1983	9.0	1.4	4.2	2.0

Source: ABS, *Social Indicators* No. 4, 1984: 320

Table 16.2 Government Outlay on Social Security and Welfare

	1968–69	1972–73	1977–78	1978–79	1979–80	1980–81	1981–82
Government outlay as % of government, all purposes	13.5	15.7	21.5	21.7	21.2	20.8	21.0
Government outlay as % of Gross Domestic Product	4.3	4.9	8.5	8.3	8.0	8.0	8.2

Source: ABS, *Social Indicators* No. 4, 1984: 329

most significant changes occurred before 1977. Changes since then mostly represent a reduction in outlays. Given that the numbers reliant on the government for support continued to increase, this means that the real level of support that people were receiving has been reduced. Table 16.3, which shows pension and benefit rates as a proportion of average weekly earnings demonstrates this to have generally been the case. The reductions for the single unemployed, particularly the young, are the most striking. The 1982 rate was less than half the real value of the 1975 figure for 16 and 17-year-olds. The 1985–86 Labor Budget announced increases which go some small way toward redressing this.

The increase in social security outlays has been a matter of concern in Australia as it has been in other OECD countries. Such has been this concern that in 1981 there was an OECD Conference on *The Welfare State in Crisis* (OECD 1981). Commentators talk of a revolt of taxpayers and a backlash against welfare, all generally meaning a reluctance of the electorate to pay the levels of taxation necessary to support redistribution (Jones 1983, Lanigan 1985: 24). This view is, however premised on the belief that it is those receiving social security who are benefiting in the redistribution stakes. In turn this belief is associated with a narrow view of welfare (Cass 1983). This is a viewpoint which must be counter-balanced by a much broader perspective which takes into account other inextricably related areas of government policy, such as fiscal policy.

Table 16.3 Age, Invalid and Widows' Pensions and Unemployment Benefits

At 30 June	Age and Invalid pensions		Widows' pensions		Unemployment benefit			
	Married rate	Standard rate	Class A	Class B	Married person	Single adult(a)	Single person 18–20 years	16–17 years
	% average weekly earnings							
1969	34.4	19.3	28.2	17.2	19.6	11.4	6.5	4.8
1972	33.4	19.1	27.9	16.7	26.1	17.7	11.5	7.8
1973	35.0	20.1	28.0	20.1	35.0	20.1	20.1	20.1
1974	36.0	20.6	27.7	20.6	36.0	20.6	20.6	20.6
1975	39.1	23.4	30.6	23.4	39.1	23.4	23.4	23.4
1976	38.2	23.0	29.4	23.0	38.2	23.0	23.0	20.1
1977	39.6	23.7	29.5	23.7	39.6	23.7	23.7	18.1
1978	39.8	23.9	29.2	23.9	39.8	23.9	23.9	16.7
1979	38.3	23.0	28.0	23.0	38.3	22.2	22.2	15.6
1980	39.4	23.6	28.1	23.6	39.4	19.9	19.9	13.9
1981	37.8	22.6	28.1	22.6	37.8	18.2	18.2	12.2
1982	37.9	22.7	27.7	22.7	37.9	17.8	17.8	11.0
1983	39.5	23.7	28.3	23.7	39.5	19.8	19.8	11.5

Source: ABS, *Social Indicators* No. 4, 1984: 322

Fiscal Welfare

Taxation is a fundamental factor in fiscal policy and one which has received a great deal of public attention over recent years. The ALP has held its tax summit and subsequently instituted some reforms. The opposition parties and the better-off sections of the public have responded, largely negatively, to the changes. Nonetheless there is considerable agreement that some form of change is necessary. Governments all over the world are looking for an electorally acceptable way of increasing revenue.

In a formal sense, the taxation system embodies the notion of equity through an apparently progressive structure of rates and the principle that taxation is not levied on an income which is sufficient only to cover the basic necessities. These principles clearly have the welfare or well-being of the poorer members of society at heart, since progressive taxation means taxing according to means. The crucial question, though, is not what the formal principles are, but what constitutes the outcome of the application of these?

In recent years in Australia, there has been a shift in the proportion of tax paid of wage and salary earners, as PAYE tax, in relation to non-PAYE taxes. Between 1975 and 1982 wages and salaries increased by 98.8 per cent; the tax paid on these increased by 148.1 per cent. Over the same period, income from rent, interest, dividends and unincorporated enterprises rose more quickly, by 125.4 per cent, but the tax paid on it rose by only 73.6 per cent (Keens and Cass 1982: 19). Essentially this change in the balance was due to the wealthier sections of the population avoiding taxation through a variety of schemes that usually did fall within the broad tax guidelines, or could be made to do so with a little expert financial advice. Despite the clear change in the distribution of the burden of taxation, because the economy has been sluggish, the wealthier have been able to mount a fairly effective case against increasing their share of taxation on the grounds of the importance of incentives.

When we look at the total taxation system, we find that certain groups of people were in a far better position than others to take advantage of a range of exemptions and deductions. Ordinary wage and lower salary earners are in the least favourable position to do this. For example, business affairs could be arranged so that certain forms of expenses such as private entertainment, holiday expenses, and even the purchase of some items for the home could, legitimately, be tax-exampt or taxed at a lower rate. As well, those who can raise capital can invest this in 'tax havens', such as farms. Here, in effect, money which would have been counted as income, for tax purposes, can be translated into a capital gain, which was not taxable. The overall effect of this network of tax exemptions was an income transfer from poorer to richer. The poorer members of the society provided vast amounts of the money which sustained the social infrastructure. Those who are wealthier, who benefit from this at least as much, often more, did not pay their share.

This was very obviously the picture, then, until the Labor government introduced its taxation reforms, which were effective from September 1986. The fringe benefit tax aims to raise more revenue, largely by collecting taxes which technically should have been paid under the former scheme. It is designed particularly to cut down on the tax-free advantages of the self-employed and those on higher incomes. The capital gains tax is similarly intended. While the government seems primarily concerned with increasing revenue, its reforms, to the extent that they are effective and not nullified by new avoidance schemes, will redress some of the inequities of the situation. In effect, the better-off have been receiving very considerable amounts of 'welfare' in the form of tax not paid. It is this part of overall government policy that Titmuss referred to as the fiscal welfare system. It is seen in purely economic terms and quite separate from welfare. This way of conceptualising government policies in itself works to the advantage of the privileged. Thus, governments have welfare policies for the poor and economic policies for everyone else. Keens and Cass who have done extensive work in this area, point out that

> fiscal welfare differs from social welfare not only in terms of the group for whom it provides but also in terms of generosity, stigma, and the extent to which expenditure is made public.
>
> (Keens and Cass 1982: 33)

Until September 1986, the tax base excluded certain items, among them inheritances and bequests, gifts not connected with employment, and realised capital where an asset had been held for more than a year (except where the sale was made with the intention of making a profit). Occupational fringe benefits were technically taxable but this was rarely enforced because of the administrative difficulties involved (Keens and Cass 1982: 17). This exempted income was significantly more likely to be advantageous to the better-off, and to men rather than women. When we look to those who are not likely to be well-off we find that, since 1976, most pensions and benefits have been included in the tax base. The major reason for their inclusion was to prevent the possibility of a person gaining more from social security sources than from paid employment. Thus we find, as Keens and Cass suggest, a tax base that 'will include most of the income of those who are relatively poor but may exclude much of the income of those who are relatively rich' (1982: 18).

It is too soon to judge the effectiveness of Labor's new tax policy which includes a capital gains component and taxes a range of fringe benefits. It is clearly an attempt to broaden the tax base to include income which accrues to the wealthier members of society. The critical question remains whether it will prove possible to collect this revenue from people who have proved adroit at avoiding taxation in the past. The systemic, even institutionalised, nature of avoidance practices is well illustrated by a full page advertisement in the *National Times* which appeared shortly after the Labor government announced its introduction of a capital gains tax in September 1985. The advertisement was for a magazine, *The Investment Advisor*, and was headlined 'Beat Keating's new real estate tax law' (13–19 September 1985: 11).

An equitable tax system must be premissed on the fact that people actually do pay what they are technically obliged to, otherwise the progressivity of the structure becomes irrelevant (Mathews 1980: 92). The issues of tax evasion and tax avoidance have been recognised as problems and received considerable attention during the months preceding the 1985 tax summit. The government's Economic Planning Advisory Council issued a communiqué claiming that 'the losers in tax reform must be the evaders and avoiders, the winners must be the needy' (ACOSS 1985: 1).

While there is considerable agreement that some reform of the tax system is necessary, there is little agreement about the appropriate method for achieving this. One proposed way forward is through indirect taxation, either through sales or value added tax, because it is more difficult to avoid these (Alchin 1982, Lanigan 1985). The official government point of view, expressed in its White Paper, and put to the summit, supported a flat sales tax on all goods, though there was by no means unanimity within the Labor Party. Those connected with the trade unions and welfare were opposed to a significant increase in indirect taxes because this ignores capacity to pay and does not support redistribution (ACOSS 1985, Institute of Family Studies 1985). They were not sufficiently reassured by the government's pledge to make up to those with low incomes the disadvantages caused by the indirect tax. In the event, the Prime Minister honoured his earlier promise, that any change in indirect taxation

> must be acceptable to the various groups in the Australian community whose response will determine whether we can maintain moderation in wage movements.
>
> (Hawke 1984)

The flat sales tax was abandoned in favour of taxing fringe benefits, though this was probably less popular with traditionally non-Labor supporters. Nonetheless the nature of an indirect tax is an issue that has also caused division within the conservative parties as they prepare a taxation policy which they hope will be electorally popular.

The personal income tax structure has facets of concern to a discussion of fiscal welfare beyond the tax base. Tax deductions, rebates and the tax threshold are also relevant. Prior to 1975 there was an extensive net of allowable deductions. The Whitlam government reformed the system to try to achieve greater equity. Instead of many of the deductions, e.g. for medical expenses and superannuation, a flat rate rebate was introduced. Because more deductions are claimed the more that is spent, and these are claimed at the marginal tax rate, deductions tend to favour high income earners whereas the rebate is the same for everyone (see Keen and Cass 1982: 20–22).

Even with the September 1985 change to taxation on fringe benefits, those deductions that can still be claimed relate mainly to expenses incurred in earning one's income and retain their capacity to advantage those with higher status and more flexible jobs. They are also likely, therefore, to be more available to male workers. There are no deductions in respect of child care, yet this could well be defined as expenditure necessarily incurred in earning income. The issue of tax deductions for child care has been a contentious one, however, with a strong feminist lobby supporting the more collectivist approach of calling for government provision of child care centres, rather than the individualistic solution through tax deductions (O'Donnell 1984, Conley 1985, Brennan and O'Donnell 1986). This approach has the decided advantage that it emphasises the need for the provision of adequate services by the government.

There is one current deduction that warrants separate mention – the one for gifts to public institutions or to approved school building funds. Presumably this was instituted to facilitate the donation of money for charitable purposes. Only the better-off have substantial amounts of money to spare for such donations, but it seems particularly anomalous to have such a deduction when gifts made directly to someone who is poor do not attract tax relief. Since we know that most help people receive is from relatives, we really have a situation which amounts to one in which if the rich help the poor (via a charity) they recoup some of the gift. If the poor help each other directly, they do not qualify for such tax relief. The Australian Council of Social Service is advocating that such concessions be abolished because of the many anomalies and inequities involved (Hunter 1985).

The pattern already established in relation to other aspects of the taxation system holds also in relation to rebates. Concessional rebates which cover a range of expenses such as medical, education and superannuation, are claimed by very few with low or moderate incomes (Keens and Cass 1982: 22). Likewise the controversial dependent spouse rebate. In 1979–80 only 21 per cent of tax payers with income below average weekly earnings, received the rebate while 43 per cent of those with higher than average earnings did. They are also very much transfers to men. Forty-five per cent of taxpayers claimed the rebate, only 2 per cent of them being women taxpayers (Keens and Cass 1982: 24).

The sole parent rebate is the one measure which contributes significantly to vertical equity. In 1979–80, 24 per cent of all female taxpayers received this rebate and 1.2 per cent of male, representing 4.5 per cent of all taxpayers. More than 70 per cent had below median earnings (Keens and Cass 1982: 24).

Another facet of a progressive tax system is to relieve low income earners of the burdens of paying tax. This is achieved by setting a threshold below which no tax is paid. If the thresholds for 1981–82 are considered in relation to the Henderson poverty line, however, we find that 'all married couples with children and sole parents with two or three children incurred a tax liability on poverty level incomes' (Keens and Cass 1982: 25). The situation for all groups has deteriorated steadily since the mid-1970s, though the 1985 tax changes (effective from late 1986) offer slight relief to those on low incomes.

It is worth considering one last issue in this consideration of fiscal welfare. This is that of taxation benefits to large corporations, and hence their principal shareholders. As Lanigan, formerly Second Commissioner for Taxation in the federal department has pointed out, the opportunities for avoidance and evasion are 'inevitably greater for those whose incomes are not readily measureable and not subject to deductions at the source' (1985: 23). Takeovers by large companies are not readily controlled but have potentially costly effects for ordinary Australians and certainly seem to have no potential for redistributing income.

In commenting on the Bond takeover of the Castlemaine-Toohey brewing company, the economics editor of the Melbourne newspaper *The Age*, added his voice to the growing number of people calling for a capital gains tax and other reforms (Davidson 1985: 13). The takeover involved $1,200 million of largely foreign money, and he suggests that the costs of this will largely be borne by the Australian people, while clearly any gains will go to a few. The effects of a major financial transaction such as this are so complex that most people will not expect to understand them.

Davidson has tried to isolate some of the flow-on effects which, he believes, include:

- upward pressure on domestic interest rates when the takeover is financed from domestic savings which in turn is an income transfer from those who are purchasing a house or would like to invest in genuine wealth- and job-creating assets;
- adding to the long-term pressure on the value of the Australian dollar (which threathens everybody's living standards) when the borrowings are from overseas;
- [and] given the tax advantages to the predator, there is probably diminished managerial efficiency as businessmen become obsessed with defensive measures at the expense of medium and long-term policies designed to strengthen their business.

(*The Age* 29 August 1985: 13)

This list of costs shows that in considering fiscal welfare we must cast our net very wide. There is a tendency even among those who expand their analysis of welfare to include occupational and fiscal welfare to fail to go beyond the official statistics. While this is understandable, it confirms the very significant advantage that comes from being able to protect one's activities from scrutiny.

As Davidson predicted, after the takeover the pressure was quickly on domestic interest rates as one after another the lending institutions raised their lending rates (Garran 1985: 3).

Occupational Welfare

The final part of Titmuss' tri-partite welfare system is occupational welfare. After the lengthy discussion of fiscal welfare, the pattern is highly predictable, though again the discussion is made difficult by the relative lack of information and the unpredictable effects of the recent changes to the tax system. Occupational welfare includes those benefits that accrue to wage and salary earners over and above their pay, i.e. fringe benefits. Most of these are now taxed, including company-provided cars, free or cheap loans, expenses paid by the employer, entertainment expenses and a proportion of living away from home allowances. As with all the changes it remains to be seen whether ways will be found around these requirements.

The evidence suggests that the biggest single side benefit reaped by income earners is from superannuation. While the information on this is by no means exact, other benefits are even more difficult to enumerate. In 1980 the Social Welfare Policy Secretariat estimated the value of taxation concessions in respect of superannuation to involve billions of dollars. (Dixon and Foster 1982). Henderson (1982: 174) comments that 'it is remarkable that even senior members of the Social Welfare Policy Secretariat can get no closer to costing this one than the range $1,000m to $2,000m'. Since then the Labor government has moved to claim some taxation on lump sum superannuation payments though as Cass points out 'significant tax advantages still remain' and savings through, for example, banks, building societies and life-insurance policies 'receive much less favourable treatment'. These forms of saving are in fact much more likely to be the forms used by low income earners (Cass 1983: 24).

Nonetheless this tax will make some impression on the situation described by Stretton in 1980. He pointed out that if he as an academic contributed to a superannuation scheme in a 'rugged individualistic way', his life-time benefit from the taxation advantage which would accrue to him would amount to five times that received by an average wage earner who takes up the age pension. This, he adds would be on top of the fact that he had already had the benefit of having earned three times as much as that of the average earner during his working life (Stretton 1981: 43–40).

The Labor government is working on a proposal to make superannuation more widely available. While this will extend the numbers benefiting from provisions that are clearly superior to the age pension, particular disadvantages will be suffered by those who do not have a continuous working life. Women make up the majority of this group (Rosenman and Leeds 1984).

Jamrozik and his colleagues undertook an analysis of occupational welfare in 1981. They used data from a survey carried out in 1979 by the Australian Bureau of Statistics of employment benefits, a survey of positions vacant in daily newspapers, and previous research findings. They present information on fourteen categories of payment outside wages or salaries. These covered: holiday costs; low-interest finance; goods and services; housing, electricity etc.; telephone; transport; medical and union dues; club fees; entertainment allowances; shares etc.; study leave; and superannuation.

They found that those earning more than $300 per week on average received 3.8 times the benefits of those earning under $180. Full-time workers do much better than part-time. No benefits were received by 52.4 per cent of part-time workers, compared with 28.1 per cent of those working full-time (Jamrozik *et al.* 1981: 97). This connection with high earnings and full-time work ensures that women are severely under-represented among those who benefit from the system (Keen and Cass 1982), and this of course relates only to women who are in the labour force. If we add to this women who work in the home, the discrepancies are even greater.

Considering trends over the ten year period from 1969, the gap between high and low income earners seems to have widened. This has occurred through an increase in provisions for executive personnel but not for workers. There has been a specific increase in those benefits with capital accumulation value (Jamrzik *et al.* 1981:77). These trends are not in a direction that will improve the redistributive effect of occupational welfare.

The evidence on occupational welfare very strongly indicates that if it is to pursue policies aimed at achieving greater equality, the Labor government was right to move to tax fringe benefits. The biggest challenge is actually to collect the revenue.

Welfare and Redistribution

From this discussion of social, fiscal and occupational welfare, it becomes clear that much government assistance goes to the wealthier. However because of the biased way in which the welfare debate is formulated, no really comparative picture is available. The transfers are in various forms and are only thoroughly enumerated and aggregated in relation to social welfare. We have a poverty line but we do not have a wealth line.

The discussion here also omits many important areas. Service usage is often greater among the middle class, tertiary education being perhaps the most striking example. To gain a complete understanding of distributional effects it would be necessary to consider all transfers from government funds, both direct and indirect. We need to ask questions such as who pays for, and how much benefit do people get, from a range of services, from education, health, and roads, to yacht harbours, opera and international banking facilities. It is not possible to consider these questions here and data are not readily available. Nonetheless, even this limited analysis does to an extent redress the view of welfare expenditure as merely a transfer from the haves to the have-nots.

If an economy expands, it is possible for the standard of living of many to improve without altering people's position in relation to one another. This can be visualised as an escalator effect, with people all standing still on their own step, but with the whole staircase moving upwards (or downwards). Thus in a time of increasing living standards people may believe that greater equality has been achieved even though relative positions have been maintained.

The evidence on income distribution that has been collected in capitalist countries this century has shown this to be the typical pattern, though the trajectory is not linear: in fact in recent years there has been a move in the opposite direction. Australia has broadly followed this pattern. Between 1972–73 and 1981–82 the proportion of people living below the poverty line increased from 8.2 to 13 per cent (Cass 1985). For the United States, the increase between 1979 and 1982 was from 11.7 to 15 per cent (Henderson and Hough 1984: 8).

In an analysis of data on the distribution of income and wealth, as measured by property left at death, taxation, cash transfers and public goods, Head (1980) came to the conclusion that whatever measure is used, very little, if any, improvement to the relative position of the poorer half of the population has occurred during this century. Between 1915 and the 1970s there does appear to have been some redistribution of wealth away from the top 1 per cent of the population but this did not go to the poor; rather the main beneficiaries were the top 30 per cent (Raskall 1978, Podder 1978, Broom and Jones 1976).

When we look at social security transfers it seems that what largely happens is that these are covered by the tax

> paid by the young, the unmarried, and the employed to the elderly, the unemployed and the parents of young families. In other words, the flow of cash payments is largely a circular intra-class transfer rather than a flow from rich to poor.
>
> (Head 1980: 49)

This same phenomenon has been remarked on for Britain and other advanced capitalist societies (Giddens 1973, Gough 1979, Townsend 1979).

While cash transfer makes a modest impression on the general distribution of income between rich and poor, they still represent the 'single most significant factor in redistributing income towards the very poor' (Head 1980: 49). If we take the lowest 20 per cent of income earners, we find that in 1967–68, they received 2.9 per cent of total pre-tax income when income security payments were not taken into account. This share increased to 6.4 per cent when such payments were included. A similar pattern held for 1975–76.

For that financial year, Harding undertook a detailed analysis of federal taxation and expenditures. She discovered that despite its apparent progressivity, the tax system was 'barely progressive' and speculates that with the growth of tax avoidance and evasion, by 1984 things were likely to have become worse. Her findings support Head's in that income security payments were the only mechanism which had a significantly redistributive effect (Harding 1984: 98).

The fact that income security payments do substantially increase the share of income of the poorest sector of the population demonstrates the point that welfare does have some clear benefits for the working class. The very poor would be even poorer without government assistance even though the fundamental issue of equality is not significantly addressed by the current system (Harding 1984: 104, Wilenski 1984: 14, Mishra 1984: 171).

Evidence that government action can be effective in improving the circumstances of particular groups can be seen in a consideration of the aged over a decade. The 1972–73 figures showed 18.3 per cent of one-person income units, which include a large proportion of aged persons, falling below the 'austere' poverty line. By 1981–82, this proportion had fallen to 11 per cent (Gallagher 1985). The decrease can be attributed largely to the improved position of the aged, and this would show up more clearly but for a marked increase of the number of 15–19-year-olds adding to those below the poverty line. During the decade, the rate of pension for those without dependent children increased in real terms (from 20.1 to 22.6 of average weekly earnings; see Table 16.3). There has been a relaxation in eligibility criteria for age pensions, somewhat compensated for by making the income taxable, by improved public housing provisions and by a more comprehensive concessions system at both Commonwealth and state levels (e.g. Victorian Parliament 1984).

The situation obviously does not allow for complacency when 11 per cent of one-person income units are still officially recognised as poor. These include the aged who do not own assets – more importantly a house – as they benefit least from the concessions system (Social Welfare Policy Secretariat 1984, Setal *et al.* 1985, Victorian Parliament 1984).

The concept of a poverty line has proved useful for monitoring the economic situation of various groups in the society. It is one developed in Australia by Henderson and his team in the late 1960s, in their work in Melbourne (Henderson *et al.* 1970). It was further refined during the federal Inquiry into Poverty which commenced in 1973 (Henderson 1975). From this Inquiry the concept was taken into fairly general currency.

Essentially the poverty line is a device for establishing a level of income below which people must be considered in very real need. The level at which the line was set was deemed 'austere', so that it 'cannot seriously be argued that those who fall below this "austere" line, who we describe as "very poor" are not so' (Henderson 1975: 13). It is based on the notion of an income unit consisting of a family or a single person. The calculations allow for the number of

Table 16.4 Poverty in Income Units by Sex of Head 1972–73 and 1981–82 (using detailed Henderson Equivalence Scale)
(N = 1,000)

Income unit type	1972–73 (excludes self-employed)			1981–82 (includes self-employed)		
	Below poverty line	Population	% in poverty	Below poverty line	Population	% in poverty
One person						
Male	59.0	535.0	11	173.1	1,526.3	11
Female	71.0	725.0	23.6	157.4	1,435.9	11
Total	230.10	1,260.0	18.3	330.5	2,962.2	11
Sole parent						
Male-headed	4.5	28.0	16.0	7.1	37.6	19
Female-headed	49.5	132.0	37.5	119.2	237.6	50
Total	54.0	160.0	33.8	126.3	275.2	46
Married couple						
No children	14.0	736.0	1.9	72.8	1,439.3	5
1 child	26.7	921.0	2.9	46.0	594.4	8
2 children	26.7	921.0	2.9	82.3	822.8	10
3 or more children	30.7	423.0	7.2	103.7	538.7	19
Total	71.4	2,080.0	3.4	304.8	3,395.3	9
All adult income units	399.4	3,916.0	10.2	761.5	6,632.8	11
All persons	781.2	9,527.0	8.2	1,905.7	14,536.8	13
All children	254.6	3,182.5	8.0	839.3	4,508.8	19

Commission of Inquiry Into Poverty, *First Main Report* (1975); Gallagher, P. *Work in Progress in Australia* (1985) (*Source*: Cass 1985)

people included and take into account some imputed facets of economic need; for example, work and accommodation status and in the detailed version, sex. It incorporates the notion that the income available to the income unit is shared, an assumption which has been challenged in recent years as evidence of poverty among women has become available.

While there are significant problems to be recognised with the poverty line concept itself (Bryson 1977, Tulloch, 1980, Social Welfare Policy Secretariat 1981, Saunders 1980), it has proved to be of great value in keeping the issue of poverty on the agenda and in providing a means for monitoring change. It is largely through this device that we are now in a position to see that the situation of the aged has improved since the early 1970s. Of course, poverty line analysis also shows that among other groups, particularly the unemployed and families with dependent children, the rates in poverty have dramatically increased (see Table 16.4). Nonetheless, the fact that an improvement in the situation of the aged can be demonstrated shows that a concerted effort by governments can make a difference. Welfare does have tangible benefits at least for groups singled out for attention.

Women as a group have also made fairly clear gains from welfare measures, though because they started so far behind there is a very long way still to go. Income maintenance provisions have provided an alternative source of livelihood to the necessity of being dependent on male partners or relatives. Despite the obvious gains, however, the situation is by no means unambiguous, and a consideration of the way in which women have fared reinforces and general proposition that welfare must be simultaneously recognised as a benefit and a restriction. As Wilson observed, 'social welfare policies amount to no less than the State organisation of domestic life' (1977: 9).

A range of welfare provisions reinforce traditional role divisions between men and women at the same time as they provide needed support. The notion of the family wage which was established in the Harvester Judgment of 1907 can be seen as one of the most fundamental of all Australian welfare state provisions. In this, the state gave recognition to the rights of men to bread-winner status and to a wage which allowed the maintenance of a wife and children. Women, whose bread-winning status was not recognised, had an official wage level established at roughly half of the male rate. This provision was not finally overtaken until 1974 when the minimum wage was extended to women and the family component was removed from wage considerations (Cass 1981: 46). However, despite formal equality of wage rates, the legacy of this wage discrimination lingers, and in December 1984 women's full-time ordinary earnings rate was still only 82 per cent of that for men (Women's Bureau 1985).

Taxation policy, which allows men a rebate for a dependent wife, is another example of the way in which income policy reinforces women's dependent status. Technically the rebate is for a spouse but the number claimed in respect of husbands is small. Such a rebate provides additional resources but there is no guarantee that people who receive the allowance make it available to their family. Pensions and benefits likewise provide for dependent spouses, usually women. The way benefits favour men and the traditional family type is illustrated by the differing rates for the sole parent rebate, which is usually claimed by women ($780), and the dependent spouse rebate, which is almost always claimed by men ($830, or $1,030 with children).

Dependent status is reinforced for women by the widow's pension, which is a strictly female entitlement, based on the notion that if a woman has no man on whom to depend, the state will step into the role (Bryson 1983). Family allowance has the symbolic and practical importance that the payment is made directly to women. Nonetheless, this is paid in respect of the traditional mother role, and the evidence clearly suggests that it is this that keeps women poor. Full-time, full-year employment is the most certain way of keeping people out of the poverty statistics (Cass 1985). While women are cast primarily in the role of mother, they will maintain their secondary status in the labour market. Thus they are likely to be much more susceptible to poverty. What is really needed to overcome this is for child care to be recognised as an equal responsibility of fathers, and one for which the society provides necessary supports.

The most recent of the social security measures, the Supporting Parent Benefit, is also paid in respect of a parenting role, though it has also established the rights of single women. In 1977, eligibility was extended to fathers though their take-up rate is quite low. In 1983, just under 11 per cent of male single parents were in receipt of a benefit, whereas almost 84 per cent of female single parents were (ABS 1984: 45, 302). Nonetheless, this does establish the legitimacy of the parenting role for fathers and the important principle that this is not merely a 'natural' role for women. Another area in which welfare tends to reinforce traditional gender divisions is in the welfare workforce, both paid and unpaid. Women take on direct caring roles e.g. foster parent, social worker, while men are more likely to be in management positions (Mowbray and Bryson 1984, Finch 1983).

To summarise, while welfare measures are of considerable benefit to those who are most economically vulnerable, the amount that is redirected to the poor is grossly inadequate. The Labor government has still not achieved its modest promise of the 1970s, which remains current, of bringing pension rates up to 25 per cent of average weekly earnings. On top of this, the amount of redistribution which does occur does not make any impression on the relative positions of people in the socio-economic hierarchy, and thus on the issue of equality. Welfare measures also tend to reinforce gender discrimination. In these senses, fiscal and occupational welfare in fact make a negative or reverse contribution to the achievement of greater economic and gender equality.

Welfare and the State

The welfare system cannot be understood in isolation. It must be seen as but one part of the total system, one form of state intervention. Theorists of the state have emphasised the way in which welfare functions to support the capitalist system. Here they are generally referring to social welfare, though the case holds even more obviously for fiscal and occupational welfare. While the details of the various theoretical positions vary considerably, the categorisation of functions adopted by O'Connor in his much-quoted book *The Fiscal Crisis of the State* (1973) provides a dual categorisation which is adequate for our purposes. The two functions he specifies are capital accumulation and legitimation. Three simplified examples of the capital accumulation function can be identified in the education system, providing training and thus relieving employers of the need to do so, or at least reducing the amount necessary; family allowance, which mean that wages can be lower than they otherwise might need to be; and the health system which keeps people fit enough to work to produce profits for their employers.

In analysing the way social welfare serves to legitimate the capitalist system, theorists point to the support of dependent persons and the relief of abject poverty as necessary to reduce the likelihood of political action by the working class to overthrow the state. It is the ransom that property pays for the security it enjoys. The way the term welfare tends to imply something for nothing, a gift, itself feeds into the legitimation process. The poor are seen as receiving benefits from the society; the benefits the rich receive are cast as their own hard-won advantages (Higgins 1982). These attitudes have been very much in evidence in the debate about capital gains.

To consider the functions welfare performs for the capitalist class is, however, to consider only part of the picture. The problem of any functional analysis is that it implies automatic rather than problematic situations and outcomes. The other side of welfare measures – at least most of them – is that they do serve the interests of the working class. Indeed, they are largely the result of working class action (Gough 1979: 58–62).

As has been demonstrated, when we consider specific measures, it becomes clear that they are very often simultaneously good and bad from the point of view of achieving a real measure of equality. Clearly, it is better to have a pension if one is unemployed through age, illness, lack of work etc. than to starve or rely on charity. Also, the fact that certain measures have been achieved provides its own impetus for change. This creates a pressure for the extension of such provisions (George and Wilding 1976: 84). Commentators such as O'Connor (1973) see this dynamic as an integral part of the present capitalist state and see the 'fiscal crisis' as a result of an imbalance between the demands for social services, and the capacity of the economy to support these, without encroaching on the interests of the dominant group. As Mishra puts it 'both the practice and the rationale of the welfare state is in jeopardy' (1984: xiii).

As has also been demonstrated, welfare transfers do, to an extent, increase the share of income accruing to the poorest. What welfare does not, and cannot, achieve is equality, yet part of its legitimation value is that is holds out hope of doing so. Essentially, all three welfare systems entrench the wage labour system as the key to a secure existence, and this inevitably involves inequality. In fact, the structure of capitalism is such that exploitation, and thus fundamental inequality, takes place automatically within the labour process as owners extract surplus value from their employees as their profit. Surplus value is that amount of value (normally translated into money terms) that is brought into a business by each worker, over the above the amount they are paid in wages or other benefits which accrue to them for their labour. This additional amount that the worker has provided is retained by owners as their profit.

The social welfare system largely makes transfers to people who deviate from the norm of being employed in a system which depends on the maintenance of profit. Wilenski makes this point in his analysis of the dilemmas facing social democrats:

> Redistribution through the welfare state can thus never totally offset this original transfer through profits to the owners of capital, since this would destroy the rationale of the capitalist system and halt investment.

> (1984: 14)

He expands on this by asserting that 'business in fact occupies a special position in relation to government' and that its 'co-operation is vital to the maintenance of the activities of the state' (1984: 15). This co-operation has proved only to be forthcoming in Australia when business has believed the government did not have the intention of seeking a revolutionary change in the form of ownership. Because capitalism is an international system, withdrawal to other countries is entirely feasible. Miliband alluded to this same process by suggesting that the operation of the capitalist economy has 'its own rationality to which any government must sooner or later submit, and usually sooner' (1973: 72).

Thus we have embedded in the notion of welfare an insoluble dilemma. Watts, in an analysis of the foundation of Australia's welfare state in the 1940s, demonstrates, using Chifley's words, how Labor's definition of social security was developed within the context of its commitment to 'full employment within a working reconstructed, efficient capitalism' (Watts 1982: 228). Thus, 'at the very moment that the Australian welfare state emerged it was relegated to a residual role' (1982: 228). That original income security structure still forms the basis of the Australian system.

Conclusion

Because of the bias involved in considering only social welfare when analysing transfers within the welfare state, perhaps the term should be dropped altogether. If this were done, perhaps it would be more difficult to ignore fiscal and occupational welfare and other state processes. This is important because the masking of the effects of other forms of transfer is detrimental to the interests of those who are most discriminated against by the current system. Whereas the term welfare state implies that the poor are the major beneficiaries, the evidence suggests that this is only marginally so.

As well, it can be suggested that we have entered a post-welfare state era. The term welfare state emphasises welfare as a separate and salient activity of the contemporary state. Yet more and more the state has expanded its intervention into a wide range of areas of people's lives. O'Malley, in a recent (1983) publication outlines the way in which the legal system has moved away from its moral stance, largely to a system of administrative regulation. Such a system blurs divisions between private and public, between state and non-state and between the various functions of the state. This is achieved through co-operative processes involving groups whose interests would previously have been seen as opposed: capital and labour. This type of state system has been termed corporatism. It 'involves an interventionist state which plays the mediating role in a tripartite alliance with capital and organised labour' (O'Malley 1983: 171). The development of this system in Australia has been highly visible since the Labor government's election in 1982, in such events as economic and tax summits; it is formalised in the Prices and Incomes Accord between the trade union movement and the government. Welfare issues have been largely incorporated into the general package in the form of a social wage, albeit as a minor issue.

Recent theorists of the capitalist state have discussed this development towards a corporate state (Jessop 1982, Mishra 1984), while earlier writers identified its essentially interventionist nature (Poulantzas 1968, Holloway and Picciotto 1977). In his analysis of corporatism, Mishra focuses specifically on welfare, and proposes the term, the integrated welfare state (1984: 103) for the system he sees as best exemplified in Austria and Sweden. He outlines the distinction between the new form and the old 'differentiated welfare state', thus:

> the differentiated welfare state refers to the notion of a set of institutions and policies added on to the economy and polity, but seen as a relatively self-contained, delimited area set apart from them. The integrated welfare state suggests that social welfare programs and policies are seen in relation to the economy and polity and an attempt made to integrate social welfare into the large society.
>
> (1984: 103)

While recognising that the integrated welfare state cannot overcome the basic inequality on which the capitalist system is based, Mishra does see this emerging state form as offering the most attractive possibilities for dealing with some equity issues and for negotiating the fiscal problems which capitalist societies are facing.

Australia has very clearly been heading in the directions outlined by Mishra, though by the standards of European states such as Austria and Sweden, corporatism is embryonic. It might partly be dismantled by a change of government and a more significant swing to the Right. Nonetheless it is critical to recognise that new alliances have been formed and new social forces activated. The Hawke Labor government has eschewed traditional Labor approaches in favour of this tri-partite co-operation. The union movement has accepted wage restraint in exchange for promises of an improvement in the economy, and some concessions such as a new taxation policy.

While it is too soon to judge the outcome of the Accord, careful monitoring is crucial. Unless current attempts to make the tax system more equitable by extracting more taxes from the wealthy, are successful, it seems likely that the unions have bought a bad bargain. Wage restraint, which the unions have agreed to, together with unemployment, alone may virtually subsidise any economic recovery. The implications of a corporate approach are fundamental. If there is a three-way alliance between state, business and unions it must be clear exactly who is benefiting and who is paying. The myopic effect of a narrow approach to welfare can only be detrimental to gaining this clear understanding of who is benefiting from the Australian 'welfare' state.

References

Abel-Smith, Brian (1958) 'Whose Welfare State?' in Norman MacKenzie (ed.) *Conviction*. London: MacGibbon & Kee.

Alchin, T. (1982) 'Indirect Taxes in Australia: the Need for Reform and Expansion', *The Australian Quarterly* 54 (3): 294–304.

Australian Council of Social Service (ACOSS) (1985) 'Editorial', *Australian Social Welfare Impact* 15 (3).

Australian Bureau of Statistics (ABS) (1984) *Social Indicators, Australia, No. 4*. Canberra: Catalogue No. 4101.0.

Baldock, C. (1983) 'Public Policies and the Paid Work of Women' in C. Baldock and B. Cass (eds) *Women, Social Welfare and the State*. Sydney: Allen & Unwin.

Brennan, D. and O'Donnell, C. (1986) *Caring for Australia's Children*. Sydney: Allen & Unwin.

Broom, L. and Jones, F.L. (1976) *Opportunity and Attainment in Australia*. Canberra: ANU Press.

Bryson, L. (1977) 'Poverty', *Current Affairs Bulletin* 54 (5).

———(1983) 'Women as Welfare Recipients' in C. Baldock and B. Cass (eds) *Women, Social Welfare and the State*. Sydney: Allen & Unwin.

Cass, B. (1981) 'Wages, Women and Children' in R.F. Henderson (ed.) *The Welfare Stakes*. Melbourne: Institute of Applied Economic and Social Research.

Cass, B. (1983) 'Divisions of Welfare in the Recession: The Political Limits to Redistribution, Revisited' in J. Jarrah (ed.) *53rd ANZAAS Congress: SWRC Papers*. University of New South Wales: Social Welfare Research Centre.

———(1985) 'Poverty in the 1980s: Causes, Effects and Policy Options', Paper presented to ANZAAS Congress, Monash University, August.

Conley, M. (1985) 'Tax Deductions for Child-care Could Force Some Women out of the Workforce', *Australian Social Welfare Impact* 15 (3): 7.

Davidson, K. (1985) 'How the Tax-payer Funds Takeovers', *The Age* 29 August: 13.

Dickey, B, (1980) *No Charity There*. Melbourne: Nelson.

Dixon, D, and Foster, C. (1982) 'Alternative Strategies to Meet the Needs of the Aged'. Canberra: Social Welfare Policy Secretariat.

Ferber, H. (1980) 'Diary of Legislative and Administrative Changes, 1975 to 1978' in R.B. Scotton and H. Ferber (eds). *Public Expenditure and Social Policy in Australia*, Vol. II, The First Fraser Years 1976–78. Melbourne: Longman Cheshire.

Gallagher, P. (1985) 'Work in Progress on Poverty in Australia, 1981–82', Paper presented to NSWCOSS Seminar, Sydney, 25 June.

Garran, R. (1985) 'Housing Rates 13 pc and Rising', *The Age* 3 September 1985: 3.

George, V. and Wilding, P. (1976) *Ideology and Social Welfare*. London: Routledge & Kegan Paul.

Giddens, A. (1973) *The Class Structure of Advanced Societies*. London: Hutchinson.

Gough, I. (1979) *The Political Economy of the Welfare State*. London: Macmillan.

Harding, A. (1984) *Who Benefits?: The Australian Welfare State and Redistribution*, Report No. 45. Sydney: Social Welfare Research Centre.

Hawke, R.J. (1984) 'Government Taxation Policy Statement', Media Release, 31 October.

Head, B. (1980) 'Inequality, Welfare and the State: Distribution and Redistribution in Australia', *The Australian and New Zealand Journal of Sociology* 16 (3): 44–51.

Henderson, R., Harcourt, A. and Harper, R.J.A. (1970) *People in Poverty: A Melbourne Survey*. Melbourne: Cheshire.

———(1975) *Poverty in Australia*, Commission of Inquiry into Poverty, First Main Report, April. Canberra: AGPS.

———(1982) 'Welfare and Taxes: Issues in the Financing of Welfare – a Comment', *The Australian Quarterly* 54 (2): 173–75.

———and Hough, D. (1984) 'Sydney's Poor Get Squeezed', *Australian Society* 3 (5): 6–8.

Higgins, W. (1982) 'To Him That Hath ... The Welfare State', in R. Kennedy (ed.) *Australian Welfare History: Critical Essays*. Melbourne: Macmillan.

Hindricks, K., Offe, C. and Wiesenthal, H. (1984–85) 'The Crisis of the Welfare State and Alternative Modes of Work Distribution', *Thesis Eleven* 10/11: 37–55.

Holloway, J. and Picciotto, S. (1977) 'Capital, Crisis and the State', *Capital and Class* 2.

Hunter, M. (1985) 'Tax Deductibility and the Tax Summit', *Australian Social Welfare Impact* 15 (3): 2.

Institute of Family Studies (1985) *Changing the Australian Taxation System*. Melbourne: IFS.

Jamrozik, A., Hoey, M. and Leeds, M. (1981) *Employment Benefits: Private or Public Welfare?* University of New South Wales, Social Welfare Research Centre.

Jessop, Bob (1982) *The Capitalist State*. Oxford: Martin Robinson.

Jones, M.A. (1983). *The Australian Welfare State*. Sydney: Allen & Unwin.

Keens, C. and Cass, B. (1982) *Fiscal Welfare: Some Aspects of Australian Tax Policy. Class and Gender Considerations*, Report No. 24. Sydney: Social Welfare Research Centre.

Kewley, T.H.)1973) *Social Security in Australia 1900–72*. Sydney: Sydney University Press.

Lanigan, P. (1985) 'Implementation of Tax Reform', *Australian Social Welfare Impact* 15 (3): 23–26.

Lawrence, G. (1985) 'The Answer Doesn't Lie in the Soil', *Australian Society* 4 (8): 18–20.

Mathews, R. (1980) 'The Structure of Taxation' in J. Wilkes (ed.) *The Politics of Taxation*. London: Hodder & Stoughton.

Miliband, R. (1973) *The State in Capitalist Society*. London: Quartet.

Mishra, R. (1984) *The Welfare State in Crisis*. Brighton: Wheatsheaf.

Mowbray, M. and Bryson, L. (1984) 'Women Really Care', *Australian Journal of Social Issues* 19 (4): 261–73.

O'Connor, J. (1973) *The Fiscal Crisis of the State*. London: St James Press.

O'Donnell, C. (1984) 'Industrial Issues for Working Parents', *Australian Left Review* 88, Winter: 12–21.

OECD (1981). *The Welfare State in Crisis*. Paris: OECD.

O'Malley, P. (1983) *Law, Capitalism and Democracy*. Sydney: Allen & Unwin.

Podder, N. (1978) *The Economic Circumstances of the Poor*, Commisson of Inquiry into Poverty, Research Reports, Consumer and Clients Series. Canberra: AGPS.

Poulantzas, N. (1968) *Political Power and Social Classes*. London: New Left Books.

Raskall, P. (1978) 'Who's Got What in Australia', *Journal of Australian Political Economy* 2: 3–16.

Roe, J. (1975) 'Social Policy and the Permanent Poor' in E.L. Wheelwright and K. Buckley (eds) *Essays in the Political Economy of Australian Capitalism*. Sydney: ANZ Book Co.

Rosenman, L. and Leeds, M. (1984) *Women and the Australian Retirement Age Income System*. University of New South Wales: Social Welfare Research Centre.

Saunders, P. (ed.) (1980) *The Poverty Line: Methodology and Measurement*. University of New South Wales: Social Research Centre.

————(1982) *Equity and the Impact on Families of the Australian Tax-Transfer System*. Melbourne: Institute of Family Studies.

Segal, L., Brous, D. and Teasdale, M. (1985) 'Government Assistance with Household Costs', Paper presented to Conference on Community Welfare Services in the Australian States, Melbourne, 16 August.

Shaver, S. (1983) 'Sex and Money in the Welfare State' in C. Baldock and B. Cass (eds) *Women, Welfare and the State*. Sydney: Allen & Unwin.

Social Welfare Policy Secretariat (1981a) *Report on Poverty Measurement*. Canberra: AGPS.

————(1981b) *Commonwealth Spending on Income Support Between 1968–69 and 1978–79 and Why it Increased*. Canberra: May.

————(1984) *Pensioner Fringe Benefits*. Canberra, June.

Stretton, H. (1981) 'Commentary' in R.F. Henderson (ed.) *The Welfare*

Stakes. University of Melbourne: Institute of Applied Economic and Social Research.

Stricker, P. and Sheehan, P. (1981) *Hidden Unemployment: The Australian Experience.* University of Melbourne: Institute of Applied Economic and Social Research.

Titmuss, R.M. (1958) 'The Social Division of Welfare: Some Reflections on the Search for Equity' in *Essays on the Welfare State.* London: Allen & Unwin.

Townsend, P. (1979) *Poverty in the United Kingdom.* Harmondsworth: Penguin.

Tulloch, P. (1980) 'The Poverty Line: Problems in Theory and Application' in P. Saunders (ed.) *The Poverty Line: Methodology and Measurement.* University of New South Wales: Social Welfare Research Centre.

Victorian Parliament, Minsterial Committee (1984) *State Government Concessions in Victoria.* Melbourne: Department of Community Welfare Services, October.

Watts, R. (1982) 'The Origins of the Australian Welfare State' in R. Kennedy (ed.) *Australian Welfare History: Critical Essays.* Melbourne: Macmillan.

Wheeler, L. (1985) 'Be in it Mate: War, Women and Welfare', PhD Thesis, University of New South Wales.

Wilenski, P. (1984) 'Dilemmas for Social Democrats', *Australian Society* 3 (1): 12–18.

Wilson, E. (1977) *Women and the Welfare State.* London: Tavistock.

Women's Bureau, DEIR (1985) *Women at Work.* Canberra: Department of Employment and Industrial Relations, January.

Chapter Seventeen

Is Australian Urbanisation Different?

Patrick Mullins

What is written on Australian urbanisation is really not about *Australian* urbanisation at all. Rather, it is about 'Western urbanisation', the urbanisation process supposedly common to all Western countries. An implicit assumption has been made within both urban sociology and urban studies generally, that the urbanisation of individual Western nations follow the same course, and the concept 'Western (or capitalist) urbanisation' is used to summarise this common process. Research findings on individual nations like Australia are of interest only if they contribute to the clarification and elaboration of this concept, with data being thrown into that large cauldron of knowledge out of which the concept was initially moulded and out of which it is now continually remodelled. If research findings ever show a country's urbanisation to deviate in either a minor or a major way from 'Western urbanisation', they are considered so idiosyncratic as to be unimportant or are ignored.

This chapter argues that Australian urbanisation is different in detail from 'Western urbanisation'. While having similarities with Western urbanisation, since like other Western countries Australia is a capitalist nation, Australian urbanisation has striking differences. This is because Australian capitalism is different, particularly when compared with that of historically powerful Western countries such as the United Kingdom and the United States. An urgent need now exists for a number of new concepts and theories which identify and explain different forms of urbanisation in different groups of Western countries, and which specifically explain Australian urbanisation.

Before elaborating this argument, we will consider the concepts, theories and methods used. The central concepts, 'urbanisation'

and 'Western urbanisation', along with their theoretical components, will first be defined, since they provide the foundation
from which the argument is constructed. Discussion will then
focus on the comparative method, since comparative urbanisation
is the tool used. It is the only one available for showing the extent
to which Australian urbanisation is similar to, or different from,
'Western urbanisation', and similar to or different from, the
urbanisation of any other country.

Urbanisation

Sociologists tend to define urbanisation in demographic rather
than sociological terms. Like other social scientists, they see
urbanisation simply as 'the proportion of the total population
concentrated in urban settlements, or else to a rise in this
proportion' (Davis 1974: 162). While having descriptive value, this
definition is inadequate because it fails to pinpoint the social
meaning of urbanisation. We must therefore add a sociological
definition, and in this context we can say that *urbanisation is the
spatial patterning of that mode of production called capitalism*. This
of course needs to be elaborated and we need to know specifically
what is meant by 'spatial patterning', 'mode of production', and
'capitalism'. We also need to understand that sociologists are – or
should be – primarily interested in the way urbanisation emerged
and in the way it changes. To do this they need to focus on those
social forces which brought urbanisation and which now constantly reshape it. These forces emerge from relations between
social classes, from actions by the state, by household and residential organisations and by social movements (see Castells 1977, 1983;
Elliott and McCrone 1982; Gregory and Urry 1985; Harvey 1985a,
1985b; Massey 1984). Although a distinctive form of capitalism
brought about Australia's different type of urbanisation, Australian capitalism was and is distinctive because historically these
four social forces have taken a somewhat different form and
it is this which brought about Australia's different brand of
urbanisation.

Now we will elaborate the sociological definition of
urbanisation.

Spatial patterning is the physical manifestation of people's use
of nature, for in exploiting nature to ensure their survival, people
constantly shape and reshape the physical environment. Each
mode of production – capitalist, feudal, socialist, etc. – exploits
nature differently and so each produces a different landscape, a

different spatial patterning. Urbanisation, as capitalism's spatial form, is characterised by the concentration of life in a limited geographic area, into particular regions of a country, and into metropolitan areas, other cities and towns, with most cities and towns being located in major regions. But, more strikingly, urbanisation represents the construction of a very large and very complex built environment – of factories, houses, etc.

Cities and towns did, of course, exist in past modes of production, but they were relatively insignificant. While present under feudalism, for example, it was 'community' (small, close-knit, localised social organisations), not urbanisation, which was feudalism's spatial form (see Mullins 1987). There are also cities and towns under socialism, yet this spatial patterning is dispersed in comparison with capitalism's. Socialist governments have also encouraged 'de-urbanisation', with people and activities being relocated out of cities into smaller centres, into the countryside and into underpopulated regions (see Bater 1980, Thrift and Forbes 1985, Murray and Szelenyi 1984, Szelenyi 1983).

A *mode of production* represents the way people organise themselves to ensure their physical survival. All modes of production have the same fundamental structure, and a distinction can be made between 'forces of production', which refer to the way people actually go about transforming the physical environment into useful items using tools, processes, etc. and 'social relations of production', which refer to relationships between people in terms of who actually does the work, who owns the means of production (land, tools, etc.), who (if anyone) directs the work, and who gets the surpluses if any are produced (see Edel 1981).

Capitalism is a mode of production based on the private ownership and control of the means of production, on producing goods for exchange rather than for subsistence, and on the pursuit of profit. It dominates the world today and encapsulates all societies, including socialist ones, into a world system (see Wallerstein 1974). Remnants of past modes of production, however, do co-exist with capitalism (and with socialism). A feudal remnant, for example, is evident in Britain today, because elements of the aristocracy (feudalism's dominant class) are present and are represented particularly by the monarchy. Since the British monarch is the Queen of Australia this feudal remnant is also present here.

Capitalism is distinguished by a marked segmentation of life. Work, home, politics, etc. are separate social spheres. In pre-capitalist societies, in contrast, life was integrated, even tightly integrated, as under feudalism. Capitalism's segmentation is readily apparent when we focus on the social forces effecting urbanisation (see Katznelson 1981). Three of them represent the most important elements of capitalist social structure – social class relates to work, the state to politics, and household and residential organisation to home. The fourth, social movements, relate to and emerge from, these and other parts of the social structure such as leisure and religion. Of course, segmentation is never total because links exist between the parts, but the degree of association varies according to different circumstances.

Now let us consider the four social forces effecting urbanisation.

Social classes exist from relationships between people over production. Under capitalism, there is one very small collection of people – one social class – which owns and controls the means of production and dominates work. This is the capitalist class or the bourgeoisie, and in controlling economic life, it controls life generally, because economic activity is central to survival. The other class is that very large collection of people who actually do the work. This is the working class (or the proletariat), a class that neither owns/controls the means of production, nor controls its own work. All it has is its work skills to sell in exchange for a wage. Exploitation is fundamental to this relationship and exists because the working class receives – in the form of a wage – only part of the total value of its work. The remaining value ('surplus value') is taken by capitalists, and after costs are deducted, captial is accumulated. Such an inequitable situation becomes the basis of class conflict. In reality, however, class structure is far more complex and these complexities are discussed fully in Chapter 3 and in Wright (1985) and Black and Myles (1986). Of all the social forces, class relationships have the most profound influence on urbanisation because they are involved in fundamental processes of survival, and are evident from actions taken by capitalists in their efforts to accumulate capital, and from the constant conflict between classes over how the wealth produced is distributed (see particularly Harvey 1985a, 1985b).

Under capitalism, *the state* is the institution of political power and is strongly influenced by the most powerful sections of society, particularity the dominant class (see for example, Alford and Friedland 1985, Clark and Dear 1984). It represents that totality of actions by government, specifically by the legislative, executive, and administrative branches, but it is also the coercive force through the judiciary, the police and the armed services. Geographically, it can operate at the local, regional (e.g. state) and national levels. It is through urban and regional planning that the state particularly influences urbanisation, with urban planning being state action to control urban change, while regional planning is state action to control regional change.

Household and residential organisation exists because of the work done – overwhelmingly by women – to reproduce workers, and involves maintaining the current workforce (e.g. with food, leisure, etc.) and maintaining and socialising children as the future workforce. It is also formed from the way people try to establish an independent life free from the oppression of class relations, from reproduction demands, and from state power. Clearly, such organisations are urban-based and thus have a profound impact upon urbanisation. Yet 'household and residential organisation' is not a concept used in sociology but is adopted here because no adequate concept is available. Sociologists have tried clumsily to adapt 'community', but as argued elsewhere (Mullins 1987), this is the spatial patterning of feudalism – and of certain other pre-capitalist societies – and so has no contemporary meaning.

A *social movement* is a shared consciousness about a certain issue, such as the environment, and is not formally organised in the way a school or a business, for example, is structured. But to be effective – to become a social force – it must have a formal organisation (e.g. a protest group) to direct its actions and to organise the means by which goals are achieved. The most significant movements associated with urbanisation are urban ones. These are primarily actions over issues of household and residential life, such as housing. There are also regional movements, such as the Scottish and Welsh secessionist movements.

Armed with these concepts we can now turn to defining 'Western urbanisation' and this will allow us to judge the distinctiveness or otherwise of Australian urbanisation. Logically, since Australia is a Western nation, its urbanisation should parallel what is described.

Western Urbanisation

Western urbanisation is the spatial patterning of Western societies, those first capitalist nations of Europe, North America and Oceania, and was established essentially as part of industrial capitalism. Mercantile urbanisation did precede this industrial urbanisation, but it was small-scale and had limited impact because pre-capitalist modes of production still dominated. Industrial urbanisation was itself superseded by corporate urbanisation, the urbanisation of the mid- to late-twentieth century, and this is now being superseded by a new, emerging form.

The transition from a mercantile to an industrial to a corporate and now to a new urbanisation, clearly shows how urbanisation is a *process*. But it is not evolutionary – rather a random development resulting from the combined impact of various social forces. Also, there is no clear-cut division between the stages of urbanisation, since each one overlaps the previous one, often by several decades. To understand Western urbanisation, then, we must examine this process, and particularly study the social forces involved.

Mercantile urbanisation is the spatial patterning of mercantile capitalism, a form based on importing and exporting. It co-existed in Europe for some time with pre-capitalist modes of production, notably feudalism. From the Middle Ages until the emergence of industrial urbanisation around 1840, a number of cities and towns grew from the marketing of imported goods. Merchant capitalists, during forays into the hinterland or overseas, bought the surpluses produced by peasants and others cheaply, and these were sold for high prices. Merchants thus accumulated capital and this was used to expand mercantile activites, used in urban land speculation, and in luxury consumption (see Gordon 1978, Watkins and Perry 1977).

Mercantile centres were clearly transportation nodes, particularly river or sea ports. They were collection sites for commodities brought from outside, and distribution centres for goods shipped elsewhere. They contained warehouses, banking, accounting and professional services, etc., and the accumulated wealth located there attracted artisans who produced luxury items for merchants and for those in power. Some merchantile cities, such as London, were also political centres. Power here and in other cities and towns rested on an uneasy alliance between the dominant but weakening authority of the pre-capitalist ruling class, and on merchants themselves who accrued power from economic exploits (see Hechter and Brustein 1980, Holton 1986).

Mercantile capitalists – unlike later ones – rarely intervened in the production process because commodities were not produced by people whose labour they hired. The goods were surplus commodities bought from producers living and working under pre-capitalist modes of production. Thus the mercantile working class was very small and was employed largely in transportation (e.g. ships, wharves) and in warehousing, etc. Capitalist class relations, then, were only partly formed, and not until industrial capitalism were they fully developed.

Spatially, mercantile cities and towns grew around wharves. Warehouses, businesses, professional activities, the owner-occupied dwellings of merchants, artisans and professionals, and other activities, were concentrated in a non-segregated way around wharves. Some employees lived with their merchant, artisan, or professional employers and this led to distinctive household and residential organisation. Here work and home overlapped, with employers being able to control employees not only at work, but at home as well (see Pahl 1984). On the outskirts lived casual seamen and other itinerants in shanties or boarding houses, and their household and residential life was unstable.

Thus, merchant capitalists, in their efforts to accumulate capital, were largely responsible for mercantile urbanisation, although the patronage and military protection given them by the (mainly) pre-capitalist state were also important. Self-employed artisans and the very small mercantile working class had relatively little influence, although towards the end of the period they were involved in a large number of social movements, ranging from revolutions to popular protests over food shortages, protests over urban inequalities, and actions taken to counter effects wrought by the dissolution of pre-capitalist societies (see Calhoun 1982, Gordon 1978, Tilly 1979). There were also movements involving mechants, such as the Boston Tea Party, which focused on restrictive trade practices.

Industrial urbanisation, the urbanisation of industrial capitalism, existed roughly from 1840 to 1940, and emerged when capitalists began hiring large numbers of workers to use machinery to produce goods. Instead of accumulating capital from selling commodities acquired cheaply through trade, capital was now accumulated directly from people hired to do the work.

The first factories were located in rural areas adjacent to sources of energy (water, and later coal) and small towns grew around each industry. Yet it was more because industrial capitalism was not conducive to pre-existing mercantile capitalism that this isolated pattern of development occurred. Institutions, laws, etc., were oriented towards mercantile activity, and so industrial capitalism was forced, socially and geographically, to keep out of mercantile cities and develop elsewhere (see Gordon 1978, Hobsbawn 1968, Watkins and Perry 1977).

These first small industrial centres offered advantages to both capitalists and the working class. Being the principal employer, capitalists were in a good position to rigorously control work processes, while the working class, in having one major employer, easily developed solidarity. The single-industry character of these towns also encouraged a close-knit household and residential organisation, and this linked closely with bonds workers forged in the workplace. Capitalists, then, fought on two fronts – against workers at the workplace, and against workers and their families in the living place. In some cases this led to the physical and social destruction of industrial towns, such as Pullman in the United States (see Buder 1967), and subsequently encouraged many capitalists to relocate their factories to – and encouraged most new industrial development within – mercantile cities. Yet this move was made possible only because mercantile society and thus mercantile cities were disintegrating: the wealth and power produced through industrial capitalism was coming to dominate. Old mercantile cities also offered capitalists other advantages, such as a plentiful labour supply, markets, sources of capital, cheaper infrastructural developments, etc. (see Harvey 1985a). In this way, manufacturing was concentrated in large cities, and these eventually merged to form industrial conurbations. In turn, these were the basis of major regions, such as the north-east/mid-west of the United States, the Midlands and North of England, and the German Ruhr.

Within industrial cities, factories were concentrated downtown, beside shopping facilities and transportation. Around them were medium to high-density housing rented by the working class, and further out and away from the grime lived capitalists and the well-off self-employed. Unlike mercantile cities, then, industrial cities were sharply segregated, clearly reflecting the increasing segmentation of capitalist life.

Working class household and residential organisation paralleled that of the first industrial towns; people lived in socially cohesive residential areas and there were close links between home and work. Bonds formed at work were reinforced in the residential area, and vice versa. Men, as the main wage labourers were primarily responsible for work solidarity, while women, as domestic labour, maintained and gave continuity to household and residential organisation. But it was industrial work which dominated people's lives. They laboured long hours, formed their friendships at work, established clubs through these friendships, etc., and this organisation has been termed the 'occupational community', or traditional working class community (see Alt 1976, Bulmer 1975). While not 'community', for reasons given above, its cohesiveness and stability relative to the rest of capitalist life, gives the impression of 'community'.

The state played a minor role in industrial capitalism and urbanisation, for this was the era when 'free enterprise' was at its 'freest'. Market forces more fully dictated the paths of economic and social life than at any other period. Nevertheless, the state did act as a regulator (e.g. with factory Acts) and began providing urban infrastructure.

Many social movements of this period focused on political representation, as with the Chartist movement. There were also some urban movements (e.g. over housing), but as indicated above, these invariably appeared in association with industrial action, as with the Glasgow rent strike of 1915 (see Castells 1983).

In summary, industrial urbanisation developed primarily from relations between social classes. Out of these conflicts cities and towns developed and changed. Household and residential organisation seemed to play an important, though hidden, part from the link with work, and the state and social movements had a lesser impact.

Corporate urbanisation is the urbanisation of monopoly capitalism. Dating from about 1945, although having its roots in the 1890s, monopoly capitalism emerged when a small group of capitalists within a few huge corporations came to own and control increasing amounts of wealth. Industrial capitalism's instability (e.g. the Depressions) initiated this change, with planning and management techniques being introduced, notably large-scale production methods demanding greater work discipline. These were tolerated by workers because resulting profits brought higher wages, thus allowing them to consume more goods such as cars, TVs, etc. (see Moorehouse 1983). In turn, workers became a large new consumer market and this stimulated production. In this way, consumption replaced work as the working class's central life interest and the occupational community was replaced by a suburban-based, loose-knit household and residential organisation which focused on consumption within owner-occupied dwellings or public housing, and in many counties home ownership became the dominant type of housing.

All these changes were aided by a huge expansion of the financial sector and by the growth of the state. The former enabled capital to move rapidly from one sector to another, and provided credit to producers so that they could expand, and to consumers so that they could buy. Equally importantly, the state provided a great range of consumption items (termed 'collective consumption'), such as schools and hospitals, with public housing estates/suburbs being the most striking urban expression of this intervention. As the state became increasingly involved in people's lives, complaints about living standards, etc., were directed increasingly at it, rather than (as in the case of industrial capitalism) at employers in the form of wage demands. Thus, from the mid-1960s to the mid-1970s, urban movements over such issues as housing and health care were widespread and invariably directed at the state, being more marked in some countries than others. Following the state's partial withdrawal from collective consumption after the mid-1970s, urban movements declined sharply (see Castells 1985, Pickvance 1985, 1986a).

Corporate urbanisation, then, is markedly different from industrial urbanisation. Apart from cities and towns being larger and containing a greater proportion of the population, manufacturing no longer dominates. The command functions based on corporate and state planning/administration are now pre-eminent and are located in skyscrapers in the downtown central business district. Furthermore, the consumption activities of the suburban household and residential organisation have had a profound impact (e.g. in demands for facilities).

Corporate cities developed in two major ways, each a consequence of a different mix of class and the state. The first rose directly out of the industrial city. Industrial capitalists relocated factories to, and developed new ones in, outlying suburbs, nearby cities and new regions. This was a response to the militancy of industrial workers and their household and residential organisation, but it resulted also from a wish by capitalists to escape congestion and increasing taxes, and occurred because transportation and communication innovations allowed the separation of production and administration. Skyscrapers housing corporations and the state replaced these factories and so the inner city became a central business district. As factories relocated, the occupational community disintegrated and the downtown retail sector followed this population into the suburbs. Although class relations initiated the transformation, the state speeded up the process with urban planning, using urban renewal as the means of rapidly destroying the built environment of the industrial city so as to allow the construction of the corporate one. The industrial built environment was very complex and was very difficult to remove, and it was for this reason that the state stepped in with urban planning. Once the destruction was completed, the state intervened again, this time to speed up the construction of the corporate city through providing, for example, transportation facilities such as freeways.

The second type of corporate city emerged from non-industrial cities and is particularly evident in the United States' Sunbelt, that underdeveloped (poor) region in the south, south-west, and west of the country. Its non-industrial cities were service centres for primary production and so lacked the complex built environment of industrial urbanisation. As a result, there was no need for significant state intervention to speed up urban change – market forces could largely achieve it independently. Moreover, these cities were attractive to capitalists because they had low land taxes and a disciplined workforce (see Mollenkopf 1983). Yet the state did intervene to speed up the construction of the Sunbelt city, but this was done indirectly, mainly through federal spending, particularly military and space expenditure during the 1940s–70s (see for example, Feagin 1984). Apart from infrastructural and other benefits this expenditure also stimulated high technology developments which, in turn, went hand in hand with booms in energy, other primary production, real estate/construction (following huge in-migrations from the north-east/mid-west), tourism, and the relocation of corporate headquarters (see Sawers and Tabb 1984, Perry and Watkins 1977).

Urban movements emerged from the state's actions to destroy the industrial city and from those to build the corporate city. Essentially these movements were defensive actions taken by household and residential organisations to protect material interests (especially housing) and social life. One type fought against urban renewal, often by remnants of the occupational community (see Gans 1962, Fried *et al.* 1973) while another directed action against the social impact wrought by the urban planning, particularly freeways, involved in corporate city construction (e.g. see Fellman and Brandt 1973).

In summary, although class relations played an important role in corporate urbanisation, the state, household and residential organisation, and social movements, made a far greater impact than in earlier stages (see Harvey 1985a).

Urbanisation is now again being transformed. This began in 1975 with the recession and when state activity contracted. Manufacturing industry was particularly hard-hit, with de-industrialisation having profound impacts on many cities and towns (see Robcrts *et al.* 1985, Sawers and Tabb 1984). Yet command activities (planning and administration) have become more important and so cities with these functions have grown stronger. Moreover, there are new developments in consumption, particularly with inner city gentrification and with tourism urbanisation (see Harvey 1985a, Smith and Williams 1986).

Comparative Urbanisation

The problem cited at the outset of this chapter for Australian urbanisation is a general one, since Australian sociology is really not about *Australian* society, but about 'Western society'. This, in fact, is an approach Australian sociology shares with sociology in all countries. The discipline has a predilection for broadly classifying social structures (e.g. 'Western society') and shows little interest in explaining specific types of social structures (e.g. *a* Western society). Individual societies seem to be of interest only if they contribute to these general concepts, although in reality 'Western society', 'Western urbanisation', etc., contain bias because they were developed from information collected on the most powerful Western societies – certain European ones and the United States. The sparse data produced on small countries like

Australia are swamped, and thus they have no impact on the concepts' meanings. This also means that we do not know the extent to which there are differences and similarities between Western societies, and how different and similar each is from 'Western society'.

Comparative analysis is the only way we can resolve this problem. It is the study of two or more cases – societies, urbanisation processes, etc. – using particular models/theories to explain the differences and similarities observed (see particularly Pickvance 1986b). Explanation is the key, for simply reporting data from two or more societies does not constitute a comparative analysis: we must know why there are differences and why there are similarities. In this chapter, then, we want to know how closely Australian urbanisation matches what has been discussed for Western urbanisation and why there are differences and similarities between the two.

Australian Urbanisation

From British colonisation in 1788, Australia has, relative to other Western societies, always been highly urbanised. In 1986, 63 per cent of the population was concentrated in the dominant south-east region, in New South Wales, Victoria and the ACT, with 39 per cent of all Australians living in Sydney and Melbourne alone. This regional concentration is less now than a couple of decades ago, because a large wave of internal migrants swelled the populations of Queensland and Western Australia during their economic booms of the 1960s and 1970s (see Rowland 1979).

Australia urbanisation is also distinguished by the concentration of population in capital cities. The state capitals, plus Darwin and Canberra, contain 62 per cent of the country's population, and each also contains a sizeable proportion of its state population. This is particularly the case with Adelaide (72 per cent), Melbourne (70 per cent), Perth (69 per cent), and Sydney (61 per cent), but is less so for Brisbane (45 per cent) and Hobart (40 per cent).

Australian urbanisation is different because Australian capitalism is different, and over recent years a number of publications – interestingly, very few by sociologists – have pointed to the distinctiveness of Australian capitalism (see Armstrong and Bradbury 1983, Denoon 1983, Duncan and Fogarty 1984, Ehrensaft and Armstrong 1981, McMichael 1984). It is quite different from that of historically powerful Western nations such as the United Kingdom and the United States, but it is similar to certain other countries, notably Argentina, Canada, New Zealand and Uruguay. What this means is that Australian urbanisation is different from the urbanisation of the former countries, but similar to the urbanisation of the latter ones.

There have been two major stages in Australian urbanisation – a mercantile stage and a corporate one. The first resulted from Australian capitalism being a mercantile capitalism, based on the export of primary produce and the importation of goods, including those already manufactured. The second results from Australian capitalism being pulled tightly into the world capitalist system. Thus, the influences which affect Australia affect other countries, and in this way Australian urbanisation has come to parallel that of other Western societies. Obviously, the distinguishing feature is that Australia had no stage of industrial urbanisation. It did, of course, industrialise but this process was not as extensive or as significant as that of dominant Western societies and its development in cities and towns did not follow that outlined for Western urbanisation (Berry 1984).

These differences in urbanisation can be explained by the different impacts of the four social forces – class relations, the state, household and residential organisation, and social movements. Firstly, Australian class relations revolved for a long period around primary production, related mercantile activities, and associated economic processes, rather than industrial production. The most pervasive feature of Australian urbanisation, then, is its mercantile character. Secondly, the role of the Australian state has been strikingly different. Whereas it was most influential in Western urbanisation during the corporate era, the Australian state was very much involved from the beginnings of European colonisation and was particularly active to about 1920. Paradoxically, it played a relatively minor role in Australian corporate urbanisation. Thirdly, if Australian class relations and the Australian state were distinctive, Australian household and residential organisations must also have been different. Most strikingly, there was no occupational community because there was no industrial urbanisation. Instead, Australia's mercantile urbanisation threw up a distinctive type of household and residential organisation. Finally, in terms of what has been discussed under Western urbanisation, the lack of an industrial urbanisation and the state's limited involvement in corporate urbanisation meant relatively few urban movements emerged. Those that did tended to be reactions against the state's involvement in establishing corporate urbanisation.

To clarify and explain these differences and similarities, we can now look in detail at the two major stages.

Australian Mercantile Urbanisation (1788–1940)

Australian mercantile urbanisation was different from the mercantile stage of Western urbanisation. At the beginning, settlements such as Brisbane, Hobart, and Sydney merely imported people (convicts) and subsistence goods, and exported little. Also, there was no link with a pre-capitalist mode of production, as happened under Western urbanisation, although (hostile) contact was made with Aboriginal hunter and food-gatherer societies. The tie with the British state was critical, since imports came from Britain, and this activity was administered locally, through state officials. Merchants played a minor role in this early commercial activity.

The second and more significant period in Australian mercantile urbanisation occurred with the growth of the export trade, and this began in the 1820s, with wool. And here was the final establishment of capitalist class relations – in the pastoral industry with pastoral capitalists and pastoral workers, and in the city with merchants and their employees. However, it was not until the export of gold in the 1850s and (particularly) the export of a great range of raw materials and foodstuffs later in the century, in response to a second wave of British industrialisation, that the mercantile city became fully developed (see McMichael 1984). In this way Australian mercantile urbanisation was largely a product of an expanding British industrial capitalism (see Clarke 1970, McCarty and Schedvin 1978, Schedvin and McCarty 1974).

A third stage followed in the 1860s–90s, when surplus British capital flooded into Australian cities, notably to Sydney and Melbourne, in search of profitable investments (see Butlin 1976). This was used to construct what became a very complex and modern mercantile city, one which had little similarity with the mercantile one of Western urbanisation. Paralleling developments in the other mercantile urbanisation, this capital was also used in urban land speculation (see Davison 1978).

Spatially, the city grew around wharves. Located nearby were warehouses, railways, mercantile companies, shopping precincts, etc. and beyond were the residential areas of workers, capitalists and the self-employed. These cities were of low density, probably because the concentration of activity (as with the industrial city) was not so crucial. There was also a clear residential segregation, of classes and status groupings, yet again this did not seem to be as marked as for the industrial city.

Unlike Western mercantile urbanisation, capitalist class relations were fully established in the Australian mercantile city, and at about the same time as in the United Kingdom. But whereas in the latter the relationship was essentially between industrial capitalists and the industrial working class, in Australia it was between mercantile capitalists and the mercantile working class.

The Australian capitalist class at this time comprised merchants, who were involved in urban activities, pastoralists, bankers and a small group of miners. While these formed a fairly integrated capitalist class, attempts by merchants to expand their interests by creating small farmers and thus small-town merchants, brought them in conflict with pastoralists – the people controlling land. Merchants were successful in this struggle and self-employed wheat, sugar, and other farmers, plus some pastoralists, and small-towns merchants and other self-employed people, were established (see Connell and Irving 1980).

The Australian working class of this period, largely male, was very distinctive and markedly different from the working class under Western urbanisation. It seems, because it was involved in mercantile, pastoral, and related activities, and because these were subject to seasons, to fluctuations due to weather, overseas prices, demand, etc., that labour mobility was considerable, and that workers seemed to lack the rigorous work discipline that was imposed upon the industrial worker through the factory system. Also, unlike in the factory system, there was not the same large-scale employment of labour. Seasonal work was significant, not only in terms of primary production (shearers, cane-cutters, etc.), but in urban employment as well – on wharves, railways, for local councils – even in factories processing primary produce, such as meatworks (see Fisher 1985). Thus, although workers received relatively good wages, could move between jobs, and had periods of voluntary and involuntary unemployment, they lacked the tightly-controlled working life of industrial workers. These characteristics have led to the impression that the Australian worker was independent, had considerable freedom and a marked self-respect. Bert Facey's (1981) autobiography well illustrates these characteristics. Thus although the efforts by capitalists to accumulate capital had a profound impact on the development of the Australian mercantile city, the distinctive nature of work life seems also to have stamped its mark on the city (see Eggleston 1932).

The state's involvement in Australian urbanisation began with British colonisation. Until the 1820s, the state dominated the economy and the society as a whole, but once capitalist class relations were fully established it became a 'partner' with capitalists in urban development specifically, and in Australian development generally. The period between 1880 and 1920 was one of very intense state involvement: an era referred to as 'colonial socialism'. Here the state was actively involved in attracting capital and labour and this, in turn, had direct impacts upon cities, towns and regions, particularly with infrastructural developments such as railways (see Butlin *et al.* 1982). Apart from maintaining integration between classes and other sections of the society, particularly through the industrial conciliation and arbitration system, the state was actively involved in the lives of the working class. It passed legislation at the turn of the century to ensure a fair wage for workers and their families (see McIntyre 1985). Indeed, there is the suggestion that institutions established to ensure this, particularly the conciliation and arbitration system, became so entrenched, that it was impossible for a welfare state to develop in the post-1940s. Welfare was seen by both capitalists and workers simply in terms of a good wage to buy housing, etc., not in terms of collective consumption (see Castles 1985).

With both class relations and state activity being distinctive, it is not surprising that working class household and residential organisation should also be distinctive. At a material level (e.g. housing), it bore no resemblance to either the comparable organisation in the Western mercantile city, except in terms of home ownership, or to the occupational community of industrial urbanisation. There was a high level of home ownership, particularly of detached houses, with about half of all housing in the 1890s being owner-occupied, although this percentage was lower in the largest cities (see Butlin 1976, Williams 1984, Kelly 1974, Jackson 1974). This seems the result of high wages, the importance of the construction industry in Australian urban development, and a finance sector (especially building societies) oriented to lending money to the working class for home ownership. The state also became involved, initially indirectly, but later directly, as a lender of home finance (see Hill 1959, Williams 1984). Yet the importance of wage levels should not be exaggerated, since cities where workers received the highest wages (Sydney and Melbourne) tended to have lower levels of home ownership, while cities (like Brisbane and Perth) which historically had the highest levels of home ownership, tended to have workers who received lower wages (see Mullins 1981a). It seems this pattern may relate to the direction in which capital was invested. The wealthier cities are – at least in Australian terms – the industrial ones, and so capital may in the past have gravitated to the more profitable manufacturing sector, while in the poorer cities, which are the most mercantile, capital seems to have gravitated to land and construction in the absence of opportunities in manufacturing. Thus, the social structures of cities like Brisbane may in the past have been more conducive to home ownership than cities such as Sydney. Indeed, this seems to be a feature applicable to Australian mercantile urbanisation generally, in contrast with industrial urbanisation.

Australian mercantile urbanisation was also characterised by a slow development in residential infrastructure – sewerage, public transport, water, sealed roads, etc. Industrial urbanisation seems to have provided this earlier, probably as a consequence of the infrastructural needs of manufacturing industry, for water, waste disposal, transport, etc. Once these were provided to industry there was a spin-off effect for residential areas. Since the built environment of Australia's mercantile urbanisation did not need the same level of infrastructural development as industrial urbanisation, there was not the same level of spin-off to residential areas (see Mullins 1981a). In fact, this pattern seems also to hold within Australia, between the more mercantile cities and the more industrial ones; residential areas in the latter had better facilities which were provided earlier (Mullins 1981a).

Socially, Australia's mercantile household and residential organisation was also quite different. There was not the close-knit structure of the occupational community, particularly its bonds between home and work. The Australian structure was loose-knit and, indeed, (employed) work did not seem to be the central life interest of the mercantile worker. Instead, it seemed to focus on domestic activity in the home and residential area, for a unique domestic economy was developed which has been called 'the urban peasantry' (Mullins 1981a, 1981b). The dwelling may have been built by the household and household land was used productively – to grow vegetables and fruit, to raise poultry, etc. – and some of it was processed in the home (see Mullins 1981a, 1981b). In addition, other goods were produced (e.g. clothes, furniture, etc.) (cf. Redclift and Mingione 1985, Pahl 1984). This very elaborate domestic economy seems to have been posible for two major reasons. Firstly, unlike the women of industrial cities, Australian women were overwhelmingly concentrated in household work and few were employed. Thus time beyond what was necessary for the reproduction of workers was devoted to this domestic economy. Women's domestic labour, then, seemed far more extensive and intensive than domestic labour in the occupational community. Secondly, men as wage labour also had time available for this because Australian workers seemed, generally, to have more non-employed time (longer holidays, 'the long weekend', etc.) to devote to the household economy. Finally, a point of qualification. It seems likely that the occupational community existed in some circumstances in Australia, around certain mines and wharves.

Although the state was heavily involved in the development of Australian mercantile urbanisation, this did not seem to spark widespread urban movements in the way it did under corporate urbanisation. This may be because the Australian state tended to intervene indirectly in terms of material aspects of household and residential life (e.g. housing, public transport, etc.). Thus, working class complaints about living standards (for housing, etc.) were directed at employers, with the state stepping in on occasions through the conciliation and arbitration system. There were, of course, numerous social movements ranging from the temperance movement to the anti-conscription one. Some urban movements have been documented (see Wheatley 1980) and there were secessionist regional movements in the outlying states, such as Western Australia.

In summary, what led to Australia's mercantile urbanisation was a unique blend of class relations and state action. Somewhat separately, household and residential organisation made a unique impact, but the role of social movements seems to have been more diffuse.

Australian Corporate Urbanisation (1945–present)

With the corporate period, Australia came, for the first time, to have an urbanisation process similar to that of 'Western urbanisation' (see Badcock 1984). This resulted because monopoly capitalism, via transnational corporations, pulled Australia more closely into the world capitalist system. In this way, the social forces effecting urbanisation (class relations, the state, etc.) took a similar form in both Australia and other Western societies.

Nevertheless, Australian corporate urbanisation had a number of distinctive features. The process of transformation to this stage was different from what happened under Western urbanisation. Whereas considerable difficulties existed, because of industrial urbanisation's complex built environment, in transforming the industrial city to the corporate one, no such difficulties existed in Australia, because the built environment of mercantile urbanisation was far less complex and so could be relatively easily transformed by market forces (i.e. by capitalists). So the Australian state did not 'need' to intervene with urban renewal. In fact, this resembles the way corporate urbanisation developed in the United States' Sunbelt, where its pre-corporate urbanisation was also non-industrial (indeed mercantile), and so the transformation was achieved relatively easily.

To a very limited extent the Australian state did intervene with urban renewal, but this occurred in those mercantile cities with the greatest amount of manufacturing – Sydney and Melbourne. Manufacturing had added complexity to their mercantile built environments and this encouraged the state to intervene (see Sandercock 1975).

The state also intervened in building the Australian corporate city (e.g. with freeways, airports, etc.) (see Neutze 1978, 1981,

Sandercock 1975, Scott 1978) but this was not as widespread as it was in the United States. In fact, the general reticence of the Australian state as an urban planner may well be linked to the relative ease by which Australian urbanisation moved from the mercantile stage to the corporate state. Urban planning seems most developed in those societies which had transformational difficulties, specifically in converting from industrial urbanisation to corporate urbanisation. Even the significant regional shift in Australia during the 1960s and 1970s – to the underdeveloped regions of Queensland and Western Australia (Australia's Sunbelt) – was not stimulated by government funding in the way the state funded the United States' Sunbelt. The Queensland and Western Australian governments have, of course, actively encouraged development by providing incentives (e.g. low taxes), but development was not initiated by huge government expenditure and planning. Capitalists essentially stimulated Australia's Sunbelt development – in mining, pastoralism, agriculture, tourism, real estate and construction (see Harman 1983, Harman and Head 1982, Mullins 1980).

The state's relatively limited involvement in urban and regional development reflects its constrained role in Australian development generally during this period. Of course, it did provide postwar reconstruction, and introduced some major projects (e.g. the Snowy River Scheme), but, relatively, these did not compare with its intervention in the nineteenth century, and it was far less than state activity in many other Western societies at the time.

Spatially, the Australian corporate city is much like other corporate cities – of low density, with skyscrapers located in the central business district, focusing on planning/administration, and consumption taking place in the suburbs. What factories there were relocated out of the city centre, and the inner city population and the retail sector went to the suburbs. The skyscrapers for planning/administration were then built and these replaced the built environment of the mercantile city (see Daly 1982, Kilmartin and Thorns 1978, Kilmartin *et al.* 1985).

Like its counterpart under the corporate stage of Western urbanisation, the Australian household and residential organisation is suburban. People owned or were buying their homes, owned cars and had stocked their dwellings with consumer durables. Consumption, then, replaced the domestic economy of the urban peasantry as the central life interest. Whereas the urban peasantry focused on domestic production within the household, suburban life focuses on consumption, also within the household (see Allport 1983, Game and Pringle 1979, Kilmartin *et al.* 1985). Socially, suburban life is loose-knit and household-based, with women continuing to play the central role, although with increasing numbers of them becoming employed, this organisation is undergoing change.

The rise of suburban home ownership was easily achieved because of increases in real wages and because credit facilities, through the finance sector and the state, were well established; having provided home loans to mercantile workers since the nineteenth century (see Hill 1959, Kilmartin and Thorns 1978). The expansion of these facilities then made the achievement of home ownership in the post-war years much easier and allowed the purchase of consumer durables.

The public housing sector (housing commission) is insignificant in Australia, particularly when compared with certain other Western societies such as Sweden (see Kemeny 1981). This seems a consequence of the general quiescence of the Australian state in urban planning, particularly in providing 'collective consumption' – welfare services, free health care, pre-school facilities, etc. But, more importantly, as suggested earlier, a number of structural factors seem to be more important in preventing full development of the welfare state (see Castles 1985).

Only in South Australia did public housing develop in any significant way. This was from the 1930s and was part of a plan to attract industrial investment to South Australia; this it did with BHP in Whyalla and with industries in Adelaide (see Aungles 1979). In fact, these efforts reflect the process of industrialisation in Australia, for the major period of development was between 1930 and 1960. Cities such as Newcastle, Wollongong, Whyalla and Geelong clearly became established as industrial cities, with the metropolitan centres of Adelaide, Sydney, and Melbourne being those with the greatest concentration of industries. Thus, Australia industrialised with corporate urbanisation.

Urban movements did not have a particularly profound impact on Australian corporate urbanisation, as they did in cities in other societies. This seems partly because the state played a very limited role in providing consumption items such as housing, which meant people did not mobilise against the state if problems arose; instead they expected increased wages to cover costs. Furthermore, housing and residential facilities were generally well provided in Australian cities. Movements which did emerge have been defensive actions, particularly over the state's involvement in constructing the corporate city, and include actions against freeways (see Mullins 1979), and in some cases against commercial redevelopment. Actions against urban renewal have been rare, because this form of urban planning has been insignificant, for the reasons given above.

Regional movements have also been evident, particularly in the 'outlands' of Tasmania, the Northern Territory, Queensland and Western Australia. These have largely been a response to problems of underdevelopment (see Mullins 1986).

There is evidence of a new urbanisation, as well, although it may simply be an extension of corporate urbanisation. There has been de-industrialisation, and industrial centres such as Wollongong have been hard hit (Stilwell 1980, Wanna 1984). There is gentrification and tourism urbanisation and these have become important for consumption (see Mullins 1982, 1984, Logan 1985). Planning/administrative functions, particularly in finance, continue to boost Sydney and Melbourne, and government funding is continuing to develop Canberra and Darwin.

Conclusion

Australian urbanisation, then, was different only during a particular period – the years to about 1940. Here, Australia had a mercantile urbanisation, while 'Western urbanisation' was industrial urbanisation. In all stages of both Australian and Western urbanisation, class relations had the greatest influence. However, in Australia the state formed a partnership with capitalists during the mercantile period and so came to play a very important role. Under Western urbanisation, considerable state involvement occurred during the corporate stage, a time when the Australian state played a far smaller role. And it seems to have been state intervention which led to considerable numbers of urban movements in the corporate stage – at least under Western urbanisation. Thus Australia's urban development is unique in a number of respects, and can be seen to reflect the particular social forces (classes, the state, household and residential organisation, and social movements), which were important in the Australian context.

References

Alford, R. and Friedland, R. (1985) *Powers of Theory*. Cambridge: Cambridge University Press.
Allport, C. (1983) 'Women and Suburban Housing' in P. Williams *Social Process and the City*. Sydney: Allen & Unwin.
Alt, J. (1976) 'Beyond Class: The Decline of Industrial Labor and Leisure', *Telos* 28: 55–80.

Armstrong, W. and Bradbury, J. (1983) 'Industrialisation and Class Structure in Australia, Canada, and Argentina, 1870 to 1980' in E. Wheelwright and K. Buckley (eds) *Essays in the Political Economy of Australian Capitalism,* Vol. 5. Sydney: Australian and New Zealand Book Co.

Aungles, S. (1979) 'The Social Consequences of Industrial Development and Decline', *Journal of Australian Political Economy* 4: 38–53.

Badcock, B. (1984) *Unfairly Structured Cities.* Oxford: Basil Blackwell.

Bater, J.H. (1980) *The Soviet City.* London: Edward Arnold.

Berry, M. (1984) 'The Political Economy of Australian Urbanisation', *Progress in Planning* 22 (1): 1–83.

Black, D. and Myles, J. (1986) 'Dependent Industrialization and the Canadian Class Structure', *Canadian Review of Sociology and Anthropology* 23 (2): 157–81.

Buder, S. (1967) *Pullman.* New York: Oxford University Press.

Bulmer, M. (ed.) (1975) *Working Class Images of Society.* London: Routledge & Kegan Paul.

Butlin, N.G. (1976) *Investment in Australian Economic Development 1861–1900.* Canberra: Department of Economic History, RSSS, Australian National University.

———, Barnard, A. and Pincus, J. (1982) *Government and Capitalism.* Sydney: Allen & Unwin.

Calhoun, C. (1982) *The Question of Class Struggle.* Oxford: Basil Blackwell.

Castells, M. (1977) *The Urban Question.* London: Edward Arnold.

———(1983) *The City and the Grassroots.* London: Edward Arnold.

———(1985) 'Commentary on G.C. Pickvance's "The Rise and Fall of Urban Movements"', *Society and Space* 3 (1): 55–61.

Castles, F.G. (1985) *The Working Class and Welfare.* Wellington: Allen & Unwin.

Clark, G.L. and Dear, M. (1984) *State Apparatus.* Boston: Allen & Unwin.

Clarke, G. (1970) 'Urban Australia' in S. Encel (ed.) *Australian Society.* Sydney: Cheshire.

Connell, R.W. and Irving, T.H. (1980) *Class Structure in Australian History.* Sydney: Longman Cheshire.

Daly, M. (1982) *Sydney Boom Sydney Bust.* Sydney: Allen & Unwin.

Davis, K. (1974) 'The Urbanisation of the Human Population' in C. Tilly (ed.) *An Urban World.* Boston: Little, Brown.

Davison, G. (1978) *Marvellous Melbourne.* Melbourne: Melbourne University Press.

Denoon, D. (1983) *Settler Capitalism.* Oxford: Clarendon.

Duncan, T. and Fogarty, J. (1984) *Australia and Argentina.* Melbourne: Melbourne University Press.

Edel, M. (1981) 'Capitalism, Accumulation and the Explanation of Urban Phenomena' in M. Dear and A. Scott, *Urbanization and Urban Planning in Capitalist Society.* London: Methuen.

Eggleston, F.W. (1932) *State Socialism in Victoria.* London: P.S. King.

Ehrensaft, P. and W. Armstrong (1981) 'The Formation of Dominion

Capitalism' in A. Moscovitch and G. Drover (eds) *Inequality*. Toronto: University of Toronto Press.

Elliott, B. and McCrone, D. (1982) *The City*. London: Macmillan.

Facey, A.B. (1981) *A Fortunate Life*. Ringwood: Penguin.

Feagin, J.R. (1984) 'The Role of the State in Urban Development: The Case of Houston, Texas', *Society and Space* 2 (4): 447–60.

Fellman, G. and Brandt, B. (1973) *The Deceived Majority*. New Brunswick, New Jersey: Transaction Books,

Fried, M. *et al. The World of the Urban Working Class*. Cambridge, Mass.: Harvard University Press.

Fisher, S. (1985) 'The Family and the Sydney Economy in the Late Nineteenth Century' in P. Grimshaw, C. McConville and E. McEwen (eds) *Families in Colonial Australia*. Sydney: Allen & Unwin.

Game, A. and Pringle, R. (1979) 'Sexuality and the Suburban Dream', *Australian and New Zealand Journal of Sociology* 15 (2): 4–15.

Gans, H.J. (1962) *The Urban Villagers*. New York: Free Press.

Gordon, D. (1978) 'Capitalist Development and the History of American Cities' in W. Tabb and L. Sawers (eds) *Marxism and the Metropolis*. New York: Oxford University Press.

Gregory, D. and Urry, J. (eds) (1985) *Social Relations and Spatial Structures*. London: Macmillan.

Harman, E. (1983) 'The City, State and Resource Development in Western Australia' in P. Williams (ed.) *Social Process and the City*. Sydney: Allen & Unwin.

———and Head, B. (eds) (1982) *State, Capital and Resources in the North and West of Australia*. Nedlands: University of Western Australia Press.

Harvey, D. (1985a) *The Urbanization of Capital*. Oxford: Basil Blackwell.

———(1985b) *Consciousness and the Urban Experience*. Oxford: Basil Blackwell.

Hechter, M. and Brustein, W. (1980) 'Regional Modes of Production and Patterns of State Formation in Europe', *American Journal of Sociology* 85 (5): 1061–095.

Hill, M. (1959) *Housing Finance in Australia*. Melbourne: Melbourne University Press.

Hobsbawn, E.J. (1968) *Industry and Empire*. Harmondsworth: Penguin.

Holton, R.J. (1986) *Cities, Capitalism and Civilisation*. London: Allen & Unwin.

Jackson, R. (1974) 'Owner-occupation of Houses in Sydney, 1871 to 1891' in C.B. Schedvin and J.B. McCarty (eds) *Urbanisation in Australia*. Sydney: Sydney University Press.

Katznelson, I. (1981) *City Trenches*. New York: Pantheon.

Kelly, M. (1974) 'Eight Acres' in C.B. Schedvin and J.B. McCarty (eds) *Urbanization in Australia*. Sydney: Sydney University Press.

Kemeny, J. (1981) *The Myth of Homeownership*. London: Routledge & Kegan Paul.

Kilmartin, L. and Thorns, D. (1978) *Cities Unlimited*. Sydney: Allen & Unwin.

———,Thorns, D. and Burke, T. (1985) *Social Theory and the Australian City*. Sydney: Allen & Unwin.

Logan, W. (1985) *The Gentrification of Inner Melbourne*. St Lucia: University of Queensland Press.

McCarty, J. W. and Schedvin, C. B. (eds) (1978) *Australian Capital Cities*. Sydney: Sydney University Press.

MacIntyre, S. (1985) *Winners and Losers*. Sydney; Allen & Unwin.

McMichael, P. (1984) *Settlers and the Agrarian Question*. Cambridge: Cambridge University Press.

Massey, D. (1984) *Spatial Divisions of Labour*. London: Macmillan.

Mollenkopf, J. (1983) *The Contested City*. Princeton: Princeton University Press.

Moorehouse, H.F. (1983) 'American Automobiles and Workers' Dreams', *Sociological Review* 31 (3): 403–26.

Mullins, P. (1979) 'The Struggle Against Brisbane's Freeways, 1966–1974', *International Journal of Urban and Regional Research* 3 (4): 542–52.

———(1980) 'Australian Urbanisation and Queensland's Underdevelopment', *International Journal of Urban and Regional Research* 4 (2): June: 212–38.

———(1981a) 'Theoretical Perspectives on Australian Urbanisation I: Material Components in the Reproduction of Australian Labour Power', *Australian and New Zealand Journal of Sociology* 17 (1): 65–76.

———(1981b) 'Theoretical Perspectives on Australian Urbanisation II: Social Components in the Reproduction of Australian Labour Power', *Australian and New Zealand Journal of Sociology* 17 (3): 35–43.

———(1982) 'The 'Middle-Class' and the Inner City', *Journal of Australian Political Economy* 11: 44–58.

———(1984) 'Hedonism and Real Estate: Resort Tourism and Gold Coast Development' in P. Williams (ed.) *Development and Change*. Sydney: Allen & Unwin.

———(1986) Queensland: Populist Politics and Development' in B. Head (ed.) *The Politics of Development in Australia*. Sydney: Allen & Unwin.

———(1987) 'Community and Urban Movements', *Sociological Review* 35 (2), May: 347–69.

Neutze, M. (1978) *Australian Urban Policy*. Sydney: Allen & Unwin.

———(1981) *Urban Development in Australia*. Sydney: Allen & Unwin.

Pahl, R.E. (1984) *Divisions of Labour*. London: Edward Arnold.

Perry, D. and Watkins, A. (eds) (1977) *The Rise of the Sunbelt Cities*. Beverly Hills: Sage.

Pickvance, C.G. (1985) 'The Rise and Fall of Urban Movements and the Role of Comparative Analysis', *Society and Space* 3 (1): 31–53.

———(1986a) 'Concepts, Contexts and Comparisons in the Study of Urban Movements: A Reply to M. Castells', *Society and Space* 4 (2): 221–31.

———(1986b) 'Comparative Urban Analysis and Assumptions about Causality', *International Journal of Urban and Regional Research* 10 (2): 162–84.

Redclift, N. and Mingione, E. (eds) (1985) *Beyond Employment*. Oxford: Basil Blackwell.

Roberts, B., Finnegan, R. and Gallie, D. (eds) (1985) *New Approaches to Economic Life*. Manchester: Manchester University Press.

Rowland, D. (1979) *Internal Migration in Australia.* Canberra: Australian Bureau of Statistics.

Sandercock, L. (1975) *Cities for Sale.* Melbourne: Melbourne University Press.

Sawers, L. and Tabb, W. (eds) (1984) *Sunbelt/Snowbelt.* New York: Oxford University Press.

Schedvin, C.B. and McCarty, J.W. (eds) (1974) *Urbanization in Australia.* Sydney: Sydney University Press.

Scott, P. (ed.) (1978) *Australian Cities and Public Policy.* Melbourne: Georgian House.

Smith, M. and Williams, P. (eds) (1986) *Gentrification of the City.* Boston: Allen & Unwin.

Stilwell, F. (1980) *Economic Crisis, Cities and Regions.* Oxford: Pergamon.

Szelenyi, I. (1983) *Urban Inequalities under State Socialism.* Oxford: Oxford University Press.

———and Murray, P. (1984) 'The City in the Transition to Socialism', *International Journal of Urban and Regional Research* 8 (1): 90–107.

Thrift, N. and Forbes, D. (1985) 'Cities, Socialism and War', *Society and Space* 3 (3): 279–308.

Tilly, C. (1979) 'Repertoires of Contention in America and Britain, 1750–1830' in M. Zald and J. McCarthy (eds) *The Dynamics of Social Movements.* Cambridge, Mass.: Winthrop.

Wallerstein, I. (1974) *The Modern World-System.* New York: Academic Press.

Wanna, J. (1984) 'Regional Development and Economic Restructuring in South Australia', *Australian and New Zealand Journal of Sociology* 20 (3): 350–64.

Watkins, A. and Perry, D. (1977) 'Regional Change and the Impact of Uneven Urban Development' in D. Perry and A. Watkins (eds) *The Rise of the Sunbelt Cities.* Beverly Hills: Sage.

Wheatley, N. (1980) 'Meeting Them at the Door' in J. Roe (ed.) *Twentieth Century Sydney.* Sydney: Hale & Iremonger.

Williams, P. (1984) 'The Politics of Property' in J. Halligan and C. Paris (eds) *Australian Urban Politics.* Melbourne: Longman Cheshire.

Wright, E.O. (1985) *Classes.* London: Verso.

Chapter Eighteen
The Mass Media
John S. Western

Communication is one of the fundamental characteristics of any social group. When, for example, a member of a small primary group such as a family shows signs of deviating from accepted patterns of behaviour, he or she becomes the focus of the group's communication until persuaded of the error of his or her ways, or until excluded from membership of the group if the behaviour is not modified. When some great event threatens society it can arouse a storm of communication via the mass media: press, radio, television and film, and when a society is making an important public decision, such as electing a government the communication channels are filled to capacity.

It is possible to distinguish between two systems of public communication: the oral and the media. In media systems of communication information or entertainment typically comes from professional communicators who have been selected for their positions on the basis of the skills they possess. Their job is to transmit information, news, commentary or entertainment, to mention but three of a number of items, through impersonal media such as print, radio, film or television to mass audiences. In oral systems of communication information usually emanates from people in positions of authority. The content of the communication is typically 'prescriptive': 'news' is less salient than 'rules' which specify correct behaviour. As the term 'oral' implies, such communication is also by word of mouth or, as it is sometimes called, 'interpersonal'. Modernising or developing societies tend to place more emphasis on oral systems of communication while 'developed' societies such as Australia tend to emphasise media systems, although in all societies both systems are present.

In the present chapter we look at Australia's media system. First we will consider matters of ownership and control. Who owns Australia's press, radio and television? Is the pattern of ownership very similar to, or different from, that found elsewhere? This leads into the second section of the chapter, a discussion of the role and effects of the mass media in society. The section starts by considering some of the theoretical arguments that have been advanced over the years and then moves on to describing how these have been dealt with in the Australian context. The problem of the changing credibility of the mass media over time is then raised. The significance of this changing credibility of press and television for media theories of 'cultural supremacy' is then considered. Finally, the future of the media in Australia is discussed in a somewhat speculative manner.

Ownership and Control

In Australia, there has developed in a relatively short space of time a media system which is highly organised, far-reaching and oligopolistic in character. Its first sign was the appearance in 1803, only fifteen years after the first settlement, of the *Sydney Gazette*, published and censored by the British authorities. Governmental control of the press was short-lived, however, and by 1824 censorship was lifted, and two years later there were already two opposition papers (Mayer 1964: Ch. 1). In 1840 the *Sydney Morning Herald* became the first regular daily, and by 1848 there were a further ten. In this period papers came and went rapidly. Typically they started as weeklies, became bi- and tri-weeklies and, finally, dailies, perhaps lasting as the last no more than 6 to 9 months. The situation had stabilised by the turn of the century, at which time there were 21 capital city daily newspapers (Western 1973).

The year 1923 saw the beginning of the end of the small proprietor. In that year there were 26 metropolitan dailies published in the capital cities and 21 separate owners (Carden 1956). By 1930, there were 20 and 12 respectively and at the present time there are 18 national and capital city dailies and 3 major owners (Table 18.1). These 3, together with a fourth group, have put, and

Table 18.1 The Rise and Fall of Press Ownership

	1903	1923	1930	1950	1960	1971	1986
Capital City and National Dailies	21	26	20	15	14	17	18
Independent Owners	17	21	12	10	7	4	3

are still putting, an indelible stamp on the system of mass communications in Australia, although it should be noted that the hegemony of the 'big four' has in recent times been somewhat weakened, particularly in the area of television.

The best-known media group is undoubtedly the Melbourne-based Herald and Weekly Times (HWT), originally presided over by Keith (later Sir Keith) Murdoch. Founded in 1902, its first paper was the *Melbourne Herald*. In 1925, Murdoch purchased the *Sun News Pictorial* which became for a long period the highest-circulation daily in Australia. The company gradually extended its influence, first to Adelaide and then to Brisbane. In Adelaide in 1929 it acquired a major interest in Advertiser Newspapers, publishers of the *Adelaide Advertiser*, and in 1953 a controlling interest in Queensland Newspapers, publishers of the *Courier-Mail* and *Telegraph*.

The actions by the *Herald* at that time resulted, as John Bushnell (1961) has suggested, 'in the concentration of a large part of Australia's mass media in the full control of one firm'. Early in 1957 the *Melbourne Argus*, which had celebrated its centenary some years before, ceased publication. The parent company, Argus and Australasian Ltd, which still published magazines, was taken over by the HWT. Five years later, through its acquisitions in Davies Brothers, they obtained a substantial interest in the *Hobart Mercury* and, in 1969, following a successful takeover bid, control of West Australian Newspapers Ltd, publishers of the two Perth dailies, the *West Australian* and *Daily News*. In 1979 they were the victim of some of their own medicine when a takeover bid was made for the company by a rising star on the media scene, Rupert Murdoch, paradoxically, perhaps, the son of the (by then) late Sir Keith. We will have a little more to say about this event later.

In addition to metropolitan dailies, the HWT is responsible for the publication of provincial papers in Victoria, Queensland and Western Australia. Six magazines, weeklies and monthlies, each with circulations over 90,000 are also produced by the HWT. The company also has interests in daily papers in Papua New Guinea, Fiji and Singapore.

In Sydney the Fairfax family became proprietors of the *Sydney Morning Herald* in 1841. They were not as expansionist as Murdoch was in the early days and their major developments have only taken place in the last twenty-five years. In 1951, the first number of the *Australian Financial Review*, at that time an ambitious businessman's weekly, appeared. In 1953 they acquired the *Sydney Sun* and in 1956 the public company, John Fairfax Ltd, was formed. In 1961 it obtained a controlling interest in Newcastle

Newspapers, publishers of the two Newcastle dailies, in 1965 purchased the *Canberra Times*, and in 1966 obtained a major interest in David Syme and Company, publishers of *The Age* in Melbourne. More recently the company has assumed complete control of *The Age* also publishing provincial dailies and national weeklies and monthlies including the *Times on Sunday, Women's Day* and *New Idea*.

Perhaps the most entrepreneurial group is the third. Known originally as News Ltd, it was formed in 1922 to publish an evening paper in Adelaide. The turning point for the company occurred in 1952 when Rupert Murdoch assumed control. At that time the Murdoch family controlled some 50 per cent of the ordinary shares. The story has it that the Murdoch family offered Rupert, Sir Keith's son, either *The News* in Adelaide or the *Courier-Mail* in Brisbane and it was the Adelaide offer that was accepted. The Murdoch story is now perhaps legend. *The News* was followed by the successful weekly *TV Week*, which commenced publication in 1957. In 1960 the company secured a controlling interest in Mirror Newspapers which published the *Sydney Daily Mirror*, the *Sunday Mirror, Sportsman*, the *Melbourne Truth* and the *Brisbane Sunday Truth*. In the same year the company acquired Cumberland Newspapers, the publisher of 16 suburban and regional papers in New South Wales. In 1963–64 a substantial interest was acquired in the Wellington Publishing Company in New Zealand, publisher of *The Dominion*; in 1964 *The Australian* was launched. In early 1969 the company gained control of the News of the World organisation in the United Kingdom and changed its name to News International Ltd. In 1969 News International acquired the London *Sun*. In 1972, the publishing rights to the *Daily Telegraph*, a Sydney daily, and the *Sunday Telegraph*, its Sunday counterpart, were purchased from Consolidated Press and the *Sunday Australian* which had appeared earlier, was merged with the *Sunday Telegraph*. Since that time, the American weekly, the *National Star*, has been launched, and the *New York Post* has been acquired as well as the *London Times* and *Sunday Times*. The company changed its name once again and is now known as News Corporation. More recently still, Rupert Murdoch, to accommodate the purchase of a television network in the United States, has become an American citizen.

Perhaps the most dramatic event in recent Australian media history was Murdoch's attempted takeover of the Herald and Weekly Times. On Tuesday, 20 November 1979, he made an offer of $4 a share for just over half the HWT shares (Western and Hughes 1983: 183). Predictably, the move was greeted with mixed reactions (Souter 1981: 572–84). Fairfax immediately began buying HWT shares. A loose association of companies known as 'the friends of the HWT' bought heavily. Ordinary shares increased to an average price of $5.27 per share. While HWT's friends were buying, Murdoch quietly began selling the shares he had already acquired so that he ended the week's trading without control of HWT but $4 million better off. On the following Thursday, Murdoch announced that the takeover bid had been abandoned, and News Limited shares in HWT sold.

Had Murdoch's bid been successful it would have given one man control of 12 of Australia's 18 metropolitan dailies and initially, at least, 6 or 7 television outlets in the capital cities, an interest in a variety of radio stations across the country and ownership of a number of magazines, weeklies and other papers. Doubtless some of these holdings would have been sold over time, but the potential for manipulation of the communications media that such control would allow would have been almost unlimited (Western and Hughes 1983: 185).

A fourth print group of note is also located in Sydney and is identified with the Packer family. The family interest in the publishing and media business dates back to the early 1920s. It was not until 1933, however, that Consolidated Press Ltd was formed. This company, presided over by Frank Packer, published the *Daily Telegraph*, the *Sunday Telegraph* and the well-known *Australian Women's Weekly*. In 1969 the company obtained a controlling interest in the *Maitland Mercury* and also all the issued capital of Bulletin Newspapers, publisher of the *Bulletin*. In 1972, however, the company moved out of daily newspaper publishing with the sale of the goodwill of the *Daily Telegraph* and the *Sunday Telegraph* to Rupert Murdoch. At the present time the major press interests of Consolidated Press Holdings are the *Australian Women's Weekly*, the *Bulletin* and *Business Review Weekly*.

To sum up, of the 18 metropolitan dailies, 8 are from the Herald and Weekly Times stable, 6 are from Fairfax and the remainder from News Corporation. Of the 13 Sunday papers, the Herald and Weekly Times controls 1 and has equal shares in 2 others, 1 with Murdoch and 1 with Fairfax. Fairfax has control of 2 and Murdoch 4. Murdoch also runs a mid-weekly, *The Melbourne Truth*, and the Herald and Weekly Times a bi-weekly, *Sporting Globe*.

As already noted, as well as the metropolitan papers, there are at least 40 provincial dailies, some 380 other provincial papers and over 250 suburban newspapers, almost all of the 'give-away' variety, and published from one to three times a week. The major companies have substantial interests in this area of newspapers as well.

There is more to the printed word than newspapers, however, for Australians support around 1,400 journals and magazines. These range from the popular women's magazines, the *Australian Women's Weekly, Women's Day* and *New Idea*, with circulations of half a million and more, to political, professional and technical journals which might have no more than 750 regular subscribers. Again, as has already been noted, the most popular of the magazines are published by one or other of the four major companies.

Radio
Since the days of the *Sydney Gazette* the press has been privately owned and despite strong tendencies in the last generation towards the concentration of press ownership into fewer and fewer hands, there has been little advocacy of public or government remedy. The situation as far as radio and television is concerned is of course different, for it is here that one can identify a public sector. This has not always been the case, for it was not until 1932, about nine years after the first radio broadcasts, that the need for some state participation in the development of radio was recognised.

Broadcasting commenced in Australia in July 1923 when the Post-Master General's Department granted licences for the establishment of wireless stations maintained by subscriptions of listeners using receivers capable of operating only on the frequency allocated to the station to which the subscription was paid. This scheme was abandoned after twelve months when only four stations commenced broadcasting, and only 1,200 listeners were licensed (Western 1973). It was replaced by a scheme which permitted the establishment of two classes of broadcasting stations, so-called Class A and Class B stations. Class A stations obtained revenue from listener's licence fees which then entitled licensees to receive programs on any station; Class B stations were maintained by revenue received from the broadcasting of advertisements.

In 1932, however, the government decided to establish a national broadcasting service and the Australian Broadcasting Commission Act heralded the establishment of the Australian Broadcasting Commisson. The Commission was empowered to take over the existing studios of the Class A stations and broadcast from these now national broadcasting stations 'adequate and comprehensive programmes' (Australian Broadcasting Control Board 1949). Parallel developments also took place among Class B stations, which became known as commercial broadcasting stations, and by 1932 along with the 8 main and 4 regional stations of the national network, were 43 commercial broadcasting stations, the majority of which were located in capital cities (Mackay 1957). The number of stations slowly increased. The national service was to move to 14 metropolitan stations, 2 in each capital city plus 1 each in Canberra and Launceston, and around 60 regional stations; 25 metropolitan commercial stations and over 80 country and regional stations also came into being.

The major breakthrough for Australian radio came in the mid-1970s. Prior to that time the Australian Broadcasting Control Board, whose principal function was to ensure the provision of adequate and comprehensive commercial radio and television services, had insisted that any scope for further development of AM radio within Australia was impossible. The AM frequency band was loaded to capacity and no further frequencies were available for additional radio stations. A report to the Minister for Post and Telecommunications at the time entitled *Australian Broadcasting* demonstrated that this was simply not the case (Green 1976). In a paper delivered at a Summer School of the Australian Institute of Political Science in 1976, the then Senator James McClelland, commenting on the situation, made the following points. He asserted that 'the technical basis of this alleged scarcity of AM frequencies was repeatedly challenged by independent experts but it was not until early last year [1975] that the Board admitted that it was possible to establish a large number of additional AM stations'.

The net result of the report *Australian Broadcasting*, which came to be known as the Green Report, after its author, was the disbanding of the Australian Broadcasting Control Board and its replacement by the Australian Broadcasting Tribunal. At the same time, AM radio multiplied rapidly and FM radio came into being in all states.

Networks play an important part in Australian commercial radio. The two chief commercial networks are perhaps the Macquarie network and the Major network. The Macquarie network has radio stations in New South Wales, Victoria, South Australia and Queensland and is closely connected with John Fairfax Ltd. The Major network has stations in Victoria, Queensland and South Australia and, in turn, is closely connected with the Herald and Weekly Times. Radio stations connected with Consolidated Press Holdings can also be found in New South Wales, Victoria and Western Australia.

Radio is not as centrally controlled as is the press. The Bell Group of Mr Holmes à Court owns four radio stations in Western Australia, and Alan Bond's Bond Corporation also has stations in Western Australia and Darwin. The Australian Broadcasting Company, not to be confused with the Australian Broadcasting

Commission, owns stations in Canberra, Queensland and New South Wales. Amalgamated Wireless Australasia owns stations in Western Australia, New South Wales, Victoria and Queensland, while Quintex Ltd, Christopher Skase's growing company, has a radio station in Brisbane. There are other smaller companies with interests in largely regional radio stations.

The ownership of radio is more diverse than newspapers partly because there are many more stations, and partly because there are legal restrictions on the number of stations any one proprietor can own. A proprietor may have what is described as a 'prescribed interest', ownership of 15 per cent or more of shares in only 1 metropolitan radio station in each state. Similarly, a proprietor can only have a total of 4 stations in each state and no more than 4 metropolitan or a total of 8 stations in Australia (Windschuttle 1985). However, despite these restrictions, it is important to note that in the 9 major metropolitan centres, Sydney, Melbourne, Brisbane, Adelaide, Perth, Hobart, Canberra, Newcastle and Wollongong, while there are 43 commercial AM and FM stations, 10 of these are owned either by Fairfax or the Herald and Weekly Times. Altogether, these 2 firms control 15 radio stations.

Television
The advent of television, Alan Davies suggested back in 1968, 'opened a choice between lessening the grip of the private proprietors, specifically the newspaper publishers, in the communication field or confirming it' (Davies 1968). The first moves towards a television service had come in June 1949 when Ben Chifley announced his Labor government's intention of introducing a national service with a television station in each of the six capital cities.

In December of the same year the Labor Party was defeated at the polls by a Liberal-Country Party coalition which had quite different ideas on the development of television. There was to be a national service established initially in Sydney, extending to the other states as experience and technical competence increased. As well, one commerical licence was to be issued in Sydney and Melbourne and in any other capital city where the applicant's capacity to provide a service justified the issue of a licence (Australian Broadcasting Control Board 1952). Little was done for several years. The prospect of Melbourne hosting the 1956 Olympic Games provided a stimulus and by the end of 1956, one national and two commercial channels were established in both Sydney and Melbourne.

It was not until the second half of 1959, however, that Brisbane and Adelaide obtained their first commercial stations. The national stations followed shortly afterwards, and by the middle of 1960, the Melbourne-Sydney pattern was reproduced. Television also moved to Perth and Hobart, but only one commercial station plus a national station, was established in each city. A further commercial station began operation in Melbourne in August 1964 and in the first half of 1965 new stations, one to each city, were established in Sydney, Brisbane, Adelaide and Perth. Between 1962 and the early 1970s, over 60 national commercial stations were established in rural and provincial areas. Currently, around 98 per cent of the Australian population has access to television.

Colour televison was slow in coming to Australia and it was not until the late 1970s that any penetration had been achieved. If we are to believe the then Senator James McClelland, tardiness in this direction can also be attributed to the Broadcasting Control Board's unwillingness to move with the times (McClelland 1976).

From the beginning, the pattern of ownership was one of concentration in the hands of a few companies. The early licences were almost all taken up by newspaper proprietors. The Herald and Weekly Times controlled a station in Melbourne, and Australian Consolidated Press, one each in Sydney and Melbourne, while Fairfax owned a Sydney station. The first group of licences issued in the other state capitals also went, importantly, to newspaper companies. The Herald and Weekly Times gained control of stations in Brisbane and Adelaide and had an interest in the only Hobart station. John Fairfax Ltd gained control of the other Brisbane station and, in conjunction with Australian Consolidated Press, controlled the Herald's Adelaide competitor. Western Australian Newspapers, a Herald and Weekly Times affiliate, obtained the licence of the only Perth station.

There was, however, as Alan Davies suggested, 'a good deal more active competition for the third commercial licence in the four larger cities and the fact that they went to non-newspaper capitalists somewhat broadened the managerial structure in private mass communications' (Davies 1968). Most involved were Ansett Transport Industries (ATI), which acquired minority interests in the new Adelaide, Sydney and Perth stations and full control of channels in both Melbourne and Brisbane.

Since the early period of television major changes have taken place in patterns of ownership. The Herald and Weekly Times now owns only two capital city stations, one each in Melbourne and Adelaide, and four provincial stations in Queensland. John Fairfax owns a Sydney channel and a Brisbane one while Consolidated Press owns a Sydney and a Melbourne channel. News Corporation sold its Brisbane holdings and now has channels in both Melbourne and Sydney. Mr Holmes à Court's Bell Group owns channels in Adelaide and Perth and the Bond Corporation has one in Perth, and has recently purchased a channel in Brisbane. Christopher Skase has recently purchased a Brisbane station.

Networks are coming to play an increasingly important role in commercial television. The Nine network is dominated by Packer family interests and includes channels in Sydney, Melbourne, Adelaide, Brisbane and Perth. The Seven network, managed jointly by Fairfax and the Melbourne Herald group, includes channels in Sydney, Melbourne and Adelaide. The Ten network has less concentration of ownership.

Both radio and television stations are coming to be attractive commercial propositions: hence the turnover in ownership that has been seen in recent times. It is likely that we will continue to see entrepreneurs such as Alan Bond, Christopher Skase and Robert Holmes à Court dealing in these media. Television and radio provide for a rapid cash flow and can support the more long-term development activities of large-scale capitalists.

Probably nowhere in the English-speaking world is the degree of concentration of ownership of the mass media as pronounced as it is in Australia. The major newspaper companies in Britain have a noticeably smaller proportion of the total market. The top three would control around two-thirds of daily circulation, a little higher on Sundays. In the United States, the major newspaper companies would control less than 10 per cent of daily circulation. Certainly television and radio networks are extensive in the United States but there is not the tie-in of the electronic media with print that we find in Australia.

What are the possible consequences of this centralised control? The *London Economist* put the case well (see Mayor 1964):

> The right to inform the public of the facts of the day and to express opinions about them is one of the safeguards of freedom; and a society in which this right becomes increasingly circumscribed (for economic reasons) forfeits one of the distinctions that set it apart from a society where the same right is curtailed by political power.

As Mayer has argued, diversity of ownership implies diversity of views, while monopoly reduced variety (Mayer 1964). This is clearly true in the abstract. Powerful groups are in a position to control in an important way what the average Australian reads, listens to and watches. The critical question, of course, is to what extent they do so. And if they do, to what extent does it matter? It would matter, of course, if, for example, watching television and reading newspapers did crucially affect the attitudes, opinions and behaviours of viewers and readers. These matters lead us to the question of 'media effects' which will be considered in the next section.

The Effects of the Mass Media

The history of pronouncements on the effects of the mass media is a recounting of varied enthusiasms and ranges all the way from convictions that effects are major, through convictions about nil or mediated effects, to convictions of grand conspiracies and 'hidden agendas'. Such a description obviously over-simplifies complex historical processes but it nevertheless highlights the major shifts in 'understanding'.

A systematic consideration of mass media effects would probably have to start with the pioneering work of Paul Lazarsfeld and Bernard Berelson in the 1940s and 1950s examining the role of the mass media in political campaigns. Lazarsfeld *et al.* (1944) and Berelson *et al.* (1954) wrote two seminal books *The People's Choice* and *Voting*. *The People's Choice* reported on a study of voting behaviour in the American 1940 presidential election and *Voting* reported on voting behaviour in the 1948 presidential election. A major concern of both studies was to examine the media's impact on the voting behaviour of the electorate. Lazarsfeld and Berelson had assumed that an election campaign was much like any major advertising campaign. They had an image of society as comprising a large number of atomised individuals who were bombarded by messages from the mass media. As there was nothing 'protecting' individual members of society from the media, messages would therefore impinge on them directly and their voting behaviour would be affected accordingly.

It was soon discovered that this was a grossly simplistic view. A major finding to come from the studies was that radio and the printed page seemed to have only negligible effects on actual voting decisions, and particularly minute effects on changes in voting decisions (Katz and Lazarsfeld 1956: 31). This is probably one of the few reported occasions in which negative or nil findings of social research have been more important in their consequences than positive findings. The negative findings caused the researchers to look for the factors which contributed to change in voting behaviour, and the 'two-step flow' notion of communication emerged as a consequence (Katz and Lazarsfeld 1956). Briefly, this argues that the effect of the mass media is typically on 'influentials' and opinion leaders in social groups who then pass on the media messages to others in their immediate environment. The mass media does have an effect on voting decisions, therefore, but an effect mediated by interpersonal relations, for when change occurs it is the result of the influence of others rather than the media. A great deal of research since that time has been undertaken to determine whether this process can be generalised to areas other than political behaviour. The findings have to some extent been controversial but it seems safe to conclude that a direct effect between exposure to the media and subsequent behaviour occurs only infrequently.

The view of the media, initially propounded by Lazarsfeld, Berelson and their supporters, was to hold sway for a great number of years and it was really not until the 1970s that a coherent review of the nil-effect claims took place. Important in this review were a number of English and European workers; among them Stuart Hall (1977), James Curran, Michael Gurevitch and Janet Woolacott (1977), Gitlin (1981) and the Glasgow University Media Group have been prominent. Their work has been strongly influenced by neo-Marxist writings and, stripped of its ideological superstructure, it has provided an important contribution to the debate on the media effect relationship. Very briefly, the argument they have developed is that the media are ideological agencies that play a central role in maintaining the domination of the ruling class.

In part their argument has been that a wrong construction has been placed upon the findings emerging from the classical empirical studies. In a state of the art paper, Todd Gitlin (1981) makes the important point that while these might have demonstrated that the media had very little influence on changeing the level of political participation, they did demonstrate the central role of the media in consolidating and reinforcing people's attitudes. Because there was an absence of conversion, Gitlin argues, there was not necessarily an absence of influence, and indeed the media were providing just that influence that the writers from the 'cultural studies' perspective (those mentioned above) have attributed to it (Gitlin 1981). In addition, Gitlin went on to argue that the Marxist assertion that the media plays a strategic role in reinforcing dominant social norms and values that legitimise the social system, was in fact borne out by the empirical studies, although this was an issue to which the earlier researchers paid little attention.

More recently still, the argument has been put forward that so-called 'dominant meaning systems' (Hall 1982) are moulded by the media and relayed to audiences who adapt and integrate these into class-based meaning systems which somehow categorise individuals. Theoretical understandings of the link between the media and political and social affairs have perhaps not come quite full circle. The view is not that the media have direct and noticeable affects on the attitudes, values and beliefs of people, but rather that the assertion of nil effects is totally misplaced. Effects there are – and these are to reinforce existing states of affairs. The media help to legitimise present social forms and structures, and the manner in which argument and debate can take place.

While the neo-Marxist response to the early empirical studies had its origins in Europe and the United Kingdom, North Americans were also reconsidering the issue. Characteristically, however, their orientation tended to be more empirical: 'agenda setting' was the means by which they approached the question. This proposes that what is emphasised by the mass media through prominence and display subsequently becomes what the public thinks is important. There is a positive causal relationship between the media agenda – what the media emphasises – and the public agenda – what the public thinks is important (Blood 1982).

The notion of agenda setting, while a reaction to the view of minimum media influence, also represents a movement away from an emphasis on direct and immediate effects of the mass media to a concern with longer-term effects. Blood (1982) has written:

> Agenda setting is concerned with examining long-term cognitive changes in media content and other influences contributing to these changes. In sum, rather than a model of limited media effects, agenda setting is more properly described as a limited model of effects.

Essentially, the argument from this point of view is that the media shape what the public thinks about; what the media judge to be important, the public learns about, while what the media regard as not newsworthy, the public is denied. People learn to have opinions, as Daniel Lerner (1958) so correctly stated, but they can only have opinions about what comes within their purview, and to a very significant extent, this is determined by the mass media.

For instance: we think about fringe benefits because the media alert us to them. We know now about bottom-of-the-harbour tax schemes because, although they have been in operation for fifty years or so, the media have only recently drawn them to our attention. We know the Prime Minister is in trouble because the media tell us he is. We learn of an upsurge of conservatism because we read about it in the press and see it on television. We are asked to consider whether the country is moving to the Right because the press and television suggest that these are matters for our consideration. So clearly, as with other things, the media structure our view of politics. They provide the upper and lower bounds, as it were, beyond which the great majority of us do not have the resources to progress.

There is another question to ask. In 1936, and in quite a different context, Karl Mannheim asked: who plans the planner? We might rephrase this question and ask: 'who sets the agenda for the agenda setter?' because clearly, while we can argue with some force, I believe, that the media set the agenda, we need to ask, on what basis is this agenda set and who determines what gets on the agenda and what doesn't? These are, I would suggest, non-trivial questions. They are, however, questions which are only starting to be asked in systematic ways in the Australian context (see, for example, Blood 1982).

The theoretical considerations reviewed very briefly in the preceding few pages have not guided Australian media research very markedly. We lack studies comparable to the ground-breaking work of Lazarsfeld and Berelson, and the two-step flow theory of communication has not been systematically examined in the Australian context. In recent times, however, the media have been approached from perspectives which have been clearly influenced by neo-Marxist writings and the writings of the so-called 'cultural studies' group.

Connell was perhaps the first to present a systematic statement of the media from this position. In a paper entitled 'The Media in Middle Class Culture' appearing in 1977, he argued that the media reflected the dominant culture, which he saw as essentially middle class. The ruling class, by its control of the media, was able to set the agenda, determining what appeared on that agenda, what form the discussion of the material took, and what the outcome of the discussion was. Essentially, Connell argued, the media operated to maintain the cultural supremacy of the ruling class.

A case study in Patricia Edgar's *The Politics of the Press* (1979) which she carried out with Alan Smith on the 1975 federal election, addressed the question of the power of the press in Australian politics and 'the possibility of press complicity in a systematic discrediting of the Labor government prior to the election campaign' (Edgar 1979: 11, quoted in Western and ughes 1983: 63). Several techniques were used to examine this issue. Firstly, the space devoted to each party was determined, and then stories relating to the parties were classified as favourable or unfavourable. In addition, discussions were held with journalists who covered the election. The evidence was quite strong that the newspapers examined favoured Fraser and the Liberal-National coalition at the expense of Whitlam, who had been dismissed from government by the Governor-General. Evidence from discussions with journalists also revealed that they had not been allowed as much freedom by their publishers to report the campaign as they saw it as they had in the election of 1974. Humphrey McQueen is in no doubt about this. In *Australia's Media Monopolies* (1977) he asserts:

> Even if all the media were completely honest, accurate and unbiased in all their political comment and reports, they would still uphold the interests of capitalism.

In more recent times, additional work has made similar claims. Influenced by the Glasgow University Media Group, which produced *Bad News* and *More Bad News*, Bell, Boehringer and Crofts (1982) produced a study entitled *Programmed Politics*. This was an examination of news and current affairs programs on the Sydney commercial television Channels 7, 9 and 10, during the 5-week period leading up to the 1980 federal election. The authors argue, on the basis of their findings, that while they do not see television as a significant cause of political and social change, they do believe that the medium amplifies, extends and consolidates socially significant kinds of change. For example, they suggest that television programs which focus on elections and party politics displace, or at least fail to take account of, a dynamic, informed and reasoning public. The electronic media, they argue (1982: 2):

> constitute an illusionary, institutional 'guarantee' for such a public sphere, in that they effectively circumscribe rather than facilitate public discussion and debate by diverse conflicting interests.

Again, the media are seen as working for the benefit of entrenched ruling class interests.

Perhaps two of the most recent studies which have come out of the tradition we are discussing are Bonney and Wilson's (1983) *Australia's Commercial Media* and Keith Windschuttle's (1985) *The Media*. In a detailed consideration of patterns of ownership and control of the Australian media, the nature of technology and economy in the press, and the place of the advertising industry in the media, Bonney and Wilson argue that media outputs are essentially cultural products. Such products cannot be regarded simply as factual material embodying no particular conceptualis- ation of reality. All media outputs are reflective of the world from a particular standpoint, 'reproducing the dominant ideology of individualism, though often tempered by the contradictory ideology of solidarity and community which tends to come to the fore during crises' (Bonney and Wilson 1983: 324). In *The Media* Windschuttle presents a comprehensive analysis of the press, television, radio and advertising in Australia in the latter part of the twentieth century. While clearly influenced by a neo-Marxist perspective or, as he terms it, the Left idealist perspective (Windschuttle 1985: 404), he argues for a broader understanding of the role of the media in society. He terms this understanding a materialist class-based perspective (Windschuttle 1985: 405).

While acknowledging the force of much of the argument generated by the Left idealist perspective, he argues that it is necessary to recognise more fully than some from this perspective have done, that the media operate within a market situation and by that very fact the first criterion of their existence is that they must satisfy the demands of their audiences. They do this, he suggests, by presenting authentic expressions of popular culture, 'a considerable volume of which 'is directly functional for working class audiences, maintaining many of the strengths and traditions of the labour movement' (Windschuttle 1985: 405). From this perspective, the media are clearly not simply a vehicle for the propagation of ruling class ideas.

Further support for this position comes from empirical studies which show quite pronounced changes in media credibility over time. If, as the 'cultural supremacists' would have us believe, the media are simply transmitting ruling class ideas to a more or less uncritical mass audience, we would not expect to find either criticism of the media or major changes in media credibility. The data which we will consider in the next section of this chapter suggest that both are occurring.

Media Use and Credibility

In any assessment of time devoted to different activities, the media rank high. Studies have consistently demonstrated people spend more hours per day in sleep than in any other activity. Next to sleep comes work (for the majority), and after work, attending to the media. Among young people in particular, television viewing occupies a substantial period of time. A related series of investigations has shown that by the time they have reached sixteen years of age, the majority of young people will have spent at least as much time in front of the television set as they have at school (Western 1973: 81, McCann and Sheehan 1985).

Such findings have caused some investigators to argue that next

to the family and school, televison is the most significant agent of
socialisation (Feschbach and Singer 1971, Baker and Ball 1969).
And, of course, the question of the effects on young people of
exposure to violence on television is a matter of perennial concern
(McCann and Sheehan 1985). Indeed, the consensus of informed
opinion now is that a positive relationship exists 'between televised
violence and aggressive behaviour' (McCann and Sheehan 1985:
40). The consensus is by no means complete, however, and some
researchers will point to different findings. Other writers also
interpret these issues in terms of the all-pervasive influence of
television and its role in reinforcing the cultural supremacy of the
ruling class. Interpretations aside for the moment, it is clear that
young people's exposure to television is substantial.

Findings from further studies help us broaden the picture a
little. We will start with the question of media use. A series of
market studies carried out over the last decade or so reveal that
more than 9 in 10 homes have at least one television set. Virtually
all homes have radio sets, and 2 out of 3 homes buy newspapers
regularly. In TV homes 93 per cent of people view commercial
television at least once a week; 86 per cent of all people listen to
some commercial radio in a week; and 85 per cent of people read a
daily newspaper on an average day. Two national surveys carried
out over a 13-year period between 1966 and 1979 reveal that in that
time exposure to the press declined, while radio and television
exposure rose. Whereas in 1966, 84 per cent of the sample
interviewed got at least one newspaper every day, in 1979 the
figure had fallen to 70 per cent. Such figures are consistent with
declines in newspaper circulation that have been evident now for
more than a decade (Western and Hughes 1983: 16).

More striking than change in circulation figures, however, is the
changing credibility of the press and television. In the two national
media studies referred to above, and conducted in 1966 and 1979,
the respondents interviewed were provided with a list of seven
items and for each were asked to indicate which of press, radio and
television was most effective with respect to it. The items were:
gives the most complete news; presents things most intelligently;
brings the latest news quickest; does the most for the public;
presents the fairest, most unbiased news; gives the clearest understanding of issues; gives the best understanding of leaders.

The data reporting the judgements of the two samples are
provided in Table 18.2. While evaluation of radio's performance
has not changed in the period 1966 to 1979, there has been a
massive shift away from the press to television. One item showed
negligible differences between the two surveys – brings the latest

news quickest. It was the only item on which radio had the advantage in 1966 and still did so in 1979. The advantage is inherent in the nature of the medium and although television has slightly improved its position *vis-à-vis* radio, it is unlikely that it will ever overtake it. However, live presentation on television of major news events does make it an effective competitor even on this item. On the other six items, television's improved position in comparison with the press is striking. Where television had been ranked about equal with the press (presents things most intelligently, gives clearest understanding of issues), or trailed slightly (does the most for the public), it is now ahead by two to one or better. Where television had the advantage (presents the fairest, most unbiased news, gives the best understanding of leaders), it is now ahead by three to one. Most dramatically of all, on the item of giving the most complete news, which had been the press's strongest in 1966, and one of the two on which a single medium had the endorsement of more than half the panel, television now has a definite edge. It is the item on which the press has a natural advantage by reason of greater space and less time constraints. Its loss of first place here shows how badly the prestige of the printed word has fallen.

Table 18.2 Rating of Media on Performance, 1966 and 1979

	Press		Radio		Television	
	1966 %	1979 %	1966 %	1979 %	1966 %	1979 %
Gives the most complete news	55	34	14	13	25	48
Presents things most intelligently	38	23	11	14	38	54
Brings the latest news quickest	7	4	58	56	30	38
Does the most for the public	39	20	17	19	27	49
Presents the fairest, most unbiased news	20	13	20	24	31	42
Gives clearest understanding of issues	36	25	10	9	33	52
Gives best understanding of leaders	33	20	6	7	41	61

n: 1966 = 1058, 1979 = 992; 'don't knows' excluded

The pattern of responses to a further item put to the respondents was also consistent with this trend. The question was 'Of newspapers, radio and television, which would you least like to go without? That is, which would you miss most, newspapers, radio or television?' The press fell as the medium which would be missed most, from 43 per cent in 1966, to 26 per cent in 1979, while radio rose from 19 per cent to 27 per cent and television from 35 per cent to 45 per cent (Western and Hughes 1983: 93).

Changes in media credibility are also suggested by the changes that have taken place in the community's views about the 'fairness' of the media. In the two studies to which we have already referred, respondents were asked their views about the 'fairness' of the press, ABC radio and television, and commercial radio and television, to the major political groupings in Australia: the Liberal-National Party coalition and the ALP. The findings from the two studies are presented in Table 18.3. There has been little change in the proportion judging commercial radio and commercial and ABC television as fair to both parties – between one-half and two-thirds report this opinion. However there has been quite a substantial change as far as judgements about the press are concerned. While nearly three-quarters saw the press as fair to the Coalition in 1966, this had dropped to a little over one-half by 1979. A similar decline, albeit from a lower starting point, exists

Table 18.3 Fairness of Media to Political Parties, 1966 and 1979

Medium	Fairness to	Yes		No		Don't Know	
		1966 %	1979 %	1966 %	1979 %	1966 %	1979 %
Press	Coalition	72	58	6	19	21	24
	ALP	55	44	21	33	22	23
ABC radio	Coalition	50	45	1	9	47	44
	ALP	48	46	3	9	47	42
Commercial radio	Coalition	51	52	3	10	45	34
	ALP	47	47	5	15	46	35
ABC TV	Coalition	64	58	1	8	32	33
	ALP	62	57	2	10	33	32
Commercial TV	Coalition	68	63	1	11	28	25
	ALP	62	57	4	16	31	25

n: 1966 = 1058, 1979 = 992; 'no answer' excluded

for the ALP. A similar decline in credibility of ABC radio in its handling of the Coalition partners can also be observed (Western and Hughes 1983: 62).

These data are important because they suggest that media audiences do not simply 'soak up' the coverage to which they are exposed. They can critically evaluate press, radio and television, and while these media may be the passive bearers of the dominant culture, the audience is inclined to somewhat more active participation in any media event.

What of the future? It would appear that there is something of a 'crisis of confidence' as far as the press is concerned. Clearly it is being replaced by televison as an information source; it has never really competed with televison as an entertainment medium. Its future must be somewhat less rosy than that of at least one of its electronic counterparts.

The Mass Media and the Future

Painting scenarios as to the future of the mass media has always been a relatively popular sport for those writing on press, radio and television in Australia. Humphrey McQueen (1977) in *Australia's Media Monopolies* was prepared to hazard a few guesses as to the nature of the change that might take place in the media industry over the next ten years. Similarly, Bonney and Wilson raise the question as to whether the press has a future. They comment (1983: 120):

> It is clear that the press cannot survive long in its present form. Costs are too high, profitability is too low and there are too many technological and industrial problems. There is a lack of diversity in the views expressed, the kinds of stories appearing and in the sources used.

They then go on to suggest that with changing computer technologies, the 'electronic newspaper' may be the way forward for the press. Newspapers have been getting too big to produce and distribute economically. With electronic newspapers, readers will be able to select sections for their own use, have these displayed on their video monitor and recalled as they wish. More generally, they believe that the upmarket press has a brighter future than the popular press (1983: 123):

It is equally clear that the upmarket press will require the services of skilled information seekers in order to survive ... there are certain prospects in at least some aspects of the press for journalists to demand more control, even if printers are forced to accept the slow death of their trade.

For some, however, the future will be in satellites and high technology (Barr 1985). Barr claims that Australia's electronic estate is composed of two inter-related economic sectors: the information technology industry, where computer hardware and software are central, and the communications industry, primarily the tele-communications and media service businesses, both private and public (Barr 1985: 13). The trend is clear, he believes. Information technology and the communications industry are now major components of the Australian economy and both will become critical indicators in determining Australian wealth and economic stability in the future (1985: 3).

We are in the early days of the information society, which, Barr (1985: 25) tells us is technologically driven, with concentration heavily on the means and techniques of distribution for ever-increasing quantities of information. New forms of information hardware are presumed to be about advancement and progress (Barr 1985: 26):

> They offer, for instance, quicker ways of being billed by electronic funds transfer, more efficient teleshopping of supermarket specials called up on screen via videotext or advanced learning at home via the computer terminal ... but do we find telebanking, teleshopping and electronic mail more satisfying? ... in broadcasting we are embarking on an expensive and technologically sophisticated national domestic satellite system which will give greater efficiency of signal distribution, allow more live broadcasting and encourage more channels to be made available. Yet will the programmes be any better or different? Will Australia's age of satellite television still continue the abysmal neglect of televison audiences? We have embarked upon profound changes in methods of communication yet have not bothered to find out about the nature of communities that these technologies are intended to serve. Media and telecommunic-ation developments concentrating so much on the conduits of delivery – cable, microwave, radiated subscription television, sat-ellite, fibre optic – that the fundamental question of what is to be delivered and why have not only gone unanswered but they have not been asked.

It is obvious that Barr raises some of the fundamental issues that must be addressed when the question of the mass media and the future is under discussion. There is clearly a tension between society's capacity to control and direct technology, and its ability to ensure that technological developments result in the attainment of social goals, and that the developments themselves are socially informed. This tension is evident in many fields. It is not beyond the capacity of human kind to land a man on the moon or direct a rocket with extraordinary precision to a far-off planet. It is beyond the capacity of human kind to ensure employment for all who want to work. If it is not beyond the capacity of human kind to produce enormous grain surpluses in the developed world, it is to ensure that these surpluses are used to reduce starvation in the Third World.

Development is technology-driven and we experience costs or benefits in a more or less random manner. This assertion holds as much for media developments as for development in any other field. Aussat, the domestic satellite, is an example *par excellence*, and in this section of the chapter, when future scenarios are our concern, the saga of Aussat clearly deserves attention.

Nothing heralds Australia's move into the so-called post-industrial society perhaps as much as the development of the country's own domestic satellite system.

The prospect of it was first introduced in October 1979 by the then Minister of Post and Telecommunications, Tony Staley. The argument for it had to do with 'the plight of those of our fellow countrymen who are seriously disadvantaged by a lack of communication services and communication dependent services' (quoted in Barr 1985: 141). There were at the time approximately 40,000 people in isolated communities in Australia who had no prospect of being connected to a telephone in the foreseeable future. There were 500,000 people who had no television service at all, and another 220,000 who had only an ABC service. A further 4,000,000 Australians had only one national and one commercial television service, 375,000 people lived beyond the normal reach of ABC radio stations, and some 4,000,000 Australians received only a third ABC network.

Barr suggests that 'an argument for the introduction of a new technology based on equity of community services obviously has merit' (1985: 141). Domestic satellites clearly have great potential in attempting to overcome communication disadvantages for Australians living in isolated areas. It was soon to be pointed out that a significant proportion of those in isolated communities were Aboriginal people. The question was raised as to whether simply transmitting programs from the major networks via satellite to Aboriginal communities was likely to meet the needs or demands of these communities. However, in the government's haste to join the satellite club, little attention has been paid to the appropriateness or otherwise of the programs and other stimuli that were to be beamed by satellite into the living rooms and other abodes of those in isolated areas.

The satellite did not come quickly. Kerry Packer of Channel 9 and Australian Consolidated Press was the driving force behind the initial activities in 1977. He had the ear of the then Prime Minister, Malcolm Fraser, and commissioned a report, *The Opportunity for Television Programme Distribution in Australia using Earth Stations* for the federal government, a report prepared by Donald Bond, an American comunications consultant. It argued from North American experience that an Australian domestic satellite would provide television coverage to areas not presently accessible to television. Within a few weeks of the release of the report, the Minister for Posts and Telecommunications set up a Commonwealth government taskforce to enquire into all aspects related to a national communications satellite system for Australia. This was chaired by Harold White, the General Manager of the Overseas Telecommunications Commission. It produced a report which indicated clearly the complexity of interests within the Australian television industry and the general lack of support for the Packer proposal (Barr 1985: 155). It also recommended the introduction of an Australian national communications satellite system as soon as possible. A great deal of political debate took place over the next eighteen months to two years. In November 1981 the next Minister for Communications, Ian Sinclair announced that the system would be officially known as Aussat. Aussat was to be a company 49 per cent owned by persons other than the Commonwealth of Australia or its authorities, with the other 51 per cent owned by the Commonwealth.

In 1983 the Hawke Labor government inherited a series of unresolved policy questions surrounding the satellite project. The new Minister of Communications, Michael Duffy, the fifth Communications Minister in six years, gained the portfolio and the Aussat brief. Shortly after taking over the reins Duffy announced that Aussat was to be retained as a Commonwealth-owned company and Telecom was to be invited to purchase up to 25 per cent of Commonwealth shareholdings, thereby revoking the earlier decision to offer 49 per cent of the Commonwealth asset to private shareholders (Barr 1985: 163).

The politics of Aussat in a number of respects was reminiscent of the politics that surrounded the introduction of television in Australia, where change in the governing fortunes of conservative and Labor governments resulted in marked changes in policy as to the manner in which a communication system should be implemented.

A great deal has transpired since 1983. Aussat became operational around October 1985 and is providing a number of services at the present time. Primary users of services are (Barr 1985: 170):

- broadcasters – the Australian Broadcasting Corporation for television and radio and the commercial television networks;
- the Department of Aviation for air navigation services;
- Telecom for remote telephone services and route diversity;
- the ABC's Remote Area Broadcasting Service;
- private secondary data and information services, including private networks.

Secondary users or services are:

- community broadcasting or radio programs distributed through the Public Broadcasting Association of Australia:
- educational programs by state-based educational organisations or out-based educational services such as the School of the Air;
- the Papua New Guinea government for television and telecommunications;
- new broadcasting systems such as radiated subscription television services or pay television.

As noted previously, the history of the emergence of Aussat mirrors quite closely the history of the emergence of television in Australia: little real planning, little solid policy development and little estimate of needs and demand and the manner in which the new service might be adjusted to respond to these factors. Once again a major new development in one area of Australia's communication system has been seen to be at the mercy of the political aspirations of whatever party happened to be in power at any particular time.

Having made that point, it is also clear that the future of communication systems in Australia will be importantly determined by advanced technology and by satellites. In 1971, with Colin Hughes, I wrote, 'We may perhaps all be living in a global village but for the time being we seem unlikely to be electronically connected' (Western and Hughes 1971: 156). That statement has not worn well. We may not yet be completely electronically connected, but by the 1990s we will be further down this path than many of us presently now suppose.

Postscript

It is a brave person who attempts to predict the future. In the last section of this chapter, I talked confidently about satellites, wired cities and the like, but paid scant attention to the immediate future which, of course, has now overtaken us.

On 4 December 1986, with this book well in production, and little chance to effect a major rewrite of my chapter, the *Courier-Mail* appeared with a banner headline: *1.8 Million Dollars King Hit*, The *Australian* also appeared with a slightly smaller headline: *Stunning HWT Takeover to Trigger Media Shakeup*. The stories below these headlines and the stories below similar ones in all other metropolitan dailies detailed an offer Mr Rupert Murdoch had made for the Herald and Weekly Times. Their chief executive, Mr John D'Arcy, recommended Mr Murdoch's bid for the Herald and Weekly Times empire to the shareholders.

The story was not, however, to end there, and on Friday 2 January 1987 Mr Holmes à Court made a counter-bid of $2 billion dollars. On 3 January, the Herald and Weekly Times board issued a qualified recommendation of Mr Holmes à Court's bid, which had been increased from $2 billion to $2.125 billion.

Queensland Press, a major element in the Herald and Weekly Times empire, was a little reluctant to accept the Holmes à Court offer. Mr Keith McDonald, the managing director of Queensland Press, saw Rupert Murdoch as a major media man and as a consequence appeared to favour the News Corporation bid. On 5 January, John Fairfax entered the fray with a bid of $910 million for Queensland Press. The papers noted that Fairfax seemed to have done a deal with Holmes à Court. On Wednesday 7 January, the chairman of Queensland Press, Mr Keith McDonald, publicly supported the News Corporation's share alternative for the Herald and Weekly Times against that of Mr Robert Holmes à Court, seemingly ruling out Fairfax's bid for Queensland Press.

On Saturday 10 January Mr Murdoch was reported as upping his offer for the Herald and Weekly Times to $2.3 billion. On Thursday 15 January, Fairfax increased its offer for Queensland Press to $1.1 billion. On Friday 16 January it was reported that *Murdoch wins Herald and Weekly Times*. Mr Holmes à Court's consolation prize was to be the Herald and Weekly Times' Western Australian papers and their Melbourne TV station, which were to be purchased from News Corporation. The apparent resolution ended six weeks of rival bidding and court actions and very clearly gave Rupert Murdoch an unassailable position in Australian media. He had a national daily, the *Australian,* and capital city dailies in South Australia, Victoria, New South Wales, Queensland, Tasmania and the Northern Territory. He also had a variety of other regional papers in the states, and television and radio stations.

The media story continues, however, because on Wednesday 21 January, newspapers across the country announced that Alan Bond had bought Kerry Packer's Channel 9 television stations in Melbourne and Sydney. The stations cost him $1 billion and the estimates were that this gave him 59 per cent of the Australian television audience, with channels in Sydney, Melbourne, Brisbane and Perth. Fairfax was not out of the fray, however, and on 22 January, they made a $2.5 billion offer for the Herald and Weekly Times. Mr Murdoch said from Los Angeles that the Fairfax organisation had made its run for the Herald and Weekly Times too late.

On 23 January, the Australian Broadcasting Tribunal announced that it would hold an urgent inquiry in February into Mr Murdoch's bid for the Herald and Weekly Times, particularly as far as it concerned television stations. It ruled that News Corporation could not register its Herald and Weekly Times shares until after the inquiry. On 29 January it was announced that Mr Murdoch had sold all the Herald and Weekly Times television and radio stations in a $387 million transaction designed to cement his takeover of the Herald and Weekly Times and to reduce the likelihood of the Australian Broadcasting Tribunal interceding in the situation.

The purchasers of the Herald and Weekly Times stations were Westfield Capital Corporation, which received two radio stations, 4BK and 4AK Toowoomba in Queensland; Mr Holmes à Court, who purchased HSV7 in Melbourne; and Mr Kerry Stokes, who purchased Melbourne radio stations 3DB and 3GL, Channel 7 in Adelaide and South Australian radio stations 5AD, 5PI and 5SE. It also appears likely that Westfield Capital, which is planning to pass the Queensland radio stations to an associated company, Northern Star Holdings, will buy the Brisbane newspapers, the *Sun* and the *Sunday Sun*, which Mr Murdoch is intending to sell.

A further press release on 29 January revealed that News Corporation was entering into agreements to sell the media group's entire radio and television interests, for around $397 million. At this time the Australian Broadcasting Tribunal withdrew its objections to the media deals.

Clearly the situation is still in flux. It is not likely that we will have a complete understanding of the structure of the Australian media until well into 1987. What is clear is that a major restructuring is taking place. There is a degree of centralised control. Clearly this is not greater than it was before the present moves took place. What appears to be apparent is that the nexus between press and television has been broken. Major press barons no longer control television networks. Whether this is a temporary or permanent position still remains to be seen. Australia still has one of the world's most highly centralised media systems but the degree of diversity is likely to be somewhat greater after the dust has settled, than it was before.

What the present range of activities has clearly underlined is the profitability of the media industry in Australia. People pay cash for their newspapers; they do not buy them on credit. Television advertising is paid for similarly. Large-scale capitalists concerned with developmental programs for which the returns may be slow in coming can finance activities on the basis of their media holdings. The impact of these considerations on the quality of the press, radio and television we are likely to receive in the future remains to be determined.

References

Australian Broadcasting Control Board (1949) *Annual Report*. Melbourne.
———(1952) *Annual Report*. Melbourne.
Baker, R.K. and Ball, S.J. (1969) *Violence and the Media: A Report to the National Commission on the Causes and Prevention of Violence*. Washington: US Government Printing Office.
Barr, T. (1985) *The Electronic Estate: New Communications Media in Australia*. Ringwood, Victoria: Penguin.
Bell, P., Boehringer, K. and Crofts, S., (1982) *Programmed Politics: A Study of Australian Television*. Sydney: Sable Publishing.
Berelson, B., Lazarsfeld, P.F. and McPhee, W. (1954) *Voting*. Chicago: University of Chicago Press.
Blood, W. (1982) 'Agenda Setting: A Review of the Theory', *Media Information Australia* 26: 3–12.
Bonney, B. and Wilson, H. (1983) *Australia's Commercial Media*. Melbourne: Macmillan.
Bushnell, J. A. (1961) *Australian Company Mergers 1946–1959*. Melbourne: Melbourne University Press.
Carden, W.M. (1956) 'Towards a History of the Australian Press', *Meanjin* 171–184.
Connell, R.W. (1977) 'The Media in Middle Class Culture' in R.W.

Connell *Ruling Class Ruling Culture*. London: Cambridge University Press.

Curran, J., Gurevitch, M. and Woolacott, J. (1977) *Mass Communication and Society*. London: Edward Arnold.

Davies, A.F. (1968) 'Communications in Australia – Mass Media' in *Anatomy of Australia*, Commonwealth Study Conference of His Royal Highness, the Duke of Edinburgh, Melbourne.

Edgar, P. (1979) *The Politics of the Press*. Melbourne: Sun Books.

Feschbach, S. and Singer, R.D. (1971) *Television and Aggression*. San Francisco: Jossey Bass.

Gitlin, T. (1981) 'Media Sociology: The Dominant Paradigm' in G.C. Wilhoit and H. Boch (eds) *Mass Communication Review Year Book*. Beverly Hills, California: Sage.

Glasgow University Media Group (1976) *Bad News, Volume One*. London: Routledge & Kegan Paul.

Green, F. (1976) *Australian Broadcasting: A Report on the Structure of the Australian Broadcasting System and Associated Matters* (the Green Report). Canberra: AGPS.

Hall, S. (1977) 'Culture, the Media and the "Ideological Effect"' in J. Curran, M. Gurevitch and J. Woollacott (eds) *Mass Communication and Society*. London: Edward Arnold.

———(1982) 'The Rediscovery of Ideology: Return of the Repressed in Media Studies' in M.B. Gurevitch, T. Bennet, J. Curran and J. Woollacott, *Culture, Society and the Media*. London: Methuen.

Katz, E. and Lazarsfeld, P.F. (1956) *Personal Influence*. Glencoe, Illinois: Free Press.

Lazarsfeld, P.F., Berelson, B. and Gaudet, H. (1944) *The People's Choice*. New York: Columbia University Press.

Lerner, D. (1958) *The Passing of Traditional Society*. New York: Free Press.

Mackay, I.K. (1957) *Broadcasting in Australia*. Melbourne: Melbourne University Press.

McCann, T.E. and Sheehan, P.W. (1985) 'Violence Content in Australian Television' *Australian Psychologist* 20: 30–42.

McClelland, J. (1976) 'Case Study No. 2: The Great Australian Scandal' in G. Major (ed.) *Mass Media in Australia*. Sydney: Hodder & Stoughton.

McQueen, H. (1977) *Australia's Media Monopolies*. Melbourne: Widescope.

Mannheim, K. (1936) *Ideology and Utopia*. New York: Harcourt Brace.

Mayer, H. (1964) *The Press in Australia*. Melbourne: Lansdowne Press.

Souter, G. (1981) *Company of Heralds: A Century and a Half of Australian Publishing of John Fairfax Limited and its Predecessors 1831–1981*. Melbourne: Melbourne University Press.

Walker, R.R. (1967) *Communicators*. Melbourne: Lansdowne Press.

Western, J.S. (1973) *Australian Mass Media: Controllers, Consumers, Producers*, AIPS Monograph No. 9. Marrickville, NSW: South Western Press.

—— and Hughes, C.A. (1971) *The Mass Media in Australia: Use and Evaluation*. St Lucia: University of Queensland Press.

—— and —— (1983) *The Mass Media in Australia*, Second Edition. St Lucia: University of Queensland Press.

Windschuttle, K. (1985) *The Media*. Ringwood, Victoria: Penguin.

Index

Aboriginal Community Councils, 200
Aboriginal Land Fund Commission, 201
Aboriginal Land Rights (Northern Territory) Bill, 200–01
Aboriginal Land Trust, 202
Aboriginal Protection Acts, 309
Aboriginal Protection and Restriction of the Sale of Opium Act, 196, 199
Aborigines, 4, 162–63, 166, 168, 172, 174, 178, 193, 235, 298, 388, 488, 530, 563–64
 and Aboriginal law, 191, 308–09
 age and, 189, 191
 as city dwellers, 204
 and crime, 389–90, 395
 definition of, 205
 division of labour, 187
 economic status of, 206
 and education, 207, 220
 as entrepreneurs, 197
 first encounters with whites, 25–26, 186, 194–95, 198–99, 309
 gender divisions and, 189
 and health, 206–07, 308–12, 319–20
 homicide and, 390
 infant death rates of, 310
 kinship and, 188–89, 205
 land and, 190
 lifestyles of, 187–88
 marriage and, 189, 191
 and missions, 197, 199
 percentage of population, 182, 187, 194–95, 201–02, 308
 political advancement of, 200–01, 208
 rate of unemployment among, 6, 197, 204
 relations with capitalism, 183–86, 195–97
 religious views of, 191–92, 308
 settlements and, 188, 202–03, 310
 social security and, 200
 social structure of, 204–05, 308–09
 and white law, 199
Aborigines and Torres Strait Islanders Act, 199

Acker, J., 109–10
Adelaide, 75, 104, 172, 204, 245, 413, 528, 536, 544–45, 550–51
Adelaide Advertiser, 544
Age, The, 449, 488, 491, 500, 545
'age of familism', 426, 435
aged, 4, 174–75, 295, 336, 350, 363, 392, 395, 490, 493, 505, 510
ageism, 115–16, 117, 449
Aitkin, Don, 216, 231, 346, 348, 355, 358, 364, 367
Albinski, H., 44
Alger, Horatio, 25
alienation, 271, 272, 281, 284, 287n, 407, 416, 429
Amalgamated Wireless Australasia (AWA), 549
American Occupational Structure, 79
American Social Science Association, 294–95
American Sociological Association, 295
Anderson, D. S., 232–33
Anglican, 177, 216, 355
Ansett, Sir Reginald, 117
Ansett Transport Industries (ATI), 550
arbitration, 34, 102
Arbitration Commission, 358
Aronowitz, Stanley, 407
Asch, S. E., 15, 17
assimilationism, 167
 as theory, 163–64
Asymmetric Society, The, 434
Aussat, 563–65
Austin, Herbert, 253
Australia
 Aborigines and, 25–26, 186–208 passim, 395
 ageing population of, 449–50
 bureaucracy in, 40–42
 capitalist development of, 30, 32, 64–65, 68, 184–86, 239, 261, 518, 528–30
 class development in, 67, 79, 83–88, 529–31
 conservative governments in, 35, 40

571